Regulating Competition in the EU

Bent Iversen
Pernille Wegener Jessen
Bent Ole Gram Mortensen
Michael Steinicke
Karsten Engsig Sørensen

Regulating Competition in the EU

Translated by Steven Harris

Djøf Publishing
2012

Bent Iversen, Pernille Wegener Jessen, Bent Ole Gram Mortensen,
Michael Steinicke, Karsten Engsig Sørensen
Regulating Competition in the EU

2. edition

Cover: Bo Helsted
Print: Narayana Press, Gylling
Binding: Jysk Bogbind, Holstebro

Printed in Denmark 2012
ISBN 978-87-574-2662-5

Published with support from

dreyersfond

Sold and distributed in Scandinavia by:
DJØF Publishing
Copenhagen, Denmark
Email: forlag@djoef.dk
www.djoef-forlag.dk

Sold and distributed in North America by:
International Specialized Book Services (ISBS)
Portland, USA
Email: orders@isbs.com
www.isbs.com

Sold in all other countries by:
The Oxford Publicity Partnership Ltd
Towcester, UK
Email: djof@oppuk.co.uk
www.oppuk.co.uk

Distributed in all other countries by:
Marston Book Services
Abingdon, Oxon, UK
Email: trade.orders@marston.co.uk
www.marston.co.uk

Content

Foreword

Our aim in writing this book has been both to explain the traditional areas of competition law – such as the prohibition of agreements which restrict competition, the prohibition of abuse of dominant position, and the rules on merger control – as well as to describe other aspects of competition law which today play an essential role in regulating the conduct of undertakings and public authorities in the market. As in the previous edition, we have sought to give a more thematically comprehensive presentation of the subject, covering most of the areas which competition lawyers may be confronted with. On this basis the most important elements of competition law as they affect public bodies have been included – elements such as State aid, the liberalised sectors and public procurement.

Since this book has a broader perspective than more traditional works on competition law, we have considered it important that it should be possible to read each chapter independently. For this reason there will inevitably be some overlaps between chapters, though we have tried to keep these to a minimum.

This text is primarily intended for use as a university textbook but it is our hope that, given its comprehensive scope, it will also be of use to practitioners.

References to Treaty articles are made using the numbering of the Treaty on the Functioning of the European Union. This also applies to the numbering of articles when referring, for example, to decisions which ante-date the current numbering, except in the case of direct quotations. Only limited changes to the law since 15 November 2011 are included.

We are grateful to Margot & Thorvald Dreyers Fond which has provided financial support for the publication of this book. We also thank Marina Møller Bitsch of the Department of Law, Aarhus University, for her editorial and administrative assistance and Steven Harris who has been responsible for the translation of the text into English.

The responsibility for each chapter is alone that of the authors of each chapter.

The authors

CHAPTER I

Competition and Union law

Michael Steinicke

Bibliography: *Damien Chalmers, Christos Hadjiemmanuil, Giorgio Monti & Adam Tomkins: European Union Law, 2006; Paul Craig & Grainne de Burca: EU Law, 2011; Josephine Steiner & Lorna Woods: Textbook on EC Law, 2009; Stephen Weatherill & Paul Beaumont: EU Law, 1999.*

1. Laws regulating markets and competition law

The basis for the creation of the European Community was a desire to establish trade cooperation so that trade between the Member States should be strengthened. This aim still plays a major role in the cooperation, even though other aims have been added to the cooperation with the formation of the European Union. Article 3(2) of the Treaty on European Union (TEU) states that among its aims, 'The Union shall establish an internal market. It shall work for the sustainable development of Europe based on balanced economic growth and price stability, a highly competitive social market economy'.

The aims of the Union are to be achieved by implementing a number of policies that are laid down in Treaty provisions, the aims of which are to ensure freedom of trade between the Member States and to promote an environment that is favourable to trade in general.

The Treaty on the Functioning of the European Union (TFEU) contains a number of rules dealing with the establishment of the internal market which has been the primary goal of the cooperation from the start. Thus in its original form (the Treaty of Rome) the TFEU primarily contained provisions on the establishment of a European market. The most important of these provisions were those on freedom of movement and those on competition. The aim of these core provisions has been to establish protection for the actors on the market so that hindrances, whether imposed by the Member States or by their public bodies, or by undertakings in the European market should be prevented or eliminated.

The primary basis for competition law in the EU is to be found in Articles 101 to 109 TFEU, with the main focus being on Article 101 (prohibition of agreements in restraint of trade), Article 102 (abuse of a dominant position), Article 106 (the grant to public undertakings or undertakings of special or exclusive rights) and Article 107 (prohibition of State aid). In addition to these rules there are a number of other provisions which contain aspects of competition law, in particular secondary regulation.[1] Thus, competition law in the EU includes considerably more than the issues which are traditionally dealt with under the heading of competition law (i.e. Articles 101 and 102).[2]

2. The structure of the Treaty

The basic structure of the Treaty is that the provisions on freedom of movement are directed at the Member States and their public bodies,[3] while the provisions on competition are directed at undertakings. There are certain exceptions to this division, see section 2.3 below. The background to this structure is that the prohibitions in the rules of freedom of movement, on the one hand, and the prohibitions in the competition rules, on the other hand, are framed in different ways. The rules on freedom of movement are framed on the basis that the prohibition laid down shall be addressed to the administrative authority and the regulatory activity and the characteristics of such kinds of activities. In contrast the prohibitions in the competition rules take account

1. For example, see the regulation of mergers, the regulation of the liberalised sectors and the directives on public procurement.
2. Articles 101 and 102 are inspired by American antitrust legislation in Articles 1 and 2 of the Sherman Act. These provisions found their way into the Treaty via German law, which in the immediately post-war years was clearly influenced by the regulation of the occupying powers in this area. These similarities between the Sherman Act and Articles 101 and 102 TFEU have given rise to comparisons of the practice on the two sets of rules.
3. The Court of Justice (CJ) has several times pointed out that these provisions are not addressed to undertakings; see for example Case 311/85, van Vlaamse. However, the CJ has also expressed the view that private undertakings cannot ignore these provisions; see for example Case 58/80, Dansk Supermarked. On the horizontal obligations of the rules on free movement, see section 2.3 below. The provisions on freedom of movement are not the primary topic of this book. For a general presentation of freedom of movement see *Weatherill & Beaumont:* EU Law; and *Damien Chalmers, Christos Hadjiemmanuil, Giorgio Monti & Adam Tomkins:* European Union Law.

of the special characteristics of carrying on commercial activities. Thus, the structure of the Treaty's system is based on the fundamental view that public bodies exercise administrative authority and they carry out regulatory activities, and that private bodies are engaged in commercial activities. In some cases this assumption is not followed, and thus the system in the Treaty is not followed (see further in section 2.3 below).

2.1. Rules directed at the Member States

The provisions on freedom of movement cover rules to ensure the free movement of goods, persons, services and capital. The rules on freedom of movement are thus structured so that they contain both prohibitions on the establishment of obstacles to the freedom of movement, and possibilities for exemptions to the prohibition, should the prohibition be infringed. The prohibition is based on the general ban on discrimination on the grounds of nationality in Article 18 TFEU and can, as such, be seen as a special expression of this prohibition. In addition to prohibiting discrimination, the rules on freedom of movement also prohibit certain hindrances that are not discriminatory, in other words, which do not affect citizens, services or goods from other Member States differently from those of the host Member State. There has been a considerable number of cases on these kinds of hindrances, and the decisions vary from one kind of freedom of movement to another.

For every prohibition there is one or more possible exception. These possibilities include a list of the circumstances which the Community considers to be acceptable potential exceptions to the prohibitions. In general, these legitimate considerations are characterised by being general societal considerations.[4] The exceptions in the TFEU include an exhaustive list of the considerations which the Member States can rely on to justify an infringement of the prohibitions. The CJ has also established a practice whereby certain infringements of the prohibitions (only infringements of a *non-discriminatory* character) can also be justified by a non-exhaustive number of considerations. However, these considerations are also characterised by being general societal considerations.

Also, in addition to the rules on freedom of movement, the Treaty's provisions on State aid are directed at public authorities. According to these rules,

4. For example, infringements of the prohibitions can be justified by reference to the fact that the national legislation protects the interests of public policy or public security.

public authorities are prohibited from giving financial support to private undertakings (for more on this, see the chapter on State aid).

In addition to the Treaty provisions, there are also a number of secondary legal acts which are discussed in this book and which are directed at the Member States despite their competition-like character. This applies to the rules on public procurement and to some extent the rules on the liberalised sectors. The rules on public procurement are concerned with purchases made by public bodies, and their authority is based on the rules on freedom of movement. The liberalisation rules are typically addressed to state-owned monopolies which have traditionally been responsible for a number of areas of service provision which are of key importance to society (such as energy supply, transport, postal services, telecommunications etc.).

In addition to the provisions on the infringement of substantive competition rules, the Member States also have a duty to ensure that the rules are effectively enforced in their courts and by their competition authorities. In this connection, there is a clear tendency for these bodies to be given increased importance in the enforcement of European competition rules, most recently with the adoption of Council Regulation (EC) No 1/2003.[5]

2.2. Rules directed at undertakings

The rules which have been laid down with a view to removing hindrances to trade between Member States would not be so effective if private undertakings were free to put in place measures which would instead create hindrances to trade and to the functioning of the internal market. The TFEU provisions for preventing private (and public) undertakings from restricting the effective functioning of the market are set out in Part Three, Title VII, Chapter 1 TFEU (see also Section 1 above).

In Case C-205/03 P, *Federación Española de Empresas de Tecnología Sanitaria (FENIN)*, the CJ stated that the activities of a public body on the market, which are not part of a commercial activity, fall outside the scope of application of the competition rules in Articles 101 and 102 TFEU, as such a body does not constitute an 'undertaking'. Thus the purchase of goods and services by a public body for the purposes of carrying out its duties or exercising its authority will not be considered an economic activity, even though

5. Moreover, this development has meant that most Member States have introduced competition rules which are inspired by the European provisions. In the present context this development means that national provisions have to a certain extent been superseded, where these are identical with or substantially the same as the Community provisions.

there is in fact a purchase agreement entered into under private law rules on the free market.[6]

2.3. Grey areas

The basis for the division of regulations into those directed to public bodies and those directed to private undertakings is the simple and usually correct assumption that private undertakings carry out economic activities in the form of business undertakings, and that public bodies carry out administrative activities and the exercise of authority. Even though this assumption is broadly correct, nevertheless there are sometimes situations in which either a public body or a private undertaking does not fit this picture. Thus in certain situations a private undertaking will carry out activities which can be characterised as regulatory or the exercise of authority, and conversely, a public body will sometimes carry on commercial activities.

Where this normal pattern breaks down, it is the *activity* which will often be decisive for which regulation will apply, rather than the formal classification of the organisation in question (i.e. whether the entity is public or private).

One example of these grey areas is the rules on public undertakings in Article 106 TFEU. The Article does not itself contain a prohibition, but rather refers to the other provisions in the Treaty which are relevant to such undertakings. There is thus scope for applying the Treaty provisions which regulate the circumstances in question (restrictions on competition or restrictive regulation). As the reference is to public *undertakings*, the competition rules will usually be used, but the provisions on free movement can also be relevant, due to the influence of public authorities on such undertakings.

Another example of where the structure is departed from can be seen in relation to establishing who is subject to the rules on free movement. In principle, all public bodies are covered by these rules.[7] However, in several cases the CJ has held that certain private bodies can be covered by the rules if they have characteristics which are normally seen in public authorities. The prima-

6. On this case, see *Ronit Kreisberger:* FENIN: Immunity From Competition Law Attack for Public Buyers?, Public Procurement Law Review 2006 NA 214; Catriona Munro: Competition Law and public procurement: two sides of the same coin', in Public Procurement Law Review 2006 p. 352; and *Albert Sanchez Graells:* Public procurement and EU Competition law, p. 150 ff. The CJ has subsequently arrived at the same conclusion in Case C-113/07 P, *Selex.*
7. The provisions refer to the Member States, and according to well established practice this is interpreted as covering all public entities in the Member States.

ry characteristic, in this context, is that the body in question has powers to lay down rules which affect others. This regulatory competence has been decisive in Case 36/74, *Walrave*, Case 13/76, *Donà*, Case C-292/92, *Bosman*,[8] and to some extent in Joined cases 266 and 267/87, *Royal Pharmaceutical Society*,[9] and Case C-292/92, *Hünermund*.[10]

An example of the reverse situation, where a public authority is subject to competition rules, is found in the practice which is referred to in American law as the 'state-action doctrine'.[11] This refers to the circumstances where the CJ applies the competition rules (primarily Article 101) to situations where public authorities adopt regulations which have the aim or consequence of prescribing or promoting agreements which are contrary to Article 101 or which reinforce the effect of such agreements, including when such an agreement is elevated to the status of law. It is characteristic of such infringements that a public authority adopts a measure which leads to an infringement. Since the competition rules are not directed at public authorities, the CJ found it necessary to supplement Article 101 (formerly Article 81) with the provisions in Article 3(1)(g) and Article 10 of the Treaty establishing the European Community. Article 3(1)(g) provided for the adoption of a system ensuring that competition in the internal market is not distorted. Article 10 contained the 'loyalty principle' whereby the Member States were required to 'abstain from any measure which could jeopardise the attainment of the objectives of this Treaty'. Even though Article 3(1)(g) has not been carried forward in the new Treaties, the case law of the CJ is still applicable; see Protocol No 27 of the TEU and TFEU on the internal market and competition. The application of Article 101 to the acts of public bodies is dealt with in further detail in Chapter II.

8. These cases concerned sports organisations which laid down employment conditions for players and others in connection with taking part in professional sports.
9. The *Royal Pharmaceutical Society and Hünermund* cases concerned trade organisations in the pharmacy sector.
10. This also played a role in the first case in which the CJ laid down a true horizontal obligation relating to the rules on the free movement of workers, Case C-281/98, *Angonese,* even though it appeared to be only one of several decisive elements. However, the facts in the *Angonese* case are not characterised by concerning a trade organisation or similar, as in the other cases, but rather an 'ordinary' undertaking, in this case a bank, which did not have any regulatory powers over others.
11. On this, see *Ulla Bøegh Neergaard:* Competition & Competences.

3. The regulation of competition in the internal market

3.1. Secondary regulation

In addition to the Treaty rules on the establishment of the internal market, the measures of undertakings and public bodies which have implications for competition law are regulated by secondary regulation. This 'secondary regulation' covers rules primarily laid down in directives and regulations.

As established by different sets of rules, the Commission has the primary responsibility for and overall competencies in competition law. These competencies allow it to take decisions in respect of concrete infringements of the competition rules and give it the power to adopt directives and regulations with the aim of carrying out general regulation of certain competition law issues.

Secondary legislative acts are defined in more detail in Article 288 TFEU. Here directives are defined as binding on each Member State to which it is adressed, as to the result to be achieved, but it leaves to the national authorities the choice of form and methods. This means that it is necessary for the Member States to implement a directive in order for it to have effect in the national legal system. In the same provision a regulation is defined as having general application. Thus, they are binding in their entirety and directly applicable in all Member States.

The question of direct applicability arises in connection with the Treaty's provisions and non-implemented (or incorrectly implemented) directives and decisions. Where a directive is correctly implemented there is no need to consider direct applicability, as the directive will have been given its intended effect in the national legal system. For regulations, under Article 288 TFEU they are directly applicable, so they have direct effect on the persons to whom they are addressed. Regulations neither can nor may be implemented in national law; see the definition in Article 288.

Direct applicability refers to the circumstances where a provision entails rights for private persons (rights which naturally give rise to corresponding obligations on others), and these rights can be relied upon before the national courts.

For the Treaty provisions, direct applicability is achieved if 1) the provision contains clear and precise obligations, 2) there are no conditions or exceptions attached to the provision, and 3) the implementation of the provision is not dependent on implementing measures by the Member States or the institutions; see Case 26/62, *van Gend en Loos*. The same conditions apply to the provisions of directives, but with the addition of a further condition that the directive provision in question does not require horizontal effects, in other words effects between undertakings or private persons within the EU. This is particularly relevant in relation to the competition rules, as these are usually directed at undertakings in particular, and are therefore intended to establish obligations for them.[12]

On the other hand, there is no reservation to allowing public bodies to be bound in connection with the direct applicability of directive provisions. This can be relevant to the competition rules directed at public authorities and undertakings, for example rules on State aid, public undertakings and public procurement.

3.2. Other sources than regulation

Some of the most important sources of European competition law are the decisions of the Commission, of the General Court and the CJ. The Commission has built up a comprehensive body of decisions in relation to several of the provisions where the Commission is (was) given exclusive powers. These decisions naturally have considerable weight as sources of law, subject to the reservation that the General Court and CJ can review the Commission's decisions. The decisions of the General Court on competition law questions also have major importance as a source of law. However, the greatest importance is attached to the decisions of the CJ, as this is the ultimate authority on the interpretation of the provisions of the TFEU and of secondary legislation, naturally including competition law issues.

In addition to the provisions laid down in the Treaty and in secondary legislation, there are also a number of non-binding sources of law in the EU, referred to as 'soft law'. Even though they may be non-binding, these acts are not entirely without legal effect and in several contexts the CJ has stated that these acts have a significant contribution, in particular in connection with the interpretation of secondary law. Thus, in Case 322/88, *Grimaldi*, in paragraph 18, the CJ stated that soft law (in this case recommendations) 'cannot therefore be regarded as having no legal effect. The national courts are bound to take recommendations into consideration in order to decide disputes submitted to them, in particular where they cast light on the interpretation of national measures adopted in order to implement them or where they are designed to supplement binding Community provisions.'

12. Where the imposition of obligations on private undertakings will constitute a hindrance to a provision having direct applicability, a private undertaking's loss of rights will prevent allowing the provision having direct applicability; see for example Case 194/94, *CIA Securities*.

Examples of the significance of soft law in the field of competition law include the many notices on the application of Articles 101 and 102 TFEU, guidelines on the different elements of aids in the area of State aid, notices on the prohibition of negotiations in the area of public procurement, as well as notices on the central concepts in the area of merger control. For more information on these sources, see the respective chapters in this book.

4. Sources of information

Information about the various rules of competition law can be found on the EU's website (europa.eu). Among other things, this website contains a comprehensive database of all the legal acts which can be relevant to the different topics of competition law which are covered in this book. This gives access to the Official Journal, and to the various legal acts both at Treaty level and secondary legislation, as well as the documentation which is prepared with a view to the adoption of new legislative initiatives in this rapidly developing area.

There is also useful material on the Commission's website (ec.europa.eu) primarily under the heading of the Directorate General for Competition, but also the Directorate General for Internal Market and Services (concerning public procurement), as well as the Directorates General for Energy and Transport , and for Enterprise and Industry (concerning the liberalised sectors). The Commission's powers to take decisions are of decisive importance in several areas of competition law.[13] These decisions can be found on the Commission's website under the heading of the Directorate General for Competition, as well as under the classification for the area of competition which each decision concerns. Judgments on the topics covered in this book from the CJ and the General Court can be found on the CJ's website (curia.eu) under the headings of competition policy, rules for undertakings (tendering), and energy, the internal market, commercial policy and transport (the liberalised sectors), as well as State aid.

13. See the amended enforcement procedure for Articles 101 and 102 TFEU in Council Regulation (EC) No 1/2003, discussed in Chapter VII.

CHAPTER II

Introduction to Article 101

Karsten Engsig Sørensen

Bibliography: *Roger J. Van den Bergh & Peter D. Camessasca: European Competition Law and Economics: A Comparative Perspective, 2006; Jonathan Faull & Ali Nikpay (eds.): The EC Law of Competition, 2007; Joanna Goyder & Albertina Albors-Llorens: Goyder's EC Competition Law, 2009; Ulla B. Neergaard: Competition & Competences, 1998; Lennart Ritter & W. David Braun: European Competition Law: A Practitioner's Guide, 2004; Richard Whish: Competition Law, 2012.*

1. Introduction

Article 101(1) of the Treaty on the Functioning of the European Union (TFEU or 'Treaty') states: 'The following shall be prohibited as incompatible with the internal market: all agreements between undertakings, decisions by associations of undertakings and concerted practices which may affect trade between Member States and which have as their object or effect the prevention, restriction or distortion of competition within the internal market'.

This is often referred to as a prohibition on agreements in restraint of trade. In order for there to be a breach of Article 81(1) a number of conditions must be fulfilled:

1. There must be an agreement, decision by an association of undertakings or a concerted practice.
2. The agreement etc. must be entered into between undertakings.
3. The agreement must be capable of affecting trade between Member States.
4. There must be a restraint of competition (prevention, restriction or distortion of competition).

Each of these conditions will be discussed in detail in sections 2 to 5 below. If there is an infringement of Article 101(1), it is possible that the agreement may nevertheless be exempted. The agreement may contain a number of advantages for consumers or for technological or economic development which outweigh its negative effects on competition. The conditions for the exemption of agreements etc. are discussed in section 6, and in section 7 there is a discussion of the sanctions which are associated with an infringement of the provision.

The aim of the present chapter is to give a general introduction to Article 101. There is more detailed consideration of different kinds of agreements in the following Chapters III to V on vertical agreements, horizontal agreements and technology transfer agreements respectively. The details of the procedures for the enforcement of Articles 101 and 102 are dealt with in Chapter VII.

2. Agreements, decisions and concerted practices

As stated, Article 101(1) refers to agreements, decisions by associations of undertakings and concerted practices. There follows a discussion of each of these three kinds of arrangements. However, it is important to emphasise that this distinction is of more theoretical than practical legal significance.[1] By including these different arrangements, Article 101 sends out a signal that it is of broad application, as in principle it covers all forms of coordination of the conduct of a commercial undertaking. The problem can therefore be to determine where the lower limit lies for an agreement etc. to be covered by the provision.

There are no special legal consequences linked to whether an issue concerns an agreement, decision or coordinated practice, since they are all equally illegal if they lead to a restraint on competition. However, as will be seen in the following, there will often be different evidential problems associated with whether there is an agreement, decision or coordinated practice, as the last named in particular gives rise to problems of proof.

In addition to this, a distinction is often made between horizontal and vertical agreements, even though these concepts are not found in Article 101. While horizontal agreements are entered into between undertakings at the

1. Thus the Court of Justice of the European Union (CJ) has accepted that an arrangement can be characterised either as an agreement or as a concerted practice, without it being necessary to decide which it is.

same level of trade (for example, between two manufacturers), vertical agreements are entered into between two undertakings at different levels of trade (for example, and agreement between a manufacturer and a sole distributor). This distinction is quite important in practice, as competition law assessments of horizontal and vertical agreements differ because the two types of agreement lead to different risks of restriction of competition.[2] Therefore this distinction will also be used in the following two chapters. The distinction is less relevant in the present chapter which concentrates on a number of more general issues.[3]

2.1. Agreements

The definition of an 'agreement' covers both oral and written agreements. They do not have to satisfy any formal requirements which may be required under national law, for example notarisation, consideration or similar. Thus there is no requirement that the agreement should be legally binding. A so-called 'gentlemen's agreement' is enough.[4] Consequently there is no requirement that the agreement can be enforced, for example by reference to the courts or to arbitration, nor is it required that sanctions should be agreed.[5] Finally, the character or designation of an agreement is not important, so, for example, a settlement in court or a protocol will be covered by the definition.[6] The fact that an agreement is entered into as part of the formation of a company (articles of association, promoters' agreements, and shareholders' agreements) does not alter the fact that the agreement may be covered by Article 101. The reader is referred to sections 7 and 8 in Chapter IV for a review of the restrictions on competition that can arise in connection with joint ventures and cooperative companies.

2. Horizontal agreements will normally have greater potential for restricting competition than vertical agreements. In Joined cases 56 and 58/64, *Consten and Grundig,* the Italian government tried to argue that Article 101 only prohibited horizontal agreements, but this was rejected by the CJ.
3. However, as will be seen in section 5.3, the distinction is key in relation to Commission decisions.
4. Case 41/69, *ACF Chemiefarma,* para. 106 et seq.
5. Commission Decision 94/599/EC PVC (OJ 1994 L 239/14), para. 30.
6. See Case 65/86, Bayer AG, para. 15, which concerned a settlement in court entered into in connection with a case on the validity of a registered utility design, and Commission Decision 94/210/EC *HOV SVZ/MCN* (OJ 1994 L 104/34), para. 46, on a protocol entered into between a number of undertakings concerning the transport of shipping containers via railways.

If an agreement is terminated, the infringement of Article 101 will also normally be terminated. However, if the parties appear to continue their conduct unaltered, the fact that the agreement has not been legally renewed is not relevant. What is decisive is the economic effect of the agreement, while its legal form is, as stated, of subordinate importance.[7]

An agreement will therefore exist where undertakings adhere to a plan which limits or is likely to limit their individual commercial conduct because it lays down guidelines for their common activity or inactivity on a market.[8] If one is to determine where the lower limit lies for when an agreement exists, there must be the following conditions: 1) there must be a plan or an understanding, 2) entered into by at least two undertakings, and 3) voluntarily. In the following the last two conditions will be considered in particular.

The requirement that there must be at least two undertakings means that the unilateral conduct of an individual undertaking cannot be condemned under Article 101. Instead, it must be assessed under Article 102, if the undertaking has a dominant position. However, the practice of the Court of Justice of the European Union (CJ) shows that conduct which, on the face of it, appears to be unilateral can in fact be an expression of an agreement. For example, in one case the CJ has held that if an undertaking adds to its invoices a prohibition on its customers exporting the goods sold, this can constitute an agreement. Even if, from the point of view of contract law, the terms printed on an invoice did not constitute part of the contract, the CJ was of the view that this was the case, when the customers must be regarded as having given tacit acceptance of the terms. The CJ found that this tacit acceptance was, among other things, evidenced by the fact that the customers subsequently placed new orders on the same terms.[9] It follows that relatively little will be required for unilateral measures in trade between undertakings which have well-established and longstanding contractual dealings to be considered to be an agreement. The question how little has been referred to the CJ in a number of cases concerning the conduct of a manufacturer towards its distributors.

7. On this, see Case 243/83, *SA Binon,* para. 17.
8. See e.g. Commission Decision 1999/60/EC, *Pre-Insulated Pipe Cartel* (OJ 1999 L 24/1), para. 129.
9. On this, see Case C-277/87, *Sandoz.* For a comparison, see also Case 25/76, *Segoura,* where in its interpretation of the Convention on Jurisdiction and the Enforcement of Judgements in Civil and Commercial matters, the CJ also held that a clause concerning the choice of forum could be valid when one of the parties in a continuing relationship sent unilateral confirmation of the agreement and the other party did not object to it.

In Case 107/83, *AEG*, AEG had refused to authorise a number of dealers. The Commission believed that this was because the dealers in question could not be assumed to follow AEG's pricing policies. AEG argued that it was a unilateral action which was therefore not covered by Article 101. The CJ rejected this argument, as it was of the view that the refusals were a part of a contractual relationship which AEG maintained with its existing dealers. The existing dealers had agreed to AEG's pricing policy, and it was part of the agreements with them that AEG refused to authorise dealers who breached this pricing policy.[10]

There was a similar example in Joined cases 25 and 26/84, *Ford*, where Ford of Europe decided that it would no longer supply right-hand drive cars to its German dealers. Ford of Europe itself sold cars on the British market through a subsidiary company and it had found that there was considerable parallel importation of right-hand drive cars from the German dealers, because the cars were cheaper in Germany. The refusal to supply was thus based on the fact that Ford wanted to support its subsidiary so that in future British customers should either buy their cars direct from the subsidiary or from one of the British dealers. The CJ considered that this refusal to supply was covered by Article 101, because the decision to refuse to supply was part of the contractual relations between Ford and its dealers.

This practice seems to mean that nearly all the decisions of an undertaking about marketing and distribution can be considered part of the undertaking's agreement with its dealers. However, in Case T-41/96, *Bayer AG*, the General Court (GC) made it clear that the concept of an agreement cannot be stretched that far. In this case Bayer AG restricted the sale of a particular medicine to its distributors in France and Spain. The background to this was that the prices in the UK were considerably higher than in these two countries, so there had been widespread parallel importation from France and Spain to the UK. In its decision, the Commission had been of the view that this was an expression of the existence of an agreement, but the GC rejected this. The GC emphasised that an agreement assumes that the two parties have a concurrence of wills. For unilateral action to be considered an agreement, the Commission had to prove that there was an express or tacit agreement from the counterparties, in other words the distributors. The GC did not believe that such evidence existed. In particular, the GC rejected the argument that the

10. Case 107/82, *AEG*, paras. 38-39.

fact that the distributors subsequently continued to trade with Bayer AG was an expression of their agreement with Bayer's policy.[11]

With exchanges of information, the Commission takes the view that if an individual undertaking gives strategic information to its competitors, this can be a breach of Article 101. Thus there is not a requirement for a mutual exchange of information, nor is it necessary to prove that there is an underlying agreement that competitors should order their market activities according to the information. On the other hand, if an undertaking unilaterally publishes information, for example in a newspaper, it will not necessarily be assumed that there is a breach of Article 101.[12]

Even though there must be at least two undertakings involved in an agreement, there is not a requirement that both must adopt some specific commercial conduct, as it is sufficient for one of the parties to do so. There was an example of such a one-sided obligation in a decision where a Japanese producer of ball bearings had promised a number of French producers that it would raise its prices on the French market. Even though it was the only party which had accepted such an obligation, the aim of the agreement was to ensure that the prices of the Japanese ball bearings approximated to the price of the French-produced ball bearings, and thereby sought to end price competition.[13]

In order for there to be a concurrence of wills, it is a requirement that the undertakings must enter into an agreement voluntarily. The fact that an undertaking feels itself forced into an agreement because it would otherwise meet with various sanctions from other undertakings (refusal to supply etc.) is

11. Case T-41/96, *Bayer AG,* in particular paras. 173-174. The judgment has since been upheld by the CJ in Joined cases C-2/01 P and C-3/01 P, *Bundesverband der Arzneimittel-Importeure, eV.* See also Case T-208/01, *Volkswagen AG,* and Case C-74/04 P, *Volkswagen AG,* where the GC and the CJ likewise held that the Commission had not shown evidence that a unilateral action was an expression of an agreement. For a more detailed discussion of these cases see *Urs Wickihalder:* The Distinction Between an "Agreement" within the Meaning of Article 81(1) of the EC Treaty and Unilateral Conduct, European Competition Journal 2006 pp. 87-117; and *Oliver Black:* Agreement: Concurrence of Wills, or Offer and Acceptance?, European Competition Journal 2008 pp. 103-125.
12. Commission Communication – Guidelines on the applicability of Article 101 of the Treaty on the Functioning of the European Union to horizontal co-operation agreements (OJ 2011 C 11/1), paras 62-63.
13. Commission Decision 74/634/EEC, *Franco-Japanese ball-bearings agreement* (OJ 1974 L 343/19).

not sufficient for Article 101 not to apply. On the other hand, if the law in a Member State requires undertakings to adopt a certain conduct, Article 101 is not applicable. For example, this will be the case, if there are pricing regulations which lay down minimum prices which all must apply. If on the other hand the pricing regulations allow for competition to a certain extent, the undertakings have no excuse for not making use of the scope for competition.[14] The fact that the law makes it easier to enter into agreements to restrict competition, or perhaps makes it easier to enforce such agreements, does not mean that such agreements fall outside the scope of Article 101. This would require that the law gives undertakings no choice.[15]

In the above it is assumed that the Member State has issued regulations that are binding on the undertakings. However, in some cases it is difficult to determine whether a 'law' has been laid down by a legislator or by the undertakings themselves. This is the case where trading terms, in particular prices, are set by a body or an organisation in which the industry is represented. In order to determine whether undertakings infringe Article 101 by complying with such 'laws' it is necessary to determine whether the organisation is acting as a legislator or as an association of undertakings.

> This is illustrated by the judgment in Case T-513/93, *Consiglio Nazionale degli Spedizionieri Doganali (CNSD)*, where CNSD was a regional council that set tariffs for the payment of customs clearance in Italy. The council consisted of nine members, selected by ballot from among persons who carried on business as customs clearers. The council was empowered by law to set the tariffs, and the same law provided that these had to be applied. The Commission believed that, in issuing rules on minimum tariffs the council had infringed Article 101, as its rules were considered to be a decision by an association of undertakings. CNSD disputed this, arguing that it had the character of a public body and thus neither the council nor the customs clearers could be found to have contravened Article 101.
>
> The GC held that CNSD was not a public body and that therefore its decisions did not have the character of a decision of the state. The members of the CNSD were thus not required to take account of general interest when they set their tariffs, and the Italian Finance Minister could

14. Case 246/86, *Balasco;* and Commission Decision in Case COMP/C.38.281, *Raw Tobacco Italy* (OJ 2006 L 353/45), paras. 315-324.
15. Joined cases C-359/95 P and C-379/95 P, *Ladbroke Racing Ltd,* paras. 33-34.

not intervene as to who might be appointed to the council and had no supervisory powers. Next, the GC considered whether the fact that the council was empowered by law to set the tariffs meant that the members had not voluntarily set minimum tariffs. However the GC found that the law did not require a specific price level or price ceiling. It was therefore the council's own decision to provide for minimum prices, which in some cases involved a price increase of 400 %. The members therefore had room for manoeuvre and this room for manoeuvre had been used to restrict competition.

In those cases where a law requires or promotes conduct which restricts competition, the question then arises as to whether the Member State itself is in contravention of Article 101; see the discussion on this in section 3.2 below.

2.2. Decisions by associations

Instead of entering into an agreement, undertakings can coordinate their conduct by means of an association. Under Article 101(1), decisions by associations of undertakings are also prohibited. Not only will the undertakings which take part in the association be in breach of Article 101, but the association itself will be in breach of the provision.

The definition of 'decision' should be interpreted broadly. It can be a decision or a recommendation to the member undertakings about some specific conduct (pricing policy, uniform trading terms etc.), or it can be terms which are included in the articles of association of the association. On this basis, obligations to supply in the articles of association of a cooperative society can be contrary to Article 101; see the discussion in section 8 of Chapter IV. However, it is clear that an association will only incur liability for a breach of Article 101 where it has played a role in the adoption of the decision. It may be that it has taken initiatives to arrange meetings between undertakings, or that it has contributed to putting into practice what the undertakings have agreed.[16]

It is not a requirement that the association should itself be an undertaking with economic activities.[17] It can therefore be a trade organisation which coordinates the members' activities. However, it is a condition that it is not a body which is in fact a public authority. If this is the case, and if its articles of

16. Joined cases T-25/95 and others, *Cimenteries CBR,* para. 1326.
17. Joined cases T-25/95 and others, *Cimenteries CBR,* para. 1320; and Case T-193/02, *Piau,* para. 71.

association have the character of legislation, Article 101 will not apply; see Case T-513/93, *CNSD*, discussed in the preceding section.[18] What is decisive is not the legal status of the body, but whether its tasks are of an economic character or whether they are merely in the nature of the exercise of public authority. The fact that an organisation has public authority in certain areas does not mean that its decisions in other areas fall outside the scope of Article 101.

2.3. Concerted practice

The CJ has defined a concerted practice as a form of coordination between undertakings, which, without having been taken to the stage where an agreement properly so-called has been concluded, knowingly substitutes for the risks of competition, practical cooperation between them.[19] The aim of introducing the concept of concerted practice was to prevent undertakings getting round the competition rules by, instead of entering into an agreement, implementing a less formal cooperation which restricts competition by, for example, informing each other in advance of the policy they intend to follow, well-knowing that the competitor will act in the same way.[20]

A concerted practice requires that the undertakings involved have the intention of coordinating their commercial conduct. This subjective requirement means that it is not enough that is can be shown that a number of undertakings have parallel conduct, for example by implementing similar price increases at the same time. Parallel conduct can have many other explanations, for example that one undertaking acts as the price leader, or that there is an oligopolistic market where it is natural that the undertakings should follow the same commercial policy. On this basis the CJ has annulled decisions where the Commission has not proved that a concerted practice was the only probable explanation for parallel conduct.[21] Parallel conduct can thus raise an assumption that there is a concerted practice, but the Commission must sup-

18. See further Case C-309/99, *Wouters,* which concerned the question of whether the Dutch Bar Association was an association of undertakings or a public authority. In Case C-519/04 P, *Meca-Medina,* the CJ held that the anti-doping rules issued by the International Olympic Committee fell outside the scope of Article 101. Even though the IOC is arguably an undertaking, the CJ found that the rules fell outside the scope of Article 101(1), to the extent that the rules were limited to what was necessary to ensure the proper conduct of competitive sport; see para. 47.
19. Joined cases 40/73 and others, *Suiker Unie,* para. 26.
20. Commission Decision 1999/60/EC, *Pre-Insulated Pipe Cartel* (OJ 1999 L 24/1), para. 130.
21. Joined cases C-89/85 and others, *Ahlström (Cellulose II),* para. 126.

port this assumption, for example by showing evidence that the parties have met, that they have exchanged competitively sensitive information etc.[22] If the Commission succeeds in finding evidence which indicates that there is a concerted practice, it is then up to the undertakings to show that there is not a concerted practice. Thus, cases on concerted practices are often highly complex and extensive from a purely evidential point of view.[23]

> Case 172/80, *Züchner*, illustrates the problem of evidence. The CJ laid down some guidelines for how national courts should assess whether there is a concerted practice. The background to the case was that a bank's customer had refused to pay a fee in connection with a transfer of money from a German bank to a bank in Italy. The fee was 0.15 % of the amount transferred. The customer claimed that this fee was set on the basis of a concerted practice between banks, contrary to Article 101, and could therefore not be demanded. The banks did not deny that the same fee was charged, but denied that there was an agreement or concerted practice. The CJ found that if the uniform fee was due to a concerted practice, it was a restraint on competition because it hindered price competition for that type of service. It was up to the referring court to decide whether there was a concerted practice, and in doing so it had to consider: 1) whether there were contacts between the banks conducting themselves in a like manner or, at least, exchanges of information on, for example, the rate of the charges actually imposed for comparable transfers or charges planned in the future, 2) whether, with regard to the conditions of the market in question, the rate of charge uniformly imposed was no different from that which would have resulted from free competition, 3) that consideration must also be given to the number and importance in the market of the banks participating in such a practice, and 4) the volume of transfers on

22. For further on when an exchange of information can most clearly be a concerted practice contrary to Article 101, see Commission Communication – Guidelines on the applicability of Article 101 of the Treaty on the Functioning of the European Union to horizontal co-operation agreements (OJ 2011 C 11/1), paras 55-104. However, it should be emphasised that not all forms of exchange of information are contrary to Article 101, see in more detail in Chapter IV, section 3.3.
23. See Joanna *Goyder & Albertina Albors-Llorens:* Goyder's EC Competition Law, 5th ed., 2009 pp. 88-96; and *Lennart Ritter & W. David Braun:* European Competition Law: A Practitioner's Guide, 2004 pp. 107-110.

which the charge in question is imposed compared with the total volume of cross-border transfers made by the banks.[24]

Apart from showing that the undertakings intended to coordinate their conduct, it must also be proved that the concerted practice has resulted in a given conduct on the market. It is also necessary to show that there is a causal link between the concerted practice and the conduct.[25] Previously the GC had adopted an interpretation according to which it was not necessary to prove that the concerted practice had led to specific conduct, as it was sufficient for there to be an infringement of Article 101 that there was an intention to restrict competition, see the word 'object' and the discussion in section 5.2 below. However, the CJ was of the view that the definition of 'concerted practice' also requires that it is possible to point to conduct. This conduct need not necessarily have restrictive effects on competition, so that an 'unsuccessful' concerted practice will also contravene Article 101.[26] Normally this condition will not present a problem in practice, as the starting point for an investigation into whether a concerted practice exists will normally be that parallel conduct has been found to exist, so that if it is possible to show that it is due to a concerted practice, both conditions will have been satisfied.

In order to find that an undertaking has contravened Article 101, evidence must be given to show that the individual undertaking has taken part in a concerted practice. While in the case of an agreement there will seldom be doubt about who is a party, in some cases it can be difficult to prove which undertakings have been sufficiently involved so as to be found to have taken part in a concerted practice. If the Commission is successful in showing that an undertaking has participated in the meetings and other activities that have led to the concerted practice, the burden of proof shifts to the undertakings to prove that they are not part of a concerted practice.[27] This means that it is not necessary to prove that the undertaking's conduct shows that it has joined a concerted practice, since passive participation in meetings etc. will be sufficient

24. Case 172/80, *Züchner,* para. 21.
25. Case C-49/92 P, *Anic,* para. 118. However, if an undertaking remains active in the market, there is an assumption that it is participating in the concerted practice; see Case C-8/08, *T-Mobile Netherlands.*
26. Case C-49/92 P, *Anic,* para. 124.
27. Joined cases T-25/95 and others, *Cimenteries CBR, paras. 1353 and 1389, and Case C-49/92 P, Anic,* para. 96. According to the CJ's statements in the succeeding paragraphs in the latter case, the Commission must also prove that the concerted practice has resulted in some specific conduct by the individual undertaking; see the condition discussed in the preceding paragraph.

in practice. If it is proved that an undertaking is part of a concerted practice, it is assumed that it participates in the whole of the concerted practice.[28] This means that it is not necessary to prove that an undertaking has been present at all meetings and thereby supported all the aspects of the concerted practice.

A concerted practice will often have the characteristics of horizontal cooperation, in other words cooperation between competitors. Many of the cases are concerned with situations where competitors coordinate their prices or agree on market sharing. However, there is nothing to prevent a concerted practice being established between undertakings at different levels of trade, for example between a manufacturer and its distributors.[29]

The Commission will often refrain from deciding whether a concerted practice has in fact amounted to an agreement. Instead, it will merely state that there is an agreement and/or a concerted practice. Since there is no great need to establish whether it is the one or the other, the CJ has accepted this practice.[30]

3. Between undertakings

The requirement that an agreement shall have been entered into 'between undertakings' ensures that the scope of application of Article 101 differs from provisions that are directed at single undertakings. In addition, it means that the exercise of authority is not, in principle, covered by the provision.

3.1. The definition of an 'undertaking'

The CJ has defined an undertaking as encompassing every entity engaged in an economic activity, regardless of the legal status of the entity and the way in which it is financed.[31] Consequently, both undertakings carried on by natural persons and undertakings carried on by legal persons are covered by the definition. This applies regardless of the form of company chosen. Furthermore, foundations or organisations which do not, in principle, have the pur-

28. The Commission has thus developed a practice where it holds the individual undertaking liable for the cartel as a whole, and the courts have accepted that an undertaking can be held liable for the whole, even if it has only taken part in certain aspects of the cartel; see Joined cases T-305/94 and others, *Limburgse Vinyl Maatschappij,* paras. 773-774.
29. Commission Decision 80/256/EEC, *Pioneer* (OJ 1980 L 60/21), paras. 79-80.
30. Case C-49/92 P, *Anic,* para. 132.
31. Case C-41/90, *Höfner,* para. 21. It appears from this paragraph that the CJ uses the same definition for both Articles 101 and 102.

pose of carrying on an undertaking will be covered, provided that they do in fact carry on an undertaking.[32] Likewise, public undertakings and authorities will be covered by Article 101, if they carry on an economic undertaking; see the next section.

The CJ has defined an undertaking as a unitary organization of personal, tangible and intangible elements which pursues a specific economic aim on a long-term basis.[33] This makes it clear that there must be certain resources present for there to be an undertaking, but the requirement is clearly not very great.

In principle it does not matter what kind of commercial activity is carried on. Article 101 covers undertakings that produce or sell goods, and undertakings that provide services.[34] The liberal professions are also covered by Article 101, and the fact that some professions are regulated and possibly subject to authorisation does not mean that they fall outside the scope of the provision. However, there are some sectors of the economy that are only covered by the competition rules to a certain extent, including agriculture and transport.[35]

Since undertakings carried on by sole entrepreneurs are covered by Article 101, it is necessary to define when a person is an independent self-employed person and when they are an employee. An employee is characterised by the fact that they are subject to the directions of an employer, and they do not normally share in the commercial risk involved in the economic activity.[36] To

32. Thus the international football association, FIFA, was found to be covered by Article 101, to the extent that it sold package tours in connection with the World Cup in 1990; see Commission Decision 92/521/EEC, *Distribution of package tours during the 1990 World Cup* (OJ 1992 L 326/31).
33. Case T-11/89, *Shell International Chemical Company,* para. 311.
34. If an organisation buys goods, it is the economic or non-economic nature of their subsequent use which determines whether the organisation is to be considered an undertaking. The CJ has held that the Spanish public health authorities are not an undertaking, even though they naturally buy many products which are used in the hospital sector; see C-205/03 P, *Federación Española de Empresas de Tecnología Sanitaria (FENIN),* para. 26.
35. *Peter Roth & Vivien Rose (eds.):* Bellamy & Child: European Community Law of Competition, 6th ed., 2008 pp. 1071-1098 and 172-180. See also Chapter XI on the liberalised sectors.
36. See Case C-22/98, *Bécu,* para. 26 as well as the discussion in *Victoria Louri:* ‘Undertaking’ as a Juristictional Element for the Application of EC Competition Rules, Legal issues of Economic Integration 2002 pp. 143-176 (especially pp. 149-151). The paragraph referred to also refers to the definition of ‘workers’ which the CJ has developed in relation to Article 45 TFEU.

the extent that it represents workers, a trade union will also not be an undertaking, and the collective agreements which are entered into on the labour market will therefore, in principle, not be evaluated under Article 101.[37]

As stated above, the legal form of an undertaking is not decisive. The CJ has stressed this by establishing that several persons and companies can constitute one undertaking. The concept of an undertaking in competition law focuses on whether there is a single economic entity. Among other things, this means that a person who controls two companies can constitute an undertaking together with their companies.[38] In addition to this, in many cases a parent company and its subsidiaries can constitute one undertaking. This is important in practice as it means that agreements which are entered into between companies in the same corporate group are typically not covered by Article 101.

> This was established in, among others, Case C-73/95 P, *Viho Europe*. A parent company, Parker Pen UK, had required its subsidiaries only to sell the company's products in the territories allocated to them. Viho complained to the Commission that this practice prevented it from buying from the subsidiary company that offered the best prices. The Commission rejected the complaint, as it believed that such agreements between parent companies and their subsidiaries fell outside the scope of Article 101, and it was this decision that Viho brought before the GC, and subsequently before the CJ. The CJ found that Parker's subsidiaries in Europe were wholly owned subsidiaries, and their sales and marketing activities were led by an area team that was appointed by the parent company, and which controlled the sales targets, gross margins, sales costs, cash flows and stocks. On this basis, the CJ found that the companies constituted 'a single economic unit within which the subsidiaries do not enjoy real autonomy in determining their course of action in the market, but carry out the instructions issued to them by the parent company controlling them'.[39]

37. Case C-67/96, *Albany International;* Case C-115-117/97, *Brentjens;* and Case C-219/97, *Maatschappij Drijvende Bokken BV,* on supplementary pensions agreed in connection with collective agreements in the Netherlands.
38. Case 170/83, *Hydrotherm,* para. 11.
39. Case C-73/95 P, *Viho Europe BV,* para. 16. In line with this, see Case C-30/87, Bodson, para. 19, and Case 66/86, *Ahmed Saeed Flugreisen,* para. 35. Hitherto, it has been assumed that the joint control which is established over a joint venture will not normally be so extensive that joint ventures would be considered as part of the participating undertakings (joint venture partners); see e.g. Commission Decision 91/335/EEC, *Gosme/Martell – DMP* (OJ 1991 L 185/23), para. 30. However, in Case

Therefore, the conclusion was that the situation was not covered by Article 101.

These arguments mean that where a parent company takes the most important decisions concerning a subsidiary, the parent and subsidiary will be considered one undertaking. Thus, every internal agreement, direction etc. will fall outside the scope of Article 101. An earlier judgment gave the impression that this exemption only applied where there was an internal division of tasks within the corporate group, but it must be assumed to be immaterial what kind of agreement is involved.[40] If, conversely, a parent company has allowed its subsidiaries a certain measure of independence, there is a risk that the parent and subsidiaries will be considered as separate undertakings, so that Article 101 will apply. This is an unsatisfactory state of law for several reasons. First, it is not clear when a subsidiary attains a sufficient degree of independence for it to constitute a separate undertaking, and second, the competition rules will act as an incentive for parent companies to exercise control over their subsidiaries. A consistent application of this approach would also mean that where a division of a company is effectively managed by its own divisional management, it too ought to be considered a separate undertaking. This would seem very difficult to enforce in practice.[41]

In the *Viho* case it was an advantage for the companies to argue that they were part of the same undertaking, as the internal agreement thereby fell outside the scope of Article 101(1), but in other cases it could be a disadvantage. In some cases parent companies seek to deny that they should be liable for the anti-competitive conduct of their subsidiaries. When the amount of a fine is set, it is a disadvantage to be part of a larger economic unit, as the fine is often set as a proportion of the turnover of the undertaking. In these cases the CJ has established a practice in which there is a presumption that a parent

T-314/01, *Avebe,* the GC held that a joint venture that is controlled by two undertakings is to be considered as part of the joint venture partners' undertakings. The judgment thereby puts in question whether it is relevant to assess whether competition between the joint venture company and the joint venture partners is restricted; see the further discussion in Chapter IV, section 7.3.

40. In line with this, see *Jens Fejø:* EU-konkurrenceret, 2009 pp. 87-88.

41. For a more detailed discussion of these arguments *Wouter P.J. Wils:* The undertaking as subject of E.C. competition law and the imputation of infringements to natural or legal persons, European Law Review 2000 pp. 99-116 (in particular pp. 106-108).

company has active control over a 100 % owned subsidiary. This presumption can be rebutted, but it is up to the parent company to do so.[42]

The concept if a single economic unit will also mean that an agent will typically have a dependent relation to its principal, and will be a part of the latter's undertaking.[43]

3.2. The exercise of public authority and public undertakings

The definition of an undertaking covers any economic entity, regardless of its legal status. On this basis it is not surprising that undertakings that are publicly owned or which are carried on in the public sector are covered by Article 101. This principle is also emphasised in Article 106 TFEU; see Chapter X.

Conversely, it is also clear that activities that are connected with the exercise of public authority are not covered by Article 101. However, it is not always easy to determine whether an activity is the exercise of authority or an undertaking. If there is an activity, such as an employment agency, which is often also carried out by private undertakings, it is not difficult to establish that there is an undertaking.[44] In other cases it is difficult to decide, and here, according to the CJ, it is necessary to take an overall view of whether, according to their nature, purpose and the rules to which they are subject, the activities are associated with the exercise of such public authority.

> On this basis, the CJ has established that the activities of Eurocontrol in relation to civil aviation cannot be considered an undertaking. On behalf of a number of countries, Eurocontrol collects route fees that are imposed on users of air space over the countries in question. It is the individual country which sets the amount of the fees; Eurocontrol collects these on behalf of the individual country and receives a proportion of the revenue. Eurocontrol is financed by contributions from the countries which set it up, and the organisation carries out its activities on behalf of these countries. According to the CJ, Eurocontrol carries out these tasks in the

42. Case C-286/98 P, *Stora Kopparbergs Bergslags,* para. 29; GCCase T-314/01, *Avebe,* para. 136; and Case C-97/08 P, *Akzo Nobel v Commission,* para. 63. Recently the CJ had the opportunity to emphasise that it is not impossible to rebut a presumption; see Case C-521/09 P, *Elf Aquitaine,* paras. 51-72. For a critical assessment of this presumptive rule, see *Laura La Rocca:* The controversial issue of the parent-company liability for the violation of EC competition rules by the subsidiary, European Competition Law 2011 pp. 68-76.
43. On this, see among others *Richard Whish:* Competition Law, 2012 pp. 621-623; and the comments in Chapter III, section 4.1 below.
44. Case C-42/90, *Höfner,* para. 22; and Case C-55/96, *Job Centre coop,* para. 22.

public interest, with the aim of contributing to the maintenance and improvement of the safety of air transport. Taking an overall view of the nature, purpose and rules to which it was subject, the CJ found that the organisation's undertaking was associated with policing air space, and that this is typically a task of the public authorities.[45]

In a number of cases the CJ has also had to assess whether a social insurance arrangement was an undertaking. In these cases the CJ has made a distinction between whether membership of an arrangement is voluntary or obligatory, as the fact that it is a voluntary scheme is an indication that there is an undertaking. In addition, the CJ has put emphasis on whether an arrangement is based on the solidarity principle or the capitalisation principle, as in the latter case there is an indication that there is an undertaking. Finally, it depends on whether the overall purpose of a scheme is a social function and whether the arrangement is subject to state control.[46]

If it is found that an activity is an exercise of public authority, it is not covered by Article 101, even if private undertakings carry out the activity.[47] In some cases it can be difficult to determine whether or not an undertaking has taken on a task of a public authority. For example, this will be the case where an association has been given authority to set the prices for a particular activity or product. It will only be the exercise of public authority if the task is car-

45. Case C-364/92, *Eurocontrol,* paras. 19-30. In Case T-155/04, *SELEX,* the General Court found that in one area (technical assistance for national administrations) Eurocontrol carried on economic activities which could be assessed pursuant to Article 102 TFEU. However, the CJ overruled this conclusion on the grounds that the activities were closely linked to Eurocontrol's activity of technical standardisation; see Case C-113/07 P, *SELEX.* Also, see Case C-309/99, *Wouters,* where the CJ did not find that the Dutch Bar Association carried out activities which, on an overall assessment, could be said to be linked to the exercise of the powers of a public authority. See also Case C-82/01 P, *Aéroports de Paris,* where the CJ held that a public body that provides airport facilities for airlines, for the payment of fees which it set itself, was an undertaking.
46. See in more detail Joined cases C-159-160/91, *Poucet;* Case C-244/94, *FFSA;* Joined cases C-264/01 and others, *AOK Bundesverband;* and Case C-350/07, *Kattner Stahlbau.*
47. See e.g. Case C-343/95, *Diego Cali,* which concerned a private undertaking which had a concession from the harbour authorities in Genoa to carry out environmental monitoring.

ried out for the purposes of the general interest and typically under public control and supervision.[48]

When a Member State exercises public authority, it must to a certain extent observe Article 101. The CJ has thus established that it is contrary to a Member State's obligations under Article 4(3) and Article 101 TFEU for it to adopt rules which require or favour the adoption of agreements which are contrary to Article 101, or to reinforce the effects of such agreements.[49]

> In Case C-2/91, *Meng*, the CJ had to decide whether a German law which prohibited an insurance intermediary from surrendering commission on health insurance was contrary to the Articles 10 and 81 (now Article 4(3) and Article 101 TFEU). The facts of the case were that in a number of instances Meng had surrendered the commission which he had received from an insurance company in connection with the writing of health insurance policies. However, Meng could not be found to have infringed the law if it was contrary to Article 4(3) and Article 101. By way of introduction, the CJ found that it would be contrary to these provisions if a Member State adopted or maintained measures, including laws, which could annul the intended effects of the competition rules. This means that a Member State is prevented from either requiring or favouring agreements in contravention of Article 101, or reinforcing the effects of such agreements. However, in the case at hand it was found that the German rules neither required nor favoured the entry into unlawful agreements by insurance intermediaries, since the prohibition laid down was sufficient in itself (in other words it was not necessary to enter into any agreement). Nor did the CJ find that the law reinforced any agreement in restraint of competition, since there was no agreement prior to the provisions of the law. Rules can only be regarded has having a reinforcing effect on an existing agreement if 'they simply reproduce the elements of

48. On this, see Case T-513/93, CNSD (summarised above in section 2.1); and Case C-185/91, *Reiff.*
49. Case 267/86, *Van Eycke,* para. 16; Case C-250/03, *Mauri,* para. 30; and Joined cases T-94/04 and T-202/04, *Cipolla,* para. 47. See also *Ulla B. Neergaard:* Competition & Competences, 1998. However, more recently the CJ has had the opportunity to reject a more extensive interpretation which would use Article 101 to challenge, e.g., rules on opening hours and prohibitions of marketing; see Case C-446/05 *Doulamis;* and Case C-393/08, *Sbarigia.*

an agreement, decision or concerted practice between economic agents in that sector.'[50]

In addition to this, a Member State could contravene the provisions referred to if it has delegated legislative competence to a private undertaking, without ensuring that, in exercising such competence, the undertaking promotes general interest and not its own interests. There are several examples where Member States have left it to associations of undertakings to set minimum prices, with the result that the Member States have been found to contravene Article 4(3) and Article 101 TFEU.[51]

If a Member State contravenes the Treaty in this way, it will incur a liability to pay compensation to the undertakings that have suffered loss as a result of agreements in restraint of competition. This follows from the general liability of Member States to pay compensation for qualifying infringements of their obligations under the Treaty.[52]

4. The effect on trade in the EU

4.1. The requirement for an effect on trade between Member States

As discussed in Chapter 1, the competition rules have the aim of ensuring the completion of the internal market. This aim can be seen, among other things, in the requirement in Article 101 that trade between Member States shall be affected, since the aim of the internal market is to remove hindrances to cross-border activities. However, the standard set for this condition to be fulfilled is not particularly high.

In 2004 the Commission issued a Notice on the effect on trade concept contained in Articles 101 and 102 of the Treaty.[53] In this Notice, the Commission points out that the conditions focus on three elements in particular.

First, trade between Member States must be affected. This means that cross-border activities between at least two Member States must be affected. The effect can be on trade in goods or in services, or it can be an effect of the

50. Case C-2/91, *Meng*, para. 19.
51. Case T-513/93, *CNSD* (summarised above in section 2.1); and Case C-185/91, *Reiff*.
52. On the liability to pay compensation for infringements of Articles 81 and 82, see *Malin Thunström, Johan Carle & Stefan Perván Lindeborg:* State Liability Under the EC Treaty Arising From Anti-Competitive State Measures, World Competition 2002 pp. 515-528.
53. Commission Notice – Guidelines on the effect on trade concept contained in Articles 81 and 82 of the Treaty (OJ 2004 C 101/81).

right of establishment in other Member States. If undertakings from different Member States enter into an agreement, the condition will often be satisfied. Also, even if they are undertakings located in the same Member State, trade can be affected if the agreement has the effect of making it more difficult for undertakings from other Member States to gain access to the market.[54]

Second, there is a requirement that the agreement etc. 'may affect' trade. The CJ has established that it is sufficient if it can be shown that it is probable that an agreement, directly or indirectly, actually or potentially, can have an influence on trade between Member States.[55] Thus it is not necessary to prove that cross-border trade is actually affected, as it is sufficient to show that it is probable that an agreement has such an effect or could have it. Even if it is shown that trade has increased, it is possible that the CJ will find that trade is affected, if trade could have increased even more without the agreement. Even an agreement that increases trade can affect trade, for example by channelling it through specific undertakings.[56] Even where trade does not yet exist for certain products, an agreement could hinder trade if it prevents trade taking place at a later date.[57] Finally, it is possible that products that are not traded are ingredients in products that are traded, so that a restriction on trade in the former will have an effect on trade in the latter.[58]

Finally, as the *third* element, there must be an assessment of whether the effect on trade is appreciable. In its Notice, the Commission states generally that Article 101 does not apply to agreements where the parties do not have a cumulative share of any market of over 5 %, and where the annual turnover of the products covered by the agreement does not exceed EUR 40 million.[59] This limit supplements the requirement for appreciability formulated in the Commission's *De minimis* Notice; see section 5.3 below.

54. Case 246/86, *Belasco;* and Joined cases C-295/04 to C-298/04, *Manfredi,* para. 45.
55. Case 56/65, *Société Technique Minière.* This formulation was later used again by the CJ in Case 8/74, *Dassonville,* in connection with the interpretation of the meaning of 'quantitative restrictions' in Article 34 TFEU.
56. Joined cases 56 and 58/64, *Consten and Grundig;* and Commission Notice – Guidelines on the effect on trade concept contained in Articles 81 and 82 of the Treaty (OJ 2004 C 101/81), para. 34.
57. Case 19/77, *Miller*, para. 14.
58. Joined cases C-89/85 and others, *Ahlström (Cellulose II),* para. 142.
59. Commission Notice – Guidelines on the effect on trade concept contained in Articles 81 and 82 of the Treaty (OJ 2004 C 101/81), para. 52. For vertical agreements the threshold is whether the supplier of the products covered by the agreement has a turnover in the EU of over EUR 40 million.

4.2. The international extent of Article 101

The purpose of Article 101 is to ensure that competition within the EU is not restricted, and consequently a restriction on competition that arises in a third country will not be covered by the provision. However, this is not to say that agreements that regulate trade with a third country and agreements between undertakings located in a third country cannot be covered by the provision.

First, an agreement which restricts the import of goods from a third country to the EU can clearly affect competition within the EU, as such import restrictions can have a direct effect on the goods offered in the EU.[60] It is less obvious that agreements on exports to third countries can affect trade within the EU. However, it is possible that if in connection with their exports to third countries, undertakings located in the EU include a requirement that the goods may not be re-exported back to the EU, this could have an effect on trade between Member States. This would probably require the export to the third country to be of a certain extent and that the competition on the product market in question in the EU is not optimal.[61]

Article 101 will also be applicable where one or more of the parties to an agreement is located in a third country. If one or more of undertakings located in a third country has subsidiaries or branches in the EU, it follows from the definition of an undertaking discussed in section 3.1 above that its branches or subsidiaries will be part of the same undertaking, and will therefore have a presence in the EU so that it is clearly covered by Article 101. Even if an agreement is entered into between undertakings that do not have a physical presence in the EU, the agreement will be covered by Article 101 if it is intended to regulate the competitive behaviour of undertakings within the EU.

> This follows from the CJ's judgment in Joined cases 89/85 and others, *Ahlström (Cellulose II)*. This case concerned a number of producers of cellulose, all located in third countries. They had coordinated their prices applicable to sales in the EU, and the Commission decided that they were thereby in breach of Article 101. The undertakings disputed the decision, as they argued that the Commission was wrong with regard to the territorial extent of Article 101, and that the Commission's application of Article 101 was contrary to public international law.

60. Case 51/75, *EMI.*
61. Case C-306/96, *Javico;* and Joined cases 29/83 and 30/83, *CRAM.*

The CJ stated that an infringement of Article 101 involved conduct with two elements, namely the formation of a cartel, and its implementation. If the application of Article 101 were dependent on the place where the cartel was formed, undertakings would easily be able to avoid the prohibition under Article 101, as they would merely have to enter into an agreement in a third country. What must therefore be decisive is where the cartel is put into practice.[62] In the case before the CJ, the undertakings had put their price cartel into practice in the EU, and it was therefore covered by Article 101. It was of subordinate importance that they had used subsidiaries, agents or branches established in the EU in order to put the cartel into practice. In other words, undertakings that do not have established representatives in the EU are covered by Article 101, provided that they are part of a cartel which is implemented in the EU. Finally, the CJ stated that such an application of the Union's competence must be regarded as being protected by the principle of territoriality, and there was therefore no conflict with public international law.

5. Restriction on competition

There will be a breach of Article 101 where an agreement has the object or effect of preventing, restricting or distorting competition within the Union. In the following chapters there will be a discussion of when a restriction on competition will be found to exist in relation to different types of agreement. But an overall assessment of whether a restriction on competition exists must be made on the basis of an evaluation of how competition would evolve if the agreement with its alleged restrictions on competition did not exist, or if the

62. The judgment was later confirmed by the General Court in Case T-395/94 *Atlantic Container* v *Commission* (TAA Agreement). The Commission has also applied it, for example in Decision of 25 June 2008 relating to a proceeding under Article 81 of the EC Treaty and Article 53 of the EEA Agreement (Case COMP/39.180 – Aluminium fluoride) (OJ 2011 C 40/22), para. 101. The effect doctrine has also been used as a basic choice of law rule in relation to certain choice of law issues arising in connection with competition law cases, for example claims for compensation. See further Regulation (EC) No 864/2007 of the European Parliament and of the Council of 11 July 2007 on the law applicable to non-contractual obligations (Rome II), Article 6(3), which is discussed in *Peter Mankowski:* Das neue Internationale Kartellrecht des Art. 6 Abs. 3 der Rom II-Verordnung, Recht der Internationalen Wirtschaft 2008 pp. 177-193.

terms in the agreement which restrict competition did not exist.[63] The evaluation must include consideration of the probable effects of the agreement on inter-brand competition (i.e. between suppliers of competing brands) and intra-brand competition (i.e. between distributors of the same brand).[64] In addition to this, the following more general considerations apply to when a restriction on competition may be found to exist.

5.1. Workable competition

Competition law is one of the areas of law in which economics has achieved greatest influence. Economic theory influences what conduct ought to be prohibited by competition rules at the overall level, and it is also acknowledged that economic theory is increasingly taken into account in the assessment of concrete competition cases.

In order to evaluate the effects of different agreements or different kinds of conduct on competition, economic theory starts from the basis of different market models. This means that, among other things, the existing market situation is compared with extreme market models: perfect competition and monopolies.[65] A monopoly describes a situation where one undertaking has the whole market, and where there are thus no competitors. Perfect competition describes the situation where there are numerous smaller undertakings on the market and these undertakings trade in a number of products which do not significantly differ from one another with regard to price, quality etc. Traditionally, perfect competition has been regarded as the optimal situation. However, it is clear that perfect competition is not a realistic goal on most markets, and the aim of legislation must therefore be based on some other ideal of competition than perfect competition. In this connection a competitive situation referred to as *workable competition* (a standard which is less strict than perfect competition and is sometimes referred to as 'effective competition') is preferred. The CJ has defined workable competition as the situation where there is 'the degree of competition necessary to ensure the ob-

63. See Case T-328/03, *O2*, where the GC set aside the Commission's decision because the Commission's decision did not include a consideration of what the competitive situation would have been if the agreement had not existed.
64. See also Commission Notice – Guidelines on the effect on trade concept contained in Article 81(3) of the Treaty (OJ 2004 C 101/97), para. 17.
65. See among others, *Doris Hildebrand:* The Role of Economic Analysis in the EC Competition Rules, 3rd ed., 2009; *Simon Bishop & Mike Walker:* The Economics of EC Competition Law: Concepts, Application and Measurement, 3rd ed., 2010; and *Roger J. Van den Bergh & Peter D. Camessasca:* European Competition Law and Economics: A Comparative Perspective, 2nd ed., 2006.

servance of the basic requirements and the attainment of the objectives of the treaty, in particular the creation of a single market achieving conditions similar to those of a domestic market.'[66]

Normally mainstream economists set a target for economic effectiveness, understood as an effective social economic use of resources. Certain parts of economic theory also point towards other goals such as consumer welfare and the protection of the economic freedom of market participants. It is not entirely clear what economic theory is used in the EU. However, as will appear from the analysis of the practice of the Commission and the CJ in the individual areas, consideration for consumers often plays a key role. In addition to this, a number of other considerations are normally taken into account in the economic theories, including consideration for the internal market and for the aims of the EU's industrial policy.[67]

5.2. 'Which have as their object or effect ...'

An infringement of Article 101 can occur both in cases where an agreement has a direct aim of restricting competition, and in cases where it is not the intention of the agreement, but where this is nevertheless the effect of the agreement.[68]

The wording means that where an agreement clearly has the aim, for example, of fixing prices between the parties to the agreement, this will be covered by the prohibition. To assess whether the intention of an agreement is to restrict competition, it is necessary to consider the content of the agreement and its objective purpose. It can also be necessary to investigate the context in which the agreement applies, as well as investigate the actual conduct of the parties on the market. Depending on the circumstances, conduct which restricts competition can be inferred from the way in which the agreement is implemented in practice.[69] However, it is emphasised that where it is clear that the agreement has a restrictive purpose, it is not necessary to consider the

66. Case 26/76, *Metro,* para. 20.
67. Commission Notice – Guidelines on the effect on trade concept contained in Article 81(3) of the Treaty (OJ 2004 C 101/97), para. 13.
68. Case C-219/95 P, *Ferriere Nord,* where the wording of the Italian translation was assessed by the CJ. In the Italian version 'or' was replaced by 'and'. The CJ stated that the provision applies either when the restriction on competition is the aim of an agreement or when it is the effect of an agreement.
69. Commission Notice – Guidelines on the effect on trade concept contained in Article 81(3) of the Treaty (OJ 2004 C 101/97), para. 22.

practical effects of the agreement.[70] Thus it is not necessary for an agreement to have been put into practice.

If an agreement is intended to restrict competition, it is not relevant that it also seeks to achieve other lawful purposes. These lawful purposes will not be given any weight when assessing whether there is a breach of Article 101(1), but they can be relevant for determining whether there is a basis for an exemption pursuant to Article 101(3).[71]

If an agreement does not have an aim of restricting competition, there must be an investigation of whether it has the effect of restricting competition. Here there must be consideration both of its actual and potential effects. There is no assumption that an agreement has restrictive effects of competition, so it must be established with a reasonable degree of certainty that the agreement can be expected to have a negative effect on prices, production, innovation, variety of goods offered or product quality on the market in question.[72]

5.3. The Commission's *De minimis* Notice

Article 101(1) does not apply if the deleterious effects on competition are found to be insignificant. The requirement for there to be an appreciable restriction was first established in the *Völk* case.[73]

Subsequently the condition that there should be an appreciable restriction was followed up by several notices from the Commission which have all specified precisely when it can be assumed that there is such a significant effect that the prohibition in Article 101 could come into play. These notices have popularly been called the '*De minimis* notices' and are in the nature of soft law. The current *De minimis* notice is from 2001.[74] It can be assumed

70. Commission Notice – Guidelines on the effect on trade concept contained in Article 81(3) of the Treaty (OJ 2004 C 101/97), para. 20. However, this does not prevent the Commission finding that there is such an effect if it exists; see e.g. Commission Decision of 1 October 2008 in Case COMP/C.39181 – Candle Waxes (OJ 2009 C 295/17), para. 304; and Commission Decision of 8 December 2010 in Case COMP/39309 – LCD (OJ 2011 C 295/8), para. 304.
71. See Case C-209/07, Competition Authority v Beef Industry Development Society, para. 21
72. Commission Notice – Guidelines on the effect on trade concept contained in Article 81(3) of the Treaty (OJ 2004 C 101/97), para. 24.
73. Case 5/69, *Völk v Vervaecke.*
74. Commission Notice on agreements of minor importance which do not appreciably restrict competition under Article 81(1) of the Treaty establishing the European Community (*de minimis*) (OJ 2001 C 368/13).

that the Commission feels an obligation not to depart from the guidelines in connection with its decisions. Thus it is expected that the Commission will not initiate proceedings against undertakings on the basis of agreements which lie below the *de minimis* thresholds. Furthermore, the Commission will not impose fines on the basis of agreements which are below the *de minimis* thresholds. On the other hand it is quite clear that neither the GC nor the CJ are bound by the notices in their application of Article 101.[75]

The principle is that horizontal agreements between undertakings (at the same level of trade) which represent a combined market share of less than 10 % will not be caught by Article 101(1).[76] For vertical agreements (between undertakings at different levels of trade) the critical threshold is a market share of 15 %. Where an agreement cannot be classified as either horizontal or vertical, it will be assessed according to the guidelines for horizontal agreements and thus must not concern a market share of more than 10 % of the relevant market.

There are specific modifications to these general guidelines as to when an agreement is considered as being covered by the prohibition in Article 101(1). *First*, the threshold values do not apply where several agreements have been entered into concerning the same issue between different suppliers or distributors (parallel networks of agreement). In these cases the critical threshold is reduced to 5 %. At the same time it is assumed that if such a parallel network has a combined market share of less than 30 %, the cumulative effects of these agreements will not result in a foreclosure effect on the market in question.[77] Second, the threshold values do not apply to agreements which contain certain serious restrictions (hardcore restrictions). These hardcore restrictions are listed in paragraph 11 and cover restrictions in both horizontal and vertical agreements. For horizontal agreements these include a

75. See para. 6 of the *De minimis* notice. It seems that in many cases the courts draw on the Commission's notices in their interpretation of the competition rules. Furthermore, in certain circumstances the principle of legitimate expectation will mean that it would be difficult to depart from a notice if it has given rise to an expectation by undertakings that their agreements would fall outside the scope of Article 101(1).
76. The assessment of market share is based on a definition of the relevant product market and relevant geographic market. The general guidelines for this (which apply to both Articles 101 and 102) are to be found in Commission Notice on the definition of relevant market for the purposes of Community competition law (OJ 1997 C 372/5). The establishment of the relevant market is dealt with in more detail in Chapter VI, section 3.2 (on Article 102) and Chapter VIII, section 3 (merger control).
77. Para. 8 of the *De minimis* Notice.

prohibition on fixing prices for sales to third parties or for allocating markets or customers. In relation to vertical agreements there are certain restrictions concerning conditions on active and passive sales, cross-deliveries and sales of components.

There is great similarity between the prohibitions of 'hardcore' conditions in, for example, Regulation (EC) No 330/2010 on vertical agreements, Article 4 and the conditions which are disallowed under paragraph 11 of the *De Minimis* Notice concerning conditions in agreements between non-competing undertakings (vertical agreements). Similarly, there is great similarity between the prohibited 'hardcore' conditions for block exemptions for horizontal agreements (for example, exemptions for categories of specialisation agreements (Regulation (EC) No 1218/2010), and research and development agreements (Regulation (EC) No 1217/2010)) and the prohibited conditions in agreements between competing undertakings (horizontal agreements), as these are listed in paragraph 11 of the *De minimis* Notice.

5.4. Rule of reason

In American antitrust practice there is a prohibition against agreements in restraint of competition corresponding to the prohibition in Article 101(1). In applying this prohibition the American courts have developed two different tests known as the *per se* test and the rule of reason test.[78] A *per se* application of the competition rules means that attention is paid solely to the character of the agreement in question, and on that basis it is decided whether there is an infringement of the prohibition. This test is applied to agreements where there is an obvious risk that they restrict competition. By contrast, in the application of the rule of reason, an infringement test is not established before an evaluation has been made between the negative effects for competition of the agreement, and any positive effects. If in connection with a rule of reason assessment the positive effects are shown to outweigh the negative effects, the agreement or conduct will not be covered by the prohibition.

In principle, rule of reason assessments are not possible under Article 101 TFEU.[79] However, there have been some cases where the CJ appears to have applied a test which has certain similarities to the rule of reason test. Several of these cases are linked to the practice on ancillary restraints which are dis-

78. For a more detailed review of the American practice, the early Community law practice and the concepts in general, see *Jens Fejø*: Monopoly law and market, 1990 Chapters IV and V.

79. The GC has stated this in Case T-112/99, *Métropole Télévision (M6),* para. 72; and Case T-328/03, *O2*, para. 69.

cussed in the next section, but as will be seen there, this practice is not identical to a rule of reason assessment.[80]

The principal reason why the rule of reason test is rejected is the structure of the European rules. Article 101 is structured with the prohibition in the paragraph 1 and with possible exemptions in paragraph 3. In connection with an examination of a case, the negative effect of an agreement is assessed under paragraph 1, and any positive effect of an agreement is assessed under paragraph 3. This splits up the two assessments (positive and negative) while under the rule of reason test they are assessed simultaneously. If the rule of reason test model were to be used in connection with Article 101(1), then Article 101(3) would lose part of its importance.[81]

In the American system the corresponding prohibition on the formation of cartels is structured differently so there are no exemptions linked to it. In such a situation there is naturally a need to be able to ease the application of the prohibition in connection with those agreements that have clear advantages and which need not necessarily be prohibited.

Against the background of the reform of the competition rules and their implementation, see Regulation (EC) No 1/2003, it could be argued that the future application of Article 101 will have a high degree of similarity to the rule of reason model. Hitherto the Commission has had sole competence to grant exemptions from the prohibition in Article 101(1); see Regulation (EEC) 17/62. Since it has not been possible for others than the Commission to grant an exemption it has not been possible to make an overall assessment, as required by the rule of reason assessment. Under the new rules, assessments of whether the conditions for an exemption under Article 101(3) are

80. However, it has previously been argued that the practice on ancillary restraints effectively introduces a rule of reason assessment; see *Richard Whish & Brenda Suffrin:* Article 85 and the Rule of Reason, Yearbook of European Law 1987 pp. 1-38. The judgment of the GC in Case T-112/99, *Métropole Télévision (M6),* seems to disprove this, since the GC both clearly rejected a rule of reason assessment while simultaneously applying the practice on ancillary restraints.

81. In the legal writing written in English, the CJ's judgment in Case 120/78, *Cassis de Dijon*, is referred to as an expression of 'rule of reason'. The Treaty system is that the existence of an import restriction is established under Article 34 TFEU, and thereafter there is consideration of whether it is justified under Article 36 TFEU. However, in *Cassis de Dijon* the CJ introduced a test for non-discriminatory import restrictions which means that, as part of deciding whether Article 34 TFEU has been contravened, an assessment is made of whether the restrictions can be justified by mandatory requirements, and thus there are many parallels with the rule of reason test which is used in American competition law.

met are left to the undertakings themselves. Thus, undertakings must themselves evaluate both whether they are covered by the prohibition, and whether the conditions for exemption are satisfied. This assessment will be made simultaneously, so there will effectively be a rule of reason assessment.[82]

5.5. Ancillary restraints

The Commission and the courts have developed a practice whereby conditions which restrict competition and which are part of a transaction which is not restricting on competition are not assessed individually, provided they are part of an agreement that is otherwise lawful. This assessment is distinguished from an assessment under Article 101(3) (and from a rule of reason assessment) by not including a weighing of the elements which promote competition against the elements which restrict competition.[83]

The background to the doctrine on ancillary restraints is found in American competition law, where the courts have developed a practice on ancillary restraints under which terms of agreements that are part of a lawful cooperation are not assessed individually, but as part of the cooperation.[84] From the mid 1970s the Commission used similar arguments to limit the scope of application of Article 101.

> One of the earliest decisions was Commission Decision 76/743/EEC, *Reuter/BASF*, where the Commission had to consider the legality of a non-competition clause which had been agreed in a transfer agreement, whereby Gottfried Reuter had disposed of his undertaking. Reuter had committed himself not to carry on a competing undertaking for a period of 8 years after signing the agreement. Reuter had himself drawn the attention of the Commission to the non-competition clause, as he hoped to be released from it. The Commission established that the transfer of the

82. For a similar argument see *James Venit:* Brave new world: The modernization and decentralization of enforcement under Articles 81 and 82 of the EC Treaty, Common Market Law Review 2003 p. 577.
83. Commission Notice – Guidelines on the effect on trade concept contained in Article 81(3) of the Treaty (OJ 2004 C 101/97), para. 30.
84. The concept was introduced by Judge Taft in the decision in *United States* v *Addyston Pipe & Steel Co.,* 85 F.271 (6th Cir. 1898) and 175 U.S. 211 (1899), where he stated, among other things, that 'no conventional restraint of trade can be enforced unless the covenant embodying it is merely ancillary to the main purpose of a lawful contract, and necessary to protect the covenantee in the full enjoyment of the legitimate fruits of the contract, or to protect him from the dangers of an unjust use of those fruits by the other party'; see 85 F p. 282.

undertaking not only included the physical assets, but also goodwill and know-how, and the latter constituted a significant part of the value of the transfer. The Commission did not believe that Article 101 was applicable if the non-competition clause was necessary in order to ensure the value of the transferred undertaking. In the actual case the Commission found that, in order to ensure that Reuter did not attract his old customer base to him immediately after the transfer, it was necessary to prevent him from competing. Since Reuter had comprehensive information about the undertaking sold, he would be an especially dangerous competitor, and this too favoured Reuter being prevented from competing. In this situation, Article 101 could not be applied to the non-competition clause 'in such cases, since it would make more difficult or even impossible transactions which are generally recognized as legitimate.'[85] However, the Commission emphasised that the prohibition on competition must not go further than necessary for protecting the value of the transferred undertaking, and the prohibition must be limited geographically and substantially to the markets where the undertaking operated prior to the transfer or where, on the basis of the evidence of significant investment, it must be considered a possible competitor. On this basis the Commission rejected the non-competition clause in the case in question, as being too extensive on a number of points.

Furthermore, in Commission Decision 90/410/EEC, *Elopak/Metal Box – Odin*, the Commission found that Article 85 [now Article 101 TFEU] did not apply to a number of terms restricting competition agreed in connection with the setting up of the joint venture Odin, as it noted that 'Since such provisions cannot be disassociated from the creation of Odin without undermining its existence and purpose, and since the creation of Odin does not fall within the scope of Article 85(1), these specific provisions also fall outside the scope of Article 85(1).'[86]

The CJ has since had to consider a number of cases on ancillary restraints. In Case 42/84, *Remia BV and others*, it confirmed that a non-competition clause which a vendor accepts in connection with the transfer of an undertaking can fall outside the scope of Article 101. The CJ emphasised that there should be an examination of how the competitive situation would be without such a

85. Commission Decision 76/743/EEC, *Reuter/BASF* (OJ L 254/40), Part II.3(a).
86. Commission Decision 90/410/EEC, *Elopak/Metal Box – Odin* (OJ 1990 L 209/15), para. 36.

clause. Since it could not be assumed that the transfer would be carried out if the vendor were free to compete, such a clause ensured that a transfer was possible and effective. As long as such clauses did not go further than was necessary for the transfer to take place, they fell outside the scope of Article 101(1).[87]

These cases confirm that ancillary restraints that are linked to the transfer of an undertaking or a joint venture are not covered by Article 101. However, the case law suggests that the practice on ancillary restraints is not only relevant in connection with agreements and transactions which involve structural changes, such as mergers and joint ventures. The practice seems to have a more general application, so that it includes terms which are a necessary part of an otherwise lawful agreement which does not constitute a restriction on competition. Such a broader application of the practice on ancillary restraints can be seen confirmed in, among others, Case 161/84, *Pronuptia de Paris*, and Case 250/92, *Gøttrup-Klim* v *Dansk Landbrugs Grovvareselskaber*, where the CJ accepted that certain terms which restricted competition were necessary in connection with a franchise agreement and a purchasing cooperative agreement respectively.[88] In these cases there was no enduring structural change to justify terms restricting trade falling outside the scope of Article 101. Nevertheless the CJ accepted that the terms did fall outside the scope of Article 101.

In order for the doctrine on ancillary restraints to apply, the restraint in question must be necessary for the (lawful) agreement with which it is connected and it must be proportional. These conditions will be fulfilled if it is concluded, from objective factors, that it would be difficult or impossible to perform the agreement or activity without the restraint in question.[89]

87. Case 42/84, *Remia BV and others,* paras. 18-20.
88. Case 161/84, *Pronuptia de Paris GmbH,* paras. 15-26; and Case C-250/92, *Gøttrup-Klim* v *Dansk Landbrugs Grovvareselskab,* para. 35. In Case C-519/04 P, *Meca-Medina,* the CJ concluded that the IOC doping rules were not contrary to Article 101(1) to the extent that the rules were limited to what was necessary to ensure the proper conduct of sporting competition and the restrictions under the rules were limited to what was necessary for the attainment of this purpose. See also Case T-112/99, *Métropole Télévision (M6),* where the GC confirmed a broad application of the doctrine on ancillary restraints.
89. Commission Notice – Guidelines on the effect on trade concept contained in Article 81(3) of the Treaty (OJ 2004 C 101/97), para. 31.

6. Possible exemptions under Article 101(3)

As seen in the preceding section, Article 101(1) contains a broad prohibition that catches many forms of agreements which restrict competition. There is therefore also a need to exclude agreements which, even if in principle they restrict competition, have more positive than negative effects from an overall perspective. This can be done either by making an individual assessment of whether there is a basis for an exemption under Article 101(3), or by considering whether the agreement falls under one of the block exemption regulations which exclude certain kinds of agreement, given that they do not contain certain conditions, and given that they do not exceed some stated thresholds for market shares.

6.1. Change to the notification procedure

Previously it was possible to have individual agreements exempted after notification to the Commission. Because of the comprehensive procedure which had to be initiated in connection with each exemption case, the Commission prepared some informal procedures so that undertakings could get a quicker response. These informal 'comfort letters' could inform an undertaking that the Commission did not regard a notified agreement to be contrary to Article 101(1).

Under Regulation (EC) No 1/2003, the notification system which had previously been a cornerstone of Union competition law was abandoned. The change meant that it was no longer possible for undertakings to notify agreements to achieve an individual exemption. Thereafter, undertakings must themselves assess whether they are covered by the prohibition under Article 101(1) and, if so, they must then assess for themselves whether the conditions in Article 101(3) are fulfilled so the agreement is exempted from the prohibition. Thus there is no requirement for a stamp of approval from the Commission before an agreement can be exempt.

The procedure for the enforcement of Article 101 is discussed in more detail in Chapter VII.

6.2. Individual exemptions – the four conditions

According to Article 101(3), it is possible to obtain an individual exemption if four conditions are fulfilled. These take the form of two positive and two negative conditions. The two positive conditions (i.e. circumstances that *must* be present) are:

1. The agreement must contribute to improving the production or distribution of goods or services etc., or promoting technical or economic progress.
2. The agreement must allow consumers a fair share of the resulting benefits.

The two negative conditions (i.e. circumstances which *must not* be present) are:

3. The agreement must not impose on the undertakings concerned restrictions which are not indispensable to the attainment of these objectives.
4. The agreements must not afford such undertakings the possibility of eliminating competition in respect of a substantial part of the products in question

The requirements that must be fulfilled before an agreement can be exempted from the prohibition in Article 101(1) were not changed by the reform of the notification procedure by Regulation (EC) No 1/2003. The conditions in Article 101(3) are cumulative, so that all must be satisfied before exemption can be obtained. It is clear that the assessment of whether the conditions have been fulfilled leaves a wide discretion. Where this discretion is exercised by the Commission or by the national competition authorities, it must be assumed that it can be subjected to a limited judicial review.[90]

90. Since, according to the GC, this involves complex economic facts, the judicial review of the legal evaluation of the factual circumstances is limited to an examination of whether the Commission's decision is a manifest error of assessment; see Case T-17/93, *Matra Hachette v Commission,* para. 104. However, the judgments of the GC in Joined cases T-185/00 and others, *Métropole Télévision (M6),* and Case T-168/01, *GlaxoSmithKline Services,* show that it does not refrain from making an examination of the Commission's assessment and setting aside an exemption if the Commission's assessment is clearly wrong. Following the entry into force of Regulation (EC) No 1/2003 in May 2004, the national authorities and courts of the Member States have had the possibility of applying Article 101(3), and therefore the Commission has most recently argued that the provision is not so discretionary and the result of such decentralised application of it will not be widely differing practice; on this see *Hans Gilliams:* Modernisation: from policy to practice, European Law Review 2003 pp. 451-474 (in particular p. 458). The fact that the Commission has issued a notice on the application of Article 101(3); see above in the text, should be seen as an attempt to establish a framework for the discretionary elements in Article 101(3), so that the exercise of discretion does not lead to the Member States developing widely differing approaches to exemptions.

In 2004 the Commission issued a more comprehensive Notice on the application of Article 101(3).[91] This Notice lays down a set of analytical frameworks for evaluating the four conditions, and it also contains a number of comments on each condition.

The *first condition* for obtaining an exemption is that the agreement should contribute to improving the effectiveness of the production or distribution of goods or services etc., or promoting technical or economic progress. For example, this could be an agreement between undertakings whereby they allocate the production of goods between them so that each concentrates on one area in which they specialise. The Commission has also had a positive approach to joint ventures as, among other things, it has found that joint ventures can contribute to the fulfilment of a number of general economic goals, including the integration of the internal market, the promotion of risk-bearing investments and innovation, the opening of new markets, and the improvement of the competitiveness of industry, not least among small and medium sized enterprises.

In its Notice, the Commission lays down some general principles for evaluating this condition. First, only objective advantages are taken into consideration, so there must be evidence of all improvements in effectiveness, so they can be tested. It should not only be possible to test the nature of the improvements, but also that there is a sufficient causal connection between the agreement and the improvements claimed.[92]

There can be different kinds of efficiency gains. For example, there can be cost savings which can be achieved through the development of new technology and production methods. Cost savings can also be made by the effects of synergy, or by two undertakings deciding to combine their production so as to gain economies of scale.

In addition to this there can be efficiency gains in the form of improved quality. The obvious example of this is agreements on joint research and development (R&D) which can result in new or improved products which the

91. Commission Notice – Guidelines on the effect on trade concept contained in Article 81(3) of the Treaty (OJ 2004 C 101/97). For a more in depth discussion of this see *Lars Kjølbye:* The New Commission Guidelines on the Application of Article 81(3): An economic approach to Article 81, European Competition Law Review 2004 pp. 566-577; and *Paul Lugard & Leigh Hancher:* Honey, I Shrunk the Article! A Critical Assessment of the Commission's Notice on Article 81(3) of the EC Treaty, European Competition Law Review 2004 pp. 410-420.
92. Commission Notice – Guidelines on the effect on trade concept contained in Article 81(3) of the Treaty (OJ 2004 C 101/97), paras. 51-52.

undertakings involved would not been able to develop individually. Qualitative efficiency gains can also be achieved by introducing more effective means of distribution.

The *second condition* for obtaining an exemption under Article 101(3) is that consumers should obtain a fair share of the benefits from the efficiency gains achieved as a result of the first condition. The requirement that consumers should get a fair share of the benefits can be seen as a sign that the agreement gives certain benefits to society, whereby one of the aims of the competition rules can also be achieved – see section 5.1 in this chapter.

There seems to be a requirement that, for the parties to an agreement to allow a reasonable share of the improvements to go to consumers, there must be a certain measure of competition in the market. If there is not such competition, whereby consumers can switch to another product if their chosen product becomes more expensive, there will not be a motivation for the undertakings to reduce prices. Where there is no such competition, it is nevertheless possible that the parties will prefer to reduce prices, in order to prevent the agreement being found invalid.

The advantage which consumers are to obtain can be expressed in various ways, for example, by lower prices, better quality, greater choice etc. The practice of the Commission suggests that there are not very high evidential requirements for showing that this condition is fulfilled, as the Commission seems to assume that the requirements will normally be satisfied where there is sufficient competition.[93]

The *third condition* means that it must be shown that the negative effects of an agreement on competition must not be unreasonable in relation to the contribution of the agreement to economic or technological progress.[94] However, in practice it can be very difficult to make such an assessment, as there are no tools for deciding how the advantages and disadvantages should be weighed, both individually and especially in relation to each other. Therefore this area is left to the wide discretion of the Commission and the other competition authorities which will in future assess whether the conditions for an exemption are fulfilled.[95] Commission Notice – Guidelines on the effect on trade concept contained in Article 81(3) [now Article 101(3)] of the Treaty

93. Commission Decision 91/301/EEC, *Ansac* (OJ 1991 L 152/54), paras. 29-30, is one of the rare examples of where the Commission did not find the condition was fulfilled.
94. Case T 17/93, *Matra Hachette v Commission,* para. 135.
95. On this see the comments of *John Temple Lang in Barry E. Hawk (ed.):* Fordham Corporate Law Institute, 2000 pp. 420-421.

(2004) does give certain guidelines for the exercise of this discretion, though without limiting it significantly.

The Notice states that it is not just the agreement as such which, reasonably enough, must achieve the effectivity gains, this also applies to the individual terms of the agreement.[96] This means that, for an agreement or a joint venture, first there must be an assessment of whether there is an alternative to the agreement/joint venture, and if it is not possible to point to such alternative, there must be an evaluation of whether the individual terms in the agreement/joint venture go further than is necessary.

The CJ has confirmed that it can be relevant to assess whether a joint venture is strictly necessary to enable the companies which set it up to enter a market.[97] This will not be the case where some of the joint venture partners could have carried out the joint venture activity on their own. This means that the assessment of the third condition can result in a conclusion that an agreement or a joint venture is unnecessary, since some other form of cooperation could lead to more or less the same effectivity gains. The consequence of this is that, when entering into their cooperation agreement, the undertakings involved must make a corresponding assessment of the alternatives to the proposed agreement or joint venture. It is clear that such an assessment can be difficult for the parties, but it must be even more difficult for the competition authorities to assess whether such an alternative is a realistic possibility. For this reason one may expect a certain reticence on this point, and this is confirmed by a reading of the Notice on the application of Article 101(3). It is stated in paragraph 75 of the Commission Notice that undertakings invoking the benefit of Article 101(3) are not required to consider hypothetical or theoretical alternatives, as the Commission will not second-guess the business judgement of the parties. The Commission will only intervene where it is reasonably clear that there are realistic and attainable alternatives.

The *fourth condition* is that it does not give the undertakings the possibility of eliminating competition in respect of a substantial part of the products in question. This assessment is based on, among other things, the market structure, the number of competitors and their size etc. This condition is closely linked to the question of abuse of dominant position. If there is no competition on the market it will be difficult for the undertakings to show that

96. Commission Notice – Guidelines on the effect on trade concept contained in Article 81(3) of the Treaty (OJ 2004 C 101/97), para. 73.
97. Case T-17/93, *Matra Hachette* v *Commission,* para. 138.

it is probable that the advantages of the agreement in question will outweigh the disadvantages.

6.3. Block exemptions

The block exemption system was established by Regulation No 19/65/EEC, and was later developed by several other authorising regulations.[98] The reason why the block exemption system was introduced was that the Commission could already see in the early 1960s that Regulation (EEC) 17/62 and the system introduced with that Regulation, with a requirement for notification to the Commission in order to obtain an exemption from Article 101(1), led to an impossibly large number of notifications, far exceeding the Commission's resources to deal with it.[99] At the same time, it was recognised that certain categories of agreements had so many advantageous effects, and so few harmful ones, that it was possible to set up an arrangement whereby all agreements within a certain category were exempted, without having to be notified to the Commission. Today the block exemptions play an important role in the EU system of competition law.

The most important block exemptions are all dealt with in this book. On block exemptions for vertical agreements, see Chapter III. On block exemptions that primarily concern horizontal agreements (agreements on specialisation, research and development) see Chapter IV. And for technology transfer agreements, see Chapter V.

7. The consequences of infringement

Chapter VII contains a more detailed description of the procedure for enforcing Articles 101 and 102, as well as the consequences of infringing these provisions. For this reason, the following comments will only illustrate some of the special consequences of infringing Article 101.

The primary consequence of an infringement of Article 101 is the invalidity of the agreement, and a fine is also normally imposed. In addition, in connection with the finding of an infringement of Article 101(1), a number of conditions can be imposed on the parties to ensure that the infringement is brought to an end, and it is also possible that the parties to an agreement can be required to pay compensation.

98. See, among others, Regulation (EEC) No 2821/71 on research and development, and Regulation (EEC) No 1534/91 on the insurance sector.
99. See the White Paper of 5 December 1999 on modernisation of the rules implementing Articles 85 and 86 of the EC Treaty, para. 25.

7.1. Invalidity

The immediate consequence of an infringement of Article 101 is that the agreement is considered invalid, in other words, it has no legal effect. The effect of invalidity does not require it to be shown that Article 101(1) has been infringed, as the invalidity applies retrospectively *(ex tunc)*. In principle, it is only those parts of an agreement that contain restrictions on competition that are affected by the invalidity. However, if it is not possible to separate the invalid terms from the rest of the agreement, the whole agreement will be invalid.[100]

The parties to an agreement which was covered by Article 101(1), but which fulfilled the conditions for exemption under Article 101(3) could previously not claim that the agreement was valid before the Commission had exempted the agreement. Since the introduction of Regulation (EC) No 1/2003, the situation is such that an agreement which fulfils the conditions in Article 101(3) will be valid, without requiring authorisation from the competent authority; see Article 1 of the Regulation.

The effect of invalidity applies in full to the relationship between the undertakings that are party to the agreement. This means that they cannot rely on the invalid agreements or conditions, and they cannot be enforced. The question whether the effects of invalidity also affect third parties is decided under national law. For example, if a joint venture agreement is declared invalid, it is clear that this can have wide-ranging consequences for third parties, such as the customers and creditors of the joint venture.[101] In principle the formation of a company can be invalidated if the formation of the company is contrary to Article 101(1).[102]

Article 101(1) has direct effect, which means that the provision may be relied upon in proceedings against an undertaking before the national courts.[103] In relation to a cartel or a joint venture, a third party who believes that the cartel or joint venture contravenes Article 101, for example because the third party undertaking is excluded from participation, can bring the question be-

100. Case C-234/89, *Delimitis,* para. 40.
101. For more detail, see *Anders Ryssdal;* Joint ventures – en konkurranserettslig analyse, 2003 pp. 309-314. However, see differently *Caroline Heide-Jørgensen* et al.: Konkurrenceretten i EU, 2009 p. 152 , where it is suggested that invalidity can also affect third parties, which can also not rely on the agreement.
102. In the case of a limited company, the effects of invalidity must be implemented in accordance with Article 12 of the First Company Law Directive (Directive 68/151/ EEC, OJ 1968 L 65/8), which requires that companies which have been invalidly formed should be liquidated by means of compulsory winding up.
103. Case 127/73, *BRT*, para. 16.

fore the national courts. A case can also be brought by one of the undertakings which is a party to the agreement if it believes that the agreement entered into is contrary to Article 101, so that it cannot be enforced between the parties. This means that in certain situations a party that wants to get out of a disadvantageous cooperation or wishes to be released from some disadvantageous terms in the agreement which forms the basis of the cooperation can do so by reference to Article 101. However, the question whether an agreement infringes Article 101 can also be raised by the national courts themselves in a case before them which concerns such cooperation.[104]

In practice, in many agreements there will be an arbitration clause, and the arbitration clause can provide that the arbitrator shall not observe the competition rules. This can be agreed between the parties to the agreement because they are aware that their agreement cannot stand up to a close examination under competition law, or because they want to avoid the uncertainty associated with such an examination. If, on the basis such a provision, an arbitrator chooses not to deal with the question of whether an agreement is contrary to Article 101, then according to the CJ, this question can be brought before the national courts which will be able to try an arbitration decision on the grounds of public policy.[105] Thus, an arbitration agreement cannot always prevent one of the parties to an agreement relying on Article 101.

7.2. Remedies and commitments

According to Article 7 of Regulation (EC) No 1/2003, in connection with bringing an infringement to an end, the Commission may impose behavioural or structural remedies on the undertakings involved. 'Behavioural remedies'

104. It depends on national law, whether there is an obligation to apply these provisions automatically, but to the extent that a national court does have a duty to enforce certain national rules automatically, the corresponding duty applies in relation to Articles 101 and 102; see Joined cases C-430/93 and C-431/93, *Van Schijndel,* para. 18. Under Regulation (EC) No 1/2003, Article 3, 'Where the competition authorities of the Member States or national courts apply national competition law to agreements ... they shall also apply Article 81 of the Treaty to such agreements.'
105. Case C-126/97, *Eco Swiss China Time v Benetton International,* para. 37. In the following paragraph the CJ stated that Article 101 is a public policy provision so it is not against the New York Convention of 10 June 1958 on the Recognition and Enforcement of Foreign Arbitral Awards, to refrain from recognising an arbitration award that has failed to apply Article 101. The judgment and its consequences are analysed in more detail in *Alison Jones & Daniel Beard:* Co-Contractors, Damages and Article 81: The ECJ Finally Speaks, European Competition Law Review 2002 pp. 246-256.

refers to conditions which require an undertaking to conduct its business in a particular way. 'Structural remedies' means that an undertaking is required to change its structure, for example, by returning it to what it was prior to entering into the unlawful agreement.[106] It is stated that structural remedies can only be imposed where there is no equally effective behavioural remedy. The possibility of imposing structural remedies as under Article 7 of the Regulation is new, and it is thus too early to evaluate how this will work in practice.

According to Article 9 of the Regulation, the Commission also has the possibility of making binding a commitment by an undertaking in connection with a finding that Article 101(1) has been infringed. It is the undertaking itself that offers the commitment in connection with the Commission's evaluation of the case, and if the Commission finds that the commitment is sufficient to remove its concerns, it can make the commitment binding on the undertaking.

7.3. Fines and compensation

In the new Regulation (EC) No 1/2003, there are more detailed rules on the possibility of imposing fines for infringements of Article 101 (and 102). The detailed rules on the calculation of fines and the possibility of exemptions or reductions are discussed in Chapter VII.

The question of compensation for breaches of Union competition law is not regulated in Union law. The questions of when compensation may be payable, what conditions must be fulfilled, and how it is calculated are thus questions which are determined under national law. However, there are certain requirements that must be fulfilled in connection with obtaining compensation on the basis of infringements of Union competition rules due to the general principle in Union law that the Member States must ensure the imposition of effective sanctions for infringements of Union law.[107] In Article 101 cases the question of compensation will normally arise in relation to third parties who are injured by the effects of the agreement which restricts competition, for example, because they have paid too much for their goods or perhaps have been excluded from the market. In principle it is also possible that one party to an agreement could seek compensation from the other parties to the agreement. However, if the party seeking compensation has gone into the agreement with open eyes, it is hard to imagine that the conditions for obtain-

106. Recital 12 in Regulation (EC) No 1/2003.

107. See in more detail *Paul Craig & Gráinne de Burca:* EU Law. Text, Cases and Materials, 5th ed., 2011 pp. 218-241.

ing compensation will exist. Nevertheless, the CJ has held that national law may not entirely exclude the possibility of compensation in cases where one party does not bear a significant responsibility for the distortion of competition. In assessing this it is necessary to focus on the economic and legal contexts of the parties, as well as their respective negotiating positions. If, accordingly, a party is in a clearly subordinate position in relation to the other party or parties, it may be possible for the subordinate party to obtain compensation.[108]

108. Case C-453/99, *Courage* v *Crehan,* paras. 31-33. See similarly Joined casea C-295-298/04, *Manfredi.* The judgments and their consequences are analysed by *Alison Jones & Daniel Beard:* Co-Contractors, Damages and Article 81: The ECJ Finally Speaks, European Competition Law Review 2002 p. 246 et seq.; *Paolisa Nebbia:* Damages actions for the infringement of EC competition law: compensation or deterrence?, European Law Review 2008 pp. 23-43; and by *Erling Hjelmeng:* Privat håndhævelse av EØS-avtalens konkurranseregler, 2003.

CHAPTER III

Vertical agreements

Bent Iversen

Bibliography: *Christopher Bellamy & Graham Child: European Community Law of Competition, 2007-2012; D.G. Goyder: EC Competition Law, 2003; Valentine Korah & Warwick A. Rothnie: Exclusive Distribution and the EEC Competition Rules, 1992; Valentine Korah & Denis O'Sullivan: Distribution Agreements under the EC Competition Rules, 2002: Mendelsohn & Rose: Distribution Agreements under the EU Competition Rules, 2002; Richard Whish: Competition Law, 2012.*

1. Introduction

In recent years vertical agreements under EU competition law have been the focus of considerable attention, not just in connection with the regulatory work of the Commission, the Council and the European Parliament, but also in the practice of the courts and in legal academic writings. The legal literature has been based on a number of specific cases where the EU's legal authorities have had to decide on the validity of contractual arrangements of this kind under EU competition law.[1]

From the point of view of the smaller Member States, this interest in the subject is due to the fact vertical agreements will often be a practical method for use by small and medium sized enterprises which wish to extend their marketing activities to the wider European market, and this is an interest

1. Even prior to the first block exemption regulation, Regulation No 67/67/EEC on the application of Article 85 (3) of the Treaty to certain categories of exclusive dealing agreements, the CJ had laid down some principles on the permissibility of and prohibition of certain key restrictive terms in these kinds of contracts. For example, see the discussion below of Case 56/65, *Société Technique Minière* v *Maschinenbau Ulm,* and Joined cases 56 and 58/64, *Consten and Grundig* v *Commission.*

which is unlikely to decrease in intensity as the market grows with the accession of new Member States.

Vertical agreements are contractual arrangements between undertakings which, according to the content of the agreements, are at different levels of the production or distribution chain. For example, this would apply to an agreement between the producer of goods and a wholesaler who buys goods from the producer with a view to selling them onwards to retailers on a particular market.[2] If the wholesale level is cut out, a vertical agreement can exist between the producer and a retailer.

In addition to this, there are *horizontal agreements*, which are agreements between undertakings which are on the same level of the production or distribution chain. Horizontal agreements are discussed in more detail in Chapter IV. Such agreements exist when they have a 'Community dimension', affecting trade between Member States etc., see Article 101(1) of the Treaty on the Functioning of the European Union (TFEU), and are considered as being a potential hindrance to the achievement of the goal of market integration. In contrast to vertical agreements, horizontal agreements have an inherent tendency to lead to market sharing, as the parties to such agreements can clearly be considered to be actual or potential competitors, and to be in a position to enforce 'naked restrictions'[3] in their part of the shared market.

2. Agreements between wholesalers and retailers are also vertical agreements. The same applies to agreements between two producers, A and B, of substitutable goods if, for example, under the agreement A appoints B as its agent in a market, without B correspondingly selling goods to A, in other words, without there being a market-sharing agreement between the parties. See the distinction made between horizontal agreements and vertical agreements in *Christopher Bellamy & Graham Child:* European Community Law of Competition, 2008 p. 140 et seq.
3. This term was used in earlier American legal practice as an expression of unilateral price setting and the exclusion of competitors from the market. In contrast to this there are 'ancillary restraints', which are restrictions on competition which are accessory to a transaction which is otherwise competitive; compare with Article 2(3) of Commission Regulation (EU) No 330/2010 of 20 April 2010 on the application of Article 101(3) of the Treaty on the Functioning of the European Union to categories of vertical agreements and concerted practices, and paragraph 31 of the Commission's guidelines on vertical restraints and the more detailed discussion in section 3 below. Ancillary restraints is a special term in common law countries which has arisen as a necessary consequence of the fact that Section 1 of the Sherman Act does not allow for a dispensation corresponding to that in Article 101(3) TFEU. Refer also to the comments below on the *rule of reason* doctrine and Case T-112/99, *Métropole Télévision (M6).* See also *Valentine Korah & Denis O'Sullivan:* Distribution Agreements under the EC Competition Rules, 2002 pp. 83-84.

Only a minority of the producers who supply the internal market undertake the distribution of their goods to the end user themselves.

Instead, producers use specialised agents who have their place of business in the chosen export market. The competition for customers will often be won by the producer who has chosen a distribution chain whose marketing is more effective and has a higher service level than that of other distributors. For example, the developments in information technology in recent years, and the use of modern 'just in time' methods, which rely on good logistics for the stockholding of goods, have meant that it is the precise planning of the demand for goods, and not for the needs of production, which are decisive for the movement of goods in the distribution chain. This puts the emphasis on closer cooperation between producers and distributors with a view to planning and sales strategies which are less demanding on resources.[4]

Among other things such developments could change the terms of an arrangement between the producer and the distribution channel, and could directly or indirectly have a knock-on effect on the ability of less competitive producers and distributors to compete for customers.

This dynamic, which characterises the distribution chain, will therefore create new demands for competition rules which the actors on the market will have to operate under. At the same time this development will bring new challenges for the authorities, both at national and Community levels, which will have to consider complaints about restrictions on competition which will arise as activities develop in the distribution chain.

4. If a producer chooses to undertake its own distribution and sales, or if it undertakes this through companies in the same corporate group (vertical integration), the assumption will be that there will not be an infringement of Article 101(1) TFEU, as there will not be any agreement between 'undertakings' within the meaning of competition law.

In mixed agreements, for example a distribution agreement between two competitors, A and B, where A undertakes to sell B's products and B undertakes to sell A's products, the horizontal nature of the agreement between the parties will be looked at first. Only if these relations fall outside the scope of Article 101(1) will it be necessary to assess whether the vertical aspects are acceptable, i.e. that they do not restrict competition.

A distribution chain can sometimes consist of three links, for example in the way that a producer has a vertical relation to one or more wholesalers, who in turn have sales arrangements with a number of dealers who have vertical agreements with the end users of the products. Article 101 applies to each of these separate agreements. Thus, depending on the circumstances, an independent assessment in relation to Article 101 must be made for each of the three arrangements.

As far as the Community is concerned both in legislation and in practice, the Council, the Commission and the Courts (both the European Court of Justice (CJ) and the General Court) are constantly aware of the possible restrictions on competition arising from parts of agreements or concerted practices between undertakings at different levels of the production and distribution chain. Competition between supply chains increases as the battle for the favour of end users is fought by an increasing number of producers and/or distributors.

2. The competition law approach to vertical restraints – Article 101(1) TFEU and the block exemption regulations

Vertically restrictive agreements are a controversial element of Union competition law. This does not only apply to determining the definition of vertical agreements as distinct from horizontal agreements; see above in section 1. Critics have questioned whether there is any general need, on grounds of competition, to intervene against vertical restraints.[5]

Among other things because of the decisions in Case 56/65, *Société technique* v *Maschinenbau Ulm*, Joined cases 56 and 58/64, *Consten and Grundig* v *Kommissionen*, and Case 32/65, *Italy* v *Council and Commission* et al., on the basis of the authorising Regulation No 65/65/EEC, the Commission adopted Regulation No 67/67/EEC, containing guidelines in abstract form regarding the circumstances under which contracting undertakings could be exempt from the provision of Article 85(3) of the EEC Treaty [now Article 101(3) TFEU]. Regulation No 67/67/EEC dealt with block exemptions for certain categories of exclusive dealing agreements. As discussed in more detail in section 2.2, Regulation No 67/67/EEC and the subsequent block exemption Regulation (EC) No 2790/1999 on the application of Article 101(3) TFEU to categories of vertical agreements and concerted practices have now been replaced by Regulation (EU) No 330/2010 on the application of Article 101(3) TFEU to categories of vertical agreements and concerted practices.

When the Court of Justice, the General Court or the Commission have had to decide on competition matters, their considerations in this respect have for

5. As early as in Joined cases 56 and 58/64, *Consten and Grundig* v *Commission* (discussed below), it was ruled that Article 101(1) could apply to both vertical and horizontal restrictions on competition.

all practical purposes been separated from the interpretation of the block exemptions, and the case law is thus still of essential importance. It is on this basis that the following review is made of the case law concerning a number of practical agreements as well as of the theoretical arguments linked to Article 101(1) TFEU and its predecessor provisions. Given the guidelines established by the courts, there is a sound basis for giving a more precise presentation of the conditions under which Regulation (EU) No 330/2010 and the exemption criteria in Article 101(3) create a 'safe harbour' for undertakings which want to keep their contractual arrangements free from intervention by the competition authorities. The development of the block exemption regulations up to the present Regulation (EU) No 330/2010 is described below in section 2.2.

2.1. Article 101(1) TFEU[6]

Elements of vertical agreements that restrict competition have traditionally been treated more leniently by the competition authorities than has been the case for horizontal restrictions. This tendency can be explained to some extent by the fact that the parties in a cross-border vertical agreement operate at different levels of trade and so they will not typically be actual or potential competitors on the market. It is also relevant that it is widely recognised that vertical agreements will often have been beneficial for effectiveness and that the terms of agreements which will, to a large extent, protect a producer from attack can sometimes be a commercial necessity for the producer wanting to sell its products in as many markets as possible in the EU.

However, in general the desire to adopt a stricter approach to restrictive agreements is supported by the fundamental reasoning behind the EU competition rules, namely that in creating a transparent and effective internal market, measures should be taken against agreements and concerted practices which restrict the potential activities of market participants. Among other things, this tendency is expressed in the Commission's guidelines on vertical restraints; see the Commission Information 2010/C 130/01, referred to here

6. In connection with the entry into force of the Amsterdam Treaty on 1 May 1999, the Treaty provisions were renumbered, so that Article 85 thereafter became Article 81, and the other key provision of competition became Article 82. The Lisbon Treaty again made changes to the numbering of the Treaty articles, so that Article 81 now appears as Article 101, and Article 82 now appears as Article 102. In terms of the wording, in two places the Lisbon Treaty changes 'common market' to 'internal market'. Apart from this no change has been made to the wording of the text, so that this has remained unchanged since the original Treaty of Rome in 1957.

as the 'Vertical Restraints Guidelines'. Given its status as an 'information', the Vertical Restraints Guidelines do not alter the exiting practice of the Court of Justice or the General Court. However, in their detailed form they are an important indicator to the area in which vertical restraints can cause problems or advantages for the creation of an effectively functioning internal market. The Vertical Restraints Guidelines are closely linked to the purpose of Article 101, which is to ensure that market participants do not use agreements (in this context, vertical agreements) to the disadvantage of one of the parties in a cross-border arrangement, for the unreasonable advantage of the other party or of end users.

In general, these considerations lead to the recognition that the competition authorities ought to intervene against vertical agreements which contain certain forms of particularly serious restrictions on trade, including certain forms of absolute territorial protection, for example where third party undertakings are prevented from trading in larger or smaller parts of the market if the area in question has been allocated to another trader as their exclusive territory. Another main area has been decisions addressing agreements where the restrictions have consisted of maintaining fixed prices in subsequent links of the distribution chain (resale price maintenance).

2.1.1. Territorial protection – dividing up markets

Article 101(1)(c) TFEU expressly prohibits the 'share markets or sources of supply'. The case law of the Court of Justice has considered this part of Article 101(1).

In Case 56/65, *Société technique* v *Maschinenbau Ulm*, the CJ established that an exclusive dealing arrangement is not automatically in breach of Article 81(1) [now Article 101(1)] if: (1) it does do not prohibit the concessionaire from re-exporting to any other markets; (2) it does not include an undertaking by the grantor to prohibit concessionaires in other Member States from selling the products in the concessionaire's territory; and (3) it does not fetter the right of dealers and consumers in the concessionaire's territory to obtain supplies through parallel imports from other Member States (other than that the concessionaire may not, without the consent of the grantor, sell goods likely to compete with the goods with which the concession is concerned).

At the same time, the CJ stated that the decision of whether there is a restriction on competition must be based on the conditions of competition as within the actual context in which it would occur in the absence of the agreement in dispute.[7] In order to be able to judge whether an agreement may be found prohibited on the grounds the restriction of competition which it is its purpose or effect, it is necessary to decide how the competition would have developed if the agreement did not exist. For this purpose it is necessary to take into account: the nature of the products that are covered by the agreement, and whether or not their quantity is restricted; the positions of the parties and the significance of the goods in question on the market; and whether the agreement is an isolated agreement or is part of a large or small network of agreements. In other words, depending on the circumstances, a commercial agreement may be found unlawful if it contains provisions that are capable of creating artificial profit-based obstacles that restrict the free flow of goods between Member States, and ultimately hold up the completion of the internal market.

The *Maschinenbau Ulm* case and the *Grundig* case were important steps towards creating clarity about the extent to which territorial restrictions could be agreed without intervention by the competition authorities, and at the same time the decisions give guidance on the content of two earlier block exemption agreements for exclusive dealing agreements: Regulation No 67/67/EEC, and its replacement Regulation (EEC) No 1983/83. Despite the fact that the *Grundig* case in particular has sometimes been over-interpreted, the decisions still stands as a leading case on Union competition law:

> In 1957, the German company Grundig entered into a contract for an unlimited period with the French trading company Consten, Paris, whereby Consten was given exclusive distribution rights for radio and television sets etc., and accessories to these in an agreed territory consisting of France, the Saar district and Corsica.
>
> Consten undertook to buy an agreed minimum quota, buy in stocks regularly in advance, maintain a repair workshop with a stock of spare parts, take on guarantee obligations and customer service, and refrain from selling similar competing products and from selling either directly or indirectly to markets in other countries. Consten's exclusive distributorship meant that Grundig was obliged to delegate to Consten retail sales within the agreed territory and to refrain from selling, directly or indirectly, to other persons in the territory. Already prior to the

7. This approach, which has been repeated in a number of subsequent decisions, is one of the most important elements in the distinction between lawful and unlawful agreements that turns upon Article 101(1).

Grundig/Consten contract, Grundig had required its German wholesalers and distributors not to supply from their own agreed territories into other territories.

In October 1957, Consten had the trade mark GINT (Grundig International) registered in France in its own name. This trade mark was registered internationally as Grundig's trade mark and was used on all Grundig's apparatus produced in Germany. In this connection, in January 1959 Consten declared that the trade mark GINT would only be used on Grundig's apparatus, and that the trade mark rights would be assigned to Grundig or be revoked when the exclusive distribution agreement with Grundig was terminated.

When Consten found out that since April 1961 another French trading company UNEF had been buying Grundig apparatus from German wholesalers (which had therefore acted contrary to the export prohibition imposed on them by Grundig) and imported them to France, Consten brought a case against UNEF for *unfair competition and infringement of trade mark rights*.

The case was brought before the Court of Appeal which adjourned its hearting until a decision was given by the Commission in a case which UNEF had brought in March 1962 claiming that the agreement between Consten and Grundig should be declared an infringement of the Treaty.

Consten also brought a case claiming unfair competition before the Tribunal de Grande Instance in Strasbourg against Leissner, a radio retailer resident there, who had also bought Grundig sets in Germany with a view to selling them in France, in breach of Consten's exclusive distribution rights. This case was also adjourned.

In accordance with the then applicable rules in Regulation 17/62, Grundig notified the Commission of its agreements with Consten and with exclusive distributors in other EC countries. After hearing the involved undertakings and the national authorities, in September 1964 the Commission gave its decision on the agreement between Grundig and Consten.

In the Official Journal in the same year (p. 2545 – there is no English version) when the case was published, it was stated:

that the exclusive distribution agreement of April 1957 and the agreement for the registration and use of the trade mark GINT was contrary to Article 85(1)[Article 101(1) TFEU] of the Treaty,

that a request for an exemption in accordance with Article 85(3) [Article 101(3) TFEU] was denied, and *that* Grundig and Consten were required to refrain from any measures which could hinder third parties or make it more difficult for them to obtain the goods covered by the agreement from wholesalers or distributors within the Community with a view to reselling them within the agreed territory.

Both Grundig and Consten referred this decision to the CJ, demanding that the decision should be repealed in its entirety. The two cases were joined in proceedings before the Court. UNEF and Leissner participated in the case on the Commission's side, while the plaintiffs' argument, which was of a general legal character, was supported by the Italian and German governments.

The Court substantially found in favour of the Commission's decision, though it did say that the Commission should either have confined itself in the operative part of the decision to declaring that an infringement only lay in those parts of the agreement which came within the prohibition, or it should have set out the reasons why those parts did not appear to be severable from the whole agreement in the preamble to the decision.[8]

In addition to this, the Court expressed the view that neither the wording of Article 81 [now Article 101] nor of Article 82 [now Article 102] give any basis for distinguishing between these two Treaty provisions with regard to the position of undertakings in the distribution chain and it therefore denied that Article 101(1) should only apply to *horizontal* agreements and not equally to *vertical* agreements. In the view of the Court, distortion of competition, within the meaning of Article 101(1), could be caused not only by agreements which restrict competition between the parties to the agreement, but also by agreements which hinder or restrict competition which would otherwise exist between a party to the agreement and a third party. In this respect too, it was not significant whether the parties were in the same economic position or functionally at the same level.

In stating its reasons for finding the agreement partially invalid, the Court laid decisive weight on the fact that, even it does not involve abuse of a dominant position, an exclusive distribution agreement can affect trade between the Member States, and it can have the object or effect of restricting or distorting competition contrary to Article 101(1). However, exclusive distribu-

8. Compare with the comments below in section 5.4 on the legal situation if invalidity under Article 101(2) affects only *part* of an agreement.

tion agreements concluded between a producer and a sole representative do not necessarily fall foul of the prohibition in Article 101(1). But an agreement between a producer and a distributor which is aimed at re-establishing national barriers to trade between Member States would be contrary to the fundamental aims of the Community. The Court hereby expressed the view, which was later expressed in general legislation [for example Article 3 of Regulation 1983/83, Article 4 of Regulation 2790/99 and now Article 4 of Regulation (EU) 330/2010)] that the Treaty, which according to its preamble and its enacting terms has the aim of removing obstacles to trade between Member States, and which has strict provisions to prevent the re-establishment of such obstacles, cannot allow undertakings to create new obstacles by means of agreements. In support of this, the Court stated – as has been repeated since – that what is decisive in relation to Article 101(1) is whether an agreement is actually or potentially calculated to affect freedom of trade and not whether such negative effects can in fact be shown to have occurred.

In assessing whether the agreement between Grundig and Consten constituted a restriction on competition contrary to Article 101(1), the Court next had to decide whether the prohibition refers to competition in interchangeable products of different brands (*inter-brand* competition), or whether it was sufficient that the agreement involved a restriction of trade in Grundig's products (*intra-brand* competition).

> On this, the Court stated that the principle of free competition must apply to all levels of trade and all forms of competition. The possibility that competition between producers in general may be more openly expressed than competition between traders in the same brand, does not necessarily mean that an agreement which restricts competition between such traders will escape prohibition under Article 101(1). In other words, when determining whether a restriction of competition existed contrary to Article 101(1), it was sufficient that the agreement was capable of restricting competition between traders in Grundig's products, in other words that there was *intra-brand* competition.[9] Therefore, in the view of the Court, the Commission was right to apply an overall assessment of the system which Grundig had constructed and on this basis determined that

9. In his Opinion, *Advocate General Roemer* proposed that the Court should reverse the Commission's decision, because the Commission had failed to take into account possible competition from other producers.

> the infringement of Article 101(1) followed from the geographic isolation which Consten had obtained under French law by means of the agreement. Within the contract territory, Consten had wished to exclude all forms of competition in the contract goods in the wholesale sector and for this purpose had used two approaches:
>
> *First*, Grundig had undertaken not to supply to third parties, either directly or indirectly, such goods as were intended for the contract territory. The effect of this obligation in restricting the territory was clearly apparent since Consten and all Grundig's exclusive agents, as well as all German wholesalers, had been prevented from exporting. *Second*, the trade mark GINT had been registered in France in Consten's name (a trade mark which Grundig applied to all its products) with the aim of strengthening protection against parallel imports to France of Grundig's products which were covered by the exclusive distribution agreement, by means of the protection given by the intellectual property (trade mark) right. Thus, no third party could sell imported Grundig products from other Member States with a view to reselling them without running considerable risk.

The Court summarised its objections to the agreement between Grundig and Consten as follows: the Commission properly took into account the whole distribution system set up by Grundig. In order to obtain a true picture of the contractual position of the contract in the economic and legal context in which it was concluded by the parties. The picture obtained showed the isolation of the French market, making it possible to charge higher prices for the products in question which were sheltered from effective competition. The more producers succeed in their efforts to render their own brands distinct in the eyes of the consumer, the more the effectiveness of competition between producers tends to diminish. It is pointless to compare the situation, to which Article 101 applies, of a producer bound by a sole distributorship agreement with a distributor of their products with that of a producer who undertakes the distribution of their own products by some means, for example by commercial representatives, to which Article 101 does not apply.

> It should not be accepted without question that the Court's assessment is correct that the agreement between Grundig and Consten restricted competition and was therefore contrary to Article 101. The fact that the aim of the agreement was to restrict trade in Grundig's products need not lead to it being categorised as a restriction on competition, since Article 101 could well have been interpreted as concerning agreements which

have the aim or effect of restricting the overall competition in the market for radios etc. With this judgment and the disfavour of later judgments for territorial divisions, the Court has gone a long way to characterising absolute territorial divisions as being prohibited per se.[10] See also the comments in *Christopher Bellamy & Graham Child:* European Community Law of Competition, 2008 pp. 142-148.

Under the doctrine of a per se prohibition, which has been developed in American antitrust law, certain specified forms of agreement, including agreements on prices, are declared to be automatically illegal. This means for example that it is not necessary to prove in each case that an agreement binding prices in subsequent levels of the distribution chain have restricted competition. And even if an agreement has certain positive effects, it is not subject to any rule of reason examination. See the comments below in section 2.1.4 on Case T-112/99, Métropole Télévision (M6).

The starting point for Article 101(1)(b) TFEU is that a distribution agreement is not covered by a block exemption if the distributor is subject to an obligation not to execute orders received from dealers situated outside the area covered by the agreement or received from a customer who is not part of the group of customers covered by the agreement.

It is not clear from Article 101(1) that there must be such a possibility for parallel trade. However, it is emphasised in paragraph 50 of the Vertical Restraints Guidelines that a provision for an exclusive distribution territory or exclusively allocated customer group must permit passive sales to such territory or customer group.[11]

10. See, among others, Case C-279/87, *Tipp-Ex* v *Commission,* Case T-41/96, *Bayer* v *Commission (Adalat),* Case 258/78, *Nungesser and Eisele* v *Commission,* and Case C-306/96, *Javico International* v *Yves Saint Laurent Parfums,* as well as decisions referred to in *Christopher Bellamy & Graham Child:* European Community Law of Competition, 2008 pp. 64-66.
11. According to paragraph 51 of the Vertical Restraints Guidelines, 'Passive' sales mean responding to unsolicited requests from individual customers including delivery of goods or services to such customers. General advertising or promotion in media or on the Internet that reaches customers in other distributors' exclusive territories or customer groups but which is a reasonable way to reach customers outside those territories or customer groups, for instance to reach customers in non-exclusive territories or in one's own territory, are passive sales.' General advertising or sales promotion campaigns are regarded as a reasonable method for reaching out to such customers, if it is profitable for the buyer to invest in them, even if they do not reach out to customers in other distributors' exclusive territories or customer groups.

A prohibition against fulfilling orders from customers outside the territory or group of customers which has been allocated to a dealer (passive sales) can be formulated as an express condition in the agreement (export prohibition) or as an obligation for the dealer to refer orders from 'foreigners' to other distributors.[12]

Indirectly, a sales prohibition can arise from special measures taken by the producer, or example by the refusal or reduction of bonuses or discounts, reductions in supplies, or threats to terminate an agreement. A number of cases before the Court and Commission in connection with infringement of the prohibition have shown that various measures have been used by producers who have breached the prohibition, see for example 93/46/EEC: Commission Decision relating to a proceeding pursuant to Article 85 of the EEC Treaty (*Ford Agricultural*) (OJ 1993 L 20/1). It does not matter whether it is the seller or the buyer who takes the initiative for including the prohibition in the agreement. The illegality consists regardless of whether the prohibition is stated in the main agreement or whether it is hidden away in the seller's standard terms, or whether it has been enforced in trade between the seller and buyer. A finding of the existence of a concerted practice likewise fulfils the conditions for finding the existence of an agreement between the parties; see Case T-49/95, *Van Megen*, paragraph 35.

See also the decision of the Court in Case T-176/95, *Accinauto* v *Commission*:

> The Belgian company Accinauto (A) was BASF's exclusive distributor for Glasurit products in Belgium and Luxembourg. The exclusive distributorship agreement contained a provision under which A was required to refer all enquiries from customers outside the agreed sales territory to BASF. It was also clear from the agreement that A could neither advertise nor have supply depots outside the territory for the sale of the contract goods. A also undertook not to sell the goods to customers

12. See for example 2001/135/EC: Commission decision relating to a proceeding pursuant to Article 81 of the EC Treaty (*Nathan-Bricolux*) (OJ 2001 L 54/1), where the Commission decided that a French undertaking, Editions Nathan, a publisher of educational books, by having exclusive distribution agreements which restricted its exclusive distributors from making passive sales outside their sales areas, and restricting the right of other dealers to make passive sales to customers within these areas, had infringed Article 101(1) TFEU. Also, one of the distributors, the Belgian company Bricolux, was fined for having refrained from selling to customers outside its exclusive distribution area and for having encouraged Editions Nathan to restrict other dealers' sales in its own exclusive territory, contrary to Article 101(1).

outside the agreed sales territory or to customers within the territory if A knew that they would sell the products on to customers outside the territory. In return, the producer bound itself to ensure that, as far as legally possible, other dealers respected A's sales territory.

The Court held that the agreement between the parties contained a covert prohibition against making passive sales outside the agreed sales territory. Furthermore, an investigation into how the agreement was carried out confirmed that the aim was to prevent imports of Glasurit products to the UK. The Commission had therefore correctly concluded that there was an infringement of Article 101(1).

The Commission had defined the relevant market as the British market for paint for car repairs. In 1991 BASF's share of this market was 16 %, of which 12 % was Glasurit products. In the view of the Court, such a market position, taken together with the fact that during the relevant period the prices for Glasurit products were higher in the UK than in other Member States, showed that the agreement could affect trade. Since, because of its purpose, the agreement already constituted a restriction on competition contrary to Article 101(1), the Court found that it was not necessary to investigate whether the agreement had appreciably affected the market; compare with the comments in section 5 below, according to which the hard-core provisions corresponding to Article 4(a) and (b) of the Regulation (EU) No 330/2010 would have effect, regardless of whether the market thresholds in Article 3 of the Regulation were exceeded.

The Court held that the infringement only came to an end when the parties revoked the provision in question. The fact that a provision which has the aim of restricting competition has not been enforced does not mean that the provision falls outside the scope of Article 101(1).

Agreed restrictions of the kind referred to can lead to the isolation of the market and hinder the integration of the market which is a fundamental aim of the EU's competition rules. In combination with other vertical restraints, for example a prohibition on a dealer carrying competing products, inter-brand competition could be restricted. Intra-brand competition could also be hindered as permanent isolation of the market could be abused as part of a price differentiation strategy.

2.1.2. Prohibition of re-export with sales to third countries

In Case C-306/96, *Javico International* v *Yves Saint Laurent Parfums*, the Court gave a preliminary ruling on whether a distributor based in a Member State, who had been entrusted with distributing agreed goods in agreed territories *outside the Community*, could be bound by the producer's prohibition on selling goods in territories other than those agreed. This includes whether the producer could validly prohibit the distributor from directly or indirectly re-exporting the goods to a territory within the Community:

In 1992, the French undertaking Yves Saint Laurent Parfums (YSLP) entered into two distribution agreements with Javico International which was based in Germany, but which was not part of YSLP's selective distribution system in Europe, for the sales of the goods to Russia, the Ukraine and Slovenia.

The distribution agreements contained conditions preventing Javico's own exports from these territories as well as obligations on Javico to impose such export prohibitions on its buyers. The referring French appeal court (Cour d'appel de Versailles) asked the Court to rule on the lawfulness of these prohibitions, in other words on their compatibility with Article 101(1) TFEU.

The Court took a step-by-step approach, as it began by stating that it was first necessary to consider whether, had they been in agreements that were only operative within the EU, the prohibitions on supply had the aim or effect of appreciably restricting competition within the Community, and whether this could affect trade between Member States. Next, the Court stated that it had itself previously established that an agreement which had the aim of preventing a distributor from freely choosing its customers by requiring the distributor only to sell to customers within an agreed territory, constitutes a restriction within the meaning of Article 101(1).[13] Moreover, the Court added that it had previously established that an agreement which obliges a distributor not to sell the contract goods outside its sales territory has the aim of hindering parallel imports within the Community and thus restricts competition in the single market.[14] On this basis, the Court concluded that conditions of the kind referred to would in themselves constitute a restriction on competition in distribution agreements within the Community.[15] However, it is only possible to intervene against such measures which restrict competition if they can affect trade between Member States. The Court pointed out that a decision, agreement or concerted practice only has such an effect if on the

13. In this connection the Court referred to Case 86/82, *Hasselblad (GB) Limited* v *Commission,* and Case C-70/93, *Bayerische Motorenwerke* v *ALD Auto-Leasing.*
14. Case C-279/87, *Tipp-Ex v Commission.*
15. Case19/77, *Miller International Schallplatten* v *Commission.*

> basis of a majority of objective, legal or actual circumstances it can be predicted with a sufficient degree of certainty that it could have a direct or indirect, actual or potential influence on trade between Member States and in such a manner as to harm the realisation of the aims of the establishment of the single market. Furthermore, this influence must be significant.[16] Finally, the Court referred to the fact that, in deciding whether an agreement had such an influence, regard had to be had for the position and strength of the parties on the market for the goods in question.[17] For example, an exclusive distribution agreement with absolute territorial protection could fall outside the scope of the prohibition in Article 101(1) if it only has an insignificant effect on the market, given the weak position of the parties on the market for the goods traded.[18]

The Court then went on to consider the agreement's compatibility with Article 101(1), given that it was to apply to an area *outside the EU*.

> On this, the Court started by stating that a provision prohibiting exports in an agreement of the kind in question should be interpreted as a provision that is not intended to prevent parallel imports and an offer for the sale of the goods on the single market. The provision should ensure that the supplier can penetrate a market outside the Community by selling a sufficient quantity of the goods covered by the agreement on the market. In the view of the Court, such an interpretation could be supported by the fact that the prohibition on sales outside the area covered by the agreement applied to all other third countries.
>
> In other words, the provisions prohibiting direct sales within the Community and against re-exports of goods to the Community must in principle be interpreted in the same way as provisions whose aim is to supply a sufficient quantity of goods to the territories covered by the agreement.[19]

On the face of it, it does not seem justifiable to draw a distinction between the situation where goods are moved from one Member State to another – in which case the existence of an export prohibition would have been contrary

16. Case 5/69, *Völk* v *Vervaecke*.
17. Case 99/79, *Lancôme* v *Etos*.
18. Joined cases 100-103/80, *Pioneer v Commission*.
19. See the comments on the case in *Christopher Bellamy & Graham Child:* European Community Law of Competition, 2008 pp. 64-66 and p. 444.

to Article 101(1) – and the situation where a distributor is allocated a territory outside the Community. In both situations the aim of exclusive distribution agreement seems to be that the distributor should concentrate its marketing efforts in the given area and not spread its efforts to other areas, whether these are within the Community or in a third country.

However, to a certain extent the Court mitigated the effect of its main argument by adding that even if the provisions in the agreement in question were not considered as having the aim of restricting or distorting competition within the Community within the meaning of Article 101(1), it was up to the national court to decide whether they did in fact have this effect. In this connection it could be relevant whether there was a significant price difference between goods sold outside the Community and goods sold inside the Community. Unlike a factor which could exclude the agreement from the scope of Article 101(1), it is noted that the Commission had previously exempted YSLP's selective distribution system from the prohibition in Article 101(1) in accordance with Article 101(3).[20]

In conclusion it must be stated that the dismissive approach to agreements giving absolute territorial protection, which the CJ adopted already in the 1960s with, among others, the *Maschinenbau Ulm* and *Grundig* cases, has in all essentials been upheld by the CJ and the Commission in the succeeding decades. Undertakings must still expect that measures will be taken against such arrangements. However, the Commission's comments in paragraphs 60-64 of the Vertical Restraints Guidelines of 2000, which are discussed below in section 2.1.5, open up the possibility that in very exceptional cases there could be a somewhat less rigorous approach to such arrangements.

2.1.3. Fixed prices – Article 101(1)(a) TFEU

The following discussion concerns the prohibition of the fixing of prices in subsequent links of the distribution chain.

The prohibition is found in Article 101(1)(a), and applies to agreements and/or concerted practices which consist of directly or indirectly fix purchase or selling prices or any other trading conditions. The prohibition ranks as a serious (hard core) restriction, and which can thus only be derogated from under Article 101(3) under exceptional circumstances.

In principle, independent undertakings have an indisputable right to agree the commercial terms for the agreements made between them. A competitive

20. See the Commission Decision on the *Yves Saint Laurent* distribution system (OJ 1992 L 12/24).

measure will only become relevant if the parties seek by their agreement to regulate trade with a third party. In other words, the prohibition affects third parties, such as a sole distributor which, as part of its business, sells on the goods that are subject to the agreement which it has bought from its counterparty, i.e. the producer or supplier of the products.

The prohibition affects *minimum sales prices*.[21] Maximum sales prices and recommended sales prices fall outside the scope of the prohibition unless they assume the character of fixed or minimum prices as a result of pressure exerted or incentives given by one of the parties. A maximum or recommended price may work as a focal point for resellers, leading to a more or less uniform application of that price level.

See further the explanation in paragraph 48 of the Vertical Restraints Guidelines, according to which the hardcore restriction referred to in Article 4(a) of the Block Exemption Regulation concerns the fixing of resale prices, i.e. agreements or concerted practices which are intended to directly or indirectly set a fixed or minimum resale price or a fixed or minimum price level which the buyer is required to comply with. With provisions in agreements or concerted practices that directly fix the resale price, the restriction is clear. However, prices can also be fixed indirectly. An example of this is an agreement setting trade margins, or setting the maximum discount that a distributor may give in relation to a given price level. Direct or indirect means of fixing prices can be made more effective if they are combined with measures to identify traders who use lower prices, for example by monitoring systems or by requiring retailers to report other members of the distribution network who do not use the fixed pricing level.

> A producer's provision of a list with recommended or maximum prices is not *in itself* regarded as leading to price fixing. However, see 96/438/EC: Commission Decision relating to a proceeding pursuant to Article 85 [Article 101 TFEU] of the EC Treaty (*Fenex*) (OJ 1996 L 181/28), according to which, by sending out recommended tariffs in the transport sector, an association of undertakings was regarded as having given expression to the association's wish to coordinate the members' pricing policies in the area concerned. This was found to constitute 'a decision by an association of undertakings' and was therefore contrary to Article 101(1) TFEU. At the same time, the Commission stated that such a result

21. The corresponding provision in the Block Exemption Regulation (Regulation (EU) No 330/2010) is in Article 4(a).

would not necessarily be linked to the sending out of information which could help undertakings calculate their own costs so that they could set their own prices. In the *Pronuptia* case (see below in section 4.2), the Court stated in paragraph 25 of the judgment that: 'Although provisions which impair the franchisee's freedom to determine his own prices are restrictive of competition, that is not the case where the franchisor simply provides franchisees with price guidelines, so long as there is no concerted practice between the franchisor and the franchisees or between the franchisees themselves for the actual application of such prices.'

See also 2001/711/EC: Commission Decision relating to a proceeding under Article 81 of the EC Treaty [Article 101 TFEU] (*Volkswagen*) (OJ 2001 L 262/14), where the Commission found that the aim of various of Volkswagen's circulars and notices to German dealers was to get them to comply with the recommended catalogue prices and submit to binding resale prices, in other words a restriction of intra-brand competition on price. The circumstances were similar in 97/123/EC: Commission Decision relating to a proceeding pursuant to Article 85 [Article 101 TFEU] of the EC Treaty and Article 53 of the EEA Agreement (*Novalliance/Systemform*) (OJ 1997 L 47/11), where all the agreements which a German company had entered into with its European distributors restricted their freedom to set their own sales prices, to a greater or lesser extent, and the distributors were required to inform the company of their policy on the granting of discounts.

The reason for the prohibition is that binding resale prices could lead to a restriction on competition between dealers who have bought goods under an agreement with the preceding link in the distribution chain. The producer's interference in the dealers' right to set their own resale prices is contrary to Article 101(1) TFEU which states that parties may not 'directly or indirectly fix purchase or selling prices', which also applies to vertical agreements. Where there are binding or minimum resale prices, the dealer can no longer compete on price for the brand concerned, which can result in the complete elimination of intra-brand competition. A series of clauses or binding prices could have the same effect as a horizontal restriction on competition and lead to market sharing.[22] As long as binding prices cover goods which a dealer imports to the area from other dealers who are not subject to corresponding

22. *Valentine Korah & Warwick A. Rothnie:* Exclusive Distribution and the EEC Competition Rules, 1992 p. 120 and p. 170.

price restrictions, that dealer will be subject to competitive restraints which do not apply to other dealers who parallel import the goods to the area.'[23] On the other hand, the prohibition of minimum prices gives rise to the 'free rider' problem, in other words the maintenance of fixed prices in a territory can sometimes be necessary to ensure that dealers in another area can cover their investments (sunk costs) made in connection with the introduction of a specific product to the market.[24]

A special approach to obtaining protection from parallel trade has been the establishment of differentiated pricing and discount systems, so that higher prices have been set for goods that have been exported than for goods destined for the home market, see for example 78/163/EEC: Commission Decision relating to proceedings under Article 85 [Article 101] of the EEC Treaty *(Distillers Company)* (OJ 1978 L 50/16), and 91/335/EEC: Commission Decision relating to a proceeding pursuant to Article 85 [Article 101] of the EEC Treaty (*Gosme/Martell – DMP*) (OJ 1991 L 185/23). See the decision of the Court in Case T-41/96, *Bayer* v *Commission* (Application for the annulment of Commission Decision 96/478/EC relating to a proceeding under Article 85 of the EC Treaty (*Adalat*) (OJ 1996 L 201/1), on a similar use of a dual pricing system.

Sometimes distributors have been subject to controls and threats of cessation of supplies or the reduction or removal of trade discounts if the contract goods are exported, see for example 88/172/EEC: Commission

23. See 73/322/EEC: Commission Decision relating to proceedings under Article 85 of the EEC Treaty (*Deutsche Philips GmbH*)(OJ 1973 L 293/40), where a German dealer was obliged to sell at prices determined by Deutsche Philips in Germany and elsewhere in the Community, regardless of whether the goods had been supplied direct from the producer in or outside Germany. See correspondingly 77/66/EEC: Commission Decision relating to a proceeding under Article 85 of the EEC Treaty (*GERO-fabriek*) (OJ 1977 L 16/8), where the distributorship agreement contained a prohibition against any departure from the fixed retail price and against any form of discount.
24. There will often be quite substantial investments and risks. In paragraph 81 of the Green Paper on Vertical Restraints in EC Competition Policy the Commission indicated that there could be grounds for treating vertical restraints more favourably, at least for an interim period, if this would ease entry into new markets or expand existing markets significantly. There is no sign in its recent decisions that the Commission is living up to this statement of policy. However, see the two year period of restriction on passive sales into an exclusive territory under Article 4(2)(b)(ii) in Commission Regulation (EC) No 772/2004 on the application of Article 81(3) of the Treaty to categories of technology transfer agreements (see below in Chapter V).

> Decision relating to a proceeding under Article 85 of the EEC Treaty *(Konica)* (OJ 1988 L 78/34) and 93/46/EEC: Commission Decision relating to a proceeding pursuant to Article 85 of the EEC Treaty (*Ford Agricultural*) (OJ 1993 L 20/1).[25]

In paragraph 118 of Commission Decision of 8 May 2001 relating to a proceeding pursuant to Article 81 of the EC Treaty Cases (*Glaxo Wellcome* and others) (OJ 2001 L 302/1), concerning the sales conditions for medicines which were sold to Spanish wholesalers, and which distinguished between prices for wholesalers who sold on the products to Spanish pharmacies with a view to their use in Spain, and higher prices for wholesalers who exported the products, the Commission expressed its view of price differentiation as follows:

> 'A pricing policy which makes it economically uninteresting for wholesalers to indulge in parallel trade must be considered to be at least as effective as an outright contractual export ban.'
>
> The Commission maintained its existing practice as it found that, in its agreements with the Spanish wholesalers, Glaxo Wellcome had infringed Article 101(1), and the Commission rejected Glaxo Wellcome's application for an exemption under Article 101(3). The Commission then drew a parallel with the *Distillers* decision,[26] according to which 'The non-applicability of price allowances on spirits for export and the application to the same customers of different prices for spirits for export and for spirits for United Kingdom consumption are clearly an attempt to impede parallel imports from the United Kingdom into EEC countries other than the United Kingdom, with the same object as a formal export prohibition and can be regarded as a more efficient way to discourage export.'[27]

25. See paragraph 48 of the Vertical Restraints Guidelines, which contains a comprehensive list of intimidatory measures which have been aimed, directly or indirectly, at ensuring that distributors comply with minimum prices.
26. Commission Decision relating to proceedings under Article 85 of the EEC Treaty (*Distillers Company*) (OJ 1978 L 50/16), and Case 30/78, *Distillers v Commission.*
27. The Commission's *Glaxo Wellcome* Decision was upheld by the Court in Joined cases C-501/06 P, C-513/06 P, C-515/06 P, and C-519/06 P, *GlaxoSmithKline Services Unlimited v Commission.*

If different price levels are set in different geographic areas for the same product, as previously stated such binding prices can only be maintained in high price areas if it is possible to prevent parallel exports to these areas, as such exports will otherwise undermine the high prices. In these and in other cases an attempt to maintain the higher prices will therefore be combined with territorial protection. The Commission has adopted a consistently critical attitude to such arrangements.[28] The basic idea behind price competition continues to be that prices should be at the lowest possible level. Only thereby will undertakings be stimulated to use their resources in such a way that consumers will have an optimal opportunity to choose products which are assessed to be the best, both as regards price and other characteristics.

The restrictions in Article 101(1) TFEU affect agreements concerning trade within the Community. As for exports from the Community or imports/re-imports from outside the Community, see above on Case C-306/96, *Javico International* v *Yves Saint Laurent Parfums*.

2.1.4. Economic analysis?

In assessing the distorting effect on competition of vertical restrictions the practice of the Commission, especially its earlier practice, has been criticised particularly in respect of sole distributorships (restrictions on inter-brand competition). Among other things, the Commission has often considered such restrictions to be contrary to the prohibition in Article 101(1) TFEU, even if an economic analysis of the market conditions would have shown that existing inter-brand competition did not make intervention necessary.

According to the critics, such an analysis would have removed vertical agreements from the scope of Article 101(1), so that there would not have been a need to undertake the sometimes more complex assessment of whether there was an exemption under Article 101(3) TFEU or one of the block exemptions then in force.[29]

> For a more detailed discussion of this criticism see, among others: *Korah & Rothnie:* Exclusive Distribution and the EEC Competition Rules, 1992 pp. 51-56, *Korah & O'Sullivan:* Distribution Agreements under the EC Competition Rules, 2002 pp. 73-76, *Richard Whish*: Regulation 2790/99: The Commission's 'New Style' Block Exemption for Veritcal

28. See *Valentine Korah & Denis O'Sullivan:* Distribution Agreements under the EC Competition Rules, 2002 p. 108 and pp. 173-175.
29. See *Korah & Rothnie:* Exclusive Distribution and the EEC Competition Rules, 1992 p. 78.

Agreements, Common Market Law Review 2000 pp. 887-924, and *Barry E. Hawk:* System Failure: Vertical Restraints and EC Competition Law Common Market Law Review 1995 pp. 973-989. The last named points out that the Commission has been all too ready to regard a restriction as being covered by Article 101(1), even though a simple economic analysis would have shown that it would be entirely wrong to apply Article 101(1). *Hawk* also refers to the Commission's historical and ongoing reluctance, both within and without distribution areas, to learn from the CJ's frequent encouragement to apply Article 101(1) only when justified by a more sophisticated economic approach. According to the criticism, the Commission has 'given up', and instead based its assessment of the competition aspects of a given agreement on an interpretation of whether the conditions for an exemption in accordance with Article 101(3) are present or not.[30] In particular, in the Commission's earlier practice, only in few cases was there a hint that the Commission was willing to listen to the views of the CJ.

However, in more recent years the Commission's decisions do seem to indicate that it has accepted the criticism to some extent.

While, in Commission Decision 93/406/EEC on *Langnese-Iglo* (OJ 1993 L 183/19), the Commission related an analysis of the market structure to Article 101(3), in connection with Commission Decision 1999/230/EC on *Whitbread* (OJ 1999 L 88/26), which concerned the validity of a competition term under Article 101(1), the Commission used a detailed economic analysis of the market conditions.[31]

Both the CJ and the General Court have adopted a more flexible approach and in a number of cases when deciding whether an agreed restriction is affected by Article 101(1), they have given weight to the actual economic and legal circumstances in which the agreement in question has been entered into, as well as an analysis of the effects of the agreement on the relevant market.[32]

30. See, among others, Commission Decision 93/405/EEC on *Schöller Lebensmittel* (OJ 1973 L 138/1).
31. On these decisions see *Valentine Korah & Denis O'Sullivan:* Distribution Agreements under the EC Competition Rules, 2002 pp. 78-80.
32. The comments in this connection have particularly concerned cases which fall outside the area of 'serious' restrictions on competition, for example cases where the parties have tried to secure absolute protection of their areas of the market, enforce maximum sales prices on distributors etc. In these areas where, except in particular

See also Case 56/65, *Société Technique Minière* v *Maschinenbau Ulm*, Case 23/67, *Brasserie de Haecht* v *Consorts Wilkin-Janssen* (No 1), and Case C-234/89, *Stergios Delimitis* v *Henninger Bräu*. An overall assessment of the market, including an investigation of inter-brand competition, was used in, among others: Case 26/76, *Metro SB-Großmärkte* v *Commission* (1), Case 161/84, *Pronuptia de Paris* v *Pronuptia de Paris Irmgaard Schillgallis*, Case 31/ 80, *L'Oréal* v *De Nieuwe AMCK*, Case 99/79, *Lancôme* v *Etos*, Case 258/78, *Nungesser and Eisele* v *Commission*, and Case 27/87, *Erauw-Jacquery* v *La Hesbignonne*.

Part of the problem that can be connected with the application of Article 101 is that it is split between, on the one hand Article 101(1), which contains a description of the circumstances which make an agreement or parts of an agreement a restriction on competition, and on the other hand Article 101(3), which sets out the circumstances that can mean that an agreement, or parts of an agreement will not after all be affected by the prohibition in Article 101(2).

Instead, according to the critics, there should first be an economic analysis of the actual or potential market structure together with a simultaneous evaluation of the positive and negative aspects of the agreement. The positive aspects will include, for example, an increase in inter-brand competition or possible consumer-related efficiency benefits connected with the restriction of intra-brand competition. If such analysis leads to the conclusion that the negative aspects of the agreement outweigh its positive aspects, the application of Article 101(3) and block exemptions could be reserved for the presumably few cases where other considerations exist which ought to justify exemption of the agreement.[33] If, conversely, such an assessment leads to the conclusion that the positive aspects outweigh the negative aspects, then according to this approach the agreement should be allowed under Article 101(1).

However, this interpretation, which is based on American antitrust practice which uses the *rule of reason* model, cannot be implemented because of the differences in structure between the American prohibition

borderline cases, the Commission has followed the line laid down by the courts, the criticism has been more muted.

33. Cf. *Barry E. Hawk:* System Failure: Vertical Restraints and EC Competition Law, Common Market Law Review 1995 p. 986.

and Article 101 TFEU.[34] If an interpretation of the agreement finds that in its economic and legal context it does in fact contain a restriction on competition, then under the European system, Article 101(1) has fulfilled its role. There is no further requirement to compare the effects of the agreement which restrict competition with the effects which promote competition. If the restriction is to be exempted, this must be on the basis that one of the elements expressly stated in Article 101(3) (for example that the cost savings and effectivity gains connected with the restriction are to the *benefit of consumers*) justifies this.[35]

The refusal to apply a rule of reason interpretation to Article 101(1) was apparently supported by the Court of First Instance (now the General Court) in Case T-112/99, *Métropole Télévision (M6) and others* v *Commission*, which concerned the establishment of a system for the digital broadcasting of television programmes via satellite to francophone viewers in Europe. On the basis referred to – the distinction between Article 101(1) and (3) – the Court expressly stated that even a number of previous decisions, in which the CJ had apparently applied a more flexible interpretation of the prohibition in Article 101(1), could not be interpreted as an expression of the application of the rule of reason.[36] Furthermore, the

34. The American prohibitions do not have exemptions corresponding to those in Article 101(3) TFEU. See also Chapter II above, in the section on the significance of the fact that in Council Regulation (EC) No 1/2003 on the implementation of the rules on competition laid down in Articles 81 and 82 of the Treaty, it is provided that undertakings themselves, and if appropriate the competition authority which hears the case, can assess whether there is a basis for applying the exemption rule in Article 101(3). In accordance with the earlier rules in Council Regulation (EEC) No 17/1962 First Regulation implementing Articles 85 and 86 of the Treaty [now Articles 101 and 102 TFEU], in relation to Article 101 the Commission had sole competence to grant an exemption under Article 101(3).
35. In the *Grundig* case, which is still considered to be a leading case in European competition law, the CJ stated that the attempt of the parties to create absolute territorial limits was sufficient grounds for regarding the group of agreements as being covered by Article 101(1), even if the enforcement of the agreement would promote inter-brand competition, in other words increase the supply of substitute products.
36. Among the decisions of interest in this context which the Court of First Instance [now the General Court] referred to were: Case 56/65, *Société Technique Minière* v *Maschinenbau Ulm,* Case 161/84, *Pronuptia de Paris GmbH* v *Pronuptia de Paris Irmgard Schillgallis,* and Case 258/78, *Nungesser and Eisele* v *Commission.*

    The Court's statement in Joined cases T-374/94 and others, *European Night Services and others* v *Commission*, that when an agreement does not have the aim of restricting competition within the terms of Article 101(1), a thorough evaluation of

Court characterised Article 101(3) as a provision in accordance with which – as an extension to Article 101(1) – an evaluation must be made of the effects of an agreement which promote competition and not of its positive effects in general, for example from the point of view of industrial policy, job creation and similar effects.[37] In the light of these comments which reject an interpretation of Article 101(1) based on rule of reason considerations, the criticism by *Hawk*, referred to above, is very much to the point in so far as it presumes that the overall economic analysis of the advantages and disadvantages is conducted within the framework of Article 101(1).

2.1.5. Further easing of restrictions?

It is clear from the preceding comments that the EU's competition authorities still take a sceptical view of undertakings' infringements of the prohibition of agreements whereby the parties, or one of them, establish absolute territorial protection; see section 2.1.1 above. The authorities take a correspondingly uncompromising approach to agreements on binding resale prices in subsequent links of the distribution chain; see section 2.1.3.

Neither the latest decisions of the CJ and the Commission, nor the latest Block Exemption Regulation (Regulation (EU) No 330/2010), on vertical agreements and concerted practices, contain any explicit indication that the EU competition authorities have changed their standpoint on these hardcore provisions.

However, some comments in the Commission's Vertical Restraints Guidelines could be understood as meaning that the Commission, at least,

the affects of the agreement both on promoting competition and restricting it, is presumably not in accordance with the judgment in Case T-112/99, *Métropole télévision (M6) and others* v *Commission.* The same applies in Case C-234/89, *Stergios Delimitis* v *Henninger Bräu,* and Case 399/93, *H.G. Oude Luttikhuis,* which the Court itself referred to. In Case T-65/98, *Van den Bergh Foods* v *Commission,* the Court repeated the view expressed in the *Métropole Télévision (M6)* case.

37. However, in Case C-309/99, *Wouters and others* v *Algemene Raad van de Nederlandse Orde van Advocaten,* on integrated cooperation between lawyers and accountants in the Netherlands, the Court used an approach where, within the framework of Article 101(1) TFEU, an overall evaluation was made as to whether there was a restriction on competition, and whether this restriction was necessary. However, the Court did not refer to the *Métropole Télévision (M6)* case and it is for this reason, among other things, that it is not safe to assume that the CJ has taken a different view from the Court of First Instance [now the General Court] in the case.

would be willing to discuss its approach to a couple of controversial matters which have created problems for a number of undertakings on the European market.

In particular, the desire to obtain protection from free riders is deeply rooted in the minds of every sole distributor. A free rider would be able to 'gather the low-hanging fruit' of a distributor's investments and marketing measures if they were able, as an unauthorised distributor, to offer the products covered by an agreement without having to bear the costs which the sole distributor incurs to introduce the products to the market and invest in facilities for after-sales service etc. (sunk costs, which cannot be recovered, and which it would be difficult to claim specific payment for, as such financial investment has no real inherent value).

If an agreement with the producer/supplier requires a sole distributor to incur costs for these tasks, it can be necessary to protect the distributor from inter-brand competition by giving protection in the form of territorial protection and fixed pricing. In particular a need to protect a sole distributor will (only?) exist in connection with the launch of a new product on the market.

In view of this, it appears that the Commission has some new thinking when, in paragraph 61 of the Vertical Restraints Guidelines, it states: 'Where substantial investments by the distributor to start up and/or develop the new market are necessary, restrictions of passive sales by other distributors into such a territory or to such a customer group which are necessary for the distributor to recoup those investments generally fall outside the scope of Article 101(1) during the first two years that the distributor is selling the contract goods or services in that territory or to that customer group, even though such hardcore restrictions are in general presumed to fall within the scope of Article 101(1).'

Where there is genuine testing of a new product in a limited territory or with a limited customer group, the distributors appointed to sell the new product on the test market or to participate in the first round of a staggered introduction may be restricted in their active selling outside the test market without falling within the scope of Article 101(1) for the period necessary for the testing or introduction of the product; see paragraph 62 of the Vertical Restraints Guidelines.

Also there has clearly been a slight change of the Commission's attitude to the prohibition of resale price maintenance. According to paragraph 223 of the Vertical Restraints Guidelines, depending on the circumstances an agreement that included resale price maintenance can fall within the scope of Article 101(3) TFEU if it can be shown that the agreement will have a positive effect on competition. According to paragraph 225 of the Guidelines, this applies in particular where a manufacturer introduces a new product. In this case, resale price maintenance during the introductory period may help stimulate demand for the product, and induce distributors to take better account of the manufacturer's interest in promoting the product.

In the same way fixed, and not merely maximum, resale prices can be necessary within the scope of a franchising scheme or equivalent distribution system based on a uniform distribution format, in order to provide for a coordinated, short-term promotional campaign that will also benefit consumers.

An agreement whereby a distributor has to pay a higher price for products that it intends to sell via the internet than for products it intends to sell via other channels (dual pricing) will normally be covered by Article 101(1); see the comments above in section 2.1.3.

However, it follows from paragraph 64 of the Vertical Restraints Guidelines that under special circumstances the Commission will allow agreements of this kind so that the conditions for the application of Article 101(3) are regarded as being fulfilled. This applies, for example, if a producer enters into an agreement with a distributor on dual pricing, because selling online can lead to substantially higher costs for the manufacturer than offline sales. For example, where offline sales include home installation by the distributor but online sales do not, the latter may lead to more customer complaints and warranty claims for the manufacturer. Conversely, it will be reasonable to ensure that an internet distributor does not have the possibility of freeloading on the costs of offline distributors' work in providing product advice etc., and thus being able to offer the goods at a lower price. It is not clear from the Guidelines whether dual pricing in these circumstances may be a general practice or whether it may only be for a limited period.

2.2. Block exemptions

The frequent questions about competition law, in the wake of the steady increase in cross-border trade in the Community, and the rapid increase in notifications to the Commission with a view to obtaining an exemption in accordance with Article 101(3) TFEU, led at an early stage in the Community's development to the adoption of Council Regulation No 19/65/EEC on application of Article 101(3) TFEU to certain categories of agreements and concerted practices, authorising the Commission to issue regulations under which certain kinds of agreements were in general exempted from the duty to notify in accordance with Article 101(3).

This authorisation was already put into effect in Commission Regulation No 67/67/EEC on the application of Article 85(3) of the Treaty [Article 101(3) TFEU] to certain categories of exclusive dealing agreements.

Council Regulation 19/65 focused exclusively on the acute problems which were the result of there being countless agreements on re-selling goods being notified to the Commission in accordance with Council Regulation (EEC) No 17/1962 First Regulation implementing Articles 85 and 86 of the Treaty [now Articles 101 and 102 TFEU].[38] Other categories of agreements, for example agreements for the provision of services, which have subsequently come to play an ever greater role, were not covered by Regulation 19/65. Some of these agreements were later covered by Commission Regulation (EEC) No 4087/88 on the application of Article 85(3) of the Treaty to categories of franchise agreements. On the other hand, neither the provision of services outside the field of franchises nor selective distribution agreements (see sections 3 and 4 below) were covered by a block exemption. With the benefit of hindsight, it would probably have been better if the Commission had limited its considerations to major cases and instead clarified the nature of the ancillary restraints to which a party to an agreement may be subject without thereby coming into conflict with Article 101(1).

Regulation 67/67 was later replaced by Commission Regulation (EEC) No 1983/83 on the application of Article 85(3) of the Treaty [Article 101(3) TFEU] to categories of exclusive dealing agreements, which could take account of the experience gained in this area and the practice which the Court had established in the meantime. In this connection, Commission Regulation (EEC) No 1984/83 on the Application of article 85 (3) of the Treaty [Article 101(3) TFEU] to categories of exclusive purchasing agreements introduced a block exemption for exclusive purchasing arrangement which had hitherto been regulated under the 1967 Regulation.[39] In Case 47/76, *de Norre* v *NV Brouwerij Concordia*, the Court stated that an exclusive purchase obligation

38. According to Article 2 of Regulation 17/62, after notification by the participating undertakings, the Commission could decide that, in the circumstances of which Commission had knowledge, there was no cause for the Commission to take measures under Articles 85(1) or 86 [now Articles 101(1) and 102 TFEU] against an agreement, decision or concerted practice (comfort letters).
39. It is characteristic of agreements that fell within the scope of Regulation 1983/83 that a dealer would be allocated an area within which the principal would not be permitted to appoint other dealers. In contrast to this, Regulation 1984/83 applied to agreements under which a supplier was subject to an exclusive obligation to purchase, but without at the same time being allocated a specific sales area and without the supplier being prevented from selling to other purchasers.

could be covered by Regulation 67/67, even if the agreement did not include any exclusive territorial provisions.

In 1999, growing criticism of the scope of application of the block exemption regulations led to all the regulations in the area of distribution being repealed and, with effect from 2000, being replaced by Commission Regulation (EC) No 2790/1999 on block exemptions for vertical restraints; see in more detail section 5 below. Regulation (EC) No 2790/1999 was replaced by Regulation (EU) No 330/2010 on the application of Article 101(3) TFEU to categories of vertical agreements and concerted practices. In all essentials, the new Regulation carries forward the approach adopted in Regulation (EC) No 2790/1999. On this basis, in the following references are made to Regulation (EU) No 330/2010 as the Regulation whose content marks the changed approach in the area of the law on block exemptions.

A block exemption regulation contains a set of rules which either directly or indirectly establish the terms for agreements in a particular category of agreements which the parties can adopt in the confidence that, even if they restrict competition, they will not be objected to. As the name suggests, the idea of the regulation is that when the conditions laid down in the regulation are met, the terms are given prior exemption from measures being taken against them, as there will be an assumption that the agreement is valid under competition law. In addition to this, the regulation sets out the terms which, if they are part of an agreement in restraint of competition, will mean that the agreement will be without legal effect in whole or in part.[40] See also the commentary on the concept of block exemptions in Chapter II above.

There can be wide-ranging consequences for undertakings if their agreement is considered to restrict competition, without it being, in accordance with Article 101(3), either individually or falling within a category (under a block exemption) of exempted agreements which are covered by Article 101(1).

To start with, as stated in Article 101(2), agreements which restrict competition contrary to Article 101(1) are void, and cannot therefore be enforced

40. According to Article 101(3), whether individual or group, exemption is conditional on the agreements contributing to improving the distribution of goods, while allowing consumers a fair share of the benefit, while not imposing on the undertakings concerned restrictions which are not indispensable for the attainment of these objectives. For a discussion of the four cumulative conditions for obtaining an exemption, see *Christopher Bellamy & Graham Child:* European Community Law of Competition, 2008 pp. 189-223 and the commentary on Article 101(3) in Chapter II above.

via the national courts. Also, by virtue of the rules of private international law (choice of law rules), a corresponding result could be reached in relation to courts in third countries (meaning courts outside the EU or EEA).

Next, an agreement to restrict competition, for example a market-sharing agreement, could lead to punishment by a fine on undertakings which are party to the agreement, and sometimes such parties may be required by national courts to pay compensation to third parties who stand outside the agreement, if it is considered that they have suffered loss as a result of the agreement between the parties.

In the EU it has predominantly been the practice that the enforcement of competition rules is a matter for the competition authorities, and not for the national courts. The sanctions applied have been prohibitions and fines, and not private law enforcement such as claims for compensation on the grounds of infringement of the competition rules. Among other things, this is due to the way in which the sanctions system is built up, including the fact that under Regulation 17/62, the Commission previously had sole competence to grant exemptions under Article 101(1) TFEU, and that under the applicable rule, undertakings had the possibility of notifying agreements which were in restraint of competition, whereby further proceedings before the national courts were excluded. The changes to Regulation 17/62 discussed below have removed these restrictions to the benefit of undertakings which believe themselves to be injured by the market conduct of a counterparty or by others who restrict competition.

In Case C-453/99, *Courage* v *Crehan*, the Court gave a clear signal that the full effect of the prohibition in Article 101(1) would be put at risk unless undertakings which have suffered loss as a result of conduct that has restricted or distorted competition can effectively enforce their rights. Since there are no provisions under Community law for the payment of compensation, it is up to the individual Member States to establish the procedural rules for cases to be brought for the protection of the rights which the direct effect Community law gives to Union citizens. The Court pointed out that such rules may not be less favourable than those that apply to corresponding cases under national law (the principle of equivalence), nor may it be impossible or unduly difficult to exercise the rights which are granted to Union citizens under Community law (the principle of effectiveness).[41] The Court expressly concluded that Article

41. See paragraph 27 in Case C-261/95, *Palmisani* v *INPS.*

101 of the Treaty prevents national laws being adopted which *prohibit* a party from claiming compensation for loss suffered solely on the grounds that the party was a party to an agreement in restraint of competition. This can be relevant, for example, in a case where a supplier establishes a network of standard agreements with a number of smaller traders, in other words where there are vertical transactions. On the other hand, Community law does not prevent there being a national law under which a party cannot rely on its own unlawful conduct with a view to obtaining compensation when this party bears a significant share of the responsibility for the restriction of competition. This decision is important, not least in relation to defining the principle of effectiveness, which in future the national courts will contribute to establishing, under a system of expanded direct effect, see immediately below.

A close examination of the provision on block exemptions can give significant guidance to an undertaking which, for example, as the producer of goods is to be party to an agreement with a trader who has undertaken to distribute the goods on a given market.

Both parties can thereby be aware of the pitfalls which can risk bringing them into the spotlight of the competition authorities, just as they can use the Regulation's statement of exempting conditions as a suitable checklist for terms which they might not have previously considered.

A block exemption regulation is built up so that the introduction – a preamble which contains a number of recitals – sets out the background to the exemption. These considerations constitute an important basis for interpretation of the operative part of the regulation, just as the recitals will often give clear indications of the Commission's policy in the area covered by the regulation.

Until the adoption of Commission Regulation (EC) No 2790/1999 on the application of Article 101(3) TFEU to categories of vertical agreements and concerted practices in the area of distribution [subsequently replaced by Regulation (EU) No 330/2010] the applicable block exemption regulations contained a number of 'whitelisted' conditions and a number of 'blacklisted' conditions.[42] The whitelisted conditions were permitted,[43] while the blacklist-

42. See, for example, Article 1 and 2 of Commission Regulation (EEC) No 1983/83 on the application of Article 85(3) of the Treaty [Article 101(3) TFEU] to categories of exclusive distribution agreements. These two Articles contained the permitted conditions which, in spite of their capacity to restrict competition, could be agreed without risk. In contrast, Article 3 blacklisted the conditions which, in addition to

ed conditions constituted significant restrictions on competition and were therefore not regarded as being suitable for prior exemption. Furthermore, a number of regulations contained a catalogue of 'grey' conditions, in other words conditions that were regarded as having been approved unless the Commission objected to them within a given period of having been informed of them. Commission Regulation (EC) No 240/96 on the application of Article 85(3) of the Treaty [Article 101(3) TFEU] to certain categories of technology transfer agreements, now repealed, contained a number of grey conditions that were subject to such objection procedure. The replacement for Regulation 240/96, Commission Regulation (EC) No 772/2004 on the application of Article 101(3) TFEU to categories of technology transfer agreements (discussed in more detail in Chapter V), does not contain any procedure for objections.

Regulation 2790/99 [now Regulation (EU) No 330/2010] contained a number of major differences from the previous block exemption regulations on exclusive distribution, exclusive purchasing and franchising.

The Regulation should be seen in conjunction with the arrangement which entered into force in 1999 whereby agreements which contain restrictions on vertical competition should no longer be notified in accordance with Article 81(3) of the EC Treaty in order to be valid, on this see section 5 below concerning Council Regulation (EC) No 1216/1999.

Regulation (EU) No 330/2010 concerns the category of 'vertical agreements', and is therefore freed from the straightjacket effect associated with the earlier block exemption regulations, and which is why each of them only covered a single type of contract, for example, sole distribution agreements. The distinction between white, grey and blacklisted conditions is departed from and instead a system is introduced with the main rule that 'everything that is not prohibited is allowed'.[44]

being invalid, included the risk of paying fines and compensation. A corresponding structure is found in Commission Regulation (EEC) No 4087/88 on the application of Article 85(3) of the Treaty [Article 101 (3) TFEU] to categories of franchise agreements.

43. Some of the whitelisted conditions were not strictly speaking restraints on competition within the meaning of Article 101(1) TFEU, but were exempted in the event that they might have had such an effect fact.
44. With effect from 1 May 2004, horizontal agreements have been subject to a corresponding arrangement, see Council Regulation (EC) No 1/2003 on the implementation of the rules on competition laid down in Articles 101 and 102 TFEU, which is discussed in various contexts below.

3. The concept of restriction of competition

The restriction on free trade which can be the result of an agreement or a concerted practice within the meaning of Article 101(1) can have an effect both on the dealings between the parties to the agreement and on third parties, whereby competitors' commercial freedom is restricted. However, a measure against free trade is not in itself a restriction on competition. The measure must also constitute a restriction either on *intra-brand* competition (competition between traders in the same product) or *inter-brand* competition (competition between traders in substitutable goods).[45]

The concept of restriction of competition, including the condition of a Community dimension etc., and the *de minimis* rule are discussed in more detail above in Chapter II.

In a number of cases on vertical arrangements involving specific contractual arrangements, the courts have taken their starting point in an assessment of whether the overall category of the agreement has been a legitimate business activity. If the result of such an analysis is in favour of the agreement in question, so it is found to be a legitimate and natural element of effective competition, the next question is whether the special conditions of the agreement are necessary for achieving its purpose. If the conditions are relevant in the given context, they could be judged to be *ancillary restraints*, as long as they are directly related to the main transaction and are not in themselves disproportionate. Such conditions would not be considered to be restrictions on competition, even if this might appear natural, if the conditions had arisen in some other context.[46] However, if the restriction has the direct aim of restrict-

45. See Case T-7/93, *Langnese-Iglo v Commission,* in which the Court, in addition to finding that an exclusive purchasing agreement and a prohibition on competition constituted an infringement of the trader's commercial freedom, stated that the two restrictions together could lead to a restriction on both intra-brand and inter-brand competition, see paragraphs 94-113 of the judgment. In the *Grundig* case the Court found that the attempt of the parties to create strict territorial limits was sufficient reason to regard the agreement as being covered by Article 101(1), even though there was a possible side-effect that in the longer term this could have the benefit of stimulating inter-brand competition, in other words it could increase the supply of substitutable products. As stated above in section 1.1, in Case C-309/99, *Wouters and others* v *Algemene Raad van de Nederlandse Orde van Advocaten,* on the integrated cooperation between lawyers and accountants (i.e. at a horizontal level) the Court seems to have come close to making a rule of reason assessment.
46. This distinction of certain ancillary restraints is a result of the general Community principle of proportionality, and the main area where this applies is under the Treaty

ing competition, it has not been accepted; see for example Case T-176/95, *Accinauto* v *Commission*, discussed above in section 2.

> Whether a condition in an agreement can be considered necessary, and therefore constitute an ancillary restraint within the definition set out, was one of the themes of the *Métropole Télévision (M6)* case referred to above, where the Court considered whether the three major French national television broadcasting companies, which were some of the participants in a joint venture to transmit satellite television to France, could undertake to refrain from providing programmes to other satellite channels. The case must be classified as concerning a horizontal agreement, but in the present context it can illustrate the condition of 'necessity' associated with ancillary restraints.
>
> Among other things, the Court referred to the fact that other undertakings had established satellite channels without adopting such exclusive conditions. Therefore, the condition could not be considered necessary, and furthermore it was found to be disproportionate, as it denied competitors access to programmes that were demanded by French viewers. The decision was based on the approach that, when deciding whether a restraint is necessary, a relatively abstract assessment must be made. If the application of a rule of reason assessment to the main transaction is excluded, see the comments above in section 2.1, it cannot be applied to an assessment of ancillary restraints, as this would involve an assessment of the commercial necessity of the restraint.[47]

Necessity, in the narrow sense that was established in the *Métropole Télévision (M6)* case, is an extension of the opinions which the Court has expressed in cases where the main transaction has been accompanied by an ancillary restraint *in order to be carried out at all*. In respect of vertical restraints on competition, such considerations have been applied, among others, in the important areas of franchising and selective distribution.

provisions on trade restrictions, but it has also been expressed in connection with the competition rules in Article 101(3).

47. See *Valentine Korah & Denis O'Sullivan:* Distribution Agreements under the EC Competition Rules, 2002 pp. 83-85. It will often be difficult to distinguish between objective and commercial necessity. The burden of proof that the condition of necessity has been satisfied rests on the undertakings. Compare with the area of merger controls, Case T-17/93, *Matra Hachette* v *Commission.*

4. Special agreements that only exceptionally fall within the scope of Article 101(1) TFEU

In the practice of the Court and the Commission it is possible to identify special types of agreements, under different conditions and for various reasons, which have been found particularly acceptable from a competition law perspective. However, individual special conditions in these agreements have received less sympathy.

These types of agreements include, among others, agency agreements, franchising agreements, and selective distribution agreements.[48]

4.1. Agency agreements

Agreements between traditionally operating commercial agents and their principals have previously been considered to be agreements which are not affected by Article 101(1) TFEU.

In Directive 86/653/EEC on the coordination of the laws of the Member States relating to self-employed commercial agents, which is directed at the law of obligations aspect of the relationship between commercial agents and principals, such agents are defined as follows:

> For the purposes of this Directive, 'commercial agent' shall mean a self-employed intermediary who has continuing authority to negotiate the sale or the purchase of goods on behalf of another person, hereinafter called the 'principal', or to negotiate and conclude such transactions on behalf of and in the name of that principal.

In a Notice of 24 December 1962, which has since lapsed and been replaced by paragraphs 12-21 of the Vertical Restraints Guidelines, the Commission expressed the view that an agent who does not undertake financial obligations in relation to third parties, other than an agreed guarantee of the solvency of the third party (*del credere*), does not for the competition purposes play a role which is different from the principal's own direct employees.

48. The comments in this section concern agreements which would not, for some other reason, be considered a restriction on competition, for example because they fall under the *De minimis* notice (Commission Notice on agreements of minor importance which do not appreciably restrict competition under Article 81(1) of the Treaty establishing the European Community (*de minimis*) (OJ 2001 C 368/13) – discussed above in Chapter II).

Paragraph 12 of the Vertical Restraints Guidelines defines the agency relationship somewhat differently, as the new wording provides that an agent can negotiate and enter into contracts on behalf of the principal either in the agent's own name or in the name of the principal, for the purchase of goods or services or the sales of goods or services that are provided by the principal. This creates the possibility that an agent can have a status corresponding to an intermediary or, as known in Danish and Continental European systems, a commission agent. In addition to this, the definition of an agent under competition law also now applies where the subject of agent's activities covers services as well as goods.[49]

The difference between the two definitions is not merely formal. The difference will presumably mean that in many more cases than previously an intermediary could be considered to have the status of an independent dealer ('non-genuine-agent') even if the intermediary otherwise has characteristics associated with a genuine agent. For the distinction between genuine and non-genuine agents, see below.

> The first real decision on the position of agents in competition law was given in Joined cases 40/73 and others, *Suiker Unie and others* v *Commission*, in which the Court stated that Article 85 of the Treaty [now Article 101 TFEU] did not apply to a non-compete obligation in accordance with which a commercial agent had undertaken to sell the principal's goods and otherwise take care of the principal's interests in the market. On the other hand, the Court found reason to state that a commercial agent who undertakes obligations which, from a financial point of view, are the same as those of an independent dealer, including the obligation to fulfil contracts entered into with third parties, cannot be regarded in competition law as an auxiliary organ. This view was repeated in Case C-266/93, *Bundeskartellamt* v *Volkswagen and VAG Leasing*, where the Court stated that it was decisive for whether the intermediary should be considered to be an agent or not, whether the intermediary took on a *financial risk* in relation to the third party. Among other things, the

49. However, in other legal systems in the EU, services are also covered by the concept of agency as it appears on the basis of Council Directive 86/653/EEC on the coordination of the laws of the Member States relating to self-employed commercial agents. For example this applies in French law and in German law; see *Agustin Jausàs:* Agency and Distribution Agreements – An International Survey, 1994, which includes a discussion of the concept of an agent in a number of European legal systems.

fact that the agent's obligations in relation to some leasing contracts expired, including at least the agent's obligation to buy back leased motor vehicles, was regarded as being sufficient to establish that the agent had taken on a financial risk.

Paragraph 15 of the Vertical Restraints Guidelines assumes that genuine agency agreements (agency agreements under which the agent merely acts in mediating agreements in which the principal carries the full financial risk) fall outside the scope of Article 101(1) of the Treaty. This is because in these cases, even if he or she is self-employed, a genuine agent is regarded as being integrated in the principal's sales organisation. The actions of the agent in the market are therefore considered to reflect that the agent acts as the extended arm of the principal in relation to third parties (the integration criterion). See also the situation referred to in paragraph 16 of the Guidelines, which point in the direction of excluding the agent from Article 101(1).

The purpose of the integration criterion is that the application of Article 101(1) TFEU will not take effect if the agent merely acts as an auxiliary organ for the principal, who does not withdraw from competition but merely uses the agent to arrange for the sale of goods in the market. A natural and probable consequence of establishing these definitions is that a genuine agent cannot be considered an 'undertaking' within the meaning of Article 101(1). Consequently, the principal can require an agent not to enter into contracts with parties to parallel trade, not to execute orders addressed to the agent by traders outside the agent's allocated territory (passive sales), and the agent must respect the instructions of the principal, among other things, not to give discounts, share sales commission with customers etc.

In contrast, in the agreements of non-genuine agents the agent takes on wider financial and commercial risks, and an assessment of the agreement in relation to Article 101(1) will often be relevant (the risk criterion).

Conceptually, the risk criterion has the function of restricting traditional agency agreements to agreements where the supplier's counterparty (the agent) acts *on his or her own account* in one or more commercially significant respects.[50] This includes taking on financial risks which are directly connected with the contracts which the agent enters into and/or negotiates on behalf of the principal, for example the building up and financing of stocks, in-

50. In such a case it will be more appropriate to consider the intermediary as an (exclusive) distributor and reserve the term 'agent' for the party who is referred to as the 'genuine agent'. Apart from this, it is probably not right to draw too wide conclusions from either the integration criterion or the risk criterion.

cluding losses on unsold goods and the lack of a right to return these goods, as well as the risks connected with market-specific investments which are necessary for the kind of undertaking which the agent is expected to make. Examples of this include investments in real property, specially trained personnel, means of transport etc. In these cases, to which could be added agreements on product liability, liability for customers' failure to fulfil their contracts etc., where the agent is more or less outside an integrated relation to the principal, the agent can be considered as an independent distributor (independent dealer), who is free to plan his own marketing strategy to cover his own contract and market-specific investments. Investments of this kind are normally irrecoverable (sunk costs) if they cannot be used in other commercial activities, or can only be sold at a loss if the agency agreement is terminated. Under these circumstances, where there can be considerable commercial risks for the agent, the agent can be classified as an independent operator in relation to Article 101(1).

In Case 311/85, *Vereniging van Vlaamse Reisbureaus* v *Sociale Dienst*, a question arose from agreements between an association of travel companies and an association of travel agents and the Court had to consider the status of intermediaries, either as an auxiliary organ or as an independent operator on the market. Among other things, the agreements, which were based on legislative provisions and administrative orders, laid down that travel agents should not sell at below the prices which had been determined by the travel companies, and that they should not provide discounts or share their sales commission with their travelling customers. As there were a large number of travel companies and a correspondingly large number of travel agencies, it was found that the travel agents were not 'agents' in the traditional sense, in other words they were not intermediaries with the status of auxiliary organs. In the view of the Court, this would have required the individual travel agent to have been engaged by a specific travel company, and not by a multiplicity of travel companies. This was not altered by the fact that, in relation to its customers, the individual travel agent acted in the name of the travel company and on its behalf.[51]

See also the illustrative example of 2002/758/EC: Commission Decision relating to a proceeding under Article 81 of the EC Treaty

51. On the practice of the Court, see *Swanson & Brown* in European Community Law Review 1991 p. 86.

(*Mercedes-Benz*) (OJ 2002 L 257/1), which considered a number of specific obligations which Mercedes-Benz had imposed on its German agents. The investigation had been initiated with a view to deciding whether the agents should be characterised as genuine agents or non-genuine dealers, because of some export restrictions which Mercedes-Benz had imposed on the agents. Among a number of other factors, the Commission emphasised that the agents had to pay considerable costs for sales promotion activities out of their own pockets, including obtaining a number of demonstration models at their own expense and risk, and subsequently selling them on under certain conditions. On the basis of these other heavy financial obligations which Mercedes-Benz imposed on its agents, Mercedes was fined EUR 72 million. See also Commission Decision – *Pittsburgh Corning Europe* (OJ 1972 L 272/35).

A more recent case in this area, Case C-217/05, *Confederación Española de Empresarios de Estaciones de Servicio* v *Compañía Española de Petróleos*, concerned agreements entered into by the CEPSA oil company and a number of petrol stations in Spain for the supply of petrol. According to paragraph 46 of the judgment, the decisive factor for the purposes of determining whether a service station operator is an independent economic operator is to be found in the agreement concluded with the principal and, in particular, in the express or implied terms of the agreement on the assumption of the financial and commercial risks linked to sales of goods to third parties. In the Court's view (paragraph 52), it is likely that the service station operator assumes the risks linked to the sale of the goods when he receives them from the supplier, that is to say, prior to selling them on to a third party. According to paragraphs 53 and 54, a corresponding assumption applies when the service station operator assumes, directly or indirectly, the costs linked to the distribution of those goods, particularly the transport costs. Furthermore, the fact that the service station operator maintains stocks at his own expense could be an indication that the risks linked to the sale of the goods are transferred to him. Finally, in paragraphs 55 and 56, there is focus on who assumes responsibility for any damage caused to the goods and whether the service station operator should pay for the fuel if he does not find a purchaser.

The question of risk must be assessed on a case-by-case basis, and in the view of the Commission the starting point will be the economic reality rather than the nomenclature which is attached more or less randomly to the intermediary stage. The terms of agreements which are usual in agency arrangements, including rights and duties to maintain stocks of goods at the expense of the principal, to provide customer service at no extra cost, to monitor the market, do not fulfil the risk criterion and therefore fall outside Article 101(1).

On the other hand, as stated an intermediary can lose the status of an agent in the traditional sense (as an auxiliary organ (genuine agent)) for the principal), if the intermediary is required to contribute to the costs of supplying/buying the agreed goods, to invest in sales promotion measures, denied the right to return unsold goods which have been carried in stock, to provide an after-sales service, repair or guarantee system without being fully recompensed by the principal, to undertake investments for the specific market, premises or specially trained personnel (see the comments above), to be responsible towards third parties for damage caused by the goods sold (product liability), and to accept general responsibility for the customers' failure to fulfil their contracts, with the exception of the agent's loss of commission.

In future it will presumably be the exception for a single factor or several individual factors to be significant from a competition law point of view, and call into use Article 101(1) TFEU in cases where an agent has not had property rights over the goods bought or sold. The condition or conditions which may perhaps fall outside the scope of a traditional agency agreement should have a significant influence on the agreement. The risks associated with the business itself, which consists in providing the normal service of an agent, including the risk of the agent's income being dependent on how well he or she carries out the work etc., or which is associated with general investments in premises and personnel, are not circumstances which in themselves make the agent more akin to some other status than that of that of an auxiliary organ for the principal. However, if the circumstances of the actual case indicate that the commercial agent has a position which is independent of the principal, whether organisationally or otherwise, the principles which regulate the assessment of vertical agreements under competition law will determine whether the agent's conduct is acceptable or prohibited. These principles, including those in Regulation (EU) No 330/2010 on the application of Article 101(3) TFEU to categories of vertical agreements and concerted practices, are discussed below.

4.2. Franchising

Neither in law nor in practical commerce is there a precise definition of what is meant by *franchising*. The term is usually used as a general concept for a *vertical* distribution system based on an agreement between *independent* undertakings.[52]

However, this abstract definition also covers sole distributorships and licensing agreements etc. It is therefore necessary to define further that franchising typically involves the franchisor providing know-how, manuals and licences to intellectual property or commercial rights etc. to the franchisee, in return for which the franchisee accepts certain restrictions on the purchase of goods, sales of competing products, the get-up of sales premises etc., and above all undertakes to pay the franchisor a regular royalty.[53] While in *sole distributorship agreements* it will typically be the distributor who provides the market knowledge to the supplier, in *franchise agreements* it is the franchisor who is responsible for systems development etc. and who has the necessary experience with regard to advertising, sales and other matters which are important for promoting awareness of the products.

Franchising is often associated with the sales of fast-food and fashion, but after franchising was introduced to Europe in the 1960s, this form of distribution has been used on a wide range of other categories of goods or, as expressed by *Joanna Goyder:* EC Distribution Law, 2003: 'it has been used to sell everything from pet dogs to hot dogs, and continues to increase in popularity as a distribution method.'

Franchising can take different forms:
With *product franchising* (sometimes called *trade mark licensing*) a producer of branded goods gives some other undertaking a licence to produce certain goods and to market them using the producer's trade mark.[54]

52. These characteristics mean that in principle franchising is treated similarly to other distribution forms that are regulated by Regulation (EU) No 330/2010; see section 5 below.
53. Compare this with Article 1(3)(a) of the now repealed Commission Regulation (EEC) No 4087/88 on the application of Article 85(3) of the Treaty to categories of franchise agreements.
54. See, among others, 78/253/EEC*:* Commission Decision relating to proceedings under Article 85 of the EEC Treaty (*Campari* – on the sale of special herbs for the manufacture of wine) (OJ 1978 L 70/69); and 90/186/EEC*:* Commission Decision relating to a proceeding under Article 85 of the EEC Treaty (*Moosehead/Whitbread* on an agreement between a Canadian brewery and a British brewery on the production and sale in the UK of a beer under the trade mark 'Moosehead') (OJ 1990 L 100/32). On these decisions see *Valentine Korah & Denis O'Sullivan:* Distriibution Agreements under the EC Competition Rules, 2002 p. 112 and pp. 140-141.

Service franchising is an agreement whereby the franchisee can offer a service under the franchisor's name or trade mark and otherwise in accordance with the franchisor's directions.[55]

Distribution franchising, as the name suggests, is an agreement to sell the franchisor's products under the franchisor's trade mark and other get-up.[56]

The *Pronuptia* case[57] was important in pointing the way for the assessment of franchise agreements under competition law and also contributed to the general assessment of the restriction on competition of special conditions on territorial limits, parallel imports and exports, cross-supplies, non-compete obligations etc; see the comments below in section 5 on Articles 4 and 5 of Regulation (EU) No 330/2010.[58]

> The background to the case was that the German *Bundesgerichtshof* had referred a question to the CJ for a preliminary ruling on the claimed breach of a franchise agreement which the French undertaking, *Pronuptia de Paris*, had entered into with a German franchisee through its representative in Germany, for the sale of bridal equipment etc. in three German towns on a franchise basis.
>
> According to the agreement, the franchisee had the sole right to use the trade mark 'Pronuptia de Paris' within the agreed territory, and undertook

55. See, for example 88/604/EEC: Commission Decision relating to a proceeding under Article 85 of the EEC Treaty (*ServiceMaster*) (OJ 1988 L 332/38).
56. See the decision in Case 161/84, *Pronuptia de Paris GmbH* v *Pronuptia de Paris Irmgard Schillgallis*.
57. See Case 161/84, *Pronuptia de Paris GmbH* v *Pronuptia de Paris Irmgard Schillgallis*.
58. The judgment in the *Pronuptia* case led to the adoption of Commission Regulation (EEC) No 4087/88 on the application of Article 101(1) of the Treaty to categories of franchise agreements. Prior to that, the *Pronuptia* judgment's detailed description of the competitive status of the franchise agreement had clearly influenced the decisions which the Commission took in the following years, and the granting of exemptions under Article 85(3)[Article 101(3) TFEU] for certain parts of notified franchise agreements, see 87/14/EEC: Commission Decision relating to a proceeding under Article 85 of the EEC Treaty (*Yves Rocher*) (OJ 1987 L 8/49), 87/17/EEC: Commission Decision in proceedings under Article 85 of the EEC Treaty (*Pronuptia* standard agreements) (OJ 1987 L 13/39), 87/407/ EEC: Commission Decision relating to a proceeding under Article 85 of the EEC Treaty (*Computerland*) (OJ 1987 L 222/12), 88/604/EEC: Commission Decision relating to a proceeding under Article 85 of the EEC Treaty (*ServiceMaster* – service franchising) (OJ 1988 L 332/38), and 89/94/EEC: Commission Decision relating to a proceeding under Article 85 of the EEC Treaty (*Charles Jourdan*) (OJ 1989 L 35/31).

to carry on the business of selling bridal equipment etc. within the territory under the name Pronuptia from premises which were approved by the franchisor and furnished and decorated in accordance with the franchisor's instructions, and using the franchisor's know-how and business methods. The franchisor undertook to help the franchisee with the furnishing and decoration of the premises, training of personnel, and in connection with the franchisee's sales promotion activities.

The franchisee had to buy the products which were the subject of the agreement exclusively from the franchisor or from suppliers approved by the franchisor. The franchisee was to have the sale of bridal equipment as its primary activity, the franchisee's status as the sole responsible proprietor of the business was emphasised, and under certain circumstances the franchisee could buy products from other Pronuptia franchisees. However, 80 per cent of the bridal equipment had to be bought directly from the franchisor. According to the agreement, the franchisor was entitled itself to sell directly into the territory by mail order sales, and to pay 10 per cent of its turnover from this to the franchisee. The franchisee was to refrain from any form of competition with other Pronuptia traders, among other things by refraining from opening shops with a similar purpose in Germany or elsewhere.

In the view of the CJ, a franchise agreement such as this could only function optimally if the franchisor was able to pass on its know-how without the risk that this knowledge would be used by competitors on the market and if the agreement could lawfully contain certain restrictions with the aim was of protecting the reputation and identity of the franchise network. The same applied to those parts of the agreement which obliged the franchisee to use the business methods developed by the franchisor, the requirements for the location of the shops, the prohibition on the transfer of the rights and duties under the agreement to a third party without the consent of the franchisor, and conditions whose purpose was to secure the franchisor's control over the goods offered for sale by the franchisee.[59]

Against the background of these considerations, the CJ necessarily came to the conclusion that the agreement's ancillary restraints – in so far as assessed – did not contain any restriction on competition contrary to Article 101(1). Likewise, these considerations led to the conclusion that the franchisee could

59. See paragraphs 44-45 of the Vertical Restraints Guidelines.

lawfully be made subject to a non-compete obligation, also for a short period after the termination of the agreement (see Regulation (EU) No 330/2010, Article 5, discussed below in section 5.4).[60]

The Court was less persuaded of the acceptability of some of the other terms in the agreement. This applied in particular to the terms which led to or could lead to the sharing of the market between the franchisor and the franchisee, or between franchisees, as well as the terms which directly or indirectly hindered their right to compete on price (improper franchise agreements).

In the view of the Court, regard for the reputation and identity of the products could not justify such terms which, in relation to a product *which was already widespread*, constituted a restriction on competition as referred to in Article 101(1) TFEU, and which *were capable of affecting trade between Member States – even though they were entered into between undertakings from the same Member State.*[61]

> The Court put special emphasis on the fact that such restrictions on competition could arise because the franchisor gave the franchisee exclusive rights within a given area, without intrusion by the franchisor or other franchisees, to use the specific know-how etc., and at the same time the franchisee (and other franchisees) were bound to carry on the activities covered by the agreement at the appointed premises and was prohibited from opening further shops.
>
> The Court also pointed out that the national courts should be alert to whether, in spite of the statement in the agreement that the franchisor's retail prices were merely *recommended*, there was nevertheless a tacit understanding which must be seen as a concerted practice to the effect that the prices could in reality be considered as *binding*.

60. See the discussion of the judgment in *Christopher Bellamy & Graham Child:* European Community Law of Competition, 2008 p. 74 et seq. and p. 174.
61. On this point the *Pronuptia* judgment can be seen as supporting the general view that, in judging whether there is a distortion of competition, the circumstances must be taken into consideration as to whether an agreement which contains a certain measure of territorial protection is necessary to enable an undertaking to penetrate a market where it has not previously been active. In support of this see Case 56/65, *Société Technique Minière v Maschinenbau Ulm,* and see *Valentine Korah & Warwick A. Rothnie:* Exclusive Distribution and the EEC Competition Rules, 1992 pp. 52-53. In the area of technology transfer, see Case 258/78, *Nungesser and Eisele* v *Commission,* which among other things concerned the transfer of an 'open exclusive licence'; for more on this case see section 4.5 below and Chapter V.

In its formulation of the conditions for the block exemption, the Commission followed the comments of the Court on the significance of binding retail prices; see most recently Regulation (EU) No 330/2010, Article 4(a). For more details on this see section 5.3.1, in which terms of an agreement, or other measures outside an agreement, which restrict a franchisee's freedom to set its own sales prices for the goods or services covered by a franchise agreement, are classified as serious (hard core) restrictions which prevent the block exemption.

The Court was aware of the possibility that a potential franchisee could be interested in participating in a franchise network if they could secure a certain degree of protection from the franchisor and the other franchisees. In the view of the Court, such a situation could be taken into account in connection with the possible application of the exemption provisions in Article 81(3)[now Article 101(3)].[62]

4.3. Selective distribution

It the starting point in the Community law-based competition rules that a producer or supplier of goods is not subject to restrictions regarding to whom or on what conditions they sell their goods. Only the provision in Article 102 TFEU on abuse of a dominant position could be applicable and lead to a different result.

In some respects selective distribution differs from this starting point. The characteristics of this form of distribution are that a producer (supplier), who trades in branded goods through a main dealer (wholesaler), seeks not only to control the dealer but also subsequent links in the distribution chain (retailers) by requiring these to be approved dealers, in other words they should satisfy certain predetermined requirements of the producer. The restriction on retail sales is not a restriction on active sales to a given territory, but a restriction on sales to retailers. Sales must thus only be made to approved retailers and to the end user.[63]

62. The Court's overall assessment of the relationship of the franchise agreement in question to Article 101(1) is made clear in paragraph 27 of the judgment.
63. According to Regulation (EU) No 330/2010, Article 1(e): ''selective distribution system' means a distribution system where the supplier undertakes to sell the contract goods or services, either directly or indirectly, only to distributors selected on the basis of specified criteria and where these distributors undertake not to sell such goods or services to unauthorised distributors within the territory reserved by the supplier to operate that system.'

> *D.G. Goyder:* EEC Competition Law, 2003 tellingly describes selective distribution as follows: 'The essence of selectivity, therefore, is not simply that the supplier selects its main distributors or wholesalers, for if this was the only restrictive element, then it would be hard to see how Article 85 [now Article 101] could apply at all to such a unilateral act of commercial policy. It is rather that the supplier limits the distribution of goods only to those wholesalers and retailers which satisfy appropriate criteria and as a result have been allowed to join the system. Wholesalers will normally sell to anyone except retail customers whereas retailers may normally sell to any level, i.e. to wholesalers, other retailers, and to consumers or users, provided that they do not sell to a dealer outside the approved list.'[64]

Principally, the risks of competition can lead to a reduction of intra-brand competition and the exclusion of certain kinds of dealers as well as a restriction in the producer's customer base.

In assessing these *restrictions on competition* by selective distribution under Article 101(1), prior to Regulation (EU) No 330/2010 the practice was to distinguish between qualitative and quantitative selective distribution.

With qualitative selection there is a selection of dealers purely on the basis of objective criteria which are regarded as necessary due to the characteristics of the products (luxury, prestige and image goods), the training of sales personnel, the capacity of the dealer to provide after-sales service (for example for technical products), as well as the presence of a certain product range in the shop which sells to the end user etc.

With quantitative selection further selection criteria are added which more directly limit the potential number of dealers, for example conditions about minimum sales levels, stockholding etc.

4.3.1. Qualitative or quantitative selective distribution systems

In the context of Community competition law, selective distributions systems were accepted with a degree of tolerance quite early on, see 70/488/EEC: Commission Decision relating to a proceeding under Article 85 of the EEC Treaty (*Omega*) (OJ 1970 L 242/22 – not officially published in English), which concerned the sale of hi-fi equipment for home entertainment systems.

64. In other words, it is characteristic for selective distribution that a number of restrictions relate to a stage in the distribution chain that is subsequent in relation to the producer's counterparty.

In a number of subsequent cases, both the Commission and the CJ have confirmed that in special circumstances a producer can practice such a form of distribution, without the restrictions which are imposed on wholesalers and retailers being affected by the prohibition in Article 101(1) TFEU.

It has been accepted that producers of, for example, luxury goods and high technology products, can have a legitimate interest in their products being exclusively sold in specialist shops or in specially fitted out departments in department stores etc.

The objective criteria for keeping a qualitative system from infringing Article 101(1) were expressed in paragraph 20 of Case 26/76, *Metro SB-Großmärkte* v *Commission*:

> 'On this view the Commission was justified in recognizing that selective distribution systems constituted, together with others, an aspect of competition which accords with Article 85(1) [Article 101(1)], provided that resellers are chosen on the basis of objective criteria of a qualitative nature relating to the technical qualifications of the reseller and his staff and the suitability of his trading premises and that such conditions are laid down uniformly for all potential resellers and are not applied in a discriminatory fashion.'

These criteria for the compatibility of a selective system with Article 101(1) – usually called the 'Metro doctrine' – have been consolidated in subsequent decisions.

> In paragraph 112 of Case T-19/92, *Groupement d'achat Edouard Leclerc* (Yves Saint Laurent) v *Commission*, the CJ laid down four conditions which must be met for the criteria to be regarded as satisfied. It required: *that* the characteristics of the product in question necessitate a selective distribution system (the necessity criterion); *that* resellers are chosen on the basis of objective qualitative criteria which are laid down uniformly for all potential resellers (the non-discrimination criterion); *that* the system in question seeks to achieve a result which enhances competition and thus counterbalances the restriction of competition inherent in selective distribution systems (the market structure criterion); and *that* the criteria laid down do not go beyond what is necessary, namely the maintenance of specialist shops which can ensure the best possible trade in the special goods (the proportionality principle.)

The necessity criterion (products of a special nature):
To illustrate this, see 85/45/EEC: Commission Decision relating to a proceeding under Article 85 of the EEC Treaty (*Ideal-Standard* distribution system) (OJ 1985 L 20/38). This decision, which concerned the sale of fittings for plumbing systems, should be seen against the background of the statement in paragraph 16 in Case 31/80, *L'Oréal* v *De Nieuwe AMCK*, according to which it is necessary to determine 'whether the characteristics of the product in question necessitate a selective distribution system in order to preserve its quality and ensure its proper use, and whether those objectives are not already satisfied by national rules governing admission to the re-sale trade or the conditions of sale of the product in question.'[65]

The Commission found it questionable, at least in relation to wholesalers, whether the products in question had such characteristics that regard for the preservation of their quality and their correct use made it necessary to use a selective distribution system. Also, the restriction on sales (only plumbing engineers could be approved as retailers) was found to be a significant restriction as it would exclude retailers who were not also craftsmen from dealing in the fittings. The disadvantages which such a restriction would lead to were found to be significantly greater than any improvement in the distribution of the goods which would be achieved by selling them through plumbing engineers.

Nor have selective systems for the sale of tobacco products or the sale of mass-produced watches been accepted, see Case 209/78, *Heintz van Landewyck and others* v *Commission*, and Case 31/85, *ETA Fabriques d'Ébauches* v *DK Investment and others*.

On the other hand, for cases where the necessity criterion has been found to be satisfied, see: Case C-376/92, *Metro SB-Großmärkte* v *Cartier*, concerning more expensive watches; Case T-19/92, *Groupement d'achat Édouard Leclerc* v *Commission* (Yves Saint Laurent), Case T-88/92, *Groupement d'achat Édouard Leclerc* v *Commission* (Givenchy), both concerning high end cosmetics; and 85/616/EEC: Commission Decision relating to a proceeding pursuant to Article 85 of the EEC Treaty (*Villeroy & Boch*) (OJ 1985 L 376/15) on a selective distribution system for the sale of ornamental and table porcelain. In this last-named Decision

65. Regulation (EU) No 330/2010, which as its starting point keeps selective distribution outside the scope of Article 101(1), does not contain a necessity criterion in relation to the nature of the products.

the Commission accepted that a selective distribution system had been built up for these products because 'some products or services, which are not simple products or services, possess certain characteristics which prevent them from being sold properly to the public without the intervention of specialist distributors.'[66] However, 91/153/EEC: Commission Decision relating to a proceeding under Article 85 of the EEC Treaty (*Vichy*) (OJ 1991 L 75/57), which was accepted by the Court in Case T-19/91, *Société d'Hygiène Dermatologique de Vichy* v *Commission*, shows that the Commission has apparently sometimes laid down stricter requirements for the special character of products for the approval of some dealers and the exclusion of others than was the case in *Villeroy & Boch*.[67]

The non-discrimination criterion:
If dealers who satisfy the qualitative conditions for taking part in a selective distribution network are excluded from participating in the network, for example on the (covert) grounds that the quota of dealers in a given area has been filled, or because the customer base is considered too small, this will not normally be compatible with Article 101(1) TFEU, see paragraph 72 of Case 75/84, *Metro SB-Großmärkte* v *Commission (Metro II)*, which expressly states that the non-discrimination criterion means that a refusal to approve distributors who satisfy the qualitative criteria of the selective distribution system must be considered unlawful.

A unilateral measure by the producer or by the main dealer, for example a failure to authorise a specific dealer in an attempt to influence pricing, cannot be treated as an infringement of Article 101(1), which only covers *agreements*, *decisions* by associations of undertakings and *concerted practices*. If, on the other hand, such measures are part of a contractual arrangement which the producer or main dealer seeks to uphold with its dealers, then there will be discriminatory measures which fall within the scope of Article 101(1), see paragraph 38 in Case 107/82, *AEG-Telefunken* v *Commission*:

'Indeed, in the case of the admission of a distributor, approval is based on the acceptance, tacit or express, by the contracting parties of the policy pursued by AEG which requires *inter alia* the exclusion from the network

66. Paragraph 22 of the decision.
67. Perhaps the decision expresses the proportionality criterion discussed below.

of all distributors who are qualified for admission but are not prepared to adhere to that policy.'

And in paragraph 39 the Court continued:

'The view must therefore be taken that even refusals of approval are acts performed in the context of the contractual relations with authorized distributors inasmuch as their purpose is to guarantee observance of the agreements in restraint of competition which form the basis of contracts between manufacturers and approved distributors. Refusals to approve distributors who satisfy the qualitative criteria mentioned above therefore supply proof of an unlawful application of the system if their number is sufficient to preclude the possibility that they are isolated cases not forming part of systematic conduct.'[68]

The Commission seems to have emphasised that there must be such an automatic acceptance procedure that the possibility of discrimination is limited. Thus, in several cases the Commission has made the approval of a selective distribution system conditional on the originally notified acceptance procedure being amended.

See for example 92/428/EEC: Commission Decision relating to a proceeding under Article 85 of the EEC Treaty (*Parfums Givenchy* system of selective distribution) (OJ 1992 L 236/11), in which the finally approved acceptance procedure included a requirement for Givenchy to decide on every application made to the company by interested dealers within specific deadlines, so that every qualified applicant is accepted in the distribution network, or if not, a reason should be given for refusing an application. This eliminated the risk of arbitrariness which was the consequence of the originally envisaged arrangement which gave Givenchy the right to decide on the acceptance of new dealers, according to its own judgement. On the other hand, the change to the arrangement meant that only dealers who were able to or willing to fit out their sales premises in the way demanded could have access to the distribution network. They did not have permission to sell the contract goods before or after the expiry of a relatively long period of notice, which could discourage many potentially qualified dealers. The duration of the deadlines was therefore found to be liable to affect competition between

68. Corresponding opinions were expressed by the CJ in Joined cases 25 and 26/84, *Ford-Werke and Ford of Europe* v *Commission.*

dealers in Givenchy products. The restriction was however exempted in accordance with Article 101(3), since the acceptance procedure was nevertheless found to ensure a smooth integration of new dealers into Givenchy's distribution network. In fact, the deadlines were found to take account of Givenchy's need to be able to organise, among other things, the inspection of the sales premises, training of personnel, the scheduling of the company's production programme and production of advertising material. The procedure was found to give retailers reasonable time to fit out their sales premises rationally, and that it was probably necessary to enable the fulfilment of the acceptance procedure laid down.

The market structure:
Though qualitative selective distribution systems are not, according to the CJ, covered by the prohibition in Article 101(1), even if a selective distribution system satisfies the qualitative requirements and does not contain any quantitative restrictions, there can be a restriction or elimination of competition where the existence of a number of systems of this kind exclude other forms of distribution which are based on other kinds of sales policies or which lead to a rigid price policy which is not balanced by other competitive parameters between products of the same brand (intra-brand competition) or by effective competition between different brands (inter-brand competition). These comments come from paragraph 40 of Case 75/84, *Metro SB-Großmärkte* v *Commission (Metro II)*, where it was also emphasised that the existence of a large number of corresponding sales systems would not in itself lead to the assumption that Article 101(1) had been infringed. In this case the Court approved the decision of 1975 by which SABA's selective distribution system had originally been approved.

If qualitative distribution systems are the norm within a given industry sector, so a serious lack of competition arises in the area these systems cover, Article 101(1) will, extraordinarily, apply to these arrangements.[69]

The proportionality principle:
The requirement for proportionality exists in various forms in several areas of EU law.

69. See *Christopher Bellamy & Graham Child:* European Community Law of Competition, 2008 p. 459 et seq. and *Valentine Korah & Warwick A. Rothnie:* Exclusive Distribution and the EEC Competition Rules, 1992 pp. 151-153.

In the present context the principle expresses that a selective distribution system which formally satisfies the qualitative conditions will nevertheless be regarded as incompatible with Article 101(1) if it goes beyond what is necessary for the appropriate sale of the products, see 91/153/EEC: Commission Decision relating to a proceeding under Article 85 of the EEC Treaty (*Vichy*) (OJ 1991 L 75/57).

> One of the requirements of the producer Vichy, that the company's cosmetics should be sold exclusively through pharmacies, was found to be disproportionate, as the sales of the products differed from that of medicines as there was no other requirement than that they should not be harmful, and control of this could not be carried out by pharmacies as they did not have precise knowledge of the composition of the products. The judgment took account of the fact that competing products were normally sold through other sales channels. While it was regarded as legitimate to require the presence of a certain level of specialist advice, for example a requirement that a pharmacist should be linked to the sales premises, it was not necessary to exclude other forms of traders in order to ensure the products' quality and correct use.
>
> The agreements were therefore contrary to Article 101(1) and the Commission also concluded that there were no grounds for granting an exemption under Article 101(3), as the conditions for granting an exemption under this provision (contributing to improving the production or distribution of goods or promoting technical or economic progress to the benefit of consumers) were not satisfied.[70]
>
> The case was referred to the CJ which upheld the decision of the Commission in Case T-19/91, *Société d'Hygiène Dermatologique de Vichy* v *Commission*.

A selective distribution system which excludes the application of Article 101(1) will be valid under competition law, even if there are no agreements for selective distribution in third countries, partially or fully. In other words, the selective distribution system in the EU must be recognised even if the goods covered by the system can be freely acquired from unauthorised dealers in third countries and can be lawfully put into circulation in the Community. A restriction of the producer's guarantee so as to cover only goods bought from authorised dealers is therefore valid. The aim is the same as that

70. For a more detailed discussion of these conditions, see Chapter II.

which lies behind the selective distribution system, which is to prevent dealers outside the system trading in the goods covered by the system, and fulfilling the guarantee obligations.[71]

4.3.2. Particular aspects of quantitative restrictions

Selective distribution agreements have been assessed from a different point of view when they have contained obligations and approval criteria which go beyond the qualitative restrictions referred to in section 4.3.1

However, it should be made clear that both qualitative and quantitative selective distribution are, in principle, covered by block exemptions granted in accordance with Regulation (EU) 33072010, see section 5.2 below, when a market share of 30 % (Article 3) is not exceeded, and when the selective system avoids one or more of the serious restrictions on competition in Article 4 and the restrictions in Article 5.[72]

The exemption applies even if the selective system is combined with other non-serious vertical restrictions,[73] such as non-compete obligations or exclusive distribution, which do not involve restrictions on sales by the approved dealers to each other or to end users. If the product's characteristics do not require the implementation of a selective distribution system, such a system will not normally be sufficiently effective so as to outweigh a significant reduction of inter-brand competition. And if there are appreciable effects on competitiveness, where a large widespread network of dealers in a market without significant inter-brand competition prevents a competitor's access to the market (cumulative effects), the block exemption will probably be put at risk.[74]

In a number of cases prior to the adoption of Regulation (EU) No 330/2010, both the Commission and the CJ found that special quantitative conditions in a selective distribution system were contrary to Article 81(1) [Article 101(1)]. In exceptional cases such systems can lose the advantages of a block exemption, see Article 29(1) of Regulation 1/2003.[75]

71. See Case C-376/92, *Metro SB-Großmärkte v Cartier.*
72. According to the above comments on the Commission's and the CJ's practice, a purely qualitative selective distribution system is not contrary to Article 101(1), so that in such cases there will not be a need for an exemption in accordance with Article 101(3) – and neither in accordance with the block exemption regulation.
73. See below in section 5.3 on Regulation (EU) No 330/2010, Article 4(a).
74. See *Christopher Bellamy & Graham Child:* European Community Law of Competition, 2008 p. 469 et seq.
75. See paragraphs 74-78 of the Vertical Restraints Guidelines and the criteria discussed for the possible repeal of an exemption under Article 29 of Regulation 1/2003.

These conditions will also be relevant if the basic market threshold in Article 3 of Regulation (EU) No 330/2010 is exceeded, as in this case an evaluation will be made of the distribution system's compatibility with Article 101(1), independently of the block exemption regulation.

Among other places, the attitude of the CJ to quantitative restrictions has been expressed in paragraph 29 of Case 243/83, *Binon* v *Agence et messageries de la presse*:

> 'In addition, access to such a system should be based on objective criteria of a qualitative nature because the use of quantitative criteria is, by definition, to be regarded as a restriction on competition within the meaning of Article 85 [Article 101]; the permissibility of quantitative criteria may only be taken into account in the context of a request for exemption under Article 85(3) [Article 101(3)] in respect of which the Commission alone is competent.'

It is not clear what should be understood as quantitative restrictions in such a case, and thus their incompatibility with Article 101(1) has not been absolutely determined. The restrictions vary from case to case, and an overall view is first obtained by putting together the restricting elements from several decisions, in which the economic and actual positions in the market in the case in question are taken into consideration.

> The control obligations imposed on the approved dealers in connection with sales to or purchases from other members of the distribution network (controlling that the customer is part of the official network), should make it possible for the producer to control the sales system. Such obligations mean that, as long as they do not go beyond what is necessary for suitable control, supplementary obligations which help ensure the fulfilment of the primary obligation are treated in the same way as the primary obligation (paragraph 27 in Case 26/76, *Metro SB-Großmärkte* v *Commission* (1)). Since a prohibition on approved dealers supplying non-approved traders would normally be regarded as a restriction on competition, this is exempted according to the practice followed and now expressed under Article 4(b) of Regulation (EU) No 330/2010, and the same is the case for control obligations which have the purpose of ensuring compliance with and supervision of this prohibition.
>
> As for the obligation to participate actively in advertising and sales promotion, in the *Metro* (1) case the Court stated that it could not be the task of a wholesaler to promote the sales of a particular producer. An

obligation of this kind is restrictive on competition as, on the one hand, it means that undertakings which satisfy the qualitative requirements but which are not able to take on further obligations are deprived of the possibility of trading in the goods concerned, and on the other hand it restricts the freedom of approved dealers to follow their own independent business policy.

However, in Commission Decision 85/404/EEC relating to a proceeding under Article 85 of the EEC Treaty (*Grundig* EEC distribution system) (OJ 1985 L 233/1) and in the *Parfums Givenchy* Decision, among others, the Commission exempted this provision in accordance with Article 101(3). The obligation was regarded as ensuring that the goods in question were only sold by dealers which could give customers professional advice and, in particular in relation to the sale of durable consumer goods, ensuring the necessary after sales service in connection with the use and maintenance of the goods.

Conditions on stockholding, in other words an obligation to invest in a stock of goods, are principally of a quantitative character, as they can mean that only those dealers who are able to take on such an obligation can be accepted in the distribution system. Such an obligation is a restriction on competition but, for example, in the *Grundig* distribution system Decision (OJ 1985 L 233/1), the *Yves Saint Laurent* distribution system Decision (OJ 1992 L 12/24), and the *Parfums Givenchy* Decision (OJ 1992 L 236/11) such a provision was nevertheless exempted out of regard for consumers in accordance with Article 101(3).

An obligation on a dealer to make a minimum purchase from the producer restricts both intra-brand and inter-brand competition, as on the one hand it means that only those dealers who are able to satisfy the condition can be admitted to the distribution network, and on the other hand it forces approved dealers to put a significant part of their sales efforts into the sale of the goods of the producer and this therefore restricts freedom of supply.

However, in the *Parfums Givenchy* Decision and elsewhere the Commission has exempted this restriction on competition in accordance with Article 101(3). The obligation to buy a minimum quantity was found to help ensure regular supplies and make it possible to concentrate distribution in the sales outlets with the widest assortment. The obligation could thus ensure better allocation of the costs associated with the sale of the products and the help provided to sales outlets.

The restrictions which are independently laid down in Regulation (EU) No 330/2010, including the prohibition on exclusive territories, and restrictions on the right to determine prices in subsequent stages of the distribution chain (hard-core restrictions) etc., and which apply in general to all vertical agreements, are discussed below in section 5.

4.4. Commercial/economic considerations?

Other than in connection and selective distribution, in special cases the Court has adopted a more commercially-based assessment of certain restrictions on competition, while the fixed attitude to other parts of an agreement have been maintained unaltered.

> In Case 56/65, *Société Technique Minière* v *Maschinenbau Ulm*, which concerned an agreement for a sole distributorship in a market where the goods in question had not previously been marketed, the CJ emphasised that the starting point must be the competitive conditions as they would have been if the agreement in question had not existed. The agreement, which neither imposed an obligation on the distributor to refrain from re-exporting the goods, nor an obligation on the producer to prohibit dealers in other EU countries from selling goods into the agreed territory, was found not to infringe Article 101(1).[76]

The *Nungesser* case[77] concerned an instance where the absence of certain provisions restricting competition would have had the effect that *new technology would not have been introduced to the market*.

The decision shows that there can be a need to allow a licensee a certain area of protection without Article 101(1) being immediately brought to bear on the ground that unlawful market-sharing has been established. The decision is discussed below in Chapter V, as is the later case of *Louis Erauw-Jacquery* v *La Hesbignonne.*[78] In this case the CJ held that a clause in an agreement on the propagation and sale of seed, under which one of the parties was the holder of certain plant breeders' rights, and which contained a prohibition on the propagating firm selling and exporting the basic seed, was compatible with Article 101(1), in so far as it was necessary to enable the plant breeder to choose authorised propagating firms, see paragraph 11:

76. The case is discussed above in section 2.1.
77. Case 258/78, *Nungesser and Eisele v Commission.*
78. Case 27/87, *Erauw-Jacqery* v *La Hesbignonne.*

> 'A provision of an agreement concerning the propagation and sale of seed, in respect of which one of the parties is the holder or the agent of the holder of certain plant breeders' rights, which prohibits the licensee from selling and exporting the basic seed is compatible with Article 85(1) [Article 101(1) TFEU] of the treaty in so far as it is necessary in order to enable the breeder to select the growers who are to be licensees.'[79]

In the part of the judgment given here, the decision expressed a point of view which is forcibly expressed in, among others, *Valentine Korah & Warwick A. Rothnie:* Exclusive Distribution and the EEC Competition Rules, 1992 p. 16 and *Valentine Korah & Denis O'Sullivan:* Distribution Agreements under the EC Competition Rules, 2002 p. 79, that there can often be a need to adopt an *ex ante* approach when assessing whether an agreement is a restriction on competition. Once success has been achieved (the product is established on the market – *ex post*), it becomes less questionable, from a competition law point of view, to allow others to forage in a previously protected area.

5. Criticism of the block exemption regulations that have applied hitherto – the Commission's response to criticism

The criticism of the rules that has applied hitherto of vertical restraints has been directed at, among others, the block exemption regulations which were issued in accordance with Regulation 19/65, in which the Council had authorised the Commission (under certain conditions, see Article 85(3) [Article 101(3)] to exempt special categories of agreements and concerted practices from the prohibition in Article 85(1) [Article 101(1)].

The dissatisfaction with these block exemption regulations[80] was particularly directed at the fact that the regulations which individually contained

79. In the *Nungesser* case the export prohibition was directed against both certified seed and basic seed, whereas the prohibition in the *Erauw-Jacquery* case only covered basic seed. The basis for the decision can therefore presumably be sought in the special nature of the exclusive right which gives the owner of that right the right to oppose the unauthorised use of the right by third parties. This decision is discussed below in Chapter V.
80. Including Commission Regulation (EEC) No 1983/83 on the application of Article 85 (3) of the Treaty to categories of exclusive distribution agreements; Commission Regulation (EEC) No 1984/83 on the application of Article 85 (3) of the Treaty to categories of exclusive purchasing agreements; and Commission Regulation (EEC) No 4087/88 on the application of Article 85 (3) of the Treaty to categories of franchise agreements.

guidelines for one particular type of contract prevented the development of new and innovative forms of distribution adapted to the dynamic which characterises contractual relations in the area of distribution (the straightjacket effect).[81] Among other things, the need was identified to draw on the guidelines of the Commission and the Courts to deal with *selective distribution*. It has also been pointed out that it was unsatisfactory that the regulations only took account of contractual relations between two undertakings, that the rules (including the Regulation on exclusive distribution agreements) were only concerned with the resale of finished products, and not equally with semi-finished products for incorporation in products for onward sale, and that the Regulation in general did not regulate the provisions of services.[82]

A constantly repeated objection to the block exemption regulations has been their inability to tackle a number of the more egregious cases of *vertical* restraints on competition. A system in which an agreement which formally satisfies the content of a number of specific whitelisted conditions is exempt from any objection will not catch those agreements where one or more of the parties has such a strong position in the market that, taken in isolation, the agreement can be considered to have the character of an abuse of dominant position.[83] Furthermore, until the new millennium such a dominant actor in the distribution chain could take advantage of the benefits associated with a *notification* of the agreement. In principle, the parties could claim exemption even if the case involved a market share of up to 100 per cent which should not have been covered by the block exemption regulations. The amendment to Regulation 17/62, First Regulation implementing Articles 85 and 86 of the Treaty, by Regulation 1216/99, under which the notification system for *vertical* agreements was scrapped and replaced by a system with exemptions determined by law together with subsequent controls of agreements which restrict competition, has taken some of the edge off the criticism. The new rules mean that an agreement which restricts competition and is caught by Article 101(1), but cannot satisfy the requirement for an exemption in Article 101(3),

81. In Case 161/84, *Pronuptia de Paris GmbH* v *Pronuptia de Paris Irmgard Schillgallis*, the CJ held that a franchise agreement did not fall within the scope of any of the then existing block exemption regulations.
82. Special rules on selective distribution, see Regulation (EU) No 330/2010, Article 4(b), (c), and (d), as well as Article 5(c) depart from the point of view that all types of vertical contracts should be subject to uniform rules.
83. On this point of view compared with a more in depth economic analysis of the market conditions, see the comments above in section 1.1.

will be unlawful and therefore without legal effect from the time when the agreement comes into being.[84]

5.1. Green Paper on Vertical Restraints in EC Competition Policy

Because, among other reasons, new distribution methods can have an effect on future competition policy, in 1997 the Commission prepared a green paper which, in addition to containing a review of the legal and economic situation with regard to vertical restraints which had applied hitherto, contained a number of proposals for amending the conditions for block exemptions. During consultations, the green paper was laid before the European Parliament, the Member States and other interested parties, including producers, distributors, employees' and consumers' organisations etc.[85] As could be expected, there was far from unanimity between the bodies consulted as to how competition policy should be shaped.

However, the Commission found that, on the basis of the responses received, it was possible to identify two main tendencies. First, there seemed to be a need in principle to depart from the formal use of whitelisted and blacklisted conditions. Second, market-share thresholds ought to be included in assessing the competitive effects of vertical restraint agreements so as to give significant weight to the actual market positions of the participating undertakings.

> With an amendment to Regulation 19/65, see Council Regulation (EC) No 1215/1999 of 10 June 1999 amending Regulation No 19/65/EEC on the application of Article 81(3) of the Treaty to certain categories of agreements and concerted practices, the Commission was given authority to replace the existing legal basis with simpler and more targeted provisions to apply to all types of vertical agreements, in other words in addition to the agreements which had been covered by the original block exemption regulations, including selective distribution, or combinations of such agreements. In addition to this, the authority covered certain non-reciprocal vertical agreements entered into between competing underta-

84. Even though, in principle, Regulation (EU) No 330/2010 no longer makes an express distinction between permitted (whitelisted) restrictions on competition and prohibited (blacklisted) restrictions, nevertheless the content of Article 4 of the Regulation (see below in section 5) effectively continues the blacklisted restrictions which applied under the earlier Regulation.
85. Green Paper on Vertical Restraints in EC Competition Policy COM(96) 721 final, of 22 January 1997.

kings, as well as vertical agreements between an association of small and medium-sized retailers and its members, or between such an association and its suppliers. In connection with this it was made clear that under the new regulation criteria should be laid down, such as market-share thresholds, to specify the circumstances where the block exemption regulation ceases to be applicable in view of the possible economic effects of the agreements. Furthermore, it was emphasised that a new block exemption regulation would in all events exclude 'certain severe anticompetitive vertical restraints' from exemption, *irrespective of the market share of the undertaking concerned*, such as the use of minimum and fixed resale prices and certain types of territorial protection. As a special amendment, the Regulation included authority for the competent authorities of the Member States to repeal the exemption in respect of that Member State's territory, or part of it; see below on Article 29(2) of Regulation 1/2003).

5.2. Commission Regulation (EU) No 330/2010

The Council's criteria for the new block exemption Regulation resulted in the adoption of Regulation 2790/99, which entered into force in 2000. As stated, Regulation 2790/99 has been replaced by Regulation (EU) No 330/2010. Apart from a couple of amendments, the content of Regulation (EU) No 330/2010 corresponds to the content of Regulation 2790/99.

The block exemption Regulation only applies to agreements which would otherwise be caught by Article 101(1) TFEU, and therefore has no effect on the Commission's *De minimis* Notice or other explanatory notices which clarify the scope of Article 101(1).

As stated, Regulation 2790/99 and Regulation (EU) No 330/2010 should be considered in connection with Regulation 1216/99, according to which the duty to notify which previously applied to both horizontal and vertical agreements which restrict competition, and which were a condition for their validity under competition law, should only apply to horizontal agreements, in other words, agreements between undertakings at the same production or distribution level. The Commission could then, regardless of whether the agreement was notified or not, exempt a vertical agreement as from the date the agreement was entered into, in other words give it retrospective effect, provided that all the conditions for notification of an individual exemption, in accordance with Article 101(3) TFEU, have been satisfied from the start.[86]

The preamble to Regulation (EU) No 330/2010 contains 16 recitals, and 11 enacting articles.

According to Article 2(1) of the Regulation (together with Article 1(1)(a)), the exemption applies to vertical restraints in agreements or concerted practices entered into between two or more undertakings which, in relation to the agreement or concerted practice, operate at different levels of the production or distribution chain, and relating to the conditions under which the parties may purchase, sell or resell certain goods or services.

In general, the 'restrictions' referred to in the provision can include the following negative effects which the EU's competition law seeks to prevent:

1. the exclusion either of other producers or other purchasers (dealers),
2. the reduction of competition either for goods of the same brand or between different brands,
3. agreements between suppliers and dealers which are promoted by the vertical restraints, and
4. the creation of hindrances to market integration, including restrictions on consumers' freedom to purchase goods or services in any Member State, according to their choice.

In relation to these restraints, in its Follow-up to the Green Paper on vertical restraints COM(98) 544 final (OJ 1998 C 365/3), the Commission made a number of general comments, as follows:

That a restraint which consists of the purchaser being induced to concentrate their orders for a particular type of good with one supplier generally has greater negative effects on competition than agreements on exclusive distribution, where the supplier only sells its products to one or a limited number of dealers. By excluding other brands the former obligations can prevent these brands being able to gain access to the market at all.

86. This amendment (of Article 4(2) of Regulation 17/62) entered into force in June 1999. The amendment is discussed in *Valentine Korah & Denis O'Sullivan:* Distribution Agreements under the EC Competition Rules, 2002 pp. 118-119. See also the comments above in section 1, where with effect from 1 May 2004 the Commission's exclusive competence to exempt horizontal agreement prohibited under Article 101(1) was repealed.

That exclusive agreements (one dealer covering all or practically all its requirements with its counterparty, so that it is prevented from buying, selling-on or using competing goods or services) are generally more harmful to competition than non-exclusive agreements. In this situation a risk can arise that the market will be isolated from competing or potentially competing suppliers, to the disadvantage of inter-brand competition.

That the possible negative consequences of vertical restraints are reinforced when not only one supplier practises certain vertical restraints with its dealers, but when other suppliers organise their trade correspondingly (cumulative effects).

It follows from Article 1(1)(a) of Regulation (EU) No 330/2010 that, in contrast to the previous situation, exemption also applies to agreements between more than two undertakings,[87] that the scope of exemption is extended to cover the purchase of semi-finished products[88] and that the agreements etc. can now concern *service provision*. On the other hand, vertical agreements with end consumers fall outside the scope of the Regulation. See the wording of Article 1(1)(a), which presumes that the parties to the agreement are undertakings which, for the purposes of the agreement, operate at a different level of the production or distribution chain.[89]

87. On the previous practice, see among others 77/100/EEC: Commission Decision relating to a proceeding under Article 85 of the EEC Treaty (*Junghans*) (OJ 1977 L 30/10), and *Valentine Korah & Warwick A. Rothnie:* Exclusive Distribution and the EEC Competition Rules, 1992 p. 87.
88. In 78/253/EEC: Commission Decision relating to proceedings under Article 85 of the EEC Treaty (*Campari*)(OJ 1978 L 70/69) a dealer bought herbs from Campari Milano and infused them in locally bought wine etc. which was thereafter sold when the herbs had been taken out. In such a case, which would today be considered as *product franchising,* the Commission was of the view that the conditions of the original block exemption regulation for exclusive distributorship, Regulation 67/67, were not fulfilled. This case would also not have been covered by the earlier, now repealed, block exemption for franchise agreements, which only regulated franchise agreements for the *distribution* of goods or services. See also *Valentine Korah & Warwick A. Rothnie:* Exclusive Distribution and the EEC Competition Rules, 1992 pp. 80-83, and in general the references above to the straightjacket effect which was associated with the application of the earlier block exemption regulations.
89. Distribution agreements in the motor vehicle industry are not covered by Regulation (EU) No 330/2010 as long as they are covered by a special block exemption agreement; see Commission Regulation (EC) No 1400/2002 on the application of

Agreements entered into between an association of undertakings and its members, or between such an association and its suppliers, are covered by the exemption subject to the conditions in Article 2(2), provided that no individual member of the association, together with its connected undertakings, has a total annual turnover exceeding EUR 50 million.

A vertical agreement which contains restraints imposed in connection with the licensing or use of *intellectual property rights*, including trademarks, patents, copyright and neighbouring rights (see Article 1(1)(f)) is only covered by the block exemption as long as these rights do not constitute the primary object of such agreements and are directly related to the use, sale or resale of goods or services, see Article 2(3). A pure sales licence, by which an intermediary obtains an exclusive right to sell a product on an export market, is comparable with a distribution agreement, and its effects are assessed in accordance with Regulation (EU) No 330/2010; see also the corresponding provision in Article 1(1)(b) of Regulation 772/2004 on technology transfer agreements.

A vertical agreement between *competing undertakings* falls outside the block exemption; see Article 2(4). However, the exemption under Article 2(1) does apply when: (1) the agreement is of a non-reciprocal nature (producer A is the distributor of producer B's products, without producer B being the distributor of producer A's products), (2) the supplier is a producer or dealer of the goods and the purchaser is a dealer who does not produce competing goods (parallel distribution), or (3) the supplier provides services at several business levels and the purchaser does not provide competing services at the business level where it buys the services.

The main difference from the earlier formal system is that Article 3 of Regulation (EU) No 330/2010 builds on the consideration expressed in recital 8 that there will not normally be a need to deny an exemption when the share of the relevant market of each of the undertakings that is a party to an agreement does not exceed 30 %.[90]

Article 81(3) of the Treaty [Article 101(3) TFEU] to categories of vertical agreements and concerted practices in the motor vehicle sector.

90. Block exemption regulations adopted after Regulation 2790/99 are likewise based on a requirement that a specific market-share threshold is not crossed. See Article 4 of Commission Regulation (EC) No 2658/2000 on the application of Article 81(3) of the Treaty to categories of specialisation agreements (20 % of the relevant market) and Article 4(2) of Commission Regulation (EC) No 2659/2000 of 29 November 2000 on the application of Article 81(3) of the Treaty to categories of research and development agreements (25 % of the relevant market).

In accordance with this, pursuant to Article 3(1), the exemption applies provided the supplier's market share does not exceed 30 % of the relevant market on which it sells the goods or services covered by the agreement, and the buyer's market share does not exceed 30 % of the relevant market where it buts the goods or services covered by the agreement.

The Regulation thus assumes that with most vertical restraints problems with competition will only arise if there is insufficient *inter-brand* competition, in other words because of the market strength of the supplier or purchaser or both. This concept includes the ability to increase prices above the level that would apply on a competitive market. An undertaking can have *market strength* without having market dominance, which is the criterion for the application of Article 102 TFEU. If several undertakings compete on a non-concentrated market, there will be an assumption that non-serious vertical restraints will not have significant negative effects.[91]

A calculation of the market share requires a definition to be made of 'the relevant market', in other words both the relevant product market and the relevant geographic market; see Commission Notice on the definition of relevant market for the purposes of Community competition law (OJ 1997C 372/5). The relevant product market includes products or services which are regarded as interchangeable or substitutable by the consumer, by reason of the products' characteristics, prices and intended use; while the relevant geographic market covers the area in which the undertakings concerned are involved in the supply of products or services, in which the conditions of competition are sufficiently homogeneous, and which can be distinguished from neighbouring areas because the conditions of competition are appreciably different. The relevant market for assessing a problem under competition law is therefore defined by a combination of the product market and the geographic market.[92]

The assumption behind the simplified procedure in Article 3, in which there is reference to the supplier's and buyer's market shares in the market

91. See paragraph 23 of the Vertical Restraints Guidelines.
92. For a more recent illustrative case see Case T-25/99, *Roberts & Roberts* v *Commission* (the *Greene King* case), on restrictions on the sale of beer from pubs and restaurants. The decision expresses considerable understanding for the special features of the individual market.

between the two parties, is that the effects in *the subsequent links* in the distribution chain will be limited when the market share is below 30 %.[93]

5.3. Agreements for specifically stated purposes – the Regulation's hard-core restrictions

While the block exemption regulations that have hitherto applied in the area of distribution have been based on certain conditions in the relations between the producer and the distributor being to the advantage of consumers (whitelisted conditions), the opposite has been the case for restrictions that have given the parties the possibility of implementing price differentiation and isolating the market. Such restrictions are considered to work counter to the market integration which has been one of the core principles behind the establishment of the internal market, and they have consistently been blacklisted, in other words they are the ultimate hindrances to the granting of block exemptions.[94]

The straightjacket effect previously referred to, which has been associated with the whitelisted conditions, necessarily requires giving up the distinction between white and black, if the aim of replacing the previous block exemption regulations with one regulation for all vertical restraints is to become a reality for the benefit of the future distribution of goods and services in the internal market.

These considerations lie behind the provision in Article 4 of Regulation (EU) No 330/2010, with its prohibition of conditions which restrict the buyer's ability to determine its sale price, and the prohibition on agreements on sales restrictions to subsequent distribution stages, which must be respected regardless of whether or not the market threshold referred to in Article 3 is crossed; see Case T-176/95, *Accinauto* v *Commission*, referred to in section 2 above.[95]

93. Any negative variations from this position could be countered via Article 29(1) of Regulation 1/2003, under which the Commission can take measures if an agreement which is subject to an exemption nevertheless has effects which are incompatible with Article 101 TFEU. This is particularly directed at situations in which competing suppliers or distributors have parallel networks of similar agreements which significantly restrict competition on the market concerned.
94. See, for example, Article 3 of Regulation 1983/83 (exclusive distribution) and Articles 4 and 5 of Regulation 4087/88 (franchising).
95. The serious restrictions in Article 4 affect agreements on trade within the Community. As for exports from the Community or imports/re-imports from third countries, see Case C-306/96, *Javico International* v *Yves Saint Laurent Parfums*. On

It is a consistent characteristic of monopolies legislation in Western countries that conditions which impose *fixed prices on subsequent stages* of the distribution chain (vertically bound prices) are considered to be harmful to competition and are therefore usually prohibited. The prohibition on fixing sales prices is maintained in Article 4(a) of Regulation (EU) No 330/2010, as a condition which will prevent the granting of an exemption. In addition to this, for the same reason the EU's competition authorities have looked very closely and very seriously into arrangements which, directly or indirectly, have the aim of restricting dealers' sales into a specific *territory* or to a specific *customer group* (agreements on market sharing), see Article 4(b).

Agreements which have been criticised by the courts have often contained both clauses on binding prices and provisions prohibiting the distributor selling outside a defined territory (exclusive rights territory). If, for the same product, different price levels are set in different geographic areas, the prohibited binding prices can only be maintained in the high-price territories if it is possible to hinder parallel exports to these territories, as such exports would otherwise undermine the higher prices. In these cases and in other cases, an attempt to maintain the higher prices will often be combined with restrictions in the form of territorial protection or customer group protection.

The prohibitions in Article 4 (a) and (b) have been the main theme of several decisions, where undertakings have attempted to counteract *parallel imports* into a protected territory.

The term 'parallel imports' is usually used to refer to imports of products which are made outside the producer's official distribution system by a third party who buys the products in area A and sells them to an unauthorised importer in area B who resells the products in area B in competition with the authorised importers. According to this definition, it is characteristic for parallel imports that there is no difference between the products which are sold to the authorised dealer and those that are sold by the unauthorised importer. The expression is sometimes used with a broader meaning to cover cases where an imported good has been produced under licence in a third country by an undertaking other than the authorised importer's supplier (the producer), so that the parallel importer's product is not of the same manufacture as that which is supplied through the authorised channels.[96]

this see *Christopher Bellamy & Graham Child:* European Community Law of Competition, 2008 pp. 311-327.

96. The term 'pirate imports' is used to refer to imports of goods which are typically of poorer quality, for example counterfeit goods, which are sold as original goods.

On a more general level, the basis for allowing parallel imports is found in Article 34 TFEU, as the sole importer's ability to rely on intellectual property rights would constitute a measure having an equivalent effect to a quantitative restriction. In the area of competition, claims of patent rights or trade mark rights could be an expression of a restriction on competition contrary to Article 101(1).

From the point of view of the authorised importer, the general acceptance of parallel imports is not always reasonable. This importer will often have incurred considerable costs in generating consumer interest in the goods, and the parallel importer will be able to benefit from this goodwill without incurring costs. This is often reasonably enough considered a gross injustice by the authorised importer. However, the view of the Commission and the Court is clear; parallel importation is a legal form of business, see the statement in Case 86/82, *Hasselblad (GB) Limited* v *Commission*:

> 'A sole distributorship agreement not containing any prohibition on exports cannot qualify for block exemption [in accordance with Article 4 of Regulation (EU) No 330/2010, corresponding to the prohibition in the original block exemption Regulation 67/67] if the undertakings concerned are engaged in a concerted practice aimed at restricting parallel imports intended for an unauthorized dealer.'
>
> See also 95/477/EC: Commission Decision relating to a proceeding pursuant to Article 85 of the EC Treaty (*BASF Lacke+Farben, and Accinauto*) (OJ 1995 L 272/16), which contains an instructive review of the Commission's approach to parallel imports and market sharing.

5.3.1. Article 4(a) – Price discrimination and selective prices

The prohibition, in Article 4(a) of Regulation (EU) No 330/2010, of agreements that restrict the buyer's ability to determine its sales price and other trading terms for goods that are covered by the agreement has a parallel in Article 101(1)(a) TFEU. The attitude of the CJ and the Commission to such restrictive agreements is reflected in the case law which is reviewed above in section 2.1.3.

Article 4(a) fulfils the aim set out in recital 10 of the Regulation, according to which the Regulation should not exempt vertical agreements containing restrictions which are likely to restrict competition and harm consumers or which are not indispensable to the attainment of the efficiency-enhancing effects, which is the purpose of the regulation of competition in the EU.

The provision expressly exempts agreements imposing a maximum sales price or recommend a sales price. This limit to the extent of the prohibition is not expressly referred to in Article 101(1)(a) TFEU, but it is fully reflected in the EU competition authorities' interpretation of the Treaty provision.

5.3.2. *Article 4(b) – Sales restrictions*

The prohibition, in Article 4(b) of the Regulation, of agreements restricting the territory into which or customers to whom a buyer party to the agreement may sell the goods or services subject to the agreement refers to Article 101(1)(b) TFEU, which is discussed and interpreted above in section 2.1.1. This provision also fulfils the aim set out in recital 10 of the Regulation.

Four restrictions linked to Article 4(b) are discussed immediately below.

5.3.2.1. *Modifications*

- The restriction in Article 4(b) of Regulation (EU) 330/2010 does not concern prohibitions against *active* sales into the exclusive territory or to an exclusive customer group reserved to the supplier or allocated by the supplier to another buyer.[97] The producer and any other dealers can therefore still be protected from another dealer who is bound by a prohibition attempting to take over their customer base, and if others of the supplier's dealers are subject to a corresponding restriction, that dealer can be protected against others trying to make inroads in their territory.
- Without reference to block exemptions, an agreement between a producer and a wholesaler may impose obligations on the wholesaler which restrict sales to end users, meaning buyers who themselves use the goods.[98]
- The third modification of the starting position relates to the free-rider problem. As previously mentioned, in the absence of a block exemption regulation in the area, following the practice of the Commission and the Courts special guidelines have been developed for selective distribution which is permissible under competition law where, as described above in

97. According to paragraph 51 of the Vertical Restraints Guidelines: ''Active' sales mean actively approaching individual customers by for instance direct mail, including the sending of unsolicited e-mails, or visits; or actively approaching a specific customer group or customers in a specific territory through advertisement in media, on the internet or other promotions specifically targeted at that customer group or targeted at customers in that territory. Advertisement or promotion that is only attractive for the buyer if it (also) reaches a specific group of customers or customers in a specific territory, is considered active selling to that customer group or customers in that territory.'
98. In such a case the wholesaler could offer a lower price to end users than a retailer who acquires the products from a wholesaler with a view to offering them to end users.

section 4, without infringing Article 101(1) a producer of special quality goods can have qualitative requirements for the distributors who sell the goods. Regulation (EU) No 330/2010 follows up this acceptance of the requirement for the image of distributors by allowing undertakings which participate in a distribution system of this kind to be subject to the condition that they may not resell the goods to *unauthorised distributors*.

The exemption applies even if, while complying with the market threshold in Article 3(1), the selective distribution system is combined with other non-serious vertical restraints, such as non-compete obligations within the scope of Article 5 (see section 5.4 below), stockholding, minimum purchases etc, in other words, conditions which, in the practice of the Court and the Commission prior to Regulation (EU) No 330/2010, had been classified as quantitative restrictions contrary to Article 101(1).

If the characteristics of the product to not require the establishment of a selective distribution system, even if this is not expressly stated in Regulation (EU) No 330/2010, such a system will not normally have sufficient effectiveness benefits to outweigh the significant reduction of intra-brand competition.[99] And if appreciable restrictions on competition arise, the block exemption will presumably be at risk. In extraordinary cases, particularly where competition is significantly restricted by the cumulative effect of parallel networks of similar vertical restraints implemented by competing suppliers or buyers, such agreements could lose the benefits associated with block exemptions; see Article 29(1) of Regulation 1/2003.

- The fourth modification of the starting position in Article 4(b) allows a supplier of components for incorporation in other products to prohibit distributors supplying such components to customers who would use them to manufacture the same type of goods as those produced by the supplier.

5.3.2.2. Article 4 (c) and (d) Selective distribution – active and passive sales. Cross-supplies

Apart from the obligation not to carry on business from unauthorised retail premises, because of the concern for the image of distributors which lies behind the selective distribution system, a retailer who is a member of a distribution system can be subject to restrictions with regard to active or passive

99. The area for selective distribution will presumably be established in line with the previous practice.

sales to end users (Article 4(c)). A corresponding hard-core restriction applies to *cross-supplies* between authorised distributors, and if the block exemption shall apply such authorised distributors must be free to execute orders received from other members of the selective distribution system, including orders from distributors operating at different level of trade (Article 4(d)). Both restrictions were established in the previous practice on selective distribution and are a counterpart to the right to restrict authorised distributors from selling products to unauthorised dealers.

5.3.2.3. Article 4(e) Components

Article 4(e) is aimed at the situation where a buyer of components, which are incorporated into its products, seeks to impose an obligation on the supplier of the components not to supply corresponding components either to end users or to other undertakings which compete with the buyer with regard to repair work on the products in which the buyer incorporates the components. The buyer's motive is thus not just related to operations on the market for finished products but also to the subsequent repair and service market. The provision means that such an agreement between the buyer and supplier of components falls outside the exemption in Article 2 of the Regulation.[100]

5.4. Restrictions that fall outside the scope of the exemption

Article 5 of Regulation (EU) 330/2010, on restrictions on competition, refers to restrictions that are non-exempt, even if the market-share threshold in Article 3 is not exceeded. As distinct from the serious restrictions in Article 4, the exemption still applies to the other parts of an agreement, as long as they can be distinguished from the non-exempt parts of the agreement.

> In English law there is a 'doctrine of severance', see *Christopher Bellamy & Graham Child:* European Community Law of Competition, 2008 p. 1434, which cites the case of *Pickering* v *Ilfracombe* from 1868, where the doctrine is expressed as follows: 'where you cannot sever the illegal from the legal part of the contract the contract is altogether void; but where you can sever them, whether the illegality be created by statute or by the common law, you may reject the bad part and retain the good.'
>
> See also paragraphs 70-71 of the Vertical Restraints Guidelines, and the example of the possibility of severance in relation to the earlier Regulation 1983/83 on exclusive distribution agreements in *Bent Iversen:*

100. See paragraph 59 of the Vertical Restraints Guidelines.

Formidlingsaftaler & EF-konkurrenceretten, 1996 p. 96. This view was confirmed by the Danish Supreme Court in a decision in 1997 which concerned the breach of a non-compete obligation in an exclusive distribution agreement. The issue of severance was also discussed in the *Grundig* case (see section 2.1.1 above).

According to the definition in Article 1(1)(d) of Regulation (EU) No 330/2010, a 'non-compete obligation' means any direct or indirect obligation causing the buyer not to manufacture, purchase, sell or resell goods or services which compete with the contract goods or services, or any direct or indirect obligation on the buyer to purchase from the supplier or from another undertaking designated by the supplier more than 80 % of the buyer's total purchases of the contract goods or services and their substitutes on the relevant market, calculated on the basis of the value of its purchases in the preceding calendar year, where such is standard industry practice.

The principal reason for Article 5 follows from Recital 11 of the Regulation, which talks about the need to ensure access to the market for competing undertakings and to prevent unlawful collusion. It is also necessary to ensure that contractual obligations which require members of a selective distribution system not to sell the brands of particular competing suppliers should be excluded from the benefit of the block exemption

On this basis, Article 5(1)(a) provides that a non-compete obligation which continues after the expiry of the agreement is not exempt if it is of indefinite duration or exceeds five years.

Non-compete obligations that are tacitly renewable beyond a period of five years are deemed to have been concluded for an indefinite duration; see Article 5(1)(c), last paragraph.[101] On the other hand there is nothing to prevent a non-compete obligation for 5 years being *renewed* for a further 5 year period if this is based on the parties' *express* agreement, and provided that there are no conditions which mean that the distributor is in fact prevented from ending the non-compete obligation at the end of the 5 year period.[102]

101. See, from the case law prior to Regulation (EU) No 330/2010, Case T-7/93, *Langnese Iglo* v *Commission,* according to which an agreement that could operate tacitly after the expiry of a certain period should be considered to be an agreement for an indefinite period.

102. If, for example, an agreement includes a 5 year non-compete obligation, and the producer extends a loan to the distributor, the repayment of this loan must not prevent the distributor from ending the obligation at the end of the 5 year period; the repayment must be made in equal or diminishing instalments, but they may not

Under Article 5(1)(b) of the Regulation, non-compete obligations which continue after the termination of an agreement normally fall outside an exemption unless, among other things, they are indispensable to protect know-how[103] transferred by the supplier to the buyer, and in this case the distributor can be bound for up to one year after the termination of the agreement; see Article 5(3)(c) and (d). Article 5(1)(b) does not prevent the imposition of a restriction of unlimited duration on the use and disclosure of know-how which has not entered the public domain; see Article 5(3), last paragraph.

In agreements that are part of a selective distribution system, a non-compete obligation which requires the distributor not to resell competing products in general will be covered by a block exemption. However, if a producer directly or indirectly prevents authorised distributors from buying products for resale from particular competing producers, then an exemption will not be allowed, see Article 5(1)(c). The aim of excluding such an obligation from exemption is to prevent a number of producers using the same selective sales channels and shutting out one or more specific competitors from distributing their products through the sales channels in question (protection of the market from a competing supplier), which would be a form of collective boycott.[104]

5.5. Withdrawal of an exemption

If a vertical agreement keeps within the market-share threshold laid down in Article 3 of Regulation (EU) 330/2010, and does not otherwise infringe either the hard-core restrictions in Article 4 or the restrictions in Article 5, there will be an assumption that the agreement is lawful, and this will normally mean that the agreement can be acted on without the risk of intervention by the competition authorities. However, in special cases this assumption can be overturned with effect from the date of the decision, either by a decision of the Commission or the competent authorities of a Member State.

The authority to withdraw an exemption was originally given in Articles 6 and 7 of Regulation 2790/99. After the implementation of Regulation 1/2003 these provisions were moved to Article 29(1) and (2) of the new Regulation.

increase over time, see paragraph 58 of the Vertical Restraints Guidelines. In any case, the distributor must have the possibility of repaying the balance if there is any outstanding debt when the non-compete obligation expires.

103. 'Know-how' is defined in Article 1(g).

104. There was an example of indirect measures with such protective effects in Commission Decision on the *Parfums Givenchy* case (OJ 1992 L 236/11).

In relation to taking concrete steps against existing agreements, the authority for the Commission and the national competition authorities to take steps against parallel networks of vertical agreements is a continuation of corresponding precautionary measures in Article 6 of Regulation 1983/83 on exclusive distribution agreements and Article 8 of Regulation 4087/88 on franchising. This authority to intervene was not in fact directly used under the previous arrangement. The Commission's authority to deny an exemption by a special regulation (see section 5.6 below on Article 6 of Regulation (EU) No 330/2010) is a new measure which did not exist in the earlier regulations.

5.5.1. Article 29.1 of Regulation 1/2003 – the Commission's withdrawal of exemption

The withdrawal of a block exemption under Article 29(1) of Regulation 1/2003 will be relevant if competing suppliers or purchasers have parallel networks of similar vertical agreements which together have the effect of significantly restricting access to the relevant market.[105]

The Commission has the burden of proof for showing that agreements fall within the terms of Article 101(1) TFEU and that the conditions do not exist for one or more of the four exemption criteria in Article 101(3). Full evidence will be relevant not only in those cases where several suppliers have arranged their distribution agreements with vertical restraints of the same kind, but also when they have used different combinations of vertical restraints. Depending on the circumstances, the withdrawal of an exemption will only concern restraints which lead to a reduction in the number of distributors, and responsibility for the cumulative effect of restrictions on competition can only be ascribed to undertakings which have contributed appreciably to it.

5.5.2. Withdrawal of exemption within the territory of an individual Member State

Article 29(1) of Regulation 1/2003 concerns the Commission's authority to act on its own initiative to withdraw exemptions for vertical agreements that

105. See Recital 13 of Regulation (EU) No 330/2010 which is repeated in paragraphs 74-75 of the Vertical Restraints Guidelines. See also the comments in paragraphs 24-26 in Case C-234/89, *Stergios Delimitis* v *Henninger Bräu.* Paragraph 76 of the Vertical Restraints Guidelines states that responsibility for an anti-competitive cumulative effect can only be attributed to those undertakings which make an appreciable contribution to it. Agreements entered into by undertakings whose contribution to the cumulative effect is insignificant are not subject to the withdrawal mechanism.

restrict competition on a geographic market which is greater than the area of a single Member State.

According to Article 29(2), *the competition authorities of individual Member States* can withdraw exemptions for agreements whose cumulative effects affect all or part of the Member State's territory, when this territory has all the characteristics of a distinct geographic market. The substantive conditions for the withdrawal are the same as those laid down in Article 29(1).

5.6. The general inapplicability of block exemptions

Article 29 of Regulation 1/2003 concerns specific cases where the Commission (or the authorities of a Member State) can intervene against existing parallel networks of vertical agreements which are found to be incompatible with an exemption granted in accordance with Article 101(3) TFEU. On the other hand, Article 6 of Regulation (EU) No 330/2010 gives general authority for not granting exemptions to such agreements so that Article 101 is applicable in its entirety.

Where parallel networks of similar vertical restraints cover more than 50 % of a relevant market, the Commission may adopt a regulation declaring that block exemptions do not apply to vertical agreements containing specific restraints relating to that market. Such restrictions can appreciably restrict access to a market, for example when a parallel selective distribution network covers over 50 % of the market, this means the choice of distributor depends on criteria which are not necessarily based on the nature of the goods concerned or which lead to different treatment of some potential forms of distribution for such goods.[106]

The scope of any regulation issued under Article 6 of Regulation (EU) No 330/2010 can be adapted by the Commission to the competition policy problems which are to be solved. For example, an assessment of the extent to which a parallel network protects the relevant market against sales of competing goods could lead to a restriction on the use of non-compete obligations or supplementary conditions for the selected distributors' obligation to take certain quantities of goods, while other restrictions which protect the market to a lesser extent may be maintained.

106. See paragraphs 79-85 of the Vertical Restraints Guidelines.

6. Conclusion

On the basis of the foregoing explanation of the Commission's preparatory legislative work, the statements that have accompanied the block exemption regulations etc., and the competition law principles which form the basis of the decisions of the Commission and the Community Courts, the conclusion must be that on competitive markets the effects of restrictions on competition which are associated with vertical restraints will only have a modest negative effect. Apart from the serious restrictions on competition referred to in Article 4 and the restrictions referred to in Article 5 of Regulation (EU) 330/2010, which the Commission and the Courts have consistently been alert to, and will no doubt be so in future, individual terms or different kinds of vertical restraints have not in themselves had a negative effect on competition or integration.

It has been seen that an analysis of a specific situation surrounding an agreement must concentrate on the *effects* of the agreement on the relevant market, rather than on the *form* of the agreement, and an important parameter of the analysis of the market will be whether the vertical agreement, in combination with their market position, gives the supplier or the distributor a possibility of imposing different prices for their products in different Member States.

The way in which the block exemption regulations are applied will show whether there are reasons to fear that there will be an increase in legal uncertainty as a result of the fact that in future it will normally be up to the parties' own judgement whether a market share is higher or lower than the permitted threshold. The certainty that existed with the earlier block exemption regulations has gone, together with the distinction between blacklisted and whitelisted conditions.

Hitherto, the Commission's legal acts or decisions have not given the highest priority to paying close attention to whether there can be significant economic risks to new and smaller undertakings' entry into new markets or the expansion of markets, in other words the establishment of new trade flows which integrate the market. However, the Commission has not been entirely unaware that such spreading of new products can often only take place if there is significant monetary or intellectual investment and that, as will be significant from a national perspective, such initiatives will seldom be undertaken unless they are given more favourable treatment, at least for a limited period.

The formulation of the special restrictions laid down in Article 5 of Regulation (EU) 330/2010 which differ from those contained in the earlier block exemption regulations, expresses the Commission's recognition that vertical restraints can have positive as well as negative effects.

The positive effects can refer both to the undertakings that are parties to a distribution agreement and consumers, and can therefore be factors which constitute the basis for an individual exemption in accordance with Article 101(3) TFEU. A combination of restrictions, for example allowing territorial protection together with a non-compete obligation for a limited period (in accordance with Article 5(a) of the Regulation) could in certain circumstances satisfy both traders and consumers, and at the same time, without being an absolute restriction on parallel trade, could help with some of the less fortunate effects (for the trader) of the free-rider problem.

At the same time, Article 5 of Regulation (EU) 330/2010 has taken account of the negative effects of non-compete obligations for unlimited periods and of quantitative restrictions linked to membership of a selective distribution system.

The response to consultation on proposed amendments to the remaining 'old' block exemption regulation, Regulation 240/96 on technology transfer agreements which has now been replaced by Regulation 772/2004 (see Chapter V below), indicated that a significant part of the business community wanted a secure arrangement before venturing into a market on an equal footing with established competitors. The response would presumably be the same from those from the new Member States who, because of the expansion of the EU, must act for the first time as equal partners in a larger market.

CHAPTER IV

Horizontal agreements

Karsten Engsig Sørensen

Bibliography: *Jonathan Faull & Ali Nikpay (eds.): The EC Law of Competition, 2007; Jens Fejø: EU-konkurrenceret, 2009; Joanne Goyder & Albertina Albors-Llorens: Goyder's EC Competition Law, 2009; Alison Jones & Brenda Sufrin: EC Competition Law, 2004; Lennert Ritter & W. David Braun: European Competition Law: A Practitioner's Guide, 2010; Peter Roth & Vivien Rose (eds.): Bellamy & Child: European Community Law of Competition, 2008; Richard Whish: Competition Law, 2012.*

1. Introduction

'Horizontal agreements' means agreements between undertakings on the same level in the market. In a competition law context the most interesting agreements are those between undertakings which are actual or potential competitors. This will be the case, for example, with agreements between two producers of the same product or two distributors of the same product.

The list of prohibited agreements in Article 101(1)(a) to (e) of the Treaty on the Functioning of the European Union (TFEU or 'Treaty') contains several examples of horizontal agreements. Thus, an agreement to fix purchasing or selling prices, or for the application of the same trading conditions will typically be entered into by competitors. Two competing producers can also have an interest in entering into an agreement to limit or control production, so as to ensure that their products can be sold at a higher price. Finally, two competitors can have an interest in market sharing, so they avoid having to compete against each other in future.

Such pricing agreements, agreements on production limits, and agreements on market sharing are classic cartel agreements, and they are often referred to as 'hardcore cartels'. In the case of such agreements it is clear that they will lead to restrictions on competition. The Commission thus assumes that such agreements will have negative effects, so that it is not necessary to undertake any further examination of how the agreements affect the competitive situation in practice.[1] The strict approach adopted towards these types of agreement is also clear from the fact that the *De minimis* Notice, does not apply to pricing agreements, agreements to limit production or market sharing agreements.[2]

Competitors can also enter into other kinds of agreements where it is not quite so obvious that the agreement has a negative effect on competition. Such agreements can include agreements on specialisation, on joint research and development (R&D cooperation), cooperation on joint purchasing etc. For these agreements there is a need for a closer examination of the effect of the cooperation on competitive conditions before it is decided whether Article 101(1) is infringed.

The Commission has published a Notice giving guidelines on the application of Article 101 to horizontal agreements.[3] These guidelines contain both general comments on the assessment of horizontal agreements, and a review of several of the most common types of agreement. The review does not include the classic cartel agreements which, as stated above, are seldom difficult to evaluate, but focuses instead on a number of commonly used agreements which are sometimes, but not always, contrary to Article 101.

By way of introduction, the following presentation will contain some general comments on the evaluation of horizontal agreements. In the following sections there will be a review of several different kinds of agreement. In the first place this review concentrates on different kinds of agreement classified according to their subject matter, in other words, whether they are pricing agreements or market sharing agreements etc. However, certain forms of horizontal agreements go beyond simple traditional cooperation agreements, as they involve setting up new undertakings or changes to the ownership of the parties to the agreement. Such horizontal agreements which

1. Communication from the Commission – Guidelines on the applicability of Article 101 of the Treaty on the Functioning of the European Union to horizontal co-operation agreements (hereinafter the 'Commission Guidelines on horizontal cooperation agreements' (OJ 2011 C 11/1), para. 160.
2. Commission Notice on agreements of minor importance which do not appreciably restrict competition under Article 81(1) of the Treaty establishing the European Community (*de minimis*) (OJ 2001 C 368/13), para. 11(1).
3. Commission Guidelines on horizontal cooperation agreements, para. 160. The 2011 Guidelines replaced the Guidelines from 2001 which were the first to deal with horizontal cooperation agreements.

affect the structure of undertakings can be more difficult to assess, and they are therefore dealt with separately in the last sections.

2. The assessment of horizontal agreements

2.1. Actual and potential competitors

The Commission's guidelines on horizontal cooperation agreements apply to cooperation established between competitors. Competitors can either be actual or potential competitors.

An undertaking is an actual competitor if it operates in the same relevant market as the other party or parties to the agreement. An undertaking is also considered to be an actual competitor if, quickly and without great cost, it is able to switch production to the relevant products.[4]

In footnote 9 of the Commission's guidelines on horizontal cooperation agreements, a potential competitor is defined as an undertaking which 'absent the agreement, this firm could and would be likely to undertake the necessary additional investments or other necessary switching costs so that it could enter the relevant market in response to a small and permanent increase in relative prices.' In addition to this, it is stated that the assessment has to be based on realistic grounds, and that the mere theoretical possibility of entering a market is not sufficient, and reference is made to the Commission's Thirteenth Report on Competition Policy, where the Commission has previously laid down guidelines for the evaluation of potential competition.[5] This means that when an assessment is made of whether an undertaking can be expected to be active on a particular market, there must be an evaluation of the following factors, among others:

- There must be an assessment of whether the undertaking has sufficient financial resources to undertake the investments necessary, and whether the undertaking is otherwise capable of doing so, for example whether it has the necessary technical know-how and whether it has access to the necessary sourcing in order to be able to make the switch in production.
- There must be an assessment of whether the undertaking has the technological capacity required, including the necessary production facilities.

4. Commission Guidelines on horizontal cooperation agreements, para. 10 with footnote 8.
5. See the Commission's Thirteenth Report on Competition Policy 1983, para. 55.

- There must be an assessment of whether there is sufficient demand so it can be profitable to switch production and whether the undertaking has access to the necessary distribution channels for the product.
- There must be an assessment of whether the undertaking would be able to bear the technical and financial risks involved in the activity.
- Finally a general assessment must be made of the hindrances to market entry in order to asses whether the undertaking would be able to overcome them on its own.

There is a further requirement that a potential entry should be able to take place relatively quickly, and the Commission Notice on horizontal cooperation agreements, footnote 3 refers to a short period of a maximum of three years.

2.2. The basic principles for evaluation under Article 101(1)

An infringement of Article 101(1) requires that the agreement involves a restriction on competition, and according to the Commission's Guidelines, this assessment must be based on an evaluation of the economic circumstances. In this connection, the Commission points in particular towards the fact that the nature of the agreement and the combined market strength of the parties, and whether the agreement contributes to creating, maintaining or strengthening market power are decisive for whether the cooperation can affect competition to a significant extent.[6]

Some categories of agreements will almost never fall under Article 101(1). This concerns cooperation between undertakings that are not competitors as defined in the previous section. The same applies to competition concerning an activity which does not influence the relevant parameters of competition.

In addition to this, there are certain agreements that in principle always fall within the scope of Article 101(1). These are the classic cartel agreements, such as pricing agreements, agreements on production limits, and agreements on market sharing which, as already stated, clearly have negative effects on the market.

For other horizontal agreements it will often be necessary to make a more detail evaluation to decide whether they involve the parties coordinating their competitive conduct. The Commission's Guidelines make it easier to analyse the following different forms of cooperation: agreements for information exchange, research and development, production agreements, purchasing

6. Commission Guidelines on horizontal cooperation agreements, para. 28.

agreements, commercialisation agreements, and standardisation agreements. Several of these forms of agreement are considered in more detail on the following sections.

The application of the Commission's Guidelines requires the placing of an agreement in one of the categories of agreement referred to. However, sometimes agreements will concern cooperation which covers several areas. In this situation the Guidelines note that it is the centre of gravity of the agreement which determines which part of the Guidelines should apply. The centre of gravity of the agreement is determined by two factors: firstly, the starting point of the cooperation, and, secondly, the degree of integration of the different functions which are combined.[7] For very complex agreements, such as strategic alliances, it may be possible to evaluate the individual elements of the agreement, according to the relevant paragraph in the Guidelines, but beyond that, one must also undertake an analysis of the overall effect of the agreement.

In addition to this, the evaluation of agreements requires an analysis to be made of the *market power* of the undertakings and the *market structure* of the relevant market. Thus, if the agreement makes it possible for the cooperating undertakings to achieve market power or to maintain market power through cooperation, the cooperation could have negative effects on the market. It will therefore be necessary to define the relevant market, which will be done in accordance with the Commission Notice on the definition of relevant market for the purposes of Community competition law.[8] Once the relevant market has been determined, market power can be estimated by measuring, in particular, the market shares of the undertakings. A small market share will normally mean that it is unlikely that the cooperation will lead to a restriction on competition. This is also in line with the Commission's *De minimis* Notice, according to which a market share of less than 10 % normally means

7. Commission Guidelines on horizontal cooperation agreements, para. 14. These not specifically operational factors are exemplified in the same paragraph. If an R&D agreement involves joint research and thereafter joint production, the agreement will normally be classified as an R&D agreement, as the production will only take place if the R&D activity is successful. The R&D activity is thus the starting point of the cooperation. However, it will be otherwise if the agreement shows an intention to carry out joint production, regardless of the joint R&D. In this case the joint production would be the centre of gravity of the agreement.
8. OJ 1997 C 372/5. These guidelines are considered in more detail in Chapters VI and VIII, in connection with the corresponding evaluation of the relevant market in the application of Article 102 and the Merger Control Regulation.

that a horizontal agreement is not covered by Article 101(1).[9] In addition to this, it can be relevant to assess market concentration, the stability of the markets shares, barriers to entry to the market, and the market power of buyers/ suppliers in order to determine the market power of the parties to a cooperative agreement.[10]

Altogether, the Commission's guidelines show that an evaluation under Article 101(1) must be based on a thorough assessment of the market, in which economic factors are of decisive importance. This is in line with the view of the General Court (GC) which has emphasised that in the evaluation of an agreement in accordance with Article 101(1) account should be taken of the actual conditions in which it operates, in particular the economic context in which the undertakings operate, the products or services covered by the agreement and the actual structure of the market concerned, unless it is an agreement containing obvious restrictions on competition such as price-fixing.[11] On several points the same judgment set aside the Commission's evaluation of a horizontal agreement, as the GC found that the Commission's decision was based on an incorrect analysis of the market, as certain points of the evaluation did not take account of the economic context, and that the decision was inadequately justified.[12] The judgment underlines the fact that there are strict requirements for the Commission's evaluation, which must be both sufficiently detailed and economically realistic, and full reasons must be given.

2.3. Exemptions under Article 101(3)

For horizontal cooperation agreements that are not classic cartel agreements (pricing agreements etc.) it will be relevant to consider whether the agreement can be exempted under Article 101(3). In connection with the

9. OJ 2001 C 368/13, para. 13(7)(a).
10. Commission Guidelines on horizontal cooperation agreements, paras. 43-47. For evaluating market concentration, in its previous Guidelines from 2001, the Commission referred to the Herfindahl-Hirsman Index (HHI Index) as an indicator for whether there is a market with high or low concentration. This index was developed by the American competition authorities in particular to calculate the effect of a merger. It involves the calculation of the sum of the squares of the market shares of all the competitors. If the sum is less than 1,000 the concentration is low, and if it is above 1,800 it is high. For a more detail account of the HHI Index; see *Roger J. Van den Bergh & Peter D. Camesasca:* European Competition Law and Economics: A Comparative Perspective, 2nd ed., 2006 pp. 352-362.
11. Joined cases T-373/94 and others, *European Night Services,* para. 136.
12. See in particular paras 142, 144, 147 and 159 of the judgment.

individual types of agreement discussed, the Commission's guidelines contain a more detailed review of what circumstances can influence assessments under Article 101(3).

For a more general review of the two positive and two negative conditions for allowing an exemption; see Chapter II, section 6.

In order to ease the assessment of special agreements, the Commission has issued two block exemption regulations which exempt agreement on research and development (R&D agreements) and specialisation agreements.[13] These kinds of agreements usually involve effectivity gains which outweigh their effects limiting competition, and they therefore fulfil the criteria in Article 101(3). Both regulations where issued under the authority of Regulation (EEC) No 2821/71 of the Council on the application of Article 101(3) of the Treaty (previously Article 85(3)). The exemption for R&D agreements is discussed in section 5, and the exemption for specialisation agreements is discussed in section 4.1.

3. Pricing agreements and agreements on other trading conditions

3.1. Agreements on purchasing or selling prices

According to Article 101(1)(a) of the EC Treaty, agreements which directly or indirectly fix purchase or selling prices could restrict competition. If competitors agree their prices, this eliminates the price competition which both ensures that prices are held down and helps ensure that there can be parallel imports and thereby economic integration of markets in the EU. A pricing agreement prevents the undertaking which has the lowest costs from lowering its prices, and such an agreement therefore normally benefits those undertakings that are party to the agreement which have the poorest control of their production costs. In the long run it thus becomes difficult to maintain cooperation on the application of common prices as there will normally be undertakings that will have an advantage from trying to reduce prices, contrary to such an agreement. Such agreements will usually contain elements to ensure that the price cartel is not breached, including mechanisms

13. Commission Regulation (EU) No 1217/2010 on the application of Article 101(3) of the Treaty on the Functioning of the European Union to certain categories of research and development agreements (OJ 2010 L 335/36); and Regulation (EU) No 1218/2010 on the application of Article 101(3) of the Treaty on the Functioning of the European Union to certain categories of specialisation agreements (OJ 2010 L 335/43).

to reveal breaches of the common pricing policy and sanctions for undertakings which do not follow the pricing policy. However, pricing agreement will be contrary to Article 101, regardless of whether there are such mechanisms, and it will not be relevant for an assessment under Article 101 whether a pricing agreement has worked in practice.[14]

The practice of the Commission shows that most agreements that are intended to influence the pricing policies of the participating undertakings are assumed to be contrary to Article 101. It is clear that agreements on fixed prices or minimum prices, or that the same price increase should be implemented, are contrary to the prohibition. A pricing agreement need not be framed so as to regulate the prices of the principal products of the undertakings, as it is sufficient that prices are agreed for certain products or services as long as these constitute a competitive parameter.[15] The prohibition also covers recommended prices, as these have the effect of enabling competing businesses to predict their competitors' pricing policies with a reasonable degree of certainty.[16] Furthermore, Article 101 covers agreements whereby the parties undertake not to sell their products at below cost price, usually referred to as dumping prices. Apart from pricing agreements of this kind being contrary to Article 101(1), there will be a further breach of the

14. In contrast to this, with an assessment of collective dominance in connection with the Merger Control Regulation, there is a requirement that there should be evidence of sanctioning mechanisms; see Chapter VIII, section 4.3.
15. Commission Decision 96/428/EC, *Fenex* (OJ 1996 L 181/28), where agreements were entered into on prices (here called tariffs) concerning a number of services which freight companies provided in addition to the provision of the transport itself. Even though the services about which agreement was entered into would normally only constitute a minor part of the overall price for the transport service, the Commission found that profit margins were generally very small and that any anti-competitive practice, even if restricted to part of the total price, affected competition; see para. 51 of the Decision. See also Case 123/83, *BNIC*, para. 29, under which an agreement on minimum prices for an intermediary product (spirits), which was not itself traded between the Member States, was a restriction on competition, because the intermediary product was a significant part of the final product (cognac) which was traded between Member States.
16. See Case 8/72, *Cementhandelaren,* para. 21, as well as Commission Decision 96/428/EC, *Fenex* (OJ 1996 L 181/28), paras 45-49. The Commission also assumed that 'target pricing' can be in breach of Article 101, since this establishes goals for the prices which undertakings are to use. Even if the prices must still be negotiated with customers and even if it is not always possible to ensure that they are applied, they have the effect of restricting the negotiating scope of the parties; see Commission Decision of 11 June 2008, in Case COMP/38695 – *Sodium Chlorate* (OJ 2009 C 137/6).

provision if the undertakings attempt to implement their pricing agreements by getting their distributors to use the agreed prices.

Discount arrangements and common discount policies are likewise covered by the prohibition, since this is merely another way of regulating the level of prices. In markets where, because of strong competition and transparency, there are uniform prices, discount arrangements can be the only competitive parameter, so that an agreement on these will restrict competition further. Also, agreements on fixed prices or minimum prices will usually, as a supplement, prevent the parties giving rebates which would prevent the application of their uniform pricing policy.[17]

> There was an example of an extensive pricing agreement in the *Belasco* case.[18] Belasco was a cooperative set up by a number of Belgian manufacturers of roofing felt. The members had an agreement which, among other things, included the implementation of price increases, and agreement about what discount margins the members could use, and a prohibition on giving gifts and selling at a loss. The Commission, and later the Court of Justice of the European Union (CJ), held that these agreements were contrary to Article 101. It was clear that the agreed prices and discounts directly affected competition, and that the prohibitions on giving gifts and selling at a loss were aimed at preventing parties getting round the agreed prices. Before the Commission, the undertakings had argued that all the price increases were a consequence of the Belgian legislation on pricing which allowed undertakings to seek collective approval of price increases. Even though the Belgian legislation required approval of price increases, it was possible for members to seek individual approval for price increases, so a certain measure of competition was possible under the Belgian legislation. Therefore, the Commission held that the legislation was not the cause of the price coordination.

17. However, it is by no means a condition that an agreement on minimum prices should be combined with an agreement to limit the use of discounts. Even if the use of discounts makes a pricing agreement less effective, it must still be assumed to have a certain effect – otherwise there would be no point in entering into it. This was the Commission's reasoning in Commission Decision 74/634/EEC concerning a *Franco-Japanese ball-bearings agreement* (OJ 1874 L 343/19), Part II, para. 3.
18. Commission Decision 86/399/EEC concerning *roofing felt* (OJ 1986 L 232/15), and the subsequent Case 246/86, *Belasco.*

Furthermore, it was held that it was irrelevant that they had not in fact succeeded in holding the members to the agreed price increases, as it was clear that the purpose of the agreement was to restrict competition on prices. The agreement was also notified to undertakings which were not party to it. The CJ found that the fact that notification of price increases had been given was intended to encourage these undertakings to bring their prices into line with the members' prices, and thereby to increase the effect of the price cartel beyond the cartel's members.

It appeared from this case that the Belgian legislation on pricing allowed undertakings to implement price increases at different times and by different amounts.[19] If on the other hand pricing legislation did in fact dictate prices, there would not be a pricing agreement, contrary to Article 101. This applies even if the undertakings themselves have proposed the prices which the legislation makes obligatory, provided that it is not in fact the undertakings which fix the prices which the legislation puts into effect.[20]

Agreements on maximum prices will not necessarily harm competition. However, it is possible to imagine that such an agreement could be aimed at forcing a competitor out of the market (predatory pricing).

If a number of undertakings agree on the maximum purchase prices they will pay their suppliers, this will be an agreement in restraint of competition.[21] The same will be the case if an agreement is made between undertakings that submit offers in connection with public tendering or public procurement, and which restricts competition by the fact that the offer of an individual undertaking is not based on its own cost calculations, but on prior

19. See also Joined cases 209 to 215 and 218/78, *van Landewyck,* and Case 260/82, *NSO*, where the CJ concluded that the Belgian and Dutch pricing rules for cigarettes still allowed competition on certain points, so that an agreement which excluded competition on these points was contrary to Article 101.
20. Case C-35/99, *Manuele Arduino,* and Case C-38/97, *Autotrasporti Librandi Snc di Librandi F & C.* If one cannot blame the undertakings for the lack of competition, one may ask whether the Member States themselves can infringe Article 101 by implementing such pricing legislation; see the comments on this in Chapter II, section 3.2.
21. Commission Decision 84/405/EEC, concerning a *zinc producer group* (OJ 1984 L 220/27), para. 66 (the purchase price of zinc ore); and Commission Decision 85/206/EEC concerning *aluminium imports from Eastern Europe* (OJ 1985 L 92/1), para. 11.1. In both cases the agreed purchase prices were part of a larger network of agreements which had the aim of restricting competition in various ways. Compare this with the comments on purchasing agreements in Commission Guidelines on horizontal cooperation agreements, paras 194-220, and see section 8 below.

knowledge of the offers of others. This can be because the undertakings exchange information about costs in connection with the offer, agree common margins, or maybe even agree on who should give the lowest offer.[22]

Instead of entering into a pricing agreement, undertakings can choose to set up a common sales company. Such a sales company will often be a commonly controlled joint venture company; section 7 below gives a review of the Commission's practice on joint ventures. However, there will seldom be economies of scale or other advantages associated with purely selling companies, and these will normally be judged on the same basis as pure pricing agreements, and not exempted from Article 101(3). This is particularly clear when the participating undertakings are obliged to sell through the joint company so they are prevented from taking individual sales initiatives and thus from practising an alternative pricing policy.[23]

Since it is clear that pricing agreements restrict competition, there is normally no reason to investigate further what effect the agreements have in practice. Pricing agreements are subject to a very strict assessment and can only very exceptionally be exempted under Article 101(3). However, an exemption has been given for banks' uniform fees for Eurocheques, as it was found appropriate to have transparency about the payment fees for precisely this kind of payment method which applied to the whole of the internal market.[24]

3.2. Agreements on other trading conditions

Article 101(1)(a) also refers to agreements on 'other trading conditions' than purchasing or selling prices. If there is uniformity of trading conditions which would otherwise act as a competitive parameter, such an agreement will mean that competition is restricted. This is obvious where an agreement on other

22. Case T-29/92, *Vereniging van Samenwerkende Prijsregelende Organisaties in de Bouwnijverheid,* Commission Decision 73/109/EEC concerning the *European sugar industry* (OJ 1973 L 140/17); Commission Decision 1999/60/EC concerning a *pre-insulated pipe cartel* (OJ 1999 L 24/1), para. 33, and Commission Decision of 28 January 2009, COMP/39406 – Marine Hoses (OJ 2009 C 168/6).
23. Commission Decision 80/182/EEC, *Floral* (OJ 1980 L 39/51), and Commission Decision 91/301/EEC, *ANSAC* (OJ 1991 L 152/54).
24. Commission Decision 85/77/EEC, *Uniform Eurocheques* (OJ 1985 L 35/43). See also Commission Decision 2002/914/EC, *Visa International* (OJ 2002 L 318/17), where the Commission likewise thought there was a basis for exempting inter-bank fees which were used by Visa.

trading conditions is a supplement to a pricing agreement,[25] but it can also be the case that where an agreement on uniform trading conditions stands alone, competition can be restricted. For example, a restriction on competition will be presumed to exist where competitors agree on common guarantee conditions, common credit conditions, common after sales service, common delivery conditions and so on.[26] In the same way, common conditions for purchasing can infringe Article 101. On the other hand, if the use of uniform conditions has only limited influence on competition, Article 101 will not be infringed and the Commission has thus accepted that banks can agree on opening hours and on uniform rules for clearing and direct debits.[27]

The result of this legal position is that attempts to apply uniform sales or purchase terms by developing standard conditions within a specific trade sector can be contrary to Article 101.[28] On the other hand, if standard conditions are drawn up by a trade organisation and individual undertakings are free to use them or not, the aim will not necessarily be to restrict competition, as it could be to create greater transparency for consumers. These can thus be assumed either to fall outside the scope of Article 101(1) or to be exempted under Article 101(3).[29]

3.3. Agreements on the exchange of information

In many case it will not be possible to prove directly that an agreement exists on the application of uniform prices etc., but it may be shown that a trade sector has entered into agreements on the exchange of information about prices, sales terms, sales turnover etc. Such agreements can very well be part of a pricing agreement, where the aim is to identify undertakings that do not

25 See e.g. Commission Decision of 28 January 2009, COMP/39406 – *Marine Hoses* (OJ 2009 C 168/6).

26. Joined cases 209 to 215 and 218/78, *van Landewyck,* paras 154-156, and Case 8/72, *Cementhandelaren,* paras 23-24.

27. Commission Decision 86/507/EEC, *Irish Banks' Standing Committee* (OJ 1986 L 295/28), paras 16-17.

28. Commission Decision 74/431/EEC concerning *Papiers peints de Belgique* (OJ 1974 L 237/3), where, in addition to an agreement on common pricing, a number of Belgian wallpaper manufacturers had agreed common terms for delivery, payment, refusal to exchange goods, the conditions for accepting complaints, and the length of rolls of wallpaper.

29. See the Commission Guidelines on horizontal cooperation agreements, para. 301. The Guidelines make reservations for two situations where such standard terms can nevertheless have the effect of restricting competition: where standard terms restrict product choice, and where standard terms are *de facto* binding; see paras 303-307.

coordinate their prices as agreed.[30] However, agreements for the exchange of such information can in themselves restrict competition, and the Commission has stated that, when assessing systems for the exchange of market information for the purposes of competition law, it also takes into account that this form of cooperation can increase market transparency for suppliers. In this way customers are deprived of the opportunity of benefiting from the secrecy in competition between suppliers which exists on oligopolistic markets.[31]

Finally, exchanges of information can lead to protection that distorts competition. The most obvious example of this is where commercially sensitive information is exchanged and this leads to significant competitive disadvantages for competitors that are not part of the exchange arrangement.[32]

Consequently, agreements for the exchange of information on prices and similar competitively sensitive information will be contrary to Article 101. This is especially so in oligopolistic markets, where undertakings have particular incentives to adapt their conduct to each other.[33] There is also greater probability of there being concerted practices where the conditions of supply and demand are stable, and where there is a symmetrical market structure and the undertakings involved cover a major part of the relevant market. Another relevant factor is, of course, the nature of the information exchanged, as distortions of competition are most likely when strategic information is involved, which an undertaking can use in framing its future strategy. It is thus less likely that exchanges of historical information will be able to harm competition, and there is less likely to be a distortion of com-

30. Commission Decision 94/601/EC, *Cartonboard (*OJ 1994 L 243/1), para. 134. See the Commission Guidelines on horizontal cooperation agreements, paras 66-67, where a distinction is made between the internal and external stability of a common understanding.
31. The Commission's Seventh Annual Report on Competition Policy, para. 7.
32 See Commission Guidelines on horizontal cooperation agreements, para. 70.
33. Commission Decision 92/157/EEC, *UK Agricultural Tractor Registration Exchange* (OJ 1992 L 68/19), where eight British manufacturers and importers of tractors had agreed to exchange information about sales volumes and market shares. This was contrary to Article 101, given the market structure, which was highly concentrated with high entry barriers, and with regard to the degree of detail of the information exchanged. In particular, the Commission attached importance to the fact that it was difficult for new competitors to enter the market, so an exemption under Article 101(3) was refused. This decision was later followed by the GC in Case T-35/92, *John Deere,* and by the CJ in Case C-7/95 P, *John Deere.*

petition where information is aggregated so that it is not possible to identify the activities of individual competitors.[34]

If the information exchanged leads to greater transparency on the market, so consumers can gain access to the information and be better informed about the supplier who gives the best terms, this would favour allowing the exchange of information.[35] It is also possible that the exchange of information can contribute to making a market more effective, even if consumers do not have access to the information.[36]

4. Agreements on production

If production is restricted and demand remains unchanged, undertakings will be able to demand higher prices, so a restriction on production will lead to a restriction on competition; see Article 101(1)(b). If an agreement means that the participating undertakings limit their production, there is therefore no doubt that it contravenes Article 101. An agreement might be framed so that each undertaking is given a quota which is has to comply with.[37] An agreement that no undertaking may increase its production without the agreement of the other undertakings will also infringe Article 101.[38] A quota agreement, or similar, can be an alternative to a pricing agreement, as a limit on production can be easier to implement and to monitor than a pricing agreement. However, a quota agreement will often be a supplement to a pricing agreement.[39]

34 See Commission Guidelines on horizontal cooperation agreements, paras 86-90.

35. The Commission's Seventh Annual Report on Competition Policy, para. 5.

36. Case C-238/05, *Asnef-Equifax,* where the CJ accepted that a system that provided for the exchange of information on customers' solvency improved the effective provision of credit, as it made it easier to identify bad payers. For further on when exchanges of information can be exempted under Article 101(3), see Commission Guidelines on horizontal cooperation agreements, paras 95-104.

37. Commission Decision 86/596/EEC, *MELDOC* (OJ 1986 L 348/50), which concerned a quota arrangement entered into by the Dutch dairy industry, mainly to do with long-life milk. The Commission also had an opportunity to investigate the Danish quota system which had been agreed between the Ministry for Health and the Danish Association of the Pharmaceutical Industry, aimed at controlling public spending on price subsidies for pharmaceuticals; see the Twenty-ninth Report on Competition Policy 199, p. 170.

38. Commission Decision 72/474/EEC, *Re Cimbel* (OJ 1972 L 303/24), para. 14.

39. Commission Decision 86/399/EEC concerning *roofing felt* (OJ 1986 L 232/15), para. 73, and Commission Decision 94/601/EC, *Cartonboard* (OJ 1994 L 243/1), para. 130.

An agreement which is merely aimed at limiting production cannot expect to be exempted under Article 101(3). However, there are a number of other agreements on production which either do not infringe Article 101(1) or are exempted under Article 101(3), because they give certain technical or economic advantages which outweigh any negative effects which restrict competition. Three different categories of such agreements are referred to in the Commission Notice with guidelines on the applicability of Article 81 of the EC Treaty to horizontal cooperation agreements. The first concerns *joint production agreements*, which are normally carried out by the cooperating parties setting up a joint venture; these are discussed in section 7. The guidelines also refer to *specialisation agreements*, where each party agrees to cease production of a product and purchase it from the other party. The third category is *subcontracting agreements*, where the contractor entrusts the production of a product to the subcontractor.[40]

The Guidelines contain some general comments on the evaluation of these agreements under competition law. It appears from this that production agreements will often have 'spill-over effects', where an agreement not only has an effect on the products that are the subject of the agreement, but the implementation of the agreement also affects upstream or downstream competition, or neighbouring markets to that of the product which is the subject of the agreement. If, for example the manufacturers of tyres agree between themselves to limit production, this can have a spill-over effect on motor car production, since cars cannot run without tyres. Problems only arise when the parties to an agreement are actual or potential competitors on at least one of the relevant markets (including spill-over markets). However, an agreement between competitors will fall outside the scope of Article 101(1) if the production agreement is the only commercially realistic way of penetrating a new market or the only way to launch a new product.[41]

40. Commission Guidelines on horizontal cooperation agreements, paras 150-186. If a subcontracting agreement is entered into between undertakings that do not compete against each other, the agreement should be assessed according to the rules for vertical agreements; see Chapter III. In addition to this, the Commission has issued Commission Notice of 18 December 1978 concerning its assessment of certain subcontracting agreements in relation to Article 85(1) (OJ 1979 C 1/2). If the subcontracting agreement can only be carried out if know-how (including intellectual property rights) is made available, it is acceptable for the subcontractor's use of this know-how to be restricted, and it can be prevented from supplying corresponding products to other undertakings.
41. Commission Guidelines on horizontal cooperation agreements, para. 163.

If the competing undertakings have a very small proportion of their cost structures in common, it is also less probable that competition will be restricted. This will be the case, for example, where a joint production agreement is entered into on an intermediary product which only accounts for a small proportion of the production costs of the final product. Production agreements which include marketing, such as joint distribution or sales, will normally be associated with a risk of coordinating prices and thus there will be an increased risk of restriction of competition. Finally, certain production agreements can prevent a third party from entering the market and thereby have an exclusive effect which restricts competition.[42]

Paragraphs 168-173 of the Commission Guidelines on horizontal cooperation agreements state that production agreements are unlikely to have restrictive effects on competition if the parties to the agreement do not have market power in the market concerned. This normally requires that the parties have a combined market share of more than 20 %. If the combined market share exceeds this, it will be necessary to make a more specific evaluation, as the market power will not necessarily be a problem if the market concerned is dynamic.

Categories of the agreements that have repeatedly been granted exemptions are agreements on specialisation, agreements to restructure a trade sector that is in crisis, and agreements on technical standards. These are discussed briefly below.

4.1. Specialisation agreements

Specialisation agreements involve two or more undertakings agreeing that the production of a particular product will be carried on by one of the undertakings or by a jointly owned undertaking. Such agreements normally contribute to the improvement of production or the allocation of goods, since the undertakings can thereby concentrate on the manufacture of certain goods, work more rationally and offer the goods at a lower price. Specialisation agreements mean that some undertakings stop production or refrain from starting competing production which is, on the face of it, contrary to Article 101(1). However, such agreements do not always restrict competition, especially when the parties are neither actual nor potential competitors. On the other hand, if the agreement is between competitors there is a clear risk of it having a restrictive effect on competition, but in this case it

42. Commission Guidelines on horizontal cooperation agreements, para. 159.

may qualify for an exemption under the Commission's block exemption Regulation on specialisation agreements.[43]

According to Article 1 of the block exemption Regulation on specialisation agreements, the following agreements are exempt: *Unilateral specialisation agreements*, where one party agrees to cease the production of certain products or the provision of a certain service, and to purchase the product or service from a competing undertaking; this covers the situation where an undertaking outsources its production. The next exempted class is *reciprocal specialisation agreements*, where two or more parties agree reciprocally to cease or refrain from producing different products or providing different services and to purchase these products or services from the other party or parties. The last form of exempted agreement is a *joint production agreement*, where two or more parties agree to produce certain products or services jointly.

According to Article 2 of the Regulation, the exemption also applies where the parties accept an exclusive purchase and/or exclusive supply obligation. This means that it is possible to agree that the party taking on a specialisation shall only sell to the other party or parties to the agreement, just as the other party or parties can be obliged to buy the product. It is also possible to agree that the sale of the products that are the subject of a specialisation agreement shall not be carried out via the participating undertakings, but shall be carried out jointly. Finally, the assignment of or grant of a licence to intellectual property rights is exempt, as long as the assignment or licence is not the main purpose of the agreement but is necessary for implementing a specialisation agreement.

Article 3 of the Regulation provides that the exemption only applies if the combined market share of the participating undertakings does not exceed 20 % of the relevant market. Article 5 deals with the market share threshold in more detail, and states, among other things, that if the market share is initially not more than 20 % but subsequently rises above this level (without exceeding 25 %), the exemption provided for in Article 1 can continue to apply for two consecutive calendar years following the year in which the 20 % threshold was first exceeded. If the market share subsequently rises above 25 %, the exemption continues to apply for one calendar year following the year in which the level of 25 % was first exceeded.

43. Regulation (EU) No 1218/2010 on the application of Article 101(3) of the Treaty on the Functioning of the European Union to certain categories of specialisation agreements (OJ 2010 L 335/43).

Article 4 of the Regulation describes the specialisation agreements that are excluded from exemption, which includes agreements which have as their aim the fixing of prices for sales to third parties, the limitation of production, and the allocation of markets. However, in all specialisation agreements it is possible to agree the quantity of the product in question that is to be produced. If there is a joint production undertaking, in other words a joint venture, it is also possible to set sales targets and fix prices for its sales to others than the participating parties.

4.2. Agreements for the restructuring of a trade sector

In principle it must be left to market forces to solve the problems of a trade sector which may have overcapacity. This is normally resolved by the least profitable undertaking in the sector being squeezed out, so the sector is 'rationalised'. Nevertheless a practice has developed whereby the Commission has exempted agreements for 'crisis cartels', whereby it is made possible for a trade sector which is hit by a structural chronic overcapacity to reduce its production capacity in accordance with a plan laid down.[44] It is a condition that the undertakings should have registered a significant fall in their capacity utilisation over a longer period, and that there should be no prospect of improvement in the longer term. Such problems may be due, for example, to the fact that new technology has made it possible to produce more effectively, or it may be due to a fall in demand.

Capacity must be cut through the coordinated efforts of the undertakings, so as to create a healthy and competitive sector in the longer term. It is a condition that the participants would not individually undertake the capacity reduction unless they had the security of knowing that their competitors will do the same, and that new production capacity would not be created.[45] An agreement to reduce capacity can either be between two competing undertakings or it can involve all the undertakings in the sector.[46] It is a condition that the agreement should contain a detailed and binding closure programme that ensures that the overcapacity is actually and irrevocably reduced. It must ensure that the closures do not go further than necessary, as

44. The Commission's Twelfth Annual Report on Competition Policy, paras 38-41.
45. Commission Decision 84/380/EEC, *Synthetic fibre* (OJ 1984 L 207/17), para. 32, and Commission Decision 94/296/EC, *Stichting Baksteen* (OJ 1994 L 131/15), para. 24.
46. See the mutual production agreement on PVC between two undertakings, which was approved because it reduced the industry's capacity by closing down certain production facilities, Commission Decision 84/387/EEC, *BPCL/ICI* (OJ 1984 L 212/1).

consumers should have sufficient choice and security of supply.[47] In addition, the Commission will ensure that the conditions for an exemption under Article 101(3) are fulfilled, so that the rationalised sector will be able to have better and more profitable production, to the advantage of consumers. Typically, the least modern factories will be closed so the overheads are reduced.[48] It is a condition that the undertakings do not otherwise restrict competition, and the agreement must ensure that the undertakings set their prices individually, and that they themselves control the production capacity which remains. Finally, the Commission states that the plan must be carried out in such a way as to secure employment in the industry in question.[49]

4.3. Agreements on common norms and technical standards

The drawing up of technical standards which undertakings can choose to follow plays a key role in the technical harmonisation which ensures the free movement of goods in the EU. As a result of this, a large number of technical standards are drawn up, most of which are drawn up by recognised national or European standardisation bodies. These standards are voluntary and can be used by all. In principle, the Commission has a positive approach to standards adopted by such bodies, provided the right to participate in setting such standards is not restricted, that the procedures for adopting the standards are transparent, and third parties can use the standards on reasonable terms and without being discriminated against.[50]

However, it is different with standards which undertakings agree upon other than within the regime of a standardisation body. Such agreements will often be aimed at ensuring that the undertakings involved produce products

47. Commission Decision 94/296/EC, *Stichting Baksteen* (OJ 1994 L 131/15), para. 30.
48. Commission Decision 94/296/EC, *Stichting Baksteen* (OJ 1994 L 131/15), para. 26.
49. The Commission's Twelfth Annual Report on Competition Policy, para. 41. The Commission expresses that this ought to be the case, so it cannot be assumed to be an absolute condition. In Commission Decision 94/296/EC, *Stichting Baksteen* (OJ 1994 L 131/15), para. 27, it was established that the agreement made it possible to carry out the restructuring of the sector on acceptable social terms and with better possibilities for the re-employment of the workers.
50. Commission Guidelines on horizontal cooperation agreements, para. 280. On certain points the latest Commission Guidelines are more critical of such open standards than the previous Guidelines; see *Marcus Glader:* Open Standards: Public Policy Aspects and Competition Law Requirements, European Competition Journal 2010 pp. 611-648. In Case T-432/05 *EMC Development,* the GC upheld the Commission's decision that the procedure for the adoption of a European cement standard fulfilled the requirements for transparency and non-discrimination, and the GC rejected the claimant's argument that the standard was *de facto* binding.

of the same quality, and standards can naturally reduce price competition on the market in question.[51] All things being equal, uniform products exclude the scope for competing on the characteristics of products.[52] The effect of such an agreement on competition depends on the extent to which the undertakings which are parties to the agreement have the possibility of developing alternative standards or alternative products. In addition to this, standardisation agreements can have the effect of creating further barriers to entry to a market. This is particularly the case where the standards are drawn up by undertakings that are dominant in the market and where the standards are not accessible to third parties.[53]

However, standards can have certain advantages which can justify them being exempted under Article 101(3).[54] Agreements can thus lead to a rationalisation of production and make it easier for consumers to make their choice of goods. In addition to this, standardisation can make products more compatible, and make it easier and cheaper for consumers to have their goods repaired. However, the Commission will normally only exempt agreements if the standards are made accessible to all undertakings that wish to enter the market and if a major part of the industry transparently takes part in setting the standards. Moreover, the standards may not restrict innovation and they should preferably be technology neutral.

51. Commission Guidelines on horizontal cooperation agreements, paras 263-269, which sets out in more detail the assessment of standardisation agreements. In para. 161 the Commission states that such agreements can lead to restrictions in two other markets: the service market for standard setting, and the distinct market for testing and certification.
52. Case 246/86, *Belasco,* where the CJ found that the agreement which ensured that all the producers of roofing felt who were members of Belasco used the same product standards, had the purpose of preventing members from differentiating their products and thereby avoiding competition between them.
53. Joined cases 96/82 and others, *IAZ International Belgium,* which involved an association of producers and distributors of washing machines and dishwashers which had agreed to use a conformity label which showed that a product fulfilled certain standards. The CJ disallowed the arrangement as, among other things, it emphasised that parallel importers did not have the possibility of being covered by the arrangement; see paras 24-25.
54. Article 1(1)(a) of Regulation (EEC) No 2821/71 on application of Article 85(3) of the Treaty to categories of agreements, decisions and concerted practices, authorises the Commission to issue block exemptions for these, but the Commission has not hitherto made use of this authorisation. Instead, there are now Commission Guidelines on horizontal cooperation agreements, paras 308-324.

There is an example of a standardisation agreement in Commission Decision 78/156/EEC concerning *Video cassette recorders*.[55] Philips had developed the VCR system which, at that time, competed with a system developed by Sony (the U-MATIC system). In order to promote the use of their systems, both Philips and Sony had allowed other undertakings to produce video recorders and video tapes using their systems. However, Philips had gone a step further and agreed with a number of major manufacturers (including Grundig and Blaupunktwerke) that they were only allowed to manufacture according to the technical standards that were appropriate for the Philips system. On the other hand, Philips made is licence rights available without charge.

The Commission was of the view that the agreement infringed Article 101(1) (then Article 85), as the participating undertakings were obliged only to produce according to Philips's standards. In view of Philips's leading position on the market, there was a clearly appreciable restriction on competition. Moreover, the Commission did not believe the circumstances justified an exemption since the agreement prevented consumers acquiring video recorders which were produced according to other standards. Thus the agreement went further than was necessary, as it would have been sufficient to require the undertakings to comply with Philips's standards when they wanted to produce according to the VCR system, but instead the agreement bound the undertakings only to produce according to this system.

On the other hand, the Commission allowed an exemption in Decision 87/69/EEC concerning *X/Open Group*.[56] In this case, a number of major European producers in the information technology sector had agreed on common use of an operating system for data handling (Unix). The aim was to overcome the problem that different machines used different operating systems, so the owner of a machine was prevented from using software that was adapted for use with another operating system, and the acquisition of a new machine could involve costs for rewriting existing programs, or even, in the worst case, the acquisition of new programs. Since the purpose of the agreement was to overcome these problems, the Commission felt that the agreement promoted technical progress and was to the advantage of consumers. The Commission emphasised that the aim of the cooperation was the establishment of an open industry standard,

55. OJ 1978 L 47/42.
56. OJ 1987 L 35/36.

> accessible to all. However, while not all undertakings could be members of X/Open, the organisation that administered the standards, the Commission accepted that there would be practical, logistical and administrative difficulties if all producers had a right to be members. It was therefore accepted that membership was reserved to major producers.

Intellectual property rights, in particular patents, can cause a number of special problems in relation to standardisation agreements. If a patent is incorporated in a standard, the use of the standard will require a licence to use the patent in question. In order to ensure that this does not make it difficult to use the standard, the patent owner must allow others to use the patent on reasonable terms and without discrimination. This is usually referred to as a 'FRAND commitment'.[57] Moreover, in its Guidelines, the Commission emphasises that there must be an intellectual property rights (IPR) policy that ensures that undertakings which take part in drawing up standards give information in good faith about their IPRs which can be significant to the standard that is being drawn up.[58]

5. Cooperation on research and development

Cooperation on research and development (R&D) will generally contribute to the promotion of technical and economic progress. Such cooperation helps prevent duplication of research that can be economically inefficient, and it is often possible to spread the high costs associated with R&D, and thus undertake research which individual undertakings would not be able to finance on their own. Also, R&D cooperation makes it possible to pool the know-how of several undertakings and thereby achieve results which either could not have been achieved by an individual undertaking or which could not have been achieved so quickly.

R&D cooperation can also have negative effects on competition. First, it can restrict innovation where it may be assumed that the undertakings which participate in R&D cooperation would have carried out the R&D on their own, had they not been party to the agreement. Next, the cooperation can lead to a concerted practice on existing markets. This is particularly likely where there is cooperation for the improvement of existing technology, though less

57. Commission Guidelines on horizontal cooperation agreements, paras 287-291.
58. Commission Guidelines on horizontal cooperation agreements, para. 286.

likely where the cooperation is aimed at developing a new product. Finally, R&D cooperation can lead to market protection.[59]

The forms of restriction on competition referred to will normally occur where the cooperating undertakings have significant strength on existing markets. On this basis, the Commission has exempted R&D agreements where the parties do not exceed a certain market share threshold, provided they fulfil a number of other conditions.[60]

The block exemption Regulation covers the situation where two or more undertakings carry out joint R&D of products, technologies or production methods; see Article 1(1). 'Research and development' is defined in Article 1(1)(c), as the acquisition of know-how and the carrying out of theoretical analysis, systematic study or experimentation, and the obtaining of intellectual property rights from the results. According to Article 1(1)(m), joint research can be carried out by a joint team, organisation or undertaking. However, it can also be carried out by delegating the research to a third party or apportioning it between the parties, according to their specialisations in research, development and exploitation. The exemption covers not only those parts of the agreement that concern joint research, but also the joint exploitation of the results of the research. This means it is possible to produce and distribute the product that results from the investment in research, or alternatively to grant a licence for the exploitation of the research results. However, it is a condition that the results that are exploited jointly are either protected intellectual property rights or constitute know-how that is of decisive importance for the production.[61] If this condition did not exist, it would be easy to camouflage joint production as being the consequence of research cooperation.

There are a number of conditions and reservations linked to an exemption. Among other things, all parties must have access to the results of the joint research; see Article 3. Where R&D agreements include the joint exploitation of the results, the exemption lasts for at least seven years, but it can continue thereafter until the parties to the agreement have a market share of 25 % of the relevant market for the products covered by the agreement; see Article 4. If an agreement is made by competing undertakings (according to Article 1(1)(r)), this includes actual or potential competitors), exemption will only be

59. Commission Guidelines on horizontal cooperation agreements, para. 127.
60. Commission Regulation (EU) No 1217/2010 on the application of Article 101(3) of the Treaty on the Functioning of the European Union to certain categories of research and development agreements (OJ 2010 L 335/36).
61 Article 3(4) of the Regulation.

granted if the combined market shares of the parties do not exceed 25 % of the product market in which the R&D cooperation is active. In addition, Article 5 lists the different kinds of agreement and conditions in agreements which will prevent an exemption being granted under the Regulation.

6. Cooperation on sales and marketing

According to Article 101(1)(c), an agreement on market sharing could have the effect of restricting competition. Such market sharing can be made by undertakings agreeing to divide the market territorially, or otherwise sharing customers. Even if the division of customers is carried out on an objective basis, and maybe even with the consent of the customers, there will be an infringement of Article 101.[62] There is a special form of market sharing where, in connection with tendering agreements, competing undertakings agree who will tender for the order in question.[63] Next, it is possible to imagine that two competing undertakings could enter into a mutual distribution agreement which is in effect an agreement on market sharing.[64]

> There was an example of a market sharing agreement in Commission Decision 1999/60/EC concerning a *pre-insulated pipe cartel*, in which a number of European undertakings had entered into a network of agreements which restricted competition.[65] A number of Danish undertakings agreed a number of basic principles for what the Commission Decision referred to as the Danish cartel. First, they agreed a number of price increases, and then they agreed a quota arrangement laying down how large a percentage market share each should have. The market sharing arrangement was based on the 'established customer' principle. Where each party was allowed to keep its existing customers, and it was not permitted to conduct an active policy to take over the customers of the other parties. The quota arrangement was supervised by the sales directors, who met regularly. One person acted as coordinator, and allocated tenders between the cartel's members. Thus it was decided, in advance, who

62. Joined cases 209 to 215 and 218/78, *van Landewyck,* paras 134-141.
63. Commission Decision 92/204/EEC relating to the *building and construction industry in the Netherlands* (OJ 1992 L 92/1), para. 80, where a cooperation agreement had been made which identified which undertaking should negotiate with the property developer.
64. Commission Guidelines on horizontal cooperation agreements, para. 232.
65. OJ 1999 L 24/1.

should 'win' the order in question. The undertaking which had the honours informed the other parties what price it intended to offer, and the other parties thereupon put forward higher bids. At the end of each year, the parties exchanged auditor certified information about the year's sales of pipes, and there was a compensation arrangement to back up the quota arrangement.

Another example of a market sharing agreement was the subject of Commission Decision 94/815/EC relating to cement.[66] The case concerned a number of agreements between European cement producers and industry associations, in which Cembureau, the European industry association, played a central role. The Commission established that there was an agreement to respect the home market principle. To the extent that there were cross-border sales, an exchange of price information ensured that the exporting undertaking could set its prices in relation to the local price leader, so as to avoid the cross-border trade in cement upsetting prices in the market in question. There were a number of other agreements between producers in particular Member States, containing further details on market sharing. An agreement between producers in Spain and Portugal decided that in principle there should not be transport of cement between the two countries.

Competitors can also cooperate on sales and marketing without this necessarily involving market sharing. The most far reaching one can imagine is that two or more undertakings agree on joint sales, for example through a joint venture sales company. As already referred to in section 3, such an arrangement would inevitably lead to the coordination of their pricing policies, and the Commission has therefore been very reluctant to accept such forms of cooperation.[67] However, it is not impossible that there could be certain effectivity gains which could justify the acceptance of such joint sales.[68]

Cooperation can also consist of joint marketing. Such cooperation can be contrary to Article 101 because it gives greater scope for the exchange of sensitive information, particularly on pricing. Also, joint marketing can in itself restrict competition where marketing costs constitute a major part of the

66. OJ 1994 L 343/1. The Decision was referred to the GC in Joined cases T-25/95 and others, *Cimenteries*.
67. Commission Guidelines on horizontal cooperation agreements, para. 234.
68. Commission Guidelines on horizontal cooperation agreements, paras 246-248; and e.g. Commission Decision 89/467/EEC, *UIP* (OJ 1989 L 226/35).

total costs, as the cooperation will remove an important competitive parameter.[69] In its Guidelines on horizontal cooperation agreements, the Commission has accepted that, provided that the marketing cooperation does not cover joint pricing, agreement between undertakings that have less than 15 % market share will not normally be covered by Article 101(1), or that an exemption can be granted under Article 101(3).[70]

If two competitors agree to refrain from marketing their products or to restrict their marketing, this can be taken as expressing a desire to limit price competition.[71]

The shared use of a trade mark can have the effect of restricting competition as products sold under the trade mark will appear to consumers to be the same, so there will no longer be competition between the products in question.[72] In the same way, agreements not to make comparative advertising can have an anti-competitive effect.[73]

If undertakings cooperate on developing joint auctions, exhibitions or trade fairs, there can be conditions which will restrict competition. This will especially be the case if the participating undertakings are prevented from taking part in other auctions etc., or if third party undertakings are, to an unreasonable extent, prevented from taking part, or are only able to take part on unreasonable terms.[74]

69. Commission Decision 85/76/EEC, *Milchförderungsfonds* (OJ 1985 L 35/35), where it was not so much that the marketing costs were harmonised, but that they had been reduced for certain undertakings. The case concerned a fund which, by voluntary contributions made by German milk producers, among other things paid for an advertising campaign for cheese in Italy. This distorted competition, as these activities supported German cheese exporters without the sales price having to bear the direct costs (because, as stated, the fund was financed by voluntary contributions); see para. 30.
70. Commission Guidelines on horizontal cooperation agreements, para. 240.
71. See Commission Decision of 13 April 2011, COMP/39579 – *Consumer Detergents.* In this case the agreement to restrict marketing was linked to pricing agreements.
72. Case 246/86, *Belasco,* para. 30, where the common use of the designation Belsaco and a collective advertising campaign was aimed at ensuring that all products had the same image, thereby removing competition between the parties to the agreement.
73. Commission Decision 1999/267/EC, *EPI* (OJ 1999 L 106/14).
74. Among others, Commission Decision 88/477/EEC, *British Dental Trade Association* (OJ 1988 L 233/1), and Commission Decision 88/491/EEC, *Bloemenveilingen Aalsmeer* (OJ 1988 L 262/27).

7. Joint ventures

7.1. The special nature of joint ventures

Many horizontal cooperation agreements are entered into in the form of a joint venture. This is clearly seen in the fact that, even though the Commission's Guidelines on the applicability of Article 101 to horizontal cooperation agreements does not, in its wording, take joint ventures as its starting point, nevertheless many of the examples given involve joint ventures.[75]

The Commission considers joint ventures to be a special institutionalised from of commercial cooperation.[76] Already in 1974 the Commission pointed out that a joint venture could involve a number of special problems in competition law, and in this connection it defined a joint venture as an enterprise that is controlled by two or more independent undertakings.[77] Subsequently the Commission has developed this definition by referring to the fact that the undertakings that control a joint venture shall be independent of each other,[78] that it is not material whether or not the joint venture is for a limited period,[79] and that the corporate form by which the joint venture is carried on is immaterial.[80]

It is clear that joint ventures can involve agreements which restrict competition and therefore ought to be judged in accordance with Article 101 TFEU. For example, a joint venture can form the framework within which two producers can agree on uniform pricing. A form of pricing agreement can be ensured by the producers agreeing that their sales shall be made though their joint venture, so there will be an automatic alignment of prices.

75. Commission Guidelines on horizontal cooperation agreements. In most cases it is directly stated that cooperation agreements of a particular kind can be established in the form of a joint venture; see para. 111 on R&D agreements, para. 150 on production agreements, and indirectly para. 194 which refers to a company which the parties jointly control in relation to purchasing arrangements.
76. Commission Notice concerning the assessment of cooperative joint ventures pursuant to Article 85 of the EEC Treaty (OJ 1993 C 43/2), para. 1.
77. The Fourth Report on Competition Policy 1974, para. 37.
78. The Thirteenth Report on Competition Policy 1983, para. 53.
79. Commission Notice concerning the assessment of cooperative joint ventures pursuant to Article 85 of the EEC Treaty (OJ 1993 C 43/2), para. 3.
80. The Thirteenth Report on Competition Policy 1983, para. 54, and Commission Notice concerning the assessment of cooperative joint ventures pursuant to Article 85 of the EEC Treaty (OJ 1993 C 43/2), para. 3.

A joint venture can also form the framework for more extensive cooperation, where two or more undertakings (joint venture partners) agree to combine resources and conduct joint activities, such as R&D, or joint production. This form of joint venture is more difficult to evaluate under Article 101 for two particular reasons: first, the formation of such a joint venture can be regarded as a partial merger, and this merger element is subject to separate evaluation; and second, such extensive cooperation gives rise to the need to assess whether the cooperation between the joint venture partners is extended beyond the setting up of a jointly owned company and can result in the coordination of other activities.

On a number of points, joint ventures are subject to special evaluation under competition law. If a joint venture has a Community dimension and is fully functioning, it should be notified under the Merger Control Regulation. As well as evaluating such a joint venture under the special merger control test, see Chapter VIII, such a joint venture may also involve some agreements which restrict competition, and in this case in must be evaluated under Article 2(4) of the Merger Control Regulation. This provision states that a joint venture that has as its object or effect the coordination of the competitive behaviour of undertakings that remain independent shall be appraised in accordance with the criteria of Article 101(1) and (3). The appraisal to which joint ventures are subject under Article 2(4) of the Merger Control Regulation are discussed in more detail in Chapter VIII, section 7. The Commission has developed a practice which differs on some points from the evaluation of joint ventures in accordance with Article 101 of the EC Treaty.[81]

If a joint venture is not covered by the Merger Control Regulation, for example because it does not have a Community dimension,[82] there must be

81. However, it is clear that the effect of joint ventures is not necessarily different, depending on whether or not they operate independently; see the Commission Guidelines on horizontal cooperation agreements, para. 21.

82. If a joint venture is fully functioning, but does not have a Community dimension, the Commission has accepted a number of restrictions on the application of Article 101 to such joint ventures. First, the Commission will not allow an exemption under Article 101(3) to a joint venture which a national authority intends to prohibit under national merger control rules. Next, the Commission only finds it relevant to apply Article 101 to restrictions on competition that occur through the joint venture partners' coordination of their commercial activities outside the joint venture, i.e. the spill-over effect; see sections 7.2.2 and 7.2.3. However, the Commission will to the greatest possible extent leave it to the Member States to assess such joint ventures. Even though the Commission has thus accepted a number of restrictions on its application of Article 101, there is not a total exclusion of the Commission's application of

an evaluation in accordance with Article 101 of whether the joint venture contains any agreements which restrict competition. The Commission has developed a special practice for the investigation of different forms of restriction of competition which can be seen in connection with joint ventures. This practice involves an investigation of the following circumstances:[83]

A. There is an investigation of whether competition between the joint venture partners is restricted. This requires it to be established that the joint venture partners are either actual or potential competitors in one or more areas. If, for example, the joint venture partners combine their existing activities in a particular area, the joint venture can have the effect of restricting competition, as two undertakings are reduced to one. Also, a joint venture can have an influence on the joint venture partners' other activities – the 'spill-over effect'.[84]
B. If a joint venture is an independent undertaking, there must be an investigation of whether there is any restriction on competition between the joint venture partners and the joint venture company.
C. Next the Commission investigates whether the setting up of a joint venture affects the position of any third parties. Depending on the circumstances, the setting up of a joint venture can have consequences for the suppliers or customers of the joint venture partners. Also, the establishment of a joint venture can mean that potential competitors are prevented from entering the market.
D. The Commission evaluates whether a joint venture is part of a network of joint venture companies, whereby the effect of the individual joint venture is reinforced.
E. Even if it is concluded that the establishment of a joint venture does not in itself lead to a restriction of competition, the Commission will also

Article 101, and an Article 101 case can be initiated by national authorities or may arise before the national courts.

83. Commission Notice concerning the assessment of cooperative joint ventures pursuant to Article 85 of the EEC Treaty (OJ 1993 C 43/2), paras 17-31. An example of an early decision which reviewed these points is Commission Decision 90/410/EEC *Elopak/Metal Box – Odin* (OJ 1990 L 209/15), which marks the new practice after the introduction of the Merger Control Regulation.
84. Sometimes the term 'group effect' is used instead of 'spill-over effect'; see e.g. Decision 94/322/EC, *Exxon/Shell* (OJ 1994 L 144/21), para. 63. Sometimes the term 'indirect effect' is used; see the Twenty-fourth Report on Competition Policy 1994, para. 165.

investigate whether the individual provisions of the joint venture partners' agreement to set up a joint venture company have the effect of restricting competition.

The following sections will review in more detail the individual elements of the Commission's analysis of joint ventures. The review will be based on the Commission's practice and the relatively few judgments there have been on the issue. In 1993 a Notice was issued on the assessment of cooperative joint ventures,[85] but this Notice was withdrawn in connection with the entry into force of the Commission's first Guidelines on horizontal cooperation agreements in 2001.[86] The 1993 Notice contains a number of more general comments on the assessment of joint ventures which have not been included in the later Notice, so the older Notice can still be of interest.

This review focuses on the Commission's practice for when a restriction on competition will be found to exist. The usual conditions, that the restriction must be appreciable and must affect trade between Member States, will not be dealt with separately in this connection, but they must, of course, be met in order for there to be an infringement of Article 101.

7.2. Restrictions on competition between joint venture partners

The key question in joint venture cases is often whether the establishment of the cooperation means that competition between the joint venture partners is restricted, either by the establishment of the joint venture, or because it can be assumed that the cooperation will affect the joint venture partners' other activities. Both of these questions will be considered below.

7.2.1. Restriction on competition by the establishment of a joint venture

The setting up of a joint venture can in itself have the effect of restricting competition, where its setting up has a direct influence on competition between the joint venture partners. This will be so if two competing undertakings set up a joint venture which is active in an area where they have previously competed. If the joint venture partners transfer their own assets in the area, in reality two or more competing undertakings will be replaced by one undertaking, and consequently competition will be restricted. If the joint venture partners continue to be active in the area, competition may not be

85. Commission Notice concerning the assessment of cooperative joint ventures pursuant to Article 85 of the EEC Treaty (OJ 1993 C 43/2) (the 'Joint Venture Notice').
86. Commission Notice – Guidelines on the applicability of Article 81 of the EC Treaty to horizontal cooperation agreements, OJ 2001 C 3/2, para. 8 together with para. 5.

immediately restricted, unless it can be assumed that setting up the joint venture will have a spill-over effect on the joint venture partners' conduct in connection with such activities; see below.

> An example of this is the *P&O Stena Line* case, where the two joint venture partners ran ferry routes between Dover and Calais, which they wanted in future to run through a jointly controlled joint venture. Since this was a joint venture between two actual competitors, its establishment was considered to be contrary to Article 101.[87] Another example was the case of *Asahi/Saint-Gobain*, where the Commission considered that the joint venture partners were both competitors in respect of the research activity which the planned joint venture should undertake. The Commission found that both joint venture partners were undertaking existing research in similar areas, and that the effect of the joint venture would therefore be to make it impossible for the joint venture partners to take individual initiatives which could give one of the partners an advantage over the other. Thereby the joint venture meant that two competing research projects were reduced to one, and competition was diminished.[88]

Competition can also be restricted if joint venture partners are potential competitors in the area in which the joint venture is active. The setting up of a joint venture means that it cannot be expected that the joint venture partners will become as active in the market where the joint venture company is active. If several joint venture partners could be expected to be active in the area where the joint venture is to be active, the consequence of setting up the joint venture will be that competition will be restricted; there will only be one player where there could have been several. The same will be the case where

87. Commission Decision 1999/421/EC, *P&O Stena Line* (OJ 1999 L 163/61), para. 61.
88. Commission Decision 94/896/EC, *Asahi/Saint-Gobain* (OJ 1994 L 354/87), in particular para. 21. It was intended that most of the research would still be carried out by the joint venture partners, even after setting up the joint venture, and one could therefore argue whether the effect referred to in the decision really was a spill-over effect on the joint venture partners' activities. However, since it was agreed that the joint venture, which should own all the rights to the technology developed by the joint venture partners while the joint venture existed, the effect was that the joint venture partners had in reality gathered their research into the joint venture. It should be emphasised that it made no legal difference whether it was considered a spill-over effect or a direct effect of the setting up of the joint venture.

one joint venture partner is an actual competitor and another is a potential competitor on the market where a joint venture is to be active.

Even if this reasoning is right in principle, the Commission's practice in this area has been subject to much criticism, because it has previously been very quick to conclude that joint venture partners were potential competitors. In order to respond to the criticisms made of its practice in this area, in the Commission's Thirteenth Report on Competition Policy 1983, the Commission stated that it was determined to use as realistic an assessment of potential competition as possible.[89] In connection with this, it formulated a number of objective criteria. These criteria have already been described in section 2.1, and as is made clear there, in its Guidelines on the applicability of Article 81 to horizontal cooperation agreements, the Commission has confirmed that these criteria are still relevant for assessing whether two undertakings are potential competitors.[90]

In many cases there does not seem to be any great doubt about whether the individual joint venture partners could carry out the production or research activity on their own. Many cases involve joint venture partners with considerable resources, and here the Commission seems merely to state briefly that the necessary financial, technical and research capacity exists.[91]

The cases where the Commission concludes that the joint venture partners are not potential competitors are, among others, cases where it is established that the individual joint venture partners do not have the necessary technology to carry out the activity on their own.[92] Next, there are a number of cases where the Commission has rejected the idea that the joint venture partners were potential competitors, because the joint venture either required such resources or was associated with such risk that it could not be expected that the individual joint venture partners would carry on the activity on their own.[93] Finally, it is possible that the individual joint venture partner does not

89. The Commission's Thirteenth Report on Competition Policy 1983, para. 55.
90. Nevertheless the GC set aside the Commission's assessment that two joint venture partners were potential competitors as unrealistic in Joined cases T-373/94 and others, *European Night Services*.
91. Commission Decision 94/986/EC, *Philips-Osram* (OJ 1994 L 378/37), para. 16, and Commission Decision 93/49/EC, *Ford/Volkswagen* (OJ 1993 L 20/14), para. 19.
92. Commission Decision 94/770/EC, *Pasteur Mérieux-Merck* (OJ 1994 L 309/1), in particular paras 65-68, where it was assessed that in the case of certain vaccines there was no certainty that any of the joint venture partners could have developed them on their own.
93. Among others Commission Decision 97/39/EC, *Iridium* (OJ 1997 L 16/87), para. 40, and Commission Decision 94/895/EC, *International Private Satellite Partners* (OJ

have enough know-how to carry out the planned activity on its own.[94] In relation to this latter, it must be assessed whether a joint venture partner could acquire the necessary know-how by buying it.[95]

7.2.2. 'Spill-over effects' on the market where the joint venture operates

In many cases the joint venture partners will refrain from competing with their joint venture after setting it up. It may be that the joint venture partners will transfer their existing assets to their joint venture, or that they will allow their joint venture the exclusive right to a particular market. Typically the joint venture partners will also be subject to a non-competition clause which will prevent them from subsequently initiating activity which will compete with their joint venture. In all these cases there cannot be a spill-over effect on the joint venture company's own market. There will also be no risk of spill-over effect in this market where the joint venture partners have agreed to terminate their operations which compete with the joint venture company within a given number of years.[96]

On the other hand, if the joint venture partners remain active on the market in which the joint venture company operates, it is clear that there is a considerable risk that they will coordinate their conduct in the area.[97] The practice of the Commission seems to be based on the assumption that there

1994 L 354/75), para. 55(b). This assessment must also include the speed of technological development in the area, as the fact that development is very rapid is a further argument against making considerable investments; see Commission Decision 88/88/EEC, *Olivetti/Canon* (OJ 1988 L 52/51), para. 41.

94. Commission Decision 86/405/EEC, *Optical fibres* (OJ 1986 L 236/30), para. 46, where the special cooperation between an undertaking which manufactured glass and a number of undertakings which manufactured cables could not have been carried on by any of the joint venture partners individually, because they did not have sufficient insight into each others' areas of activity.
95. Commission Decision 87/100/EEC, *Mitchell Cotts/Sofiltra* (OJ 1987 L 41/31), para. 19, according to which one of the joint venture partners entirely lacked the necessary know-how and research and development facilities to develop a component which was of core importance to the planned activity. It could not be assumed that this joint venture partner could have bought or obtained a licence for the production of these products.
96. JV.44, *Hitachi/NEC – DRAM/JV*, Decision of 3 May 2000, para. 32, where the Commission dismissed the idea that the market was a candidate market for coordination since both parent companies would eventually withdraw from the market.
97. If only one joint venture partner remains active, the question is whether the risk of there being coordination between this joint venture partner and the joint venture company can be contrary to Article 101; see section 7.3.

will be coordination of their operations, without it always being necessary to show why this should be the case. However, in its Decision in the *Exxon/Shell* case, the Commission gave more detailed reasons for why it assumed that a spill-over effect would arise in the situation where both joint venture partners operated in the same product market as the joint venture company (polyethylene production):

> 'It has in particular to be pointed out that the flow of information between Exxon and Shell allowed by the joint venture structure is the basis on which each partner can plan its polyethylene production and adapt it to the choices of the other partner. This interdependence has a direct effect on the Exxon and Shell joint venture production plans (allowing, as was established by a Commission verification of the practical functioning of the joint venture, a perfect equalization of the quantities produced by the two ventures or a contemporaneous halting of the joint venture's production), but also an indirect effect (spill-over or group effect) on the polyethylene production plans of the Exxon and Shell groups as a whole. In fact any increase, reduction or halt in production decided by one partner in order to adjusts its behaviour to the other partner's choices in the joint venture entails a general reconsideration of the production plans of all polyethylene sites belonging to that partner's group.'[98]

This reasoning explains how the insight of the partners into the circumstances of the joint venture company and their participation in the planning of its operations can very easily lead to a coordination of the conduct of the joint venture partners. The reasoning is especially obvious with production joint ventures, but it is clear that similar effects can arise with other kinds of joint ventures. Even though in many cases it may be natural to assume that there can be a concerted practice contrary to Article 101, this should not always be assumed without closer evaluation. In particular, there should be an evaluation of how important the joint venture is for the joint venture partners, since a very small joint venture would perhaps not give the joint venture parties the incentive to coordinate their conduct. However, if the joint venture partners themselves have very large market shares, their general incentive for

98. Commission Decision 94/322/EC, *Exxon/Shell* (OJ 1994 L 144/21), para. 63.

a concerted practice will be greater, so that even a joint venture with modest operations can form the framework for a concerted practice.[99]

7.2.3. 'Spill-over effects' on other markets

The fact that joint venture partners cooperate in connection with a joint venture operation can mean that they may also coordinate their operations in other areas. In principle such coordination may take place in areas which have absolutely nothing to do with the joint venture activity, but in such a case it seems difficult to see the establishment of a joint venture as being the true cause of the partners trying to coordinate their activities. For this reason, the evaluation of spill-over effects will be concentrated on the markets which are more closely linked to the market in which the joint venture operates. This will typically be markets that are upstream or downstream in relation to the joint venture company's market, as well as related markets that are closely connected to the joint venture company's market.[100]

The decisions taken in accordance with Article 101 point to a number of special circumstances which mean that a particular joint venture cooperation can have a spill-over effect. One of the circumstances which has been emphasised in a number of decisions is that the participation of the joint venture partners in the management of the joint venture company makes it possible for them to exchange confidential information.[101]

In addition to this, it will be significant to assess what connection there is between the operations of the joint venture and the operations of the joint venture partners.

1. If a joint venture operates downstream as a sales channel for the products of the joint venture partners, this will by its very nature automatically diminish competition between the joint venture partners on the market in

99. See also *Jonathan Faull & Ali Nikpay (eds.):* The EC Law of Competition, 2nd ed., 2007 pp. 674-675.
100. Commission Guidelines on horizontal cooperation agreements, para. 156, which states that spill-over effects can be assumed to occur if the markets are linked by interdependencies. In this connection, the relevant closely connected markets are defined in the same way as in the Merger Control Regulation, Article 2(4), and in the note connected with it there is an express reference to this provision.
101. Commission Decision 93/49/EC, *Ford/Volkswagen* (OJ 1993 L 20/14), para. 21.

question. Furthermore, such a joint venture can create entry barriers to new competitors.[102]

2. If, in contrast, the joint venture operates upstream from the joint venture partners, it will depend on an evaluation of the importance of the input supplied by the joint venture. For example, if a joint venture produces certain components which are included in the products of the joint venture partners, this could reduce competition between the products of the joint venture partners, if the components are an important part of the finished product.[103] If the main part of a product is produced by a joint venture company, the joint venture partners will find it difficult to differentiate their products with regard to price and quality. This effect will naturally be reinforced if the joint venture partners supply the raw materials/intermediary products which a joint venture company processes and then delivers back to the joint venture partners. A similar effect can arise where a joint venture is responsible for the purchase of raw materials or components which are included in a product which several joint venture partners sell. The joint purchasing means that one of the factors which could contribute to price differentiation is no longer present.[104] A concerted practice is most probable if the joint venture is the only source for the joint venture partners of the product in question (for example, because they have undertaken to buy only from their joint venture). At the same time, this gives an insight into the sales of the other joint venture partner.[105]
3. If a joint venture is to operate in another territorial market than the ones where the joint venture partners compete, a concerted practice would be

102. Commission Notice concerning the assessment of cooperative joint ventures pursuant to Article 85 of the EEC Treaty (OJ 1993 C 43/2), para. 38, and Commission Decision 93/50/EEC, *Astra* (OJ 1993 L 20/23), para. 6.
103. Commission Decision 94/322/EC, *Exxon/Shell* (OJ 1994 L 144/21), para. 55. In Commission Decision 94/986/EC, *Philips-Osram* (OJ 1994 L 378/37), the Commission dismissed the idea that spill-over effects would arise in the market for lamps, where both joint venture partners competed, as the components produced by the joint venture company only constituted 2-3 % of the costs of producing a lamp; see para. 18. The standardisation brought about by the use of common components was thus not sufficiently significant to be a restriction on competition.
104. Commission Notice concerning the assessment of cooperative joint ventures pursuant to Article 85 of the EEC Treaty (OJ 1993 C 43/2), para. 39 with reference to this practice. See also Commission Guidelines on horizontal cooperation agreements, para. 201.
105. See *John Temple Lang* in *Barry E. Hawk (ed.):* Fordham Corporate Law Institute, 2000 pp. 381-464 (in particular pp. 398-399).

natural. By coordinating prices, the joint venture partners and the joint venture can help ensure that it is not attractive for parallel importers to operate, and this can contribute to maintaining divisions into several different territorial markets.[106]

4. If a joint venture operates in a related or neighbouring market to the markets where the joint venture partners are active, there may be a spill-over effect where these markets are closely connected. Previously the practice seems to have been to assume that there should be a relatively close connection between the activities, for example that the products on the different markets were complementary.[107] However, the more recent practice seems to be for the Commission to be satisfied by establishing that the product markets are related, without the Commission appearing to find it necessary to argue that the markets are interdependent.[108]

Many joint ventures involve several types of activity and therefore cannot be made to fit any of the situations referred to. The previous Joint Venture Notice provided that an overall assessment should be made in the case of such mixed joint ventures.[109] The same appears from the Commission's Guidelines on horizontal cooperation agreements. These provide that, in

106. See *John Temple Lang* in *Barry E. Hawk (ed.):* Fordham Corporate Law Institute, 2000 pp. 381-464 (in particular p. 405); and *Joseph F. Brodley:* Joint Ventures and Antitrust Policy, Harvard Law Review 1982 p. 1523.

107. Commission Notice concerning the assessment of cooperative joint ventures pursuant to Article 85 of the EEC Treaty (OJ 1993 C 43/2), para. 41. One of the few cases in which the Commission extended its investigation to neighbouring markets was in Commission Decision 93/49/EC, *Ford/Volkswagen* (OJ 1993 L 20/14), where the Commission found that the joint production of MPVs could have a spill-over effect on the market for estate cars and light goods vehicles.

108. This development of the practice has been clearest in those cases which the Commission has decided in accordance with the Merger Control Regulation, Article 2(4). See e.g. JV.19, *KLM/Alitalia,* Decision of 11 August 1999, where the effects of a joint venture between KLM and Alitalia to coordinate scheduled flights was also assessed in relation to the market for charter flights, the market for aircraft maintenance and the market for ground handling services. See also JV.22, *Fujitsu/Siemens,* Decision of 30 September 1999, where the effects of cooperation for the production of DRAM (dynamic random access memory) were also assessed in relation to the markets for financial and retail workstations, hardware maintenance services and global account IT services. In neither of these two decisions were further arguments given for why these markets are related.

109. Commission Notice concerning the assessment of cooperative joint ventures pursuant to Article 85 of the EEC Treaty (OJ 1993 C 43/2), para. 41.

principle, an attempt should be made to determine the centre of gravity of the cooperation, and where it is possible to find this centre of gravity, the relevant parts of the Guidelines should be applied.[110]

7.3. Restrictions on competition between the joint venture and the joint venture partners

If a joint venture is an independent undertaking, it will be relevant to assess whether in the relationship between a joint venture and a joint venture partner restrictions are agreed which contravene Article 101. If one joint venture partner controls the joint venture company, it follows from the concept of an undertaking which is given in Chapter II that they are considered to be one undertaking, and it is thus not relevant to apply Article 101 to the relationship between the two. However, the Commission has adopted the assumption that where a joint venture is controlled jointly by several joint venture partners, the joint venture is considered to be an independent undertaking.

> This follows from Commission Decision 91/335/EEC, *Gosme/Martell – DMP*, which concerned a joint venture, owned in equal shares by two joint venture partners. The Commission was of the view that in this situation the joint venture was not part of the same undertaking as one of the joint venture partners, Martell, as the Commission did not believe that Martell could control the joint venture's commercial activities. In this, it emphasised that both joint venture partners had 50 % of the voting rights, and appointed half the members of the board of directors of the joint venture company. The joint venture company also distributed products which did not belong to the joint venture partners, and the joint venture company had its own sales team. Since this joint venture was sufficiently independent in relation to the joint venture partners, the Commission was of the view that an agreement between the joint venture company and Martell was contrary to Article 101, since it was intended to restrict parallel imports.[111]

This practice is perhaps challenged by the GC in Case T-314/01, *Avebe*, where the GC had to decide whether a joint venture partner could be made

110. Commission Guidelines on horizontal cooperation agreements, paras 13-14.

111. Commission Decision 91/335/EEC, *Gosme/Martell – DMP* (OJ 1991 L 185/23), para. 30. In line with this; see Commission Decision 91/562/EC, *Eirpage* (OJ 1991 L 306/22), para. 9, and the Decision of 21 December 2005 in Case COMP/F/38.443 – *Rubber chemicals* (OJ 2006 L 353/50), para. 263.

liable for the fact that the joint venture company was part of a cartel. The GC established that the joint venture was subject to the joint control of the joint venture partners. In this situation the GC held that it could be assumed that the joint venture partners had in fact exercised control and were thus liable for the conduct of the joint venture company. The GC concluded that the joint venture and the two joint venture partners constituted a unit in relation to the concept of an undertaking; see paragraph 141. The consequence of this conclusion was that Avebe, as a joint venture partner, could be held liable for the conduct of the joint venture company, and that agreements between the joint venture company and the joint venture partners fell outside the scope of Article 101.

However, this was a radical break with the previous practice, so there are reasons for suggesting that the decision might be interpreted narrowly. It appears from the judgment that the joint venture was purely contractual, and there was no independent legal person. It was managed by two people appointed by the joint venture partners, and had premises with one of the joint venture partners. Thus, in this case there were a number of circumstances which meant that it was not so obvious that the joint venture was an independent undertaking. In order to establish that a joint venture is an independent undertaking, there must be certain requirements for a joint venture to have certain resources. The courts have previously expressed that an undertaking is 'a unitary organization of personal, tangible and intangible elements which pursues a specific economic aim on a long-term basis'.[112] This statement confirms first that an economic activity must be carried on, but it can also be understood as meaning that certain resources must be made available to a joint venture. It is possible that the finding in the *Avebe* judgment can be based on the fact that the joint venture did not have sufficient resources, even though this is not clearly stated in the judgment. On the other hand, it is clear that if it appears from the circumstances that a joint venture is established with a view to representing the joint venture partners in a cartel, there is nothing to prevent the joint venture partners being held liable for the conduct of their joint venture.[113]

There is a clear possibility that competition between a joint venture and one or more joint venture partners will be restricted if they are competitors. This is confirmed by the fact that the joint venture partners will often have agreed

112. Case T-11/89, *Shell International Chemical Company,* para. 311, and Case T-9/99, *HFB-Holding,* para. 54.
113. The Commission thus named a joint venture and its two joint venture partners in Commission Decision COMP/F/38.899 – *GAS INSULATED SWITCHGEAR* (OJ 2008 C 5/7), and on the basis of an overall assessment, the Commission assumed that the joint venture partners had elected to participate in a cartel via their joint venture; paras 389-402.

to a non-competition clause, whereby they will not compete with their joint venture. Moreover, the fact that the joint venture partners have joint control over their joint venture is assumed to protect them against the joint venture company entering into unexpected and undesired competition with them.[114]

If several joint venture partners are actual or potential competitors to their joint venture, it follows from the review in section 7.2 that the Commission will investigate whether the competition between the joint venture partners will be restricted. If it is concluded that this is the case, it will less significant whether competition between the joint venture partners and their joint venture will be restricted. If competition between the joint venture partners is not restricted, for example because the market structure is not optimal for a concerted practice, the conditions for a concerted practice between the joint venture partners and their joint venture are also unlikely to be optimal. Therefore, there is the greatest independent significance for undertaking an evaluation of restrictions on competition between the joint venture and the joint venture partners in the situation where only one joint venture partner competes with the joint venture company.

If one looks at the existing decisions, only few of them include an evaluation of restrictions on competition between a joint venture and the joint venture partners. The decisions which do contain such an evaluation restrict themselves to evaluating the restrictions on competition which are the direct consequence of the various contractual provisions concerning the joint venture company, such as non-competition clauses, supply clauses etc. These are considered below in section 7.6. On the other hand, there are no examples of cases where the Commission has assessed whether there is a specially high risk of there being a concerted practice between a joint venture and the joint venture partners, contrary to Article 101. The fact that this is so can probably be explained by the Commission not having a real expectation that a joint venture partner will compete with its joint venture, so the Commission is content with looking into any contractual terms which seem to be unnecessarily restrictive.

7.4. The effects on third party undertakings

A joint venture can also restrict competition by affecting the position of a third party. This will typically be the case where a joint venture achieves a certain economic strength which affects undertakings which compete with the

114. See *John Temple Lang* in *Barry E. Hawk (ed.):* Fordham Corporate Law Institute, 2000 p. 395.

joint venture company.[115] However, it is not enough to establish that a joint venture has economic strength; it must also be shown that one or more third party undertakings is, as a result, put in a position where it cannot compete, typically because it is excluded from the market.

Even though there are a number of decisions that include an assessment of the effect of a joint venture on third party undertaking, there are only a few where this is the decisive element. This will typically be one of many effects restricting competition that are found to exist in connection with a joint venture.

First of all, the effects restricting competition for third parties can be established in relation to the customers or suppliers of a joint venture. Where joint venture partners combine their sales in a joint venture, this can mean there are significantly fewer choices for customers.[116] Similarly, a purchasing cooperation can mean that such a great purchasing strength is created that it has a serious negative effect on competition.[117] If a third party undertaking cannot receive deliveries, for example because the joint venture partners has the exclusive right to supply from the joint venture, this can constitute an infringement of Article 101(1), if there is market concentration.[118] In many cases the joint venture will have bound itself to take deliveries of raw materials or components from the joint venture partners, so that other suppliers are excluded from supplying in competition with the joint venture partners.[119]

Next, a restriction on competition can be found to exist in relation to undertakings that compete with the joint venture company or the joint venture partners. For example, a purchasing cooperation can obtain such economic strength that competitors are effectively unable to compete with the joint venture partners that are part of the cooperation.[120] A joint venture can also

115. Commission Notice concerning the assessment of cooperative joint ventures pursuant to Article 85 of the EEC Treaty (OJ 1993 C 43/2), para. 23.
116. Commission Notice concerning the assessment of cooperative joint ventures pursuant to Article 85 of the EEC Treaty (OJ 1993 C 43/2), para. 24.
117. On the assessment of purchasing cooperation, see Commission Guidelines on horizontal cooperation agreements, paras 194-220.
118. Commission Decision 88/88/EEC, *Olivetti/Canon* (OJ 1988 L 52/51), para. 45.
119. Commission Decision 88/88/EEC, *Olivetti/Canon* (OJ 1988 L 52/51), para. 47, where it was found that the restriction on competition was not appreciable, as the situation was only that the joint venture partners had a preferential status in the supply of components to their joint venture, as long as the joint venture partners' components were competitive.
120. Commission Decision 93/403/EEC, *EBU/Eurovision* (OJ 1993 L 179/23), para. 51.

have developed and produced a unique product which others than the joint venture partners must have access to in order to compete.[121] For example, this can be because the joint venture has acquired the sole right to exploit some particular technology,[122] or because a joint venture has a production which can prevent third parties from supplying because there are not (enough) alternative supply channels.[123] In these cases it is often decisive whether the third party can participate in the cooperation, or can at least obtain supplies on non-discriminatory terms.[124] In several cases the Commission has provided for such conditions as will ensure this; see section 7.7.

In other cases the essential question is whether a joint venture creates barriers to entry which potential competitors cannot be expected to be able to surmount. In these cases the Commission appears to be satisfied with finding that very large economic strength is created, and if this means that there are

121. E.g. this can be the case where a joint venture has control of an 'essential facility'. As pointed out by *John Temple Lang* in *Barry E. Hawk (ed.):* Fordham Corporate Law Institute, 2000 pp. 406-407, a denial of access to such facilities, together with the fact that a dominant joint venture uses discriminatory pricing are typically factors that will be contrary to Article 102. Therefore, it can be argued that it is not necessary for this to be considered in an assessment under Article 101, as it can be expected that the joint venture will be found to be abusing its dominant position, and action can be taken against this under Article 102. However, the Commission has never accepted that the possibility of applying Article 102 should make it unnecessary to include this aspect in an Article 101 assessment of a joint venture.
122. Commission Decision 94/770/EC, *Pasteur Mérieux-Merck* (OJ 1994 L 309/1), paras 70-71, where the joint venture partners had agreed they would only supply vaccines and grant licences via their joint venture. However, it was judged that even though this could affect other producers, as they were thereby prevented from acquiring the technology they needed from the joint venture partners, the restriction on competition was not significant, as there were other potential suppliers of this technology.
123. Commission Decision 94/986/EC, *Philips-Osram* (OJ 1994 L 378/37), para. 17, where the Commission assessed that the setting up of a joint venture could give the joint venture partners the possibility of preventing independent manufacturers getting hold of lead glass. However, as it was shown that there was overcapacity, the Commission found this was not the case.
124. Commission Decision 2001/696/EC, *Identrus* (OJ 2001 L 249/12), para. 46, where the Commission found that other undertakings could become shareholders in the company, provided they fulfilled a number of objective criteria.

barriers to entry to the market, the Commission will be disinclined to approve the joint venture.[125]

> An example of this is Commission Decision *LH/SAS*, where the Commission found that the proposed cooperation between Lufthansa and SAS to establish an integrated air transport network between the two companies would give them an economic strength which would act as a significant barrier to access to the market on all routes between Scandinavia and Germany.[126] Another example is Commission Decision *Astra*, where the Commission emphasised that the customers who had signed contracts with the joint venture, which was to be responsible for running the new Astra satellite, were bound for a period of 10 years, and that during this period others were excluded from access to this market.[127]

7.5. Networks of joint ventures

If a joint venture is part of a network of joint venture companies, this can reinforce the individual joint venture companies' effect on the joint venture partners' business policies and the position of third parties. For this reason, such joint ventures are assessed with regard to the overall effect of the network of joint ventures.[128]

The fact that many joint ventures are set up between the same joint venture partners is an indication that the joint venture partners work closely together, and that it is therefore probable that they cooperate in other areas.[129] In addition to this, with a network of joint ventures it is necessary to include the restrictions on competition that arise in the relationships between the different joint ventures. For example, if the joint venture partners set up several joint ventures which operate on the same product market, but in different territorial markets, it is often clear that competition between the joint ventures will be restricted. Competition will also be restricted where the joint venture partners set up a number of joint venture companies for comple-

125. Commission Decision 91/130/EEC, *Screensport/EBU Members* (OJ 1991 L 63/32), para. 63, Commission Decision 91/562/EEC, *Eirpage* (OJ 1991 L 306/22), para. 12, and Commission Decision 96/546/EC, *ATLAS* (OJ 1996 L 239/23), para. 40.
126. Commission Decision 96/180/EC, *LH/SAS* (OJ 1996 L 54/28), para. 54.
127. Commission Decision 93/59/EEC, *Astra* (OJ 1993 L 20/23), para. 17.
128. Commission Notice concerning the assessment of cooperative joint ventures pursuant to Article 85 of the EEC Treaty (OJ 1993 C 43/2), para. 27.
129. See *John Temple Lang* in *Barry E. Hawk (ed.):* Fordham Corporate Law Institute, 2000 p. 409.

mentary products which the joint venture partners themselves prepare. Finally, the Commission assumes that there can be restrictions on competition if competing joint venture partners set up a network of joint ventures which produce non-complementary products, provided that the joint venture partners themselves sell the products in question.[130]

> The Commission tried to apply this reasoning in Commission Decision 94/663/EC, *Night Services*, which involved a joint venture company set up between a number of railway companies with a view to running night trains for passengers between Britain and the Continent via the Channel Tunnel. The Commission found that this joint venture restricted competition between the joint venture partners, and made it more difficult for other transport undertakings to gain access to the market. Furthermore, the Commission concluded that the restrictions on competition were strengthened by the fact that the joint venture partners had set up a network of joint ventures for the transport of freight and passengers, including via the Channel Tunnel.[131] However, this part of the Decision was subsequently overruled by the GC.[132] The GC stated that it was not clear from the Decision which joint ventures were set up with a view to passenger transport, and the Commission was not able to point to such during the proceedings before the Court. There were a number of joint ventures between the joint venture partners in the area of freight transport, but as this was a non-complementary product in relation to passenger transport, according to the joint venture Notice, there would only be a restriction of competition where the joint venture partners themselves undertook the sales of the non-complementary products. However, there was no evidence that the joint venture partners sold these products, and the GC therefore found that the Commission's Decision on this point was not sufficiently justified.

Where there is a network of joint ventures, in each of which different joint venture partners participate, this can be seen as an expression that there is considerable interdependence between the joint venture partners on the

130. Commission Notice concerning the assessment of cooperative joint ventures pursuant to Article 85 of the EEC Treaty (OJ 1993 C 43/2), para. 29.
131. Commission Decision 94/663/EC, *Night Services* (OJ 1994 L 259/20), paras 49-53.
132. Joined cases T-373/94 and others, *European Night Services,* paras 157-159.

market where these compete.[133] This can mean that there is a considerable risk that the joint venture partners will coordinate their conduct, not least where the existence of many joint ventures can contribute to the exchange of commercially sensitive information between the joint venture partners.[134]

A joint venture between joint venture partners who do not compete will not normally constitute a restriction on competition, but if a joint venture is part of a network of joint ventures, it is possible that a restriction on competition could arise, if these joint ventures have been set up in the same product market.

> This was the case in the Commission Decision on *Optical fibres*, where the American company Corning Glass Works had set up three joint ventures together with European undertakings located in different EU Member States. It was the intention that all three joint ventures should produce optical fibres, which was a newly developed product which could be used for communications technology. Since the new product was intended to replace more traditional cables, Corning had chosen to enter into joint venture agreements with companies that produced cables. Since Corning itself was primarily involved in the production of glass and ceramic products, the joint venture partners in the three joint ventures were not its competitors. For this reason the Commission did not find that the individual joint ventures restricted competition. However, restrictions on competition arose between the three joint ventures, since they were involved in the same production, and together they created an oligopolistic market. Because of Corning's financial involvement and the fact that Corning occupied the key technical and financial position in all three joint ventures, the Commission found that Corning was able to coordinate the conduct of the three joint venture companies. It could therefore be expected that the notified joint venture agreements would result in restrictions on competition.[135]

133. Commission Notice concerning the assessment of cooperative joint ventures pursuant to Article 85 of the EEC Treaty (OJ 1993 C 43/2), para. 31.
134. See *John Temple Lang* in *Barry E. Hawk (ed.):* Fordham Corporate Law Institute, 2000 p. 409, referring to Case C-7/95 P, *John Deere*.
135. Commission Decision 86/405/EEC, *Optical fibres* (OJ 1986 L 236/30), paras 47 and 56.

7.6. Special provisions

Even where it is found that the setting up of a joint venture does not restrict competition, and that there are no restrictions between the joint venture partners or in relation to third party undertakings, in some cases the Commission has undertaken an assessment of the agreements made in connection with the setting up of a joint venture company, with a view to seeing whether these contain contractual terms that restrict competition. This practice means that even if in principle the Commission has no objection to a joint venture, it retains the right to assess the terms agreed in the joint venture agreement, the articles of association of the joint venture company, and any other agreements associated with the cooperation.

The terms which the Commission eliminates in this way are often terms which restrict competition between the joint venture company and the joint venture partners. However, the Commission has admitted that some terms are necessary for the establishment and operation of a joint venture. Such restraints are therefore ancillary to the setting up of a joint venture and cannot be challenged.[136]

In 2005 the Commission issued a Notice on ancillary restraints in relation to the Merger Control Regulation.[137] According to its wording, this Notice is limited to cases under the Merger Control Regulation, and no corresponding notice has been issued in relation to the assessment of joint ventures under Article 101. The Joint Venture Notice from 1993 contained a number of guidelines for the assessment of ancillary restraints, but these were not repeated in the Commission's Notice on horizontal cooperation agreements. For this reason, a review of what constitutes an ancillary restraint under Article 101 must be based on the Commission's decisions.[138]

In general, the Commission seems to accept that a non-competition clause, which prevents the joint venture partners and the joint venture company competing with each other, is ancillary, even if it applies for the whole duration of the joint venture agreement. According to the Commission, the prohibition on competition is merely a concrete expression of the joint

136. For more detail on the practice on ancillary restraints, see section 5.5 in Chapter II.
137. Commission Notice on restrictions directly related and necessary to concentrations (OJ 2005 C 56/24). For more on this, see Chapter VIII, section 6.
138. However, there are certain general comments on the assessment of ancillary restraints in Communication from the Commission – Notice – Guidelines on the application of Article 81(3) of the Treaty (OJ 2004 101/97), paras 28-31.

venture partners' enduring and mutual commitment to their joint venture.[139] The Commission has even allowed that the duration of a non-competition clause may be extended so that it binds a joint venture partner for a short period after it has sold its ownership interest in the joint venture company, on the grounds that the exiting joint venture partner would otherwise have an unreasonable competitive advantage because of the know-how acquired through participation in the joint venture company.[140] On the other hand, it is obvious that the Commission cannot be expected to accept terms whereby the joint venture partners restrict competition between them in areas which are outside the area of activity of the joint venture company.[141] Nor will the Commission accept that a joint venture partner which does not have a share in the control of the joint venture company can be bound by a non-competition clause.[142]

139. Commission Decision 94/986/EC, *Philips-Osram* (OJ 1994 L 378/37), para. 20, Commission Decision 96/546/EC, *ATLAS* (OJ 1996 L 239/23), para. 42, and Commission Decision 1999/242/EC, *TPS* (OJ 1999 L 90/6), para. 97. The Commission also accepted an open-ended non-competition clause in Commission Decision 94/5789/EC, *BT-MCI* (OJ 1994 L 223/36), para. 46, and Commission Decision 96/547/EC, *PHOENIX/GlobalOne* (OJ 1996 L 239/57), para. 53, but here the Commission seems to have required there to be special circumstances relating to the joint venture company's market in order for an open-ended non-competition clause to be acceptable. In particular, this can be the case where substantial investments and risks are associated with the joint venture. In Commission Decision 1999/242/EC, *TPS* (OJ 1999 L 90/6), para. 99, the Commission only accepted a non-competition clause in the start-up phase, specifically 3 years. Commission Decision 93/48/EEC, *Fiat/Hitachi* (OJ 1993 L 20/10), is difficult to reconcile with this practice, as para. 21 of the Decision seems to conclude generally that a non-competition clause is contrary to Article 101, without determining whether it was ancillary or not. However, the agreements were exempted under Article 101(3). The decision must be regarded as incorrect on this point.
140. Commission Decision 94/823/EC, *Fujitsu AMD Semiconductor* (OJ 1994 L 341/66), para. 35, in which the Commission accepted that the non-competition clause should be extended for two years following the sale, provided that this took place within 10 years of setting up the joint venture company. See also Commission Decision 1999/781/EC, *British Interactive Broadcasting/Open* (OJ 1999 L 312/1), paras 125 and 148, where the Commission accepted that the prohibition on competition applied for 12 months after a joint venture partner had sold its controlling shareholding, provided that this took place within the first three years.
141. See *Jonathan Faull & Ali Nikpay (eds.):* The EC Law of Competition, 2007 p. 677.
142. Commission Decision 1999/781/EC, *British Interactive Broadcasting/Open* (OJ 1999 L 312/1), para. 125.

The Commission also seems to accept terms whereby a joint venture company or joint venture partner take on purchase and supply obligations to each other. Thus, in several cases the Commission has accepted an obligation, limited in time, for joint venture partners to take the joint venture company's products, since, among other things, this helps to ensure the effective and economic use of the joint venture company's production capacity, and can create a stable financial basis for the operations of the joint venture company.[143] In this connection, the Commission has accepted agreements whereby joint venture partners are given priority in receiving supplies,[144] and it has also accepted favouritism provisions which ensure that the joint venture partners obtain the best prices.[145] If joint venture partners not only have an obligation to fulfil their own needs for the product by buying it from the joint venture company, but also have the status of sole distributors, the Commission will look more critically at whether this constitutes an ancillary restraint. The Commission seems to hold the view that a non-exclusive distributorship is sufficient to secure the interests of the joint venture company.[146]

In connection with the setting up of a joint venture, the sole right to exploit certain know-how will often be granted to the joint venture, or the joint venture will be granted a licence to use some technology. This will not be contrary to Article 101, even if certain restrictions are imposed on the joint venture in connection with how the licence can be used, for example by restricting it to sales to a certain territory or preventing the joint venture company from producing products that compete with the licensed products.[147] It is more questionable whether the Commission will accept an exclusive licence which excludes the joint venture partners themselves from

143. Commission Decision 96/546/EC, *ATLAS* (OJ 1996 L L239/23), para. 42.
144. Commission Decision 94/986/EC, *Philips-Osram* (OJ 1994 L 378/37), para. 20. See also Commission Decision 1999/573/EC, *Cégétel + 4* (OJ 1999 L 218/14), paras 52-55.
145. Commission Decision 94/895/EC, *International Private Satellite Partners* (OJ 1994 L 354/75), para. 61.
146. Commission Decision 96/547/EC, *PHOENIX* (OJ 1996 L 239/57), para. 53. However, the Commission accepted such an exclusive distribution right in Commission Decision 97/39/EC, *Iridium* (OJ 1997 L 16/87), para. 49.
147. Commission Decision 90/410/EEC, *Elopak/Metal Box-Odin* (OJ 1990 L 209/15), para. 30. See also Commission Notice concerning the assessment of cooperative joint ventures pursuant to Article 85 of the EEC Treaty (OJ 1993 C 43/2), paras 72-73.

using some specific technology. However, the Commission seems to accept such a restriction during the start-up period.[148]

7.7. Exemptions and conditions

The practice of the Commission shows many examples where a joint venture is assumed to be contrary to Article 101(1), but which will normally be exempted under Article 101(3). However, in many cases the Commission attaches terms and conditions to an exemption. An exemption can also be granted on the basis of a block exemption regulation, and here reference is made to the review of the block exemption regulations on specialisation agreements and R&D agreements, given above in sections 4.1 and 5 respectively.

If one looks at the Commission's practice, it is characterised by the fact that the Commission accepts that joint ventures can contribute to the improvement of production and distribution in many different ways. This is the case with joint ventures which it is assumed will bring forth a new or significantly improved product.[149] Therefore, the Commission is usually very positive about R&D joint ventures whose main purpose is the development of new products.[150] This applies even if the Commission finds that several joint venture partners could have developed a corresponding product on their own, provided that it is either considered less likely that the joint venture partners would have taken on the risks and costs associated therewith,[151] or if it is assumed that the joint venture partners would be able to develop the product more effectively, economically and quickly than they would have been able to on their own.[152] In cases of R&D joint ventures, the Commission has also

148. Commission Decision 87/100/EEC, *Mitchell Cotts/Sofiltra* (OJ 1987 L 41/31), para. 23.

149. Commission Decision 93/48/EEC, *Fiat/Hitachi* (OJ 1993 L 20/10), para. 25, Commission Decision 94/322/EC, *Exxon/Shell* (OJ 1994 L 144/20), para. 67, Commission Decision 94/770/EC, *Pasteur Mérieux-Merck* (OJ 1994 L 309/1), para. 82, Commission Decision 96/6546/EC, *ATLAS* (OJ 1996 L 239/23), paras 48-50, and Commission Decision 97/781/EC, *Uniworld* (OJ 1997 L 318/24), paras 68-75.

150. The Commission's Twenty-fourth Report on Competition Policy 1983, para. 155.

151. Commission Decision 77/781/EEC, *GEC-Weir/Sodium Circulators* (OJ 1977 L 327/26), p. 33, and Commission Decision 2000/182/EC, *GEAE/P&W* (OJ 2000 L 58/16), para. 80. However, it is noted that, in more recent practice, the fact that there are major risks and investments associated with an activity will normally lead to the conclusion that the joint venture partners are not potential competitors, so the joint venture in question may not in fact infringe Article 101(1).

152. Commission Decision 91/562/EEC, *Eirpage* (OJ 1991 L 306/22), para. 14; Commission Decision 77/781/EEC, *GEC-Weir/Sodium Circulators* (OJ 1977 L 327/26), p.

relied on the fact that the product which it is sought to develop has great economic significance,[153] or can otherwise be considered as contributing to progress.[154]

Some of the same advantages can be associated with a production joint venture. These can lead to the introduction of new production methods,[155] and they can contribute to introducing new or increased production capacity.[156] There can also be cost savings associated with such joint ventures, but the Commission is normally reluctant to accept that such an advantage can outweigh the disadvantages associated with joint ventures.[157]

In contrast, the Commission looks much more critically at joint ventures that are primarily concerned with sales. Even though in certain circumstances a sales joint venture can support market penetration, the Commission will normally judge them negatively, unless the sales cooperation is part of a wider cooperation in which there are other elements which are persuasive that there are advantages.[158] A purchasing joint venture can also give a number of economic benefits, such as economies of scale in connection with transaction costs, transport, and warehousing, and these advantages can outweigh the reservations to which these kinds of joint ventures can give rise, because they can give greater purchasing power to the joint venture in question.[159]

More generally, in its notices the Commission states that most efficiency gains arise from a combination and integration of different forms of know-

33; and Commission Decision 2000/182/EC, *GEAE/P&W* (OJ 2000 L 58/16), para. 80.

153. Commission Decision 86/405/EEC, *Optical fibres* (OJ 1986 L 236/30), para. 59.
154. Commission Decision 94/770/EC, *Pasteur Mérieux-Merck* (OJ 1994 L 309/1), paras 83-84.
155. Commission Decision 93/49/EC, *Ford/Volkswagen* (OJ 1993 L 20/14), para. 25.
156. Commission Decision 94/322/EC, *Exxon/Shell* (OJ 1994 L 144/20), para. 67, and Commission Decision 94/986/EC, *Philips-Osram* (OJ 1994 L 378/37), para. 25.
157. Thus, in Commission Guidelines on horizontal cooperation agreements, para. 185, the Commission rejects the idea that cost savings that are due to a reduction in production or to market sharing, or which are due to the exploitation of strength in the market, can be allowed any influence. However, cost savings were accepted as being relevant in Commission Decision 94/986/EC, *Philips-Osram* (OJ 1994 L 378/37), paras 26-27, and in Commission Decision 1999/421/EC, *P&O Stena Line* (OJ 1999 L 163/61), paras 62-63.
158. Commission Notice concerning the assessment of cooperative joint ventures pursuant to Article 85 of the EEC Treaty (OJ 1993 C 43/2), para. 60.
159. Commission Guidelines on horizontal cooperation agreements, para. 217.

ledge and resources.[160] Therefore it is relevant to evaluate the know-how and other resources which the individual joint venture partners contribute, and the extent to which the joint venture involves their integration. However, it is difficult to see from the practice of the Commission how it evaluates this integration, apart from the fact that it evaluates what know-how and resources the joint venture partners possess. The Commission does not appear to have found a method for measuring whether it is in fact possible to integrate these.

The Commission has the possibility of attaching conditions to its individual exemptions, both concerning the structure and the conduct of a joint venture (structural and behavioural conditions).[161] In contrast to the case with the Merger Control Regulation, the Commission has not issued a notice giving a more detailed explanation of its practice.[162]

> A structural condition was accepted by the joint venture partners in Commission Decision 1999/781/EC, *British Interactive Broadcasting/Open*, where the Commission was concerned that there might be cross-subsidising between the activities of the joint venture company, to the injury of third party undertakings. These concerns were met when the joint venture partners accepted the splitting up of the two activities to be conducted in two separate companies. Each company was to have its own day-to-day management, and nobody could sit on the board of both companies. Both companies had to present annual accounts, and the auditors of the companies had to confirm that all transactions between the companies were carried out on an arm's-length basis.[163]

160. Commission Communication from the Commission – Guidelines on the application of Article 81(3) of the Treaty [now Article 101(3) TFEU] (OJ 2004 101/97), para. 60.
161. Under Article 9 of Regulation (EC) No 1/2003, the Commission also has the possibility of imposing conditions when it assesses whether an agreement can be exempted.
162. Commission Notice on remedies acceptable under Regulation (EC) No 139/2004 on the control of concentrations between undertakings (the EC Merger Regulation) (OJ 2004 L 24/1) and Regulation (EC) Regulation (EC) No 802/2004 implementing Regulation (EC) No 139/2004 (OJ 2004 L 133/1) , discussed in more detail in Chapter VIII, section 5. The Notice is clearly directed at solutions for dealing with dominant position.
163. Commission Decision 1999/781/EC, *British Interactive Broadcasting/Open* (OJ 1999 L 312/1), paras 126-127.

In several cases the Commission has accepted conditions which are of a more behavioural character, and which are aimed at ensuring that there is no spill-over effect on other markets.

> In Commission Decision 2000/182/EC, *GEAE/P&W*, this led to the Commission imposing conditions that the joint venture in question might not be involved in the development of a specific product (an aero engine intended for an aircraft capable of carrying more than 450 passengers). In order to ensure compliance with this condition, a number of requirements were imposed, including 1) that the Commission was to be informed of all changes to the cooperation, 2) that the joint venture activity should be carried out by a separate legal entity, which should act in its own name and independently of the joint venture partners (i.e., at arm's-length), and 3) that the exchange of confidential information should be restricted to what was necessary for the joint venture to operate.[164]

There have been other decisions where the Commission has laid down conditions that the joint venture partners should not exchange information, as this may lead to a concerted practice. However, the problem is to ensure that the condition is complied with.[165] In one decision the Commission attempted to solve this problem by making it a condition that the joint venture partners and the joint venture company itself should undertake not to exchange competitively sensitive information.[166]

Another way of countering concerted practices is to seek to restrict the scope for the joint venture partners to exercise influence over the joint venture company. This is a more radical intervention, as it disturbs the balance between the joint venture partners, but nevertheless the Commission has used conditions of this kind in some cases.

164. Commission Decision 2000/182/EC, *GEAE/P&W* (OJ 2000 L 58/16), paras 92-96.
165. However, it is also possible that the exchange of information is prevented by company law and competition law rules, and this may be enough in itself to satisfy the Commission's concerns; see Commission Decision 96/547/EC, *PHOENIX/Global-One* (OJ 1996 L 239/57), para. 51.
166. Commission Decision 86/405/EEC, *Optical fibres* (OJ 1986 L 236/30), para. 83. See also JV.15, BT/AT&T, Decision of 30 March 1999, para. 187, where the Commission did not immediately accept that the 'firewall' arrangements proposed were sufficient protection against a concerted practice.

> In the Commission Decision 86/405/EEC, *Optical fibres*, one of the joint venture partners (Corning) accepted a restriction of its rights in the three joint venture companies in which it was a participant in the European market. Among other things, Corning accepted that its voting rights in the German joint venture company should be reduced so that Corning no longer had a veto right, and Corning also agreed to withdraw all its representatives from the board of the German joint venture company and to reduce the number of its representatives on the board of the British company. Corning also restricted its right to appoint leading personnel in the joint venture companies, and only retained the possibility of appointing the technical director (who had to come from Corning as it provided the essential know-how) as well as an internal auditor.[167]

In several cases the Commission has imposed conditions to ensure that a joint venture does not restrict competition in relation to third party undertakings. This is ensured by imposing a requirement on the joint venture partners or the joint venture company to make certain facilities available to potential competitors, so they have the possibility of surmounting the barriers which exist.[168] In many cases, where it is important for other undertakings to receive supplies from the joint venture company, the Commission has laid down conditions that such deliveries must be made on fair and non-discriminatory terms.[169] It is also possible to impose conditions to regulate other aspects of

167. Commission Decision 86/405/EEC, *Optical fibres* (OJ 1986 L 236/30), paras 63-65.
168. Commission Decision 96/180/EC, *LH/SAS* (OJ 1996 L 54/28), where the conditions are set out in paras 86-114. In Commission Decision 94/663/EC, *Night Services* (OJ 1994 L 259/20), paras 80-81, the Commission laid down a number of conditions to ensure that new competitors who wanted to run a train service should have the right to be provided with a number of services.
169. See, among others, M.1327, *NC/Canal+/CDPQ/Bank America,* decision of 3 December 1998, para. 40, Commission Decision 96/547/EC, *PHOENIX/GlobalOne* (OJ 1996 L 239/57), para. 31, Commission Decision 94/663/EC, *Night Services* (OJ 1994 L 259/20), para. 82, and Commission Decision 96/546/EC, *ATLAS* (OJ 1996 L 239/23), para. 28. However, it is possible that the Commission will find that the prohibition on discrimination already applies under national law, so it is not necessary to make further conditions; see Commission Decision 1999/781/EC, *British Interactive Broadcasting/Open* (OJ 1999 L 312/1), para. 131, and Commission Decision 94/579/EC, *BT-MCI* (OJ 1994 L 223/36), para. 57. It could be objected that a prohibition on discrimination also applies under Article 102 TFEU, so it is not necessary for the Commission to impose conditions on this. However, imposing conditions is probably more effective than applying Article 102, and not all joint ventures have a dominant position so as to be covered by this provision.

the joint venture activities, including ensuring that there is no cross-subsidising, that there are no requirements for bundling, that confidential information is not passed on etc.[170]

One way to ensure that joint venture partners and joint venture companies comply with the Commission's conditions is to require an audit to be carried out to confirm a number of facts, typically including that the trade between the joint venture partners and the joint venture company takes place on an arm's-length basis.[171] Also, there can be a condition that the Commission has the right, upon request, to have access to monitor the companies' accounts etc., and the companies can be required to report to the Commission on certain matters.[172]

8. Cooperatives

A cooperative company is characterised by the fact that its business is based on trade with its members. For example, a cooperative company buys the members' production (for example flowers, cereals, pigs etc.) and sells these on after having carried out a measure of processing. There can also be a purchasing cooperative, where the cooperative company buys goods and sells them on to the members. In many of the EU Member States cooperatives are a special form of company, characterised by the fact that the company's profits are distributed to the members in proportion to their share of the turnover, and similar forms are found in other countries.[173] However, it is clear that for the purposes of evaluation under competition law, the form of incorporation is largely irrelevant, and a purchasing cooperation will in principle be evaluated in the same way, whether it takes the form of a limited company or a cooperative company.

Many cooperatives are active in the area of agriculture. In principle, agriculture is excluded from the competition rules of the Treaty, see Article 42 TFEU, unless the Council decides otherwise. In Regulation No 26 of

170. Commission Decision 97/780/EC, *Unisource* (OJ 1997 L 318/1), paras 56-67, and Commission Decision 96/546/EC, *ATLAS* (OJ 1996 L 239/23), para. 29.
171. Commission Decision 97/780/EC, *Unisource* (OJ 1997 L 318/1), para. 105, and Commission Decision 96/546/EC, *ATLAS* (OJ 1996 L 239/23), para. 30.
172. Commission Decision 97/780/EC, *Unisource* (OJ 1997 L 318/1), para. 105, and Commission Decision 96/546/EC, *ATLAS* (OJ 1996 L 239/23), para. 30.
173. In order to make it easier for cooperative companies to merge and to cooperate across borders in the EU, the Council adopted Regulation (EC) No 1435/2003 on the Statute for a European Cooperative Society (SCE) (OJ 2003 L 207/1).

1962, the Council decided that to a large extent the competition rules should apply in the area of agriculture, but in Article 2(1) of the Regulation a reservation is made that 'Article 85 (1) of the Treaty [now Article 101] shall not apply to such of the agreements, decisions and practices referred to in the preceding Article as form an integral part of a national market organisation or are necessary for attainment of the objectives set out in Article 39 of the Treaty. In particular, it shall not apply to agreements, decisions and practices of farmers, farmers' associations, or associations of such associations belonging to a single Member State which concern the production or sale of agricultural products or the use of joint facilities for the storage, treatment or processing of agricultural products, and under which there is no obligation to charge identical prices, unless the Commission finds that competition is thereby excluded ...'[174] This provision means that it is also possible to adopt restrictions on competition in cooperative companies established between farmers.[175]

A cooperative company can infringe the competition rules in various ways. First, the company's undertaking may have a dominant position on the market, so that its conduct may infringe Article 102. But, because the company's activities are closely linked to the activities of its members, the company can also be assessed under Article 101. For example in a purchasing cooperation, it can have a restrictive effect on the market for purchases if the company acquires considerable market strength on this market. In addition, purchasing activities can have a spill-over effect on the members' competition on the market where they sell their products. For example, if there is purchasing cooperation for shops, the fact that they buy most of their goods from the same place will make it less likely that the shops will compete with each other.[176]

In principle, the evaluation of the activities of cooperative companies does not differ from the evaluation of other horizontal cooperation agreements for

174. EEC Council: Regulation No 26 applying certain rules of competition to production of and trade in agricultural products (OJ 30, 20.4.1962), p. 993, English special edition: Series I Chapter 1959-1962 p. 129.
175. For further details see Case C-399/93, *H.G. Oude Luttikhuis*, paras 27-31. For a more detailed review of the application of the competition rules to agriculture, see *Peter Roth & Vivien Rose (eds.):* Bellamy & Child: European Community Law of Competition, 6th ed., 2008 pp. 1172-1180.
176. On purchase agreements, see Commission Guidelines on horizontal cooperation agreements, paras 194-220. In para. 208 it is stated that if the parties to an agreement have a market share of less than 15 %, it is unlikely that that there will be a significant restriction on competition.

the same activities. However, cooperative companies do have a special position in that their existence is based on modest capital contributions from the members, but in return the members are subject to a number of different obligations. These obligations will normally be laid down in the articles of association of the company, and they can include an obligation to supply, an obligation to purchase, and a prohibition on membership of other cooperatives, a general prohibition on competition, and special terms for leaving the cooperative etc. As most of these conditions can have the effect of restricting competition, it is relevant to consider whether they infringe Article 101.[177]

In a number of cases the CJ and GC have had an opportunity to assess various different provisions and obligations in the articles of association of cooperative companies. In this, they have taken as their starting point that there is nothing in principle that makes the organisation of an undertaking in the form of a cooperative a restriction on competition, but that nevertheless such a cooperative can be capable of influencing the business conduct of the members of the cooperative and thereby restrict competition.[178] Some of these restrictions may be necessary to enable the cooperative to operate, and these can be compatible with Article 101, provided that the restrictions do not go further than is necessary to ensure the effective running of the cooperative.

> On this basis, in Case T-61/89, *Dansk Pelsdyravlerforening*, the GC found that it was natural that members should be subject to an obligation to supply, so they had a duty to sell their production through the cooperative company. In principle, the obligation to supply can be justified by the fact that a cooperative company has only a small capital base, so it would be difficult for it to finance its activities unless there was certainty that the members would supply their products to the company. In the case in question, the members were subject to a non-competition clause, which in the opinion of the GC went further than could be considered reasonable, because of its general and unlimited character.[179]
>
> In Case C-250/92, *Gøttrup-Klim*, the CJ had to consider the articles of association of Dansk Landbrugs Grovvareselskab (DLG). The members

177. The conditions for membership can also be contrary to Article 102, e.g. where a cooperative company with a dominant position has unreasonable conditions for admitting new members, or has an unreasonably long period of notice for leaving.
178. Case T-61/89, *Dansk Pelsdyravlerforening,* para. 51, and Case C-399/93, *H.G. Oude Luttikhuis,* para. 12
179. Case T-61/89, *Dansk Pelsdyravlerforening,* in particular paras 72-77.

were divided into different categories, and for B and D members it was provided that they could not be members of or otherwise participate in undertakings which competed with DLG in the distribution of fertiliser and plant protection. If the members did not comply with this obligation, they could be excluded from DLG. The CJ found that it could undermine the cooperatives ability to achieve its aims if some members also participated in other cooperative purchasing associations. Such double membership could make it difficult to carry on the cooperative undertaking satisfactorily, and diminish its bargaining power with producers. On the other hand, the non-competition clause was a restriction on competition, so it was necessary to ensure that it did not go further than was necessary for ensuring the satisfactory running of the cooperative. The CJ did not find that this was so in the case in question, as the non-competition clause was first of all limited so as to cover fertilisers and plant protection preparations, which are the only bulk goods where there is a direct relationship between quantity and price, and where it was thus clear that it would damage DLG if members bought part of their needs elsewhere. Next, it was possible for members to buy fertiliser and plant protection preparations other than through DLG, as long as it was not through some organised cooperative. In connection with this, the CJ noted that non-members could also buy from DLG at the same prices as members. Finally, the CJ did not find that the conditions for exclusion were unreasonably strict.[180]

In Case C-399/93, *H.G. Oude Luttikhuis*, the CJ had to assess a number of the terms of the articles of association of some Dutch dairy cooperative companies. The members were obliged to supply all their milk to the cooperative company (which was in turn obliged to buy all their milk). In addition, in the event of withdrawal or exclusion from the cooperative, a fee had to be paid amounting to 2 % of the amount which the member had received for the milk he had supplied over the preceding five years. The CJ commented that the combination of a supply obligation and a very high fee upon withdrawal could cause the market to become very rigid, and it could give the cooperative a market power which made it very difficult for others to enter the market. The CJ refrained from passing judgment on the

180. Case C-250/92, *Gøttrup-Klim,* in particular paras 32-42.

concrete case, as it was a referral for a preliminary ruling from a national court.[181]

9. Acquisition of minority shareholdings

If undertaking A acquires shares in undertaking B, this can result in A controlling B. This will be the case if a controlling shareholding is acquired, for example where more than half of all voting rights are acquired, or if so many voting rights are acquired as to give A effective control. This is also possible if A's shareholding allows A to exercise joint control with another shareholder with whom A has an agreement. If control or joint control is acquired in this way, notification of it must be given in accordance with the Merger Control Regulation, provided that the other conditions of the Regulation are fulfilled; see Chapter VIII.

If a minority shareholding is acquired there will not be a merger, but instead it can be considered whether the acquisition should be assessed in accordance with Article 101.[182] The acquisition of a shareholding can thus be seen as a step towards establishing an agreement or concerted practice, whereby two undertakings align their business policies. This can particularly be the case where the undertakings are competitors. If two undertakings mutually acquire such minority shareholdings (cross-holdings) it will be natural to assess whether such an ownership structure gives cover for conduct which restricts competition. In the *Philip Morris* case, the CJ confirmed that the acquisition of a minority shareholding can infringe Article 101.[183]

Philip Morris had originally intended to enter into a joint venture with the Rembrandt Group to run Rothman Holdings, which had hitherto been 100 % owned by Rembrandt. Philip Morris and Rothmans were competitors in the tobacco industry. The plan was that Philip Morris should own 50 % of the holding company which controlled Rothmans. Philip Morris and Rembrandt should have the right to appoint equal numbers of Rothmans's management. However, as the Commission objected to this joint venture under both Articles 101 and 102, the

181. Case C-399/93, *H.G. Oude Luttikhuis,* in particular paras 12-20.

182. Depending on the circumstances, the acquisition of a minority shareholding can also constitute an infringement of Article 102, see Commission Decision 93/252/EEC, *Warner-Lambert/Gilette* (OJ 1993 L 116/21).

183. Joined cases 142 and 156/84, *British-American Tobacco & R.J. Reynolds* v *Commission.*

agreement was changed so that Philip Morris should instead only acquire a minority shareholding giving control of less than 25 % of the voting rights in Rothmans, and an undertaking was given that Philip Morris would not be entitled to appoint members to Rothmans's board or otherwise have access to strategic information about Rothmans's business. The Commission thereafter decided not to object to the agreement, but this decision was referred to the CJ by some competing undertakings in the tobacco industry.

The CJ confirmed the decision of the Commission, but on the basis of some ambiguous reasons.

In paragraph 31 of the judgment it is stated that, since the acquisition of shares in Rothmans International was the subject-matter of agreements between companies which remained independent after the entry into force of the agreements, the issue had to be examined under Article 101. In paragraph 37 it is stated that, although the acquisition by one company of an equity interest in a competitor does not in itself constitute conduct restricting competition, it may nevertheless serve as an instrument for influencing the commercial conduct of the companies in question so as to restrict or distort competition. Thereafter, paragraph 38 continues:

'That will be true in particular where, by the acquisition of a shareholding or through subsidiary clauses in the agreement, the investing company obtains legal or de facto control of the commercial conduct of the other company or where the agreement provides for commercial cooperation between the companies or creates a structure likely to be used for such cooperation.'

This decision gave rise to a debate about whether Article 101 could be used for the control of mergers, especially where one undertaking acquired control over another. However, the actual case did not involve a merger, and paragraph 31 emphasises that Article 101 requires the parties to remain independent of each other. However, paragraphs 37-38 suggest that Article 81 also applies where one undertaking acquires control of another, even if this is normally understood to mean that the undertakings are no longer independent.[184] The debate particularly concerns the question whether acquisition of effective control can be covered by Article 101. On the other

184. For a summary of the discussion see *D.S. Nava*: The Policy of the EEC on Concentrative Joint Ventures, Leiden Journal of International Law 1992 pp. 57-67; and *Barry E. Hawk & Henry L. Huser*: Europcan Community Merger Control, 1996 pp. 346-360.

hand, there is less doubt about whether acquisitions of minority shareholdings which give the shareholder a certain measure of control, though without giving full control, can be a clear indication that an agreement exists which restricts competition. The question is whether it is enough to establish that there has been such a share acquisition, or whether there must be additional elements for Article 101 to have been infringed, for example in the form of underlying agreements or overlapping personnel on the boards of directors.[185] There is therefore still considerable uncertainty in assessing when Article 81 is applicable to the acquisition of minority shareholdings. One can also question whether it would not be more appropriate to consider such acquisitions under the Merger Control Regulation.[186]

185. Commission Decision 94/771/EC, *Olivetti-Digital* (OJ 1994 L 309/24), where the Commission assessed Digital's acquisition of a minority shareholding in Olivetti of 8 % which was established in connection with technology cooperation, as well as a shareholder agreement that secured Digital the right to representation on Olivetti's board. For a more detailed review of the assessment of the acquisition of minority shareholdings from a competition law point of view, see *Robin A. Struijlaart:* Minority Share Acquisitions Below the Control Thresholds of the EC Merger Control Regulation: An Economic and Legal Analysis, World Competition 2002 173-204; *John Temple Lang in Barry E. Hawk (ed.):* Fordham Corporate Law Institute 1999, 2000 pp. 426-427; *Francesco Russo:* Abuse of Protected Position? Minority Shareholdings and Restriction of Markets' Competitiveness in the European Union, World Competition 2006 pp. 607-633, and *Fausto Caronna:* Article 81 as a tool for controlling minority cross-shareholdings between competitors, European Law Review Vol. 29 (4) 2004 pp. 485-500.

186. The Commission has previously considered whether the acquisition of minority shareholdings should be covered by the Merger Control Regulation; see the Commission Green Paper on the Review of Council Regulation (EEC) No 4064/89, COM(2001) 745 final, paras. 106-110. So far, the Merger Control Regulation has not been expanded to cover such acquisitions.

CHAPTER V

Technology transfer agreements. Commission Regulation (EC) No 772/2004

Bent Iversen

Bibliography: *Steven D. Anderman: EC Competition Law and Intellectual Property Rights, 1998; Valentine Korah: Franchising and the EEC Competition Rules, 1989; Valentine Korah: Technology Transfer Agreements, 1996.*

1. The EC Treaty and intellectual property rights

The following is a review of the competition law assessment of technology transfer agreements, in other words, agreements under which a licensee obtains a right to exploit the technology of another (the licensor).

The purpose of this chapter is to cast some light on the conditions under which such licences may be compatible with the EU competition rules.

The subjects of the agreements referred to, i.e. patents, copyright etc., are traditionally dealt with under the heading of *intellectual property law*, which, in respect of most of these rights, is based on laws which give intellectual or industrial property rights the character of legally protected *exclusive rights*.[1]

At the regional level (meaning the area of the European Union) the provisions in Articles 34 and 36 of the Treaty on the Functioning of the European Union (TFEU) are particularly relevant. These provisions state as follows:

1. The comments that follow will primarily concern patent licence agreements. Licence agreements concerning know-how and software copyright will be touched on when relevant in respect of Regulation (EC) No 772/2004, particularly when the rules differ because of the differences in the kinds of rights referred to.

Article 34

'Quantitative restrictions on imports and all measures having equivalent effect shall be prohibited between Member States.'

Article 36

'The provisions of Articles 34 and 35 shall not preclude prohibitions or restrictions on imports, exports or goods in transit justified on grounds of public morality, public policy or public security; the protection of health and life of humans, animals or plants; the protection of national treasures possessing artistic, historic or archaeological value; or the protection of industrial and commercial property. Such prohibitions or restrictions shall not, however, constitute a means of arbitrary discrimination or a disguised restriction on trade between Member States.'

These two provisions should be understood in the light of the fact that the legal regulation of intellectual property is still primarily a matter for *national* law, and is not based on Community legislation.[2]

In principle it is still national authorities that determine the content and exercise of intellectual property rights; see Article 345 TFEU, according to which systems of property ownership are not affected by the Treaties.

However, national rules on intellectual property must be so framed that they may only prevent the free movement of goods if the prevention is justified by the protection of the rights that constitute the specific subject matter of the intellectual property right (the existence of the right rather than its exercise); see further below on this distinction.

The restriction on the content of national rules on intellectual property rights first arose in connection with Community competition law in Joined cases 56 and 58/64, *Consten and Grundig* v *Commission*, and has since reappeared in different forms in a number of judgments of the Court of Justice of the European Union (CJ).[3]

2. However, there are certain important exceptions to this, e.g. see the implementation of the First Council Directive 89/104/EEC of 21 December 1988 to approximate the laws of the Member States relating to trade marks (the Trade Marks Directive) (OJ 1989 L 40/7). However, this Directive was not aimed at implementing a complete harmonisation of the Member States laws on trade marks, but was restricted to dealing with national provisions that were believed to have the most direct effect on the functioning of the internal market, including the exhaustion of rights referred to in Article 7(1) of the Directive; see below on the content of this principle in relation to patent rights.
3. The *Grundig* case, which is referred to above in section 2.1 of Chapter III, and which contained the Commission's and the CJ's criticisms of measures for achieving complete territorial protection, is illustrative in the present context, primarily because it found that a French sole distributors use of Grundig's trade mark was contrary to

The essence of these decisions relating to, for example, *patent law* is that the 'specific subject matter' of patent rights is to *secure for the patent owner the sole right to exploit an invention* by being the first to put a product on the market and thereby, depending on the circumstances, make it possible for the inventor to obtain a financial *reward for the inventors creativity* and to *compensate for the costs* of developing the product to the stage where it can be traded. There are also other aspects of the specific subject matter, including the *right to issue licences* to third parties and the right to *oppose the sale of copies* of the product.

> See for example Case 15/74, *Centrafarm BV and Adriaan de Peijper* v *Sterling Drug*, in particular paragraph 9: 'In relation to patents, the specific subject matter of the industrial property is the guarantee that the patentee, to reward the creative effort of the inventor, has the exclusive right to use an invention with a view to manufacturing industrial products and putting them into circulation for the first time, either directly or by the grant of licences to third parties, as well as the right to oppose infringements.'
>
> See also Case 187/80, *Merck* v *Stephar*.

When there is no exploitation of an intellectual property right, particularly where there is an agreement or a concerted practice between the owner of a right and an undertaking about the latter's taking a licence to exploit the right, the agreement will fall outside the scope of Article 101(1). The abuse provision in Article 102, which relates to an undertaking's abuse of a dominant position and does not typically refer to an agreement between two or more undertakings, will not be widely applicable. However, see section 2.2 on, among other things, the *Volvo*, *Renault* and *Magill* cases.

Outside the area of agreements, the CJ's decisions have primarily considered the question in relation to national laws and other measures on whether national prohibitions of hindrances to trade and/or other measures are compatible with Articles 34 and 36 TFEU.

See for example Case 15/74, *Centrafarm and Adriaan de Peijper* v *Sterling Drug*, and paragraph 22 in Case 19/84, *Pharmon BV* v *Hoechst AG* (on the principle of exhaustion of rights, discussed below):

Article 101(1) TFEU, as it could hinder parallel imports to France to the extent that under the applicable French law.

'It must be recalled that the Court has consistently held that Articles 30 and 36 of the EEC Treaty [now Articles 34 and 36] preclude the application of national provisions which enable a patent owner to prevent the importation and marketing of a product which has been lawfully marketed in another Member State by the patent proprietor himself, with his consent, or by a person economically or legally dependent on him.'

See also Case 24/67, *Parke, Davis & Co.* v *Centrafarm*, where the referring Dutch appeal court wanted the CJ's opinion on whether a patent owner would be acting contrary to, among other things, Article 101(1) TFEU by exercising the rights granted to a patent owner under Dutch law with regard to medicines, in order to prevent the import to the Netherlands of similar products which were manufactured in a country where, at that time, medicines could not be patented. The Dutch rules, which the CJ did not find to be contrary to the Treaty, gave the owner of a patent registered in the Netherlands the possibility of imposing an injunction against patent protected products from another Member State where patent protection was not granted to these products or to the method for their production. See likewise the CJ's decision in Case C-23/99, *Commission* v *France*, where it stated: 'by implementing, pursuant to the Code de la Propriété Intellectuelle, procedures for the detention by the customs authorities of goods lawfully manufactured in a Member State of the European Community which are intended, following their transit through French territory, to be placed on the market in another Member State where they may be lawfully marketed, the French Republic has failed to fulfil its obligations under Article 30 of the Treaty [now Article 36 TFEU].' The French Republic tried to justify the detention of the products by reference to French law on design rights. But in the view of the Commission, which was accepted by the CJ, goods in transit are not covered by the specific subject matter of a design right, and the detention of the goods was not found to be justified by regard for the protection of intellectual property rights.

While the acknowledgement of the existence of intellectual property rights is an expression that competition law must accept these rights for what they are, the problem changes when it comes to the exercise of these rights.[4]

4. The distinction between the existence of a right (the rights specific subject matter) and its exercise must not be given exaggerated importance, as it would probably not stand up to a jurisprudential analysis. A warning should be given against drawing binding conclusions from whether something is characterised as being the content of

Regional competition law (EU competition law) is based on the goal of integration. Undertakings must not, by making agreements, be able to recreate barriers which it is the aim of the single market to remove; see also section 2.

There are two aspects of the interests of society. On the one hand there is consideration for the owners of rights and their exploitation of their own productions, and thereby the spread of useful knowledge and technology. On the other hand, there is consideration for the goal of market integration. These interests can conflict.

However, intellectual property law has to a certain extent itself sought to make good some of its inherent restrictions to integration.

For example, a source of conflict, which would otherwise arise from the restrictions to integration that are inherent in intellectual property law, is that an owner of intellectual rights might refuse to grant a licence to another, is countered on a European basis by provisions in the intellectual property legislation itself. In the case of patent law, see the Danish Patents Act §§ 45-50 on the conditions for granting a compulsory licence. A patent owner's refusal to grant a licence is kept outside the realm of competition law, except that in extraordinary circumstances it can be relevant to the application of the abuse of dominant position provisions in Article 102 TFEU (see section 2.2).

Another example of where the problem of the restrictions to integration which are inherent in intellectual property law has been suppressed before it could cause harm is the intellectual property doctrine of exhaustion of rights. This principle is included, among others in the Danish Patents Act § 3.3 second indent, and accordingly the exclusive right of a patentee does not in-

a right or its exercise. The distinction is found elsewhere, e.g. in German law (the Immanenz doctrine) and in US law (the Inherency doctrine). See also *Valentine Korah:* Technology Transfer Agreements and the EC Competition Rules, 1996 pp. 36-40. The distinction has been claimed as being a method for helping objectify the result of the CJ's balancing of different interests in concrete cases, between on the one hand consideration for maintaining respect for the arrangements of intellectual property law, and on the other hand the considerable weight which must be attached to the attempts to break down artificial barriers which are injurious to the establishment of the internal market. See also the comments of *Claus Gulmann* in his capacity as Advocate General in Joined cases C-241/91 P and C-242/91 P, *Radio Telefis Eireann* v *Commission* (generally referred to as the *Magill* case), which is discussed below in section 2.2. On the development from the earlier practice up to the more refined presentation of the distinction in more recent cases on the existence of rights and their exercise, see *Steven D. Anderman:* EC Competition Law and Intellectual Property Rights, 1998 pp. 8-16.

clude trade in products which have been put on the market by the patent owner or with his consent in Denmark or in another Member States within the European Economic Area (EEA). Once the products have been put on the market (by the patent owner, or a licensee or by others who may lawfully market the products), neither the patent owner nor the licensee may restrict the further circulation of the products in the market.[5]

For example, a purchaser may not be required not to resell products to a distributor who intends to export the products to another area within the internal market. In other words, the doctrine of exhaustion of rights supports the Commission's and the CJ's well known principle of allowing parallel imports.

The EU's goal of market integration requires that the right of the owner of rights (the patent owner) and others to control the circulation of products in the market ceases once the product has been marketed in one of the Member States with their consent.

National exhaustion of rights would not satisfy this goal, and the CJ has previously interpreted Articles 34 and 36 so that putting a product on the market in one Member State results in regional (EU-wide) exhaustion of rights.[6] For example, as stated the Danish Patent Act § 3.3 has followed this line. Under this provision, the exhaustion of rights arises upon the marketing of a product in Denmark or in another Member State in the European Economic Area (EEA).

Exhaustion of rights requires that the product is put on the market 'by the patent owner or with his consent'. The principle of exhaustion therefore does not apply when a product is put on the market by virtue of a compulsory licence, or upon the import of counterfeit products or other copies (pirate imports).[7]

5. See also the comments above on Article 7(1) of the Trade Marks Directive.
6. See Case 15/74, *Centrafarm BV and Adriaan de Peijper* v *Sterling Drug,* in which Sterling Drugs attempt to prevent the Dutch company Centrafarm importing the medicine NEGRAM to the Netherlands from Germany and England, was found to be contrary to Articles 34 and 36. The medicine had been bought in Germany and England, where it had been marketed by Sterling Drugs local marketing companies. Concerning the exhaustion of rights in respect of trade marks, see Case C-355/96, *Silhouette,* according to which Article 7(1) of the Trade Marks Directive must be interpreted as expressing regional (EU) exhaustion of rights, and not global exhaustion.
7. By contrast, the original product may compete against copied products that are manufactured in a Member State where they have not been granted patent protection,

See Case 19/84, *Pharmon BV* v *Hoechst AG*, where an English company, which had been granted a compulsory licence to exploit the invention of a medicine in the UK, for which Hoechst had a patent in force in Germany and parallel patents in the Netherlands and the UK. In breach of an export prohibition, the English company sold a large batch of the medicine to the Dutch medicine firm Pharmon, which intended to resell the goods in the Netherlands. The question which the referring Dutch Supreme Court laid before the CJ for a preliminary ruling was whether it would be contrary to the provisions of the Treaty (now Articles 34 and 36 TFEU) on the free movement of goods, if Hoechst used the authority of the applicable Dutch laws to prevent the marketing of the products in the Netherlands. The clear message from the CJ was that it must be regarded as necessary that a patent owner, who in the case of a compulsory licence would not normally have given consent, could still have the possibility of preventing the import and marketing of the products. Only in this way was it possible to secure for the patent owner the sole right to be the first to put a patented product on the market and thus to 'obtain the reward for his creative effort.'

See also Case 35/87, *Thetford Corporation* v *Fiamma SpA*, where the CJ found in favour of Thetford, which had a UK patent for the production of portable toilets, and wished to prevent Fiamma, which did not have any licence from Thetford, from selling toilets which Fiamma imported from Italy. The CJ found that a prohibition could be imposed without the English law on this thereby coming into conflict with the Treaty rules on free movement of goods, and regardless of the fact that the British patent, under a special British recognition of the patent law principle of 'relative novelty', had been published more than 50 years before the current patent application.

The specially emphasised condition, that the product should have been marketed by the patent owner or with the patent owners consent, will be fulfilled as long as either the owners of the rights in the exporting and importing countries are identical, or they have such a close economic connection with each other that the product is put on the market by an undertaking in the same corporate group or by a licensee; see Case 15/74, *Centrafarm BV and Adriaan de Peijper* v *Sterling Drug*.

see paragraph 11 in Case 15/74, *Centrafarm BV and Adriaan de Peijper v Sterling Drug*.

There was a special situation in Case 187/80, *Merck* v *Stephar*:

Merck, which was the owner of two Dutch patents for medicines, put a medicine on the market in Italy where it could not be patented, because of the then applicable prohibition under Italian law on the granting of patents for medicines or methods for producing medicines. The medicine was bought in Italy by Stephar and imported to the Netherlands, where it was put on the market in competition with Merck. The referring Dutch court wanted to know whether Merck would infringe Article 30 of the EC Treaty [now Article 36] if, with the support of the national Dutch rules which prohibited the import, Merck opposed the parallel import of the medicines to the Netherlands in the circumstances described. In its answer, the CJ stated that it is up to the patent owner whether it will market its product or not, and it must be assumed to have full knowledge of the conditions under which it can market the products, including when this is on a market where patent protection does not apply. If it decides to undertake such marketing, it must accept the consequences of its choice and accept that its control over the further circulation of the product is exhausted.

In Joined cases C-267/95 and C-268/95, *Merck* v *Primecrown*, the result was in line with the first *Merck* case, though the CJ added that, to the extent that under national or Community rules the patent owner had a legal obligation to market its goods in a Member State where its exclusive rights were not protected, it could lawfully oppose the import to and marketing of the products in a Member State where they were protected; see *Valentine Korah:* Technology Transfer Agreements and the EC Competition Rules, 1996 pp. 42-43.

2. Licence agreements and EU competition law

2.1. The relationship to Article 101 TFEU

When the individual intellectual property rights grant an 'exclusive right', it is obvious – especially if 'the exclusive right to the commercial exploitation of an intellectual property right' is rewritten as a 'monopoly' – that competition law should be brought into play to protect against abuse of the monopoly. This is particularly indicated at the regional (EU) level, since exclusive rights are, by definition, calculated to hinder the integration which is the goal of the internal market.

Among other things, the EU-based competition rules are aimed at regulating agreements and concerted practices which may affect competition between undertakings within the Community when such agreements etc. can affect trade between the Member States and hinder the integration of the markets [Article 101(1) TFEU].

In connection with the exploitation of an intellectual property right, for example when entering into a licence agreement, both the licensor and the licensee can have an interest in laying down certain restrictions on the other party's exploitation of the licence.

From a competition law point of view, some of the restrictions will be neutral in relation to society's ideal of promoting the effective us of resources through effective competition.

Competition law will not normally be concerned with purely contractual issues between the parties, for example the fees for a licensee to exploit the licensors invention or know-how for a certain period. The same will apply to the territorial extent of a licence – whether the licensee has the right to use the licence in one or more countries, or maybe only in a limited part of a single country – at least in so far as the conditions on territorial extent are not combined with other terms which restrict the licence out of consideration for third parties, including other licensees, or if the licensor itself that wishes to operate on the market and therefore has an interest in restricting the extent of the first licensees activities.

However, experience has shown that there will be a need for the competition authorities to intervene against more or less sophisticated terms which are aimed taking care of concerns other than the due recognition of the parties' rights to take part in the free competition on a given market, without seeking to impose restrictions on competition, whether unilaterally or by agreement.

One example could be a term whereby the licensor restricts the quantity of products which the licensee may produce under the licence, since this may restrict the availability of products which a third party might buy and export to a territory where the licensor has agreed to help another licensee as part of a policy of pricing differentiation in order to maintain a higher price for the products.[8]

Examples of restrictions on competition of the kind described and other kinds are legion, and these will be discussed below. However, the comments so far have already shown that an undertaking will often need to know in advance, and with a reasonable degree of certainty, whether the terms which it wishes to include in a contract can be expected to be accepted by the competition authorities, which in this instance means the Commission, the CJ and

8. See the comments below in section 6.1.2.

the Court of First Instance (now the General Court), and the national competition authorities.[9]

In this context, Regulation (EC) No 772/2004 on the application of Article 81(3) of the Treaty [now Article 101(3) TFEU] to categories of technology transfer agreements (block exemptions for licence agreements) (for more detailed discussion see section 5) will be an invaluable tool for undertakings which want to avoid the effects of Article 101(1) TFEU ('safe harbours').

2.2. The relationship to Article 102 TFEU

Article 102 is the other key provision on competition rules laid down in the Treaty. Article 102, which is discussed in detail in Chapter VI, concerns the prohibition of the abuse by one or more undertakings of their dominant position in the internal market.

It is emphasised in section 1 above that the competition rules do not usually affect the exclusive right of, for example, a patent owner to decide for itself whether it will exploit its rights by granting a licence or not, since this is part of the 'specific subject matter' of the patent, in respect of which the Treaty does not give authority to intervene. In other words, the competition rules do not usually provide for compulsory licensing, which would thereby highlight the fundamentally opposed aims previously referred to of the competition law principle of free access to the market, and the exclusive rights provided for in intellectual property law.[10]

These basic considerations in principle on the balance to be struck between competition law and intellectual property law has also been the

9. The practice which is built up by the national courts plays a special role after the implementation of the amendment to Council Regulation 17/62. See now Council Regulation (EC) No 1/2003 on the implementation of the rules on competition laid down in Articles 81 and 82 of the Treaty (OJ 2003 L 1/1), according to which with effect from 1 May 2004 the Commission's sole authority to grant exemptions from Article 101(1) TFEU is repealed, so that the whole of Article 101, including the right to grant exemptions under Article 101(3), can be applied by the national courts and other national authorities. See more on this above in Chapters II and III.
10. The right of an owner of a right to decide whether it will grant another party a licence to its exclusive right must not be confused with the situation where the owner of rights refuses to supply the products which are subject to the protection of intellectual property rights. If the owner of the exclusive right has first established itself on an open market, the reference to the specific subject matter of the exclusive right will not usually justify different treatment of potential purchasers of the products. Such refusal to supply is dealt with under the ordinary rules of competition, including Article 102 TFEU.

basis of the CJ's practice; see Case 238/87, *Volvo* v *Veng*, and Case 53/87, *Maxicar* v *Renault*, which both considered – and accepted – that the owner of a protected design for car bodywork had the right to object to others producing products which were covered by the design right, with a view to selling the products on the domestic market or on export markets (the 'specific subject matter of the exclusive right'). To prevent the application of national law in such circumstances would effectively be the same as putting the existence of such a right in doubt. Consequently, a refusal to give a third party a licence to produce the protected elements of the bodywork – even upon payment of a reasonable royalty – could not be considered an abuse of a dominant position.

However, the CJ held that in the three instances described (paragraph 9 in the *Volvo* case, and paragraph 16 in the *Renault* case) the refusal of the owner of the rights to grant a licence could be covered by the prohibition in Article 102 TFEU. This was, particularly the case where (1) the owner of the rights relatively arbitrarily refuses to supply spare parts to independent repair workshops, (2) sets unreasonably high prices for spare parts, or (3) stops production of spare parts for a model of motor car of which a large number are still found on the roads.[11]

Thus the two cases recognise that in very special circumstances, a compulsory licence can be imposed under competition law.

In Joined cases C-241/91 P and C-242/91 P, *Radio Telefis Eireann* v *Commission* (generally referred to as the *Magill* case), which is the result of three cases decided by the Court of First Instance (now the General Court), the CJ upheld the Commission's decision that for three television broadcasting companies to refuse to make previews of television programmes available to Magill, who was the publisher of a TV guide, was an infringement of Article 102.

In other words, the case concerned the extent to which the owner of copyright could be required to give a licence to exploit the work protected by copyright. The CJ upheld the view of the Commission and of the General Court that the

11. Only the last named situation (termination of production of spare parts) concerns an intervention in the specific subject matter of the exclusive rights, since the car manufacturer must either meet demand by maintaining production itself, or by granting a licence to a third party to do so. On the other hand, according to the practice of the CJ on refusal of supply and Article 102(a) TFEU, the first two situations constitute an abuse of dominant position, regardless of any sole right to produce the spare parts in question.

three companies had been wrong in assuming that their conduct (laying down a prohibition) towards Magill, who had published programme previews in a weekly magazine, fell within the scope of the specific subject matter and was thus excluded from any assessment under Article 102.

The *Magill* case seems to have gone a step further than the previous practice (*Volvo* and *Renault*), as Magill had not previously had the right to print the whole of the weeks previews and therefore (in contrast to the dealers in the *Volvo* and *Renault* cases) had not based his business on this. In addition, the product which Magill wanted to produce was a 'new product' (a weekly guide to television programmes). Furthermore, in the *Magill* case the CJ seems to have stated that the refusal to grant a licence could, in itself, constitute a restriction contrary to Article 102.

If the line in the *Magill* case is followed in relation to intellectual property rights other than copyright, and if the case is not merely dependent on the concrete circumstances, then a considerable breach has been opened in the previously accepted view of the relationship between exclusive intellectual property rights and the abuse of dominant position provisions in Article 102.

The judgment is discussed in *Valentine Korah:* Technology Transfer Agreements and the EC Competition Rules, 1996 p. 18 and pp. 51-54.

3. Licence agreement in general

In this context a licence agreement is an agreement between a licensee and the owner of a patent, know-how, or software copyright, or a mixed licence concerning patents, know-how, and software copyright; see Regulation 772/2004, Article 1(1)(b), which makes it possible for a licensee to exploit the intellectual property rights which can otherwise only be exploited by the owner of these rights.

With a licence agreement there is a partial transfer of an exclusive right by the owner of that right. The property right in the intellectual property remains with the owner of those rights which means, among other things, that the licence agreement lapses at the end of the licence period.

There is no standard formula for licence agreements for the transfer of technology, and there are few places in legislation where such an agreement is touched on; see for example the Danish Patents Act §§ 43-50.

There are no special forms provided for licence agreements, but in the nature of things, it is not advisable to rely on an oral contract. In relation to patent licences it is relevant to point to the practical rules in the Danish Patents Act § 44 whereby, upon request, a patent is entered on the patent register.

The lack of direct legislative treatment might lead one to suppose that a licence agreement is subject to the principle of freedom of contract, and that the parties to the agreement are therefore free to determine the content of their agreement without being bound by anything other than the terms they agree between them.

In the relationship between the licensor and the licensee there are several factors under the principles of the law of obligations which affect the agreement and its legal effects.

> Among other things this applies to the terms on the amount of the royalty which the licensor is to receive – whether a royalty is to be paid according to the number of units produced, or as a proportion of the gross or net earnings or otherwise.[12] The same applies to a licence agreements territorial and temporal extent, with the restriction that follows from the period of validity of the right and the rules on the effects of breach of the agreement by late payment of royalties, including the conditions for revoking the agreement, compensation and repayment of royalties paid, for example if the licensor cannot grant the licensee the intended right etc. The same applies, i.e. terms are not contrary to Article 101(1) TFEU, if the terms concern confidentiality obligations concerning the transferred technology, obligations not to use the transferred technology after the expiry of the licence, provided that the transferred technology is still valid and in use, obligations to help the licensor enforce the intellectual property rights in respect of which the licence is granted, obligations to use the licensor's trade mark or to state the licensor's name on the product etc.; see paragraph 155 of Commission Notice – Guidelines on the application of Article 81 of the EC Treaty [now Article 101 TEUF] to technology transfer agreements.
>
> It is also a natural consequence of the general principles of the law of obligations that, without a special agreement thereon, the licence rules will

12. However, it is a requirement that the obligation to pay a royalty should not be equivalent to price fixing, since this would be a hardcore restriction which would fall foul of Article 4(1)(a) of the Regulation (see section 6.1.1 below), e.g. if competitors pay each other ongoing royalties, even if there is no real licence arrangement. In this case the agreement will not normally serve the purpose of integrating complementary technologies or some other purpose which promotes competition; see paragraph 157 of Commission Notice – Guidelines on the application of Article 81 of the EC Treaty [Now Article 101 TEUF] to technology transfer agreements (OJ 2004 C 101/02). These Guidelines are discussed below in section 4.

not give the licensee a legal claim to reward and competitiveness in connection with the use of the licence. Nor does the licensee have an automatic right to exploit any know-how related to a patent. Correspondingly, the principles of the law of obligations apply when in § 43 of the Danish Patents Act it is provided that when the licensor has given another the right to commercially exploit the invention (licence), the licensee cannot, without a special agreement, transfer the licence to others. Likewise it may be assumed that the licence agreement may not be transferred to third parties by other means, for example by making a claim for distraint before the courts with a view to auctioning the right or by including the licence in the licensee's bankruptcy estate.

In principle licensors and licensees – at least typically in their own view – are not competitors, but two undertakings that have the same aim, namely to obtain as high a turnover as possible from the same product. In other words they have a shared aim which is to a certain extent in line with the interests of society in disseminating useful technology.

However, consideration for the interests of society in disseminating useful technology will not always carry weight in relation to that aspect of competition law which is concerned with licence agreements not being unduly restrictive of the commercial opportunities of the parties to the agreement or affected third parties.

The distinction between acceptable and unacceptable contractual terms which follows from Articles 4 and 5 of Regulation 772/2004 and which essentially reflect the view of the Commission and the European courts on restrictions on competition, shows that in a number of cases freedom of contract must give way not only out to consideration for the parties to a contract, but also to consideration for third parties, in other words, competing undertakings. The introductory comments on Articles 34 and 36 TFEU, as well as Article 101, give hints of this, just as the competition rules and their relation to intellectual property law are the main themes in the interpretation of Regulation 772/2004.

Partly in accordance with American and German theory, at the European level it has also been suggested that certain restrictions on competition in patent licensing agreements should not be covered by prohibitions corresponding to those in Article 101(1) TFEU, as they are covered by the specific subject matter of the patent. On this basis a distinction has been proposed between the 'patent law effects' of licence restrictions, which are not affected by competition law, and the 'independent contract law' effects of licence restrictions which are subject to Article 101(1) TFEU.

These considerations are linked to the fact that the legislator has recognised intellectual property law rights, and that as a result only the owner of the right has a right to decide about the time and place of their exploitation.

It is also possible to see a connection between this theory and the related doctrine of implied powers (that a greater right implies the existence of a lesser right). When the owner of a right has an absolute right to decide that it does not want to exercise that right by granting a licence, then it ought also to have the 'lesser' right of exploiting the patent on special terms – without that right being affected by competition law. It is argued that there would be a conflict between regulatory systems if competition law included a general prohibition of such an effect of patent law, but this would not be the case with the contract law effects of restrictions, in other words restrictions that are not derived from the patent (exclusive rights).

The categorical view that certain licensing restrictions are *per se* immune from intervention under competition law does not accord with the practice of the Commission. Already in the predecessor to Regulation (EC) No 240/96 (Regulation (EEC) No 2349/84, on block exemptions for patent agreements) the distinction seems to have been pushed into the background. The distinction between restrictions under patent law and under contract law were only significant as starting points which did not prevent a relevance-based examination of whether the licence restrictions did in fact lead to a restriction which was harmful to competition within the terms of Article 101(1) TFEU. Such an examination ought naturally to take account of the fact that a patent is in itself an expression of a legitimate restriction on competition.

A more radical and perhaps more effective solution would be to give up the distinction between the two types of licence restrictions. The contractual restrictions which, in German law, are considered as belonging to the specific subject matter of the patent, see § 17 in the GWG *(Gesetz gegen Wettbewerbsbeschränkungen),* is in reality arbitrarily chosen and unsuitable for supporting a dynamic competition law assessment aimed at achieving 'workable competition'.

4. Block exemptions – the development of the legal basis

As is the case of distribution agreements (see above in Chapter III), over a number of years a number of regulations have been drawn up concerning block exemptions for technology transfer agreements.[13] The latest of these is Commission Regulation (EC) No 772/2004 of 27 April 2004 on the application of Article 81(3) of the Treaty [now Article 101(3) TFEU] to categories of technology transfer agreements. Associated with this Regulation is Commission Notice – Guidelines on the application of Article 81(3) of the Treaty [now Article 101(3) TFEU] (OJ 2004 C 101/2), referred to in this Chapter as the 'Guidelines'. These Guidelines are indispensable for an understanding of the Regulation and will be referred to frequently in the following.

With effect from 1 May 2004, Regulation (EC) No 772/2004 replaced Regulation (EC) No 240/96 which in its turn had replaced Regulation (EEC) No 2349/84 and Regulation (EEC) No 556/89.

> In relation to the earlier regulations, Regulation (EC) No 240/96 was an expression of considerable liberalisation of the assessment of licence agreements. This was evident, among other things, in the increased number of 'white-listed' provisions (Article 2) and the decreased number of 'blacklisted' provisions (Article 3). Thereby it was reflected that a less strict assessment of when an agreement would be considered to restrict competition would also apply in the area of licences. Article 4 of the Regulation introduced an opposition procedure, as an agreement containing one or more 'grey conditions' [meaning conditions which were not automatically covered by Articles 2 or 3] was exempted if the agreement was notified to the Commission and the Commission did not oppose such exemption within a period of four months from the date of notification in accordance with the procedure described in the Regulation. Such an agreement was assumed to be valid until the Commission's decision was made known.
>
> Regulation (EEC) No 2349/84 applied to patent agreements and agreements which were a combination of a patent licence and a know-how licence, where in the licence or the patents this was necessary to achieve the goal of the transfer of technology. A condition for the application of the Regulation was that the licensed products should be protected by parallel patents in all Member States where the licence applied. This

13. The concept of a block exemption is discussed above in Chapters II and III.

condition restricted the scope of the Regulation, as an agreement which granted a patent licence in one Member State could often contain provisions in relation to other Member States where the same technology had not received a patent, but was only covered by the know-how agreement.

Regulation (EEC) No 556/89 applied to pure know-how licences as well as mixed know-how and patent licences that were not exempted under Regulation (EEC) No 2349/84.

Regulation (EC) No 772/2004 is structured according to the same pattern as Regulation (EC) No 330/2010 on block exemptions for vertical distribution agreements and concerted practices, discussed above in Chapter III. This means that black, white and grey conditions are abandoned in favour of exemption criteria which are based on the market strength of the parties to the agreement; see below in section 5.1.5 on Regulation (EC) No 772/2004, Article 3.

In December 2001, in connection with drawing up the new block exemption Regulation, the Commission sent out an evaluation report, which was later followed up by a round of consultations. The responses from the trade organisations involved etc. indicated that a substantial part of the business sector believed there was a need for a change to the regulatory basis.

According to Article 13 of Regulation (EC) No 240/96, the Regulation was intended to stay in force until 31 March 2006.

Meanwhile, the consultation of the undertakings affected by the Regulation showed that there was already a significant need to change to a different 'safe harbour' than that hitherto provided under the Regulations distinction between black, white and grey-listed obligations.

There has not yet been any official decision which could help with the interpretation of the new Regulation. However, in describing the Regulation, see sections 5-8 below, a number of Commission decisions and decisions of the European courts are discussed, and it is assumed that they still express the applicable law. Naturally, this applies primarily to those parts of the new Regulation's operative provisions whose content is the same as the provisions which applied under the previous regulations.

The Regulation has the same substantive scope as Article 101(1) TFEU. This means that only those agreements which can affect trade between Member States under the conditions referred to in Article 101(1) (direct or indirect, actual or potential) are covered by the rule. If an agreement only has effects in a single Member State, it will be assessed under national law. Nor are agreements whose full effects take place in a third country (i.e. outside the EEA) covered by the Regulation.[14]

As is the case with block exemption regulations in general, see Chapter III above on Regulation (EU) No 330/2010 on the application of Article 101(3) TFEU to categories of vertical agreements and concerted practices, Regulation (EC) No 772/2004 is only directed at restrictions on competition which, if they were not exempted by Regulation (EC) No 772/2004, would infringe Article 101(1) TFEU. Therefore if, according to its content, an agreement or a condition in an agreement is not covered by Article 101(1) [because the agreement or condition in question is not found to be an expression of a restriction on competition], there is no need for an exemption under a block exemption regulation.

On the other hand, if the content of an agreement is contrary to Article 101(1), but is covered by one of the grounds for exemption in Regulation (EC) No 772/2004, the parties can normally confidently perform their agreement, as there will be an assumption in favour of the validity of the agreement under competition law.[15] The grounds for block exemptions constitute the safe harbour for the parties to the agreement. On the other hand, there is no assumption that agreements that restrict competition and that are not covered by one of the grounds for exemption in Regulation (EC) No 772/2004 will automatically fall within the scope of Article 101(1). Whether or not this will be the case will depend on whether an individual evaluation of the agreement finds that there is a basis for an exemption under Article 101(3), as discussed in Chapter II.

Regulation (EC) No 772/2004 has 10 articles, with 20 recitals in the preamble which forms part of the Regulation, and the Guidelines which are associated with the Regulation contain important aids to the interpretation of the substantive rules. In the review of the individual provisions in Regulation (EC) No 772/2004 below in section 5, there will be extensive references to these aids to interpretation.

14. Compare this with the comments on Case C-306/96, *Javico International* v *Yves Saint Laurent Parfums,* in section 2.1.2 of Chapter III above.
15. Paragraph 34 of the Guidelines.

5. Regulation (EC) No 772/2004 – block exemptions for technology transfer agreements

5.1. Agreements

According to Regulation (EC) No 772/2004, Article 1(1)(b), cf. Article 2(1) the agreements covered by exemptions are technology transfer agreements entered into between two undertakings permitting the production of contract products, as follows:

Patent licensing agreements, know-how licensing agreements, software copyright licensing agreements or mixed patent, know-how or software copyright licensing agreements. The Regulation also covers agreements containing provisions relating to the sale and purchase of products, or which relate to the licensing of other intellectual property rights or the assignment of other intellectual property rights. However, this only applies if those provisions do not constitute the primary object of the agreement and are directly related to the production of the contract products, i.e. the products which are produced using the licensed technology; see the definition in Article 1(1)(f). The same applies to assignments of patents, know-how, software copyright or a combination thereof where part of the risk associated with the exploitation of the technology remains with the assignor. This will particularly be the case where the sum payable for the assignment is dependent on the turnover obtained by the assignee from the products produced using the assigned technology, the quantity of such products produced or the number of operations carried out using the technology

The following are comments on the individual elements of this area:

5.1.1. 'Entered into between two undertakings'

This condition is satisfied even if the agreement lays down conditions for more than one level of trade; see recital 19 in the preamble to the Regulation. For example, this situation will exist if the licence agreement requires the licensee to set up a special distribution system or sets out obligations which the licensee shall or may impose on distributors of the product produced under licence. However, it will be a requirement that such obligations must be compatible with the rules of competition law relating to supply and distribution agreements. They may not, for example, contain any of the hardcore restrictions referred to in Article 4 of Regulation (EU) No 330/2010 or any of the restrictions referred to in Article 5 of the Regulation; see Chapter III on Articles 4 and 5.

If the licensee exercises a right to grant sub-licences, then the block exemption regulation applies in its entirety to agreements between the licensee and the sub-licensee.[16]

If the licensor wishes to exercise control over any sub-licensees, this must be provided for in the agreement with the licensee. The licensor cannot be a party to an agreement between the licensee and a sub-licensee since Article 2(1) of the Regulation only allows for exemptions between two undertakings.

> Agreements between parent companies and their subsidiaries will not normally constitute an agreement between two undertakings within the meaning of the Regulation, as long as the two companies are integrated parts of an economic unit; see the statement of the CJ in Case 15/74, *Centrafarm and Adriaan de Peijper* v *Sterling Drugs*, according to which a subsidiary company's organisational relationship to a parent company means that it does not have any real freedom to take decisions on its own, so that agreements with the parent company cannot restrict competition when an agreement concerns the internal allocation of tasks between the companies. This is in line with the aim of the EU competition rules, which is to ensure the existence of workable competition in the internal market by the regulation of agreements between independent undertakings.
>
> On the other hand, if a subsidiary company can operate independently on a market, or if the matter concerns something other and more than an internal allocation of tasks, the parent and subsidiary could be regarded as two independent undertakings.

5.1.2. The concept of an 'undertaking'

The concept of an 'undertaking' is not expressly defined in Regulation (EC) No 772/2004, but it may be assumed to correspond to the meaning of 'undertaking' as interpreted in relation to the use of this term in Articles 101 and 102 TFEU; on this see Chapter II. In addition to this, Article 1(2) of Regulation (EC) No 772/2004 adds that the terms 'undertaking', 'licensor' and 'licensee' include their respective connected undertakings; see the full provisions in Article 1(2)(a)-(e).

16. A prohibition on the licensor giving a licence to another undertaking is not a restriction on competition and is therefore not contrary to Article 101(1) TFEU; see paragraph 155(b) of the Guidelines.

5.1.3. *'Transfer' of technology*

According to recital 7 of Regulation (EC) No 772/2004, the term 'transfer', in the context of 'technology transfer agreements', should be understood as meaning that the technology flows from one undertaking to another in the form of a licence agreement whereby the licensor, upon payment of a licence fee, allows the licensee to use it technology.[17] The agreement must concern the production of the contract products, in other words, the goods or services produced with the licensed technology; see Article 1(1)(f) of the Regulation. Pure sales, in other words, a transfer in the form of a sale of the technology, are thus not covered by the block exemption Regulation. The same applies to pooling agreements, the purpose of which is cooperation between two or more undertakings to pool technologies, for example with the aim of licensing the created package of intellectual property rights to third parties; see recital 7. On the other hand, individual licences which the pool may grant to third parties are dealt with in the same way as other licensing agreements.[18]

If the purpose of an agreement is that the licensor transfers technology to the licensee, who is then obliged to produce certain products for the licensor, then such a subcontracting agreement is also covered by the exemption.

A subcontracting agreement can also mean that the licensor provides *equipment* for the production of the goods or services which are covered by the agreement. However, it is the transferred technology and not the transferred equipment which must be the principal purpose of the agreement.

As already stated, if the licensee is entitled to grant sub-licences of the transferred technology, such an agreement is covered by the exemption, provided that in this case too the production of the contract products is the principal purpose of the agreement. If this is not the case, the Commission will apply the principles of the Regulation by analogy to such 'master licensing agreements' between licensor and licensee; see paragraph 42 of the Guidelines.

5.1.4. *The transferred technology*

The transferred technology constitutes primarily the licence for the rights referred to in section 5.1, in other words the patents, know-how and software copyright or mixed agreements for the exploitation of these rights. 'Technology' is an input which is integrated either in a product or a production process.

17. See the Guidelines, paragraph 48.
18. See the Guidelines, paragraph 212.

A patent right is a right which is created by legislation and is protected for a number of years; see for example Danish Patents Act § 40 under which a patent can be maintained for up to 20 years from the date on which the patent application is made. This applies regardless of whether the patent owner has exploited the patent or not.

The Regulation's definition of a 'patent' is based on patent legislation, in the case of Denmark on the Patents Act, according to which a patent is an *exclusive right* created by virtue of the registration of an invention which is novel in relation to what was known before the submission of the patent application, and which is sufficiently different from it; see Patents Act § 2.1 on *novelty* and the *degree of invention*.

The Regulation applies to the grant of licences for the national patents of the Member States and licences for European Patents.

The definition of a patent also includes patent applications, utility models, applications for registration of utility models, designs, topographies of semiconductor products (chips), supplementary protection certificates for medicinal products or other products for which such supplementary protection certificates may be obtained and plant breeders certificates; see Article 1(1)(h) of the Regulation.

According to the definition in Article 1(1)(i), 'know-how' means a package of non-patented practical information, resulting from experience and testing, which is:

i. secret, that is to say, not generally known or easily accessible,
ii. substantial, that is to say, significant and useful for the production of the contract products, and
iii. identified, that is to say, described in a sufficiently comprehensive manner so as to make it possible to verify that it fulfils the criteria of secrecy and substantiality.

The connection between patents and know-how is operative in the sense that the confidentiality of special know-how can be a precursor to a later patent application, and even if such an application is later made, there will often be some additional knowledge about processes etc. Under a strict interpretation of the patent rules, *specific production guidelines* need not be included in the patent application. Such guidelines will often be one of the main areas of know-how.

If the owner of some know-how, for example the process for the production of a chemical compound, is doubtful about whether the method can be patented, they can sometimes keep their knowledge confidential until it may later be clarified whether the conditions for a patent application exist (novelty and the degree of invention). Or they can instead publish a so-called 'patent prophylaxis', so that when the process is later made public, a patent cannot be granted either to a competitor or the owner of the right themselves. However, this means that the process is surrendered, since anyone can now use it. If the patent holder decides to keep the process secret, the period of the patent can be extended, as long as the process is secret. The product may be put into the market, but the process can remain secret.[19]

A licensee can take on and exploit both the conceptual idea which is expressed in the patent and the technical knowledge, which is expressed in the know-how. There is nevertheless a fundamental difference between the two types of rights, which is also reflected in competition law. Unlike patents, know-how is not protected by special laws and its value ceases when the knowledge about the processes etc. which constitute the substance of the know-how is no longer secret.[20]

The term 'software' is not defined either in the Regulation or the Guidelines. According to the general view of the character of this intellectual property right it is natural to consider it as concerning computer programs, in other words instructions or information presented in whatever form or by whatever medium, which are intended, directly or indirectly, to enable a computer to carry out a particular function or achieve a particular result.

As stated above, the Regulation primarily exempts licence agreements relating to patents, know-how, or software copyright, or a mixed licence for these rights. On the other hand, agreements containing provisions for the grant of a licence or assignment of other intellectual property rights are only covered by the Regulation if these provisions do not constitute the primary purpose of the agreement.[21] From this it follows that these other

19. An alternative to a patent application can be the registration of an industrial design, in other words a product which can be used industrially but which does not in fact constitute a solution to a technical problem.
20. In Danish law know-how enjoys protection against unjustified use by previous employees and similar parties who have previously had the possibility of using the know-how in question.
21. See Regulation (EC) No 772/2004, Article 1(1)(b), and paragraph 50 of the Guidelines.

rights only qualify for a block exemption if they enable the licensee to better exploit the transferred technology. For example, a trade mark licence may enable the licensee to exploit the technology better as it may give consumers the impression that there is a direct connection between the goods offered and the characteristics they have been given via the transferred technology. Likewise, an obligation to use the licensors trade mark can serve to promote the dissemination of the technology, where the licensor is identified as the source of the underlying technology. On the other hand, if the transferred technology is of limited value to the licensees, because they already use identical or very similar technology, and if the core element of the agreement is the trade mark itself, then Regulation (EC) No 772/2004 does not apply.[22]

5.1.5. Definition of the relevant market

Where the undertakings party to the agreement are competing undertakings, the block exemption is conditional on the *combined market share* of the parties not exceeding 20 % of the relevant technology and product market; see Article 3(1). Where the undertakings party to the agreement are not competing undertakings, the *individual market shares* of each of the parties may not exceed 30 % of the relevant market; see Article 3(2).[23]

The *product market* is defined by the products which buyers consider are interchangeable with or substitutable for the contract products which incorporate the transferred technology, by reason of their characteristics, price or intended use.[24] Product markets also include the products which are produced by means of the transferred technology.

22. Compare with Commission Decision 90/186/EEC, *Moosehead/Whitbread* (OJ 1990 L 100/32), where the trade mark rather than the other parts of the agreement were found to constitute the commercial centre of gravity of the agreement. On this decision, see among others*: Terence Prime & David Booton:* European Intellectual Property Law, 1998 p. 49 and p. 64; *Valentine Korah:* Technology Transfer Agreements and the EC Competition Rules, 1996 pp. 68-71 and 116-121; and the commentary on Article 2(3) of Regulation (EU) No 330/2010 in Chapter III, section 5.2.
23. Article 3 includes both the technology market and the product market in the definition of the relevant market because the technology market provides an input which is integrated either in the product or the production process; see paragraph 20 of the Guidelines. Technology transfer can thus affect competition on both the input and output markets.
24. Paragraph 21 of the Guidelines.

The *technology market* consists of the technology transferred to the licensee and alternatives to it, in other words other technologies which are regarded by licensees as interchangeable with or substitutable for the licensed technology, by reason of its characteristics, royalties and intended use. Starting from the technology which is marketed by the licensor, it is necessary to identify the other technologies to which licensees could switch in response to a small but permanent increase in relative prices, i.e. the royalty payments.[25]

When the relevant markets have been defined, the market shares can be allocated to the different sources of competition on the market and used as an indication of the relative strengths of the market participants, which Article 3 emphasises as being relevant to distinguishing between competitors and non-competitors.

In connection with technology markets, the market shares can be calculated on the basis of each technology's share of the total licence revenue. However, this would be a purely theoretical and impractical method for calculating market shares, since there would usually be a lack of clear information about royalty incomes etc.[26] For this reason, among other things, in practice it will be *the product market* that will be indicative for the different legal effects referred to in Article 3 of the Regulation and whether a technology transfer agreement will covered by the block exemption or not.

According to Article 8(1), the market share is calculated on the basis of information about the turnover on the market for the previous calendar year. The calculation is made according to the generally applicable competition law principles.[27] If initially the market share referred to in Article 3(1) or (2) does not exceed 20 % or 30 % respectively, but subsequently crosses these thresholds, then the exemption referred to in Article 2 continues to apply for the two calendar years following the year in which the 20 % or 30 % threshold was first exceeded; see Article 8(2).

The abandonment of the system with white-listed, blacklisted and grey-listed restrictions on competition in favour of a system which makes the application of the block exemption dependent on certain market share thresholds not being crossed (market strength) has meant that a number of restrictions on

25. Paragraph 22 of the Guidelines.
26. Paragraph 23 of the Guidelines.
27. Commission Notice on the definition of relevant market for the purposes of Community competition law (OJ 1997 C 372/5), see Chapter III, section 5.2 above.

competition which were expressly stated to be black or grey now fall within the block exemption.

Among other things, the focus on market strength has meant that *tie-in sales* in agreements that do not exceed the market share thresholds referred to in Article 3 are covered by the block exemption.[28] Tie-in sales are not included in either Article 4 or 5 (see section 6 below) as restrictions which exclude the granting of exemptions, regardless of whether Article 3 is complied with or not.[29]

This may seem surprising, given that in Article 101(1)(e) TFEU particularly exemplifies tie-in sales as the kind of agreement that can affect trade between Member States, and which is incompatible with the aims of the internal market if the conditions in Article 101(1) are otherwise fulfilled.[30]

In relation to technology transfers, there will be a tie-in sale if the licensor makes the grant of a licence for a technology (the primary product) conditional on the licensee accepting a licence on some other technology or buying a particular product from the licensor or from an undertaking appointed the licensor (the tied product). The same exemption applies to 'bundling', where two technologies or a technology and a product are only sold together as a pack. Both tie-ins and bundling are concerned with special technologies in the sense that, on the relevant market, there is a distinct demand for the individual products included in the tie-in sale or pack. There will not normally be such a tie-in if the technologies or products are necessarily bound together in such a way that the transferred technology cannot be used without the tied-in product, or if neither of the products in the package can be used without the other.[31]

28. On tie-ins, see *Valentine Korah:* Technology Transfer Agreements and the EC Competition Rules, 1996 pp. 173-180.
29. However, Regulation (EC) No 240/96, which was the predecessor to Regulation (EC) No 772/2004, had already indicated that the Commission would adopt a milder stance towards such tie-ins, since the prohibition was included in Article 4(2)(a) as part of the grey list, i.e. terms which were subject to an opposition procedure, see section 4 above. Previous block exemption regulations had classified tie-in clauses as blacklisted; see the practice of the Commission in Commission Decision 79/86/EEC, *Vaessen/Morris* (OJ 1979 L 19/32), *Valentine Korah:* Technology Transfer Agreements and the EC Competition Rules, 1996 pp. 176-178; and *Steven D. Anderman:* EC Competition Law and Intellectual Property Rights, 1998 pp. 57-63.
30. See also Article 102(2)(d) TFEU, which is discussed in Chapter VI.
31. Paragraph 191 of the Guidelines.

The market share thresholds apply to each relevant technology and product market affected by the licence agreement, including the market for a tied product.[32]

If the market thresholds in Article 3(1) or (2) of the Regulation are exceeded, the block exemption does not apply, and it will therefore be necessary to evaluate the restrictions on competition and the competition promoting effects of the tie-in sale and bundling before it can be decided whether sales on these terms are contrary to Article 101(1).

5.1.6. Competing and non-competing undertakings

The idea behind many of the provisions in Regulation (EC) No 772/2004 is that agreements between competitors constitute a greater threat to competition than agreements between non-competitors; see the comments above in section 5.1.5 on the market thresholds that are triggered at a lower level of market share for agreements between competitors than they are for agreements between non-competitors, and see further in section 6 on the hardcore restrictions – Article 4(1) compared with Article 4(2) of the Regulation.

On the other hand, the intra-technology competition between licensees, i.e. competition between undertakings that use the same technology, will lead to lower prices for the products that incorporate the technology in question, which should not only be a direct and immediate advantage to the consumers who use these products, but also intensify the competition between undertakings that use the competing products. In connection with licence agreements it is also necessary to be aware that licensees sell their own products and do not, as in the case of distributors covered by Regulation (EU) No 330/2010 on vertical agreements, resell the products of another undertaking. There are thus better opportunities for product differentiation than there are in connection with vertical agreements for the re-sale of products; see paragraph 26 of the Guidelines.

In order to determine the competitive situation between a licensor and a licensee it is first necessary to evaluate whether, *without the agreement*, the parties would have been actual or potential competitors; see the distinction below. If, without the agreement, the parties would not have been actual or

32. Paragraph 192 of the Guidelines.

potential competitors on the relevant market affected by the agreement, they are considered to be non-competitors.[33]

The parties are thus not competitors in relation to Regulation (EC) No 772/2004 if the licensor is neither an actual or potential supplier of products on the relevant market and the licensee, who must already be active on the product market, does not grant the licensor a licence on competing technology, even though it owns competing technology and produces on the basis thereof. However, the parties become competitors if the licensee subsequently begins to grant licences on its technology, or if the licensor becomes and actual or potential supplier of products on the relevant market. In this case, the hardcore restrictions discussed in section 6 continue to apply to the agreement, unless the agreement is materially amended on its important points which do not correspond to the context in which it was entered into; see Article 4(3) of the Regulation.

According to Article 1(1)(j) of the Regulation (see paragraphs 28, 28, 67 and 68 of the Guidelines) the parties are *actual* competitors when they are both active on the same product market and the same territorial market on which the products are sold which incorporate the transferred technology.[34] They are also regarded as competitors (*potential* competitors) if on the basis of realistic considerations it is likely that they will be prepared to invest in the costs of organising their production with the aim of penetrating the relevant product and/or territorial markets within a reasonably short period, in response to a small and permanent increase in relative prices.

5.1.7. Reciprocal contra non-reciprocal agreements

The distinction between reciprocal contra non-reciprocal agreements is relevant to several of the restrictions referred to in Article 4 of the block exemption Regulation. The difference is seen in the fact that non-reciprocal agreement are treated more advantageously in competition law than reciprocal agreements; see Article 4 (1)(b) and (c), and the more detailed discussion in section 6. Reciprocal agreements and non-reciprocal agreements are defined in Article 1(1)(c) and (d).

33. Paragraphs 27 and 68 of the Guidelines.
34. Products are goods and services, including both intermediary goods and services and finished goods and services. On intermediary products, see Chapter III, section 5.

According to the definition in Article 1(1)(c), a reciprocal agreement is a technology transfer agreement where two undertakings grant each other, in the same or separate contracts, a patent licence, a know-how licence, a software copyright licence or a mixed patent, know-how or software copyright licence and where these licences concern competing technologies or can be used for the production of competing products (cross licences).[35]

According to the definition in Article 1(1)(d), a non-reciprocal agreement means a technology transfer agreement where one undertaking grants another undertaking a patent licence, a know-how licence, a software copyright licence or a mixed patent, know-how or software copyright licence, or where two undertakings grant each other such a licence but where these licences do not concern competing technologies and cannot be used for the production of competing products.

5.1.8. The duration of the block exemption

According to Regulation (EC) No 772/2004, a block exemption lasts as long as the intellectual property rights covered by the agreement have not lapsed, expired or been invalidated.[36] However the period of validity of the Regulation expires on 30 April 2014, see Article 11.

In particular with regard to know-how, the exemption lasts as long as the know-how covered by the licence remains confidential from the outside world, unless it becomes generally known as a result of the actions of the licensee, in which case the exemption applies for the duration of the agreement. The block exemption applies for each of the intellectual property rights covered by the technology transfer agreement, and expires on the date on which the last of the intellectual property rights which constitute the technology covered by the block exemption Regulation expires, is declared invalid or enters the public domain; see paragraph 55 of the Guidelines.[37] Even though the block exemption only applies as long as the technology is valid and in use, the parties can normally agree to extend the obligation to pay royalties for the intellectual property rights beyond the period of validity, without infringing Article 101(1).

35. An agreement is not reciprocal merely because the agreement contains a grant back obligation or because the licensee licenses back its own improvements of the licensed technology. Grant back is discussed in section 7.2.
36. See paragraph 54 of the Guidelines.
37. Compare with the comments on the individual rights in section 5.1.4.

Once these rights expire, third parties can legally exploit the technology in question and compete with the parties to the agreement; see paragraph 159 of the Guidelines.

6. Hardcore restrictions in respect of the block exemption Regulation

Article 4 of Regulation (EC) No 772/2004 contains certain 'hardcore restrictions' which if one or more of them is agreed between a licensor and a licensee, will nearly always mean that the agreement in its entirety will not qualify for the exemption provided for in Article 2.[38]

The restriction can be expressed either in the purpose of the agreement itself, or in the specific circumstances of an individual case, without it being necessary to give evidence of concrete effects on the market for the purposes of the application of Article 101(1) TFEU.[39] Moreover, it is unlikely that an agreement containing one or more of these restrictions would be exempted under Article 101(3) TFEU.[40]

Article 4 distinguishes between competing undertakings and non-competing undertakings, and for a number of the restrictions a distinction is made between reciprocal and non-reciprocal agreements; on the latter distinction, see section 5.1.7, with the emphasis on the fact that reciprocal agreements (cross-licences) are treated more strictly in competition law than non-reciprocal agreements.

38. In other words, for the application of the block exemption Regulation hardcore restrictions are not separated from the rest of the agreement so that the agreement can continue with the hardcore restriction excised. The doctrine of severance does not apply to hardcore restrictions; see the comments above in Chapter III, section 5.4, on distribution agreements, and section 7 below on Article 5 of the Regulation.
39. See Case C-49/92, *Anic,* paragraph 99, on hardcore cartels.
40. Paragraph 75 of the Guidelines.

6.1. Agreements between competitors[41]

When the parties to an agreement are undertakings which compete with each other, the exemption provided for in Article 2 of the Regulation does not apply to agreements which, directly or indirectly, in isolation or in combination with other factors under the control of the parties, contain the restrictions set out in Article 4(1)(a)-(d) of the Regulation.

6.1.1. Agreements on the pricing of the contract products

Article 4(1)(a) of the Regulation concerns the restriction on a party's right to determine its prices for the sale of its products to third parties, including sales prices for products which incorporate the transferred technology. It does not matter whether the restriction concerns fixed prices, minimum prices, maximum prices or recommended prices; see paragraph 79 of the Guidelines.[42]

Article 4(1)(a) concerns one of the key considerations of block exemption regulations in general: an undertaking (the licensee) that acts as an intermediary between the principal (the licensor) and a customer must be free to determine for itself the pricing policy it will apply in relation to third parties. A provision on binding prices which apply to downstream levels of trade has always been characterised as a restriction on trade in the legal practice on licence agreements; see for example Case 27/87, *Erauw-Jacquéry* v *la Hesbignonne*, paragraph 15:

41. In the following account of the hardcore restrictions in Article 4, it is important to bear in mind that, as appears from its wording, the comments in section 6.1 (concerning Article 4.1) relate to agreements between competing undertakings, while section 6.2 (Article 4.2) relates to agreements between non-competing undertakings. When the undertakings to an agreement do not compete with each other at the time of entering into an agreement, but subsequently become competing undertakings, the rules relating to the relationship between non-competing undertakings (section 6.2) apply to the agreement for the whole of the period, unless the agreement is subsequently materially amended; see Article 4.3. However, the distinction between reciprocal and non-reciprocal agreements is operative in each of the two parts.
42. On this point the wording of Regulation (EC) No 772/2004 is stricter than the corresponding provision in the vertical agreements regulation; see Chapter III, section 5.3.1 on Regulation (EU) No 330/2010, Article 4(a), which only contains a prohibition on the setting of binding minimum prices, whereas in principle maximum sales prices and recommended prices fall outside the prohibition. On the other hand, see section 6.2 below on Article 4(2)(a), which concerns agreements between non-competing undertakings and which allows agreements on resale prices as long as these are not fixed prices or minimum sales prices.

> 'In this connection it must be pointed out that article 85(1) [now Article 101(1) TFEU] of the Treaty expressly mentions as being incompatible with the common market agreements which "directly or indirectly fix purchase or selling prices or any other trading conditions". According to the judgment of the national court the plaintiff in the main proceedings concluded with other growers agreements identical to the contested agreement, as a result of which those agreements have the same effects as a price system fixed by a horizontal agreement. In such circumstances the object and effect of such a provision is to restrict competition within the common market.'[43]

A pricing agreement can, for example, take the form of a direct agreement on the exact price, or a price list with the maximum permitted discounts which the licensee can allow third parties. The pricing conditions can also be imposed indirectly, via measures which are intended to warn off the licensee from departing from the agreed pricing, for example by stating that the royalty will be increased if the price for the products is reduced below a certain level.

Article 4(1)(a) also affects agreements in relation to which royalties are calculated on the basis of total sales of products, whether or not they use the transferred technology.[44] Such agreements generally restrict competition as it could make it more expensive for the licensee to use its own technology and restrict the competition which existed prior to entering into the agreement.[45]

43. For a commentary on this case, see *Valentine Korah & Denis O'Sullivan:* Distribution Agreements under the EC Competition Rules, 2002 pp. 81-83; and *Valentine Korah:* Technology Transfer Agreements and the EC Competition Rules, 1996 pp. 16-19 and 190-194.
44. Agreements of this kind are also affected by Article 4(1)(d) (see section 6.1.3.4 below), under which the licensor may not prevent the licensee using its own technology.
45. On one particular method of calculation, see Case 193/83, *Windsurfing International* v *Commission,* paragraph 67, where the CJ found that it was contrary to Article 101(1) TFEU to calculate the license fee based on the sales of a product which was not covered by the licensed technology, in the case in question sailboards without rigs. For a commentary on this case *see Valentine Korah:* Technology Transfer Agreements and the EC Competition Rules, 1996 pp. 145-148 and *Terence Prime & David Booton:* European Intellectual Property Law, 1998 pp. 53-54.

6.1.2. Production restrictions

The hardcore restriction referred to in Article 4(1)(b) concerns reciprocal production limitations and production limitations imposed on the licensor with regard to its own technology. On the other hand, production limitations imposed on a licensee in a non-reciprocal agreement or a limitation which is only imposed on one of the licensees in a reciprocal agreement are not covered by the provision. Such a restriction is therefore, in this respect, covered by the block exemption; see paragraph 82 of the Guidelines.[46]

A production limitation is a limitation on the quantity that an undertaking may produce and sell. When competing undertakings enter into an agreement under which both the licensor and the licensee accept obligations to limit production, this will often be an indication that they intend to restrict output on the market – and presumably succeed in doing so.

If a licensee in a non-reciprocal agreement is willing to accept a unilateral restriction of its production, the reason can be that it wishes to implement the integration of complementary technologies or the integration of the licensors more advanced technology in the licensees own production. In a reciprocal agreement an output restriction on one of the licensees is likely to reflect the higher value of the technology licensed by one of the parties and may serve to promote pro-competitive licensing.[47]

6.1.3. The allocation of markets or customers (sales restrictions)

6.1.3.1. The allocation of markets

Both exclusive licences and sole licences refer to activities within the territory of the relevant market.

An *exclusive licence* means that the licensee is the only one who is permitted to produce on the basis of the licensed technology within a given territory. The licensor thus undertakes not to produce itself, using the licensed technology, or license others to produce within the given territory.[48]

By granting a licensee a *sole licence*, the licensor undertakes not to licence third parties to produce within a given territory, but the licensor is not itself prevented from using the technology in question.[49]

46. In all agreements between non-competing undertakings (including reciprocal agreements) all sales restrictions which otherwise fulfil the conditions of the Regulation, including that they are below the threshold in Article 3(2), are covered by the block exemption; see paragraph 172 of the Guidelines and section 6.2 below.
47. Paragraph 83 of the Guidelines.
48. Paragraph 162 of the Guidelines.
49. Paragraph 162 of the Guidelines.

Reciprocal exclusive licences between competing undertakings are categorised as a hardcore restriction in Article 4(1)(c), with the consequence that the whole agreement is invalid.

Sole licences between competing undertakings are covered by the block exemption up to the market share threshold of 20 % (see the definition of the market in section 5.1.5 above). The exemption applies regardless of whether the agreement is reciprocal or non-reciprocal; see Article 4(1)(c)(iii) and recital 10.[50]

6.1.3.2. Sales restrictions (allocation of customers)

Restrictions on one or both of the parties active and passive sales, as part of a reciprocal agreement between competing undertakings, constitute hardcore restrictions on competition and are prohibited in Article 4(1)(c).[51] Sales restrictions of this nature in a reciprocal agreement will normally be considered as evidence of market sharing, as the restriction will prevent the party concerned from either actively or passively selling into the territories and thus to customers which the party already sells to or could realistically sell to if the agreement did not prevent it from doing so.

By contrast, the assessment of sales restrictions in non-reciprocal agreements is quite liberal, as will appear from several of the qualifications on the extent of Article 4(1)(c) discussed immediately below in section 6.1.3.3, with reference to Article 4(1)(c)(i)-(vii).[52]

6.1.3.3. Permitted restrictions pursuant to Article 4(1)(c)

Article 4(1)(c)(i)

> According to this provision, which carries forward the corresponding provision in Regulation (EC) No 240/96, Article 2(1)(8), the hardcore restriction in Article 4(1)(c) does not cover a requirement for licensees only to produce with the licensed technology within one or more technical fields of use, or one or more product markets.

50. Paragraph 163 of the Guidelines.
51. Paragraph 169 of the Guidelines. On the meaning of active and passive sales, see the comments on Article 4(b) in the Regulation (EU) No 330/2010 on vertical agreements in Chapter III, section 5, and in paragraph 51 of the guidelines on vertical agreements referred to there, as well as section 6.1.3.3 below on Article 4(1)(c)(iv) and (v).
52. See also Article 4(2)(b)(i) and (ii), on agreements between non-competing undertakings (section 6.2 below).

For example, with the aim of exploiting the special expertise of one or more of its licensees, a licensor can divide up a given area of technical application or a given product market by, for example, granting a licence to the licensee in question to exploit the technology for one purpose, perhaps for producing some veterinary medicine, while reserving to another licensee or to itself the exploitation of the medicine for human purposes – provided of course that the medicine could be used by humans in unaltered form.[53] Restrictions of this kind enjoy a block exemption up to the market share threshold of 20 %; see Article 3(1), regardless of whether the agreement is reciprocal or non-reciprocal. However, restrictions may not go further than the scope of the licensed technology, and limits may not be put on the licensee's use of its own technology, as this would amount to market sharing.[54]

On the other hand, the provision does not allow the licensor to impose limitations on the licensee with regard to which particular customer groups it may sell to, see below with regard to Article 4(1)(b)(iv) which allows the possibility of non-reciprocal agreements addressing this need.

Article 4(1)(c)(ii)

The exception under sub-subparagraph (ii) concerns cases where, as part of a non-reciprocal agreement, the licensor grants the licensee an exclusive licence to produce products on the basis of the licensed technology within a specific territory, and thereby binds itself not to produce the contract products in the territory in question or to supply the contract products from this area. Such agreements are not considered as hardcore agreements, regardless of the size of the area concerned. The aim of such agreements may be to give the licensee an incentive to invest in and develop the licensed technology, and not necessarily to share markets.[55]

Article 4(1)(c)(iii)

Sub-subparagraph (iii) concerns the obligation on the licensor not to license the technology to another licensee in a particular territory.

Such an agreement, where the licensor appoints a licensee to be the sole licensee in a given territory, and thus excludes third parties from obtaining a licence to produce products based on the licensed technology is, regardless of whether the agreement is reciprocal or non-reciprocal, a sole licence which is covered by Article 2 of the block exemption regulation. This is because the agreement does not affect the parties' unlimited ability to exploit their own technology in their respective territories; see the definitions of exclusive and sole licences in section 6.1.3.1 above.[56]

53. The distinction between an area of technical application and a product market does not seem to have any practical importance.
54. Paragraph 90 of the Guidelines.
55. Paragraph 86 of the Guidelines.
56. Paragraph 88 of the Guidelines.

Article 4(1)(c)(iv)

The restriction which, according to Article 4(1)(c)(iv), is exempted under Article 2 is not considered as market sharing, as it would be if the restriction were reciprocal. The provision refers to a part of a non-reciprocal agreement which is a restriction on the licensee's and/or the licensor's active and/or passive sales into the exclusive territory or to the exclusive customer group reserved for the other party, i.e. the licensee or the licensor.

Article 4(1)(c)(v)

The purpose of this qualification under Article 4(1)(c)(v) is that a restriction, in a non-reciprocal agreement, on active sales by the licensee into the exclusive territory or to the exclusive customer group allocated by the licensor to another licensee will fall outside the scope of the hardcore restrictions, provided the protected licensee was not a competitor to the licensor at the time when the agreement was entered into.[57] By allowing a licensor to protect a licensee who has been introduced at a later point from the active sales of competitors to the licensee who may be expected to be already established on the market, such restrictions are likely to induce the licensee to exploit the licensed technology more efficiently.[58] On the other hand, if the licensees were to agree between themselves to refrain from active or from passive sales into specific territories or to specific customer groups, this would be a cartel agreement between the licensees which, as it would not involve the transfer of any technology, see Article 2(1), would fall outside the scope of the block exemption.

Article 4(1)(c)(vi)

According to Article 4(1)(c)(vi), a licensor can, without affecting the block exemption, restrict the licensee's production so as only to produce the contract products for its own use.[59] If the contact product is a component, the licensee can be required only to produce the component in question for incorporation in the products which it produces

57. On the meaning of active sales see paragraph 51 in the guidelines referred to in section 6.1.3.2 for Regulation (EU) No 330/2010 on vertical agreements, according to which active sales are understood as being direct approaches to individual customers who are covered by another's exclusive sales territory or exclusively allocated customer group, e.g. by mail, personal visit, media advertisements and other sales promotion methods etc. which are specifically directed towards customers in the exclusive sales territory or exclusively allocated customer group. Passive sales means responding to unsolicited approaches from individual customers from the territory allocated to another distributor, including supplying goods or services to these customers. For further discussion of active and passive sales, see Chapter III, section 5.
58. Paragraph 89 of the Guidelines.
59. Paragraph 91 of the Guidelines.

itself. However, the restriction will only apply as long as the licensee is not at the same time prevented from actively or passively selling the contract products as *spare parts* for the licensee's own products.

The permissibility of the restriction under sub-subparagraph (vi) is justified by, among other things, consideration for the dissemination of technology, particularly between competitors. The provision does not cover sales of the contract products with a view to their incorporation in other producer's products. These restrictions are covered by the block exemption up to the market share threshold of 20 %; see paragraph 186 of the Guidelines.

Article 4(1)(c)(vii)

According to Article 4(1)(c)(vii), in a non-reciprocal agreement a licensee can be obliged to produce the contract products only for a particular customer, where the licence is granted in order to create an alternative source of supply for that customer.

The provision is aimed at situations where an undertaking is granted a licence to produce spare parts and other components. If this undertaking is a sub-contractor to the producer of the principal product, for example motor cars, an interruption of supply, for example a strike, which affects the licensee's business could develop so that the producer of the principal product is unable to produce and may be required to halt production for a shorter or longer period, with corresponding financial consequences.[60] The basis for Article 4(1)(c)(vii), under which a (second) licensee can be obliged to supply only a limited quantity of the contract goods to a specific customer, is therefore not primarily to restrict the delivery quantities of the second (new) licensee, but to procure for the customer in question a further source of supply. The risk that such agreements will result in market sharing is limited when a licence is granted with the aim of supplying one specific customer.[61]

The provision also covers cases where more than one undertaking is granted a licence for the same specific customer.

6.1.3.4. Exploitation of own technology etc.[62]

According to the hardcore restriction in Article 4(1)(d), the licensee must not be prevented from using its own competing technology, provided the licensee does not use the technology licensed by the licensor in connection with this. With regard to the use of its own technology, the licensee must be free to de cide how and how much it will produce and sell, and at what price. It must likewise be free to grant licences of its technology to third parties.

60. According to *Valentine Korah:* Know-how Licensing Agreements and the EEC Competition Rules, Regulation 556/89, 1989 p. 170, the provision was originally included at the wish of the motor car industry.
61. Paragraph 93 of the Guidelines.
62. Paragraph 95 of the Guidelines.

The restriction also applies to the right of one of the parties to the agreement to carry out research and development, unless such a restriction is indispensable to prevent the disclosure of the licensed know-how to third parties.

The basis for the provision is clear: if a licensee is subject to restrictions on the use of its own technology or in the area of research and development, its technology will be less competitive on the existing product and technology markets, and it will reduce its incentive to invest in the further development of its technology.

6.2. Agreements between non-competing undertakings

When the parties to an agreement are undertakings which do not compete with each other, the exemption provided for in Article 2 of the Regulation does not apply to agreements which, directly or indirectly, in isolation or in combination with other factors under the control of the parties, contain the restrictions which are set out in Article 4(2)(a)-(c) of the Regulation.

6.2.1. Agreements on the pricing of contract products – Article 4(2)(a)

The hardcore restriction in Article 4(2)(a) concerns the fixing of sales prices when selling products produced using the licensed technology to third parties; for the reasons for this provision see the comments in section 6.1.1 on the corresponding provision in Article 4(1)(a) relating to agreements between competing undertakings.

While Article 4(1)(a) covers all kinds of pricing (ability to determine its prices), Article 4(2)(a) expressly allows for the possibility for a block exemption of agreements both on maximum sales prices and recommended prices, provided they do not amount to a fixed or minimum sales price as a result of pressure from, or incentives offered by, any of the parties.[63]

> Paragraph 97 of the Guidelines refers to a number of examples of agreements which have as their direct or indirect object the establishment of a fixed or minimum selling price or a fixed or minimum price level to be observed by the licensor or the licensee when selling products to third parties.
>
> In the case of agreements that directly establish the selling price, the restriction is clear-cut. However, the fixing of selling prices can also be achieved through indirect

63. By the use of this wording the provision corresponds to the provisions in Article 4(a) in Regulation (EU) No 330/2010 on vertical agreements, discussed above in Chapter III, section 5.3.1, where there is also a discussion of various decisions which, depending on the circumstances, can be interpreted as decisions which have the purpose of casting a veil over whether there is an intended sales policy between the parties, contrary to Article 4(a).

means which can be difficult to see through, whether this is the purpose of the agreement or it is due to special measures linked to the sales price. Examples of this are agreements that fix the sellers margin, agreements that fix the maximum level of discounts in connection with setting the sales price, agreements linking the sales price to the sales prices of competitors, threats to restrict supplies, or measures outside the scope of the agreement such as threats, intimidation, warnings, penalties, or contract termination in relation to observance of a given price level. The direct or indirect means of achieving price fixing can be made more effective if, for example, they are combined with a hidden price monitoring system, or the obligation on licensees to report deviations of prices from the fixed price level, or are combined with a most-favoured-customer clause, i.e. an obligation to grant to a customer any more favourable terms granted to any other customer.[64]

However, the provision of a list of recommended prices to or the imposition of a maximum price on the licensee by the licensor is not *in itself* considered as leading to fixed or minimum selling prices.[65]

6.2.2. Sales restrictions Article 4(2)(b)

The core of Article 4(2)(b) is the hardcore restriction which restricts a licensee's passive sales to specific territories or to specific customer groups. The aim or consequence of an agreement or concerted practice with the licensor binding the licensee by such an obligation is a division of the market which is contrary to Article 101(1)(c) TFEU.

The obligation can be in the form of a direct order not to sell to customers in a specific territory or to customers of a particular customer group, or a requirement to pass on orders received from such customers to another licensee who has been given exclusive rights to the specified territory or customer group from which the order has been received.[66]

The obligation of licensees to refrain from making passive sales can also arise in the form of indirect measures which have the effect of countering the licensees' sales to such customers, for example financial incentives and the establishment of a control system that can be used to verify where the prod-

64. On most-favoured-customer clauses, see *Valentine Korah:* Technology Transfer Agreements and the EC Competition Rules, 1996 pp. 199-200.
65. Compare with the provisions in the area of distribution agreements in paragraph 111 of the guidelines for vertical agreements referred to above in Chapter III, section 5.3.1, and Commission Decision 96/438/EC, *Fenex* (OJ 1996 L 181/28), Commission Decision 2001/711/EC, *Volkswagen* (OJ 2001 L 262/14), and Commission Decision 97/123/EC, *Novalliance/Systemform* (OJ 1997 L 47/11).
66. The view that a combination of agreements on territorial protection and intellectual property rights could artificially contribute to the maintenance of national markets was established as early as in Case 56 and 58/64, *Grundig and Consten* v *Commission,* which is referred to above in Chapter III.

ucts in fact end up. The same applies to quantitative restrictions which can be used to restrict passive sales, for example if there are quantitative adjustments over time with the aim of only covering the local demand, if the quantitative restriction is combined with an obligation for the licensee to sell a certain minimum quantity to the allocated territory, or if the requirement for the payment of a certain minimum on royalties is linked to sales in the allocated territory etc.; see paragraph 98 of the Guidelines.

Article 4(2)(b) does not affect agreed sales restrictions which a licensee imposes on a *licensor*, and all such restrictions agreed between the licensee and the licensor are therefore covered by the block exemption up to the market share threshold of 30 %; see Article 3(2).[67] The block exemption likewise applies to all restrictions on the licensees active sales, without regard for whether measures such as advertising campaigns in another licensee's territory originate from a licensee that has not been allocated an exclusive territory or an exclusive customer group.

The statement of intent on exclusions from the block exemption (at the introduction to Article 4(2)), and the introductory wording to Article 4(2)(b) are diluted by a number of exceptions, see Article 4(2)(b)(i)-(vi). These exceptions are discussed in section 6.2.3 below.

In addition to this, there still seems to be a lack of clarity in the judicial practice about the importance that should be attached to the views on exclusive licences that were expressed in the *Nungesser* case, which is discussed immediately below.

It has always been the Commission's view that an exclusivity clause that protects a licensee against competition both from the licensor and from parallel imports from licensees in other territories is contrary to Article 101(1). The Commission has argued that even if a licensor could grant or refrain from granting a licensee the right, for example, to use a patent, this could not in itself justify the licensor undertaking not to grant *other licensees* the right to use their patents. In the view of the Commission, such a restriction would lead to full territorial protection, contrary to Article 101(1) TFEU.

However, a possibly decisive break with this practice occurred with the CJ's decision in Case 258/78, *Nungesser and Eisele* v *Commission*, which concerned a new technology for producing hybrid maize. The decision can be read as a recognition that there can be a legitimate need to allow a licensee a certain measure of territorial protection, without Article 101(1) being immediately brought to bear under a claim of an unlawful market sharing.

67. Paragraph 99 of the Guidelines.

The CJ had to consider a reference for a preliminary ruling on an agreement between a French research institute, INRA, and a German undertaking, Nungesser, for the use of seed for hybrid maize varieties which had been developed by INRA.

Nungesser had been given an exclusive licence for Germany, and INRA bound itself not to sell or produce in Germany either itself or through other licensees. In addition to this, INRA bound itself to prevent all direct or indirect exports to Germany. In one clause in the licence agreement it was stated that INRA bound themselves to do 'everything in their power to prevent the export' of the varieties of seeds in question to Germany, and for its part, Nungesser undertook not to export the products.

In its reasoning the CJ made a distinction between the two types of obligation, as the first restriction (Nungesser's exclusive right in relation to the licensor and the other licensees appointed by the licensor) was classified as an 'open exclusive licence', where the exclusivity only concerned the relations between the licensor and the licensee, and therefore, 'having regard to the specific nature of the products in question ... the grant of an open exclusive licence, that is to say a licence which does not affect the position of third parties such as parallel importers and licensees for other territories, is not in itself incompatible with article 85(1) [now Article 101(1) TFEU] of the Treaty'.

The CJ justified this on the grounds that when, as in the case before it, there was a licence for an invention that had been recently developed in a Member State, an undertaking located in another Member State might be reluctant to take on the financial risks of cultivating the product and putting it on the market unless is was granted such protection against other licensees or the licensor itself. In the view of the CJ, this would be injurious to the spread of new technology and thus also for competition between the new product and equivalent existing products in the Community.

As for the obligation to prevent exports to the licensees territory – the CJ referred to this as an exclusive licence, or a sole licence with absolute territorial protection – the CJ only expressed itself in relation to the case as presented, which only concerned the attempt of the parties to restrict parallel imports/exports of products which had already been put on the market by INRA, in other words a case where there had been *exhaustion of rights* (see section 1 above for a discussion of this concept).

Parallel importers and exporters that offered INRA's seed to German buyers had been subject to civil proceedings and other pressure from INRA and Nungesser to protect Nungesser's position as the exclusive producer and distributor on the German market. In addition, the CJ found that, according to well established practice, full territorial protection with a view to controlling and restricting parallel imports was incompatible with Article 101(1) TFEU, and such measures would clearly lie outside the scope of what could be exempted under Article 101(3).

On the other hand, the CJ did not directly address the question of whether Nungesser, as licensee, would be bound by a provision which prevented the undertaking from exporting to potential customers in other licensees' territories, or whether licensees in other territories could be bound not to export to customers in Germany.

It is presumed that, following the CJ's reasoning, such a prohibition would be covered by Article 101(1), since the CJ apparently considered a restriction on parallel imports and an export prohibition on the licensee to be equivalent. In paragraph 58 the CJ stated that the grant of an open exclusive licence, which in the view of the CJ was not in itself incompatible with Article 101(1) TFEU, 'does not affect the position of third parties such as parallel importers and licensees for other territories'. See also the careful statement in recital 11 in Regulation (EC) No 240/96 (in other words, the technology transfer regulation prior to Regulation (EEC) No 772/2004), according to which the exemption of export bans on the licensor and on the licensees does not prejudice any developments in the case law of the CJ with respect to Articles 30 to 36 (now Articles 34 and 36 TFEU) and Article 85(1) (now Article 101(1) TFEU).

However, in the later Case 27/87, *Erauw-Jacquéry* v *la Hesbignonne*, the CJ found that a clause in an agreement on the propagation and sale of seed, under which one of the parties was the owner of certain breeding rights, and which included a prohibition on the propagator selling or exporting basic seed, was compatible with Article 101(1), in so far as the agreement was necessary for the plant breeder to choose authorised propagators. As emphasised in paragraph 11 of the judgment: 'Therefore, the answer to the first part of the question referred by the national court must be that a provision of an agreement concerning the propagation and sale of seed, in respect of which one of the parties is the holder or the agent of the holder of certain plant breeders' rights, which prohibits the licensee from selling and exporting the basic seed is compatible with Article 85(1) [now Article 101(1) TFEU] of the Treaty in so far as it is

> necessary in order to enable the breeder to select the growers who are to be licensees.'[68]

However, it is doubtful, both after the *Nungesser* case and the *Erauw-Jacquéry* case, whether the courts would hold that an open exclusive licence is only exempted when it refers to *new* technology, or whether the scope of the judgment could be stretched to *other* technology than the specific technology relating to seed. However, it is presumably reasonable to interpret the fact that the *Nungesser* case so strongly emphasised the importance of new technology being spread as an expression that, given the many other circumstances that could be linked to such heavy costs of implementing technology in a new area, it ought to be possible, at least in an introductory period, to give a licensee some protection, whether the exclusivity in question relates to new or previously proven technology. In accordance with this, see *Valentine Korah*: Technology Transfer Agreements and the EC Competition Rules, 1996 p. 50, and the comments in section 6.2.3 below relating to Article 4(2)(b)(ii). According to its content this provision seems to be influenced by the statements in the *Nungesser* case about having consideration for the dissemination of new technology.[69]

6.2.3. Permitted restrictions pursuant to Article 4(2)(b)

Article 4(2)(b)(i)

> According to Article 4(2)(b)(i), the restriction on passive sales into an exclusive territory or to an exclusive customer group that is reserved for *the licensor* is not a hardcore restriction on competition. Agreements of this nature are therefore covered by the block exemption, as long as the market share threshold laid down in Article 3(2) is not exceeded. In paragraph 100 of the Guidelines it is presumed that such restrictions, if they restrict competition, will contribute to the dissemination of technology which will promote competitiveness and the integration of such technology into the production of the licensee. It is not important whether the licensor does in fact produce by means of the licensed technology in the territory in question or for the customer group in question, as this territory or customer group could be reserved to the licensor for later exploitation.

68. The case is discussed in, among others, *Valentine Korah:* Technology Transfer Agreements and the EC Competition Rules, 1996 pp. 16-18.
69. In footnote 46, relating to paragraph 101 of the Guidelines (concerning Article 4(2)(b)(ii)) there is an express reference to the *Nungesser* case.

Article 4(2)(b)(ii)

The restriction on a licensee's passive sales into an exclusive territory or to an exclusive customer group allocated to another licensee is exempted during *the first two years* in which this other licensee sells the products incorporating the licensed technology in that territory or to that customer group.

The rationale of the provision in Article 4(2)(b)(ii) is that a licensee often has to make considerable investments in production capacity and marketing in order to create and develop a new sales territory, and would therefore be reluctant to enter into a licence agreement without being protected from the active and passive sales of other licensees in that territory; see paragraph 101 of the Guidelines. This appears to be an expression of a new approach in the Commission's assessments in this area.[70] However, see Commission Decision 1999/6/EC, *Sicasov* (OJ 1999 L 4/27), where in paragraph 72 the Commission stated that the prohibition on exporting certified seeds does not correspond to any of the obligations mentioned in Article 1(1) of Regulation (EC) No 240/96 (the predecessor to Regulation (EC) No 772/2004, which set out the scope for block exemption agreements in its Article 1(1)). However, the Commission exempted the export prohibition under Article 101(3) as the licensee's obligation not to export seed directly was not found to enable the seed producer to prevent competition. The Commission emphasised that most new seed varieties compete with existing varieties, which are well-known to customers and which therefore constitute an alternative source of supply. Next, the Commission bore in mind that there would continue to be freedom to make parallel imports from the licence territory, so that even during the launch period any customer located in another Member State could have access, even if indirect, to the French varieties.[71]

In this connection, see also the comments on the *Nungesser* case and the *Erauw-Jacquéry* case at the end of section 6.2.2 above.

Article 4(2)(b)(iii)

The content of Article 4(2)(b)(iii) corresponds to the provision in Article 4(1)(c)(vi) (see section 6.1.3.3 above) so that in this respect (restriction to producing the contract products only for own use) the same legal considerations apply to agreements between non-competing undertakings as to agreements between competing undertakings.

Article 4(2)(b)(iv)

70. It is expressly stated in paragraph 101 of the Guidelines that after the expiry of this two-year period, restrictions on passive sales between licensees will be considered hardcore restrictions. Such restrictions will generally be caught by Article 101(1) TFEU and are unlikely to fulfil the conditions of Article 101(3).
71. With this last comment the Commission has presumably had in mind the effects of the principle of exhaustion of rights.

This provision (for ensuring the existence of alternative sources of supply) corresponds to Article 4(1)(c)(vii) (see section 6.1.3.3 above). In paragraph 103 of the Guidelines it is added that in the case of agreements between non-competitors, such restrictions are unlikely to be caught by Article 101(1) TFEU.

Article 4(2)(b)(v)

Article 4(2)(b)(v) provides for a block exemption for an obligation on a licensee only to sell the contract products to retailers, and not to end users of the products. The provision makes it possible for the licensor to grant the licensee a distribution function at the wholesale level; see paragraph 104 of the Guidelines, and such a restriction will normally fall outside the scope of Article 101(1) TFEU.

Article 4(2)(b)(vi)

Article 4(2)(b)(vi), under which a licensee can be required not to sell to non-authorised distributors, has a counterpart in Article 4(b) in Regulation (EU) No 330/2010 on block exemptions for vertical distribution agreements. The block exemption for an obligation of this kind makes it possible for the licensor, while complying with the provisions of the Regulation on vertical distribution agreements, to bind a licensee to participate in a *selective distribution system* (see recital 19 in Regulation (EC) No 772/2004 referred to in section 5.1.1 above). [

7. Restrictions which fall outside the scope of the block exemption

7.1. Article 5 of Regulation (EC) No 772/2004

Article 5 of Regulation (EC) No 772/2004 contains four restrictions which are excluded from the block exemption, and which therefore require individual assessment of their effects on restricting and promoting competition before a decision can be taken about their effect; see paragraph 107 of the Guidelines.

Corresponding to the effect associated with Article 5 of Regulation (EU) No 330/2010 on block exemptions for vertical distribution agreements, it follows from the wording of Article 5 of Regulation (EC) No 772/2004 that even if a licence agreement contains one or more of the restrictions referred to therein, this does not automatically mean that the block exemption will not be applicable to the remaining part of the agreement. In accordance with, among other things, the doctrine of severance in English law, any invalidity of an agreement under competition law only affects the specific restriction, but will not necessarily affect the whole agreement so as to be considered an infringement of the provisions on hardcore restrictions under Article 4.[72] Thus, if a restriction covered by Article 5 can be separated from the agreement, the rest of the agreement will continue to be valid.

7.2. Article 5(1)

Article 5(1) covers both agreements between competing undertakings and agreements between non-competing undertakings.

The restriction in Article 5(1)(a) and (b), on grant-back agreements, is directed at obligations for the licensee to grant the licensor, or a third party appointed by the licensor, an exclusive licence to its own severable improvements to or its own new applications of the licensed technology. The same applies to obligations for the licensee to assign, in whole or in part, to the licensor or to a third party designated by the licensor, rights to its own severable improvements to or its own new applications of the licensed technology. Grant-back agreements are therefore only covered by the block exemption if they are non-exclusive and do not prevent the licensee from itself exploiting improvements to or new applications of the licensed technology.[73]

> A 'severable improvement' means an improvement made by the licensee that can be exploited without infringing the licensed technology; see paragraph 109 of the Guidelines. As referred to in Article 5(1)(a) and (b) and in recital 14, such obligations could be a disincentive to innovation and the appropriate application of intellectual property rights, if, because of the restrictions, the licensee had no prospect of itself being able to exploit any improvements, including via a licence entered into between the licensee and a third party. This would be the case if there were a severable improvement that concerned the same application as the licensed technology or newly developed applications of this technology.
>
> The block exemption will be excluded, regardless of whether the licensor gives the licensee payment or an exclusive licence for the improvements: see paragraph 110 of the Guidelines; and, pre-dating Regulation (EC) No 772/2004, Commission Decision 85/410/EEC,

72. See Chapter III, section 5.4 and the references made there to the doctrine of severance.
73. See Commission Decision 88/143/EEC, *Rich Products* (OJ 1988 L 69/21), which pre-dated Regulation (EC) No 772/2004, on the assignment of the sole right to know-how about the production of yeast.

> *Velcro/Aplix* (OJ 1985 L 233/22); and *Valentine Korah:* Technology Transfer Agreements and the EC Competition Rules, 1996 pp. 160-161.[74]

The general principles of interpretation seem to lead to the conclusion that the licensor has a right to use improvements that are not severable from the licensed technology, without being required to allow the licensee to use the now improved technology after the expiry of the licence agreement.[75]

According to Article 5(1)(c), neither direct nor indirect hindrances may be put in the way of the licensee's possibility of challenging the validity, or the confidential or significant character of the licensor's intellectual property rights within the internal market (non-challenge clause).

The purpose of excluding non-challenge clauses from the block exemption is to avoid disputes arising about whether an intellectual property right is valid at all. It will normally be the licensee who will have the best qualification for assessing whether an intellectual property right is valid and if the licensee does not have the possibility of intervening, a non-challenge clause will contribute to creating a fluid and uncertain situation. The right in question could still serve outwardly as a means for blocking competition and unjustifiably give the licensor who claims that the rights should validly remain in force, competitive advantages at the expense of others. The right to challenge intellectual property rights, which has been a topic of particular interest in patent law, reflects the ideal of a system based on well-defined and well-controlled property rights.[76]

> A condition that the licensor will have the right to terminate a contract if the licensee challenges the validity of one or more parts of the licensed technology is covered by the block exemption; see the reservation in Article 5(1)(c). The licensor is thus not forced to continue dealing with a licensee who challenges the very subject matter of the licence agreement; see paragraph 113 of the Guidelines. If, after termination of the licence,

74. If payment of a fee is provided for in connection with a grant-back obligation, the amount of the fee could be a relevant factor for assessing whether an exemption could be granted outside the scope of application of the block exemption regulation, i.e. under Article 101(3) TFEU.
75. However, for a contrary view, see *Valentine Korah:* Technology Transfer Agreements and the EC Competition Rules, 1996 p. 171.
76. On the Commission's changing approach to non-challenge clauses, see *Valentine Korah:* Technology Transfer Agreements and the EC Competition Rules, 1996 pp 180-186, and Case 65/86, *Bayer and Hennecke v Süllhöfer.*

the licensee continues to use the challenged technology, this will be at its own risk. The significance of Article 5(1)(c) is thus primarily that it ensures that the block exemption does not cover contractual obligations that prevent the licensee from challenging the licensed technology. In this case, the licensor will have the possibility of suing the licensee for breach of contract and thus deter the licensee from further challenging the validity of the intellectual property rights. The provision thus ensures that the licensee's position is equivalent to that of any third party.

7.3. Article 5(2)

Article 5(2) provides that the exemption provided for in Article 2 does not apply to any direct or indirect obligation in technology transfer agreements between non-competing undertakings which limits the licensee's right to exploit its own technology or limits the ability of any of the parties to the agreement to carry out research and development. However, this restriction does not apply, if it is necessary for preventing the disclosure of the licensed know-how to third parties.

The restriction in Article 5(2) corresponds to the hardcore restriction referred to in Article 4(1)(d), relating to agreements between competing undertakings; see section 6.1.3.4 above. As regards agreements between non-competing undertakings, it is the Commission's view that it cannot be assumed that such restrictions generally have a negative effect on competition, or that the conditions in Article 101(3) TFEU are generally not fulfilled; see paragraphs 14 and 114 of the Guidelines. Therefore in these cases there is a need for an individual assessment.

8. Withdrawal of the block exemption in individual cases

8.1. Article 6 of Regulation (EC) No 772/2004

Corresponding to the provisions in Articles 6 and 7 of Regulation (EC) No 2790/99 [the predecessor to Regulation (EU) No 330/2010] on the possibility for the Commission and the competition authorities in the individual Member States to withdraw exemptions given under the Regulation, under Article 6(1) of Regulation (EC) No 772/2004, in accordance with Article 29(1) of Council Regulation (EC) No 1/2003, the Commission can withdraw a block exemption if in the individual case it finds that a technology transfer agreement in fact gives rise to effects which are incompatible with the conditions in Article 101(3) and which, according to Article 6(1), of the Treaty, and in particular where:

a. access of third parties technologies to the market is restricted, for instance by the cumulative effect of parallel networks of similar restrictive agreements prohibiting licensees from using third parties' technologies;
b. access of potential licensees to the market is restricted, for instance by the cumulative effect of parallel networks of similar restrictive agreements prohibiting licensors from licensing to other licensees;
c. without any objectively valid reason, the parties do not exploit the licensed technology.

8.2. Article 6.2.

According to Article 6(2), corresponding to the powers given to the Commission under Article 6(1), the competition authority of *a Member State* may withdraw a block exemption if a technology transfer agreement has unintended effects in the territory of the Member State, or a part thereof which has all the characteristics of a distinct territorial market.

According to paragraph 121 of the Guidelines, the reason for the rules in Article 6 is that Articles 4 and 5, on hardcore restrictions and provisions that are not covered by the block exemption, does not sufficiently take account of the effects of an agreement on third parties. Depending on the circumstances, a licence agreement could lead to the exclusion of third parties, both as licensors and as licensees.

The exclusion of other licensors from the market can stem from the cumulative effect of networks of licence agreements which oblige licensees not to use competing technologies. The exclusion of other licensees from the market can also be the result of the cumulative effect of licences which oblige the licensor not to grant licences to other licensees, so that other potential licensees are denied access to the necessary technology.

It is also possible, see paragraph 122 of the Guidelines, that the Commission will withdraw the benefit of the block exemption where the parties *refrain from* exploiting the licensed technology. The aim of granting the block exemption, that there will be efficiency enhancing activities, will thus not be realised, and in the case of licensing between competitors, the fact that the parties do not exploit the licensed technology may be an indication that the arrangement is a disguised cartel.

In paragraph 122 of the Guidelines the Commission states that for these reasons it will examine very closely cases of non-exploitation.

If a block exemption is withdrawn in accordance with Article 6, which will presumably be a seldom used safety valve, the burden of proof is on the authority withdrawing the exemption to show that the agreement falls within the scope of Article 101(1) TFEU and does not fulfil the conditions of Article 101(3).[77]

8.3. Article 7

According to Article 7 of Regulation (EC) No 772/2004, the Commission may by a regulation declare that, a block exemption does not apply where parallel networks of similar technology transfer agreements cover more than 50 % of a relevant market. Such a measure is not directed against individual undertakings, but concerns all undertakings whose agreements are defined in the regulation withdrawing the block exemption. A regulation withdrawing a block exemption adopted in accordance with Article 7 would merely annul the block exemption in relation to the restrictions and markets in question, so that Article 101(1) and (3) TFEU would again apply in full; see paragraphs 123 and 124 of the Guidelines.

77. As far as can be determined, the withdrawal of an exemption, or the threat of such, has only been practised by the Commission in Case T-51/89, *Tetra Pak Rausing* v *Commission,* where the Commission persuaded Tetra Pak to surrender an exclusive licence which the undertaking had acquired from a competing undertaking, and would thereby have been in a position to make a number of users of Tetra Pak's products dependant on Tetra Pak. The decision thus raised the question of whether Article 86 [now Article 102 TFEU] of the Treaty could have been applied, even if the block exemption had not yet been withdrawn. The CJ answered this in the affirmative, as the block exemption would otherwise mean that Tetra Pak would be protected from sanctions under Article 86 [now Article 102 TFEU].

CHAPTER VI

Abuse of dominant position

Pernille Wegener Jessen

Bibliography: *Ivo Van Bael & Jean-Francois Bellis: Competition Law of the European Community, 2010; Christopher Bellamy & Graham Child (consultant eds.): European Community Law of Competition, 2007-2012; Jonathan Faull & Ali Nikpay (eds.): The EC Law of Competition, 2007; D.G. Goyder: EC Competition Law, 2009; Giorgi Monti: EC Competition Law, 2007; Lennart Ritter & W. David Braun: European Competition Law: A Practitioner's Guide, 2009; Richard Whish: Competition Law, 2012.*

1. Introduction

Article 102 of the Treaty on the functioning of the European Union, together with the other competition rules, is part of a system which is intended to ensure that competition in the internal market is not distorted. The competitive concerns which relate to dominant undertakings are that as such an undertaking's position in the market is strengthened, so the self-regulatory forces in the market are weakened. Such undertakings are therefore able to use a dominant position to restrict supplies to the market or obtain a supernormal profit and act in a way which is harmful to effective and non-distorted competition in the internal market. Article 102 of the Treaty therefore states that:

'Any abuse by one or more undertakings of a dominant position within the internal market or in a substantial part of it shall be prohibited as incompatible with the internal market in so far as it may affect trade between Member States.

Such abuse may, in particular, consist in:

a. directly or indirectly imposing unfair purchase or selling prices or other unfair trading conditions;
b. limiting production, markets or technical development to the prejudice of consumers;

c. applying dissimilar conditions to equivalent transactions with other trading parties, thereby placing them at a competitive disadvantage;
d. making the conclusion of contracts subject to acceptance by the other parties of supplementary obligations which, by their nature or according to commercial usage, have no connection with the subject of such contracts.'

The specific conditions for the application of the prohibition in Article 102 to the unilateral conduct of an undertaking are thus: 1) that there is an undertaking; 2) that the undertaking has a dominant position in a substantial part of the internal market; 3) that this dominant position is abused; and 4) that this abuse affects trade between the Member States.

While Article 101 is directed at multilateral conduct, based on agreements between undertakings, Article 102 is directed at unilateral conduct which has negative consequences for competition and trade within the internal market, as a result of the market dominance of an undertaking.[1] Article 102 is thus only directed at cases where an undertaking abuses its dominant position. There is no prohibition on an undertaking having or acquiring a dominant position, nor is the strengthening of a dominant position prohibited by Article 102,[2] as long as it is not strengthened as a result of abuse of the dominant position. Thus, for example, a dominant undertaking will lawfully be able to have a pricing policy which increases its market share, as long as the prices cannot be characterised as an abuse for example in the form of unlawful predatory pricing.[3]

Article 102, second paragraph, lists forms of conduct which constitute an abuse covered by the prohibition. However, this list is not exhaustive, and is supplemented by other forms of abuse which appear from the practice of the Court of Justice of the European Union (CJ). In contrast to Article 101, Article 102 does not make provision for exemptions from the prohibition for certain kinds of conduct.[4] If an undertaking's conduct can be characterised as

1. For a more detailed discussion of the distinction between unilateral and multilateral actions; see Chapter II, section 2.1.
2. However if a dominant position is created or strengthened in connection with a merger, the merger can be declared to be incompatible with the internal market and therefore prohibited if the merger significantly impedes effective competition within the internal market or a substantial part of it; see Council Regulation (EC) No 139/2004 on the control of concentrations between undertakings (the Merger Control Regulation), Article 2(2) and (3) (OJ 2004 L 24/1). The Merger Control Regulation is discussed in more detail in Chapter VIII, section 4.
3. On the limits to predatory pricing, see section 4.1.2.
4. Joined Cases T-191/98 and T-212/98 to T-214/98, *Atlantic Container Line and others* v *Commission,* para. 1455.

abuse, it will not be possible to allow the abuse, and it will be prohibited in all circumstances.

Nevertheless, according to a number of decisions, it is possible that some disputed conduct may be objectively justifiable.[5] This means that a dominant undertaking can, for example, take measures to protect its trading interests when these are threatened, as long as it complies with the principle of proportionality.[6] Such objectively justified conduct is not characterised as abuse, and therefore does not fall within the scope of application of Article 102.[7]

The fact that a dominant undertaking's conduct leads to efficiency advantages can also mean that such conduct will not be characterised as abuse. When assessing the application of Article 102 of the Treaty to exclusionary abuses, the Commission will therefore include efficiency improvements in its analysis.[8]

Article 102 only prohibits the abuse of a dominant position to the extent that trade between the Member States is affected. This condition limits the scope of the provision in relation to national law.

Article 102 has direct effect in national law. Thus it is possible for natural and legal persons to rely on the provision directly in national courts, and national courts have jurisdiction and an obligation to apply the provision in order to protect the rights which Article 102 gives to the parties involved.[9] In addition to this, national competition authorities have powers to apply Article 102 in individual cases.[10] This means that the authorities do not have powers to lay down general rules on the application of the Treaty provisions, such as the block exemption regulations laid down by the Commission in relation to Article 101 of the Treaty.

5. Case C-163/99, *Portugal* v *Commission,* para. 53; Case T-83/91, *Tetra Pak II,* paras 115, 136 and 207; and Case C-52/09, *TeliaSonera,* para. 31.
6. Case 27/76, *United Brands,* paras 189-190.
7. See the Opinion of Advocate General Jacobs in Case C-53/03, *Syfait,* point 72.
8. Communication from the Commission – Guidance on the Commission's enforcement priorities in applying Article 82 of the EC Treaty to abusive exclusionary conduct by dominant undertakings (OJ 2009 C 45/7). While such an interpretation of Article 102 was rejected in Case T-191/98, *TACA*, see paras 1111-1122, Case T-193/02, *Laurent Piau,* might possibly open up for such an interpretation, see para. 119.
9. Case 123/73, *BRT II;* and Council Regulation (EC) No 1/2003 on the implementation of the rules on competition laid down in Articles 81 and 82 of the Treaty, Article 6 (OJ 2003 L 1/1).
10. Article 5 of Regulation (EC) No 1/2003. For a further discussion of the powers of national authorities and courts, see Chapter VII, section 4.2.

As will be shown below, the CJ interprets Article 102 in the light of its purpose, in other words to prevent dominant undertakings abusing their market position. This means that a broad interpretation of the scope and conditions of the provision is generally applied.

2. The meaning of an *undertaking*

In relation to Article 102 and the other provisions on competition, the term *undertaking* is defined by the CJ as covering any entity which carries on economic activity, regardless of the legal status of the entity or the method by which it is financed.[11] In this context, any activity which consists of offering goods or services for sale on a market constitutes an economic activity.[12] It is not necessary to separate an activity which consists of purchasing goods from the subsequent use of the goods in order to assess whether an activity is an economic activity. It is the economic or non-economic nature of the subsequent use of a product which necessarily determines the nature of the activity.[13]

In order to fall within the scope of the concept of an undertaking, it will be sufficient if the undertaking in fact carries on economic activity. This means that the CJ does not require that the activities of the undertaking should be carried on for profit.[14] This means that non-profit organisations[15] are also covered by the term *undertaking*.

Both private and public undertakings can be an undertaking for the purposes of competition law. This follows not only from the practice of the CJ,

11. Case C-41/90, *Hoefner & Elser,* para. 21; and Case C-280/06, *ETI* et al., para. 38. The concept of an undertaking in relation to Article 102 does not differ from the concept of an undertaking in relation to Article 101. For further discussion of the concept, see Chapter II, section 3.1; and *Ivo Van Bael & Jean-Francois Bellis:* Competition Law of the European Community, 2010 pp. 17-19.
12. Case T-155/04, *Eurocontrol,* para. 50; and Case T-81-83/07, *Jan Rudolf Maas,* para. 178.
13. Case C-113/07 P, *Selex,* para. 102; and Case C-205/03, *FENIN,* para. 26
14. Case C-41/90, *Höefner & Elser,* paras 19-23.
15. Case C-437/09, *AG2R,* para. 65.

but also from Article 106 TFEU, and the Transparency Directive,[16] which states that public undertakings are subject to the Treaty's competition rules.[17]

The CJ does not make any special demands as to the legal form of undertakings. This means that public limited companies, private limited companies, trusts, mutual institutions, one-man businesses etc. are all covered by the concept of an undertaking. For public bodies, for the purposes of the definition of an undertaking, it does not matter whether the body in question is a separate legal entity, or whether it is part of the central government administration.[18] However, the concept of an undertaking does not cover the exercise of public authority, for example the collection of air navigation fees from airlines,[19] or carrying out tasks of a social character such as the administration of health insurance and pensions arrangements.[20]

3. Dominant position

In order for conduct to be in breach of Article 102, an undertaking must have a dominant position in the internal market or in a substantial part of the internal market. The term *dominant position* is defined by the CJ as:

16. Commission Directive 2006/111/EC on the transparency of financial relations between Member States and public undertakings as well as on financial transparency within certain undertakings (OJ 2006 L 318/17). Article 106 is discussed in more detail in Chapter IX.
17. Subject to the reservation for undertakings covered by Article 106(2). Moreover, under Article 345 of the Treaty, public and private undertakings must be treated equally under the competition rules, as the Treaties do not affect systems of property law in the Member States.
18. Case 118/85, *Commission* v *Italy,* para. 13; Case C-69/91, *Decoster,* para. 15; and Case C-92/91, *Taillandier,* para. 14.
19. Case C-364/92, *Eurocontrol,* para. 30.
20. Joined Cases C-264, 306, and 354-355/01, *AOK*, paras 47 and 55; and Case T-319/99, *FENIN,* paras 38-39. See also Case T-155/04, *Eurocontrol,* where the Court held that Eurocontrol's activities concerning technical standardisation were not an economic activity, (para. 69), nor were the research and development activities which Eurocontrol financed (para. 82), while Eurocontrol's activities in the form of providing technical support for national authorities was an economic activity (paragraph 92). See also, in more detail, the distinction between the exercise of public authority and the concept of an undertaking in Chapter II, section 3.2, as well as *Jonathan Faull & Ali Nikpay (eds.):* The EC Law of Competition, 2007 sections 3.38-3.46.

> 'a position of economic strength enjoyed by an undertaking which enables it to prevent effective competition being maintained on the relevant market by affording it the power to behave to an appreciable extent independently of its competitors, its customers and ultimately of the consumers.'[21]

What is decisive is the ability of the undertaking concerned to behave to an appreciable extent independently of its competitors, its customers and ultimately of the consumers. The assessment of this is made on the basis of the economic circumstances that apply at the time of the alleged abuse.

The legal definition of when an undertaking can be considered to be dominant has been criticised as being unusable in practice. The reason for this is that the ability of a dominant undertaking to act independently of its competitors, customers and consumers does not differ significantly from the ability of a non-dominant undertaking to act independently.[22]

The ability to act independently in the terms described depends on the market strength of an undertaking in the relevant market. The undertaking should thus have a market strength which enables it 'if not to determine, at least to have an appreciable influence on the conditions under which that competition will develop, and in any case to act largely in disregard of it so long as such conduct does not operate to its detriment.'[23]

Whether or not an undertaking has the necessary market strength depends on the undertaking's market share, as well as on a number of other factors such as the barriers to entry to the market, the relative market shares of competitors etc. The market strength of an undertaking will thus be the result of a combination of these different factors, though without these factors necessarily being decisive in themselves. However, where an undertaking has a comprehensive market share this will be highly relevant to the assessment of dominance.[24] On the other hand, the smaller the market share of an undertaking, the more significant seems to be the role of the other factors, so there is a need to assess whether the other elements indicate the existence of a dominant position.

21. Case 85/76, *Hoffmann-La Roche,* para. 38; Case T-193/02, *Laurent Piau,* para. 109; and Case C-52/09, *TeliaSonera,* para. 23.
22. See *João Pearce Azevedo & Mike Walker:* Dominance: Meaning and Measurement, European Competition Law Review 2002 pp. 363-367.
23. Case 85/76, *Hoffmann-La Roche,* para. 39.
24. Case 85/76, *Hoffmann-La Roche,* para. 39; and Case T-340/03, *France Télécom,* para. 100.

3.1. One or more undertakings – collective dominance

According to Article 102, the provision is applicable to the abuse of a dominant position by *one or more undertakings*. In a narrow sense, this wording covers, first an individual undertaking's abuse of a dominant position. Next, it covers abuse of a dominant position which is the result of the collective conduct of several independent legal entities which belong to the same group of companies and which therefore constitute a collective economic entity which is considered to be a single entity for the purposes of competition law.[25]

It is also clear from the practice of the courts that the reference to more than one undertaking can be understood so that several entities which are financially and legally independent of each other, and which are therefore not considered as one undertaking for the purposes of competition law, can together have a dominant position.[26] If such undertakings act collectively there will not be genuine competition between the parties.[27]

In deciding whether Article 102 is applicable in this context, an assessment must first be made of whether the undertakings concerned constitute a collective entity. If this is the case, it is next necessary to examine whether the collective entity does in fact have a dominant position, and thirdly, whether this dominant position is abused.[28]

Collective dominance can exist where, in economic terms, two or more economic entities which are legally independent of each other present themselves or act together on a particular market as a collective entity.[29]

In assessing this an examination is made of the mutual economic cooperation and the mutual economic relations between the undertakings concerned, among other things in order to determine whether such economic cooperation exists between the undertakings, and whether they act independently of their competitors, customers and, ultimately, their consumers.[30]

The case law does not clearly define what forms of economic activity (and legal relationships) are decisive for this assessment, but in this connection the CJ has emphasised that collective dominance cannot be established solely on

25. Case 6/72, *Continental Can.*
26. Joined Cases T-68, 77 and 78/89, *Italian Flat Glass,* para. 358.
27. Case C-96/94, *Centro Zervizi Spediporto,* para. 34.
28. Joined Cases C-395-396/96 P, *CMB,* para. 39.
29. Joined Cases C-395-396/96 P, *CMB,* para. 36. On collective dominance, see also*: Ivo Van Bael & Jean-Francois Bellis:* Competition Law of the European Community, 2010 pp. 104-108.
30. Joined Cases C-395-396/96 P, *CMB,* para. 41.

the basis that there may be an agreement, decision or concerted practice between the parties involved, within the meaning of Article 101(1).[31] However, when such an agreement etc. is implemented, this can mean that the undertakings involved are bound with regard to their conduct on a given market so as to act on the market as a collective entity.[32] Thus, depending on the nature or wording of an agreement, from the way in which it is implemented, and the consequent cooperation and relations between the undertakings, a collective dominant position can be found to exist.[33]

However, there need not be an agreement or other legal connection between the undertakings involved in order for a collective entity to be found to exist. Such a collective entity can be found to exist on the basis of other relations between the undertakings involved, and requires an economic assessment to be made, as well as an assessment of the structure of the relevant market.[34]

In practice, collective dominance may be found to exist both on a contractual basis, and on the basis of an economic connection between the undertakings involved. In the *Italian Flat Glass* case the CJ gave the example that an economic connection can exist where, through agreements or licences, two or more independent undertakings jointly have a technological lead affording them the power to act independently to an appreciable extent.[35] Other examples could be cross-shareholdings, common directorships, family links,[36] and the pursuit of a common marketing strategy or sales policy.[37]

Where several undertakings are found to constitute a collective entity, it is the collective entity as such which must fulfil the conditions for the existence of a dominant position in a substantial part of the internal market, as well as the conditions for the existence of abuse of that dominant position. Thus, there can be an infringement of Article 102 even if the individual undertakings could not in themselves be considered dominant within the meaning of Article 102, and regardless of whether all the undertakings or only one of the

31. Joined Cases C-395-396/96 P, *CMB,* para. 43.
32. Joined Cases C-395-396/96 P, *CMB,* para. 44. See also case T-193/02, *Laurent Piau,* discussed below in section 3.1.1.
33. Joined Cases C-395-396/96 P, *CMB,* para. 45.
34. Joined Cases C-395-396/96 P, *CMB,* para. 45.
35. Joined Cases T-68, 77 and 78/89, *Italian Flat Glass,* para. 358. See also Case T-193/02, *Laurent Piau,* discussed below in section 3.1.1.
36. See the Opinion of Advocate General Fennelly in Joined Cases C-395-396/96 P, *CMB,* point 28.
37. Case C-393/92, *Almelo,* para. 42; Case 30/87, *Bodson;* and Joined Cases 40-48, 50, 54-56, 111, 113 and 114/73, *Suiker Unie.*

undertakings engages in conduct which can be characterised as an abuse of the collective dominance.[38]

3.1.1. Oligopolistic market structure

The possibility of using Article 102 to sanction undertakings' abuse of a collective dominant position is particularly relevant where the market structure is characterised by having few large market participants, and where the Commission is unable to prove that apparently coordinated conduct between the undertakings concerned is due to a concerted practice covered by Article 101, rather than by the oligopolistic market structure.[39]

On such oligopolistic markets, there will be assumed to be a collective dominant position as long as three cumulative conditions are fulfilled:

> 'First, each member of the dominant oligopoly must have the ability to know how the other members are behaving in order to monitor whether or not they are adopting the common policy; second, the situation of tacit coordination must be sustainable over time, that is to say, there must be an incentive not to depart from the common policy on the market; thirdly, the foreseeable reaction of current and future competitors, as well as of consumers, must not jeopardise the results expected from the common policy'.[40]

On this basis, in Case T-193/02, *Laurent Piau*, the CFI held that FIFA had a collective dominant position.

> 'In the present case, the market affected by the rules in question is a market for the provision of services where the buyers are players and clubs and the sellers are agents. In this market FIFA can be regarded as acting on behalf of football clubs since, as has already been stated ... it constitutes

38. Case T-228/97, *Irish Sugar*, para. 66, confirmed by the ruling of the CJ in Case C-497/99 P. See also Case C-393/92, *Almelo*, para. 51.
39. See *Chris Withers & Mark Jephcott:* Where to now for E.C. oligopoly control?, European Competition Law Review 2001 pp. 295-303. See also Chapter VIII, section 4.3, on collective dominance in relation to merger control.
40. Case T-193/02, *Laurent Piau*, para. 111. The judgment refers to the conditions which were laid down in connection with assessment of collective dominance for the purposes of the Merger Control Regulation in Case T-342/99, *Airtours*, para. 62, as confirmed in Case T-374/00, *Verband der freien Rohrwerke*, para. 121. On collective dominance in connection with the Merger Control Regulation, see Chapter VIII, section 4.3.

an emanation of those clubs as a second-level association of undertakings formed by the clubs.

A decision like the FIFA Players' Agents Regulations may, where it is implemented, result in the undertakings operating on the market in question, namely the clubs, being so linked as to their conduct on a particular market that they present themselves on that market as a collective entity vis-à-vis their competitors, their trading partners and consumers.

Because the regulations are binding for national associations that are members of FIFA and the clubs forming them, these bodies appear to be linked in the long term as to their conduct by rules that they accept and that other actors (players and players' agents) cannot break on pain of sanctions that may lead to their exclusion from the market, in particular in the case of players' agents. ... such a situation therefore characterises a collective dominant position for clubs on the market for the provision of players' agents' services, since, through the rules to which they adhere, the clubs lay down the conditions under which the services in question are provided.'[41]

However, the CFI did not find that it had been established that FIFA had abused its dominant position, as the rules did not lay down quantitative restrictions on the right to act as a players' agent which were harmful to competition, but rather that the restrictions were qualitative and could be justified in the circumstances.[42]

3.2. Relevant factors for assessing market dominance

An undertaking's dominant position on the relevant market is generally due to a combination of a number of factors, which are not necessarily decisive in themselves.[43] If an undertaking has a large market share, this will be a strong indication that it has market dominance,[44] but both the market shares of competitors, and barriers to market entry by actual or potential competitors could overturn an assumption of market dominance.[45] The same can apply if

41. Case T-193/02, *Laurent Piau,* paras 112-114.
42. Case T-193/02, *Laurent Piau,* para. 118.
43. Case C- 250/92, *Gøttrup-Klim,* para. 47.
44. Case C- 250/92, *Gøttrup-Klim,* para. 48.
45. Communication from the Commission – Guidance on the Commission's enforcement priorities in applying Article 82 of the EC Treaty to abusive exclusionary conduct by dominant undertakings, point 7 (OJ 2009 C 45/7).

the undertaking's customers have negotiating strength such that the undertaking cannot act autonomously.[46]

3.2.1. Market share

The structure of a market can mean that an undertaking is in possession of the whole market, because of a monopoly in law or in fact.[47] Where such an undertaking is not exposed to actual or potential competition, it will be assumed that it has a dominant position within the terms of Article 102.[48]

In other cases too, the possession of a very large market share will also, in itself, be regarded as evidence that an undertaking has a dominant position, unless there are unusual circumstances.[49]

> In Case T-83/91, *Tetra Pak II* the CFI found that the undertaking concerned, with 90 % market share, had a dominant position. Likewise, in Case 85/76, *Hoffmann-La Roche*, where the undertaking had a market share of 75 %, it was found to have a dominant position in the relevant market for vitamins.[50]

In this context, a *very large market share* appears to include market shares of 50 % or more of the relevant market, so that a market share of this size can, in itself, be regarded as evidence of an undertaking's dominant position.[51] However, regardless of this, the CJ will often assess whether other factors, in particular the relative market shares of competitors, indicate that the undertaking has a dominant position,[52] so there only appears to be a strong presumption.[53]

Depending on the circumstances, an undertaking that has a market share of less than 50 % of the relevant market can also be considered to be domi-

46. Communication from the Commission – Guidance on the Commission's enforcement priorities in applying Article 82 of the EC Treaty to abusive exclusionary conduct by dominant undertakings, points 12 and 18 (OJ 2009 C 45/7).
47. See Commission Decision COMP/C-3/37.792, *Microsoft,* point 435, where Microsoft's market share of more than 90 % was an actual monopoly.
48. Case 127/73, *BRT II;* and Case C-260/89, *ERT.*
49. Case 85/76, *Hoffmann-La Roche,* para. 41.
50. Case 85/76, *Hoffmann-La Roche,* paras 41 and 56.
51. Case C-62/86, *Akzo,* para. 60; Case T-340/03, *France Télécom,* para. 100. See also *Jonathan Faull & Ali Nikpay (eds.):* The EC Law of Competition, 2007 section 4.49.
52. Case 322/81, *Michelin,* para. 52; and Case T-30/89, *Hilti,* paras 92 and 93.
53. *Ivo Van Bael & Jean-Francois Bellis:* Competition Law of the European Community, 2010 pp. 109-110.

nant. However, this will often require other relevant factors to support the finding.[54]

However, the Commission regards it as unlikely that there will be a dominant position if an undertaking has a market share of less than 40 % of the relevant market, unless there are special circumstances.[55]

If an undertaking has a market share of less than 25 %, it is unlikely it could be considered to have a dominant position.[56] As for market shares of less than 10 %, these are clearly insufficient for the undertaking concerned to be considered as dominant.[57]

Undertakings which, in accordance with the above, are not regarded in themselves as having a dominant position for the purposes of Article 102, are not excluded from the possibility of having a collective dominant position, together with other undertakings, as discussed in section 3.1.

However, it is not only an undertaking's absolute market share that is relevant to an assessment of dominance. In certain cases it will also be relevant to examine the relative market share of an undertaking, in other words an undertakings market share compared with its competitors' market shares.[58] The structure of the market can thus be relevant to the size of a market share for assessing dominance.

For example, this will be the case where the market is characterised by having many participants, and where the undertaking concerned has a market share which is relatively greater than its competitors. The smaller the competitors' market shares in relation to the share of the undertaking concerned, the greater will be the probability that the undertaking will be considered to have a dominant position.[59] In this context, the collective relative market share of

54. In Case 27/76, *United Brands,* the CJ found that a market share of 40-45 % was not in itself sufficient for an undertaking to be regarded as dominant; see para. 48. See also Case 85/76, *Hoffmann-La Roche,* paras 57-58.
55. There can be special cases below this threshold where competitors are not sufficiently able to restrict the conduct of an undertaking and where there can therefore be dominance. Communication from the Commission – Guidance on the Commission's enforcement priorities in applying Article 82 of the EC Treaty to abusive exclusionary conduct by dominant undertakings, point 14 (OJ 2009 C 45/7).
56. In relation to mergers, this is indicated in Recital 32 of the Merger Control Regulation. See also *Ivo Van Bael & Jean-Francois Bellis:* Competition Law of the European Community, 2010 p.111.
57. Case 75/84, *Metro SB-Großmärkte* v *Commission (Metro II),* paras 85 and 86.
58. See e.g. Joined Cases T-24/93 and others, *CMB,* para. 78.
59. Thus, given that its closest competitors' market shares were 14.8 % and 6.3 %, in Case 85/76, *Hoffmann-La Roche,* the CJ found that the undertaking had a dominant position in the market for Vitamin C when it had a market share of 64.8 %.

several undertakings can form the basis for a finding of the existence of collective dominance.

Another factor that can be significant for deciding whether an undertaking is dominant is how the market share has developed over time.[60] If over a longer period an undertaking has had a very large market share, and undertakings with considerably smaller market shares are unable quickly to meet a demand which the undertaking in question no longer wishes to meet, this can mean that the undertaking is an indispensable business connection for its customers, and is therefore dominant.[61]

In Case 85/76, *Hoffmann-La Roche*, on the basis of an investigation into market shares over a period of three years, the CJ found that the undertaking had a dominant position. However, the practice of the courts has not defined precisely what is meant by a *longer period*, but seems to emphasise that it is relevant the undertaking has shown an ability to maintain a high market share for a sufficiently long time that it can have the kind of conduct that is characteristic of a dominant position.[62]

3.2.2. Other factors

In practice, when assessing whether an undertaking can be considered to have a dominant position on the relevant market, it is seldom sufficient to look only at the market share of the undertaking. Market share is thus calculated with regard to the actual competitive pressure which the undertaking is subject to. An assessment of an undertaking's market strength will often require other factors, which may express the potential competitive pressure, to be taken into consideration. While 'actual competition' refers to competition from undertakings which already produce or can switch at short notice to produce the relevant (substitutable) products and market them,[63] 'potential competitors' covers undertakings which only have the possibility, over the medium to long

60. Communication from the Commission – Guidance on the Commission's enforcement priorities in applying Article 82 of the EC Treaty to abusive exclusionary conduct by dominant undertakings, point 13 (OJ 2009 C 45/7).
61. Case 85/76, *Hoffmann-La Roche,* para. 41; and Case T-83/91, *Tetra Pak II,* para. 109.
62. Case 85/76, *Hoffmann-La Roche,* para. 41. However, the maintenance of a market share over a longer period does not automatically mean that the undertaking is dominant; Case 85/76, *Hoffmann-La Roche,* para. 44.
63. This is supported in point 20 of Commission Notice on the definition of relevant market for the purposes of Community competition law (OJ 1997 C 372/5).

term, of switching to the production of relevant (substitutable) products, as well as new entrants to the market.[64]

Potential competitive pressure from new competitors will be limited by barriers to entry to the market. The existence of such barriers is thus necessary for an undertaking to be able to maintain a dominant position, as the undertaking would not be able, in the longer term, to abuse its position in order to obtain a supernormal profit, without potential competitors thereby being attracted to a freely accessible market.[65]

When assessing whether an undertaking has a market share which makes it dominant within the meaning of Article 102, it is necessary to take into consideration whether there are any legal or actual barriers to entry to the market which make it difficult or impossible for potential competitors to enter the market in question in the longer term.

Such barriers to entry can be, for example, a monopoly based on law,[66] intellectual property rights,[67] or public regulation of the conduct of business in the market concerned.[68] The cost and competitive advantages of undertakings that are already established on a market will also be barriers to entry. For example, this can be the case with capital intensive investments (high sunk costs),[69] technological advances,[70] vertical integration – including a well developed distribution system,[71] and consumer preferences.[72] Finally, by its conduct on the market an undertaking can create barriers to entry, for example by entering into exclusive distribution arrangements, agreeing tied sales, giving loyalty discounts and by refusal of supply.

64. Argument by exception from point 20 of Commission Notice on the definition of relevant market for the purposes of Community competition law (OJ 1997 C 372/5).
65. Communication from the Commission – Guidance on the Commission's enforcement priorities in applying Article 82 of the EC Treaty to abusive exclusionary conduct by dominant undertakings, point 11 (OJ 2009 C 45/7)
66. Case 311/84, *CBEM,* para. 18; and Case C-260/89, *ERT*, para. 31.
67. Joined Cases C-241 and 242/91 P, *Magill,* para. 46.
68. Commission Decision *Decca Navigator System* (OJ 1989 L 43/27); and Commission Decision *British Midland/Aer Lingus* (OJ 1992 L 96/34).
69. Case 85/76, *Hoffmann-La Roche,* para. 33; and Case 27/76, *United Brands,* paras 122 and 123.
70. Case T-83/91, *Tetra Pak II,* para. 110; and Case 27/76, *United Brands,* paras 52-54.
71. Case 27/76, *United Brands.*
72. Commission Decision on interim measures in *BBI/Boosey & Hawkes,* para. 18 (OJ 1987 L 286/36).

3.3. The relevant market

The assessment of an undertaking's dominance of a market requires a definition to be made of the market in which, given its market share and the other relevant factors, the undertaking can have a dominant position. This market is referred to as the *relevant market*.

The relevant market is defined both by reference to the relevant product market and the relevant geographic market. In certain circumstances it can also be necessary to define the relevant market from a time perspective. The purpose of defining the relevant market is to identify the undertaking's actual competitors, in other words to define who, on the basis of effective competitive pressure, is able to restrict the conduct of the undertaking in question and thereby prevent it from acting independently. This determines whether there are in fact any competitors who can, at short notice, act as alternative sources of supply for the customers of the undertaking in question, both with regard to the relevant products and services, and with regard to the geographic location of the suppliers.[73]

The competitive pressure which is taken into consideration when defining the relevant market is, in particular, demand substitution and, under certain circumstances, supply substitution.[74] In economic terms, demand substitution is considered to be the competitive pressure which has the greatest disciplinary influence on an undertaking's pricing.[75] If an undertaking's customers can find alternative suppliers or substitutable products without difficulty, then that undertaking will not be able to behave independently in its pricing.

Supply-side substitution is taken into consideration if it has the same effective and direct effect as demand substitution. According to the Commission Notice on the definition of relevant market, this means that 'suppliers are able to switch production to the relevant products and market them in the short term without incurring significant additional costs or risks in response to small and permanent changes in relative prices'.[76] Conversely, it means

73. Commission Notice on the definition of relevant market for the purposes of Community competition law, point 13 (OJ 1997 C 372/5).
74. Potential competition, which constitutes the third cause of the restrictions on competition to which an undertaking is subject, is not taken into consideration in the definition of the relevant market; see Commission Notice on the definition of relevant market for the purposes of Community competition law, points 13 and 24 (OJ 1997 C 372/5). On the other hand, it is relevant in assessing the market strength of an undertaking in the relevant market.
75. Commission Notice on the definition of relevant market for the purposes of Community competition law, point 13 (OJ 1997 C 372/5).
76. Commission Notice on the definition of relevant market for the purposes of Community competition law, point 20 (OJ 1997 C 372/5).

that supply-side substitution is not taken into consideration when this 'would entail the need to adjust significantly existing tangible and intangible assets, additional investments, strategic decisions or time delays'.[77]

In determining whether there are any easily available alternative sources of supply for the customers of the undertaking in question, a test is made – the SSNIP test – which examines whether a hypothetical small permanent increase of 5-10 % of the relative price of the products concerned in the area concerned would make the undertaking's customers switch to substitution products or to other suppliers.[78] If the level of substitution is enough to make the price increase unprofitable because of the resulting loss of sales, additional substitutes and areas are included in the relevant market. This is done until the set of products and geographical areas is such that small, permanent increases in relative prices would be profitable. If on the other hand the increase means that the undertaking's customers switch to competing alternative sources of supply, and the price increase is unprofitable in relation to the fall in sales, the substitutable products and the alternative suppliers are part of the relative market.[79]

Once the relevant market has been defined, it is possible to calculate the market share of the undertaking concerned,[80] and thereby get a significant indication of the undertaking's market strength with a view to deciding whether it can be regarded as having a dominant position. The definition of the relevant market is thus central to the assessment of whether an undertaking has a dominant position. It is for this reason that the Commission's definition of the

77. Commission Notice on the definition of relevant market for the purposes of Community competition law, point 23 (OJ 1997 C 372/5). On supply-side substitution, see also points 20-23 of the Notice.
78. Commission Notice on the definition of relevant market for the purposes of Community competition law, point 17 (OJ 1997 C 372/5). The test is usually called the SSNIP test – 'small but significant non-transitory increase in price'. The Commission can also use other tests for evaluating demand substitution; see Commission Notice on the definition of relevant market for the purposes of Community competition law, point 39, including e.g. cross-price elasticities of demand for a product (OJ 1997 C 372/5).
79. Commission Notice on the definition of relevant market for the purposes of Community competition law, point 17 (OJ 1997 C 372/5). When there is a concentration of purchasing power, a corresponding test is carried out, but with the supplier as the starting point rather than the customers; see also point 17 of the Notice.
80. On the calculation of market shares, see Commission Notice on the definition of relevant market for the purposes of Community competition law, points 53-55 (OJ 1997 C 372/5).

relevant market will often be disputed in cases brought before the court for the annulment of decisions.

3.3.1. The relevant product market

The purpose of defining the relevant product market is to define which products are suitable for competing with the products of the undertaking in question. The key word in determining the product market is therefore *substitution* – seen from the consumer's point of view.[81] The relevant product market is therefore defined as 'all those products and/or services which are regarded as interchangeable or substitutable by the consumer, by reason of the products' characteristics, their prices and their intended use'.[82]

When considering which products or services should be regarded as substitutes for the products or services of the undertaking concerned, importance is attached to the physical similarities, characteristics and qualities,[83] differences in price, previous substitutions between products, the views of customers and competitors, consumer preferences, the obstacles and costs of redirecting demand to potential substitutes, as well as differences in the end use of the products.[84] Regardless of whether products can be regarded as substitutes on the basis of their characteristics and prices, they will only be considered part of the relevant market if there is such a degree of interchangeability

81. Commission Decision *British Sugar,* point 42 (OJ 1988 L 284/41), according to which liquid sugars and syrups were not substitutes for granulated sugar from the customer's point of view.
82. Commission Notice on the definition of relevant market for the purposes of Community competition law, point 7 (OJ 1997 C 372/5). See also Case 322/81, *Michelin,* para. 37; and Case C-333/94 P, *Tetra Pak II,* para. 63. For a more detailed statement of the basis for assessing the relevant product market, see points 35-43 of the Commission Notice, and the special considerations on Article 102 in point 56.
83. Case 85/76, *Hoffmann-La Roche,* according to which the individual vitamin groups which the undertaking produced constituted separate product markets, as the vitamins had different effects on the metabolism, and could therefore not be substituted by other vitamin groups. However, differences in product characteristics are not in themselves sufficient to exclude demand substitution, as this depends to a large extent on consumer perceptions of the different characteristics; see Commission Notice on the definition of relevant market for the purposes of Community competition law, point 36 (OJ 1997 C 372/5).
84. Commission Notice on the definition of relevant market for the purposes of Community competition law, points 37-43 (OJ 1997 C 372/5), where further factors are also listed.

for the same purposes that there is effective competition between the products.[85]

In determining whether two products can be substituted on the demand side, it is not always sufficient to concentrate exclusively on the characteristics and purposes of the products. Differences in competitive structure can thus result in the establishment of two separate product markets – for example, this is the case with the markets for original components and spare parts for cars.[86]

3.3.2. The relevant geographic market

The purpose of defining the relevant geographic market is to define which undertakings located in other geographic areas can be characterised as competitors to the undertaking concerned. The relevant geographic market is thus defined as 'the area in which the undertakings concerned are involved in the supply and demand of products or services, in which the conditions of competition are sufficiently homogeneous and which can be distinguished from neighbouring areas because the conditions of competition are appreciably different in those area.'[87]

The assessment of the extent of the relevant market for a product or service for the purposes of Article 102 will not necessarily be the same as an assessment for the purposes of the Merger Control Regulation. In examining a merger, the assessment of the relevant geographic market looks at future circumstances, in contrast to the assessment for the purposes of Article 102, where the assessment is based on the circumstances existing at the time when the disputed conduct arose.[88]

The relevant geographic market in relation to Article 102 will often cover the whole of the internal market. However, various factors can mean that the relevant market is narrowed to a limited part of the internal market, for example to an individual Member State, or regional[89] or local areas or facilities.[90] Nevertheless, in order to fall within the scope of Article 102, the relevant ge-

85. Case 322/81, *Michelin;* and Case C-62/86, *Akzo.*
86. Commission Notice on the definition of relevant market for the purposes of Community competition law, point 36 (OJ 1997 C 372/5).
87. Commission Notice on the definition of relevant market for the purposes of Community competition law, point 8 (OJ 1997 C 372/5).
88. Commission Notice on the definition of relevant market for the purposes of Community competition law, point 12 (OJ 1997 C 372/5); and see Chapter VIII, section 3.
89. Joined Cases 40/73 and others, *Suiker Unie,* concerning parts of Germany.
90. E.g. harbours, see Case C-179/90, *Porto di Genova;* and Case C-242/95, *GT-Link.*

ographic market must at least constitute a significant part of the internal market.

A restriction of the relevant geographic market so as only to cover part of the internal market will be due to the fact that the special competitive conditions which apply in the respective areas effectively limit the area where the undertaking competes. This will be the case where there is an appreciable difference in the competitive conditions on the relevant market and the conditions in the surrounding geographic areas. Thus, disproportionate transport costs[91] and special import arrangements[92] will limit the geographic market to a greater or lesser part of the internal market, just as national or local preferences in customers' purchasing habits,[93] sole rights provided by law,[94] and limits inherent in the subject of the case[95] will justify such a limitation.[96]

3.3.3. The relevant temporal market

In order to define which actual competitors are able to compete effectively with the undertaking in question, in some cases it is not enough to define the relevant market in the terms of the product market and the geographic

91. The transport costs associated with a product set a natural limit to how far it can be profitable to transport it. See also Commission Notice on the definition of relevant market for the purposes of Community competition law, point 57 (OJ 1997 C 372/5).
92. See Case 27/76, *United Brands,* where the Commission's definition of the relevant geographic market for bananas excluded the Member States which had special import arrangements for the benefit of selected banana-producing countries, because in these Member States the undertaking in question competed on different terms than in the Member States where there was an open market for bananas.
93. Case T-504/93, *Tiercé Ladbroke,* paras 103-107, which concerned the definition of the geographic market for sound and picture transmission of horse races. In this connection the CJ held that the competitive conditions in this market were determined by the conditions in the main market for betting, which was in turn characterised by a close geographic link between gamblers and bookmakers, as the gamblers' mobility was regarded as limited and marginal. On this basis the geographic market could be restricted to the national market.
94. Where an undertaking acquires a sole right, granted by law, to carry on a specific undertaking in a given area, the assumption must be that the geographic market is coextensive with this area. See Case 26/75, *General Motors;* and Case 226/84, *British Leyland.*
95. Joined Cases C-241 and 242/91 P, *Magill,* where the relevant geographic market for TV programme listings was limited to the area where it was possible for viewers to see the programmes referred to.
96. Commission Notice on the definition of relevant market for the purposes of Community competition law, points 29 and 44-52 (OJ 1997 C 372/5).

market, as it can also be necessary to assess the relevant time during which the relevant market exists.

Competitive and market conditions on the relevant market can change over time and this can be relevant to how the market should be defined.[97] Seasonally determined variations in the demand for the relevant product can be relevant to whether other products can exert effective competitive pressure and be regarded as substitutes.

> There was such a situation in Case 27/76, *United Brands*, where the CJ examined the relevant market for bananas. This product was offered on the market throughout the year. The CJ therefore found that only other fresh fruits which competed throughout the year, and did not provide only seasonal competition, could be regarded as substitutes for bananas. However, the CJ found that neither of the other fruits which were on the market throughout the year – apples and oranges – could be regarded as substitutes for bananas.

3.4. A substantial part of the internal market

As previously stated, the relevant geographic market for the purposes of Article 102 can be defined as the whole of the internal market or a greater or lesser part of it. According to the provision, for the application of Article 102 there is a requirement that the area which is defined as the relevant market should at least be a *substantial part* of the internal market. This requirement means that Article 102 does not apply to an undertaking which has a dominant position in an insignificant part of the internal market, and it therefore seems to have the same effect as the appreciability requirement in relation to Article 101.[98]

In assessing whether an area is big enough to constitute a substantial part of the internal market, the CJ takes into account the structure and extent of production and consumption of the product in question, as well as the cus-

97. Case 77/77, *BP*. Because of the shortage of supply during the oil crisis in 1973, it was not possible for BP's customers to get supplies from alternative sources. The Commission limited the duration of the relevant market so as to cover the period 1973-1974, and found that in this period BP had had a dominant position with regard to its customers. The CJ did not make a ruling on the definition of the market on this basis, but annulled the Commission's decision on the grounds that there had been no abuse.

98. See *Richard Whish:* EC Competition Law, 20129, p. 189; and *Jonathan Faull & Ali Nikpay (eds.):* The EC Law of Competition, 2007 section 4.135.

toms and economic possibilities of buyers and sellers.[99] The assessment of substantiality is thus not based purely on the geographic extent of the area in relation to the European Union as a whole,[100] but also on an assessment of the product market in the geographic area in question. Basically, this assessment involves a quantitative assessment of the market's economic importance in relation to the internal market as a whole.[101]

Where an undertaking is found to have a dominant position on the internal market as a whole, the substantiality requirement is naturally considered to be satisfied. This also seems to be the case where the market is defined as being the territory of a Member State,[102] regardless of the size of the Member State.[103] The CJ has also accepted that a dominant position in part of a Member State can fulfil the substantiality requirement.[104] Furthermore, due to their importance for transport, local facilities such as harbours and airports have been regarded as a substantial part of the internal market.[105]

4. Abuse

Under Article 102 of the Treaty, the conduct of an undertaking which is found to have a dominant position on the relevant market is restricted to the

99. Joined Cases 40/73 and others, *Suiker Unie,* para. 371.
100. See *Richard Whish:* EC Competition Law, 20129, p. 189. See also *Jens Fejø:* EU-konkurrenceret, 2003, where it is argued that it is not always clear whether the assessment of substantiality is made purely on the basis of the size of the territory, or whether an assessment of the economic position of the market in question is also included, see p. 188.
101. See *Jonathan Faull & Ali Nikpay (eds.):* The EC Law of Competition, 2007 section 4.136. See also Joined Cases 40/73 and others, *Suiker Unie,* where the CJ found that the market for sugar in Belgium and Luxembourg constituted a substantial part of the internal market.
102. Case 322/81, *Michelin,* para. 28; Case C-7/97, *Bronner,* para. 36; and Case C-340/99, *TNT Traco,* para. 43.
103. See *Jonathan Faull & Ali Nikpay (eds.):* The EC Law of Competition, 2007 section 4.137.
104. See, e.g. Joined Cases 40/73 and others, *Suiker Unie,* where the CJ found that the South German market constituted a substantial part of the internal market; and Case 22/78, *Hugin,* where the City of London was also considered to be a substantial part of the internal market.
105. With regard to harbours, see Case C-179/90, *Porto di Genova;* and Case C-242/95, *GT-Link.* See also Commission Decision 94/119 (OJ 1994 L 55/52), concerning Rødby harbour.

extent to which such conduct can be considered to be an abuse of its dominant position.

In Case 85/76, *Hoffmann-La Roche*, the CJ defined the concept of *abuse* as follows:

> 'The concept of abuse is an objective concept relating to the behaviour of an undertaking in a dominant position which is such as to influence the structure of a market where, as a result of the very presence of the undertaking in question, the degree of competition is weakened and which, through recourse to methods different from those which condition normal competition in products or services on the basis of the transactions of commercial operators, has the effect of hindering the maintenance of the degree of competition still existing in the market or the growth of that competition.'[106]

It is clear from this that the definition of abuse is an objective definition. Conduct which can be characterised as abuse is therefore covered by Article 102, regardless of whether the disputed conduct has in fact resulted in distortion of competition, and regardless of whether the undertaking concerned has intended the conduct whereby it abuses its dominant position.[107]

As stated in the introduction, Article 102 does not prohibit an undertaking either from acquiring or having a dominant position, nor does it prohibit an undertaking from strengthening its market position, as long as this is not a result of the abuse of its dominant position.

The special obligations which Article 102 imposes on dominant undertakings not to conduct themselves in a way which harms effective and undistorted competition in the internal market,[108] means that conduct, such as entering into exclusive purchasing arrangements or the use of discriminatory discount schemes, which could be considered normal and legitimate if carried out by non-dominant undertakings, can constitute abuse if there is the same conduct

106. Case 85/76, *Hoffmann-La Roche,* para. 91; and Case C-52/09, *TeliaSonera,* para. 27.
107. This means that the intentions of a dominant undertaking cannot excuse its conduct, but it can be relevant in connection with the setting of the amount of any fine. See the guidelines for the Commission's calculation of fines in Article 23(2)(a) in Council Regulation (EC) No 1/2003 on the implementation of the rules on competition laid down in Articles 81 and 82 of the Treaty, according to which the Commission can impose a fine, whether an undertaking infringes Article 102 intentionally or negligently. See also Chapter VII, section 6.1.
108. Case 322/81, *Michelin,* para. 57. See also *Ivo Van Bael & Jean-Francois Bellis:* Competition Law of the European Community, 2010 pp. 800-801.

on a market on which competition has already been weakened as a result of the existence of a dominant undertaking.[109] This means that a dominant undertaking cannot justify its conduct, for example in the form of tied sales, by claiming that its conduct is in accordance with trade practice.[110]

However, this special obligation does not mean that, in order to avoid infringing Article 102, dominant undertakings must remain altogether passive in the face of aggressive marketing by their competitors. Thus, the CJ recognises that a dominant undertaking is entitled to protect its commercial interests – 'meet competition' – by taking measures which are proportionate and appropriate in the circumstances.[111]

In Case 27/76, *United Brands*, the CJ thus stated:

> 'Although it is true, as the applicant points out, that the fact that an undertaking is in a dominant position cannot disentitle it from protecting its own commercial interests if they are attacked, and that such an undertaking must be conceded the right to take such reasonable steps as it deems appropriate to protect its said interests, such behaviour cannot be countenanced if its actual purpose is to strengthen this dominant position and abuse it.
>
> Even if the possibility of a counter-attack is acceptable that attack must still be proportionate to the threat taking into account the economic strength of the undertakings confronting each other.
>
> The sanction consisting of a refusal to supply by an undertaking in a dominant position was in excess of what might, if such a situation were to arise, reasonably be contemplated as a sanction for conduct similar to that for which UNC blamed Olesen.'[112]

An undertaking which, together with other undertakings, can be considered as collectively dominant is likewise restricted by this special obligation, regardless of whether the undertaking cannot in itself be considered dominant within the terms of Article 102.[113]

109. Case T-65/89, *BPB Industries*, paras 65-71 and 94.
110. Case T-83/91, *Tetra Pak II*, para. 137.
111. Case 27/76, *United Brands*, paras 189-190; Joined Cases T-24 to 26 and 28/93, *CMB*, para. 148; and Case T-228/97, *Irish Sugar*, para. 189.
112. Case 27/76, *United Brands*, paras 189-191. See also Case T-340/03, *France Télécom*, para. 185.
113. See the discussion in section 3.1.

The forms of abuse that are covered by Article 102 include both structural abuse and exploitative or exclusionary abuse, or a combination of these. 'Exploitative abuse' means behaviour which affects the dominant undertaking's immediate trading partners, such as unreasonable sales or purchasing prices or tied sales. In contrast, 'exclusionary abuse' affects the dominant undertaking's actual or potential competitors so that competition from these competitors is weakened or their access to the market is impeded. Such behaviour can include, for example, refusing to supply, or predatory pricing. In the last resort, both exploitative and exclusionary conduct can be harmful for consumers, as it can lead to a limited offering of goods on the market or abnormally high pricing. Finally, structural abuse can harm effective competition on the market. Structural abuse will exist where, for example, a dominant undertaking takes over competing undertakings and thus effectively eliminates the competition.[114]

When it is established that an undertaking has abused its dominant position, the Commission has the powers to order the undertaking in question to bring the abuse to an end.[115] In this connection the Commission is empowered, while complying with the principle of proportionality, to impose on undertakings the necessary behavioural or structural remedies. However, structural remedies should only be imposed if there are no less burdensome behavioural remedies that are equally effective. Thus, changes to the structure of an undertaking, as it existed before the infringement of Article 102 was committed, will only be proportionate in relation to the infringement if there is a material risk of continual or repeated infringements which are caused by the undertaking's structure.

4.1. Examples of abuse

The second paragraph of Article 102 of the Treaty contains a non-exhaustive list of examples of conduct that may constitute abuse covered by the provision.[116] There follows a presentation of the different kinds of abuse covered by the provision, and examples are also given of other forms of abuse which can likewise be covered by Article 102 according to the practice of the courts.

4.1.1. Article 102, second paragraph, sub-paragraph (a)

According to Article 102, second paragraph, sub-paragraph (a), abuse may consist of the dominant undertaking directly or indirectly imposing unfair

114. Case 6/72, *Continental Can.* Such mergers may be subject to an assessment under the Merger Control Regulation – see the discussion in Chapter VIII.
115. Council Regulation (EC) No 1/2003 on the implementation of the rules on competition laid down in Articles 81 and 82 of the Treaty (OJ 2003 L 1/1).
116. Case C-52/09, *TeliaSonera,* para. 26.

purchase or selling prices or other unfair trading conditions on trading partners.

Unreasonably high selling prices

A dominant undertaking can be tempted to exploit its market position and impose unreasonably high selling prices on its customers for goods or services, or, where a purchaser has a dominant position, to require unreasonably low prices from its suppliers. This typical form of abusive conduct, whereby the dominant undertaking takes an above normal profit, falls under Article 102, second paragraph, sub-paragraph (a).

In judging whether the price of goods or services is unreasonable, in its practice the CJ attaches importance to the relationship between the price and the economic value of the product – the price must thus be reasonable in relation to the economic value of the product or of the service performed.[117]

The assessment of whether this is the case involves an objective judgment, whereby the sales price of the product in question is compared with its production costs.[118]

However, it is not possible to calculate the production costs of a product with sufficient certainty in all cases. In such cases the price of the product can be compared with the price of equivalent products from other undertakings or in other Member States in order to obtain an indication of whether the undertaking has abused its dominant position by setting an unreasonably high price for the product.[119]

In relation to intellectual property rights, the assessment whether the price for a protected product is unreasonably high must take into account the entitlement of the owner of the right to cover the production costs, to obtain a reasonable profit, and to cover the costs of research and development.[120] This entitlement may thus, to some extent, explain any price difference between the product and equivalent products in other Member States.

In practice, the provisions of Article 102, second paragraph, sub-paragraph (a) have only occasionally been applied in this context. Among other things this is because it is difficult to determine whether a price is unreasonable, and

117. Case C-242/95, *GT-Link,* para. 39; and Case C-385/07, *Der Grüne Punkt,* para. 142.
118. Case 27/76, *United Brands,* para. 251.
119. Case 24/67, *Parke Davis;* Case 40/70, *Sirena;* and Case 78/70, *Deutsche Grammophon.* See also Joined Cases 110/88 and others, *Lucazeau;* and Case 395/87, *Tournier.*
120. Case 53/87, *Renault,* para. 17. See also Case 24/67, *Parke Davis.*

market forces will normally be sufficient in themselves to press unreasonably high prices down to a normal level.

Other unfair trading conditions

Other unfair trading conditions can be imposed by a dominant undertaking, both in its capacity as a purchaser[121] and as a seller.[122] In assessing whether trading conditions are unfair, an overall assessment is made, where among other things there is a focus on the burdensome element in relation to the advantages which the trading partner obtains on the basis of the trading agreement, as well as the interest of the dominant undertaking in maintaining the trading conditions.[123]

For example, there can be unfair trading conditions where the trading partner binds itself to obtain permission from the dominant undertaking for the transfer of equipment bought from the dominant undertaking,[124] or where the members of an association impose restrictions on the conduct of their business to a greater extent than is necessary for the association to achieve its aims.[125]

4.1.2. Predatory pricing

A dominant undertaking can try to force competitors out of the market or prevent new competitors entering the market by setting prices at below the level of the undertaking's costs.[126] Once competitors have been excluded, the undertaking can then raise its prices to a level which lies above that which would apply in a competitive market, and recover the losses suffered by the price reduction.[127] According to the practice of the courts, such predatory

121. Case 127/73, *BRT II.*
122. See for example the Commission Decision in *Tetra Pak II* (OJ 1992 L 72/1).
123. Case 127/73, *BRT II.*
124. Commission Decision in *Tetra Pak II* (OJ 1992 L 72/1).
125. Case 127/73, *BRT II,* where the CJ held that there could be abuse in cases where a copyright protection association required a new member to transfer all existing and future copyright to the association, and the right to exploit these rights would remain with the association for five years following the termination of membership. See also Case 247/86, *Alsatel;* and Case C-250/92, *Gøttrup-Klim.*
126. Communication from the Commission – Guidance on the Commission's enforcement priorities in applying Article 82 of the EC Treaty to abusive exclusionary conduct by dominant undertakings, point 63 (OJ 2009 C 45/7).
127. However, in order to establish the existence of predatory pricing it is not necessary to prove that the loss can be recovered. See Case T-340/03, *France Télécom,* para. 228; and Case T83/91, *Tetra Pak II,* para. 150.

pricing can constitute an abuse which is covered by Article 102.[128] The CJ has stated in Case C-62/86, *Akzo*:

> 'Prices below average variable costs (that is to say, those which vary depending on the quantities produced) by means of which a dominant undertaking seeks to eliminate a competitor must be regarded as abusive. A dominant undertaking has no interest in applying such prices except that of eliminating competitors so as to enable it subsequently to raise its prices by taking advantage of its monopolistic position, since each sale generates a loss, namely the total amount of the fixed costs (that is to say, those which remain constant regardless of the quantities produced) and, at least, part of the variable costs relating to the unit produced.'[129]
>
> 'Moreover, prices below average total costs, that is to say, fixed costs plus variable costs, but above average variable costs, must be regarded as abusive if they are determined as part of a plan for eliminating a competitor. Such prices can drive from the market undertakings which are perhaps as efficient as the dominant undertaking but which, because of their smaller financial resources, are incapable of withstanding the competition waged against them.'[130]

Thus, if a dominant undertaking sets *prices that are lower than the average variable costs* (AVC), there will be an assumption that there is predatory pricing which is contrary to Article 102.[131] However, this assumption can be overturned if it can be shown that the conduct is due circumstances other than the wish to eliminate a competitor, for example the wish to reduce stocks of perishable goods, or to match a competitor's offer.[132] However, a dominant undertaking cannot claim a general or absolute right to match its competitors' prices as a justification for its conduct,[133] but in relation to specific customers it will have the possibility of matching the prices at which another producer would be able to supply.[134]

128. Case 298/83, *CICCE.*
129. Case C-62/86, *Akzo,* para. 71.
130. Case C-62/86, *Akzo,* para. 72.
131. Case T-83/91, *Tetra Pak II,* para. 150; and Case T-340/03, *France Télécom,* para. 130.
132. See *Jonathan Faull & Ali Nikpay (eds.):* The EC Law of Competition, 2007 section 4.287.
133. Case T-340/03, *France Télécom,* para. 187.
134. Case T-340/03, *France Télécom,* para. 179, with reference to Commission Decision 83/462, *Akzo.*

If prices are *above the average variable costs*, but *below the average total costs* (ATC), and thus not profitable in the longer term, the Commission must show that the undertaking has the intention of eliminating a competitor, before Article 102 becomes applicable.[135]

In this connection, setting *prices that are higher than the average total costs* will not be considered an abuse under the terms of Article 102, but could be regarded as abuse in connection with a selective price reduction.

While in the *Akzo* case the CJ used both AVC and AVT methods for calculating costs,[136] in its 2009 Communication the Commission stated that it would use average avoidable cost (AAC) and long-run average incremental cost (LRAIC) as cost benchmarks.[137]

Among other things, the use of LRAIC as a benchmark leads in some cases to certain commercial sectors having cost structures which mean that the *Akzo* test is not suitable for determining the existence of predatory pricing. For example, in the telecommunications, oil and gas industries, the cost structures are characterised by having very high fixed costs and very low variable costs, so the average variable costs are so low that it is virtually impossible for there to be predatory pricing.[138]

The Commission applied this standard for covering costs in the *Deutsche Post* case and assessed as follows:

> 'In the period 1990 to 1995 DPAG's revenue from mail-order parcels was below the incremental costs of providing this specific service (see table 3). This means that in the period 1990 to 1995 every sale by DPAG in the mail-order parcel services business represented a loss which comprises all the capacity-maintenance costs and at least part of the additional costs of

135. Such an intention to exclude a competitor was established in Case T-83/91, *Tetra Pak II,* see para. 151. The decision was confirmed by the CJ in Case C-333/94 P.
136. This practice has subsequently been confirmed in, among others, Case T-340/03, *France Télécom,* para. 130, a decision upheld in Case C-202/07 P, *France Télécom.* Similarly the Commission has previously used these methods in Commission Decision COMP/38.233, *Wanadoo Interactive,* where the Commission concluded that Wanadoo Interactive had abused its dominant position in the market for household access to high-speed internet access with predatory pricing of its services.
137. Communication from the Commission – Guidance on the Commission's enforcement priorities in applying Article 82 of the EC Treaty to abusive exclusionary conduct by dominant undertakings, points 26 and 64 (OJ 2009 C 45/7). For further on the different costing methods and calculations, see *Caroline Heide-Jørgensen* et al.: Konkurrenceretten i EU, 2009 pp. 708-712.
138. See *Richard Whish:* EC Competition Law, 2012, pp. 747-748.

providing the service. In such circumstances, every additional sale not only entailed the loss of at least part of these additional costs, but made no contribution towards covering the carrier's capacity-maintenance costs. In the medium term, such a pricing policy is not in the carrier's own economic interest. This being so, DPAG had no economic interest in offering such a service in the medium term. DPAG could increase its overall result by either raising prices to cover the additional costs of providing the service or – where there is no demand for this service at a higher price – to discontinue providing the service, because revenue gained from its provision is below the additional costs incurred in providing it. However, DPAG, by remaining in this market without any foreseeable improvement in revenue restricted the activities of competitors which are in a position to offer this service at a price that covers their costs.'[139]

On this basis the Commission concluded that in the period 1990-1995, Deutsche Post had infringed Article 102 by supplying parcel services at prices below the additional costs of providing those services.[140]

4.1.3. Article 102, second paragraph, sub-paragraph (b)

According to Article 102, second paragraph, sub-paragraph (b), a dominant undertaking can be found to have abusive conduct if it limits production, marketing or technical development to the prejudice of consumers. Thus, depending on the circumstances, the provision can cover abuse in the form of refusal to supply,[141] restriction of production with a view to creating the possibility for increasing prices and profits,[142] imposing an obligation on a dealer to restrict its exports,[143] and by hindering technical development.[144]

139. Commission Decision COMP/35.141, *Deutsche Post,* para. 36 (OJ 2001 L 125/27).
140. Commission Decision COMP/35.141, *Deutsche Post,* para. 30 (OJ 2001 L 125/27).
141. Joined Cases C-241 and 242/91 P, *Magill;* and the Commission Decision in *Sabena* (OJ 1988 L 317/47).
142. See e.g. the Commission Decision in *British Sugar* (OJ 1988 L 284/41); the Commission Decision in *Sabena* (OJ 1988 L 317/47); and Commission Decision in *BPB Industries* (OJ 1989 L 10/50).
143. Case 40/73, *Suiker Unie,* paras 396-402.
144. Case T-51/89, *Tetra Pak;* and Case C-179/90, *Porto di Genova.*

Refusal to supply

In principle undertakings are free to choose their trading partners. However, if a dominant undertaking refuses to supply a trading partner, with the result that competition is significantly restricted, this could constitute abuse within the meaning of Article 102, unless the refusal is objectively justified.[145] In such a case, with a view to promoting competition in the short term and depending on the circumstances, it may be possible to order the dominant undertaking to supply the trading partner in question.

However the breach of the principle of freedom to choose trading partners is not without problems. Thus, there is a risk that competition will be weakened in the longer term as, out of concern that trading partners can obtain their goods, undertakings will be deprived of the incentive to make investments in developing new production or distribution facilities or production methods, just as trading partners, who can gain access to the goods of other producers on the basis of Article 102, will lose the incentive to invest themselves in competitive facilities and methods.[146] The obligation to supply should thus be imposed with care, having regard to intervention in the freedom of contract of the dominant undertaking, and only after carefully weighing regard for competition in the short term against consideration for promoting competition in the longer term.

A refusal to supply can relate to products, services, information,[147] the issue of licences,[148] as well as denial of access to important facilities or infrastructure,[149] and it can be directed at both existing and new customers.[150]

145. Case T-201/04, *Microsoft,* para. 319.
146. Communication from the Commission – Guidance on the Commission's enforcement priorities in applying Article 82 of the EC Treaty to abusive exclusionary conduct by dominant undertakings, point 75 (OJ 2009 C 45/7).
147. Commission Decision, *Decca Navigator System* (OJ 1989 L 43/27); the XIVth Report on Competition Policy, 1984, points 94-95 concerning *IBM;* and the XXXth Report on Competition Policy, 2000 p. 164 concerning *Microsoft.*
148. See e.g. Case T-201/04, *Microsoft,* para. 331, concerning the refusal to supply information to competitors about interoperability; and the preliminary ruling of the CJ in Case C-418/01, *IMS Health/ NDC Health,* para. 38, on the refusal to grant a licence to use a copyright protected brick structure used to supply regional sales data for pharmaceutical products in a Member State.
149. Commission Decision 94/19/EC, *Sea Containers* v *Stena Sealink* (OJ 1994 L 15/8); and Commission Decision 92/213/EEC, *British Midland* (OJ 1992 L 96/34).
150. Communication from the Commission – Guidance on the Commission's enforcement priorities in applying Article 82 of the EC Treaty to abusive exclusionary conduct by dominant undertakings, point 84 (OJ 2009 C 45/7).

Where a refusal to supply affects an existing customer, the refusal can constitute abuse if, for example, the refusal to supply involves a clear risk that competition from a customer in a downstream stage of distribution[151] or on a related market[152] will be eliminated, or if the existing customer is prevented from establishing itself on the supplier's market.[153] However, there can also be abuse where a dominant undertaking refuses to supply an existing customer who does not compete directly with the dominant undertaking, for example with a view to preventing the trading partner starting to trade with a competing product.[154] In this context, instead of refusing to supply, a dominant undertaking can restrict competition by means of a margin squeeze, whereby the dominant undertaking demands a price for the product in the upstream market which, in relation to the price taken by the dominant undertaking in the downstream market, would not give an equally effective competitor the possibility of carrying on long-term profitable trading in the downstream market.[155]

If a refusal to supply affects new trading partners, with a view to preventing their entry into the market, Article 102 will also be applicable. This is so regardless of whether the new trading partner is an actual or potential competitor to the dominant undertaking.[156]

In determining whether there is a refusal of supply contrary to Article 102, the Commission will have regard for (1) whether the refusal concerns a product or a service that is objectively necessary for enabling an undertaking to compete effectively in a down stream market, (2) whether the refusal is capable of preventing effective competition on the down stream market, and (3) whether the refusal will be to the disadvantage of consumers.[157]

151. Joined Cases 6 and 7/73, *Commercial Solvents,* para. 25.
152. Case 311/84, *CBEM;* and Case C-18/88, *RTT.*
153. Commission Decision in *BBI/Boosey & Hawkes* (OJ 1987 L 286/36); and Commission Decision in *British Sugar* (OJ 1988 L 284/41).
154. Case 27/76, *United Brands,* para. 182.
155. Communication from the Commission – Guidance on the Commission's enforcement priorities in applying Article 82 of the EC Treaty to abusive exclusionary conduct by dominant undertakings, point 80 (OJ 2009 C 45/7).
156. Joined Cases C-241 and 242/91 P, *Magill;* Commission Decision in *Sabena* (OJ 1988 L 317/47); and Commission Decision in *British Midland* (OJ 1992 L 96/34).
157. Communication from the Commission – Guidance on the Commission's enforcement priorities in applying Article 82 of the EC Treaty to abusive exclusionary conduct by dominant undertakings, point 81, with further discussion in points 83-88, (OJ 2009 C 45/7).

The application of Article 102 presupposes that the refusal to supply cannot be objectively justified,[158] or are otherwise justified by relevant effectivity gains.[159] In this context, a dominant undertaking's desire to remove existing customers from the market because it wishes to begin production of products corresponding to those of the customer is not an objective justification for refusing supply.[160] The same was the case in relation to refusal to supply because the repair of the products (cash machines) required special technical skills,[161] as well as the desire to avoid losing market share to a new competitor.[162] On the other hand, lack of capacity or the customer's payment problems will be objectively justified grounds for refusing to supply.

Essential facilities
An essential facility is defined by the Commission as being some facility or infrastructure to which it is necessary for competitors to have access in order to be able to provide services to their customers.[163]

Where the owner of such a facility – for example a harbour or a telephone network – denies an actual or potential competitor access to the facility in question, or gives the competitor access but on discriminatory terms, then under certain circumstances this can constitute an abuse of a dominant position under Article 102, so that the owner can be required to give the trading partner access to the facilities on the same terms as those that are used for the dominant undertaking's own service provision.

As stated above, such an intervention in the freedom of contract of the owner of the facility should be made with care, and only after a careful assessment of whether consideration for promoting competition in the short term, by giving a trading partner access to the facility, outweighs the possible harmful effects on competition in the longer term, because of the reduced in-

158. A dominant undertaking can take reasonable and proportionate measures necessary to protect its own trading interests; see Joined Cases C-468-478/06, *GlaxoSmithKline,* paras 69-71, on the refusal to supply medicinal products to wholesalers that were engaged in parallel exporting.
159. On the more detailed assessment of effectivity gains in connection with refusals of supply, see Communication from the Commission – Guidance on the Commission's enforcement priorities in applying Article 82 of the EC Treaty to abusive exclusionary conduct by dominant undertakings, points 89-90 (OJ 2009 C 45/7).
160. Joined Cases 6 and 7/73, *Commercial Solvents.*
161. Commission Decision in *Hugin* (OJ 1978 L 22/23).
162. Commission Decision in *British Midland* (OJ 1992 L 96/34).
163. Commission Decision on interim measures in *Sea Containers/Stena Link,* point 66 (OJ 1994 L 15/8).

centive to invest in the development and construction of such essential facilities.

The principle of essential facilities is closely connected with the question of refusal of supply, and the Commission assesses it on the basis of the same principles referred to above.[164] The application of the principle of essential facilities presupposes that the facilities in question are *essential*, in the sense that it is necessary for an undertaking's access to the market that it should have access to the facilities in question.[165] It must thus be either impossible or extraordinarily difficult, due to physical, geographic or legal restrictions, or there must be an insurmountable financial burden for the competitor to create a corresponding facility.[166]

It is also a requirement for the application of the principle of essential facilities that there is no objective justification for denying a trading partner access to the facility in question. Security or technical reasons, as well as limited capacity, will presumably be legitimate grounds.

The application of the principle concerning essential facilities has been raised in several cases concerning the denial of access to transport facilities. This has especially concerned harbours, where the Commission has assessed denial of access in relation to Rødby Harbour,[167] Helsingør Harbour,[168] Roscoff Harbour,[169] as well as Holyhead Harbour.[170] Access to facilities in the air transport sector has also been assessed in several of the Commission's decisions; see for example access for the provision of ground handling services,[171] access to underground pipes for providing fuel to aircraft,[172] and access to a computerised reservation system.[173] The principle concerning essen-

164. Communication from the Commission – Guidance on the Commission's enforcement priorities in applying Article 82 of the EC Treaty to abusive exclusionary conduct by dominant undertakings, point 78 (OJ 2009 C 45/7).
165. Case C-7/97, *Bronner,* where the CJ did not accept Bronner's claim that the facility was essential.
166. See the Opinion of Advocate General Jacobs in Case C-7/97, *Bronner.*
167. Commission Decision in *Rødby Havn* (OJ 1994 L 55/52).
168. XXVIth Report on Competition Policy, 1996 point 131.
169. XXVth Report on Competition Policy, 1995 pp. 120-121.
170. Commission Decision on interim measures in *Sea Containers/Stena Link* (OJ 1994 L 15/8).
171. Commission Decision in *Flughafen Frankfurt/Main* (OJ 1998 L 72/30).
172. See the *Disma* case in the XXIIIth Report on Competition Policy, 1993 points 223-224.
173. Commission Decision in *Sabena* (OJ 1988 L 317/47). See, conversely, in the rail transport sector, Joined Cases T-374 and 375, 384 and 388/94, *European Night Services.*

tial facilities can also be relevant in the liberalised sectors, where the Commission has in particular set out the principles relating to access agreements in the telecommunications sector.[174]

4.1.4. *Article 102, second paragraph, sub-paragraph (c)*

According to Article 102, second paragraph, sub-paragraph (c), a dominant undertaking can abuse its market dominance if it applies dissimilar conditions to equivalent transactions with different trading partners, thereby placing a trading partner at a competitive disadvantage. The provision covers discriminatory pricing as well as other forms of discrimination, for example in the form of refusal to supply or discriminatory business terms.

This means that a dominant undertaking's pricing policy can be an expression of abuse covered by Article 102. For example, if an undertaking practises discriminatory discount or bonus schemes, or if the undertaking sets unreasonably high or low prices, or even predatory prices, this can have both an exploitative and an exclusionary effect.

Discriminatory pricing can be directed against specific customers or groups of customers with the aim of increasing the undertaking's profits by making customers who value the product most pay a higher price than others. Discrimination can also be based on the nationality of trading partners,[175] or involve geographic price discrimination by applying different prices in different Member States.[176]

Likewise, depending on the circumstances, a dominant undertaking's use of selective pricing can be covered by Article 102. Selective pricing can be seen, for example, in the form of price reductions, whereby the undertaking reduces its prices for certain trading partners with a view either to retaining an existing customer or to capturing a chosen customer from a competitor.[177]

Discount arrangements

Undertakings often offer their customers various forms of discounts or bonuses as part of ordinary customer care and price competition. Such discount and bonus arrangements can involve price discrimination which is covered by

174. Notice on the application of the competition rules to access agreements in the telecommunications sector – framework, relevant markets and principles (OJ 1998 C 265/2).
175. Case T-83/91, *Tetra Pak II.*
176. Case 27/76, *United Brands.*
177. Case T-228/97, *Irish Sugar;* Case T-30/89, *Hilti;* and Joined Cases C-395 and 396/96 P, *CMB.*

Article 102, in the form of applying dissimilar conditions – in this case dissimilar prices – to equivalent transactions with other trading partners. However, there will not only be price discrimination where a dominant undertaking uses *differing prices*. The application of the *same prices* in circumstances that are not comparable will also involve price discrimination. This can be the case where an undertaking uses the same price for goods delivered carriage free, without regard for where the customer is located in relation to the producer, so that a customer located closest to the producer does not have the opportunity of taking advantage of the low transport costs.[178]

It must nevertheless be assumed that a dominant undertaking can use the same prices for trading partners in comparable situations, as it can hardly be required that the dominant undertaking should take into account individual differences in each customer's cost profile.[179]

A discount or bonus scheme which, on the face of it, seems to involve different treatment for the customers of an undertaking will not be considered discriminatory as long as the differences in treatment are objectively justified by the market situation or can otherwise be justified on the grounds of effectivity gains.[180] Thus, it is not considered to be discriminatory if a discount reflects cost savings which the dominant undertaking has in relation to the customer. Depending on the circumstances, a dominant undertaking can offer a discount which is based on lower transport costs, cash payment, quantity, differences in the costs of maintaining a distribution network in different areas etc.

Quantity discounts, which are offered automatically according to the quantity which a customer buys from a dominant undertaking, will usually be an expression for a normal difference in prices which does not involve a discriminatory difference in treatment of the undertaking's customers. Where such discounts merely reflect the cost savings obtained by the dominant undertaking in selling the quantity in question, compared with selling smaller quantities, the scheme will not normally be objectionable under Article 102. However, quantity discounts could be covered by Article 102 where the quantity which a customer must buy in order to benefit from the discount amounts to the greater part of the customer's needs, or where the discount

178. Commission Decision in *British Sugar* (OJ 1988 L 284/41).

179. See *Katja Høegh:* Hvor snævre grænser gælder for større virksomheder og dominerende virksomheders rabat og bonussystemer?, UfR 2002B.32, at p. 37.

180. Communication from the Commission – Guidance on the Commission's enforcement priorities in applying Article 82 of the EC Treaty to abusive exclusionary conduct by dominant undertakings, point 46 (OJ 2009 C 45/7).

scheme is so arranged that, for example, only certain larger trading partners can in fact benefit from the scheme.[181]

In addition to being discriminatory, discount and bonus schemes can also have the effect of tying-in the undertaking's customer base. Thus it may be that loyalty discounts are only given on condition that the customer buys all or most of its purchases from the dominant undertaking.[182] In this way the dominant undertaking deprives its trading partners of any financial incentive to switch to a competing supplier as this would only be beneficial to the customer if the competitor could offer discounts which would compensate for the discounts which the customer would lose by switching supplier.[183] This form of discount thus has, *de facto*, the same effect as an exclusive purchasing agreement.[184] Loyalty discounts do not relate to cost savings and will therefore usually fall foul of the prohibition in Article 102.

The effect of loyalty discounts in tying-in customers can also be achieved by, among other things, 'top slice' discounts and discounts related to specific purchase targets, as such discounts give great incentives to customers to buy all their purchases from the dominant undertaking.

Top slice discounts are used when a trading partner has bought its core quantity from the dominant undertaking and, by offering a particularly large discount, the dominant undertaking seeks to give the trading partner the incentive to buy additional quantities from it – extra quantities which the trading partner might otherwise have bought from a competitor.[185]

Discount schemes which are tied to the customer reaching a specific purchase target do not necessarily require the trading partner to make all or a large part of its purchases from the dominant undertaking. Therefore, the

181. See for example the case of *Brussels Airport,* in the Commission's XIXth Report on Competition Policy, 1989 para. 50.
182. See e.g. Commission Decision COMP/37.990, *Intel.*
183. Communication from the Commission – Guidance on the Commission's enforcement priorities in applying Article 82 of the EC Treaty to abusive exclusionary conduct by dominant undertakings, point 40 (OJ 2009 C 45/7).
184. Case 85/76, *Hoffmann-La Roche,* para. 89. See also Joined Cases 40/73 and others, *Suiker Unie,* paras 518-528. According to the Commission, an exclusive purchasing obligation is one which 'requires a customer on a particular market to purchase exclusively or to a large extent only from the dominant undertaking'; see Communication from the Commission – Guidance on the Commission's enforcement priorities in applying Article 82 of the EC Treaty to abusive exclusionary conduct by dominant undertakings, point 33 (OJ 2009 C 45/7). See e.g. Case 322/81, *Michelin,* para. 210; and Case T-65/89, *BPB Industries,* paras 65-77.
185. Commission Decision *Solvay* (OJ 1990 L 152/21).

compliance of such discount schemes with Article 102 will often depend on the length of the reference period against which the discount is calculated, and on whether the conditions for obtaining the discount are objective and transparent. In this context, a reference period of one year will not be acceptable, while a reference period of three months seems to be acceptable.[186]

The question of dominant undertakings' use of marketing contributions does not seem to have been assessed in relation to EU law. However, the question has been the subject of consideration by the Danish competition authorities in connection with the *Arla* dairy products company's use of such contributions. The Danish competition authorities found that such contributions should be assessed according to the same principles as those used in relation to the evaluation of discount schemes. Thus the Danish Competition Council has stated that:

> 'Just as dominant undertakings can give their customers various discounts, when this is justified on cost grounds, in certain situations it must also be possible for dominant undertakings to give customers various forms of marketing contributions. On the basis of analogy, different marketing contributions can be given when it can be shown that the contribution primarily benefits the supplier – and not the retailer – and when it is neither the purpose nor the consequence of giving the contribution that other suppliers are excluded.'[187]

4.1.5. Article 102, second paragraph, sub-paragraph (d)

According to Article 102, second paragraph, sub-paragraph (d), there will also be abuse where a dominant undertaking makes the entering into a contract subject to acceptance by the other party of supplementary obligations which, by their nature or according to commercial usage, have no connection with the subject of such contracts.

Tied sales

Tied sales can take various forms. 'Tying' covers sales whereby, in order to obtain a right to buy the product or service required (the primary product), a

186. Case 322/81, *Michelin,* concerning a reference period of one year; and Commission Decision, *Coca-Cola* (OJ 1997 L 218/15), where the reference period was voluntarily reduced to three months.
187. Decision of the Danish Competition Council of 30 March 2005, *Arla Foods rabatter og markedsføringstilskud,* Journal No: 3/1120-0289-0055, para. 66 (unofficial translation).

trading partner must also agree to buy supplementary products or services (the secondary product). 'Bundling' refers to the usual way in which products are offered for sale and priced, including situations where products are only sold together in fixed ratios, and where products can be bought individually, but the combination of individual prices is higher than the 'bundled' price.[188]

Tied sales may occur where an undertaking has a dominant position on the market for the tying product (the primary product), and can exploit this dominant position to reserve to itself a derived or associated market, by forcing contracting parties to accept supplementary products or services (the secondary product). The undertaking will not necessarily have a dominant position on the market for the secondary product, but can use tying-in arrangements to strengthen its position on secondary market, at the expense of consumers and competitors. Thus, in certain circumstances, the conduct of a dominant undertaking on markets other than the one in which it is dominant can constitute abuse contrary to Article 102.[189]

First, the supplementary transaction in a tied sale can consist of the contracting trading partner agreeing to buy other products from the dominant undertaking – the tied products. This kind of tied sale is referred to as a 'tie-in agreement'. The price of the tied-in products will often be above the market price, so that not only is the trading partner forced to buy the tied-in products, but it is also forced to buy them on less favourable terms than could be obtained elsewhere.

Second, the supplementary transaction can consist of the contracting trading partner agreeing not to buy the tied products from other specified suppliers. This exclusionary conduct thus shuts out competitors from the derived or associated market. This type of tied sale is referred to as a 'tie-out agreement'.

Tied sales agreements can thus contain elements which are both exploitative and exclusionary.

For the prohibition in Article 102 to apply in connection with tied sales, the conditional supplementary transaction should not by its nature, or by commercial usage, be connected to the subject of the agreement.

In determining this, in connection with *products that are not new*, attention is paid to whether, from a consumer's point if view, the tying and the tied products are regarded as the same product or as separate products. According

188. Communication from the Commission – Guidance on the Commission's enforcement priorities in applying Article 82 of the EC Treaty to abusive exclusionary conduct by dominant undertakings, point 48 (OJ 2009 C 45/7).
189. Case C-52/09, *TeliaSonera,* para. 85.

to the Commission, it will be assumed that there are separate products if, from the purchasers point of view if 'in the absence of tying or bundling, a substantial number of customers would purchase or would have purchased the tying product without also buying the tied product from the same supplier, thereby allowing stand-alone production for both the tying and the tied product'.[190] For example, if a media player and an operating system are sold together, this will be a tied sale,[191] while it is natural to buy shoes and shoelaces together.[192] However, the result of this assessment can change over time, in line with product developments and changes to trade customs and consumer preferences. For example, while it was previously usual to buy surf boards and rigs as a composite product, this is no longer the case.

With *new products*, for example in the fields of IT or multimedia, it is naturally not possible to apply the same consumer perspective. In these cases the decision will probably depend on whether the tied sale is objectively justified.[193]

Regardless of whether it is found that, because of the nature of the products or because it is in line with commercial usage, the tied products are sold as a whole, the tied-in sale could be covered by Article 102 if the dominant undertaking cannot show that the tied-in sale is objectively justified and is in accordance with the principle of proportionality.[194] For example, the sale may be justified by regard for efficiency, whereby the dominant undertaking can reduce its costs or obtain technical or qualitative advantages.[195] However, it seems that this bears a high evidential burden.[196]

190. Communication from the Commission – Guidance on the Commission's enforcement priorities in applying Article 82 of the EC Treaty to abusive exclusionary conduct by dominant undertakings, point 51 (OJ 2009 C 45/7).
191. Case T-201/04, *Microsoft,* paras 917, 921 and 922.
192. Case T-30/89, *Hilti,* on tied sales of cartridge magazines and nails for nail guns; and Case T-83/91, *Tetra Pak II,* concerning tied sales of filling machines and cartons for the packaging of liquid foods.
193. See *Richard Whish:* Competition Law, 2012, p. 692.
194. Case 333/94 P, *Tetra Pak II,* para. 37; and Case T-201/04, *Microsoft,* para. 942.
195. Communication from the Commission – Guidance on the Commission's enforcement priorities in applying Article 82 of the EC Treaty to abusive exclusionary conduct by dominant undertakings, point 62 (OJ 2009 C 45/7).
196. Case 333/94 P, *Tetra Pak II,* para. 138.

5. The effect on trade

An undertaking's abuse of its dominant position is only prohibited to the extent that trade between the Member States is affected by the abuse; see Article 102. In this context, the effect on trade covers not only traditional cross-border trade in goods and services, but any form of effect on cross-border economic activities between at least two Member States, including an effect on the competitive structure of the market.[197] The application of the criterion is independent of how the relevant geographic area is defined – trade between Member States can thus be affected even though the relevant market is defined as national or sub-national.[198]

As previously stated, this condition limits the scope of application of Union law in relation to national law.[199] Thus, if a dominant undertaking's conduct is only relevant to the national market, then whether the conduct should be prohibited should be assessed according to national law.[200]

The requirement in Article 102 for there to be an effect on trade is interpreted broadly,[201] and it is therefore relatively easy to meet the requirement. Conduct which directly or indirectly, actually or potentially affects trade between Member States will thus fall within the scope of the provision. If the conduct has an effect on trade flows and competition in the internal market, for example, where the abusive undertaking hinders competitors' access to

197. Commission Notice – Guidelines on the effect on trade concept contained in Articles 81 and 82 of the Treaty, paras 19-21 (OJ 2004 C 101/81).
198. Commission Notice – Guidelines on the effect on trade concept contained in Articles 81 and 82 of the Treaty, para. 22 (OJ 2004 C 101/81).
199. The concept of effect on trade acts as a jurisdiction criterion which defines the scope of application of the EU's competition rules, see Joined Cases 56 and 58/64, *Consten & Grundig;* Joined Cases 6 and 7/73, *Commercial Solvents;* as well as Commission Notice – Guidelines on the effect on trade concept contained in Articles 81 and 82 of the Treaty, para. 12 (OJ 2004 C 101/81).
200. There is an example of the lack of an effect on trade in Case 22/78, *Hugin.* Where trade is affected, national courts and competition authorities must apply the EU competition rules; see Council Regulation (EC) No 1/2003 on the implementation of the rules on competition laid down in Articles 81 and 82 of the Treaty, Article 3(1), (OJ 2003 L 1/1). However, it is possible for national competition rules to be applied in parallel, see Chapter VII.
201. Joined Cases 6 and 7/73, *Commercial Solvents;* and Case 22/79, *SACEM,* para. 11. However, the need for a broad interpretation in order to ensure the implementation of the EU's competition policy has been gradually diminished as the competition laws of the Member States have increasingly been based on the Treaty's competition provisions.

the market, it is irrelevant for the application of Article 102 whether the conduct complained of exclusively takes place within the territory of a single Member State.[202]

Where the abusive conduct consists of several elements, in this context it is not necessary to make a separate assessment of these individual elements, but rather the conduct should be assessed as a whole. This means that if a dominant undertaking uses different kinds of abusive behaviour for the realisation of a strategy, for example to eliminate its competitors, Article 102 applies to all these kinds of conduct if just one of them can affect trade between Member States.[203]

As is the case in relation to Article 101, the effect on trade must be appreciable.[204] The broad interpretation of the requirement for an effect on trade means that it is not necessary to give evidence of an actual appreciable effect on trade, but it is sufficient to show that the disputed conduct *could* affect trade appreciably.[205] Where a dominant undertaking practices conduct which can mean that a competitor is eliminated, it is not necessary to examine more closely whether the conduct directly affects the pattern of trade between Member States (imports and exports), but it is sufficient to establish that the structure of competition in the internal market will be changed if the competitor is eliminated.[206]

202. Case 322/81, *Michelin,* para. 103.
203. Commission Notice – Guidelines on the effect on trade concept contained in Articles 81 and 82 of the Treaty, para. 17 (OJ 2004 C 101/81). See Case 85/76, *Hoffmann-La Roche,* paras 126 and 127.
204. Commission Notice – Guidelines on the effect on trade concept contained in Articles 81 and 82 of the Treaty, para. 13 (OJ 2004 C 101/81); see the CJ's judgment in Case 22/71, *Béguelin,* para. 16. See also paras 44-57 and 97-99 of the Commission Notice.
205. Joined Cases C-241 and 242/91 P, *Magill,* para. 69; and Case C-41/90, *Höfner & Elser,* para. 32.
206. Case 6 and 7/73, *Commercial Solvents,* para. 33; and Joined Cases T-24/93 and others, *CMB,* para. 203.

CHAPTER VII

Procedure and enforcement Regulation (EC) No 1/2003

Pernille Wegener Jessen & Michael Steinicke

Bibliography: *Christopher Bellamy & Graham Child (consultant eds.): European Community Law of Competition, 2007-2012; Jonathan Faull & Ali Nikpay (eds.): The EC Law of Competition, 2007; D.G. Goyder: EC Competition Law, 2009; Ioannis Lianos & Ioannis Kokkoris (eds.): The Reform of EC Competition Law, 2010; Giorgi Monti: EC Competition Law, 2007; Richard Whish: Competition Law, 2012.*

1. Introduction

In recent years the procedural and enforcement system associated with Articles 101[1] and 102 is characterised by a high degree of decentralisation. Thus enforcement takes place partly at EU level where it is taken care of by the Commission, subject to the judicial review of the Court of Justice of the European Union (CJ), and partly at national level, where the national competition authorities and courts are involved.

Such a decentralised enforcement system requires close cooperation between all the authorities involved, both to ensure the uniform interpretation of Articles 101 and 102, and to ensure that the proper division of competence is complied with. The framework for the division and implementation of this competence and for cooperation to ensure the uniform application of the rules is laid down in Council Regulation (EC) No 1/2003 on the implementation of the rules on competition laid down in Articles 101 and 102 of the Treaty on

1. Including the associated block exemption regulations discussed in more detail in Chapters II to V.

the functioning of the European Union.[2] Among other things, the Regulation contains rules on the relevant authorities' powers of investigation, and what types of sanctions can be imposed in connection with infringements of its provisions.

Regulation (EC) No 1/2003 constitutes the key legal framework for the enforcement of Article 101 and 102. However, the Regulation does not stand alone; it is supplemented by a number of non-binding guidelines and notices issued by the Commission. Among other things, these guidelines and notices are aimed at clarifying and defining the key concepts, the frameworks for co-operation between the authorities involved, as well as the setting and imposition of fines and penalties.[3] The enforcement of Articles 101 and 102 is also based on a number of implementing provisions in the national legal systems in areas which do not fall under the heading of EU legal cooperation, but where it remains a matter for the Member States to lay down the detailed rules.

Regulation (EC) No 1/2003 entered into force on 24 January 2003 and has applied since 1 May 2004[4] as the basis for dealing with cases on anti-

2. OJ 2003 L 1/1. Parts of the Regulation are implemented by Commission Regulation (EC) No 773/2004 relating to the conduct of proceedings by the Commission pursuant to Articles 81 and 82 of the EC Treaty (OJ 2004 L 123/18).
3. See Guidelines on the method of setting fines imposed pursuant to Article 23(2)(a) of Regulation (EC) No 1/2003 (OJ 2006 C 210/2), Commission Notice on Immunity from fines and reduction of fines in cartel cases (OJ 2006 C 298/17), Commission Notice on cooperation within the Network of Competition Authorities (OJ 2004 C 101/43), Commission Notice on the co-operation between the Commission and the courts of the EU Member States in the application of Articles 81 and 82 EC (OJ 2004 C 101/54), Commission Notice on the handling of complaints by the Commission under Articles 81 and 82 of the EC Treaty (OJ 2004 C 101/65), Commission Notice on informal guidance relating to novel questions concerning Articles 81 and 82 of the EC Treaty that arise in individual cases (guidance letters) (OJ 2004 C 101/78), Commission Notice – Guidelines on the effect on trade concept contained in Articles 81 and 82 of the Treaty (OJ 2004 C 101/81), Communication from the Commission – Notice – Guidelines on the application of Article 81(3) of the Treaty (OJ 2004 C 101/97), Commission Notice on the rules for access to the Commission file in cases pursuant to Articles 81 and 82 of the EC Treaty, Articles 53, 54 and 57 of the EEA Agreement and Council Regulation (EC) No 139/2004 (OJ 2005 C 325/7), Commission Notice on agreements of minor importance which do not appreciably restrict competition under Article 81(1) of the Treaty establishing the European Community (*de minimis*) (OJ 2001 C 368/13), and Commission Notice on the definition of relevant market for the purposes of Community competition law (OJ 1997 C 372/5).
4. Regulation (EC) No 1/2003, Article 45.

competitive agreements and cases on abuse of a dominant position. From this date the Regulation has replaced the previous enforcement Regulation No 17/62,[5] which represented a central enforcement system under the authority of the Commission as the central and sole competent authority.

The aim of this chapter is to present the basic elements on which the enforcement system relating to Articles 101 and 102 is based. The enforcement system in Regulation (EC) No 1/2003 is specifically related to the application and implementation of Articles 101 and 102 of the Treaty, but the system is also based on the same legal principles as apply to the enforcement of the Treaty's other competition provisions.

1.1. Regulation (EC) No 1/2003 – structure

Regulation (EC) No 1/2003 consists of 45 articles divided into 11 chapters under the following headings:

Chapter I:	Principles (Articles 1-3)
Chapter II:	Powers (Articles 4-6)
Chapter III:	Commission decisions (Articles 7-10)
Chapter IV:	Cooperation (Articles 11-16)
Chapter V:	Powers of investigation (Articles 17-22)
Chapter VI:	Penalties (Articles 23-24)
Chapter VII:	Limitation periods (Article 25-26)
Chapter VIII:	Hearings and Professional secrecy (Articles 27-28)
Chapter IX:	Exemption regulations (Article 29)
Chapter X:	General provisions (Articles 30-33)
Chapter XI:	Transitional, amending and final provisions (Articles 34-45)

1.2. 2001 – the modernisation of the enforcement of Articles 101 and 102

From the mid 1990s onwards the system for the enforcement of the competition rules was subject to detailed consideration. This led to the publication, in 1999, of the Commission's White Paper on the modernisation of the rules implementing Articles 101 and 102 of the Treaty which had the aim of presenting the main outlines of the changes which the Commission was consid-

5. EEC Council: Regulation No 17: First Regulation implementing Articles 85 and 86 of the Treaty (OJ 1962 13/204) (English special edition: Series I Chapter 1959-1962 p. 87).

ering proposing as reforms of the enforcement system.[6] The background to the desire for reform was the existence of a number of unintended consequences and restrictions in connection with the application of the system that had been established under the then applicable implementation Regulation No 17/62.[7]

Under the Regulation then in force, upon application by the undertakings concerned, the Commission could certify that, on the basis of the facts in its possession, there were no grounds for action on its part in respect of the conduct of the undertakings.[8] Similarly, on the basis of a notification to the Commission concerning their agreements, decisions and practices the undertakings concerned could seek individual exemption under Article 101(3).[9] Regulation No 17/62 required the Commission to concentrate its efforts on dealing with notifications received, rather than concentrating on more proactive control functions, which was the role which the Commission preferred to play in relation to Articles 101 and 102. This was so, even though the Commission had put in place several measures to reduce the number of notifications, such as introducing informal procedures which were less demanding on resources than the formal procedures (comfort letters), as well as establishing a fixed *de minimis* threshold which excluded certain agreements from the scope of Article 101, thus removing them from the notification process.

Another factor was that, even with the increase in the number of EU Member States, no amendment had been made to Regulation No 17/62. So it was the view of the Commission that there was a need to bring the Regulation up to date, as the accumulated effects of increased market integration, the accession of new Member States, the entry into agreements with third countries, and the globalisation of the economy since the 1960s had led to a significant expansion of the role of the Commission and the number of cases which the Commission was required to deal with.[10]

6. Commission White Paper of 5 December 1999 on modernisation of the rules implementing Articles 85 and 86 of the EC Treaty, COM(1999) 101 final (OJ 1999 C 132/1).
7. EEC Council: Regulation No 17: First Regulation implementing Articles 85 and 86 of the Treaty (OJ 1962 13/204) (English special edition: Series I Chapter 1959-1962 p. 87).
8. EEC Council: Regulation No 17, Article 2.
9. EEC Council: Regulation No 17, Articles 4(1) and 5(1).
10. Paras 19-23 of the White Paper.

The conduct of undertakings was also relevant. The Commission noted that undertakings quickly discovered that they could benefit from the opportunity to make notifications because they knew that, due to their large number, the Commission's processing of notifications was long drawn out, while being aware that during the processing period, i.e. after notifications were made, they obtained immunity from fines.

At the same time, the developments in the EU and in relation to the competition rules meant that the need for an enforcement system had gone beyond the central enforcement system laid down by Regulation No 17/62. This was primarily because in the practice of the Commission, in notices and suchlike, as well as in the cases decided by the CJ and the General Court (GC), such a large body of information about the competition rules had been accumulated that, on the basis of this material, undertakings and their advisers would themselves be able to assess whether they were covered by the scope of the competition rules.[11]

These considerations formed the background to the drafting of Regulation (EC) No 1/2003. The Regulation retains certain of the procedural rules which were previously found in Regulation No 17/62, while making a number of key changes.

The most obvious changes in Regulation (EC) No 1/2003 in relation to Regulation No 17/62 were: 1) the notification system was abandoned in favour of a system by which, in the first instance, undertakings must themselves assess whether there is an infringement; 2) the Commission was given increased scope for controls and increased powers for obtaining information; and 3) Member States' bodies (competition authorities and courts) were given the possibility of applying the exemptions under Article 101(3) of the Treaty.[12]

11. Para. 51 of the White Paper.
12. For a further discussion of Regulation (EC) No 1/2003, see *Jonathan Faull & Ali Nikpay:* The EC Law of Competition, 2007, Chapter 2, and *James Venit:* Brave new world: The modernization and decentralization of enforcement under Articles 81 and 82 of the EC Treaty, Common Market law Review 2003 pp. 545-580.

2. The relationship between Union competition law and national competition law

2.1. Direct applicability

The CJ has previously established that both Article 101(1) and Article 102 are directly applicable.[13] Thus, both natural and legal persons can rely on these provisions directly before national courts, and the national courts have an obligation to apply the provisions in order to protect the rights which Article 101(1) and Article 102 ascribe to the parties involved.

The direct applicability of these rules is further emphasised and expanded by Regulation (EC) No 1/2003 since, according to Articles 5 and 6 of the Regulation, national courts and competition authorities are given powers to apply the provisions, including the right of an exemption under Article 101(3).

While under the previous Regulation the Commission had sole powers to decide on the right to an exemption under Article 101(3), the direct applicability of the provisions means that an agreement which is covered by Article 101(1) and which satisfies the conditions for an exemption in accordance with Article 101(3), is considered lawful without it being necessary for a competition authority to make a decision on this.[14]

In contrast, abuse covered by Article 102, as well as agreements covered by Article 101(1) which do not fulfil the conditions for exemption under Article 101(3), are considered prohibited, though likewise without it being necessary for a competition authority to make a decision on this.[15]

2.2. The framing and application of national competition law in relation to Articles 101 and 102 of the Treaty

The provisions of national competition law apply in cases where cartel agreements or an undertaking's abuse of a dominant position does not affect trade between Member States. However, regardless of whether trade between Member States is affected, under certain conditions it is possible for the national competition authorities to apply national competition law to a situation.

Where the competition authorities or courts of a Member State applies national competition law to an agreement etc., as referred to in Article 101(1), or to the abuse of a dominant position under Article 102, which can affect

13. Case C-453/99, *Courage,* para. 23.
14. Regulation (EC) No 1/2003, Article 1(2).
15. Regulation (EC) No 1/2003, Articles 1(1) and 3.

trade between Member States, as referred to in the article concerned, they must also apply Article 101 or Article 102, as appropriate, to such agreement or abuse.[16]

However, under no circumstances may the application of national competition law lead to agreements etc. which can affect trade between Member States, but which are not covered by the prohibition in Article 101, being prohibited.[17] National rules on prohibitions of agreements which can affect trade between Member States may thus not be more restrictive than the rules of Union law. There is not a corresponding rule against there being stricter national regulation prohibiting or penalising unilateral conduct, and therefore in this context the Member States can adopt more restrictive national competition rules.[18]

Since the question of the effect on trade is thus central, not only in relation to which set of competition rules is applicable to given circumstances, but also in relation to the obligations to which national courts, competition authorities and legislators are subject, as part of its reform package the Commission has published a Notice giving guidelines on the effect on trade concept in Articles 101 and 102 of the Treaty.[19] Apart from giving an account of the principles which the courts have developed in relation to the interpretation of the concept of trade, the Notice sets out the 'non-appreciable affectation of trade rule' or 'NAAT-rule', which can be used by the courts and competition authorities of the Member States as guidance for establishing when agreements can in general be assumed to affect trade between Member States appreciably.[20]

16. Regulation (EC) No 1/2003, Article 3(1). See e.g. the Decision of the Danish Competition Authority of 26 October 2011, *Dansk Brand- og Sikringsteknisk Instituts retningslinie 001*.
17. This is so regardless of whether the reason why the situation is not covered by the prohibition in Article 101(1) is due to the fact that competition is not restricted in accordance with Article 101(1), that the conditions for exemption under Article 101(3) are fulfilled, or that the agreement is covered by a block exemption.
18. Regulation (EC) No 1/2003, Article 3(2). Article 3(1) and (2) do not in principle apply to the application of national rules on merger control by national authorities and courts, nor national rules which have some other primary purpose than that pursued by Articles 101 and 102 of the Treaty; see Article 3(3).
19. Commission Notice – Guidelines on the effect on trade concept contained in Articles 81 and 82 of the Treaty (OJ 2004 C 101/81).
20. Commission Notice – Guidelines on the effect on trade concept contained in Articles 81 and 82 of the Treaty, point 3 (OJ 2004 C 101/81).

3. Allocation of competence, powers and uniformity

As referred to above, the enforcement of Articles 101 and 102 of the Treaty is the task both of the Commission and the national competition authorities and courts. This enforcement is carried out through close cooperation between the authorities involved. In addition to helping to ensure the uniform application of Articles 101 and 102, this cooperation also helps both to ensure that specific cases are dealt with by the authority which has the competence to do so, and to prevent several authorities which have the competence to deal with the same case from initiating parallel proceedings.

For this purpose the Commission and the competition authorities of the Member States are part of a competition network which constitutes a forum for discussion and cooperation on the implementation and enforcement of Articles 101 and 102, and within which the authorities can exchange information about, for example, investigations which they have initiated and cases they have concluded.[21]

Cooperation between the Commission and the national courts also involves exchange of information about, among other things, decided cases, and the national courts have the possibility of obtaining the opinion of the Commission on the application of Articles 101 and 102.[22]

It should also be noted that self-regulation by undertakings plays a role in the overall enforcement of Articles 101 and 102. This self-regulation is not explicitly referred to in Regulation (EC) No 1/2003, but it is a direct consequence of the ending of the notification system and the full direct applicability of the provisions. Thus today many large undertakings have formulated compliance programmes which are directly focused on ensuring that they act in accordance with Articles 101 and 102.

In cases where there is a dispute about whether the competition rules have been infringed, according to the CJ's decision in Case C-185/95 P, *Baustahlgewebe* v *Commission*, it is up to the Commission to show evidence of an infringement and that the circumstances which constitute such infringement do in fact exist.[23]

21. Regulation (EC) No 1/2003, Article 11. See also Commission Notice on cooperation within the Network of Competition Authorities (OJ 2004 C 101/43).
22. Regulation (EC) No 1/2003, Article 15. See also Commission Notice on the cooperation between the Commission and the courts of the EU Member States in the application of Articles 81 and 82 EC (OJ 2004 C 101/54).
23. Case C-185/95 P, *Baustahlgewebe* v *Commission,* para. 58.

This rule on the burden of proof has now been codified in Regulation (EC) No 1/2003, Article 2, and has been extended so as to cover the other authorities which enforce the competition rules with a view to ensuring the effective enforcement of the competition rules, while respecting the fundamental right of a party to defend themselves.[24] Thus, the burden of proof to show that there is an infringement of Article 101(1) and Article 102 rests on the party or the authority which asserts the existence of such infringement.

In contrast, the burden of proof for satisfying the conditions of Article 101(3) rests on the undertakings or associations of undertakings which claim the benefit of the exemption in question.[25]

The requirements which, in a concrete case, are made as to the standard of proof or to the enforcing authority's obligation to ascertain the relevant facts of a case are not regulated in the Regulation, but are governed by the rules which apply in the legal systems within which the respective authorities operate, whether this concerns the EU Commission or the national competition authorities or courts.[26]

3.1. The Commission's competences

The Commission's powers in relation to the application of Articles 101 and 102 are laid down in Regulation (EC) No 1/2003,[27] which defines the powers of the Commission in respect of, among other things, initiating proceedings, dealing with complaints, the form and content of decisions, and the right to carry out control inspections. In principle, the Commission's involvement with actual competition cases and the subsequent application of the competition rules arises either from a complaint or from taking up a case on its own initiative.

24. Regulation (EC) No 1/2003, recital 5.
25. Regulation (EC) No 1/2003, Article 2. The provision expresses the general principle on the allocation of the burden of proof; if any person makes a claim about some circumstances (e.g. that they infringe the competition rules), they have the burden of proof for showing that this is so. At the same time, the burden of proof relating to Article 101(3), requires that, in accordance with the general rules on exemptions in Union law, an undertaking has the burden of proof for showing the existence of circumstances which justify the exemption claimed.
26. Regulation (EC) No 1/2003, recital 5.
27. Regulation (EC) No 1/2003, Article 4.

Thus, if on the basis of a complaint[28] or on its own initiative the Commission finds that there is an infringement of Article 101 or 102, it can make a decision requiring the undertakings or undertakings concerned to bring such infringement to an end.[29] In this connection the Commission has the possibility of imposing *behavioural remedies* on undertakings, in other words in practice to stop certain conduct and to refrain from it in future.

The Commission also has powers to impose *structural remedies* on the undertakings concerned under Article 7(1), second sentence of Regulation (EC) No 1/2003, for example the disposal of a subsidiary or part of an undertaking. The imposition of such obligations is also a key power in relation to the Merger Control Regulation.[30]

However, in Article 7(1) it is stated that structural remedies can only be imposed either where there is no equally effective behavioural remedy or where any equally effective behavioural remedy would be more burdensome for the undertaking concerned than the structural remedy.

Prior to making a final decision about an infringement of Article 101 or 102, the Commission has the possibility of deciding on interim measures on the basis of a *prima facie* finding of infringement. However, this only applies if there is a risk of serious and irreparable damage to competition; see Article 8(1) of Regulation (EC) No 1/2003.[31]

Where the Commission intends to adopt a decision to bring to an end an infringement of the competition rules, the undertakings concerned may offer commitments to meet the concerns of the Commission. Where undertakings give such commitments, the Commission may decide to make them binding on the undertakings. Such a decision may be adopted for a specified period and it must be concluded in the decision that there are no longer grounds for action by the Commission; see Article 9(1), second sentence of Regulation (EC) No 1/2003. However, reasons may nevertheless arise for the Commission to reopen the proceedings either upon request or on its own initiative: (a) if there has been a material change in any of the facts on which the decision was based; (b) if the undertakings concerned act contrary to their commit-

28. According to Article 7(2) of Regulation (EC) No 1/2003, a complaint can be lodged by a natural or legal person who can show a legitimate interest, or by a Member State.
29. Regulation (EC) No 1/2003, Article 7.
30. See in more detail in Chapter VIII.
31. A decision on interim measures will apply for a specified period but may be renewed if necessary and appropriate.

ments; or (c) if the decision was based on incomplete, incorrect or misleading information provided by the parties.[32]

Finally, where the 'Community public interest relating to the application of Articles 101 and 102 of the Treaty so requires', the Commission, acting on its own initiative, may decide that Article 101 or Article 102 is not applicable to an agreement in a specific case.[33]

3.2. The competences of the national competition authorities and courts

According to Article 5 of Regulation (EC) No 1/2003, the competition authorities of the Member States have the power to apply Articles 101 and 102 of the Treaty in individual cases. Conversely, this means that the authorities do not have powers to apply the provisions generally, for example to grant a block exemption. In connection with the treatment of a specific case, national competition authorities can require infringements to be brought to an end, and decide on interim measures, accept commitments, impose fines, periodic penalty payments or any other penalty provided for in the national law of the Member State concerned.

However, national authorities lose their powers to apply Articles 101 and 102 if the Commission itself initiates proceedings in relation to infringements of the competition rules. Where a national competition authority is already dealing with a case, the Commission will first initiate proceedings after having consulted the competition authority in question.[34]

Where several national competition authorities have jurisdiction to deal with a specific case, it will be sought to have the case dealt with by the most suitable authority.[35] But in certain cases it may be most appropriate to have the case dealt with in parallel by more than one national competition authori-

32. Regulation (EC) No 1/2003, Article 9(2). See e.g. Commission Decision of 26 November 2008 in Cases COMP/39.399 & COMP/39.389, *E.ON.*, and Commission Decision of 18 March 2009 in Case COMP/39.402, *RWE*.
33. Regulation (EC) No 1/2003, Article 10. No more specific definition has been given of what is meant by the 'Community public interest'. However, it may be possible to draw on the term 'the interests of the Community', which is found in Article 106(2), last sentence of the Treaty. Under this provision it is possible that the Community public interest means an interest which is in line with the purposes of the Community set out in Article 3 of the Treaty on European Union.
34. Regulation (EC) No 1/2003, Article 11(6).
35. Commission Notice on cooperation within the Network of Competition Authorities, points 7 and 8 (OJ 2004 C 101/43).

ty.[36] Where a competition authority of a Member State receives a complaint about a case which is already being dealt with by another competition authority, it may reject it.[37]

In relation to national courts, their jurisdiction is established by Article 6 of Regulation (EC) No 1/2003 to the effect that: 'National courts shall have the power to apply Articles 81 and 82 [now Articles 101 and 102] of the Treaty.'

In contrast to the earlier Regulation No 17/62, under Regulation (EC) No 1/2003 both the national competition authorities and the national courts have jurisdiction to apply Article 101(3) of the Treaty. There is a risk that delegating jurisdiction for the enforcement of the competition rules to national competition authorities and courts will lead to the loss of the uniformity which was guaranteed by the sole jurisdiction of the Commission.[38] On this basis, Article 16 of Regulation (EC) No 1/2003 includes a provision to the effect that when national courts rule on agreements, decisions or practices under Article 101 or Article 102 of the Treaty which are already the subject of a Commission decision, they cannot make decisions which run counter to the decision adopted by the Commission. National courts must also 'avoid giving decisions which would conflict with a decision contemplated by the Commission in proceedings it has initiated.'[39] If the Commission has already made a decision in a case, the national competition authorities cannot make decisions

36. Commission Notice on cooperation within the Network of Competition Authorities, point 12 (OJ 2004 C 101/43).
37. Regulation (EC) No 1/2003, Article 13(1).
38. This problem is at two levels. First, there can be consequences for the uniform application of the law when the courts and competition authorities of the 27 Member States can apply the rules so that the practice in relation to Articles 101 and 102 can depend on the Member State where the case is considered. Second, there is a risk that the same case may be dealt with by competition authorities in different Member States, with differing outcomes. While Regulation (EC) No 1/2003 lays down provisions for ensuring that the decisions of the competition authorities do not conflict with the decisions of the Commission (see Article 16), there are no rules about how the conflicting application of the provisions by different national authorities should be dealt with.
39. Since it can be difficult for the national courts to predict what decision the Commission will make, it is pointed out in Article 16(1) of the Regulation that they may assess whether it is necessary to stay their proceedings. It is also made clear in Article 16(1) that the obligation of the national courts under the Regulation is without prejudice to the rights and obligations of courts to make referrals for preliminary rulings under Article 267 of the Treaty.

which would run counter to the decision of the Commission in a case concerning the same facts.[40]

Where there is doubt about the interpretation of competition law, the national courts can make referrals to the CJ for preliminary rulings in accordance with Article 267 of the Treaty. Against the background of the *Syfait* case,[41] it is hardly likely that a national competition authority will be considered as being entitled to make a referral for a preliminary ruling, but it is possible that a national competition appeal tribunal might be allowed to make such a referral.[42]

3.3. Self-evaluation and decisions on inapplicability

Regulation (EC) No 1/2003 departed from the notification system which was previously the cornerstone of Union competition law. This change meant that it was no longer possible for undertakings to give notifications to the Commission with a view to obtaining clarification on the assessment of an agreement under competition law. In relation to exemptions under Article 101(3) of the Treaty, the situation is thus that undertakings must themselves apply the whole of Article 101 and assess for themselves whether they are, on the one hand, covered by Article 101(1), and if so whether the conditions of Article 101(3) are satisfied so the undertaking is exempted from the prohibition. Thus there is no requirement for a stamp of approval from the Commission in order to obtain an exemption.[43]

However, there is always a risk that an undertaking will make a wrong assessment of the compatibility of a given agreement with Article 101. Both the Commission and the national competition authorities may assess the situation differently, so that a decision will be made that the undertaking has infringed Article 101. The undertaking's assessment is thus by no means binding on the enforcing authorities. However, it can be an element which is taken into account in connection with the assessment of the seriousness of an infringement, and thereby the size of a fine which may be imposed on the undertaking for the infringement.

However, Article 10 of Regulation (EC) No 1/2003 allows the possibility for the Commission to decide, on its own initiative, that Article 101(1) does not apply to an agreement etc. This scope for the Commission to make a

40. Regulation (EC) No 1/2003, Article 16(2).
41. Case C-53/03, *Syfait.*
42. See *Morten Broberg:* Hvornår er en ret en ret?, Advokaten 10/2006.
43. Regulation (EC) No 1/2003, Article 1(2).

'Finding of inapplicability'[44] in relation to a specific agreement can be based either on the grounds that the conditions for applying Article 101(1) do not exist, or that the conditions for granting an exemption under Article 101(3) do exist.

Undertakings cannot rely on the Commission making such a finding of inapplicability in relation to their agreements on its own initiative. There is thus not the same direct possibility of obtaining a formal declaration that the enforcement authorities do not regard the agreement in question to be contrary to Article 101, and undertakings must thus rely on their own assessments of the lawfulness of their agreements.

4. Powers of investigation

4.1. The Commission's powers of investigation

In connection with the investigation of whether an undertaking's conduct is in accordance with Article 101 or Article 102 on the basis of Regulation (EC) No 1/2003, the Commission has powers to conduct general investigations of sectors of the economy, and to make more specific investigations on the premises of undertakings and certain private premises, as well as obtaining relevant information and taking statements in order to throw light on a case. These powers can be used individually or together, depending on the actual case and on what is proportionate in the context in question.[45]

According to Article 17 of Regulation (EC) No 1/2003, the Commission can conduct inquiries into a particular sector of the economy or into a particular type of agreement across various sectors if, for example, the development of trade between Member States or the lack of price elasticity provokes the suspicion that competition is restricted or distorted.[46] In this connection the Commission may request the undertakings or associations of undertakings concerned to supply the information necessary for the application of the competition rules.[47]

In addition to the cases where there is a suspicion of a restriction on competition, the Commission can, by a request or a decision, require undertakings

44. The heading of the Article.
45. See Case T-145/06, *Omya AG,* para. 34, and Case T-340/04, *France Télécom SAT,* para. 147
46. For example, in this connection the Commission has examined the European electricity and gas sectors; see COM(2006) 851 final.
47. According to Article 17(1) fourth sentence, the Commission may publish a report on the results of its inquiries and invite comments from interested parties.

to provide all necessary information, where this is required in order to carry out the duties assigned to it by the Regulation.[48]

The more detailed rules for the Commission's request for information are laid down in Article 18 of the Regulation. Regardless of whether the Commission uses a request or a decision to obtain the information, the document in question must state:[49] 1) the legal basis and the purpose of the request; 2) what information is required; 3) the time-limit within which it is to be provided; 4) and the penalties for providing incorrect or misleading information.[50] Where information is sought on the basis of a decision, it must also be stated that the decision can be referred to the CJ.

Information can be required from owners of the undertakings or their representatives.[51] In the case of legal persons, companies, or associations the persons authorised to represent them by law or by their constitution must supply the information requested.

Finally, lawyers duly authorised to act may supply the information on behalf of their clients. However, the clients remain fully responsible for the information supplied being complete, correct and not misleading.

If the Commission so requests, the governments and competition authorities of the Member States are obliged to provide the Commission with all the necessary information for carrying out the duties assigned to it by the Regulation.[52]

In addition to obtaining information, the Commission also has the power to take statements.[53] The Commission may interview any natural or legal person who consents to be interviewed.[54] The aim of such an interview is to obtain information about the circumstances in a particular case. Where an interview is conducted on the premises of an undertaking, the Commission must

48. Regulation (EC) No 1/2003, Article 18(1).
49. Regulation (EC) No 1/2003, Article 18(2) and (3).
50. According to Article 23(1)(a), fines can be imposed for giving incorrect or misleading information in response to a request made pursuant to Article 17 or Article 18(2). Likewise, under Article 18(1)(b), fines can be imposed for giving incorrect, incomplete or misleading information or failing to give information within the required time-limit. Furthermore, where information is obtained from undertakings on the basis of decision, under Article 24(1)(d) periodic penalty payments can be imposed with a view to getting undertaking to supply complete and correct information which has been requested.
51. Regulation (EC) No 1/2003, Article 18(4).
52. Regulation (EC) No 1/2003, Article 18(6).
53. Regulation (EC) No 1/2003, Article 19.
54. On the other hand, there is no right to force people to take part in an interview.

inform the competition authority of the Member State where the interview takes place and, at its request, representatives of the competition authority of that Member State may assist the officials of the Commission at the interview.[55]

However, the principle that a person may not be obliged to incriminate themselves does limit the Commission's powers to obtain information to a certain extent. Thus, an undertaking is not obliged to confess to an infringement of Articles 101 or 102,[56] but an undertaking is obliged to provide information and documents, even if this information may be used against it.[57]

4.2. The Commission's inspections

4.2.1. The Commission's inspections of undertakings

The Commission is empowered to carry out all necessary inspections of undertakings and associations of undertakings in order to carry out the duties assigned to it by Regulation (EC) No 1/2003.[58]

These powers include the right:

a. to enter any premises, land and means of transport of undertakings and associations of undertakings;
b. to examine the books and other records related to the business, irrespective of the medium on which they are stored;
c. to take or obtain in any form copies of or extracts from such books or records;
d. to seal any business premises and books or records for the period of the investigation and to the extent necessary for the inspection;
e. to ask any representative or member of staff of the undertaking or association of undertakings for explanations on facts or documents relating to the subject-matter and purpose of the inspection and to record the answers.

55. Regulation (EC) No 1/2003, Article 19(2).
56. Regulation (EC) No 1/2003, recital 23; and Case 374/87, *Orkem*, para. 35.
57. Case 374/87, *Orkem,* paras 34-35; Joined Cases T-236/01, T-239/01, T-244 to 246/01, and T-251 and 252/01, *Tokai and* others v *Commission,* paras 402-403; and Case C-301/04 P, *Commission* v *SGL,* paras 41-42. See also Commission notice on best practices for the conduct of proceedings concerning Articles 101 and 102 TFEU (OJ 2011 C 308/60).
58. Regulation (EC) No 1/2003, Article 20(1).

There are certain formal requirements for the documentation on which an inspection is based. Thus, the Commission's representatives and others who accompany them and who are authorised by the Commission to carry out an inspection must show a written authority. This must specify the subject matter and purpose of the inspection and the penalties applicable if there is incomplete provision of the books required or other records related to the business, or if the answers given to questions asked under Article 20(2) are incorrect or misleading.[59]

The Commission must give notice of the inspection to the competition authority of the Member State where it is to be conducted in good time before the inspection is carried out.

Representatives of the competition authorities as well as persons authorised or appointed by the competition authorities of the Member State where the inspection is to be carried out must, at the request of the competition authority concerned or of the Commission, actively assist the Commission's representatives and others who accompany them and who are authorised by the Commission.

Undertakings have an obligation to submit to inspections to which the Commission has subjected them by a decision. The decision must state the subject matter and purpose of the inspection, the date for the commencement of the inspection, and give information about the penalties applicable,[60] as well as the right to refer the decision to the CJ. The Commission takes such decisions after consulting the competition authorities in the Member State where the inspection is to be carried out.

If the Commission's representatives and those accompanying them who are authorised by the Commission establish that an undertaking opposes an inspection ordered in accordance with the Regulation, the Member State concerned must give them the necessary assistance to enable them to conduct their inspection. This may include requesting the assistance of the police or of an equivalent enforcement authority.[61]

If, under national rules, such assistance requires authorisation from a judicial authority, such authorisation shall be applied for. Upon such an application being made, the national court can control that the Commission's decision is authentic and that the coercive measures envisaged are neither arbitrary nor excessive having regard to the subject matter of the inspection. In its

59. Regulation (EC) No 1/2003, Article 20(3).
60. Regulation (EC) No 1/2003, Articles 23 and 24.
61. Regulation (EC) No 1/2003, Article 20(6).

control of this, the national court may ask the Commission, directly or through the Member State's competition authority, for detailed explanations of the grounds which the Commission has for suspecting infringement of Articles 101 and 102 of the Treaty, as well as of the seriousness of the suspected infringement and the nature of the involvement of the undertaking concerned. However, the national court may not call into question the necessity for the inspection, nor demand that it be provided with the information in the Commission's file. In this context, the CJ has sole jurisdiction to examine the lawfulness of the Commission's decisions.

4.2.2. Inspections in private homes

Regulation (EC) No 1/2003 gives the Commission powers to carry out inspections other than on the premises of an undertaking, including in private homes; see Article 21. Mostly these inspections follow the same rules as normal inspections.

If the Commission believes that there is a reasonable suspicion that books or other records related to the business and to the subject-matter of the inspection, which may be relevant for proving the existence of a serious violation of Article 101 or Article 102 of the Treaty, are being kept in any other premises, land or means of transport, including the homes of directors, managers and other members of staff, the Commission can, by a decision, order an inspection of such other premises, etc. to be carried out.

As is the case for normal inspections[62] the Commission's decision must specify the subject matter and purpose of the inspection, appoint the date on which it is to begin, and indicate the right to have the decision reviewed by the CJ.[63]

Also, and in particular, the Commission must state the reasons that have led it to conclude that books or other records related to the business are being kept in any other premises than those of the undertaking. The Commission must take any decision referred to in Article 21(2) of the Regulation after consulting the competition authority of the Member State where the inspection is to be conducted. A decision under Article 21(1) may not be carried out without the prior permission of a national court of the Member State in question; see Article 21(3).

62. Regulation (EC) No 1/2003, Article 20(4).
63. Regulation (EC) No 1/2003, Article 21(2), first sentence.

As with a normal inspection,[64] in this connection a national court may not call into question the necessity for the inspection, nor demand that it be provided with the information in the Commission's file, as the CJ has sole jurisdiction to examine the lawfulness of the Commission's decisions.

However, the national court can control that the Commission's decision is authentic and that the coercive measures envisaged are neither arbitrary nor excessive having regard to the subject matter of the inspection. In its control of this, the national court may take account of the seriousness of the presumed infringement and the importance of the evidence sought, the involvement of the undertaking concerned, and the reasonable likelihood that business books and records relating to the subject matter of the inspection are kept on the premises for which the authorisation is requested. In this connection, the national court may ask the Commission for detailed explanations concerning those elements which are necessary to allow it to assess the proportionality of the measures envisaged.[65]

4.3. The powers of the Member States to carry out investigations

One of the aims of Regulation (EC) No 1/2003 is to establish better possibilities for cooperation between the competition authorities of the different Member States, among other things in relation to the investigation and clearing up of competition cases.[66] It was thus also necessary to lay down rules on the powers of national competition authorities to carry out investigations, as regards investigations carried out at the request of other Member States or the Commission. Against this background, Article 22 of the Regulation lays down that the competition authority of a Member State may, in its own territory, carry out any inspection or other fact-finding measure under its national law on behalf and for the account of the competition authority of another Member State, in order to establish whether there has been an infringement of Article 101 or Article 102 of the Treaty. Any exchange and use of the information collected must comply with Article 12 of the Regulation. This means that it is possible to exchange evidence on any matter of fact or of law, including confidential information.[67] The information exchanged may only be used in evidence for the purpose of applying Article 101 or Article 102 and

64. Regulation (EC) No 1/2003, Article 20(8).
65. Regulation (EC) No 1/2003, Article 21(3).
66. Commission White Paper of 5 December 1999 on modernisation of the rules implementing Articles 85 and 86 of the EC Treaty, paras 91-98.
67. Regulation (EC) No 1/2003, Article 12(1).

only in respect of the subject-matter for which it was collected; see Article 12(2) of the Regulation.

At the request of the Commission, the competition authorities of the Member States undertake such inspections as the Commission considers necessary or has ordered by a decision (for both situations see Article 20 of the Regulation). Those who are responsible for carrying out these inspections exercise their powers in accordance with national law.[68] In connection with inspections carried out at the request of the Commission, the national competition authorities can be assisted by representatives for the Commission.

5. The consequences of infringement

Where there is an infringement of the prohibition in Article 101 of the Treaty, the consequence of this is invalidity of the agreement.[69] However, in the context of agreements that restrict trade, invalidity is not a very effective sanction. This is because in principle none of the parties to the agreement will have an advantage from claiming invalidity. On the contrary, the parties to such an agreement are often more interested in maintaining the agreement which is a true expression of the parties' wishes in relation to their conduct in the market. Thus, in addition to invalidity, other sanctions can be applied to infringements of Article 101. The most important sanction – also in relation to Article 102 – is a fine, but it is also possible to impose periodic penalty payments, as well as to award damages for losses suffered because of an agreement which restricts competition.

5.1. Fines

Regulation (EC) No 1/2003 lays down detailed rules on the possibility of imposing fines for infringements of Articles 101 and 102. Such fines are not of a criminal law nature; see Article 23(5).

The Commission's scope for imposing fines is set out in Article 23. Fines can be imposed in two situations: first, in connection with the infringement of the formal rules which apply to enforcement; and second, in connection with substantive infringements of the competition rules in the Treaty. For infringement of the rules which apply to enforcement, the Commission can impose on undertakings and associations of undertakings fines not exceeding 1 % of the total turnover in the preceding business year. The culpability for

68. Regulation (EC) No 1/2003, Article 22(2).
69. For further discussion of invalidity, see Chapter II, section 7.1.

applying such a fine is based on intention or negligence. Fines can be imposed if an undertaking gives incorrect or misleading information in reply to a request made in accordance with Article 17 or Article 18(2) of Regulation (EC) No 1/2003; if in response to a request made by a decision adopted pursuant to Article 17 or Article 18(3), an undertaking gives incorrect, incomplete or misleading information or fails to supply information within the required time-limit; if seals affixed in accordance with Article 20(2)(d) by officials or other accompanying persons authorised by the Commission have been broken.

Furthermore, fines can be imposed where undertakings subject to investigation in accordance with Article 20 of the Regulation produce the required books or other records related to the business in incomplete form or refuse to submit to inspections ordered by a decision adopted pursuant to Article 20(4).

Finally, it is possible to impose fines where, in response to a question asked in accordance with Article 20(2)(e), an undertaking gives an incorrect or misleading answer; fails to rectify within a time-limit set by the Commission an incorrect, incomplete or misleading answer given by a member of staff; or fails or refuses to provide a complete answer on facts relating to the subject-matter and purpose of an inspection ordered by a decision adopted pursuant to Article 20(4).

In relation to substantive infringements of the competition rules, for each undertaking which participates in the infringement, a fine may not exceed 10 % of its total turnover in the preceding business year.[70]

When calculating the amount of a fine, regard shall be had both to the gravity and to the duration of the infringement, see Article 23(3) of Regulation (EC) No 1/2003.[71] Moreover, there is a possibility of exemption from a fine or a reduction of a fine in accordance with the Commission's Guidelines.

The Commission's Notice on immunity from fines in cartel cases must be taken into account.[72]

Regulation (EC) No 1/2003 does not mean there is any harmonisation of fines for infringements of Articles 101 and 102, and the setting of the

70. Regulation (EC) No 1/2003, Article 23(2). Detailed guidelines for the calculation of fines are laid down in the Commission's Guidelines on the method of setting fines imposed pursuant to Article 23(2)(a) of Regulation (EC) No 1/2003 (OJ 2006 C 210/2).
71. See the Commission's Guidelines on the method of setting fines imposed pursuant to Article 23(2)(a) of Regulation (EC) No 1/2003 (OJ 2006 C 210/2).
72. Commission Notice on Immunity from fines and reduction of fines in cartel cases (OJ 2006 C 298/17).

amounts of fines thus follows national rules and procedures when cases are dealt with by the competition authorities of the Member States.

In addition to fines, it is also possible to impose periodic penalty payments to the extent than this can compel undertakings to:[73]

a. put an end to an infringement of Article 101 or Article 102 of the Treaty, in accordance with a decision taken pursuant to Article 7 of Regulation (EC) No 1/2003;
b. comply with a decision ordering interim measures taken pursuant to Article 8 of the Regulation;
c. comply with a commitment made binding by a decision pursuant to Article 9 of the Regulation;
d. supply complete and correct information which it has requested by decision taken pursuant to Article 17 or Article 18(3) of the Regulation; and
e. submit to an inspection which it has ordered by decision taken pursuant to Article 20(4) of the Regulation.

The CJ has unlimited jurisdiction to review decisions whereby the Commission has fixed a fine or periodic penalty payment; see Article 31 of Regulation (EC) No 1/2003. According to the practice of the CJ, the GC also has unlimited jurisdiction in this respect.[74]

While there are no formal deadlines within which the Commission can commence an investigation of conduct that restricts competition contrary to Articles 101 and 102, there are rules on limitation periods for the Commission's powers to impose fines and periodic penalty payments and to enforce decisions on this.

The power of the Commission to impose fines or periodic penalty payments ends three years after an infringement of provisions concerning requests for information or the conduct of inspections.[75] This period of limitation is in principle calculated from the date on which the infringement is committed, while the period in cases where there is a continuing or repeated infringement is calculated from the date when the infringement ends.[76] The period of limitation is interrupted each time the Commission, or the competition authorities of a Member State, takes steps to investigate or prosecute the

73. Regulation (EC) No 1/2003, Article 24.
74. Case C-219/95 P, *Ferriere Nord* v *Commission,* para. 31.
75. Regulation (EC) No 1/2003, Article 25(1).
76. Regulation (EC) No 1/2003, Article 25(2).

infringement, and thereafter the period starts afresh, just as the period of limitation will be suspended as long as a case on the Commission's decision is pending before the CJ.[77]

The Commission's powers to enforce decisions on fines and periodic penalty payments expire after five years.[78] This period is calculated from the date on which the decision is made final, and will in certain circumstances be interrupted or suspended.[79]

5.2. Damages

The EU rules do not lay down what possibilities there are for obtaining damages in connection with infringements of the competition rules. However, it must be assumed that, in accordance with the duty to provide effective sanctions for breaches of the competition rules, the Member States must ensure the possibility for obtaining damages where undertakings suffer loss as a result of infringements of the competition rules.

The question of damages is not something that belongs under the heading of EU competition law, but falls instead under the jurisdictions of the Member States. Thus, the questions of when damages can be awarded, what conditions must be fulfilled, and how they should be calculated are questions which are decided under the laws of the Member States.

However, there are certain EU rules on the conditions which must be fulfilled in connection with obtaining damages on the grounds of infringements of EU competition rules. This is subject to the general principle of EU law that the Member States must ensure the effective sanctioning of infringements of EU law.[80]

Among other things, the CJ has stated that: 'As regards the possibility of seeking compensation for loss caused by a contract or by conduct liable to restrict or distort competition, it should be remembered from the outset that, in accordance with settled case-law, the national courts whose task it is to apply the provisions of Union law in areas within their jurisdiction must ensure that those rules take full effect and must protect the rights which they confer on

77. Regulation (EC) No 1/2003, Article 25(5) and (6). According to Article 25(5), the period of limitation expires 'at the latest on the day on which a period equal to twice the limitation period has elapsed without the Commission having imposed a fine or a periodic penalty payment. That period shall be extended by the time during which limitation is suspended pursuant to paragraph 6.'
78. Regulation (EC) No 1/2003, Article 26(1).
79. Regulation (EC) No 1/2003, Article 26(2) to (5).
80. In relation to the competition rules see Case C-453/99, *Courage.*

individuals.' The CJ continued: 'The full effectiveness of Article 85 of the Treaty and, in particular, the practical effect of the prohibition laid down in Article 85(1) would be put at risk if it were not open to any individual to claim damages for loss caused to him by a contract or by conduct liable to restrict or distort competition.'[81] The more detailed requirements for damages is laid down by the CJ which has stated that 'in the absence of Community rules governing the matter, it is for the domestic legal system of each Member State to designate the courts and tribunals having jurisdiction and to lay down the detailed procedural rules governing actions for safeguarding rights which individuals derive directly from Community law, provided that such rules are not less favourable than those governing similar domestic actions (principle of equivalence) and that they do not render practically impossible or excessively difficult the exercise of rights conferred by Community law'; see Case C-453/99, *Courage*, paragraph 29.

81. Case C-453/99, *Courage,* paras 25 and 26. On the duty to pay damages, see also Chapter III, section 1.2.

CHAPTER VIII

Merger control

Karsten Engsig Sørensen

Bibliography: *Morten P. Broberg: The European Commission's jurisdiction to scrutinise mergers, 2006; John Cook & Christopher Kerse: EC Merger Control, 2009; Jonathan Faull & Ali Nikpay (eds.): The EC Law of Competition, 2007; Barry E. Hawk & Henry L. Huser: European Community Merger Control, 1996; Lennart Ritter, W. David Braun & Francis Rawlinson: EC Competition Law: A Practitioner's Guide, 2004; Michael Rosenthal & Stefan Thomas: European Merger Control, 2010; Peter Roth & Vivien Rose (eds.): Bellamy & Child: European Community Law of Competition, 2008; Ulrich Schwalbe & Daniel Zimmer: Law and Economics in European Merger Control, 2009; E. Navarro Varona, A. Font Galarza, J. Folguera Crespo & J. Briones Alonso: Merger Control in the European Union, 2002; Richard Whish: Competition Law, 2012.*

1. Introduction

1.1. Introduction to the topic

In the years leading up to the adoption of the first Merger Control Regulation in 1989, the Commission had to a certain extent attempted to control mergers by using Articles 101 and 102 of the Treaty on the Functioning og the European Union (TFEU or the 'Treaty'). This problem was the subject of a comprehensive report prepared by the Commission in 1966.[1] In its report the Commission concluded that Article 101 was not suitable for regulating concentrations, among other things because it required the existence of two independent undertakings, and many concentrations result in only one undertak-

1. See the report, Das Problem der Unternehmenskonzentration im Gemeinsamen Markt, Kollektion Studien, Reihe Wettbewerb No 3, 1966.

ing remaining.[2] As for Article 102, it was stated in the report that this could be applicable to a concentration where one of the merger parties had previously had a dominant position, and the merger further eliminated competition. This view was later confirmed by the Court of Justice of the European Union (CJ) in its Decision in Case 6/72, *Continental Can*. Article 102 can thus be used for *ex post* control of certain concentrations, but in practice the provision has been shown to be of limited significance in this area.

In recognition of the fact that the two provisions were inadequate to ensure effective control of concentrations, already in 1973 the Commission put forward a proposal for a merger control regulation.[3] However, it was not before 1989 that agreement was reached on Council Regulation (EEC) No 4064/89 on the control of concentrations between undertakings, commonly called the Merger Control Regulation (MCR).[4] A number of amendments were implemented in 1997, including changes to the threshold values which determine when a concentration is considered to have a Community dimension, as well as changes to the special rules on joint ventures.[5] In 2004 a completely new regulation was adopted (Regulation (EC) No 139/2004), which included amendments to the test to which mergers are subject.[6]

The MCR introduces an obligation to notify mergers and full-function joint ventures, where these have a certain size (Community dimension). There is a more detailed definition of this in section 2 below. If a concentration is notified, it must be assessed whether it significantly impedes effective competition, in particular as a result of creating or strengthening a dominant position. In order to evaluate whether this is the case, it is first necessary to define the relevant market (see section 3), and next there must be an investi-

2. The possibility of applying Article 101 to mergers was also considered by the CJ in Joined cases 142 and 156/84, *British American Tobacco (BAT) & R.J. Reynolds Industries* v *Commission*. The CJ indicated that Article 101 can be used where one undertaking acquires a certain level of control over another undertaking through the acquisition of a minority shareholding, but without the control being so extensive that the two undertakings should be treated as a single undertaking for the purposes of competition law. However, the extent of the applicability of the judgment is somewhat doubtful; see the discussion in Chapter IV, section 9.
3. OJ 1973 C 92/1.
4. OJ 1990 L 257/13.
5. Regulation (EC) No 1310/97 (OJ 1997 L 180/1).
6. Council Regulation (EC) No 139/2004 on the control of concentrations between undertakings (OJ 2004 L 24/1). Since this Regulation codifies the regulation of merger controls, it is this legal act which is referred to when referring to the Merger Control Regulation (MCR) in the following.

gation of the effect of the concentration on that relevant market (see section 4). A concentration will seldom be totally prohibited as the Commission often uses the possibility of laying down different terms and conditions for the approval of a concentration instead. This issue is dealt with in more detail in section 5. If a concentration is approved, this raises the question of which terms of the agreement should still be assessed according to Article 101, on the grounds that they are not an essential part of the concentration; see section 6. In the case of joint ventures, there can also be a need to evaluate whether, in connection with the setting up of a joint venture company, there is cooperation on other activities, and if so, such cooperation has to be evaluated in accordance with Article 2(4) of the MCR; see section 7. Finally, section 8 contains a brief review of the procedure for the notification of concentration.

1.2. The sources of law

The following review will largely be based on the practice of the Commission in its decisions. Only the decisions of the Commission taken under Article 8 of the MCR in the second phase are published in the Official Journal of the European Union.[7] The decisions taken in the first phase, under Article 6, are only published on the Commission's website (ec.europa.eu/comm/competition/mergers/cases/), where they are typically available in English and in some cases in French or in German. Since the first Merger Control Regulation entered into force, cases which have been notified have been given the prefix M followed by a serial number. During the period 1998-2002, instead of M the prefix JV was used for joint ventures which were notified, and they were independently numbered. In this chapter references are made using the relevant M or JV number, or where a decision has been published in the Official Journal, there is a reference to the OJ number.

In addition, references are made to several of the Commission's notices issued in connection with the MCR. Even though these are only claimed to be 'guidelines', they have a certain value as sources of law, in part because they have been drawn up on the basis of the practice of the Commission, as can be seen from the fact that they refer to the relevant decisions, and in part because the Commission refers to its notices in its decisions, which must be seen as an expression of the fact that the Commission itself feels bound to follow its own guidelines.[8] The most important notice is the Jurisdictional Notice from

7. For more details on the procedural rules, see section 8 below.
8. M.604, *Albacom,* decision of 15.9.1995, para. 13; and JV.12, *Ericsson/Nokia/ Psion/ Motorola,* decision of 22.12.1998, para. 13.

2007, which deals with the question of which mergers and joint ventures must be notified.[9] In addition, the Commission has issued a Notice on restrictions directly related and necessary to concentrations (ancillary restraints), Guidelines on the assessment of horizontal mergers and Guidelines on the assessment of non-horizontal mergers, which are discussed below.[10]

In recent years there has been a sharp increase in the number of cases referred to the CJ and the General Court (GC) (formerly the Court of First Instance) concerning the MCR, due not least to the introduction of a 'fast track' procedure, which makes it more attractive for the parties to a merger (and their competitors) to appeal against the Commission's decisions.[11] Both courts have adopted the starting position that several of the provisions in the MCR allow the Commission discretion with regard to economic assessments, and the judicial review of the Commission's decisions show respect for the fact that the Commission is allowed a certain margin for discretion.[12] However, it is mainly in the assessments made under Article 2 of the MCR that

9. Commission Consolidated Jurisdictional Notice under Council Regulation (EC) No 139/2004 on the control of concentrations between undertakings (hereinafter referred to as the 'Jurisdictional Notice') (OJ 2008 C 95/1).
10. These are published in OJ 2005 C 56/24, OJ 2004 C 31/5 and OJ 2008 C 265/6 respectively. The Guidelines on non-horizontal mergers was prompted by the fact that in 2005 the Commission partially lost two cases on conglomerate mergers; see Case C-12/03 P, *Tetra Laval,* and Case T-210/01, *General Electric.*
11. See *Alessandro Nucara: Schneider/Legrand and Tetra Laval/Sidel:* Fast Track Towards Merger Reform?, European Business Law Review, 2003 pp. 193-200.
12. Joined cases C-68/94 and C-30/95, *France and others* v *Commission (Kali & Salz),* paras 223-224; Case T-22/97, *Kesko* v *Commission,* para. 142; Case T-102/96, *Gencor* v *Commission,* paras 164-165; and Case T-221/95, *Endemol Entertainment* v *Commission,* para. 106. See also Case T-290/94, *Keysersberg* v *Commission,* para. 182, according to which 'It is not for the Community judicature, in the context of annulment proceedings, to substitute its own appraisal for that of the Commission', which was followed in almost identical wording in Case T-3/93, *Air France v Commission,* para. 113. See further, in relation to the Commission's assessment of commitments in Case T-119/02, *Royal Philips Electronics.* The fact that the Commission has discretion means that the courts will only set aside a decision of the Commission where its assessment is clearly mistaken. Nevertheless, this has happened in a number of cases, see among others Case T-342/99, *Airtours plc.* The Commission was of the view that the GC had gone too far in examining the Commission's exercise of its discretion in Case T-5/02, *Tetra Laval/Sidel,* but the CJ rejected this on appeal. The EC thereby underlined that the GC was entitled to examine information of an economic nature which formed the basis of the Commission's decision.

both courts have accepted that the Commission has such a margin for discretion; see sections 3 and 4.

2. Concentrations with an obligation to notify

If the following conditions are fulfilled, there is an obligation to notify a concentration:

1. There must be a concentration, as defined in the Regulation. This also covers the situation where one or more undertakings acquire control of another undertaking. The concept of a concentration and the concept of control are reviewed in more detail in sections 2.1 and 2.2.
2. If there is a joint venture, there is only an obligation to notify if it has full-function status (i.e. it operates independently); see section 2.3.
3. For a concentration to be notifiable, it must have a Community dimension; see section 2.4, as concentrations without a Community dimension are subject to different rules; see section 2.5.
4. Finally, there is a requirement that the concentration shall have some geographic connection to the EU; see section 2.6.

2.1. The concept of a concentration

The MCR involves an obligation to notify concentrations which is very broad term and includes measures which can lead to a permanent change to the structure of an undertaking.[13] A concentration is defined in Article 3(1) of the MCR as either the true merger of undertakings, or the situation where one or more undertakings directly or indirectly acquire control over one or more other undertakings.

A true merger occurs when there is a merger as understood in company law, whereby a company transfers all its assets and liabilities to another company and the first company ceases to exist. It has long been possible to carry out such mergers between companies situated in the same Member State, and since October 2004 it has also been possible to carry out cross-border mergers of public limited companies.[14] It is also possible to create a concentration

13. Recital 23 in the preamble to the original Regulation.
14. Since October 2004 it has been possible to set up an SE company by means of a cross-border merger; see Regulation (EC) No 2157/2001 on the Statute for a European company (SE) (OJ 2001 L 294/1). From December 2007 it became possible for all companies to carry out cross-border mergers; see Directive 2005/56/EC on cross-border mergers of limited liability companies (OJ 2005 L 310/1).

when two or more undertakings, without carrying out a true merger, establish an economic entity with common management, where in one way or another there is a sharing of profits and losses between the different undertakings in the entity. In certain countries such arrangements can be established by entering into wide-ranging cooperation agreements, by establishing cross-shareholdings etc.[15]

A concentration can also occur when one undertaking acquires control of another, meaning the acquisition of sole control. Such acquisition can take many forms, but it will typically be through the acquisition of shares which carry a majority of the voting rights. An acquisition of shares in this way can take place following the making of a takeover bid.

A joint venture can also constitute a concentration which is covered by the MCR, provided it meets a number of conditions. First, it must be under the joint control of the participating undertakings (the joint venture partners), next it must be an independently operating undertaking (full-function), and finally it must be set up on a lasting basis. These conditions are discussed in more detail below.

It is not only the setting up of a new joint venture company that can constitute a concentration under the MCR. It can also be that an existing company comes under joint control,[16] or that a joint venture that has hitherto been under joint control becomes subject to sole control.[17] This can have the practical consequence that the dissolution of a joint venture can involve an obligation to notify.

An arrangement whereby there is a change to the joint control, but without there being a move to sole control, can also amount to a concentration which must be notified. This will be the case if there is a change to the composition of the group of joint venture partners,[18] or if there is an increase in the number of joint venture

15. Jurisdictional Notice, para. 10.
16. M.2840, *Danapak/Teich/JV,* decision of 30.8.2002, para. 8.
17. M.23, *ICI/Tioxide,* decision of 28.11.1990, para. 2; M.2838, *P & O Stena Line (Holding) Limited,* decision of 7.8.2002, para. 4; and Jurisdictional Notice, para. 89.
18. M.376, *Synthomer/Yule Catto,* decision of 9.9.1993, where one of two joint venture partners was changed. A consistent application of the view that a change of joint venture partners constitutes a merger means that if the control of a joint venture partner changes hands, there is then indirectly a new joint venture partner and therefore a merger which must be notified. *Morten P. Broberg:* The European Commission's jurisdiction to scrutinise mergers, 2006 p. 44 states that the Commission will not normally deal with such indirect changes in joint control, unless the purpose of the takeover is to obtain control of the joint venture.

partners.[19] The new Jurisdictional Notice states that a change in the activity of a joint venture may constitute a concentration. This is the case where the joint venture partners decide to enlarge the joint venture, for instance transferring additional assets, know-how etc. if this results in an extension of the activities of the joint venture into new markets.[20]

There is a special form of joint venture formation where the aim of the acquisition of joint control is to make an immediate distribution of the assets of the joint venture. In this situation the arrangement is considered as a whole, so that it is considered as two mergers, whereby the acquiring companies acquire sole control over their respective parts of the assets of the joint venture. Such an arrangement should still be notified (provided the other conditions of the MCR on turnover etc. are fulfilled), but it is not notified and processed as a joint venture.

A concentration necessarily involves at least two undertakings. This is why the starting point in Article 3(1)(a) of the MCR is that a concentration involves two or more previously independent undertakings. According to subparagraph (b) in the same Article, there can also be a concentration where a person who already controls at least one undertaking acquires control of another undertaking

The MCR does not provide a specific definition of an 'undertaking'. However, it must be assumed that this should be interpreted very broadly, so as to include any entity that carries on some commercial activity, regardless of its corporate form. It must also be assumed that the case law of the CJ and the GC on the definition of an undertaking in relation to Articles 101 and 102 TFEU applies to the interpretation of the concept of an undertaking under the MCR.[21]

In situations where public bodies participate in a concentration by taking over control of an undertaking or by participation as a joint venture partner, the public body will be treated as equivalent to a person that controls other undertakings.[22] As for the situation where a state controlled undertaking takes part in a merger or in the setting up of a joint venture, it appears from recital 22 to the MCR that the calculation of the turnover of an undertaking should take account of undertakings making up an economic unit with an independent power of decision.

19. M.902, *Warner Bros/Lusomundo/sogecable,* decision of 12.5.1997; and M.1014, *British Steel/Europipe,* decision of 26.2.1998, where in both cases the number of joint venture partners was increased from two to three.
20. Jurisdictional Notice, paras 106-109.
21. See Chapter II for commentary on this practice.
22. M.157, *Air France/Sabena,* decision of 5.10.1992, para. 11c.

Finally, Article 3(5) of the MCR contains a list of special exceptions where the acquisition of control is not covered by the MCR. This applies to temporary (12 months) acquisitions by financial institutions, office-holders' acquisitions in connection with liquidations, insolvencies and suchlike, as well as acquisitions by financial holding companies. The list of exceptions is exhaustive and will be interpreted very restrictively.[23]

2.2. The definition of control

In practice, the great majority of concentrations are carried out by one or more undertakings acquiring control over another undertaking, and for this reason the definition of control is central to the MCR.

There is an overall definition of control in Article 3(2) of the MCR, as the possibility of exercising decisive influence on another undertaking. The definition is defined more precisely in a number of other respects in the same provision, as it states that influence can be exercised in the following ways, among others:

- by the controlling undertaking obtaining ownership or the right to use all or part of the assets of an undertaking;
- by the controlling undertaking securing decisive influence on the composition, voting or decisions of the organs of an undertaking.

In practice in its decisions the Commission uses the terms *de jure* and *de facto* control. These terms show that control must be assessed from all factual and legal points of view. Several times the Commission has stressed that the definition of control in the MCR is not identical with the definition of control used in other areas of legislation.[24]

While the concept of control is defined in Article 3(2), there is no corresponding definition of the terms 'sole control' or 'joint control'. In Article 3(1)(b), it is stated that a merger occurs when one or more persons acquires control of another undertaking, and this implies that the concept of control

23. See *Jonathan Faull & Ali Nikpay (eds.):* The EC Law of Competition, 2007 p. 432.
24. Jurisdictional Notice, para. 23. More specifically, in a decision the Commission has rejected the idea that the concept of control is the same as the threshold for the obligation to make a mandatory takeover bid under the British City Code on Takeovers and Mergers; see M.754, *Anglo American/Lonrho* (OJ 1998 L 149/21), para. 40.

includes both kinds of control. The term 'joint control' is used in the MCR,[25] though without this being defined, and the term sole control is not used. However, to a certain extent the terms have been defined in the practice of the Commission, and the key elements are reviewed in the following.

2.2.1. Sole control

Sole control means that one undertaking takes over control of the strategic commercial decisions of another undertaking. This can either be by the first undertaking acquiring assets which together constitute an undertaking, or by the undertaking otherwise acquiring control of the target undertaking. Sole control often arises through the purchase of shares in another undertaking, whereby the acquirer either obtains control of a majority of the voting rights in the company or obtains control of an effective majority. An effective majority will exist where a shareholder does not in fact have a majority of the voting rights in the company, but where there is a high probability that they will be able to secure a majority of the votes at a general meeting of the company. This is particularly relevant in companies with dispersed ownership, as in this case it is unlikely that all small shareholders will exercise their voting rights.[26] A minority shareholding can also give sole control where special rights are attached to the shares which give the minority shareholding decisive influence, for example by giving the right to appoint more than half the members of the board.[27]

> There was an example of *de facto* control through ownership of an effective majority in Decision M.1046, *Ameritech/TeleDanmark*, decision of 5.12.1997, where in the first instance Ameritech acquired 34 % of the voting rights in TeleDanmark. By acquiring the State's remaining shares Ameritech could acquire control of 42 % of the voting rights. This was sufficient to give Ameritech *de facto* control, particularly as (i) the remaining shares in TeleDanmark had dispersed ownership, and no other shareholder owned more than 7.5 % of the company's shares, and (ii) in

25. Article 4(2). In Article 5 there are several references to the situation where undertakings together have certain rights and powers.
26. This form of effective majority existed in, among others, M.754, *Anglo American/ Lonrho* (27.47 % of the voting rights) (OJ 1998 L 149/21) and in M.5469, *Renova Industries/Sulzer,* (31.1 % of the votes), decision of 17.6.2009, but it was rejected in M.197, *Laporte/Interox,* decision of 30.4.1992. In all three cases the Commission investigated how votes had been cast in previous general meetings of the companies.
27. Jurisdictional Notice, para. 57.

the latest three years no more than 54 % of the voting rights had been represented at the company's general meeting, so Ameritech could expect to have a *de facto* majority.

There can also be *de facto* control where an undertaking has a purchase option, which enables it to acquire shares in another company so that *de jure* control can be acquired later. The Commission has adopted the view that an option to purchase shares or an option to convert securities to shares does not in itself give a basis for control, unless the option will be exercised in the near future.[28] In Case T-2/93, *Air France* v *Commission*, the GC accepted that the Commission did not take into account an option which had not yet been exercised, and where furthermore it had not been substantiated that the owner of the option intended to exercise the option.[29] On the other hand, there have been several cases where the Commission has assessed that option/conversion possibilities of this kind can create or contribute to creating *de facto* control.

In Decision M.397, *Ford/Hertz*, decision of 7.3.1994, a stock conversion right was in itself enough to demonstrate *de facto* control. Ford owned 49 % of the voting rights in Hertz and had a right to appoint 4 out of the 9 members of the board. Even though Ford had a veto right over certain decisions, the veto right did not include strategic commercial decisions, so that Ford did not have *de jure* control. However, according to an agreement with the other investors in Hertz, Ford had a right to convert its C class shares into B class shares, which would mean that Ford would be entitled to appoint two further members of Hertz's board, and Ford would thereby have a majority on the board. The Commission was of the view that Ford had therefore acquire *de facto* control, as the conversion right could be exercised at very short notice and did not require Ford to make further investments or otherwise pay for the exercise of this right. The decision was thus unusual, as the conversion right enabled *de jure* control to be acquired at any time, but an option or conversion right will not typically be so effective for securing control. For this reason, in other

28. Jurisdictional Notice, para. 60.
29. Case T-3/93, *Air France v Commission.*

cases the Commission has merely stated that such rights are one of several elements which point towards the existence of *de facto* control.[30]

Control does not necessarily mean that the controlling undertaking is a shareholder of the target company. An undertaking may have control or a share in control if it has *de facto* control of a shareholding via a shareholder who is formally the holder of the rights, but only acts as a vehicle.[31] It is also possible for an undertaking to acquire considerable influence on the running of another company via other legal means than ownership. The most obvious example is a management agreement which can give the managing undertaking considerable influence and, depending on the circumstances, it can also obtain a share of the joint control.[32] It is clear that what matters is not the category of an agreement, but its effect.[33]

The Commission has adopted the view that a situation of economic dependence can result in *de facto* control. For example, this can be due to wide-ranging long term supply agreements, or credit provided by suppliers or customers, combined with structural links.[34] So far, when the Commission has assessed whether there is *de facto* control on this basis, it has refrained from finding that control has existed.[35]

In certain cases legislation can secure influence in a company for a public authority, employees or other groups. Even though such public prerogatives can secure others than the shareholders *de jure* control over a company, the Commission has adopted the view that this form of influence does not amount to control for the purposes of the MCR.[36]

30. M.967, *KLM/Air UK,* decision of 22.9.1997, para. 12.
31. Jurisdictional Notice, para. 13.
32. See *C.J. Cook & C.S. Kerse:* EC Merger Control, 5th ed., 2009 p. 50. In German law a range of different types of contract has been developed which can all lead to an undertaking securing control of another company.
33. M.890, *Blokker/Toys'R'Us* (OJ 1998 L 316/1), where the Commission stated that the fact that a franchise agreement existed between the parties did not exclude the possibility that, in the context of other agreements, the agreement could involve a merger; see para. 14 of the Decision.
34. Jurisdictional Notice, para. 20.
35. This was the case in M.258, *CCIE/GTE,* decision of 25.9.1992, where the Commission denied that the fact that Siemens had financed CCIE's takeover of the undertaking IL was sufficient for it to be said that Siemens had control over either CCIE or IL. In M.697, *Lockheed Martine/Loral Corporation,* decision of 27.3.1996, the Commission likewise denied that there was control in a situation where an undertaking (LMC) which owned non-voting shares in another company (LSCL), had provided guarantees for LSCL for up to $250 million, had granted LSCL a number of important licences, and where there was an overlap of personnel in several important positions in LMC and LSCL.
36. Jurisdictional Notice, para. 22.

If an undertaking has control, this is enough to establish that there is an obligation to notify under the MCR. The fact that the undertaking does not use its influence is irrelevant; what matters is that the undertaking has the possibility of exercising controlling influence.[37] However, there is a special exception for credit institutions and other financial undertakings that trade in securities as part of their usual business, as well as certain holding companies; see Article 3(5) of the MCR. Even though these undertakings acquire a controlling shareholding, there will not be a merger, provided that the undertakings do not exercise their voting rights to determine the undertaking's competitive conduct, i.e. its business strategy.

2.2.2. Joint control

Joint control means that two or more undertakings together have control over another undertaking. What is decisive is that the joint venture partners need to agree on important matters, so that joint control is in fact a (qualified) veto right.

When assessing a joint venture, it is first necessary to establish whether the joint venture partners together have the necessary control to exercise decisive influence on the running of the joint venture. This assessment corresponds largely to the assessment of the rights which give sole control over a company. In many cases it will be obvious that there is the necessary control, for example where the joint venture partners together own all the shares in the company. To establish the existence of joint control it is next necessary to investigate whether there are veto rights so that control can only be exercised if all the joint venture partners agree.

In the case of a 50/50 joint venture, where two joint venture partners have the same voting rights, there will normally be joint control. In such a joint venture, either party can block any decision in the joint venture, and thus have a negative decision-making influence on the running of the company.[38] In a joint venture where the joint venture partners do not have equal voting rights, it will often be laid down in agreements etc. that the parties will have a

37. M.330, *McCormick/CPC/Rabobank/Ostmann,* decision of 14.9.1993, where a bank was secured wide veto rights in a joint venture. Even though the bank stated that it would not become involved in important business decisions, the Commission held that the bank had a share in the joint control; see *C.J. Cook & C.S. Kerse:* EC Merger Control, 5th ed., 2009 p. 38.
38. This presupposes that there are no special rules giving one of the joint venture partners a casting vote, or similar.

veto right in relation to certain decisions, and in this situation the question arises as to whether the veto rights are sufficiently extensive.

According to the Jurisdictional Notice, the Commission believes that it is decisive whether veto rights concern strategic decisions on the joint venture company's business policies. The Commission's Notice paragraph 67 states that 'veto rights which confer joint control typically include decisions and issues such as the budget, the business plan, major investments or the appointment of senior management'. The Commission's view is that a veto right on the business plan, or on the amendment of an already adopted business plan can in itself be enough for it to be found that joint control exists.[39] In Case T-2/93, *Air France* v *Commission*, the GC accepted that the Commission had assessed that there was joint control, as it emphasised that important decisions required the support of at least one of the members of the board appointed by each of the two joint venture partners, just as it emphasised that a business plan containing the most important directions for the running of the joint venture company could only be amended with the agreement of both joint venture partners.[40] However, budgets and business plans are not the only important strategic decisions. Depending on the actual circumstances, other decisions can be just as strategically significant.

In Decision M.998, *OBS! Danmark*, decision of 10.11.1997, the Commission emphasised that even relatively small investments required unanimity. Since the joint venture in question had to take a decision about the modernisation of its shops, and thus make a number of investments, the veto right was especially important.[41] However, this decision should be contrasted with Decision JV.46, *Blackstone/CDPQ/Kabel Nordrhein-Westfalen*, decision of 19.6.2000; and Decision JV.50, *Blackstone/CDPQ/ Kabel Baden-Württemberg*, decision of 1.8.2000, where the Commission

39. Jurisdictional Notice, para. 70.
40. Case T-3/93, *Air France v Commission,* para. 65. In its practice hitherto, the GC had accepted the Commission's assessment of whether there is joint control or sole control. See also Case T-221/95, *Endemol Entertainment Holding;* and Case T-102/96, *Gencor,* where the GC agreed with the Commission that the case concerned sole control and not joint control, paras 167-194. This last case is particularly interesting since the GC went into considerable detail in assessing the question of control, which suggests that the GC will not always uncritically accept the Commission's assessment.
41. See also Case T-102/96, *Gencor,* where the GC pointed out that marketing policy was a very important aspect of the competitive strategy of the joint venture in question, see para. 178.

did not accept that a veto right which included investments and sales of a certain size was sufficient to establish the existence of joint control. The Commission referred to the fact that the veto right did not cover business plans and budgets, and that there was nothing to prevent the joint venture partners making investment alongside their joint venture.

In several cases the Commission has found that the veto rights which ensure joint control go further than the veto rights that are normally allowed to minority shareholders.[42] Since the content of minority rights varies from country to country, it can be difficult to assess the extent of this statement.[43] In Case T-221/95, *Endemol Entertainment Holding BV*, it was agreed that the most important strategic decisions had to be put before the general meeting, and it was also agreed that decisions taken at a general meeting had to be adopted unanimously. The GC thus found that the requirement for unanimity went further than was required for the protection of the interests of minority shareholders; see paragraph 163. These decisions must be seen as an acceptance of the Commission's point of view that ordinary minority shareholders' rights are, in principle, not enough for establishing that there is joint control, but it does not otherwise contribute to establishing the content of the concept of 'ordinary' or 'normal' minority rights.

When joint venture partners wish to regulate their influence in their joint venture in more detail, they will typically make an agreement on the composition of the management or supervising body, including giving each joint venture partner a right to appoint a given number of board members. By combining this with a provision that all important strategic decisions shall be put before the board, it is possible to ensure that the individual joint venture partners acquire an indirect veto right. This will be the case if there is a requirement for unanimity, or if a measure requires the support of at least one member appointed by the different joint venture partners. In these cases the joint venture partners try to establish the veto right in the board rather than in the general meeting. However, the Commission has accepted that a veto right at this level corresponds to a veto right at a higher level in the decision-making hierarchy of the company.

42. M.10, *Conagra/Idea,* decision of 30.5.1991 para. 14; and M.308, *Kali+Salz/MdK/Treuhand* (OJ 1994 L 186/38).
43. See *C.J. Cook & C.S. Kerse:* EC Merger Control, 5th ed., 2005 p. 37. Minority rights are still not fully harmonised in the EU. However, certain minority rights in connection with company capital, mergers etc. have already been harmonised.

While such a composition of the management or supervising body is an important part of assessing the existence of joint control, it is less important how the day-to-day management is composed. In many companies the day-to-day management will not be concerned with taking strategic decisions, but will 'only' be concerned with implementing them. This means that the fact that one joint venture partner takes care of the day-to-day running of the company does not exclude the possibility of there being joint control, as long as the strategic decisions require unanimity.[44]

In other cases the joint venture partners bind themselves to exercise their voting rights in a specific way, thereby establishing a 'pooling' agreement. A pooling agreement means that several shareholders bind themselves to exercise their voting rights in cooperation with each other. In this way, two minority shareholders who cannot individually exercise control can acquire control jointly, so they both partake of the joint control.[45] Instead of entering into an agreement about the exercise of voting rights, joint venture partners can choose to set up a holding company to which they transfer their ownership rights in the joint venture company. By establishing the decision-making process in this way, the owners of the holding company can exercise a veto right in connection with the holding company's exercise of its voting rights in the joint venture, and achieve the same result as in a pooling agreement.

> This is illustrated by Decision M.141, *UAP/Transatlantic/Sun Life*, decision of 11.11.1991, where the undertakings involved pooled their shares in Sun Life in a jointly owned holding company whose only activity was to own a majority of the shares in Sun Life. Each of two joint venture partners owned 50 % of the holding company, and the Commission held that the holding company was merely a vehicle used by the joint venture partners to secure their joint control over Sun Life.

44. M.269, *Shell/Montecatini* (OJ 1994 L 332/48), paras 9-10. It is also clear from the Jurisdictional Notice, para. 81, that the fact that one joint venture partner has specialist knowledge about the activities of the joint venture company, and the other joint venture partner therefore plays no role in the day-to-day management, does not exclude there being joint control.
45. JV.2, *ENEL/FT/DT,* decision of 22.6.1998, where two shareholders who each had 24.5 % of the voting rights in a joint venture ensured themselves a share in the joint control by entering into a pooling agreement; and JV.4, *VIAG/Orange UK,* decision of 11.8.1998, where two participants each had 35 % of the voting rights in a joint venture likewise ensured that they jointly acquired control by entering into a pooling agreement.

There will also be joint control where minority shareholders act collectively on a *de facto* basis – in other words, without having entered into a pooling or similar agreement. According to the Jurisdictional Notice, paragraph 76, it is only 'very exceptionally' that there will be such a *de facto* basis for collective action, as it requires there to be 'strong common interests' which prevent the minority shareholders acting against each other. This can be indicated by previous connections between the shareholders, by the fact that they have acquired their shareholdings at the same time with a coordinated acquisition, that they have set up the joint venture in question together, or the fact that all the minority shareholder have invested essential assets in the joint venture, or have made some other vital contribution.[46]

> There is an example of where the Commission has found there to be such a collective *de facto* control in Decision M.382, *Philips/Grundig*, decision of 3.12.1993, where Grundig was controlled through a company which was 40 % owned by Philips, while the other 60 % of the voting rights were divided between three banks. The Commission found that the three banks together had *de facto* control, even though none of the banks individually had a veto right. The Commission emphasised that according to the articles of association of the company, the banks appointed one of the two managing directors of the company. Since the banks did not have the expertise required to run a company like Grundig, the Commission found that it was most probable that the banks would follow the advice of the managing director jointly appointed by them, so it was probable that they would act collectively.

The establishment of joint control requires that the joint venture partners have the possibility of exercising control over a longer period. This means that if joint control only lasts for a limited period, and is replaced by sole control, the Commission will consider that sole control was established from the start. There have been many examples of this in practice, where the partners have established a temporary joint venture, but where the agreements provide for the joint venture to be controlled by one of the parties after a given number of years.[47]

46. Jurisdictional Notice, paras 77-80.
47. M.425, *BS/BT*, decision of 28.3.1993; and M.604, *Albacom*, decision of 15.9.1995, where it was only for the first three years that one of the parties had extensive veto rights, and this was not long enough for it to be considered that there was joint control.

Some joint venture agreements or articles of association include special provisions which are intended to deal with the deadlock problem which can lead to a joint venture being paralysed. These solutions necessarily mean that the veto right of one of the joint venture partners is restricted, since consideration for the interest of the activities of the joint venture means that a joint venture partner cannot maintain its veto unconditionally. To a large extent the Commission has accepted that such deadlock provisions do not alter the fact that there is joint control. It has readily accepted solutions whereby decisions on which agreement cannot be reached are referred to a group of experts or to an arbitrator.[48] This practice also seems to have been accepted by the GC.[49]

2.3. Full-function joint ventures

According to Article 3(4) of the MCR, the Regulation only applies to 'a joint venture performing on a lasting basis all the functions of an autonomous economic entity'. According to the judgment in Case T-87/96, *Assicurazioni Generali and Unicredito*, the determination of the existence of a full-function joint venture involves the putting together of assets and/or activities so that a new undertaking is created alongside the joint venture partners. The practice of the Commission shows that it takes account of a number of different elements when assessing whether a joint venture has full-function status. Even if the Commission has not made such clear distinctions, it seems that the conditions can be divided into the following four categories:

1. According to the Jurisdictional Notice, in order to fulfil the requirement a joint venture must have access to *sufficient resources*, including finance, staff, and assets (tangible and intangible).[50]

   In several cases the Commission has considered whether a joint venture has sufficient financial resources to be able to operate autonomously, in other words, without being dependent on credits and/or injections of cash from the joint venture partners. The financial resources will normally be secured in the form of investments by the joint venture partners which are either already invested upon the formation of the company, or which the joint venture partners have committed themselves to invest as the need arises.[51] However, financing can also be obtained indirectly, by the joint venture

48. M.683, *GTS-Hermes Inc./HIT Rail,* decision of 5.3.1996 para. 10; and M.662, *Leisure Plan,* decision of 21.12.1995, (para. not numbered).
49. Case T-221/95, *Endemol Entertainment* v *Commission,* para. 162.
50. Jurisdictional Notice, para. 94.
51. M.222, *Mannesmann/Hoesch* (OJ 1993 L 114/34), para. 8, where the joint venture partners had committed themselves to make further investments if their joint venture

partners helping their joint venture to establish a bank loan; see Decision JV.36, *TXU Europe/EDF-London Investment*, decision of 3.2.2000, paragraph 17. On the other hand it would be less appropriate if the joint venture's credit facilities essentially consisted of a loan from the joint venture partners, see Decision M.722, *Teneo/Merill Lynch/Bankers Trust*, decision of 15.4.1996, paragraph 14, where the Commission decided that the joint venture in question did not have full-function status.

If a joint venture has sufficient financing it will usually buy the assets it needs. Some assets, in particular registered intellectual property rights and know-how, can only be made available to the joint venture by one of the joint venture partners, and the Commission therefore investigates whether this is the case. If the rights and the necessary know-how are transferred to the joint venture, there will naturally be no problem.[52] However, in many cases the joint venture partners do not want to transfer their rights, as they want also to exploit them themselves. A common solution for this is to grant the joint venture a licence to use the technology. In its recent practice the Commission has accepted that a licence can be equivalent to an assignment of the rights.[53] However, this requires the licence to be irrevocable, though the licence can be for a predetermined period.[54] It is also a requirement that the licence should be given without conditions which would significantly restrict the joint venture's possibility of exploiting the rights.

The Commission has also accepted that a major part of the personnel who work for the joint venture are made available by the joint venture partners.[55] As for particularly important resources, the Commission sometimes makes an evaluation of the reasons why they are not transferred to the joint venture.

did not have sufficient finances, provided it was not possible to obtain more advantageous financing from third parties.

52. See e.g. M.310, *Harrisons & Crosfield/Akzo,* decision of 29.4.1993, para. 13. In this situation there seems to be nothing to prevent one or more of the joint venture partners receiving a licence from their joint venture to exploit the technology; see e.g. M.527, *Thomson/Deutsche Aerospace,* decision of 2.12.1995, para. 10
53. M.527, *Thomson/Deutsche Aerospace,* decision of 2.12.1995, para. 10, which seem to treat an assignment of rights and a licence which applies for the duration of the joint venture's existence as being equivalent.
54. M.1049, *AKZO/PLV-EPL,* decision of 4.12.1997, para. 7 (10 years); and JV.11, *Home Benelux B.V.,* decision of 15.9.1998, para. 9 (number of years not disclosed).
55. M.994, *Dupont/Hitachi,* decision of 24.10.1997, where there had not been time to transfer the personnel. The Commission accepted this, but also found that the personnel were under the management of the joint venture. There was another example in M.1049, *AKZO/PLV-EPL,* decision of 4.12.1997, para. 10, where it appears from the decision that the personnel had not wanted to be transferred. But see in contrast, M.551, *ATR/BAe,* decision of 25.7.1995 para. 17, where the Commission apparently used the fact that the personnel were loaned out by one of the joint venture partners as one of several arguments for finding that there was not a full-function joint venture.

2. In addition to resources, the Jurisdictional Notice requires a joint venture to have *management* dedicated to its day-to-day operations.[56] It is clear that the requirement does not require the joint venture to be independent of the joint venture partners, as what is decisive is whether there is sufficient autonomy from an organisational point of view. Thus there is a requirement that the joint venture should have a management, and that the management of the joint venture should not be left entirely to a joint venture partner.

   If one looks at the practice of the Commission, it seems that the requirement for an autonomous management plays only a minor role. In its more recent practice the Commission has begun to establish whether a joint venture has 'its own management dedicated to day-to-day operations'.[57] In most cases the Commission does not make a more detailed analysis, other than finding that there is such management. However, there have been individual decisions where it has looked in more detail.

An example of a case which addressed the question more explicitly is Decision M.3576, *ECT/PONL/EUROMAX*, decision of 22.12.2004. In this case the joint venture partners argued that there was not a full-function joint venture, among other things because the management of the joint venture had limited decision-making powers. The joint venture partners referred in particular to the fact that the management board of the joint venture had to obtain the consent of the supervisory board for a number of decisions. However, the Commission did not find that these decisions meant that the management did not have some autonomy. It is not clear from the Decision what kind of decisions of the joint venture required consent, but it is clear that the Commission attached importance to the fact that the supervisory board did not have direct influence on the joint venture's commercial relationships with its customers; see paragraph 12. Since the management of the joint venture was still responsible for that part of the day-to-day management, the Commission found there was sufficiently autonomy.

56. Jurisdictional Notice, para. 94.
57. JV.14, *Panagora/DG Bank,* decision of 26.11.1998 para. 12; JV.22, *Fujitsu/Siemens,* decision of 30.9.1999 para. 11; JV.23, *Telefonica/Portugal Telecom/MEDI Telecom,* decision of 17.12.1999 para. 13; JV.36, *Sydkraft/HEW/Hansa Energy Trading,* decision of 30.9.1999 para. 17; and JV.44, *Hitachi/NEC-Dram/JV,* decision of 3.5.2000, para. 11.

3. In addition to this, there is a requirement that a joint venture must carry on *autonomous business activities*. This means that there must be an initial evaluation of whether the planned activities correspond to an activity which is normally carried on by an undertaking in the business sector in question.[58] If a joint venture only takes on one specific function for the joint venture partners, it will merely have an auxiliary function in relation to them, and it will thus not be operating autonomously. According to the Commission, this will be the case if a joint venture is only concerned with research and development, or with production.[59] A joint venture which primarily undertakes the sales of the joint venture partners' products will often also not fulfil the requirement.[60]

There have been a number of cases on the question of whether a joint venture which does not itself have a distribution system can have full-function status. However, there is not a strict requirement that a joint venture must have its own distribution system. It is presumably acceptable for part of its sales to be made by one or more of the joint venture partners acting as a distributor, and buying the joint venture's products with a view to their resale.[61] However, if the joint venture partners act as distributors and buy the major part of the joint venture's production, and thereby also determine the pricing, it is less likely that the join venture will be considered to have full-function status.[62]

In many cases doubt has been raised about whether a joint venture has full-function status because the planned activity of the joint venture is based to a large extent on trade with the joint venture partners. The Commission accepts that a joint venture can be dependent on the joint venture partners either as suppliers or as customers during a

58. Case T-87/96, *Assicurazioni Generali and Unicredito,* para. 73; and the review of the Commission's practice in *Matthias Karl:* Der Zusammenschlussbegriff in der Europaischen Fusionskontrollverordnung, 1996 pp. 276-277.
59. Jurisdictional Notice, para. 95. Such an assessment appears to have been persuasive for the result in M.168, *Flachglas/Vegla,* decision of 13.4.1992; and M.904, *RSB/TENEX/Fuel Logistic,* decision of 2.4.1997, which both concluded that joint ventures had an auxiliary function, see expressly para. 13 of the former Decision (*Hilfsfunktion*) and para. 10 in the latter Decision.
60. There was an example in M.58, *Baxter/Nestle/Salvia,* decision of 6.2.1991. See also M.551, *ATR/BAe,* decision of 25.7.1995, where the Commission did not believe that a joint venture would develop new products, so it was most probable that it would merely function as a sales agency for the joint venture partners.
61. M.441, *Daimler Benz/RWE,* decision of 20.6.1994 para. 17, where the Commission emphasised whether the cooperation between the joint venture and the joint venture partners was on arm's length terms.
62. M.353, *British Telecom/MCI,* decision of 13.9.1993 para. 6. See also *Adrian Brown:* Distinguishing between Concentrative and Cooperative Joint Ventures: Is It Getting Any. Easier, European Competition Law Review, 1996 pp. 240-249 (in particular p. 244 et seq.)

start-up period which is normally up to three years.[63] Next, the Commission normally requires the trade to be on arm's length terms. Finally, in some cases the Commission has attached importance to whether the joint venture is contractually bound to the trade, i.e. whether it has the possibility of finding other suppliers or customers.[64]

In some situations the Commission accepts that a joint venture acts as sales agent for one or more of its joint venture partners. This is the case where the joint venture operates in a trade market where there are undertakings which specialise in sales and distribution without being vertically integrated with the undertakings which produce the goods and where different sources of supply are available.[65]

4. Finally, there is a requirement that a joint venture must be set up on a *lasting basis,* in other words it is not merely of a temporary character. This requirement is presumed to be satisfied if a joint venture is set up for an indeterminate period, e.g. without it being expressly provided that it will terminate at a given date. Naturally, in such joint ventures it will often be possible for the joint venture to be wound up if disagreements arise or if the project fails. This does not alter the conclusion that a joint venture is established on an enduring basis.[66] The fact that a joint venture agreement can be terminated by one of the joint venture partners after a certain period also does not mean that it is not set up on a lasting basis. What is important is that, when setting it up, the partners intend that it should be lasting.

   A joint venture can also be set up for a specific period, and the question here is how long the period must be in order for the joint venture to be considered as being enduring. The Commission's practice is not clear, but it can be assumed it must be for at least five years.[67]

63. Jurisdictional Notice, para. 97. See however M.168, *Flachglas/ Vegla,* decision of 13.4.1992 para. 21, where the Commission seems to have accepted a start-up period of 5 years.
64. M.179, *Spar/Dansk Supermarked,* decision of 3.2.1992 para. 8.
65. Jurisdictional Notice, para. 102
66. Jurisdictional Notice, para. 103.
67. The practice in the decisions of the Commission is ambiguous. It appears from M.722, *Teneo/Merill Lynch/Bankers Trust,* decision of 15.4.1996, and M.3858, *Lehman Brothers/SCG/Starwood/Le Meridien,* decision of 25.7.2005, that three years is too short. On the other hand, 6½ years was sufficient in M.259, *British Airways/TAT,* decision of 27.11.1992 para. 10. In this decision the Commission emphasised that the business sector in question was in a permanent state of change, and this fact favoured acceptance of a joint venture of a shorter duration. This means that when assessing whether the joint venture has a lasting character, one must consider the rate of change in the business sector in question.

The way in which a joint venture is set up is important for the way in which the Commission makes its assessment. Many joint ventures are set up by the joint venture partners establishing joint control over an existing company. If, in this way, the joint venture has hitherto been an independent undertaking, typically owned by one of the joint venture partners, the Commission will assume, *prima facie*, that the joint venture will continue to have full-function status.[68] Where a joint venture is set up as a start-up, in other words where it does not take over existing activities or a package of assets and resources, there is no assumption as to whether it is a full-function joint venture. As the joint venture partners will not yet have established such a joint venture (and may not establish it prior to notification), the Commission's assessment is based on the agreements and the information submitted by the joint venture partners. The Commission's assessment will often involve an assessment of how the joint venture will develop after the start-up period. The Commission accepts that during a start-up period of normally 2-3 years, a joint venture can be dependent on the joint venture partners, among other things by them buying most of its production etc. and it can also be planned that the joint venture will, over time, be supplied with additional resources.

It could be considered whether the form of incorporation chosen for the joint venture is significant for the assessment of whether a joint venture has full-function status. Unsurprisingly, the Commission does not rely on such formal factors in its practice. The fact that a joint venture is set up as an independent legal person does not exclude the possibility of it being found not to be full-function for the purposes of the MCR.[69] Conversely, a joint venture can be a full-function joint venture, even if it is not set up as a company, in other words if it is a 'contractual joint venture'.[70]

68. See e.g. M.58, *Baxter/Nestle/Saliva,* decision of 6.2.1991; M.222, *Mannesmann/Hoesch* (OJ 1993 L 114/34); M.249, *Northern Telecom/Matra Telecommunication,* decision of 10.8.1992; and more recently, JV.3, *BT/Airtel*, decision of 8.7.1998; JV.17, *Mannesmann/Bell Atlantic/OPI,* decision of 21.5.1999; JV.24, *Bertelsmann/Planeta/Bol Spain,* decision of 3.12.1999; and JV.37, *B SKY B/Kirch Pay TV,* decision of 21.3.2000.
69. However, it should be mentioned that in M.293, *Philips/Thomson/Sagem,* decision of 18.1.1993, para. 12, the Commission seems to have given weight to the fact that the joint venture 'will be a separate legal entity'. However, this case can probably not be taken as establishing an independent argument for the fulfilment of the full-function requirement. See the discussion in *Karsten Engsig Sørensen:* Joint ventures – struktur og regulering, 2006 pp. 225-226.
70. Such was the situation in JV.19, *KLM/Alitalia,* para. 11.

2.4. Community dimension

According to Article 1(1) of the MCR, the Regulation applies to all concentrations with a Community dimension. The Community dimension is defined by reference to certain threshold values which require that merging companies have a turnover of a certain size and a certain cross-border element. According to the original threshold values in Article 1(2) of the MCR, a concentration has a Community dimension where:

a. the combined aggregate worldwide turnover of all the undertakings concerned is more than EUR 5,000 million; and
b. the aggregate Community-wide turnover of each of at least two of the undertakings concerned is more than EUR 250 million,

unless each of the undertakings concerned achieves more than two-thirds of its aggregate Community-wide turnover within one and the same Member State.

This definition was the result of a compromise between those Member States that wanted merger control, and those Member States that did not think it appropriate for the Commission to be given further powers in this area.[71] The 'one-stop shop' principle means that mergers or concentrations that have a Community dimension can only be examined by the EU, thereby excluding the competence of the Member States.[72]

From the beginning, it was intended that the MCR's original turnover threshold should be revised after the start-up period. In 1996 the Commission published a Green Paper, setting out different possible solutions.[73] The result of this consultation was the addition of new threshold values in Article 1(3), which were added in Regulation (EC) No 1310/97.[74] These thresholds were as follows:

a. the combined aggregate worldwide turnover of all the undertakings concerned is more than EUR 2 500 million;

71. See *Morten P. Broberg:* The European Commission's jurisdiction to scrutinise mergers, 3rd ed., 2006 pp. 3-5.
72. Under Article 9 of the MCR the Commission can, in certain specified circumstances, refer a notified case to the competition authorities of the Member States.
73. COM(96) 19 final.
74. Regulation (EC) No 1310/97 on the control of concentrations between undertakings (OJ 1997 L 180/1).

b. in each of at least three Member States, the combined aggregate turnover of all the undertakings concerned is more than EUR 100 million;
c. in each of at least three Member States included for the purpose of point (b), the aggregate turnover of each of at least two of the undertakings concerned is more than EUR 25 million; and
d. the aggregate Community-wide turnover of each of at least two of the undertakings concerned is more than EUR 100 million;

unless each of the undertakings concerned achieves more than two-thirds of its aggregate Community-wide turnover within one and the same Member State.

This provision expands the scope of application of the MCR so as to include concentrations between smaller undertakings. The focus is directed towards concentrations where the participating undertakings have their sales across at least three Member States. The turnover threshold is applied by seeing first whether the threshold in paragraph (b) has been met, and if not, then by seeing whether the threshold in paragraph (c) is met.

The application of the above threshold requires it to be established which undertakings are the participating undertakings concerned, and how their turnover should be calculated, including its relation to different areas.

2.4.1. Undertakings concerned

The turnover threshold presumes that it is determined which undertakings are taking part in a concentration. Where one undertaking takes over another undertaking, it is on the face of it unproblematic to determine which are the undertakings concerned. However, in cases which involve joint ventures it can sometimes be difficult to decide this.

If two or more undertakings acquire control of a newly established company, the undertakings concerned are those which have a share of the control, i.e. the joint venture partners.[75] If a joint venture is set up by the acquisition of joint control of an existing undertaking, the undertakings concerned are the joint venture partners and the joint venture itself. However, the joint venture company itself is not an undertaking concerned where it is an existing undertaking subject to the sole control of one of the joint venture partners prior to the establishment of joint control. The reason for this difference is that in this case the joint venture company's turnover will be counted with that of the original owner which, as one of the joint venture partners, is one of the under-

75. Jurisdictional Notice, para. 139.

takings concerned. If there is an existing joint venture, a change from joint control to sole control will normally constitute a concentration, and in this case the undertakings concerned will be the remaining (acquiring) joint venture partner together with the joint venture company.

If a joint venture acquires control of another undertaking, the undertakings concerned will be assumed to be the joint venture and the acquired undertaking. In certain situations it may seem somewhat formalistic to adopt this view, as it is effectively the joint venture partners that are behind the acquisition and which therefore ought to be considered the participating undertakings. For example, this is the case where undertakings A and B set up a joint venture (C) with the sole aim of taking over undertaking D. This transaction is equivalent to the situation where A and B take over control of D themselves, and therefore both A and B ought to be considered as undertakings concerned. The difficult question to decide is when a joint venture is considered to be an undertaking concerned, and when the joint venture partners are the undertakings concerned. According to the Jurisdictional Notice, the Commission will normally consider the joint venture company to be the undertaking concerned where the joint venture is a full-function joint venture.[76] This refers back to the definition of a full-function joint venture developed in relation to Article 3(4) of the MCR. In addition to this, in its Notice the Commission has listed a number of circumstances which indicate that a joint venture is merely being used by the joint venture partners as a vehicle for carrying out a takeover, so that it is the joint venture partners that ought to be included as the participating undertakings. In paragraph 147, the Notice refers to the following circumstances:

- where the joint venture is set up especially for the purpose of acquiring the target company,
- where the joint venture has not yet started to operate,
- where an existing joint venture has no full-function character.

2.4.2. Calculation of turnover

According to Article 5(1) of the MCR, in principle the basis for calculating turnover is the sale of products and the provision of services falling within the undertakings' ordinary activities in the preceding financial year, after deduction of sales rebates and of value added tax and other taxes directly related to

76. Jurisdictional Notice, para. 146.

turnover.[77] Article 5(3) of the MCR contains special rules for credit institutions and other financial institutions. By focusing on sales, it is clear that a merger in a business sector where there are large sales turnovers but low margins will exceed the thresholds more easily than a merger in a business sector with low turnovers and high margins. Since the consequences for competition will not necessarily be different in the two kinds of sectors, the thresholds may be inappropriate in some respects. However, the Commission has chosen to focus on turnover because this is relatively easy to establish and because turnover can be used as a measure of the financial resources and activities covered by a concentration.

According to Article 5(1), the geographic allocation of turnover is determined by focusing on where the customer is located, regardless of where the customer receives the goods or services. This information will not always be apparent from the official accounts. The Commission will usually be satisfied with the calculations made by the undertakings themselves.[78]

When the participating undertakings are part of a larger corporate group it can sometimes be necessary to include the turnover of associated companies as part of the turnover of the undertaking concerned. This is regulated in more detail in Article 5(4) and (5) of the MCR.

Article 5(4)(b) of the MCR defines the subsidiary companies whose turnover should be included in the calculation of turnover. These are undertakings in which the undertaking concerned, directly or indirectly:

i. owns more than haf the capital or business assets, or
ii. has the power to exercise more than half the voting rights, or
iii. has the power to appoint more than half the members of the supervisory board, the administrative board or bodies legally representing the undertakings, or
iv. has the right to manage the undertakings' affairs.

This definition is used in several places in competition law, and is found, among others, in the *De minimis* Notice from 2001, as well as in several of the block exemption

77. The definition closely follows the definition in Article 28 in the Fourth Company Law Directive (OJ 1978 L 222/11). In practice, the calculation of turnover is based on the latest audited annual accounts, unless more recent figures are available which can have a decisive influence, see *C.J. Cook & C.S. Kerse:* EC Merger Control, 5th ed., 2009 p. 90; and *Jonathan Faull & Ali Nikpay (eds.):* The EC Law of Competition, 2nd ed., 2007 p. 448.
78. Jurisdictional Notice, para. 195.

regulations.[79] In Article 5(4)(c) of the MCR it is stated that those undertakings which have the rights or powers listed in subparagraph (b) are also included. This means that the parent company of an undertaking concerned is included. The same can apply to sister companies; see subparagraph (d). To the extent that an undertaking concerned is part of a corporate group, as defined in Article 5(4), its turnover from transactions between group companies is included.

If the undertaking concerned is a joint venture, for example where a joint venture takes over another undertaking, the question then arises whether the joint venture partners' turnover should be added to the turnover of the joint venture company. Here it is necessary to investigate whether the individual joint venture partner fulfils the criteria in subparagraph (b). There seems to be agreement that the different sub-subparagraphs in subparagraph (b) do not exclude each other. They are alternatives to the extent that it must be investigated whether each of the joint venture partners fulfils one of them.[80]

However, the Commission has adopted an even wider interpretation of subparagraph (c), according to which the joint venture partners which exercise joint control are included, regardless of whether each of the joint partners individually fulfils the criteria in the sub-subparagraphs to subparagraph (b).[81] The Commission's extended interpretation of subparagraph (c) in this way has been criticised.[82] The Commission's interpretation means that even very small joint ventures can exceed the turnover threshold, provided the joint venture partners have a sufficiently large turnover.

Article 5(4)(e) deals with the situation where a joint venture is set up by several companies in the same corporate group. The turnover of such a joint venture should also be included in the turnover of the participating undertaking.

According to its wording, Article 5(5) deals with the situation where a joint venture is jointly controlled by the undertakings concerned. This will be the case where two

79. Commission Notice on agreements of minor importance which do not appreciably restrict competition under Article 81(1) of the Treaty establishing the European Community (*de minimis*) (OJ 2001 C 368/13), para. 12; Regulation (EU) No 1217/2010 on the application of Article 101(3) TFEU to certain categories of research and development agreements, Article 1(2) (OJ 2010 L 335/36); Regulation (EU) No 330/2010 on the application of Article 101(3) TFEU to categories of vertical agreements and concerted practices, Article 1(2) (OJ 2010 L 102/1); and Regulation (EC) No 772/2004 on the application of Article 81(3) of the [EC] Treaty to categories of technology transfer agreements, Article 1(2) (OJ 2004 L 123/11).
80. See *Barry E. Hawk & Henry L. Huser:* European Community Merger Control: A Practitioner's Guide, 1996 p. 105; *C.J. Cook & C.S. Kerse:* EC Merger Control, 5th ed., 2009 p. 102; and *Morten P. Broberg:* The European Commission's jurisdiction to scrutinise mergers, 3rd ed., 2006 p. 96.
81. Jurisdictional Notice, para. 182.
82. See *Morten P. Broberg:* The European Commission's jurisdiction to scrutinise mergers, 3rd ed., 2006 pp. 104-105; *C.J. Cook & C.S. Kerse:* EC Merger Control, 4th ed., 2009 p. 104; and *Barry E. Hawk & Henry L. Huser:* European Community Merger Control: A Practitioner's Guide, 1996 p. 104.

undertakings which merge or which wish to set up a joint venture already have a joint venture. Article 5(5) provides that the calculation of the turnover of such a joint venture does not include the turnover which is derived from sales between the joint venture and the joint venture partners (and with companies in the same corporate group as them). Finally, according to Article 5(5)(b), the turnover of the undertakings concerned is to be allocated in proportion to their participation. For example, if two joint venture partners already have a joint venture, half the turnover in the joint venture is to be allocated to each joint venture partner. The Commission has used the principle in Article 5(5)(b) in cases where an undertaking concerned controls a joint venture together with a third party undertaking.

2.5. Concentrations without a Community dimension

If a concentration does not exceed the thresholds in Article 1(2)-(3), it does not have a Community dimension and therefore cannot, in principle, be assessed under the MCR. However, this does not mean that such concentrations are never subject to an assessment under competition law.

First, Article 22(3) of the MCR contains the so-called 'Dutch clause', whereby one or more Member States can request the Commission to deal with a concentration which does not have a Community dimension. The Commission can intervene under Article 8, if a concentration creates or strengthens a dominant position with the effect that competition is actually significantly restricted in one or more Member States. There is also a requirement that the concentration should affect trade between Member States. This condition should be interpreted in the same way as the condition concerning the effect on trade between Member States in Articles 101 and 102 TFEU.[83]

Next, the undertakings concerned can request the Commission to consider a concentration, even if it does not have a Community dimension. This possibility was introduced in the revision of the MCR in 2004; see Article 4(5). There is a requirement that the concentration must be capable of being reviewed under the national competition laws of at least three Member States. A Member State that has competence to deal with the concentration under its national competition law can object to the case being referred to the Commission, and if it does so the reference will not be made.

In addition, in principle the Commission has the possibility of applying Articles 101 and 102 TFEU to mergers without a Community dimension. According to Article 21(1) of the MCR, Council Regulation No 17 (EEC): First Regulation implementing Articles 85 and 86 of the [EC] Treaty and Regulation (EC) No 1/2003 does not apply, so that such enforcement would have to

83. Case T-22/97, *Kesko v Commission,* paras 103-110.

be under the provisions in Article 105 TFEU. In its commentary on Article 22 of the original MCR the Commission has declared that under no circumstances does it intend to intervene against a concentration which has a global turnover of less than EUR 2 billion, or a minimum turnover at EU level of less than EUR 100 million, since concentrations below this level will not normally have an appreciable influence on trade between Member States.[84] This limit can be especially relevant to the application of the Dutch clause, and it can also restrict the application of Articles 101 and 102 TFEU.

The amendments to the MCR in 1997 meant that, among other things, several joint ventures were covered by the Regulation, including autonomously operating joint ventures with cooperative elements. As a result, Article 21(1) was amended so that it is now stated that Regulation No 17 (EEC) and Regulation (EC) No 1/2003 still applies to joint ventures without a Community dimension, if their establishment has the aim or consequence of coordinating the competitive behaviour of undertakings which continue to be autonomous. In this way the Commission has secured full access to apply Article 101 (and in principle Article 102, though this normally less relevant) to joint ventures, where there is a concerted practice between the joint venture partners. However, in a declaration recorded in the minutes of a Council meeting, the Commission has stated that it is normally the job of the national competition authorities to control full-function joint ventures which do not have a Community dimension.[85]

It is also clear that the national competition authorities have the possibility to apply their own competition rules to concentrations which do not have a Community dimension.

2.6. The territorial scope of application of the MCR

Apart from the turnover threshold laid down in its Article 1(2) and (3), the MCR does not have any requirements as to the link which a concentration must have to the EU in order to be covered by the Regulation. This raises the question of whether there are any limits to the territorial reach of the MCR.

In its practice the Commission has applied the MCR to concentrations between undertakings outside the EU,[86] and it has also dealt with the establishment of joint ventures located outside the EU between joint venture partners

84. See the commentary on Article 22 of the MCR published in Bull. Suppl. 2/90.
85. See document 9296 of 20 June 1997.
86. See e.g. M.877, *Boeing/McDonnell Douglas* (OJ 1997 L 336/16).

who were not located in the EU.[87] It thus appears that the starting point is that, if the turnover threshold laid down in Article 1 of the MCR is met, the concentration should be notified and assessed in accordance with the MCR.[88]

The application of the MCR has to respect the principles of public international law which set a limit to the territorial extent of regulations of this nature. However, legal theorists do not agree on where the boundaries are according to public international law, and even though the GC has had an opportunity to judge the question in a single case, it cannot be said that the state of the law on this is entirely clear.[89]

> The problem came before the GC in Case T-102/96, *Gencor* v *Commission*. The case concerned a South African company, Gencor, which owned another South African company, Impala, which was responsible for the group's activities concerning platinum. The intention was that Impala should be transferred so as to be controlled jointly by Gencor and the English company Lonrho. This concentration had been notified to and

87. See e.g. M.346, *JCSAT/SAJAC,* decision of 30.6.1993; and M.994, *Dupont/Hitachi,* decision of 24.10.1997.
88. For the sake of completeness it should be mentioned that under Article 57 of the EEA agreement, the EFTA Surveillance Authority has powers to deal with concentrations which have an EFTA dimension; see the more detailed review in *Morten P. Broberg:* The European Commission's jurisdiction to scrutinise mergers, 3rd ed., 2006 pp. 193-211.
89. See, among others, the discussion in *Andre R. Fiebig:* International Law Limits on the Extraterritorial Application of the European Merger Control Regulation and Suggestions for Reform, European Competition Law Review, 1998 pp. 323-331; and *Morten P. Broberg:* The European Commission's jurisdiction to scrutinise mergers, 3rd ed., 2006 pp. 232-240. For analysis of the economic advantages and disadvantages of the extraterritorial application of the MCR, see *Ariel Ezrachi:* Limitations on the Extraterritorial Reach of the European. Merger Regulation, European Competition Law Review, 2001 pp. 137-146.

    In particular, the question of the territorial application of the MCR has given rise to problems in relation to the USA, not least in the wake of the merger between Boeing and McDonnell Douglas. In 1991 the USA and the EU entered into a cooperation agreement (OJ 1995 L 95/47), which among other things means that the competition authorities must give each other notice of cases which are being dealt with by one of the parties, which affect important interests of the other party. In practice it is mostly merger cases of which notification is given in this way; see COM(96) 479 final, Annex 1. In 1998 the cooperation was extended, but this did not apply to merger control; see Decision 98/386 (OJ 1998 L 173/26). For a review of these cooperative relations, see *Mads Andenas & Anestis Papadopoulos:* Antitrust Law and International Companies, European Business Law Review, 2002 pp. 193-216.

approved by the South African competition authorities, but upon its subsequent notification to the Commission, the Commission declared that the concentration was incompatible with the internal market in accordance with Article 8(3) of the MCR. Gencor challenged this decision under various headings, including that the concentration did not fall within the jurisdiction of the MCR. Gencor pointed out that the planned concentration concerned economic activities in the territory of a third country and according to the international law principle of territoriality, the MCR was not applicable.

On the scope of application of the MCR, the GC stated that Article 1 of the MCR does not require the undertakings concerned to be established in the EU or that the production activities covered by the concentration to be located in the EU, see paragraph 79 of the judgment. The GC refused to interpret the preamble to the MCR as requiring there to be some link to the EU, over and above that the undertakings should have sales, and thus turnover, in the EU.

Next, the GC stated that, under public international law, if a concentration would have direct and significant effect in the EU, there was an entitlement to apply the MCR. The GC thereby stated that the so-called 'effects doctrine' applies when deciding what limits public international law puts on the territorial application of the MCR. This principle has primarily been developed in American law, so it is surprising that the GC applied it without further comment.[90]

In the *Gencor* decision, the GC next assessed whether the three international law criteria, that the effect should be direct, significant and predictable, were fulfilled in this case. The GC held that this was the case. The GC's application of these three criteria in the actual case shows that they are characterised by having a very wide margin for discretion. For this reason it is difficult to establish precisely the requirements under public international law which must be fulfilled in order for a concentration to have a sufficient link to the EU. The GC found that it was

90. See *G. Porter Elliott:* The Gencor judgment: collective dominance, remedies and extraterrioriality under the Merger Regulation, European Law Review, 1999 pp. 638-652 (especially p. 641); and *C.J. Cook & C.S. Kerse:* EC Merger Control, 5th ed., 2009 p. 14. This result is surprising, not least in the light of the decision in the *Cellulose* case (Joined cases C-89/85 and others, *Ahlström (Cellulose II)*) where the CJ apparently chose not to apply the effects doctrine, but instead chose to develop a principle following the implementation, see *Jacques H.J. Bourgeois* in the Yearbook of European Law, 1990 pp. 103-132 (especially p. 115).

not a problem in this case, but it did not make it clear in what situations it would be contrary to public international law to apply the MCR.

3. The relevant market

In order to measure the effects of a concentration on competition, the Commission starts by defining the relevant market. The definition of the market is necessary in order to calculate the market shares of the merging undertakings, but in addition, the definition of the market is also a prerequisite for enabling other aspects of the competition in a given area to be analysed; see further on this in section 4.[91]

In principle, the relevant market is the market where the merging undertakings are active, or in the case of a joint venture, the markets where the joint venture company is active.

The Commission has published a Notice on the definition of the relevant market.[92] This Notice applies equally to the definition for the purposes of Articles 101 and 102 TFEU, and the MCR. While the market definition for Article 102 is aimed at judging whether an undertaking had a dominant position at the time when it has had certain conduct (abuse), the aim of the market definition under the MCR is to assess whether the merging undertakings can in future be assumed to acquire or to strengthen a dominant position. This difference can be the reason why market definitions can differ, especially as the geographic extent of the market for the purposes of the MCR will be affected by developments which can be expected in the near future.[93]

Defining the relevant market means that the Commission must determine both the relevant product market and the relevant geographic market. Nor-

91. The definition of the market was previously an obligatory part of the Commission's assessment under the MCR. This was also confirmed by the CJ in Joined cases C-68/94 and C-30/95, *France and others* v *Commission (Kali & Salz),* para. 143; and by the GC in Case T-2/93, *Air France v Commission,* para. 80. Following the reform of the MCR in 2004 it has been possible to prohibit certain concentrations, even if they do not create a dominant position (see more on this in section 4), so it is no longer clear that it is necessary to make a definition of the market in all cases. However, it seems that since 2004 the Commission has retained the practice of always starting by defining the relevant market.
92. Commission Notice on the definition of relevant market for the purposes of Community competition law (OJ 1997 C 372/5) (hereinafter 'Commission Notice on the definition of relevant market').
93. Commission Notice on the definition of relevant market, para. 12, and see the comments on this in section 3.2 below.

mally the Commission will make a final determination of the market, but sometimes the Commission leaves the question partially open. This will be the case where the Commission can see that regardless of whether it chooses the narrowest possible product market or the narrowest possible geographic market, the concentration will under no circumstances create or strengthen a dominant position.

3.1. The relevant product market

The 'relevant market' means all those products and/or services which are regarded as interchangeable or substitutable by the consumer, by reason of the products' characteristics, prices and intended use.[94]

The definition of the relevant market is made by the Commission taking into account such market analysis as exists, and the Commission itself undertakes an analysis of customers, competitors etc. There is thus no fixed procedure for how the Commission tackles cases, as the Commission decides from case to case what investigations should be included.[95]

The key issue in defining the relevant market is to investigate which products/services are considered substitutable on the demand side. This can be done on the basis of market analysis which shows which products consumers typically regard as substitutable, or it can be deduced from how the goods are sold. The Commission has said that it uses a conceptual experiment where it evaluates what effect a price increase would have on consumption. The test involves evaluating whether a hypothetical price increase in the range of 5-10 % in the relative price of product A would make so many of A's consumers shift to product B as to make the price increase unprofitable for the suppliers of A.[96] If the price increase is unprofitable, this means that A and B are in the same market. Thereafter a new hypothetical test is made to see whether a price increase of both A and B would be profitable or not. If, for example, it is judged that consumers would not shift to product C, then C is not considered part of the relevant product market, and this is so regardless of

94. Commission Notice on the definition of relevant market, para. 7.
95. Over time, the Commission has dealt with several cases within the same sector, so it has developed an established practice for how the product markets are divided up. See the review in *Peter Roth & Vivien Rose (eds.):* Bellamy & Child: European Community Law of Competition, 6th ed., 2008 pp. 295-301.
96. Commission Notice on the definition of relevant market, para. 17. This test is based on the 'SSNIP test' (Small but Significant Non-transitory Increase in Price), see *Peter Roth & Vivien Rose (eds.):* Bellamy & Child: European Community Law of Competition, 6th ed., 2008 pp. 254-258.

why consumers cannot be expected to shift. For example, this can be because of consumer preferences, or because the products are not comparable in price or function.

However, in many cases the Commission makes an assessment of which products are substitutable on the demand side on the basis of a number of less structured evaluations of the circumstances of the market in question.

> The market for beverages, in which the Commission has had the opportunity to define the relevant market in several cases, can be used to illustrate the Commission's practice. First, the Commission has rejected the idea that it is possible to adopt a narrow functional approach where it is argued that all beverages belong to the same product market because they all quench thirst.[97] Even though it is normally relevant to distinguish products that have the same function,[98] this cannot be a stand-alone criterion. The Commission has stated that carbonated and non-carbonated soft drinks cannot be assumed to belong to the same product market. There are differences in patterns of consumption which mean they cannot be said to belong to the same market. While mineral water and fruit juices in particular are used at breakfast, carbonated soft drinks are often used on other occasions, particularly in fast food restaurants and at social gatherings.[99] Another difference is that some beverages, such as milk and fruit juice, satisfy nutritional needs, while others, such as mineral water, have a consumer image as a natural product and are associated with good health and a healthy lifestyle.[100] Consumers do not associate any of these qualities with fizzy drinks. The fact that there are different product markets is also confirmed by statements of consumers and the fact that supermarkets do not put fizzy drinks on the same shelves as coffee, juice or milk, for example.[101] If one looks at pricing developments it is also possible to see that the prices of different beverages have developed independently of each other. On this basis the Commission has concluded that the market for bottled mineral water constitutes a separate product market.[102] Fizzy drinks with cola flavouring also constitute a market

97. M.190, *Nestlé/Perrier* (OJ 1992 L 356/1), para. 9.
98. See also M.580, *ABB/Daimler-Benz* (OJ 1997 L 11/1), para. 13.
99. M.794, *Coca Cola/Amalgamated Beverages GB* (OJ 1997 L 218/15), para. 30.
100. M.190, *Nestlé/Perrier* (OJ 1992 L 356/1), para. 10.
101. M.833, *The Coca Cola Company/Carlsberg* (OJ 1998 L 145/41), para. 36.
102. M.190, *Nestlé/Perrier* (OJ 1992 L 356/1), para. 19.

which is distinct from other beverages, including other fizzy drinks.[103] Finally, beers constitute a separate market, as they cannot be substituted with non-alcoholic soft drinks.[104]

The market for spirits is clearly different from markets for other beverages, but the Commission has gone further and denied that all forms of spirits are part of the same market.[105] Nor does the Commission accept that spirits should be divided between a market for 'white' spirits and a market for 'brown' spirits, as it is of the view that, on the basis of consumer demand and preferences, the product markets must be divided according to the type of spirit. As well as each type of spirit belonging to a separate product market, for some kinds of spirits a further division of product markets is made, as among other things the Commission has found that there are separate markets for whiskeys of different origins (Scotch, Irish, Canadian and American), and there are also whiskeys of differing prices and qualities which can hardly be assumed to belong to the same product markets.

In addition to distinguishing between product markets on the basis of product characteristics, there can also be a basis for distinguishing between different groups of consumers if the competitive conditions differ in relation to the different groups of consumers. Thus, in relation to the market for fizzy drinks with cola flavour, the Commission considered whether the product market could be divided into thee different segments, depending on the consumers: one for sales of colas to multiple retailers for home consumption, one for sales of colas to pubs and restaurants for on-premises consumption, and one for sales to small independent grocers etc.[106] The Commission chose not to decide on this question in the case in question, but in another case it has decided that sales of beer for retail sales and sales of beer to hotels and restaurants are two different markets.[107] The Commission has developed similar

103. M.794, *Coca Cola/Amalgamated Beverages GB* (OJ 1997 L 218/15), para. 26. See also M.289, *Pepsico/KAS,* decision of 21.12.1992, para. 5.1.2, where the Commission was inclined to say that the market for fizzy drinks should be divided up according to flavour, so that in addition to a market for cola flavour there was a market for lime/citrus, orange, tonic water etc. However, the Commission refrained from making a final decision on this question.
104. M.582, *Orkla/Volvo* (OJ 1996 L 66/17), para. 28.
105. M.938, *Guinness/Grand Metropolitan* (OJ 1998 L 288/24).
106. M.794, *Coca Cola/Amalgamated Beverages GB* (OJ 1997 L 218/15), para. 26.
107. M.582, *Orkla/Volvo* (OJ 1996 L 66/17), para. 32.

practices in other areas where it has found that a product is sold on different terms to different customer groups.[108]

In addition to assessing the substitution of demand, the Commission sometimes also considers the supply situation when defining the relevant product market. If, in reaction to small permanent changes to relative prices, a supplier can switch to production of the relevant products and market them in the short term without incurring significant extra costs, this can have a disciplinary effect on the behaviour of the undertakings involved. The Commission gives the example of the situation where there is production of a product with a range of different qualities, for example paper. Even if the different paper qualities are not substitutable from the consumer's point of view, they can be considered as part of the same product market because the producers can switch production from one paper quality to another at short notice and without incurring major costs.[109]

3.2. The geographic market

The relevant geographic market is a defined geographic area where the product in question is marketed and where the competitive conditions are sufficiently uniform for all undertakings so that it is possible to make a reasonable assessment of the effect on competition of the notified concentration.[110] By determining the geographic area, one also physically limits the undertakings which are actual or potential competitors to the merged undertaking. Undertakings which are located outside the area will thus normally be prevented from competing, since they will not be able to gain access to the market in the short term or without incurring major costs.

The geographic market will typically be either global or national. However, it can also be regional so that it either covers several Member States (or even the whole of the EU/EEA) or perhaps only a part of a Member State.

108. The authors of *Barry E. Hawk & Henry L. Huser:* European Community Merger Control: A Practitioner's Guide, 1996 pp. 126-129, are critical of this, believing that the Commission's practice is wrong as it only focuses on whether there are different prices in relation to different groups of customers, without investigating whether the price differences are due to the different costs associated with the different groups of customers.

109. Commission Notice on the definition of relevant market, paras 20-23.

110. Joined cases C-68/94 and C-30/95, *France and others* v *Commission (Kali & Salz),* para. 143, where the CJ refers to its decision in Case 27/76, *United Brands,* paras 11 and 44. In Case T-151/05, *NVV*, a competitor tried, unsuccessfully, to challenge the Commission's decision approving a merger, alleging that the Commission had made a number of mistakes in its definition of the geographical market.

There could typically be a global market for advanced technology products where there are relatively few suppliers. This is the case with the market for aircraft and for landing gear for aircraft.[111] Even simple products can have a global market, as in the case of platinum.[112]

In many cases the Commission will find circumstances which indicate that the geographic market is smaller.[113] This can be seen from an analysis of price differences, as major price differences in different areas suggests that these areas do not belong to the same geographic market.[114] Finally, and analysis of trade flows and of developments in trade flows can be used to define the geographic market. If there is only a small quantity of exports/imports to or from an area, this suggests that it is a self-contained geographic market. In this connection the Commission has rejected the application of the *Elzinga-Hoharty* test which is used by the US competition authorities.[115] According to this test it is decisive whether imports or exports are on or above 10 % of the total production or consumption. The Commission did not believe the test was suitable, as it says nothing about mutual market penetration between the areas in question. It is thereby decisive whether there are both exports and imports of a certain volume.

However, the finding of pricing differences and the lack of trade between different geographic areas cannot stand on their own. It is also necessary to investigate the cause of the apparent division of the markets, and in particular to assess whether such division is only short term. For example, there can be historical reasons for why markets are divided nationally with large national

111. See respectively M.877, *Boeing/McDonnell Douglas* (OJ 1997 L 336/16), para. 20; and M.368, *Snecma/TI,* decision of 17.1.1994, para. 21.
112. M.754, *Anglo American Corporation/Lonrho* (OJ 1998 L 149/21), para. 94.
113. As pointed out by *Ulf Bernitz & Irina Gutu:* The Effect of EU Merger Policy on Large Multinationals based in Sweden and Other Smaller EU Member States: Is the Policy Discriminatory?, European Competition Law Review 2003 pp. 19-29, the fact that the Commission often finds that a geographic market is limited to individual national markets prevents undertakings in smaller countries, such as Denmark, from consolidating. A Danish undertaking will have limited opportunities for growing by taking over its closest Danish competitors, as it would soon acquire a dominant position in Denmark. By comparison, a German undertaking has better opportunities for growing through consolidation before giving rise to problems of competition on the German market. This means that the German market is better suited than the Danish market for developing large undertakings which are able to compete on the global market.
114. The CJ seemed to accept this reasoning in Joined cases C-68/94 and C-30/95, *France and others v Commission (Kali & Salz),* para. 148.
115. M.315, *Mannesmann/Vallourec/Ilva* (OJ 1994 L 102/15), para. 33.

producers. Even though producers may still have large market shares in their home markets, barriers to trade may have since been removed, so the markets belong to the same geographic area.[116]

On the other hand, if the reason for the pricing differences and/or the lack of trade between areas is due to more substantial barriers to market access, this suggests that the geographic market cannot be extended beyond these barriers. Such barriers to market access can be due to a number of factors, including consumer preferences, culture, language, restricted access to the distribution network, and legislative barriers. Finally, they can be due to physical factors, such as very high transport costs that can be reason why a product cannot be sold at a great distance from where it is produced.[117] The Commission's analyses of the retail sector often result in findings of very small geographic areas, as consumers cannot be expected to travel far to do their shopping.[118]

116. See e.g. .308, *Kali+Salz/MdK/Treuhand* (OJ 1994 L 186/38), para. 44, where the producers' very large market shares on their home markets did not influence the definition of the geographic market.

117. Among other things, transport costs have played a role in the assessment of the geographic market in several of the cases concerning beverages. Since it is expensive to transport beer and soft drinks, this restricts geographic markets so these are generally national markets; see M.582, *Orkla/Volvo* (OJ 1996 L 66/17), para. 43; and M.794, *Coca Cola/Amalgamated Beverages GB* (OJ 1997 L 218/15), para. 97. According to M.358, *Pilkington-Techint/SIV* (OJ 1994 L 158/24), para. 16, even high transport costs do not always prevent there being trade between national markets. The case concerned float glass which is expensive to transport, and it was shown that 80-90 % of float glass was sold within a radius of 500 km from where it was produced. However, at the time when the case was decided, there were 36 production plants in the EU, and they therefore lay so close that their radiuses of activity overlapped. For this reason, the relevant market was considered to be the EU. Such considerations were also relevant in JV.29, *Lafarge/Readymix,* decision of 20.12.1999, which concerned the market for ready mixed cement. This can only be transported for about one hour, so the extent to which the radiuses of the producers overlapped was decisive. The Commission started from where the planned joint venture should be located, and concluded that the overlap could only be considered to exist in the Rhine-Ruhr area. The Commission left open the final decision of the definition of the geographic market; see para. 14 of the decision.

118. M.784, *Kesko/Tuko* (OJ 1997 L 110/53), para. 21, according to which the relevant geographic market for a supermarket is the distance that consumers can travel in 20 minutes. On the other hand, if a retail market consists of a chain of stores, these can be considered as a whole, so the geographic market will typically be nationwide; M.890, *Blokker/Toys 'R 'Us* (OJ 1998 L 316/1), para. 38.

As examples of the Commission's practice, the market for television broadcasts will often be national, since cultural, linguistic and legislative conditions mean that the broadcasts of programmes and advertisements in one country cannot be broadcast to other countries.[119] Similarly the market for beverages will often be defined as being national. In addition to transport costs, this can be due to consumer preferences, problems with getting access to the distribution network, and legislative requirements (for example the Danish requirements for the use of returnable bottles, the special rules in Norway on the state monopoly on sales of alcohol, and the Norwegian taxation on disposable packaging).[120]

I many cases the legal conditions have resulted in a market being considered as national. Thus, differences in accounting rules and tax law mean that the market for accountancy and tax advice remains national.[121] Perhaps some products cannot be sold because technical harmonisation has still not been implemented, or because the necessary technical standards have still not been created at European level.[122] However, in many cases the Commission has found the beginnings of harmonisation that will liberalise the market in question. In these cases the question is whether the liberalisation can be assumed to create uniform competitive conditions throughout the EU within a relatively short period (normally 2-3 years).[123] In order to assess the expected devel-

119. M.553, *RTL/Veronica/Endemol* (OJ 1996 L 134/32), para. 25.

120. See decisions M.582, *Orkla/Volvo* (OJ 1996 L 66/17), paras 42-55; M.794, *Coca Cola/Amalgamated Beverages GB* (OJ 1997 L 218/15), paras 95-107; M.833, *The Coca Cola Company/Carlsberg* (OJ 1998 L 145/41), paras 44-48; and M.938, *Guinness/Grand Metropolitan* (OJ 1998 L 288/24), paras 24-29.

121. M.1016, *Price Waterhouse/Coopers & Lybrand* (OJ 1999 L 50/27), para. 63. In this same decision the Commission left open the question of whether the market for management consultancy was greater, which is naturally connected with the fact that this market is not so dependent on national laws.

122. See e.g. M.222, *Mannesmann/Hoesch* (OJ 1993 L 114/34), paras 79-85, where the Commission concluded that, despite Directive 89/106/EEC (the 'Construction Products Directive'), and despite the mandate given to the European Committee for Standardization (CEN), the market for steel tubes was still dominated by national standards, so that Germany was considered a separate geographic market.

123. M.580, *ABB/Daimler-Benz* (OJ 1997 L 11/1), para. 43, where the Commission seems to have stated that the evaluation of potential competition and the evaluation of the geographic market should, in principle, be based on what can be expected in the coming 2-3 years. In the case in question, however, the Commission accepted that the evaluation should look 5 years forward. See also M.477, *Mercedes-Benz/Kässbohrer* (OJ 1995 L 211/1), para. 41, where the Commission accepted that there was an

opments in the near future, the Commission will often focus on how far the harmonisation process has reached in a particular area. However, in many cases it will be relevant to look at the influence of the directives on public procurement, as these directives often contribute towards opening national markets.[124] Finally, it is clears that a tariff which is imposed on the import of goods to the EU can have the effect of being a barrier to access which protects the EU from the rest of the world.[125]

4. The substantial appraisal of concentrations

4.1. From the dominance test to appraisal of whether effective competition would be significantly impeded

Under the previous wording of Article 2(2) and (3), a concentration should either be declared compatible or incompatible with the common market depending on whether or not the concentration creates or strengthens a dominant position so that effective competition would be significantly impeded within the common market or in a substantial part thereof. The wording indicated that there are two separate parts to the dominance test, first whether a dominant position would be created or strengthened, and next whether effective competition would be significantly impeded. A reading of the Commission's decisions gives the impression that the dominance test only consists of a single step. However, the practice of the CJ established that there were two independent conditions.[126]

The Commission's practice and the practice of the CJ gave rise to another important element in the definition of the dominance test, as it was established that collective dominance was also covered. Collective dominance exists in the situation where the merged undertaking does not itself have a dom-

internationalisation of the market for buses in process, but nevertheless the Commission was of the view that this internationalisation would take so long that it did not alter its conclusion that the market was national.

124. The public procurement directives have been assessed in the following decisions: M.221, *ABB/Brel,* decision of 26.5.1992, para. 11 (railway equipment); M.222, *Mannesmann/Hoesch* (OJ 1993 L 114/34), paras 85-86 (steel tubes); M.477, *Mercedes-Benz/Kässbohrer* (OJ 1995 L 211/1), paras 95-100 (buses); and M.580, *ABB/Daimler-Benz* (OJ 1997 L 11/1), para. 32 (railway equipment).

125. M.315, *Mannesmann/Vallourec/Ilva* (OJ 1994 L 102/15), para. 37, where the EU market for steel tubes was protected by a 10 % tariff. See also M.269, *Shell/Montecatini* (OJ 1994 L 332/48), para. 46.

126. Case T-3/93, *Air France* v *Commission,* para. 79; and Case T-5/02, *Tetra Laval/Sidel*, para. 120.

inant position, but it would obtain a dominant position together with one or few other undertakings. If it is assumed that, after a concentration, these undertakings will coordinate their competitive behaviour, the concentration can be said to create a dominant position for the group of undertakings. The problem of collective dominance will be discussed in more detail in section 4.3.

In 2001 the Commission commenced work on a major reform of the MCR. In this connection, the Commission considered whether it ought to change the dominance test, and perhaps replace it with the SLC test (substantial lessening of competition), which is known from American and English competition law. However, the Commission concluded that there was no great difference between the two tests, so there would be no great benefit in giving up the dominance test.[127] Instead, the Commission proposed to create greater clarity about the dominance test in the Regulation by defining the dominance criterion in a new Article 2(2). However, not all the Member States agreed with the Commission's assessment. In particular, there was a discussion as to whether the existing test, in addition to covering the dominance of individual undertakings and collective dominance, could be used to regulate concentrations in oligopolistic markets where, after a concentration, there would not be a prospect of the remaining undertakings on the market coordinating their conduct (non-coordinated oligopolies). Such concentrations can be declared to be contrary to the US/English SLC test, if it can be shown that there is a restriction on effective competition, even if it cannot necessarily be said to create a dominant position.[128] The Commission be-

127. COM(2001) 745. See also the discussion in *Ulf Böge & Edith Müller:* From the market dominance test to the SLC test: Are there any reasons for a change, European Competition Law Review 2002 pp. 495-498.

128. In particular, the judgment of the GC in Case T-342/99, *Airtours,* discussed in more detail below in section 4.3, has been seen by many as confirmation that there is such a lacuna in the dominance test. In the *Airtours* case the GC stated that collective dominance requires there to be shown that it is probable that, after the concentration, there will be coordination between the remaining undertakings, and that it is therefore natural to conclude that where it cannot be assumed that such a coordination will take place, the dominance test cannot apply. For a more detailed review of the debate which preceded the introduction of the new test see, among others: *Francisco Enrique González Diaz:* The Reform of European Merger Control*: Quid Novi Sub Sole?,* World Competition 2004 pp. 177-199; *Rhodri Thompson:* Goodbye to 'The Dominance Test'? Substantive appraisal under the new UK and EC Merger Regimes, Competition Law 2003 pp. 332-346; *Ioannis Kokkoris:* The reform of the European Control Merger Regulation in the aftermath of the Airtours case. The eagerly expected debate: SLC v Dominance test, European Competition Law Review 2005 pp. 37-47; *Vijay S.V. Selvam:* The EC Merger Control Impasse: Is There a Solution to

lieved that the original dominance test could be used in cases where a concentration results in non-coordinated oligopolies, but the fact that several people pointed out that there could be an 'enforcement gap' made it necessary to consider making a change to the test.

This debate led to a change of the wording of Article 2(2) and (3), so that the test now is whether a concentration would 'significantly impede effective competition in the common market or in a substantial part of it, in particular as a result of the creation or strengthening of a dominant position ...'.[129] It is notable that the new test has many similarities with the old test, as the only significant change is that the two steps have been switched around. However, such reformulation means that it is no longer a necessary condition that a concentration will create dominance. The creation of dominance is merely an example of how effective competition can be impeded; see the use of the words 'in particular'. Since this is not merely a cosmetic change to the provision, it is necessary to consider what the consequences of the new test are.

The first question which must be considered is whether the new formulation of Article 2(2) and (3) affects the dominance test developed under the previous formulation of the same provision. The fact that it was decided to repeat the dominance test in the new Article 2(2) and (3) must mean that in principle it has not been changed. This is also confirmed by the fact that several of the decisions which the Commission has given under the new test are entirely in accordance with the practice which the Commission developed before the new Regulation entered into force on 1 May 2004.[130]

Even if, in principle, the finding and evaluation of the dominance of individual undertakings and collective dominance seem to be the same, it is natural that in future it will be easier to argue that efficiency gains, which are a justification for allowing concentrations, create dominance. This is indicated by the fact that the dominance test is made subsidiary to an assessment of the concentration's effect on the market, and it is confirmed in the Commission's

This Predicament?, European Competition Law Review 2004 pp. 52-67; and *Kyriakos Fountoukakos & Stephen Ryan:* A New Substantive Test for EU Merger Control, European Competition Law Review 2004 pp. 277-296.

129. A 'significant impediment to effective competition' (SIEC).

130. See also the Commission's Guidelines on the assessment of horizontal mergers under the Council Regulation on the control of concentrations between undertakings (OJ 2004 C 31/5), para. 4, (hereinafter the 'Commission's Guidelines on the assessment of horizontal mergers') according to which the Commission has chosen to retain the guidance that can be drawn from past practice.

Guidelines on the assessment of horizontal mergers, which makes reference to 'efficiency gains'. This is discussed in more detail below in section 4.5.

The next question to be considered is what new forms of restrictions on competition are covered by the new formulation of Article 2(2) and (3). The wording suggests that the Commission has wide discretion to step in against concentrations that impede competition, even if they do not create dominance. Thus a textual interpretation seems to indicate that the new Article 2(2) and (3) have not only been introduced to close the 'enforcement gap' in relation to non-coordinated oligopolies which may have existed under the old dominance test. On the contrary, recital 25 of the Regulation indicates that the new test should be used to catch all cases where non-coordinated oligopolies restrict competition. By way of introduction, this recital sets out why it can be necessary to take action to maintain effective competition on oligopolistic markets, 'even in the absence of a likelihood of coordination between the members of the oligopoly'. According to the recital, the European courts have not to date expressly interpreted the MCR as covering such non-coordinated concentrations. Out of regard for legal certainty, the new Regulation makes it clear that these types of concentrations can also be prohibited where they significantly impede effective competition. The Council has hereby made it clear that the test has been changed primarily in order to close the enforcement gap which may have existed in the dominance test. Recital 25 then continues:

"The notion of 'significant impediment to effective competition' in Article 2(2) and (3) should be interpreted as extending, beyond the concept of dominance, only to the anti-competitive effects of a concentration resulting from the non-coordinated behaviour of undertakings which would not have a dominant position on the market concerned."

This formulation, especially the use of the word 'only', indicates that, in addition to cases of dominance (individual or collective), the new test can only be used to prohibit concentrations that create restrictions on competition which can arise as a result of the existence of non-coordinated oligopolies. Preambles are often used by the European courts for the interpretation of legal acts, so it seems natural to assume that the new test cannot be used other than in cases of non-coordinated oligopolies.[131] If one looks at the practice of the

131. See *Jessica Schmidt:* The new ECMR: 'Significant impediment' or 'significant improvement'?, Common Market Law Review 2004 pp. 1555-1582 (at p. 1469).

Commission following the introduction of the new test, there are no examples of cases where a concentration has been prohibited without either the presence of dominance or a non-coordinated oligopoly. The Commission's Guidelines on the assessment of horizontal mergers also indicate that, apart from cases of dominance, the new test only covers non-coordinated oligopolies, as these are the only kind of restrictions referred to.[132]

The Commission has issued Guidelines both on the assessment of horizontal mergers and on the assessment of non-horizontal mergers. As the former constitute mergers between actual or potential competitors, it is clear that this form of merger is more likely to create problems. Normally, a merger between undertakings that are not competitors[133] does not involve the creation or strengthening of a dominant position, though in some cases it can create a barrier whereby competitors to the merged undertakings are denied access to supplies or to markets. Moreover, it is conceivable that undertakings that have not previously coordinated their activities will do so following a merger. A merger can also make it easier for undertakings that have coordinated their activities prior to a merger to continue to do so. In the following, the focus will be on horizontal mergers, as it is these that can most clearly create problems for competition.

The following review will begin by looking at what is required for there to be a finding of the existence of dominance, both individual and collective; see sections 4.2 and 4.3 respectively. In section 4.4 there is an examination of how the MCR can be applied to non-coordinated oligopolies. Finally, in section 4.5 there is a focus on what role efficiency gains play in cases which are assessed under the MCR.

However, for a contrary view, see *Francisco Enrique Gonzales Diaz:* The Reform of European Merger Control: *Quid Novi Sub Sole?,* World Competition 2004 pp. 177-199 (in particular at pp. 188-189).

132. Even though the Commission has thus had the possibility of intervening against several mergers, it must be noted that the number of cases in which the Commission has intervened against mergers has fallen. This indicates greater reticence on the party of the Commission, presumably due to the strict requirements for evidence which the European courts have repeatedly demanded; see *Michael Rosenthal & Stefan Thomas:* European Merger Control, 2010 p. 87.

133. In its Guidelines on non-horizontal mergers, the Commission distinguishes between two types: vertical mergers, between companies operating at different levels of the supply chain; and conglomerate mergers, between firms that do not compete in the same market, but are active in closely related markets; see the Guidelines in OJ 2008 C 265/6, paras 4-5.

4.2. The creation or strengthening of a dominant position

Until 2004 the MCR was only focused on whether a concentration created or strengthened a dominant position. Even after the amendment to the MCR in 2004 this has been the theme of most of the Commission's decisions. As stated above, the 2004 amendment does not mean that the assessment of a dominant position has been changed, and the practice from before 2004 is still good law.

In assessing whether a dominant position exists, it is necessary to take a number of factors into account. These factors are listed in Article 2(1) of the MCR, which was not changed in the 2004 amendment:

'a. the need to maintain and develop effective competition within the common market in view of, among other things, the structure of all the markets concerned and the actual or potential competition from undertakings located either within or outwith the Community;

b. the market position of the undertakings concerned and their economic and financial power, the alternatives available to suppliers and users, their access to supplies or markets, any legal or other barriers to entry, supply and demand trends for the relevant goods and services, the interests of the intermediate and ultimate consumers, and the development of technical and economic progress provided that it is to consumers' advantage and does not form an obstacle to competition.'

As can be seen, there are many factors which can potentially be included in the assessment. In practice, the most important factors are the market shares of the merging undertakings, other signs of strength, the position of competitors and the position on the demand side. Each of these is commented on below.

4.2.1. Market share

Normally the Commission will start by calculating the market shares in the markets which are affected by the concentration. The first question this raises is which markets are affected by the concentration, and the next question is how market shares are calculated.

In a merger, the Commission will usually concentrate on the markets where most of the merging undertakings are active. In special cases it can also be relevant to investigate markets where there is a vertical integration which can strengthen the position of the undertakings; see the comments on this in section 4.2.2. The calculation of market share is done by simply adding together the market shares which the merging companies had before the merger.

With a joint venture, the Commission's investigations will normally focus on the activities which the joint venture partners put into their joint venture company. If, for example, two joint venture partners both transfer their production of a particular product to their joint venture, then the market shares of these two production units is added together in order to evaluate the market share of the new joint venture. If one or more of the joint venture partners has retained a production unit in the same sector, then the market share for which that production unit is accountable is also included in the calculation of the market share of the new joint venture.[134]

When adding together the market shares of the merging undertakings and the market shares of the joint venture and the joint venture partners, in some cases it can be difficult to decide which companies should be allocated to which merging undertaking or joint venture partner. This problem has certain parallels with the question of which undertakings should be allocated to the undertakings concerned when calculating whether a merger has a Community dimension. As discussed in section 2.4.2, this is regulated by Article 6(4) and (5) of the MCR. However, the corresponding problem of calculating the collective market shares should be carried out independently of the rules referred to, as the Commission has more discretion when deciding on the effect of a concentration.[135] In these cases the Commission will focus on whether the joint venture partners or the merging undertakings have a sufficient degree of influence over another undertaking.

The calculation of market shares will typically be based either on turnover or on the number of units sold. While the Commission normally uses turnover in its calculations, there can be cases where it is more correct to use the

134. M.774, *Saint-Gobain/Wacker Chemie/NOM* (OJ 1997 L 247/1). One could question whether, in situations where there is no indication that the joint venture and the joint venture partners will coordinate their activities, they should be considered as a whole. However, there has not hitherto been much sign that such an argument would be accepted; see *Karsten Engsig Sørensen:* Joint ventures – struktur og regulering, 2006 pp. 307-311.

135. Case T-22/97, *Kesko* v *Commission,* para. 139, where the GC held that the Commission, when assessing the effect of a merger on competition, was not obliged to apply the conditions for control in Article 3 of the MCR. In the underlying M.794, *Coca Cola/Amalgamated Beverages GB* (OJ 1997 L 218/15), para. 98, the Commission assessed that the market shares for a number of retailers which were part of a chain should be allocated to the merging parties, because they exercised significant influence on the retailers.

number of units sold. This depends on the concrete circumstances.[136] For the same reasons, in some cases the Commission will focus on entirely different factors, such as the number of viewers.[137]

The market shares of the merging undertakings are probably the most important factor in assessing whether a dominant position is created or strengthened. If the market share is below 25 % there is a clear presumption against the existence of a dominant position.[138] This is also supported by recital 15 of the original preamble to the MCR. The practice suggests that a market share must be up around 40-45 % before the existence of a dominant position is considered probable.[139]

Conversely, it is not possible to point to an upper limit, where a market share is so high that there is necessarily considered to be a dominant position. In Decision M.477, *Mercedes-Benz/Kässbohrer* (OJ 1995 L 211/1), paragraph 65, the Commission stated:

"High market shares do not in themselves justify the assumption of a dominant position. At any rate, they do not allow a dominant position to be assumed if other structural factors are detectable which, in the foreseeable future, may alter the conditions of competition and justify a more relative view of the significance of the market share of the merged companies ... Such structural factors could, for example, be the ability of actual competitors to constrain the action of the new entity, the expectation of a significant increase in potential competition from powerful competitors, the possibility of a quick market entry or the buying power of important customers. In the present case, the market shares of the merged companies are relativized by the fact that it

136. See the comments in M.190, *Nestlé/Perrier* (OJ 1992 L-356/1), para. 40; and M.430, *Procter & Gamble/VP Schickedanz* (OJ 1994 L 354/32), paras 113-117, where in both cases the Commission reached the conclusion that calculation according sales volumes was more correct.

137. M.553, *RTL/Veronica/Endemol* (OJ 1996 L 134/32).

138. M.289, *Pepsico/KAS,* decision of 21.12.1992, para. 6.3.

139. See the Commission's Tenth Annual Report on Competition Policy, 1981 para. 150. See also M.315, *Mannesmann/Vallourec/Ilva* (OJ 1994 L 102/15), para. 51, where 36 % market share did not indicate market dominance; and M.344, *Codan/ Hafnia,* decision of 28.5.1993, where 33 % market share did not indicate market dominance. Finally the threshold of 40 % may be seen confirmed in M.1016, *Price Waterhouse/Coopers & Lybrand* (OJ 1999 L 50/27), para. 85, where the Commission stated, by way of introduction, that the merger would not give a market share of over 40 % in any Member State, so that a dominant position was not created.

may be expected that there will be substantial actual and in particular potential competition, as explained in the following sections."

As is clear from this quotation, the Commission cannot be expected to find that there is a dominant position solely on the basis of the calculated market share, as it will normally also assess the actual and potential competition as well as the situation on the demand side; see the following sections. On the other hand, it must be assumed that a very high market share can give rise to an assumption that there is a dominant position.[140]

If a merger or a joint venture only leads to a very small increase in market share, or even no increase at all, this is an indication that a dominant position is neither created nor strengthened.

In practice, prior to 2004 the Commission was dismissive of the use of the *Herfindahl-Hirschman Index* (HHI) as an indicator of the extent to which a market is concentrated and thereby creates a dominant position. However, in its Guidelines on the assessment of horizontal mergers, the Commission suggested that it would use the HHI to a greater extent.[141] This index can be used to measure the extent of market concentration before and after a concentration is carried out. The HHI uses the sum of the squares of the market shares of all undertakings on the market in question. If the merger is carried out, the HHI predicts whether the merger will lead to a high concentration which ought, in principle, to be prohibited, or to a low concentration which means that there is no risk of market strength or abuse thereof. Where the concentration is of a certain degree, it depends on how much the merger leads to increased concentration according to the HHI. According to the Commission's

140. The Commission also seems to assume this in some of its decisions. See, e.g. M.222, *Mannesmann/ Hoesch* (OJ 1993 L 114/34), para. 91, where it stated: 'High market shares represent an important factor as evidence of a dominant position provided they not only reflect current conditions but are also a reliable indicator of future conditions'. See also M.890, *Blokker/Toys 'R' Us* (OJ 1998 L 316/1), where a retail chain obtained a market share of 55-65 %, on which the Commission commented (para. 59): 'This high market share in itself creates a presumption of dominance, especially when compared to the fragmented structure of the rest of the market.' See also M.1229, *American Home Products/Monsanto,* decision of 28.9.1998, para. 24. This also seems to have been assumed by the GC which, in Case T-102/96, *Gencor,* para. 205 stated: 'although the importance of the market shares may vary from one market to another, the view may legitimately be taken that very large market shares are in themselves, save in exceptional circumstances, evidence of the existence of a dominant position.' See the similar statement in Case T-342/07, *Ryanair,* para. 41.

141. The Commission's Guidelines on the assessment of horizontal mergers, para. 16 (OJ 2004 C 31/5).

Guidelines, an HHI of less than 1000 is an indication that the merger does not create problems for competition. If the merger creates an HHI of between 1000 and 2000, and the increase in the index is below 250, it is unlikely that the merger will create problems for competition. If the HHI is above 2000 and the increase is below 150, it is also assumed that there are no problems. However, in the last case the Commission makes the reservation that there can nevertheless be circumstances which make the merger problematic. The rules laid down by the Commission are thus only 'safe harbour rules' for mergers that result in an HHI of less than 1000. For mergers with an HHI of over 1000, the Commission's guidelines create doubts and mean that the HHI is less suitable for guiding undertakings. There has also been criticism that the limits set by the Commission are stricter than the corresponding limits laid down in US anti-trust law, where the HHI has been used for many years.[142]

4.2.2. Other indications of market strength

Apart from market shares, the Commission can also focus on other factors concerning the merging undertakings which indicate whether they occupy a dominant position. For example, sometimes the Commission refers to the fact that the merging undertakings have a far superior financial position than their competitors.[143] In the case of joint ventures it is not so much the financial strength of the joint venture as that of the joint venture partners which is assessed.[144] In addition, the Commission can attach weight to the fact that a new entity has a strong position because of the patents and know-how of the undertaking.[145] The fact that an undertaking is able itself to produce a com-

142. See *Stefan Voigt & André Schmidt:* Switching to Substantial Impediments of Competition (SIC) can have Substantial Costs – SIC!, European Competition Law Review 2004 pp. 584-590 (in particular at pp. 589-590); and *Mette Alfter, Simon Bishop & Eric Mahr:* The Commission's Draft Notice on Horizontal Mergers: An Opportunity for Change, Lawyers' Europe, Business Law International 2004 pp. 385-399 (in particular at p. 390).
143. M.12, *Varta/Bosch* (OJ 1991 L 320/26), para. 32; and M.580, *ABB/Daimler-Benz* (OJ 1997 L 11/1), para. 64.
144. M.469, *MSG Media Service* (OJ 1994 L 364/1), para. 60 et seq., where the Commission emphasised that all the joint venture partners had great prior market strength in a number of different areas.
145. See e.g. M.877, *Boeing/McDonnell Douglas* (OJ 1997 L 336/16), para. 102.

plete or very broad product range can also indicate that is has a dominant position.[146]

Finally, sometimes the Commission focuses on vertical integration as an indicator of a dominant position. In these cases the Commission looks at whether the concentration can contribute to creating or strengthening vertical integration, and whether this in itself contributes to creating or strengthening a dominant position.[147] In its practice the Commission is particularly alert to situations where vertical integration which results from a merger leads to third parties being excluded from a market.[148]

4.2.3. Actual and potential competitors

Even though the assessment of the existence of a dominant position must necessarily take the planned merger as its starting point, it is clear that the assessment must also take into account the new undertaking's position relative to its competitors – both actual and potential.

If the nearest competitors only have very small market shares, and do not otherwise have a strength which makes it likely they will be able to offer the merged undertaking much competition, this indicates the existence of a dominant position. If, on the other hand, the nearest competitors are of a corresponding size to the merging undertaking, this indicates that there is not a dominant position. However, if it is possible that, after the merger, two or three undertakings will dominate the market in question, a collective dominance may be found to exist; see section 4.3.

When assessing the nearest competitors' possibilities for competing effectively, it is again relevant to focus on their market shares. Even if the competing undertakings have relatively modest market shares, they may nevertheless

146. M.222, *Mannesmann/Hoesch* (OJ 1993 L 114/34), para. 99; M.580, *ABB/ Daimler-Benz* (OJ 1997 L 11/1), para. 65; and M.938, *Guinness/Grand Metropolitan* (OJ 1998 L 288/24), para. 86.

147. See e.g. M.833, *Coca Cola Company/Carlsberg* (OJ 1998 L 145/41), where the Commission held that the fact that Coca Cola entered into at joint venture with Carlsberg on bottling, effectively strengthened Coca Cola's dominant position. This joint venture meant that Coca Cola went from being a licensor to also being the co-owner of a bottling plant, and this vertical integration increased Coca Cola's market strength; see paras 50 and 83-90. See also M.469, *MSG Media Service* (OJ 1994 L 364/1), where in relation to several of the joint venture partners, the planned joint venture would strengthen their dominant position on markets which were related to the joint venture's own market.

148. See the Commission Guidelines on the assessment of non-horizontal mergers (OJ 2008 C 265/6).

have a position which means that they can be expected to compete effectively. When assessing this, the Commission takes into account, among other things, their financial strength, their technical know-how, their distribution systems and their production capacity. If, for example, the competitors have filled their production capacity, it cannot be expected that they will be able to compete effectively,[149] but if there is excess capacity this can be an indicator against a finding of the existence of a dominant position.[150] If there is a competitor with a very strong financial position, this can be an argument against the existence of a dominant position, even if for the time being the competitor only has a modest market share.

In Decision M.12, *Varta/Bosch* (OJ 1991 L 320/26), the Commission changed its assessment of a concentration which concerned the market for car batteries, as in the course of the proceedings it became clear that Fiat had taken over the next largest competitor. Even though the merged undertaking would have a market share of 44 % and the Fiat-controlled competitor only had 10 % of the market, the Commission found that Fiat's entry in the market would ensure effective competition.

If for a longer period the nearest competitor has tried to compete but without gaining market share, this can indicate that it is not in a position to ensure that there will be effective competition.

This was the case in M.877, *Boeing/McDonnell Douglas* (OJ 1997 L 336/16), where the Commission did not believe that Airbus, with a market share of 30 %, would be able to ensure effective competition if the merger between the two American aircraft manufacturers were permitted, as it emphasised that throughout the 1990s Airbus had been unable to increase its market share.

149. See e.g. M.1313, *Danish Crown/Vestjyske Slagterier,* decision of 9.3.1999, para. 122, where it was found that the other pig slaughterhouses in Denmark made full use of their capacity, so they could not compete effectively with the merged undertaking. See also M.358, *Pilkington-Techint/SIV* (OJ 1994 L 158/24), where the closest competitor had reached its full capacity, para. 43.
150. Even if the competitors have overcapacity, this does not automatically mean they can in fact use it to gain market share. This was the case in M.582, *Orkla/Volvo* (OJ 1996 L 66/17), where the two small breweries may have had reserve capacity, but the Commission nevertheless did not believe they could use it, as they could not overcome the distribution costs associated with this, and they would find it difficult to get access to the shelf space in the retail trade; see paras 64-67.

If there have been previous signs that competition does not function effectively, this can indicate that there is a dominant position.

If there are no current significant competitors, potential competitors may be able to prevent a merged undertaking exploiting its market strength. Potential competitors can either exist among the undertakings that have the possibility of switching their production apparatus to serve the market concerned, or among undertakings that are active in other geographic markets. The Commission assesses whether it is realistic (or meaningful)[151] in terms of competition that other undertakings will seek to enter the market and whether this will be of such an extent and at such a price level that it would rapidly and effectively put a stop to any attempt by the merging undertakings to exploit their market strength by, for example, maintaining a price level which is far above what would otherwise apply under conditions of effective competition.[152]

Potential competitors will often be found in the same geographic market as the merging undertakings. In many cases the geographic market is defined by reference to whether there are barriers to market access, see section 3.2 above, so it seems logical that undertakings that are active in other markets cannot immediately be considered as potential competitors. Where there are special cultural or legal circumstances which mean that a market is considered a separate geographic market, the same circumstances naturally make it less likely that a foreign producer will be able to penetrate the market in question.[153] However, the Commission's assessment of how a geographic market should be defined and its assessment of potential competition need not go hand in hand.

> For example, this was not the case in Decision M.315, *Mannesmann/Vallourec/Ilva* (OJ 1994 L 102/15), where the geographic market was defined as being Western Europe, but the Commission nevertheless assumed that there was no risk of there being a collective dominant position, since both Japanese and Eastern European producers were considered potential competitors.

151. See the choice of words in M.430, *Procter & Gamble/VP Schickedanz* (OJ 1994 L 354/32), para. 175.
152. M.190, *Nestlé/Perrier* (OJ 1992 L-356/1), para. 91.
153. M.582, *Orkla/Volvo* (OJ 1996 L 66/17), paras 78-79, on the potential for Swedish brewers to gain access to the Norwegian market.

The assessment of potential competitors concentrates in particular on investigating whether there are barriers to market access and if so, whether these can be surmounted within a reasonable period. This can be on the basis of an empirical assessment, as in a number of cases the Commission has attached importance to whether there has previously been entry into the market, or whether on the contrary there have been many failed attempts to do so.[154] However, in most cases the question is assessed on the basis of considering what barriers to entry exist and what is necessary in order to overcome them. Where the Commission can identify potential competitors, the Commission will also assess their concrete possibilities for gaining access to the market.[155]

There can be various forms of barriers to entry. For example, a high level of customer loyalty can prevent potential competitors gaining market access to a market, which will typically be the case in markets which are characterised by the existence of strong brand franchises.[156] There can also be a need for access to special technology or means of distribution in order to gain access to a market.[157] If the existing competitors operate with a special discount system, this can make it difficult for new competitors to gain access.[158] Finally, various kinds of exclusive agreements can make market access difficult if not impossible.[159]

Even if it is possible to gain entry to a market in principle, this can be associated with such major costs that there is almost an assumption that it will not happen. For example, this is the case where there would be a requirement for significant investment

154. M.477, *Mercedes-Benz/Kässbohrer* (OJ 1995 L 211/1), para. 73 (repeated examples of foreign undertakings entering the German market); M.737, *Ciba-Geigy/Sandoz* (OJ 1997 L 201/1), para. 161 (several new competitors); and conversely M.430, *Procter & Gamble/VP Schickedanz* (OJ 1994 L 354/32), para. 178 (repeated examples of failure to enter the market).
155. M.774, *Saint-Gobain/Wacker Chemie/NOM* (OJ 1997 L247/1), where the Commission judged that there were potential competitors in China and in Eastern Europe.
156. See for example the cola market, which is characterised by there being very few brands and where it would be very difficult to build up a new brand with an image and brand recognition corresponding to those of the established brands; M.833, *The Coca Cola Company/Carlsberg* (OJ 1998 L 145/41), para. 72 et seq. The market for sanitary towels is also characterised by a high level of brand loyalty among consumers, so it is difficult for a new competitor to gain access; M.430, *Procter & Gamble/VP Schickedanz* (OJ 1994 L 354/32), para. 126.
157. M.833, *The Coca Cola Company/Carlsberg* (OJ 1998 L 145/41), para. 74, according to which a new producer of fizzy drinks would either have to make considerable investment in its own distribution network, or negotiate with a competitor in order to gain access to their network.
158. M.190, *Nestlé/Perrier* (OJ 1992 L-356/1), para. 95.
159. M.1313, *Danish Crown/Vestjyske Slagterier,* decision of 9.3.1999, para. 125, where there was an obligation to supply which the Danish pig slaughterhouses imposed on their cooperative members and which made it difficult for foreign slaughterhouses to enter the market.

in research or in production capacity in order to start production.[160] Where a market is characterised by having strong brand loyalties, there will be a requirement for substantial marketing investment in order to launch a new product.[161] In particular where these investments are in the nature of 'sunk costs' (investments which cannot be recovered if the attempt to enter the market is unsuccessful), the Commission will assume that it is less likely that new competitors will attempt to enter the market.[162]

For the Commission to consider a potential competitor to be a guarantee for effective competition requires that such barriers to entry can be overcome within a reasonable period, normally two years.[163] In order to assess whether this is the case, it is first necessary to evaluate how market conditions can be expected to develop, and sometimes also to assess whether the potential competitors have the ability to overcome the barriers sufficiently quickly. For example, the Commission can decide that harmonisation is necessary in order to ensure the market access of potential competitors within this time horizon.[164] If entry to a market requires the development of know-how or patents, this can take so long that it is not realistic for there to be potential competition.[165] The same is the case if switching production[166] or the construction of new production plant would take several years.[167]

160. M.877, *Boeing/McDonnell Douglas* (OJ 1997 L 336/16), para. 49, where it would require investments in the order of $ 10 billion to develop an aircraft from the ground up; and M.358, *Pilkington-Techint/SIV* (OJ 1994 L 158/24), para. 44, where it would costs something in the order of EUR 100 million in order to build a new plant for the production of float glass.
161. M.430, *Procter & Gamble/VP Schickedanz* (OJ 1994 L 354/32), para. 145.
162. M.430, *Procter & Gamble/VP Schickedanz* (OJ 1994 L 354/32), para. 147 (advertising investment as 'sunk costs'); M.190, *Nestlé/Perrier* (OJ 1992 L-356/1), para. 97 (advertising investment as 'sunk costs'); and M.358, *Pilkington-Techint/SIV* (OJ 1994 L 158/24), para. 44 (costs of new production plant as 'sunk costs').
163. Commission's Guidelines on the assessment of horizontal mergers, para. 74.
164. M.222, *Mannesmann/Hoesch* (OJ 1993 L 114/34), paras 107-114, where the Commission assessed that the public procurement directives as well as the implementation of technical harmonisation of the rules on gas pipes within a period of 2 to 4 years would ensure access for new competitors. Therefore, even if a merger immediately created a dominant position, it would only exist for a limited period, and therefore the merger would not create a dominant position.
165. M.269, *Shell/Montecatini* (OJ 1994 L 332/48), paras 85-91.
166. M.774, *Saint-Gobain/Wacker Chemie/NOM* (OJ 1997 L247/1), paras 217-219, where the producers in Eastern Europe could not be expected to raise their levels of production quality to Western European levels within a period of three years. Therefore the Commission concluded that these producers could not be considered as potential competitors of the merged undertaking.
167. M.358, *Pilkington-Techint/SIV* (OJ 1994 L 158/24), para. 44, where it was emphasised that a new float glass production plant would take more than two years to construct, as merely getting planning permission was difficult because of the environmental problems involved.

> In some situations the barriers to access cannot be overcome, and in this case potential competitors can be disregarded. For example, this can be the case if there are legal or actual monopolies.[168]

If a merger or a joint venture eliminates a potential competitor, this can in itself be an indication of the creation or strengthening of a dominant position. This will be the case, for example, if one or more of the joint venture partners are potential competitors to the newly established joint venture, and it is assessed that if the planned joint venture were not realised, then one or more of the joint venture partners could have carried through the project on their own.[169]

4.2.4. The position on the demand side

If customers for the products on the market concerned have a strong negotiating position, this can help prevent the merged undertakings from abusing their market strength. In order for the customers to adopt such a position there must either be a buying monopoly or at least a limited number of customers. While examples of buying monopolies are rare, they do exist.[170] There will normally be several customers, and the question will be whether they have sufficient strength and a sufficient interest in pushing the merged undertaking to compete effectively. For example, there can be pricing regulations which man that no-one has any special interest in putting downward pressure on prices.[171] If there is no other supplier, then even the strongest customer group cannot be expected to exploit its market strength. For example, this can be the

168. M.754, *Anglo American Corporation/Lonrho* (OJ 1998 L 149/21), para. 118, where it was found that nobody had yet discovered a platinum mine which was not being worked and there could therefore not be expected to be any potential competitors.
169. M.469, *MSG Media Service* (OJ 1994 L 364/1), paras 56-59.
170. M.580, *ABB/Daimler-Benz* (OJ 1997 L 11/1), where Deutsche Bahn was the only customer for railway equipment on the German market.
171. M.582, *Orkla/Volvo* (OJ 1996 L 66/17), para. 76, where the buyers of beer on the Norwegian market may have had a strong market position, but they nevertheless lacked the incentive to put pressure on the producers as the many restrictions on the sale of beer in Norway meant that they did not effectively profit from their sales of beer. Another reason why buyers can lack an incentive to put pressure on produces can be because they buy such small amounts that the effort is disproportionate to the return.

case with certain branded goods which retailers absolutely have to have on their shelves.[172]

> In M.1313, *Danish Crown/Vestjyske Slagterier*, the Commission did not believe that the fact that two Danish retail chains (FDB and Dansk Supermarked) took 50 % of the merging undertakings' sales of pork was sufficient to find that a dominant position would not result from the planned merger of the slaughterhouses.[173] First, the Commission did not think that the fact that the two supermarket chains had a strong negotiating position, was in itself enough to ensure that there was not an abuse of the dominant position. The two supermarket chains would not have been able to prevent the slaughterhouses exploiting their position in relation to other customers. Next, the Commission pointed out that, while the supermarkets were virtually bound to buy their pork from the merged slaughterhouses, the slaughterhouses themselves could, without great difficulty, export the pork which the supermarkets did not buy. This meant that the negotiating position of the slaughterhouses was stronger than that of the supermarkets. See also M.190, *Nestlé/Perrier* (OJ 1992 L-356/1), where the Commission likewise assessed that the producers' position was stronger, even though four large retail chains took 50 % of the mineral water production from the merging undertakings.[174]

The position of buyers can also be strong in markets where retailers market products under their own brands. For example, this is the case with packaged processed nuts, where the retailers' own brands are stronger than those of the producers. Since retailers can relatively easily switch suppliers, it would be difficult for a producer to acquire a dominant position, even if they had a high market share.[175]

4.3. Collective dominance (coordinated effect)

As stated above, in assessing a dominant position, it will often be relevant to assess the status of the nearest competitor to the merging undertakings. If the

172. M.430, *Procter & Gamble/VP Schickedanz* (OJ 1994 L 354/32), para. 169 (sanitary towels); and M.833, *The Coca Cola Company/Carlsberg* (OJ 1998 L 145/41), para. 79.
173. M.1313, *Danish Crown/Vestjyske Slagterier,* decision of 9.3.1999, paras 171-173.
174. M.190, *Nestlé/Perrier* (OJ 1992 L-356/1), paras 77-89.
175. JV.32, *Granaria/Ültje/Interschnack/May Holding,* decision of 28.2.2000, paras 41-48.

nearest competitor is of almost the same size as the merged undertaking, this is an indication that there is not a dominant position. However, in this situation it is possible that the merged undertaking and its nearest competitors together have a dominant position. This will be the case if a small group of undertakings is able to a large extent to act independently of the existing or potential competitors, customers or ultimately the consumers.[176] This was originally referred to as collective dominance. In the Commission's Guidelines on the assessment of horizontal mergers this is referred to as 'coordinated effects', but here the term 'collective dominance' is retained.

The Commission has assessed whether collective dominance exists in a number of cases. However, it was first in a judgment in 1998 that the CJ had an opportunity to confirm that collective dominance can also be prohibited under Article 2(3) of the MCR. The CJ found that the interpretation of the provision according to its purpose leads to this conclusion since the opposite conclusion would lead to the provision losing a significant part of its effect.[177] However, in this judgment it was emphasised that the Commission has a heavy burden of proof in such cases, and the CJ did not believe that the Commission had satisfied the burden of proof in the actual case. In 2002, the GC gave judgment in Case T-342/99, *Airtours plc*, where it had the opportunity to lay down in more detail the conditions which must be satisfied for collective dominance to be found to exist. In particular, the GC emphasised that there must be sufficient deterrents to ensure that each member of the oligopoly has no interest in departing from parallel conduct with the other members.

In its Guidelines on the assessment of horizontal mergers, the Commission has had an opportunity to summarise what elements indicate the existence of collective dominance. First it must be possible to establish the conditions for coordination. Here it is relevant to look at the structure of the market, as col-

176. M.315, *Mannesmann/Vallourec/Ilva* (OJ 1994 L 102/15), para. 53. Purely in principle, it can be debated whether it is more appropriate to counteract this risk by preventing such collective dominance existing (i.e. by application of the MCR) or to prevent undertakings on oligopolistic markets coordinating their actions; see the discussion in *Antoine Winckler & Marc Hansen:* Collective dominance under the EC merger control regulation, Common Market Law Review 1993 pp. 787-828 (in particular at p. 791). The background to this discussion is that Article 102 TFEU has also been used against cases of collective dominance; see among others, the review above in Chapter IV, and *Giorgio Monti:* The Scope of Collective Dominance under Articles 82 EC, Common Market Law Review 2001 p. 131 et seq.

177. Joined cases C-68/94 and C-30/95, *France and others v Commission (Kali & Salz)*, para. 171.

lective dominance will normally require there to be few actors in the market sector, a homogeneous product and relatively stable conditions of supply and demand. The second condition is that the coordination must be sustainable.

In assessing whether the market structure makes it easy to establish coordinated conduct, the Commission starts from the basis of the economic theory on oligopolistic markets.[178] These are markets with few suppliers which, because of the nature of the market, have an incentive not to compete. On the basis of economic theory the Commission has sought to define what characterises oligopolistic markets. First, it is characteristic that there are few suppliers on the market. In most cases of collective dominance two undertakings dominate the market, but in one case the Commission has concluded that there was collective dominance between three undertakings.[179] Collective dominance between more than three or four undertakings would be far too complex and unstable to be sustainable.[180] Next, the two or three dominant suppliers should have a large combined market share and that their individual

178. See *Erik Kloosterhuis:* Joint Dominance and the Interaction Between Firms, European Competition Law Review 2001 pp. 79-92; *Derek Ridyard:* Economic Analysis of Single Firm and Oligopolistic Dominance under the European Merger Regulation, European Competition Law Review, 1994, pp. 255-262. *Ioannis Kokkoris:* The Development of the concept of Collective Dominance in the European Community Merger Regulation. From its Inception to its Current Status, World Competition 2007 pp. 419-448; and *Antoine Winckler & Marc Hansen:* Collective dominance under the EC merger control regulation, Common Market Law Review 1993 pp. 787-828, also give accounts of the American practice that has been the model for the Commission's practice. There is a simplified but illustrative analogy given by *G. Porter Elliott:* The Gencor judgment: collective dominance, remedies and extraterrioriality under the Merger Regulation, European Law Review 1999 pp. 638-652 (in particular at p. 645), which compares the situation to two sumo wrestlers living in a cupboard. Neither of them will be inclined to fight, as they both know this will merely result in them both suffering cuts and bruises, while ending up just where they started.

179. M.1524, *Airtours/First Choice,* decision of 22.9.1999. This decision was later reversed by the GC in Case T-342/99, *Airtours plc,* not so much because there were too many participants in the collective dominance, but because on a number of points the Commission had not produced enough evidence in support of its claims and because the Commission had made a number of wrong judgements.

180. M.1016, *Price Waterhouse/Coopers & Lybrand* (OJ 1999 L 50/27), para. 113. In the same decision the Commission decided that the merger between Coopers & Lybrand and Price Waterhouse would not create a situation of collective dominance since there would be five major undertakings on the market after the merger; see para. 119. However, in M.1383, *Exxon/Mobil,* decision of 29.9.1999, the Commission decided that 7 undertakings together had collective dominance.

market shares should be similar (i.e. the market should be symmetrical).[181] A large collective market share will be an indication of the existence of collective dominance,[182] but this is not enough in itself. The factors which further support a finding of the existence of an oligopolistic market are as follows, on the demand side and on the supply side, respectively:[183]

On the *demand side* there is only moderate growth, and demand is inelastic. If on the other hand there is significant concentration on the demand side, this can indicate that suppliers will compete with each other.[184]

The *supply side* is, as stated above, strongly concentrated. Next, the market must have a high degree of transparency, as transparency is a prerequisite for suppliers being able to see whether the others overstep tacit pricing agreements. If there is a commodity such as platinum, potash or mineral water, the condition will be fulfilled in principle, but it can be more difficult to evaluate this with more complex products.[185] Next, the Commission will have regard for whether the production technology is well developed, as the fact that further developments can be expected will make it less likely that the suppliers will have parallel competitive conduct.[186] Conduct that restricts competition will also be more likely if there are high barriers to entry to the market (with high sunk costs). The Commission will often investigate wheth-

181. See also the Commission's Guidelines on the assessment of horizontal mergers (OJ 2004 C 31/5), para. 48. In M.358, *Pilkington-Techint/SIV* (OJ 1994 L 158/24), the fact that the market positions of the five remaining float glass producers were asymmetric was one of the main reasons why the Commission did not think that parallel conduct in restraint of competition would occur; see para. 63 of the decision.
182. Case T-102/96, *Gencor* v *Commission,* para. 206.
183. M.619, *Gencor/Lonrho* (OJ 1997 L 11/30), para. 141; M.1016, *Price Waterhouse/ Coopers & Lybrand* (OJ 1999 L 50/27), para. 96; and M.1524, *Airtours/First Choice,* decision of 22.9.1999, para. 87, where the Commission summarised the most important factors it will investigate when assessing whether there is an oligopolistic market.
184. M.580, *ABB/Daimler-Benz* (OJ 1997 L 11/1), where Deutsche Bahn's market strength as a buyer meant that it was most probable that the planned joint venture and Siemens would compete with each other on a number of the market sectors for railway equipment; see para. 137.
185. For example, the Commission has assumed that the market for auditing work is transparent. It believes that there is a homogeneous service as each auditing task will require uniform control, analysis, reports and whatever else is required under national laws. It was therefore easy to compare services, and the Commission found that in practice the major auditing firms knew their competitors' fee rates; see M.1016, *Price Waterhouse/Coopers & Lybrand* (OJ 1999 L 50/27), para. 100.
186. Commission's Guidelines on the assessment of horizontal mergers (OJ 2004 C 31/5), para. 45.

er the undertakings have the same cost structures. If not, this can mean the parties will be less likely to accept a tacit coordination of their pricing policies.[187] On the supply side the Commission will also have regard for how competition on the market has previously developed. Thus, if there have previously been examples of competition not functioning optimally, because cartels have been formed or because there have been high price levels, this can be taken as evidence that the market already has oligopolistic characteristics.[188]

The Commission will also investigate whether there are *structural links* between producers which will make it less likely they will compete. For example, such structural links can be the existence of joint ventures or cross-shareholdings between the companies.[189] There was previously some discussion as to whether there was a requirement for such structural links to exist, but the GC has established that this is not a requirement, but merely one of the factors which point towards the existence of collective dominance.[190]

An example of the Commission's practice is Decision M.190, *Nestlé/Perrier* (OJ 1992 L-356/1), which was one of the first cases in

187. M.190, *Nestlé/Perrier* (OJ 1992 L-356/1), para. 125. In M.315, *Mannesmann/Vallourec/Ilva* (OJ 1994 L 102/15), para. 68, the Commission emphasised that there must be large cost differences before it will be interesting for producers to break away from parallel conduct. Even though in the actual case there were differences in cost structures, especially as one of the two producers of steel pipes was vertically integrated, the Commission did not believe that the differences were in fact big enough to rebut the assumption that there was an oligopolistic market; see paras 68-79. In its Guidelines on the assessment of horizontal mergers, para. 48, the Commission emphasises that it can also be relevant whether undertakings are the same on other points, for example with regard to their capacity levels and their degree of vertical integration.
188. This was the case with the market for platinum; see M.619, *Gencor/Lonrho* (OJ 1997 L 11/30), paras 165-172, where it was found that there was a very high price level and a poor competitive environment even before the merger. See also M.1524, *Airtours/First Choice,* decision of 22.9.1999, paras 128-138.
189. The existence of joint ventures between producers was emphasised in the following cases: M.308, *Kali+Salz/MdK/Treuhand* (OJ 1994 L 186/38), para. 58; M.619, *Gencor/Lonrho* (OJ 1997 L 11/30), para. 156; and M.942, *Veba/Degussa* (OJ 1998 L 201/102), para. 55. See also the Commission's Guidelines on the assessment of horizontal mergers (OJ 2004 C 31/5), para. 48.
190. Case T-102/96, *Gencor* v *Commission,* paras 273-278. The question was previously debated e.g. in M.1313, *Danish Crown/Vestjyske Slagterier,* decision of 9.3.1999, para. 179, where the merging undertakings argued that the Commission had to prove that there were structural links.

which the Commission found there was collective dominance. The decision concerned the merger of two undertakings which were both active on the French market for mineral water. After the merger the new undertaking and BSN would jointly have considerable market shares on the French market for mineral water, e.g. 75 % of the market by volume, and over 82 % of the market by value.[191] The Commission found that the merger meant that the number of suppliers would be reduced from three to two, and thus rejected the argument that it would merely be a cosmetic change to the market structure.[192] Next, the Commission found that the following factors were indicative of the existence of an oligopolistic market: first, there was a market with great homogeneity and transparency, as the undertakings regularly exchanged price lists and information about turnover. The two remaining producers would have more or less the same capacity and market shares, so there would be a symmetrical duopoly, and this mutual dependence was a strong incentive to seek to maximise their profits by entering into a coordinated practice in restraint of competition. There was a relative lack of price elasticity on the demand side, as consumers usually had strong loyalty towards their normal brands. Finally, the two producers had more or less the same cost structures, so it was to be expected that they would have an interest in following the same pricing policy. In particular, in this area there was no prospect that any of the producers would be able to establish a technological advantage, as the market used well-established technology. Furthermore, there were significant barriers to access to the market and the existing competitors were too small to be able to prevent the two major producers from exploiting their market strength. On this basis the Commission was of the view that the merger would create a collective dominance, and the merging undertakings had to undertake to dispose of sources of water and brand names, as well as bottling capacity, to a competitor before the Commission accepted the merger.[193]

191. Para. 119.
192. Para. 120.
193. See para. 136 of the Decision, and see also section 5 on conditional approvals.

Next, there is an examination of whether the *coordination is sustainable*. There are three conditions which must be fulfilled for a coordination to be sustainable:[194]

1. The first condition is that the coordinating undertakings must be able *to control* whether the terms of their coordination are complied with. To a large extent this is a question of the degree of market transparency. Normally, the fewer the actors on the market, the more transparent the market will be. It can also depend on how transactions on the market are carried out. If it is fully open to the public, for example by public auctions, it is easy to control, but it is more difficult if the transactions are made with customers in confidence. Where markets are less transparent, undertakings may have instituted exchanges of information, which makes control easier, just as having people from other undertakings as members of the board of directors can be used as a method of mutual monitoring.
2. Next, it must be possible to apply *credible deterrents* if deviations are found to exist. If such measures cannot be applied with a degree of certainty, rapidity and force, it is unlikely that the coordination will be sustainable. The deterrent mechanisms can consist, for example, of the other undertakings instituting a price war or significantly increasing production, with a view to penalising the undertaking that has breached the coordination. The retaliation need not take place on the market where there is coordination, as it can also be applied on other markets. For example, it is possible that undertakings will dissolve joint ventures entered into with an undertaking which breaches the coordination, or they may refuse to enter into new joint ventures.[195]

194. The conditions are set out in the Commission's Guidelines on the assessment of horizontal mergers (OJ 2004 C 31/5), paras 49-57.
195. A joint venture as retaliation was considered by the Commission in M.3333, *Sony/BMG,* decision of 19.7.2004. In this case the Commission had to consider the consequences of the fact that Sony and Bertelsmann put their music activities together in a joint venture. This led to concentrations on several music-related product markets which were dominated by 5-6 major actors. The Commission investigated whether this gave rise to collective dominance on the market for recorded music. In assessing whether there was retaliation, the Commission found that it was possible to penalise undertakings which breached the coordinated conduct by refusing to allow undertakings to take part in compilation joint ventures, which are joint ventures put together by several music producers to produce CDs on a particular theme, or the hits of a certain period. For such CDs several producers have to cooperate since an individual producer would not normally have control, on their

3. Finally it is a requirement that *third party* undertakings and customers cannot put the coordination at risk. This condition requires that neither actual nor potential competitors, nor customers are able to put at risk the expected results of the coordination. See the review in section 4.2.3 and 4.2.4.[196]

These three conditions were formulated by the GC in Case T-342/99, *Airtours*, where the Court set aside the decision of the Commission because the Commission had not produced evidence to prove that there were sufficient deterrent mechanisms. This was a major blow for the Commission and not surprisingly it led to a change of practice so that in subsequent cases the Commission investigated whether there were such deterrents. In Decision M.3333, *Sony/BMG*, decision of 19.7.2004, the Commission reached the conclusion that there was insufficient evidence to show that a reduction in the number of undertakings from five to four would result in collective dominance. This decision was set aside by the GC in Case T-464/04, *Impala*. Among other things, the GC found that the Commission was wrong to conclude that there had not already been collective dominance prior to the merger. The GC pointed out that the Commission's assessment of whether there was evidence of the existence of the three conditions formulated in the *Airtours* case could be 'established indirectly on the basis of what may be a very mixed series of indicia and items of evidence relating to the signs, manifestations and phenomena inherent in the present of a collective dominant position'.[197] The GC also found that the Commission's assessment of whether the conditions for sustainable coordination existed after the merger was highly inadequate.[198] However, this judgment was overturned by the CJ in Case C-413/06 P, *Bertelsmann & Sony*. The CJ did not find that the GC was wrong in that identifying the three conditions can be established indirectly, but that the GC had not examined the matter correctly. According to the CJ, it is it is necessary to avoid a mechanical approach examining each criterion in

own, of the necessary songs (hits etc.). On the other hand, since it is a very profitable form of issuing CDs the exclusion of a producer from participation in these joint ventures would be an effective sanction. However, the Commission could not establish that such exclusions had previously been practised; see paras 114-118.

196. In M.315, *Mannesmann/Vallourec/Ilva* (OJ 1994 L 102/15), the Commission believed that, in principle, the conditions for collective dominance were fulfilled, but as there were both actual and potential competitors of a certain strength, the Commission found that there was not dominance.

197. Para. 251.

198. See especially para. 528.

isolation. Instead, the examination should be carried out carried out using the mechanism of a hypothetical tacit coordination, which the GC had failed to do.[199] The CJ thus adopted a stricter assessment of whether there was collective dominance than that adopted by the GC.[200]

4.4. Non-coordinated oligopolies

The concentrations which the new test is particularly aimed at are mergers on oligopolistic markets which eliminate important competitive pressures which previously existed between the merging parties, so that competition is weakened even where coordination between the oligopolistic undertakings is not likely.[201] This will typically be in the situation where a market consists of 3 or 4 undertakings which produce similar but differentiated products. If two undertakings on such a market merge, and customers can easily switch to the remaining undertakings, the merged undertakings do not have the possibility of raising prices. However, if the customers of the two merged undertakings have the products of the two undertakings as their first and second choice, it is less likely that the customers will switch supplier even if the merged undertaking raises prices. In this situation there could therefore be a restriction of competition after the merger, even if the remaining undertakings do not coordinate their conduct.[202] Usually such a restriction on competition arises when numbers two and three undertakings on the market merge, so as to have a market share just below that of the biggest undertaking on the market.

199. See paras 117-133.
200. The Commission has since attempted to follow the directions of the CJ, on the first occasion in M.4980, *ABF/GBI Business,* decision of 23.9.2008.
201. The Commission's Guidelines on the assessment of horizontal mergers (OJ 2004 C 31/5), para. 25.
202. For a more detailed review of the circumstances that can lead to such non-coordinated restrictions on competition, see *Ben Dubow, David Elliott & Eric Morrison:* Unilateral Effects and Merger Simulations Models, European Competition Law Review 2004 pp. 114-117; *Vincent Verouden, Claes Bengtsson & Svend Aalbaek:* The Draft EU Notice on horizontal mergers: A further step toward convergence, Antitrust Bulletin 2004 pp. 243-285; *Sven B. Völcker:* Mind The Gap: Unilateral Effects Analysis Arrives In EC Merger Control, European Competition Law Review 2004 pp. 395-409; *Simon Baxter:* Unilateral effects under the European Merger Regulation : How big is the gap?, European Competition Law Review 2005 pp. 380-389; and *Simon Baxter:* Collective dominance under EC merger control – after airtours and the introduction of unilateral effects is there still a future for collective dominance?, European Competition Law Review 2006 pp. 148-160. This situation is often referred to as 'unilateral effects', which is the term used for the corresponding situation in US anti-trust law.

In its Guidelines on the assessment of horizontal mergers the Commission points to a number of factors which can indicate the existence of this kind of restriction on competition, for example that the merging parties have large market shares, that they are two close competitors (the higher the degree of substitution, the more probable it is that the undertakings can raise prices without customers switching suppliers), as well as whether it is unlikely that competitors will increase supplies if prices are raised.[203]

There have been some decisions where the Commission has applied these criteria to assess the effect of non-coordinated conduct on an oligopolistic market. In many of these cases the Commission has assessed both the coordinated and the non-coordinated (unilateral) effects, so the decisions on collective dominance and on non-coordinated effects support each other.[204]

In Decision M.3465, *Syngenta CP/Advanta*, decision of 17.8.2004, the Commission found that there were non-coordinated restrictions on competition in an oligopolistic market. The case involved a merger between two undertakings which were among the major actors on the European market for seeds. The Commission indicated that the geographic markets for the different kinds of seeds were national, though the exact definition of the market was left open; see paragraph 30. The Commission found that there were differences in how large a market share the merged undertaking would have in the different national markets for sugar beet seed. The Commission found that this market was dominated by 5 major actors, and that the merged undertaking would have market shares varying from 20 % in some markets (in Denmark 20-30 %) up to 80 % in others (Finland). According to the Commission the merger would lead to further concentration in an already concentrated market. On the basis of an analysis of market conditions, the Commission believed that on some markets the merger would lead to the establishment of a dominant

203. The Commission's Guidelines on the assessment of horizontal mergers (OJ 2004 C 31/5), paras 26-38.

204. In addition to the decision referred to in the text, the Commission has investigated both coordinated and non-coordinated effects in, among others, M.5549, *EDF/SEGEBEL,* decision of 12.11.2009 (OJ 2010 C 57/9) M.3817, *Wegener/ PCM/JV,* decision of 7.7.2005; M.3653, *Siemens/VA Tech* (OJ 2006 L 353/19); M.3625, *Blackstone/Acetex* (OJ 2005 L 32/60); M.3765, *Amer/Salomon,* decision of 12.10.2005; and M.3829, *Maersk/PONL,* decision of 29.7.2005. Even before the MCR was amended in 2004 there were decisions in which the Commission investigated whether there were non-coordinated effects, e.g. M.3216, *Oracle/Peoplesoft,* decision of 26.10.2004.

position, while on the French and Belgian markets it would lead to non-coordinated restrictions on competition in an oligopolistic market; see paragraph 52. The markets where the Commission found that a dominant position would be created were markets where the merged undertaking would be more than twice as big as its nearest competitor. On the French and Belgian markets the merged undertaking would be the market leader with market shares of 40-50 % and 50-60 % respectively, though the merged undertaking would not be so far ahead of the closest competitor for it to be considered in a dominant position. The closest competitor would have a market share of 40-50 % in Belgium and 30-40 % in France; see paragraph 42. Since there would not be a dominant position in Belgium and France, the question was whether the restrictions on competition would arise as a result of market concentration on a market which was already concentrated, and the Commission's investigation showed that this would be the case; see paragraph 45.

4.5. The positive effects of mergers

In principle it can be argued that there are so many positive effects from mergers that they counteract the fact that a merger can lead to a high level of concentration in the relevant market. This argument is often referred to as the 'efficiency defence' – a term borrowed from US anti-trust law.[205]

In European law only a limited assessment is made of the positive effects of concentration. In most cases the Commission concentrates on evaluating the negative effect, and any positive benefits are not considered at all.

However, following the amendment of the MCR in 2004 it seems that efficiency gains ought to play a more central role. According to recital 29 of Regulation (EC) No 139/2004 on the control of concentrations between undertakings, in evaluating a merger 'it is appropriate to take account of any substantiated and likely efficiencies put forward by the undertakings concerned'. The recital goes on to say that it is possible that the efficiencies brought about by the concentration will counteract the effects on competition, and the Commission is encouraged to issue guidelines on this. However,

205. For a comparison of US and EU law, see *Pierre-Emmanuel Noël:* Efficiency considerations in the assessment of horizontal mergers under European and U.S. antitrust law, European Competition Law Review 1997 pp. 498-519; *Peter D. Camesasca:* The Explicit Efficiency Defence in Merger Control: Does it Make the Difference, European Competition Law Review 1999 pp. 14-28; and *Peter D. Camesasca:* European Merger Control: Getting the Efficiencies Right, 2000.

there is no particular discussion of efficiency gains in the enacting terms of the MCR, other than the reference in Article 2(1)(b).[206]

However, there is no doubt that the rewording of the test in Article 2(2) and (3) of the provision will give efficiency gains a more central role in future.[207] This is also confirmed by the Commission in its Guidelines on the assessment of horizontal mergers, where there is a reference to how efficiency gains will in future be included in appraisals of such mergers. However, if one looks at the practice following the amendment of the MCR, there is no reason to believe that efficiency gains will play a very prominent role in future.[208]

In its Guidelines, the Commission lays down three conditions for taking account of efficiency claims – they must:[209]

1. Benefit consumers

This condition presumably means that only certain forms of efficiency gains can be considered. The Commission's Guidelines particularly refer to cost savings which lead to a reduction of the variable or marginal costs as these will most likely lead to lower prices and thereby benefit consumers; see paragraph 80.[210] Consumers can also benefit from new or better goods or services as a result of efficiency gains in research and development. Here the Com-

206. According to Article 2(1)(b), in its appraisal the Commission must have regard for 'the development of technical and economic progress provided that it is to consumers' advantage and does not form an obstacle to competition'. On the face of it this provision seems to suggest that a more detailed evaluation should be made of the positive effects of a merger. However, if one looks at the practice of the Commission prior to the amendment to the MCR in 2004, the Commission has interpreted Article 2(1)(b) so as to attach very little significance to it.

207. See *Jessica Schmidt:* The new ECMR: 'Significant impediment' or 'significant improvement'?, Common Market Law Review 2004 pp. 1555-1582 (in particular at p. 1572); and *Liam Colley:* From 'Defence' to 'Attack'? Quantifying Efficiency Arguments in Mergers, European Competition Law Review 2004 pp. 342-349.

208. See *Mitja Kocmut:* Efficiency Considerations and Merger Control – Quo Vadis, Commission?, European Competition Law Review 2006 pp. 19-27.

209. The Commission's Guidelines on the assessment of horizontal mergers (OJ 2004 C 31/5), para. 78. The three conditions are set out in more detail in paras 79-88. On these three conditions, see also *Hanne Iversen:* The Efficiency Defence in EC Merger Control, European Competition Law Review 2010 pp. 370-376.

210. Given the very large market share that Ryanair would obtain in certain markets through a merger with Aer Lingus, the Commission did not believe that there was a prospect of any efficiency gains benefitting consumers. The GC accepted this view in Case T-342/07, *Ryanair,* para. 441.

mission refers to the fact that a joint venture which is set up to develop a new product can have such efficiency gains; see paragraph 81.

2. Be merger-specific

The condition that the efficiency gains must be merger-specific means that the Commission assesses whether there are alternatives to the merger which are less harmful to competition. For example, the Commission refers to the fact that the setting up of a cooperative joint venture or a concentrative joint venture can be an alternative to a merger.[211] It thus seems that the Commission will make an assessment of whether a joint venture could be an alternative way to realise the efficiency gains and if so the Commission will disallow the merger and refer the parties to the alternative. In fact, the Commission will go so far as to evaluate which kind of joint venture would be best (a cooperative joint venture or a concentrative joint venture). The practice of the Commission can thus put pressure on businesses to get them to consider joint ventures as alternatives to mergers. The Commission emphasises that it only considers alternatives that are reasonably commercially practical in the situation of the merger parties. However, it is often difficult to assess whether a concentration in the form of a merger or a joint venture is right, and such an evaluation makes great demands on the Commission's insight into commercial life. It may therefore be expected that the Commission will be reticent in pointing out alternatives to the form of transaction which the parties themselves have chosen.

3. Be verifiable

Finally, it is a condition that the efficiency gains should be verifiable. It is thus often difficult, if not impossible, to give conclusive proof of such gains, and often it is difficult to quantify the size of these gains.

Apart from efficiency gains of various kinds, it is possible to imagine that some concentrations can have other positive effects, such as creating jobs or environmental benefits. The wording of Article 2 of the MCR does not suggest that the Commission will be able to take such considerations into ac-

211. The Commission's Guidelines on the assessment of horizontal mergers (OJ 2004 C 31/5), para. 85. In M.4000, *Inco/Falconbridge,* decision of 4.7.2006, the Commission found that the synergies identified by the parties which would realised by the merger could equally well be realised by the setting up of a joint venture that was limited to mining and processing, and this would be an alternative which would be less harmful to competition than the proposed full merger; see paras 538-542.

count when evaluating concentrations. However, it does seem that the possibility of taking account of other considerations was opened up in thirteenth recital of the original preamble to the MCR (Regulation (EEC) No 4064/89), according to which the Commission must place its appraisal within the general framework of the achievement of the fundamental objectives referred to in Article 3 TFEU, including the strengthening of the Union's economic and social cohesion, referred to in Article 174 TFEU. In particular, the reference to Article 174 supports the suggestion that the Commission should have regard for whether certain regions may be less developed in its appraisal of a merger.[212] The reference to Article 3 TFEU also means that a number of other goals (social, industrial policy and environmental) can be included.[213] This has been confirmed by the GC which has assumed that the thirteenth recital opens the way for the Commission to include consideration of the consequences of a merger for employees, including the effect on the level of employment or the terms of employment.[214]

Several cases have concerned the situation where an undertaking which is in difficulties can be saved by being taken over by another undertaking. Even though such a takeover can create or strengthen a dominant position, the question is whether there are other positive effects of such a concentration which can make up for this. If the alternative to the takeover is that the undertaking in difficulties has to be declared insolvent and close its business, the concentration can have positive effects by avoiding the dismissal of (some of) the employees and by preserving the resources and know-how which exist in the undertaking. On this basis the Commission has accepted the 'failing firm defence' – sometimes called a 'rescue merger'.

In the first decision on the failing firm defence the Commission laid down the following three conditions for this defence: 1) the acquired undertaking would be forced out of the market in the near future if not taken over by another undertaking, 2) the acquiring undertaking would take over the market share of the acquired undertaking if it were forced out of the market, and 3)

212. It is this element which the Commission particularly reads from the thirteenth recital; see the Commission's comments on the MCR, Article 2, published in Bull. Suppl. 2/90.

213. See the discussion in *David Banks:* Non-Competition Factors and their Future Relevance under European Merger Law, European Competition Law Review 1997 pp. 182-186.

214. Case T-96/92, *Comité Central D'entreprise de la Société générale des grandes sources et al* v *Commission,* para. 28.

there is no less anti-competitive alternative takeover option.[215] These conditions were subsequently accepted by the CJ in Joined cases C-68/94 and C-30/95, *France and others v Commission* (*Kali & Salz)*. In the same case the CJ stated that there is a requirement for there to be a causal link between the dominant position and the fact that effective competition is restricted, and if it can be assumed that the acquiring undertaking itself would have taken over the acquired undertaking's market share if it had not taken over the company, then the merger will not have been the cause of the creation or strengthening of dominance.[216] On this basis, the failing firm defence is not so much an expression of the Commission allowing a merger because it has positive benefits, but because the merger is not in itself the true cause of the creation or strengthening of dominance.[217]

The second condition which the Commission laid down for accepting the failing firm defence sets very narrow limits to the scope of the defence. Unless there were a duopoly, where only the two merging undertakings were active in the market, it would be improbable that the acquiring undertaking would, in all circumstances, acquire the whole of the market share of the undertaking which is in difficulties. The Commission has rephrased the condition in a later decision so that instead it must be assessed whether the assets of the undertaking in difficulties, and thus its production capacity, would inevitably leave the market unless the merger were allowed.[218] In the case in question, the Commission assessed that if the merger were not allowed, the assets of the undertaking in difficulties would be lost and this would result in a lack of production capacity in the market. Thus the negative effects of not allowing the merger would outweigh the negative effects of allowing it.

215. M.308, *Kali+Salz/MdK/Treuhand* (OJ 1994 L 186/38). As a further argument in favour of the merger, at the conclusion of the decision the Commission stated that the closure of the acquired undertaking would have serious consequences for the eastern German regions, so the decision to allow the merger was in line with the thirteenth recital.
216. See paras 109-124 of the judgment.
217. For a more detailed review of the arguments see *Giorgio Monti & Ekaterina Rousseva:* Failing Firms in the Framework of the E.C. Merger Control Regulation, European Law Review 1999 pp. 38-55; *Patrick Fiedler:* EG-Kommission erleichtert Voraussetzungen für Sanierungsfusionen, Europäisches Zeitschrift für Wirtschaftsrecht 2001 pp. 585-589; and *Ioannis Kokkoris:* Failing Firm Defence in the European Union. A Panacea for Mergers?, European Competition Law Review 2006 pp. 494-509.
218. M.2314, *BASF/Eurodiol/Pantochim,* decision of 11.7.2001, paras 149-163.

In its Guidelines on the assessment of horizontal mergers, the Commission has confirmed that it will accept the failing firm defence if 1) the failing firm would be forced out of the market in the near future because of financial difficulties if it were not taken over, 2) that there are no alternatives to the notified merger which would be less harmful to competition, and 3) if the failing firm's assets will inevitably leave the market if the merger is not carried through.[219]

5. Conditional approval

If the Commission judges that a merger or a joint venture would significantly impede effective competition, it can declare that the concentration is incompatible with the common market, so that the concentration may not be made. In practice this only happens in a few cases, as the Commission will instead allow the merger, subject to certain conditions.[220]

The possibility of attaching conditions or obligations has always existed in Article 8(2) of the MCR, which concerns the second phase of the merger process. Article 6(2) of the MCR was amended by Regulation (EC) No 1310/97, so it is now also possible to apply such conditions for the approval of a concentration in the first phase. Different deadlines apply for proposing conditions in the two phases, but apart from this there is no clear distinction in the MCR as to when conditions are applicable in the two phases.

According to the wording of the MCR, it is the undertakings which propose commitments and the Commission which accepts them, either as conditions or as obligations. If the Commission makes its approval conditional on compliance with certain commitments, the failure to comply with these can make the undertaking subject to a fine under Article 14(2)(d). Failure to comply with a condition also means that the approval can lapse. In practice, the Commission will normally make key commitments conditions, and not merely obligations.[221]

219. Para. 90 of the Guidelines.

220. Since the introduction of Article 2(4) of the MCR, it is also possible to lay down conditions to meet the concerns of the Commission on competitive aspects linked to a joint venture. This problem is dealt with in more detail in section 7.

221. However, the duty to report to the Commission is only a duty, just as the other implementation measures that are necessary to fulfil the conditions are normally only obligations; see Commission notice on remedies acceptable under Council Regulation (EC) No 139/2004 and under Commission Regulation (EC) No 802/ 2004 (OJ 2008 C 267/1), para. 19 (hereinafter 'Commission Notice on remedies acceptable under the MCR').

Sometimes the parties propose commitments which, for one reason or another, the Commission does not accept. This means that these become neither formal conditions nor obligations, but the Commission merely notes them. This raises doubts as to the legal status of such commitments. Unless there are good reasons to the contrary, such commitments must be regarded as non-binding, so the approval of the concentration is not conditional on compliance with them.[222]

Different kinds of commitments can be given; in particular, a commitment can be of a structural or behavioural character.[223] It is clear that a *structural commitment* that ensures that the structure of a given market is changed so a dominant position is neither created nor strengthened can be accepted. This applies in particular to measures by which a new competitor is created (typically by disposing of part of an undertaking – so-called divestment commitment), or where connections with competitors are severed.

1. If the sale of part of an undertaking creates competition, the activity which is disposed of must consist of a viable business. The divestment commitment will include a more general description of what the undertaking is committed to dispose of. If several activities from different locations are gathered together, there must be a broad description of the activities included in the disposal, typically including the intellectual property rights and personnel involved. Other cases may involve a party disposing of its shares in an existing (subsidiary) company, and in this

222. As such commitments are non-binding, they can also not be the basis of a suit for annulment; see Joined cases C-68/94 and C-30/95, *France and others* v *Commission (Kali & Salz),* paras 60-69; and Joined cases T-125/97 and 127/97, *Coca-Cola Company* v *Commission,* paras 96-106. In particular, according to the latter case the GC will make a more detailed investigation of the commitments before concluding that they have no binding effect.
223. In October 2005 the Commission published a report on the conditions which had been used in 40 cases in the period 1996-2000. There was a clear predominance of cases in which there had been structural commitments. For a review of the report see *Penelope Papandropoulos & Alessandro Tajana:* The Merger Remedies Study – In Divestiture We Trust?, European Competition Law Review 2006 pp. 443-454; and *David Went:* The Acceptability of Remedies Under the EC Merger Regulation: Structural Versus Behavioural, European Competition Law Review 2006 pp. 455-475.

case there is no need for any further description of the assets that are to be disposed of.[224]

For the disposal to have the desired effect, there may be a requirement for the assets to be transferred to a suitable buyer approved by the Commission. The buyer will normally be a viable actual or potential competitor which is independent of the merging undertakings. There is a further requirement that the buyer should have the necessary financial means and professional know-how to carry on the business.[225]

The Commission has also developed a more detailed procedure for carrying out the divestment.[226] It must be agreed that the divestments will be made by a certain deadline. There is not agreement about the price at which the disposal is to be made, as the merging undertakings must naturally be allowed to sell at the best price they can get from an approved buyer. If the price is not acceptable the condition for the merger cannot be fulfilled and the approval for the merger will lapse.[227] During the period up to the sale, the Commission will also require a commitment that the activities to be divested of are kept separate from the merging undertakings' own activities. This means that such activities should be carried on independently and in particular that the merging undertakings refrain from acquiring know-how or commercially confidential information.[228] Next, the parties commit themselves to carry on the separated activities on ordinary terms, i.e. with responsible management, and sufficient capital and salary framework. In order to ensure that this happens, the Commission approves the appointment of a trustee to oversee the parties' compliance with such commitments (a so-called 'hold-separate trustee').[229]

224. M.833, *The Coca Cola Company/Carlsberg* (OJ 1998 L 145/41), para. 110, where Carlsberg undertook to dispose of its shares in Dansk Coladrik (Jolly Cola) and Jyske Bryg, which it controlled.
225. Commission Notice on remedies acceptable under the MCR (OJ 2008 C 267/1), para. 48. The Commission states in a footnote that it does not accept seller-financed disposals, as this would naturally make it less likely that competition would be generated.
226. See *Simon Holmes & Sarah Turnbull:* Remedies in merger cases: Recent developments, European Competition Law Review, 2002, pp. 499-511.
227. On the other hand, if the uncertainty surrounding the disposal is due to circumstances over which the merging parties have no control, e.g. prior purchase rights or uncertainty about the transfer of important contracts, the Commission accepts that the parties should propose an alternative to the disposal. However, such an alternative must be at least as appropriate for establishing effective competition, and will often mean that a 'crown jewel' must be disposed of; Commission Notice on remedies acceptable under the MCR (OJ 2008 C 267/1), para. 45.
228. M.190, *Nestlé/Perrier* (OJ 1992 L-356/1), para. 136 sub-para. b); and M.833, *The Coca Cola Company/Carlsberg* (OJ 1998 L 145/41), para. 109 sub-para. 9.
229. Commission Notice on remedies acceptable under the MCR (OJ 2008 C 267/1), para. 112.

The divestment itself can also be regulated by commitments. Apart from the criteria for approval of the buyer, there can be requirements for periodical reporting and conditions for the approval of prospectuses or advertising materials. As the Commission cannot be directly involved in overseeing compliance with such interim preservation measures on a daily basis, it approves the appointment of a divestiture trustee for this task, and this will often be an investment bank, a financial consultant or an accountancy firm. It is the parties who propose and pay the trustee, but the Commission must approve the appointment and approve the mandate given to the trustee. Normally the trustee should only monitor the attempts of the merging undertakings to dispose of the part undertaking, but if these are not successful, the trustee will take on this task.[230]

2. Another way to ensure increased competition is to remove all structural links which may exist between the merging undertakings and their competitors. In several cases the Commission has accepted commitments whereby the parties bind themselves to sell or to wind up a joint venture which they have together with competitors,[231] commitments to sell minority shareholdings in competing undertakings[232] or commitments to terminate other kinds of cooperation.[233] In other cases the Commission has accepted commitments whereby the merging undertakings agree to limit their scope for exercising influence on competing undertakings.[234] This can be by agreeing to reduce their shareholding in competing

230. Commission Notice on remedies acceptable under the MCR (OJ 2008 C 267/1), paras 117-127.
231. M.269, *Shell/Montecatini* (OJ 1994 L 332/48), para. 117; M.942, *Veba/Degussa* (OJ 1998 L 201/102), paras 56-57; M.1467, *Rohm and Haas/Morton,* para. 41; M.1082, *Allianz/AGF,* decision of 8.5.1998, para. 72; JV.56, *Hutchinson/ECT,* decision of 29.11.2001, para. 47; and M.3436, *Continental/Phoenix,* decision of 26.10.2004, para. 220.
232. M.2416, *Tetra Laval/Sidel,* decision of 30.1.2002, para. 97.
233. See M.1229, *American Home Products Monsanto,* decision of 28.9.1998, paras 53-54, where the Commission accepted a commitment to terminate a distribution agreement which one of the merging undertakings had on the French market for a medicinal product which competed with a product which was produced by another undertaking which was included in the merger. By terminating the distribution agreement this opened the possibility that the distributorship would be given to an undertaking which would compete with the merged undertaking.
234. M.754, *Anglo American Corporation/Lonrho* (OJ 1998 L 149/21), para. 126, whereby the merging undertakings agreed to reduce their shareholdings in the closest competitor to a maximum of 9.99 % of the share capital.

undertakings, or by surrendering specific rights, for example the right to appoint a member of the board of a competing company.[235]

The effect of a *behavioural commitment* is more questionable. If an undertaking gives a commitment to refrain from some particular form of conduct, it is difficult to monitor that such a commitment is honoured, and for this reason alone this type of commitment is less suitable for ensuring effective competition. In its previous practice the Commission had established that it would not accept any commitments of a behavioural nature.[236] However, this practice was to some extent overruled by the GC in Case T-102/96, *Gencor* v *Commission.* The GC did not find that a commitment could be accepted whereby the merging undertakings promised not to abuse their dominant position, since Article 2 of the MCR requires the Commission to refuse mergers which create a dominant position.[237] However, in general the GC did not exclude the possibility of commitments of a behavioural nature which could contribute to preventing the creation or strengthening of a dominant position. It accepted that, in principle, commitments of a structural nature are preferable because they change the structure of the market once and for all, and therefore do not require controlling measures. The CJ has subsequently gone a step further and held that it was wrong of the Commission not to take account of commitments of a behavioural nature when these are proposed by the parties.[238]

If one looks at the more recent practice of the Commission, one will find a number of decisions in which an undertaking is required to take certain steps which are expected to improve competitive conditions, without these measures being of a purely structural character.[239] For example, if a sector of business has exclusive agreements, the termination of these can often open up the market for competitors. This will typically come about if the merging un-

235. M.1082, *Allianz/AGF,* decision of 8.5.1998, para. 66; and M.1080, *Thyssen/Krupp,* decision of 2.6.1998, para. 35. However, a commitment of this kind was rejected by the Commission in M.3440 *ENI/EDP/GDP,* decision of 9.12.2004, para. 759 et seq.
236. M.619, *Gencor/Lonrho* (OJ 1997 L 11/30), para. 216.
237. Case T-102/96, *Gencor* v *Commission,* para. 317.
238. Case C-12/03 P, *Tra Laval,* para. 89.
239. See *Katri Paas:* Non-structural Remedies in EU Merger Control, European Competition Law Review 2006 pp. 209-216; and *Ariel Ezrachi:* Behavioural Remedies in EC Merger Control – Scope and Limitations, World Competition 2006 pp. 459-479; and *Jonas S. Brueckner & Thomas Hoehn:* Monitoring Compliance with Merger Remedies – The Role of the Monitoring Trustee, Competition Law International 2010 pp. 73-79.

dertakings release their suppliers from exclusive agreements,[240] but increased competition can also be created by freeing distributors and their customers from certain obligations.[241] Where a merging undertaking possesses some key technology, a commitment to allow others a licence to use the technology can be enough to ensure effective competition. In such cases the merging undertaking will normally commit itself to giving licences to suitable undertakings on fair and reasonable terms, and the commitment often states that the licence fee will not exceed a certain percentage of the turnover obtain by using the licence.[242] Finally, the merging undertakings may have some essential facility at their disposal and they can give a commitment that they will allow competitors access to it.[243]

In some individual cases the Commission has sought to improve competition by accepting commitments that part of an undertaking will be carried on independently from the merging undertakings or joint venture partners. In these cases the separation is not just for a short period, until a sale is carried out, but is for a longer period.

> In M.1168, *DHL/Deutsche Post*, decision of 26.6.1998, Deutsche Post agreed to keep separate accounts for two divisions in order to ensure that there were no cross-subsidies.[244] There was a special situation in M.877, *Boeing/McDonnell Douglas* (OJ 1997 L 336/16), where the Commission

240. M.986, *Agfa-Gevaert/DuPont* (OJ 1998 L 211/22), para. 110(a); and M.1313, *Danish Crown/Vestjyske Slagterier,* decision of 9.3.1999, para. 200, where the two slaughterhouses accepted the partial release of their members from their obligations to supply, as they would be free to supply up to 15 % of their weekly production to other slaughterhouses. In M.5046, *Friesland Foods/Campina,* decision of 17.12.2008, the merging cooperatives undertook to give financial support to members who agreed to supply milk to other companies. A looser commitment was given in M.877, *Boeing/McDonnell Douglas* (OJ 1997 L 336/16), para. 119, where Boeing committed itself not to put pressure on its suppliers to refrain from supplying competing undertakings.
241. M.1168, *DHL/Deutsche Post,* decision of 26.6.1998, para. 110(b) and (c), whereby distributors were made freer; and M.877, *Boeing/McDonnell Douglas* (OJ 1997 L 336/16), para. 116, where Boeing committed itself to allowing their customers more freedom.
242. M.986, *Agfa-Gevaert/DuPont* (OJ 1998 L 211/22), para. 110(a); M.737, *Ciba-Geigy/Sandoz* (OJ 1997 L 201/1), para. 275; and JV.37, *B sky B/Kirch Pay TV,* decision of 21.3.2000, annex para. 8.
243. M.259, *British Airways/TAT,* decision of 11.12.1992, and M.5440 *Lufthansa/ Austrian Airlines,* decision of 28.8.2009 (both concerning landing slots at airports).
244. M.1168, *DHL/Deutsche Post,* decision of 26.6.1998, para. 34 with annex.

accepted that it was not possible to find a buyer for McDonnell Douglas's aircraft division. In order to ensure a certain measure of competition the Commission therefore accepted a commitment that this division should be kept separate, in a separate legal entity, for 10 years. However the company was only given limited independence by this, as it was also stated that Boeing had management rights which it could exercise in its capacity as owner of all the shares in the new company. The aim was to ensure the continued separate legal existence of the division so it was stated how Boeing should give the division certain possibilities for carrying on its business.[245]

In some cases the Commission has also given consideration to commitments intended to ensure that information about competitors is not given to some of the undertakings involved in the concentration. For example, this is the case where an acquired undertaking possesses information about competitors and where, in order to ensure competition, it is necessary to restrict the acquiring undertaking's access to this information. However the Commission seems reluctant to accept this kind of commitment, which may be linked to the fact that it is very difficult to monitor whether such a condition is complied with.[246]

The Commission's practice with regard to such commitments has given rise to a number of cases in which claimants have either argued that the Commission has made a formal error, or made an incorrect assessment of the facts. It seems clear that, especially in relation to the latter, the Commission has wide discretion to decide what commitment is sufficient to overcome the competitive concerns to which a merger gives rise.[247] For the same reason, it will be difficult to recover damages from the Commission on the basis of a claim that it is in error.[248]

245. M.877, *Boeing/McDonnell Douglas* (OJ 1997 L 336/16), para. 115.
246. See *Massimo Motta, Michele Polo & Helder Vosconcelos* in *Francois Lévêque & Howard Shelanski (eds.):* Merger Remedies in the American and European Union Competition Law, 2003 p. 106 et seq. (in particular from p. 116). In M.3440, *ENI/EDP/ GDP,* decision of 9.12.2004, para. 799, the Commission rejected such measures as inadequate. On the other hand the Commission did accept such measures in M.2268, *Pernod Ricard/Diageo/Seagram Spirits,* decision of 8.5.2001, para. 51.
247. See the decision of the GC in Case T-342/07, *Ryanair,* paras 447-526.
248. See Case T-212/03, *MyTravel Group.*

6. Ancillary restraints

If a concentration is approved as being compatible with the common market, then according to Article 6(1)(b) and Article 8(2) of the MCR, such a decision will also clear restrictions which are directly related and necessary to the implementation of the concentration. These are normally called 'ancillary restraints'.

The definition of what restraints are ancillary to a concentration is relevant to when Article 2(4) is applicable to the various terms of an agreement which is part of the setting up of a joint venture and whether Article 101 TFEU is applicable to some of the terms agreed in relation to other mergers. If a condition is a necessary part of a concentration, it cannot be challenged even if it may restrict competition between undertakings. The corresponding problem arises with joint ventures which are assessed in accordance with Article 101, and reference is made to the review of this in Chapter IV, section 7.6. Since the practice in the two areas has developed somewhat differently, it is best to give a short review of the practice that applies under the MCR.

In 1990 the Commission published a Notice on restrictions directly related and necessary to concentrations, and the Commission's latest revised notice was published in 2005.[249] In 2001 the Commission stated that it would no longer make an appraisal of all the different restraints in its merger decisions.[250] In the previous decisions the Commission had evaluated each of the actual terms of the agreement, as they appeared from the notifications. The new practice means that the parties themselves have to determine whether various terms are ancillary or not, and this determination must be made on the basis of the Commission's previous practice which is now summarised in the new Notice.

The conditions for accepting that a term is an ancillary restraint are that it must be a term which 1) constitutes a restraint, 2) which is directly linked to the merger, and 3) is necessary for carrying out the merger.

The first of these conditions means that the freedom of action of one or more of the parties involved must be restricted. In the absence of this there is no restrictive effect on competition.

249. OJ 1990 C 203/5 and OJ 2005 C 56/24 respectively.

250. This practice was criticised by the GC, as Article 8 of the MCR provided that the Commission has an obligation to assess ancillary restraints; see Case T-251/00, *Legardére SCA and Canal+ SA* v *Commission,* para. 90. As a consequence of this judgment, Articles 6 and 8 of the MCR were amended so as to make it clear that the Commission does not have an obligation to assess such restraints.

The second condition means that the term must have a connection with the merger. Thus, a term which is wholly unrelated to the concentration is not covered.[251] The condition also means that the restraint must be agreed at the same time as the merger.[252] If the agreement is entered into prior to the merger or the formation of the joint venture, or if it is entered into after the merger then in principle it is not ancillary.

The third condition means that either the concentration could not be implemented or could only be implemented under considerably more uncertain conditions, at substantially higher cost, over an appreciably longer period or with considerably less chance of a successful outcome.[253] This makes it clear that the Commission has a certain scope for discretion. However, the Commission tries to make the assessment as objective as possible, as it has stated that restrictions are not directly related and necessary to the implementation of a concentration simply because the parties regard them as such.[254]

In addition to assessing whether it is necessary to have a term with the restriction in question, there is also a requirement that the restriction should not go further than is reasonably necessary. The Commission's Notice states that in its subject matter and geographic field of application, a restriction may not go further than is necessary, thereby clearly aiming at non-competition clauses. It is also stated that where there are effective alternatives available for attaining the legitimate aim pursued, the undertakings must choose the one which is objectively the least restrictive of competition.[255] Thus, the proportionality principle has found its way into the regulation of ancillary restraints.

The Commission's Notice focuses on non-competition clauses, licensing agreements, and purchasing and supply obligations, as well as on certain terms related to the establishment of joint control:

251. M.1298, *Kodak/Imation,* decision of 23.10.1998, para. 75, where the Commission noted that a clause that the merger parties should resolve some disputes concerning the ownership of some intellectual property rights was 'completely unrelated to the transaction at stake and therefore is not covered by the present decision'.
252. Commission Notice on restrictions directly related and necessary to concentrations (OJ 2005 C 56/24), para. 14.
253. Commission Notice on restrictions directly related and necessary to concentrations (OJ 2005 C 56/24), para. 13.
254. Commission Notice on restrictions directly related and necessary to concentrations (OJ 2005 C 56/24), para. 11.
255. Commission Notice on restrictions directly related and necessary to concentrations (OJ 2005 C 56/24), para. 13.

1. The Commission's latest Notice from 2005 contains detailed guidelines as to what *non-competition clauses* are ancillary, and it distinguishes between a condition that is imposed on the seller upon the sale of an undertaking and non-competition clauses that are imposed on joint venture partners upon the setting up of a joint venture. The Commission is more receptive to such clauses in joint ventures than upon the disposal of an undertaking.

   With a transfer of an undertaking which includes both goodwill and know-how, the Commission normally accepts non-competition clauses which last for 3 years, but a period of 2 years is normally considered reasonable if only goodwill is involved.[256] The Commission can accept clauses for longer periods, but it is difficult to argue for a longer period.[257] For joint ventures the Commission generally accepts non-competition clauses that apply for as long as the lifetime of the joint venture.

   In the case of joint ventures there is the further question of whether the non-competition clause can be extended to apply after the dissolution of the joint venture or after the date when a joint venture partner no longer participates in the joint venture. The Commission previously accepted that such a clause could apply to a period after the dissolution of a joint venture.[258] However, subsequently the Commission has rejected such clauses.[259]

   A non-competition clause will typically mean that the joint venture partners or the selling undertaking are prevented from competing with the joint venture or the transferred undertaking. In this respect, the Commission ensures that such clauses do not go further than necessary in the products or geographic areas they cover.

   Non-competition clauses will often cover both the undertakings themselves, and the companies they control.[260] According to the Commission's Notice, a non-competition clause can bind the undertaking's agents, but it cannot bind third parties, for example

256. Commission Notice on restrictions directly related and necessary to concentrations (OJ 2005 C 56/24), para. 20.
257. See *C.J. Cook & C.S. Kerse:* EC Merger Control, 5th ed., 2009 p. 76.
258. M.523, *Akzo Nobel/Monsanto,* decision of 19.1.1995, para. 50, where a restriction was accepted during the lifetime of the joint venture and for two years thereafter.
259. M.1113, *Nortel/Norweb,* decision of 18.3.1998, para. 31; M.1132, *BT/ESB,* decision of 19.5.1998, para. 20; JV.2, *Enel/FT/Wind,* decision of 22.6.1998, para. 42; and JV.36, *TXU Europe/EDF-London Investments,* decision of 3.2.2000, para. 53
260. Where a joint venture partner or a selling undertaking is itself controlled, it is sometimes accepted that the non-competition clause can be extended to the shareholders; see *C.J. Cook & C.S. Kerse:* EC Merger Control, 5th ed., 2009 p. 76.

distributors or customers. Clauses prohibiting undertakings from investing in competing undertakings may be accepted.

In addition to preventing competing business itself, the Commission also accepts joint venture partners binding themselves not to contact customers and employees of the joint venture, which can be particularly relevant where a joint venture partner has transferred part of its undertaking to the joint venture. Finally, the Commission accepts confidentiality clauses whereby the joint venture partners may not disclose confidential information which they have or acquire about the activities of the joint venture.[261]

2. The Commission considers *licence agreements* between joint venture partners for the exploitation of intellectual property rights and know-how as ancillary, regardless of whether they are exclusive or not, and regardless of whether they are for a limited period or not.[262] It is not unusual for joint venture partners to allow their joint venture to use all the intellectual property rights that are necessary for the joint venture's activities, and this is often without the payment of a licence fee.[263] The Commission has also accepted terms whereby a joint venture allows one or more of the joint venture partners a licence to the rights which it either has or expects to obtain.[264] On the other hand, the Commission will not, in principle, accept licence agreements between joint venture partners as ancillary restraints.[265]

   With transfers of undertakings, the Commission accepts that licence agreements can be necessary where the seller will not transfer some of the rights or know-how, so the buyer must be allowed a licence to these in order to be able to make full use of the transferred assets. It is also possible that a seller will agree to transfer the rights, but needs a licence

261. Commission Notice on restrictions directly related and necessary to concentrations (OJ 2005 C 56/24), para. 41. However, a confidentiality clause can be limited so as only to cover sensitive information, such as know-how, while information of a more general nature is not accepted as ancillary; see M.1167, *ICI/Williams,* decision of 29.4.1998, para. 22.
262. Commission Notice on restrictions directly related and necessary to concentrations (OJ 2005 C 56/24), para. 42. See also M.1137, *Exxon/Shell,* decision of 8.7.1998, para. 27, where the Commission noted that licence agreements are a substitute for a transfer of rights.
263. M.310, *Harrisons & Crosfield/Akzo,* decision of 8.5.1993, para. 39.
264. M.310, *Harrisons & Crosfield/Akzo,* decision of 8.5.1993, para. 40.
265. Commission Notice on restrictions directly related and necessary to concentrations (OJ 2005 C 56/24), para. 43.

itself in connection with activities other than the transferred activities. The Commission also accepts that such licence agreements can be entered into without a time limit, but it will not accept restrictions which are aimed more at protecting the licensor than the licensee.[266] Nor, in connection with the transfer of intellectual property rights, does the Commission accept the imposition of restrictions on the seller that are intended to protect the intellectual property rights where the buyer already has the necessary protection under intellectual property law.[267]

3. *Buying and selling agreements* can be ancillary both in connection with the transfer of an undertaking and the setting up of a joint venture. The Commission's Notice lays down a number of conditions for accepting such agreements, and these conditions are the same in both situations. First, the buying and selling agreements must be necessary to ensure continuity of supply of the products. Therefore, if the products concerned can be easily acquired from other suppliers, this would be an argument against there being an ancillary restraint.[268]

   In principle the Commission only accepts such agreements if they are entered into for a limited period, as the aim of such agreements is to ensure continuity of supply during a transition period.[269] In its latest Notice the Commission has stated that this transition period can be for up to five years; see paragraph 33 of the Notice. In its practice the Commission has acknowledged that the assessment of what can be an acceptable period depends in part on an assessment of how long it would take to find or create alternative sources of supply, and – in accordance with the principle of proportionality – the effect of the agreement on third parties.[270]

   The Commission has an assumption that buying and selling obligations for unlimited quantities are not ancillary, and the opposite assumption if the agreements are for specific amounts.[271] However, it is difficult to

266. Commission Notice on restrictions directly related and necessary to concentrations (OJ 2005 C 56/24), para. 30.
267. M.1188, *Kingfisher/Wegert/Promarkt,* decision of 18.6.1998, para. 22.
268. JV.50, *Blackstone/CDPQ/Kabel Baden-Würtember,* decision of 1.8.2000, para. 52.
269. JV.15, *BT/AT&T,* decision of 30.3.1999, paras 209-212, where the Commission systematically restricted the duration of all the buying and selling agreements.
270. M.550, *Union Carbide/Enichem,* decision of 13.3.1995 para. 96.
271. Commission Notice on restrictions directly related and necessary to concentrations (OJ 2005 C 56/24), para. 34.

reconcile this with the practice, as it is seldom apparent from the decisions that quantitative restrictions are associated with such agreements.

Finally, the Commission will often set aside exclusive buying and selling agreements which it considers too extensive.[272] This does not mean that exclusive agreements are never accepted, merely that they must be justified by the circumstances of the case.[273] In many cases it is agreed that the one party will make its purchases from a particular source as far as possible and these less binding terms seem to be accepted, even though they are presumably just as effective in the context of a cooperative joint venture.[274]

4. The Commission's Notice contains a number of comments on the terms which are ancillary in connection with the situation where two or more undertakings agree together to acquire control of another undertaking, and where the aim is to share the assets between them. In this situation the Commission accepts a number of restraints which are necessary for carrying out the joint acquisition of control, as well as restraints aimed at the sharing out of the assets.[275]

7. Assessment of coordinated practice in joint ventures

As stated in the review given in Chapter IV, section 7, joint ventures can include a number of restrictions on competition which can be contrary to Article 101 TFEU. The same applies to joint ventures which contain elements of concentration and which are notified under the MCR. Previously there was an attempt to distinguish between those joint ventures where it could be assumed that the cooperation would cover activities outside the actual joint venture in question (these are also referred to as cooperative joint ventures, as distinct from concentrative joint ventures). However, it was very difficult to distin-

272. Commission Notice on restrictions directly related and necessary to concentrations (OJ 2005 C 56/24), para. 34
273. M.102, *TNT/Canada Post et al.,* decision of 13.12.1991, para. 61, where exclusivity was accepted; and M.1298, *Kodak/Imation,* decision of 23.10.1998, para. 74 and JV.22, *Fujitsu/Siemens,* decision of 30.9.1999, para. 83, where the Commission found that exclusivity was not justified.
274. M.951, *Cable and Wireless/Maersk Data – Nautec,* decision of 10.7.1997, para. 21 ('will use Nautec as their preferred channel for the supply of'); and M.409, *ABB/Renault Automation,* decision of 9.3.1993, para. 20 ('shall endeavour to satisfy its demand for').
275. Commission Notice on restrictions directly related and necessary to concentrations (OJ 2005 C 56/24), paras 15-16.

guish these joint ventures and so in 1997 the MCR was amended so that authority was introduced to make an assessment of joint ventures with cooperative aspects under Article 101, as part of the merger control procedure. This was done with the introduction of Article 2(4) and (5) which state as follows:

"4. To the extent that the creation of a joint venture constituting a concentration pursuant to Article 3 has as its object or effect the coordination of the competitive behaviour of undertakings that remain independent, such coordination shall be appraised in accordance with the criteria of Article 81(1) and (3) of the Treaty, with a view to establishing whether or not the operation is compatible with the common market.
5. In making this appraisal, the Commission shall take into account in particular:

   - whether two or more parent companies retain, to a significant extent, activities in the same market as the joint venture or in a market which is downstream or upstream from that of the joint venture or in a neighbouring market closely related to this market,
   - whether the coordination which is the direct consequence of the creation of the joint venture affords the undertakings concerned the possibility of eliminating competition in respect of a substantial part of the products or service in question."

It is immediately clear that, not only is there a reference to the applicability of Article 101, but there seems to have been an adaptation or clarification of how the Commission should make its assessment. However, to a large extent the wording reflects the practice which the Commission has developed under Article 101, see Chapter IV, section 7, as the previously developed practice only appears to have been departed from on certain points. However, the provision assumes that it is not relevant to assess any coordination between the joint venture and some of the joint venture partners where these are active on the same market, as there is a requirement for two or more joint venture partners to be active on a market for it to be necessary to assess whether any restriction on competition exists. Thus, on this point Article 2(4) of the MCR seems to depart from the Commission's practice on Article 101.[276]

276. See *Francisco Enrique González-Diaz in Marianne Dony & d'Aline de Walsche (eds.):* Mélanges en hommage á Michel Waelbroeck, vol. II, 1999 pp. 1019-1069 (in particular at p. 1046); and *John Temple Lang in Barry E. Hawk (ed.):* Fordham Corporate Law Institute, 2000 pp. 404 and 446.

In addition to Article 2(4) providing for a different evaluation on some points, it can be seen that in the cases decided, the Commission has chosen to adopt a different approach in its assessments. Very early on the Commission established that it would first assess which markets are likely candidates for a concerted practice, candidate markets being those markets where the joint venture and at least two joint venture partners are active, or a closely related market to the joint venture's market where at least two joint venture partners are active.[277] In assessing whether there is a coordination on the candidate markets identified, 'it is necessary that the co-ordination of the parent companies' competitive behaviour is likely and appreciable and that it results from the creation of the joint venture, be it as its object or its effect'.[278] In this test the Commission seems to have added a number of further conditions which it had not previously consistently taken account of in its assessments under Article 101. First, it must assess whether coordination is 'likely', which suggests that the assumption must have a secure basis. Then, the coordination must be 'appreciable'. Next, there is a requirement for a causal connection – i.e. the coordination must 'result' from the creation of the joint venture.

Some comments must be made on these three steps of the assessment:

1. First, there is an assessment of whether it is the aim or the effect of the creation of a joint venture that there is coordination on the candidate markets. Since it is not normally the direct aim of a joint venture to ensure that there is such coordination, the decisions have concentrated on deciding whether it is the effect of a joint venture. In assessing whether such coordination is likely, the Commission takes account of the following circumstances: 1) the structure of the candidate markets, 2) the market shares of the parties on the candidate markets, and 3) the structural changes resulting from the creation of a joint venture.

The practice shows that in the assessment of market structure, a number of factors can be included as indicators of the existence of coordination. In Decision JV.22, *Fujitsu/Siemens*, the Commission listed no fewer than six reasons why the market for dynamic random access memory (DRAM) semiconductor chips was not suitable for coordination. First, pricing on the market was not transparent. Next, the buyers were all large undertakings with strong negotiating positions; and third, price developments were highly unpredictable. Fourth, the market was constantly swinging between undersupply and oversupply; and fifth there was an ongoing adjustment of supply and

277. JV.1, *Telia/Telenor/Schibsted,* decision of 27.5.1998, decided immediately after the new provisions entered into force.
278. JV.1, *Telia/Telenor/Schibsted,* decision of 27.5.1998, para. 28.

demand. Finally, the DRAM market was a market in which there was rapid technological development, and consequently there was strong competition with regard to innovation. By comparison, in the same decision it was found that the market for financial workstations was suitable for coordination, among other things because the market was highly concentrated and the technology was well developed and mature.[279] It can also be relevant to assess whether the barriers to access to the market are high or low, as in the latter case coordination would be less likely.[280] Finally, the fact that a market is characterised by rapid growth,[281] and that buyers have a strong negotiating position,[282] can be indicators that there is not coordination.

If the market shares of joint venture partners on the candidate market are very small, this can be an argument against the assumption of coordination.[283] Coordination is also unlikely if, for example, one of the joint venture partners is entirely new to the market, and would therefore be assumed to work hard to achieve a certain market share.[284] If there are many competitors, this will also contraindicate coordination.[285] The Commission thus assumes that the parties to a coordination have a certain market strength on the candidate market.[286] If it is found that the joint venture partners have a position on the candidate market which effectively gives them collective dominance, this clearly indicates that there will be coordination. This was the case in Decision JV.22, *Fujitsu/Siemens*, where the Commission found that one of the candidate markets was concentrated, and the two joint venture partners and their closest competitor had a market share of about 70 %. In addition, the two joint venture partners and their closest competitor had nearly symmetrical market shares, and none of the other competitors had a market share of over 10 %.[287] If only one joint venture partner has a significant market share it will not be assumed that parties with very different market shares will coordinate their behaviour.[288]

Finally, in several cases the Commission has attached weight to how extensive the joint venture activity is in relation to the other activities of the joint venture partners. If a joint venture is of relatively modest extent, it cannot be assumed that it will lead to

279. JV.22, *Fujitsu/Siemens,* decision of 30.9.1999, para. 63.
280. JV.1, *Telia/Telenor/Schibsted,* decision of 27.5.1998, para. 43; and JV.35, *Beiselen/Bay WA/ MG Chemag,* decision of 1.2.2000, para. 29.
281. JV.1, *Telia/Telenor/Schibsted,* decision of 27.5.1998, para. 43.
282. JV.11, *@ HOME Benelux,* decision of 15.9.1998, para. 38.
283. JV.7, *Telia/Sonera/Lithauanian/Telecommunications,* decision of 14.8.1998, para. 31, according to which a market share of less than 10 % made coordination less likely.
284. M.1327, *NC/Canal+/CDPQ/Bank America,* decision of 3.12.1998, para. 32.
285. JV.22, *Fujitsu/Siemens,* decision of 30.9.1999, para. 61, according to which coordination was not considered likely where the joint venture partners had a market share of 15 % and where there was a relatively large number of competitors.
286. See this expressly stated in JV.21, *Skandia/Storebrand/Pohjola,* decision of 17.8.1999, para. 37.
287. JV.22, *Fujitsu/Siemens,* decision of 30.9.1999, para. 63.
288. JV.35, *Beiselen/Bay WA/ MG Chemag,* decision of 1.2.2000, para. 28.

coordinated conduct in the areas where the joint venture partners have significant activities.[289]

2. Many cases have been decided on the basis of an assessment that, even though it is assumed that there will be restrictions on competition, these would not have an appreciable effect. If the collective market shares of the joint venture partners are less than 10 %, the Commission will not normally make any more detailed examination of whether setting up the joint venture would lead to a concerted practice on the market in question.[290] In some cases the Commission even seems to accept that there will be no appreciable effect even if the joint venture partners have more than 10 % market share.[291]
3. In some cases the Commission has had the opportunity to make a closer examination of the requirement for there to be a causal connection. Thus, there have been several cases where the Commission has found that the joint venture partners do not seem to have competed on a candidate market before the establishment of a joint venture and in these cases the Commission has rejected that the creation of the planned joint venture should be the cause of the lack of competition.[292] It is thus clear that if the parties have previously set up some cooperation, the joint venture cannot be the cause. As stated above, in several cases the Commission has pointed out that the fact that a joint venture is of a very modest extent compared to the joint venture partners' other activities makes it less likely that the joint venture partners will use the formation of the joint venture as an occasion to undertake coordination. In several decisions the Commission has justified this conclusion by the lack of a causal

289. JV.6, *Ericsson/Nokia/PSION,* decision of 11.8.1998, para. 38; JV.7, *Telia/Sonera/ Lithuanian/Telecommunications,* decision of 14.8.1998, para. 30; and JV.29, *Lafarge/Readymix,* decision of 20.12.1999, para. 20.
290. JV.1, *Telia/Telenor/Schibsted,* decision of 27.5.1998, para. 41; and JV.5, *Cegetel/CANAL+/AOL/Bertelsmann,* decision of 4.8.1998, paras 35-37.
291. JV.8, *Deutche Telecom et al.,* decision of 28.9.1998, para. 30 (commercially confidential information, but less than 20 %); JV.11, *@ HOME Benelux,* decision of 15.9.1998, para. 38 (11.8 % and 11.6 %); JV.17, *Mannesmann/Bell Atlantic/ OPI,* decision of 21.5.1999, para. 20 (11 %).
292. JV.35, *Beiselen/Bay WA/ MG Chemag,* decision of 1.2.2000, para. 30; JV.23, *Telefonica/Portugal Telecom/Medi Telecom,* decision of 17.12.1999, para. 29; and JV.2 *ENEL/FT/DT/WIND*, decision of 22.6.1998, paras 37 and 39.

connection between the formation of a joint venture and any concerted practice.[293]

On the other hand, in its practice the Commission does not seem to require it to be shown that the actual cooperation is arranged in such a way as to make it probable that it will lead to a concerted practice.[294] The Commission is normally satisfied by establishing that cooperation on a market can be expected to result in an effect on other markets. Thus, the assessment is often based on an evaluation of the market rather than on an evaluation of the individual elements of the cooperation.

The new method for evaluation which is followed in Article 2(4) cases has generally been welcomed in the legal literature, where it has been seen as expressing a more realistic method for evaluating joint ventures under Article 101 TFEU.[295] The Commission previously said that it will issue guidelines on the application of Article 2(4) of the MCR, but this has not yet happened.[296]

8. Merger control procedure

The MCR contains a number of rules on the procedure to which notified mergers are subject. Besides the MCR, there are a number of supplementary rules in Regulation (EC) No 802/2004,[297] and the Commission has further issued a number of notices on certain procedural questions.[298] The following review is chronologically structured; the first section looks at the different

293. JV.23, *Telefonica/Portugal Telecom/Medi Telecom,* decision of 17.12.1999, para. 29.
294. See the view on this in *John Temple Lang* in *Barry E. Hawk (ed.):* Fordham Corporate Law Institute, 2000 p. 428.
295. See *Jonathan Faull & Ali Nikpay (eds.):* The EC Law of Competition, 2nd ed., 2007 p. 515; *Francisco Enrique González-Diaz* in *Marianne Dony & d'Aline de Walsche (eds.):* Mélanges en hommage à Michel Waelbroeck, vol. II, 1999 pp. 1019-1069 (in particular at p. 1061); and *Alison Jones & Brenda Suffrin:* EC Competition Law, 3rd ed., 2008 p. 1073.
296. See note 3 in Commission Notice on the concept of full-function joint ventures (OJ 1998 C 66/1).
297. Regulation (EC) No 802/2004 implementing Council Regulation (EC) No 139/ 2004 on the control of concentrations between undertakings (OJ 2004 L 133/1). This note has not been repeated in the Jurisdictional Notice which has replaced this notice.
298. See the Commission's 'Best Practices on the conduct of EC merger control proceedings' from January 2004, published on the Commission's website (DG Competition), and Commission Notice on a simplified procedure for treatment of certain concentrations under Council Regulation (EC) No 139/2004 (OJ 2005 C 56/32).

steps in the normal procedure, and there is thereafter a discussion of the special rules for the simplified procedure.

8.1. The duty to notify

If there is a concentration which has a Community dimension, as defined in detail in section 2 above, then according to Article 4(1) of the MCR, it must be notified. Prior to 2004, according to the MCR, notification had to be made within one week of the entry into the merger or joint venture agreement, but this deadline has been removed. It is now up to the parties to assess how long they need to give notification, but as they may not carry out their merger or set up their joint venture before the concentration is approved, in practice they will have an interest in giving notification in good time. Under the previous rules it was necessary to decide when the duty to notify arose and therefore when the period for notifying began to run. Since there is no longer any deadline, there is not the same need to determine precisely when the duty to notify arises.

The parties will often be interested in having their merger or joint venture assessed before they make a final agreement. For this reason, before 2004 it was not unusual for the parties to contact the Commission prior to official notification with a view to discussing how the notification should be carried out, as well as to get some idea of how the Commission would appraise the proposed merger.[299] The business community found this form of informal contact satisfactory, and the view was expressed that it ought to be possible to give notification prior to the point when there was a binding agreement etc. Thus, in the 2004 amendment, a provision was included making it possible to give notification 'where the undertakings concerned demonstrate to the Commission a good faith intention to conclude an agreement', see Article 4(1). It is not absolutely clear how advanced the parties' negotiations should be for the condition to be satisfied. A certain help to interpretation is given in recital 34 to the new MCR, where it is stated that it is a condition that the intended merger 'is sufficiently concrete, for example on the basis of an agreement in principle, a memorandum of understanding, or a letter of intent signed by all undertakings concerned'. It is thus clear that most agreements should be in place.

299. In its Best Practices on the conduct of EC merger control proceedings, the Commission has laid down some guidelines on how such a meeting is conducted and what is normally discussed at such meetings.

There is a further possibility for voluntary notification of concentrations without a Community dimension in Article 4(5); see the discussion on this in section 2.5 above.

Finally, according to Article 7(1) of the MCR, the implementation of a concentration must be suspended until the Commission has declared the concentration compatible with the common market, or its compatibility can be established on the basis of the presumption in Article 10(6) of the MCR. On the face of it, this seems to mean that the entry into force of agreements and any transfers may first take effect when such approval has been given.[300] However, this interpretation does not fit well with Article 4, under which the obligation to notify first arises when the agreement has been entered into, or when a controlling shareholding has been acquired. An interpretation of Article 7 in the light of Article 4 therefore leads to the conclusion that the controlling shareholding can be acquired before the merger is notified and assessed, and in this situation it is therefore not possible to maintain the suspension under Article 7.[301]

If the parties ignore or forget the suspension obligation, this can result in a fine under Article 14(2)(a). The civil law effects of such an infringement are only partly regulated by Article 7(4), where it stated that the validity of any transaction carried out in contravention of the suspension obligation will dependent on a decision pursuant to Article 6(1)(b) or Article 8(1), (2) or (3). Next, it is stated that the provision does not have any effect on the validity of transactions in securities admitted to trading on a regulated market such as a stock exchange, unless the buyer and seller knew or ought to have known that the transaction was carried out in contravention of Article 7(1). This means that mergers that are carried out by the transfer of securities listed on a stock exchange can only be declared invalid if both the buyer and the seller act in bad faith. Conversely it must be assumed that mergers and joint ventures which come into existence by other means must in principle be declared invalid, given that there is a decision by the Commission which declares the merger to be incompatible with the common market. If the Commission makes such a decision, the starting point must be that all agreements made in contravention of the suspension obligation are invalid, regardless of whether or not the parties have acted in good faith.

300. However, according to Article 7(2), public take-over bids can be implemented as long as the acquirer does not exercise the voting rights associated with the acquired shares, or only exercises such rights with a view to protecting the full value of the investment.

301. See *C.J. Cook & C.S. Kerse:* EC Merger Control, 5th ed., 2009 p. 150.

According to Article 7(3), the merging parties have the possibility of seeking a derogation from the suspension obligation. This will normally be possible if the parties have good commercial reasons for wishing the concentration to be carried out quickly in order to avoid negative consequences for the parties or for third parties, and if the concentration does not significantly affect competition. Article 7(3) is thus most relevant to concentrations that are notified under the simplified procedure; see section 8.4. However, the Commission has so far been very reluctant to allow such derogations, and it must be assumed that it will continue to be reluctant in future.[302]

Where a merger is carried out or a joint venture is set up contrary to the suspension obligation under the new Article 8(5) the Commission may take appropriate interim measures to restore or maintain conditions of effective competition.

The more detailed requirements for the content of the notification are set out in Regulation (EC) No 802/2004. According to Article 3(1) of this Regulation notifications must contain the information and documentation prescribed by Form CO as set out in Annex I to the Regulation. In addition to information about the form of the concentration, including attaching the final documents on the merger, the parties have to give comprehensive information about the product markets affected by the concentration. For joint ventures there is also an obligation to give information about the effects on cooperation; see Section 10 of Annex I. The parties' information is intended to give the Commission the information necessary to assess the concentration under Article 2 (1)-(3) as well as – for joint ventures – to assess them under Article 2(4). The notification may be made in one of the official languages, but in practice most notifications are made in English, and this is the language for the further processing of cases.

The Commission can give a dispensation from the obligation to give some of the information required in Form CO, see Regulation (EC) No 802/2004, Article 4(2), and this is often the subject of discussion at meetings held with the Commission prior to notification.[303] In addition, the Commission has decided that certain smaller joint ventures can be notified in short form, see Article 3(1). This applies if they fulfil the following conditions: 1) the joint venture's turnover and/or the turnover of the allocated activities is less than EUR 100 million in the EEA, and 2) the assets transferred to the joint venture have a total value of less than EUR 100 million in the EEA. Form CO states in more detail what information must be given when notifying such joint ventures.

302. See *Jonathan Faull & Ali Nikpay (eds.):* The EC Law of Competition, 2nd ed., 2007 p. 545.
303. See the Commission's Best Practices on the conduct of EC merger control proceedings.

8.2. The first phase of the merger control procedure

The first, introductory phase of the merger control procedure must, in principle, be concluded within 25 working days after the Commission receives notification; see MCR Article 10(1).[304] If the Commission does not decide otherwise within the period provided, the concentration will be considered as approved, see Article 10(6).

In this phase, the Commission's investigations will be based on the information which the parties give in their notification. The Commission can demand further information from the parties and there will often be negotiations with the parties concerning various commitments; see Article 6(2). The first phase can result in a decision that the case should proceed to the second phase, because the concentration is covered by the MCR and there is serious doubt as to whether it is compatible with the common market; see Article 6(1)(c). Moreover, the Commission can take one of the following decisions, which means that the case is concluded in the first phase:

1. According to Article 6(1)(a), the Commission can conclude that the concentration notified does not fall within the scope of the MCR. For example, this can be because the parties have estimated incorrectly when calculating that the turnover thresholds have been fulfilled. More typically it will be due to a decision that the parties have incorrectly assessed that the notified joint venture would be a full-function joint venture.
2. According to Article 6(1)(b), the Commission can decide that the concentration notified does not raise serious doubts as to its compatibility with the common market. If there are found to be restrictions on competition which are not ancillary restraints, these will be assessed under Article 2(4). These decisions are decided by another section than the Merger Task Force. However, the assessment under Article 2(4) is made within the deadlines laid down in the MCR.[305]

8.3. The second phase of the merger control procedure

The relatively few concentrations which pass on to the second phase of the merger control procedure are subject to a very thorough analysis, under

304. However, according to the same provision this period can be extended to 35 working days, i.a. in cases where following the notification the undertakings concerned offer commitments pursuant to Article 6(2) with a view to rendering the concentration compatible with the common market.

305. See *Lennart Ritter & W. David Braun:* European Competition Law: A Practitioner's Guide, 3rd ed., 2004 p. 679.

which the effect of the concentration on competition is assessed. In this assessment the Commission will often make use of its powers to obtain further information. This can be by requesting information under Article 11 of the MCR, either from the Member States or from undertakings, including the participating undertakings. It is also possible for the Commission to undertake inspection visits of the undertakings under Article 13.

The parties will be consulted at every stage of the second phase procedure. According to Article 18(1) of the MCR, before the Commission takes any decision under Article 8, the parties will have had the chance to make their views known on the objections concerning the effect of the concentration on competition. The Commission may not base its decision on objections to which the parties have not had an opportunity to submit their observations; see Article 18(3). Normally the hearing of the parties will be in writing, but there can be an oral hearing if the parties so request.

Under Article 18(4) the Commission can also obtain the views of other natural or legal persons. Persons are also entitled to be heard if they so request and if they have a legitimate interest. The Commission often consults third parties on the commitments which the participating undertakings make in order to satisfy the Commission's concerns about the compatibility of the concentration with the common market.[306] It is not entirely clear what rights of access to documents such third parties have, but it must be assumed that they can obtain such a right unless this would undermine the protection of commercial interests of other undertakings, including the merging undertakings.[307] However, it is clear that much information will be in the nature of commercially confidential information, and this cannot be disclosed in connection with a right of access to documents. There can even be information of a confidential nature in the final decision which is not made public, typically information on market shares.[308]

According to Articles 14 and 15 of the MCR, the Commission can impose fines, including periodic penalty fines. Among other things, the Commission can impose fines on parties who fail to notify a concentration or who have given incorrect information when giving notification or in responding to a request to information under Article 11.

306. See *C.J. Cook & C.S. Kerse:* EC Merger Control, 5th ed., 2009 pp. 165-166.
307. See *Jonathan Faull & Ali Nikpay (eds.):* The EC Law of Competition, 2nd ed., 2007 pp. 564-565.
308. There was a somewhat special case in M.951, *Cable and Wireless/Maersk Data – Nautec,* decision of 10.7.1997, para. 14, where the A.P. Møller Group was allowed to keep information about its total turnover confidential.

The second phase may last a maximum of 90 working days from the date when it is begun. In exceptional circumstances this period can be suspended; see Article 10(4). Before a decision is made as a conclusion of the phase, the Advisory Committee on concentrations must be consulted. This is a committee which consists of representatives of the competent authorities of the Member States.[309] According to Article 8, the decisions which the Commission can take are as follows:

1. A concentration can be approved as being compatible with the common market, as set out in Article 8(2), which is what happens in the great majority of cases which reach the second phase. Approval can be given on the basis of changes which the parties have made to their merger plan, or by reference to various kinds of commitments which the parties may have made. The various kinds of commitments, and the conditions and obligations associated with these are discussed above in section 5. Where there is a cooperative joint venture, approval will be dependent on the notified concentration fulfilling the criterion for an exemption under Article 101(3) TFEU.
2. A concentration can be declared incompatible with the common market under Article 8(3), and this can be because the concentration either significantly impedes effective competition, or because a joint venture contains restrictions on competition which are not exempt under Article 101(3) TFEU. Such a decision means that the parties cannot carry out the concentration as it stands.
3. If a concentration is declared incompatible with the common market under Article 8(3), and it has already been carried out, then under Article 8(4) of the MCR the Commission can require the undertakings concerned to dissolve the concentration, including requiring the joint control to be terminated or requiring any other measure to be taken which can restore effective competition.[310]

309. Article 19(3)-(7) of the MCR.

310. The GC has held that the logical consequence of a decision that a merger is incompatible with the common market is that the undertakings should be split again, in other words the restoration of the *status quo ante;* see Case T-80/02, *Tetra Laval,* para. 36. In the latest amendment to the MCR, it is stated in Article 8(4) that such a measure is within the Commission's powers.

In accordance with the general obligation in Article 296 TFEU, the Commission has an obligation to state the reasons for its decisions.[311] The decisions may be brought before the CJ by a Member State, or before the GC by the parties or by an individual third party who is affected.[312]

If the parties infringe a decision made in accordance with Article 8(3) or (4), or fail to comply with an obligation imposed in a decision under Article 8(2), the Commission can impose a fine in accordance with Article 14(2) for up to 10 % of the undertaking's total annual turnover. Next, in the event of an infringement of a condition imposed under Article 8(2), the Commission can take measures for dissolution etc. under Article 8(4). Under Article 8(5), the Commission can now take interim measures, for example by requiring joint venture partners not to exercise their joint control. Under Article 15(2) periodic penalty payments can be imposed on the parties until they comply with an order or comply with a decision for the restoration of effective competition under Article 8(4) or 8(5).

8.4. The simplified procedure

In 2005 the Commission issued a Notice in which it set out its practice concerning a simplified procedure for dealing with certain kinds of concentrations.[313] The simplified procedure is reserved for those kinds of mergers and joint ventures which, in the experience of the Commission, only rarely give rise to problems of competition.[314] The simplified procedure means that the Commission does not make the investigations which it normally makes in the first phase of the merger procedure. Upon receipt of a notification, a short notice is published in the Official Journal, stating among other things that the case will be dealt with according to the simplified procedure. Unless special circumstances apply, the simplified procedure will be concluded by the Commission making a decision under Article 6(1)(b) within 25 working days, or by refraining from taking a decision which, as stated above, indicates tacit approval.

311. In Case T-290/94, *Keysersberg,* paras 141-152, the GC made clear the requirements for the Commission's statement of reasons in merger control cases.
312. If the validity of conditions imposed is challenged, the CJ or the GC can decide to nullify the conditions associated with the decision, provided the conditions are separable from the other parts of the decision; see Article 10(5) of the MCR, and Joined cases C-68/94 and C-30/95, *France and others* v *Commission (Kali & Salz),* para. 256. In the latter case the CJ annulled the decision in its entirety.
313. Commission Notice on a simplified procedure for treatment of certain concentrations under Council Regulation (EC) No 139/2004 (OJ 2005 C 56/32).
314. See para. 5 of the Notice.

Three different forms of concentrations are covered by the procedure. First, there are smaller joint ventures which fulfil the following conditions: i) the joint venture company or the transferred activities have a turnover of less than EUR 100 million within the EEA, and ii) the total value of the assets which are transferred to the joint venture company is less than EUR 100 million within the EEA. Next, there are mergers or joint ventures where none of the participating undertakings are active on the same market or markets which are in an upstream or downstream trading relation to each other. Finally, there are the mergers or joint ventures in which the participating undertakings are active on the same market (horizontal connections), but where they do not jointly have a market share of 15 % or above, and vertical connections where the parties do not have a market share of 25 % or above.[315] The Notice states that there can be cases where there may nevertheless be problems of competition, so that in these cases the Commission reserves the right to implement the usual first phase procedure.[316]

315. See para. 5 of the Notice. A vertical connection will exist where a party to a merger is active on a market which is upstream or downstream from a product market where one of the other participants in the merger is active.
316. See paras 7-12 of the Notice.

CHAPTER IX

State aid

Pernille Wegener Jessen

Bibliography: *Mona Aldestam: EC State aid rules applied to taxes – An analysis of the selectivity criterion, 2005; Andrea Biondi, Piet Eeckhout & James Flynn: The Law of State aid in the European Union, 2004; Leigh Hancher, Tom Ottervanger & Piet Jan Slot: EC State aids, 2006; Gustavo Luengo Hernández de Madrid: Regulation of Subsidies and State aids in WTO and EC Law, 2007; Heidenhain: European State aid Law, 2010; Pernille W. Jessen: Forbuddet mod statsstøtte i EU, 2003; Phedon Nicolaides, Mihalis Kekelekis & Maria Kleis: State aid Policy in the European Community, 2008; Conor Quigley: European State aid Law and Policy, 2009; Luca Rubini: The Definition of Subsidy and State Aid, 2009; Erica Szyszczak (ed.): Research Handbook on European State aid Law, 2011; Peter L. Vesterdorf & Mogens Uhd Nielsen: State aid law of the European Union, 2008.*

1. Introduction

The provisions on State aid in Articles 107-109 in the Treaty on the functioning of the European Union are part of the legal basis for ensuring the establishment of an internal market in which competition is not distorted. In this context the special role of the provisions on State aid is to erect a barrier against the disruptive effects which the provision of State aid by the Member States can have on the proper functioning of the internal market. Thus, in contrast to Articles 101 and 102, the provisions on State aid are directed at the conduct of the Member States and not at the conduct of undertakings.

The Member States can use State aid as an effective instrument of financial control to promote, for example, employment policies, social policies or environmental aims. Where such aid is directed towards specific undertakings or sectors rather than to the Member State's undertakings in general, the aid could distort competition in the relevant market. The undertakings or sectors which receive aid thus obtain a financial advantage which puts them in a better competitive position than their competitors both in the same Member State and in other Member States.[1]

Article 107(1) thus states that any aid granted by a Member State or through State resources, in any form whatsoever, which distorts or threatens to distort competition by favouring certain undertakings or the production of certain goods is incompatible with the internal market, in so far as it affects trade between Member States. Accordingly, Article 107 does not cover all forms of aid granted by Member States, but only such measures as distort the conditions which normally apply to competition between undertakings and which affect trade between Member States.

Article 107(1) is not framed as an absolute prohibition, but merely states that State aid is in principle incompatible with the internal market. However, the Court of Justice of the European Union (CJ) seems to apply Article 107(1) as a prohibitory provision, so that in this chapter the Article is referred to as containing a prohibition.[2]

The application of Article 107(1) as a prohibitory provision is based on the fact that the consequences that follow from the fact that a State aid is in principle incompatible with the internal market largely correspond to the consequences that generally follow from a provision which is framed as a prohibition.[3] State aid measures that are found to be incompatible with the internal market are thus either repealed or amended, and aid paid out under such measures must be repaid.

The prohibition of State aid is not absolute, but is modified to a certain extent both by other parts of the provisions on State aid and by other provisions of

1. 'In order to favour the aided enterprise, taxes must be levied on the rest of the economy. Thus not only are enterprises in other Member States put at a competitive disadvantage by the aid because the aided enterprises are favoured in a way outside the normal fiscal or social security systems that contribute to the equilibrium between the Member States, but also enterprises not receiving aid in the same Member State are disadvantaged and pay higher taxes directly or indirectly.' Second Survey on State aids in the European Community in the Manufacturing and Certain Other Sectors, at p. 7, SEC(90) 1165/3, 10 July 1990.
2. See e.g. the CJ's application of the provision in Case 78/76, *Steinike & Weinlig;* and Case C-354/90, *FNCE.*
3. However, in contrast to what is normally the case with prohibition provisions, Article 107(1) does not have direct effect; see Case 78/76, *Steinike & Weinlig,* para. 10.

the Treaty.[4] Thus, in certain circumstances the Commission has powers to approve State aid measures subject to Article 107(1). This power stems from Article 107(2) which lists certain forms of support which *are* compatible with the internal market, and Article 107(3) which lists certain forms of aid which *may be considered* to be compatible with the internal market. Furthermore, under Article 108(2), third paragraph, the Council has powers to decide that a specific aid measure is to be considered as compatible with the internal market.

The scope of the prohibition of State aid depends on how the term *incompatible State aid* – in other words, State aid that is incompatible with the internal market according to Article 107(1) – is interpreted. The interpretation of this is decisive for whether a measure is covered by the Commission's exclusive competence to assess the compatibility of a State aid measure with the internal market. In such a case the Member States have an obligation to notify the measure to the Commission and await the Commission's approval before implementing it.

The Commission thus has powers to use the rules on State aid to control parts of the Member States' financial support for business. The more broadly the term is defined, the broader is the scope of the Commission's powers, at the expense of the powers of the Member States. For this reason the definition of the term *incompatible State aid* will often be the cause of political tension, prompted on the one hand by the Member States' desire to retain the freedom to implement their chosen economic and social policies, and on the other hand by the Commission's desire to secure an effective internal market against State aid which distorts competition, by being able to sanction any measure that has the least hint of State aid that could be incompatible with the internal market.

In order to ensure effective control of national State aid measures, the Member States must give notification of new State aid measures to the Commission, whereas the compatibility with the internal market of existing State aid measures is subject to constant evaluation by the Commission.[5] There are detailed provisions on the notification of State aid and the legal

4. 'Save as otherwise provided in the Treaties ...' – Article 107(1). The provisions are modified by Articles 38-44 (agriculture), Article 106(2) (services of a general economic interest), Article 93 (transport), Article 107(2) and (3), Article 108(2), third paragraph, Articles 143-144 (difficulties as regards balance of payments), and Article 346 (protection of essential security interests).
5. However, State aid covered by the block exemption regulations are exempt from the duty to notify; see more on this in section 2.2.1.

consequences in Article 108 of the Treaty and in the Procedure Regulation.[6] These lay down more detailed rules on the Commission's scope to control and react, as well as the procedure that applies in the event that a Member State does not comply with the obligation to notify or to prohibit implementation (the standstill requirement).

The Procedure Regulation was adopted by the Council under Article 109 which gives the Council authority to make appropriate regulations for the application of Articles 107 and 108. Article 109 also gives the Council authority to determine the conditions in which Article 108(3) is to apply and the categories of aid exempted from the obligation to notify and the procedure associated with this. In accordance with this, the Council has adopted Regulation (EC) No 994/98, which gives the Commission powers to adopt block exemption regulations in relation to certain identified forms of horizontal State aid.[7] Such regulations may now also be adopted by the Commission on basis of Article 108 (4).

2. State aid procedure

In assessing the compatibility of a State aid measure with the internal market, the Commission has to follow the procedure provided for in Article 108 of the Treaty. In 1999 the practice and principles which had been developed over time and established by the CJ and the Commission were codified in the Procedure Regulation, which created a much-needed if not entirely comprehensive overview of the procedure in the area of State aid.[8]

6. Council Regulation (EC) No 659/1999 laying down detailed rules for the application of Article 93 [now Article 108] of the Treaty (OJ 1999 L 83/1) (hereinafter the 'Procedure Regulation').
7. Council Regulation (EC) No 994/98 on the application of Articles 92 and 93 of the Treaty establishing the European Community to certain categories of horizontal State aid (OJ 1998 L 142/1). On this basis the Commission has adopted Commission Regulation (EC) No 1998/2006 on the application of Articles 87 and 88 of the Treaty to *de minimis* aid (OJ 2006 L 379/5) and Commission Regulation (EC) No 800/2008 declaring certain categories of aid compatible with the common market in application of Articles 87 and 88 of the Treaty (General block exemption Regulation) (OJ 2008 L 214/3), which, in addition to consolidating five previous block exemption regulations in one regulation, includes State aid for environmental protection, risk capital investments, and research and development.
8. Council Regulation (EC) No 659/1999 (OJ 1999 L 83/1). The Regulation was implemented by Commission Regulation (EC) No 794/2004 (OJ 2004 L 140/1), as amended. (On 27 June 2007 the Commission proposed an amendment to Regulation (EC) No 794/2004.) For more detail on the Procedure Regulation, see *Adinda*

The procedure which the Commission has to follow in relation to a specific State aid measure depends on whether the measure is classified as a new State aid measure or an existing State aid measure. Existing aid measures are governed by Article 108(1) and (2), while new aid measures are subject to the procedure in Article 108(2) and (3).

2.1. Existing State aid measures

The term *existing aid* is defined in Article 1 of the Procedure Regulation. The term covers all forms of aid that existed before the Treaty's entry into force in the Member State concerned. This means that aid that is provided in accordance with individual aid measures[9] or general aid schemes[10] which a Member State has implemented prior to the Treaty's entry into force in the Member State, and which are still in force, are considered to be existing aid.

Next, existing aid includes existing aid schemes and individual aid which has been approved by the Commission or by the Council in accordance with Article 108(2), third paragraph. Third, aid is considered to be existing aid if it is approved in accordance with Article 4(6) of the Procedure Regulation, or under the corresponding procedure which applied before the Procedure Regulation entered into force,[11] or as a result of the Commission exceeding the deadline for taking a decision, or the Commission's failure to react to a Member State's subsequent notification that the measure is being implemented.

Sinnaeve: Der Kommissionsvorschlag zu einer Verfahrensverordnung für die Beihilfenkontrolle, Europäische Zeitschrift für Wirtschaftsrecht 1998 pp. 268-273; *Adinda Sinnaeve & Piet Jan Slot:* The New Regulation on State Aid Procedures, Common Market Law Review 1999 pp. 1153-1194; *Adinda Sinnaeve:* Die neue Verfahrensverordnung in Beihilfensachen, Europäische Zeitschrift für Wirtschaftsrecht 1999 pp. 270-277; and *Heidenhain:* European State Aid Law, 2010 pp. 573-705.

9. *Individual aid* is defined in the Procedure Regulation as 'aid that is not awarded on the basis of an aid scheme and notifiable awards of aid on the basis of an aid scheme'; Article 1(e).
10. *Aid scheme* is defined in the Procedure Regulation as 'any act on the basis of which, without further implementing measures being required, individual aid awards may be made to undertakings defined within the act in a general and abstract manner and any act on the basis of which aid which is not linked to a specific project may be awarded to one or several undertakings for an indefinite period of time and/or for an indefinite amount'; Article 1(d).
11. The previous procedure meant that, after notifying the Commission, a Member State could implement measures after the expiry of a deadline of 2 months; see e.g. Case 120/73, *Lorenz,* para. 4; and Case C-312/90, *Spain* v *Commission,* para. 18.

Fourth, aid which the Commission can no longer require to be repaid, because of the expiry of the 10 year period of limitation in Article 15 of the Procedure Regulation, is considered to be existing aid.[12]

Finally, aid is considered to be existing aid if it can be shown that, upon the introduction of the aid, it was not aid within the meaning of Article 107(1), and that the measure later came to be considered as aid because of the development of the internal market, without the Member State having made any changes to the measure.[13] However, measures that acquire the character of State aid as a result of the EU's liberalisation of an activity are not considered to be existing aid after the date on which the liberalisation takes effect, but is regarded as new aid.[14]

In accordance with Article 108(1), existing aid schemes are subject to continuing control carried out in cooperation between the Commission and the Member States. In principle such aid is considered to be compatible with the internal market, and can be implemented until the Commission states that it is incompatible with the internal market.

2.2. New aid measures

In the Procedure Regulation *new aid* is defined as all 'aid schemes and individual aid, which is not existing aid, including alterations to existing aid'.[15] The Regulation thus defines the term negatively in relation to existing aid.

New aid measures are subject to prior controls which are in part based on a duty to notify,[16] and in part on a standstill obligation.[17] The obligation to notify means that the Member States must inform the Commission of any proposed introduction of or change to an aid measure so that the Commission has the opportunity to give its opinion on the aid measure before it is put into

12. See in more detail in section 2.7.
13. See e.g. the Commission's assessment of the Irish corporation tax where, in 1980, the Commission found that the favourable treatment of the manufacturing sector was a general measure, while in its Decision of 22 July 1998, State aid E/2/98 (OJ 1998 C 395/19), the Commission found that the measure involved State aid. The Commission therefore proposed that, in accordance with Article 108(1), the arrangement should be repealed and replaced by a uniform tax rate for both the manufacturing and the service industries; see also the XVIIIth Report on competition policy, 1999, para. 21.
14. Procedure Regulation, Article 1(b)(v).
15. Procedure Regulation, Article 1(c). Changes to an existing arrangement thus mean that the scheme will be considered new, which gives rise to certain procedural consequences.
16. Article 108(3), first paragraph, of the Treaty and the Procedure Regulation, Article 2.
17. Article 108(3), third paragraph, of the Treaty and the Procedure Regulation, Article 3.

effect. The obligation is supplemented by a standstill obligation which means that a Member State may not put a proposed measure into effect before the Commission gives its final approval or can be regarded as having approved it. This prevents aid which is incompatible with the Treaty from being instituted and having a damaging effect. In Case 120/73, *Lorenz*, the CJ established that, as the only such part of the State aid provisions, the standstill clause has direct effect.[18]

In principle, new State aid measures are regarded as being incompatible with the internal market and are therefore considered unlawful if they are not notified or suspended in accordance with the above.[19] Subject to certain procedural modifications, such unlawful aid is dealt with in the same way as notified State aid measures.[20]

2.2.1. Notifiable measures

According to Article 108(3), Member States have a duty to notify the Commission of any plans to alter existing aid schemes and any proposal to introduce new aid schemes.[21] The aim of this is to give the Commission the possibility of controlling whether an aid scheme is compatible with the internal market before the measure is implemented.

However, the duty to notify is not without exceptions. On the basis of Council Regulation (EC) No 994/98, the Commission has the possibility of declaring that certain forms of aid either do not fulfil the criteria in Article 107(1), or are regarded as being compatible with the internal market in accordance with Article 107(3), and are therefore exempted from the notification obligation under Article 108(3).[22] On the basis of this authority, the Commission has adopted Regulation (EC) No 1998/2006 on *de minimis* aid and the General block exemption Regulation, which exempt certain forms of aid from the obligation to notify.[23]

18. Case 120/73, *Lorenz,* para. 8, which refers to Case 6/64, *Costa/ENEL,*
19. See the definition of *unlawful aid* in the Procedure Regulation, Article 1(f).
20. Procedure Regulation, Article 13(2).
21. Procedure Regulation, Article 2 (see Article 1(c)). It has also been proposed that recipients of State aid should have the possibility of notifying the aid to the Commission; see *Vincent J.G. Power:* A Proposal for State Aid Reform: Beneficiaries of Potential State Aid Should be Able to Notify the European Commission of the Proposed Aid, European Competition Law Review 2005 26(1) pp. 1-3.
22. Articles 1 and 2 of Council Regulation (EC) No 994/98 (OJ 1998 L 142/1). See also Article 108(4).
23. Article 2(1) of Commission Regulation (EC) No 1998/2006 on the application of Articles 87 and 88 of the Treaty to *de minimis* aid (OJ 2006 L 379/5); and Article 3 of

Individual aid which is given in accordance with an approved aid scheme need not be notified to the Commission, unless a reservation to this effect is made in the Commission's decision giving approval.[24] In this case the aid will be treated procedurally in the same way as existing aid. The reason why there is not a general duty to notify is that the circumstances which the Commission has taken into account in connection with approving an aid measure will be the same as those the Commission would have to assess in relation to individual aid which is granted as part of the implementation of the general aid scheme. Where there is no requirement for notification as a condition for the approval of an aid measure which is associated with an existing aid scheme, the Member State nevertheless has a duty to send annual reports to the Commission with a view to controlling whether the aid scheme is used correctly.[25]

2.3. Unlawful aid measures

In Article 1(f) of the Procedure Regulation, *unlawful aid* is defined as new aid put into effect in contravention of Article 108(3) of the Treaty. As previously stated, Article 108(3) imposes on Member States both a notification obligation and a standstill obligation. New aid which has not been notified in accordance with Article 108(3), first paragraph, is thus considered unlawful aid. The same applies to new aid which has been correctly notified in accordance with Article 108(3), first paragraph, but which has been put into effect prior to notification, or subsequent to notification but prior to the Commission's approval, and aid has therefore been paid in breach of the standstill requirement in Article 108(3), third paragraph.[26] Aid that is paid without the approval of the Commission is dealt with in the same procedural context as non-notified aid, regardless of whether the aid has in fact been notified to the Commission,[27] and it is considered unlawful in line with other non-notified aid.

Commission Regulation (EC) No 800/2008 declaring certain categories of aid compatible with the common market in application of Articles 87 and 88 of the Treaty (General block exemption Regulation) (OJ 2008 L 214/3).

24. Case C-47/91, *Italy* v *Commission,* para. 21.
25. Procedure Regulation, Article 21(1).
26. The expression *unlawful aid* thus refers to the fact that the aid has not been notified and/or has been paid without approval, and does not refer to the compatibility of the aid with the internal market under Article 107(1).
27. See e.g. the Commission Decision in Case C-23/2000, *Ojala-Yhtymä* (OJ 2000 C 278/2), where the case was treated as non-notified aid, as a part of the planned aid had

2.4. The procedure for existing aid

As stated above, aid schemes that are characterised under the Procedure Regulation as existing schemes, are considered compatible with the internal market. However, the gradual growth and development of the internal market can mean that such an aid scheme will no longer be considered as compatible with the internal market. For example, if overcapacity arises in a particular business sector, it would not serve the interests of the Union if aid continued to be given under an existing aid scheme for an expansion of production capacity in the sector in question. In order to prevent such situations arising, the Member States and the Commission together undertake a constant review of the aid schemes in each of the Member States.[28] However, such reviews are not only undertaken with a view to identifying existing aid schemes which have become incompatible with the internal market, but also with a view to identifying existing aid schemes which were never compatible with the internal market. If such a scheme is identified, the Commission will, after giving the Member State an opportunity to give its opinion,[29] propose suitable measures to change an aid scheme to make it compatible with the internal market by amending the content of the aid scheme, introducing procedural requirements or repealing the aid scheme.[30]

If the Member State concerned accepts the Commission's recommendation, the Member State is bound by its acceptance.[31] On the other hand, if the Member State does not accept the Commission's recommendation, the Commission can initiate a formal examination procedure.[32] Member States are not subject to a standstill obligation in relation to existing aid, and the aid may continue to be paid until the Commission decides that the aid is incompatible with the internal market.

2.5. The procedure for notified aid

According to the Treaty, notified aid is subject to a two-part procedure, namely the preliminary examination and the formal investigation procedure.

already been allocated and paid to the undertakings in question at the date when the aid was notified.

28. Article 108(1).
29. Procedure Regulation, Article 17(2). The Member State has a deadline of one month to give its views. This deadline can be extended by the Commission if there are good grounds for doing so.
30. Procedure Regulation, Article 18.
31. Procedure Regulation, Article 19(1).
32. Procedure Regulation, Article 19(2) (cf. Article 4(4)).

Under the *preliminary examination*, within two months,[33] the Commission must form a preliminary view of the compliance of the aid arrangement with the provisions on State aid[34] and take a decision accordingly.

The Commission thus has the possibility of deciding that the measure in question does not involve State aid, or it can approve a measure which does involve State aid but which is considered compatible with the internal market.[35] A decision to approve an aid measure must be unconditional, so that, unlike the case of the formal investigation procedure, the Commission does not have the possibility of making the approval subject to special terms or conditions.

If the 2 month deadline for making a decision is exceeded, the aid scheme is considered as having been approved by the Commission. However, the Member State in question must give the Commission notice before an aid measures is implemented, and the Commission then has 15 working days from receiving such notice in which to take any decision in accordance with Article 4.[36] In order to prevent the implementation of aid schemes that are contrary to the provisions on State aid, the standstill obligation has effect throughout the whole of the preliminary examination procedure.[37]

The Commission can also decide to initiate the *formal investigation procedure*. This will occur where, after the preliminary examination, the Commission is in doubt about the compatibility of an aid measure with the internal market,[38] and there is therefore a need to gather full information as a basis for making a decision about the aid measure, as well as consulting the interested parties.[39]

33. The deadline of 2 months begins on the day following the receipt of notification of an aid scheme or individual aid; see the Procedure Regulation, Article 4(5), which also states that: 'The notification will be considered as complete if, within two months from its receipt, or from the receipt of any additional information requested, the Commission does not request any further information'.
34. Case 120/73, *Lorenz,* para. 2; and Case C-367/95 P, *Sytraval,* para. 38.
35. Procedure Regulation, Article 4(2) and (3).
36. Procedure Regulation, Article 4(6).
37. Case 84/82, *Germany v Commission,* para. 11.
38. Procedure Regulation, Article 4(4), as well as Article 108(2), second paragraph, of the Treaty. The procedure is also initiated where, in accordance with Article 9 of the Regulation, the Commission intends to revoke a decision based on incorrect information which was a determining factor.
39. The Commission publishes its views on aid measures in the Official Journal, inviting the Member State in question and other interested parties to comment. Such comments must be made within a deadline laid down, which is normally not longer than one month; Procedure Regulation, Article 6(1).

As a conclusion to the formal investigation procedure, the Commission can decide that the measure does not constitute a State aid – possibly after the Member State in question has made some change to the measures. The Commission can also take a positive decision that the aid measure can be approved as being compatible with the internal market. Such a decision will contain a reference to the provision in the Treaty that is used as authority for exempting the measure from the prohibition of State aid. The Commission can make the approval conditional on compliance with certain specified requirements, as well as instituting control measures enabling the Commission to monitor compliance with the decision. Finally, the Commission can take a negative decision, that the aid is incompatible with the internal market.[40]

As soon as the Commission is no longer in doubt about the compatibility of a measure with the internal market, it makes one of the decisions referred to above. As far as possible, this decision is taken within 18 months of the initiation of the procedure.[41]

If the Commission does not decide within the 18 months deadline, the Member State concerned can request the Commission to decide on the basis of the existing information within 2 months or, if the existing information is insufficient, to take a negative decision.[42] It is not clear from Article 7(7) of the Procedure Regulation whether the Commission's inaction means – as it does in relation to Article 4(6) of the Regulation – that after the expiry of the 2 months the Member State has a right to implement the aid measure. However, there seems little purpose in a Member State triggering this deadline if the expiry of the deadline does not result in a right to implement the aid measure. However, the Procedure Regulation does not contain such an express authorisation, so it must be left to the CJ to decide whether such a meaning can be ascribed to Article 7(7).

2.6. The procedure for unlawful aid

It is not all Member States that live up to the obligation to notify planned aid measures. Such non-notified aid measures can come to the attention of the Commission on the basis of information about them or of complaints received from other Member States or competitors. The Commission must then investigate the measures in question in more detail.[43] This investigation is concluded with a decision in accordance with Article 4(2), (3) or (4) of the Procedure Regulation or, in the event of a decision to initiate the formal

40. Procedure Regulation, Article 7(2)-(5).
41. Procedure Regulation, Article 7(6).
42. Procedure Regulation, Article 7(7).
43. Procedure Regulation, Article 10.

investigation procedure, by a decision in accordance with Article 7 of the Regulation.[44]

The procedure for unlawful State aid thus corresponds generally to the procedure for notified aid. However, there is the important difference that in dealing with unlawful State aid the Commission is not bound by any of the deadlines for processing the case.[45] In practice, the deadlines for non-notified measures will not vary much from those that apply to notified measures, among other things out of regard for good administrative practice to complete the processing of cases within a reasonable time.

2.6.1. Interim legal measures

As a non-notified aid measure is characterised as unlawful, in special circumstances the Commission can apply interim measures. Thus, the Commission can order the Member State concerned either to suspend the aid measure, or to recover aid already paid out, or both.[46] Since these measures are of an interim nature, they only have effect up to the point when the Commission makes its final decision on the compatibility of the aid measure with the internal market.

The power given in Article 11(2) of the Regulation, to order recovery of non-notified aid can only be used in special circumstances. According to the established practice, first there must be no doubt about the nature of the aid in question; second, it must be necessary to take immediate steps; and third the measure must involve a serious risk of substantial and irreparable damage to a competitor.[47] These provisions can only be applied if all the conditions are fulfilled. This is assumed to apply in only very few cases, and thus the provision is not of great practical importance.

2.7. Recovery of unlawful aid

The Commission's powers to require recovery

Since 1973 the CJ has recognised that, under the authority of Article 108(2) of the Treaty, the Commission can require the recovery of unlawful aid. This was established in Case 70/72, *Kohlengesetz*, where the CJ concluded that the

44. Procedure Regulation, Article 13(1). On these provisions, for the preliminary examination see Article 4, and for the formal investigation procedure see Article 7.
45. Procedure Regulation, Article 10(2).
46. Procedure Regulation, Article 11(1) and (2), according to which the Commission may require the Member State to suspend and to recover any unlawful aid. If the Member State fails to comply with a suspension injunction or a recovery injunction, the Commission can refer the matter to the CJ directly and apply for a declaration that the failure to comply constitutes an infringement of the Treaty; the Procedure Regulation, Article 12
47. Procedure Regulation, Article 11(2).

Commission's right to require a Member State to suspend or abolish an aid measure which is found incompatible with the internal market implies authority to require that payment made which is contrary to the provisions on State aid should be recovered.[48] This is necessary in order to ensure that a decision of the Commission to abolish or alter an aid scheme can be effective in practice.

If a Member State does not comply with a Commission decision on the recovery of incompatible State aid, that Member State can be subject to an action for breach of the Treaty.[49]

The Commission's powers to recover State aid which is incompatible with the Treaty is now codified in Article 14 of the Procedure Regulation. According to this, where the Commission takes a negative decision in a case of unlawful aid, the Commission will decide that payments made must be recovered, provided that such a decision is not contrary to general principles of Union law.[50] If the conditions for requiring repayment of State aid are fulfilled, the Commission has a duty to seek recovery of the aid. In contrast to the situation under previous practice, the exercise of the Commission's power to require repayment is no longer a matter of the Commission's choice, it is an obligation.[51]

The conditions for requiring recovery

The Commission can only require recovery under Article 14 of the Procedure Regulation in special circumstances. Thus, the recovery requires that the aid measures should be classified as new aid,[52] the aid must be unlawful,[53] the aid must be incompatible with the internal market, payments must have been made in accordance with the aid scheme, that the period of limitation in Article 15(1) of the Procedure Regulation must not have been exceeded, and the requirement for repayment must not be contrary to general principles of Union law.

48. Case 70/72, *Kohlengesetz,* para. 13.
49. Case 70/72, *Kohlengesetz,* para. 13. See also Case C-24/95, *Alcan,* para. 22.
50. E.g., the principle of proportionality and the principle of legitimate expectations, which are discussed further below.
51. The Commission explains its policy towards the implementation of recovery decisions in a notice: Towards an effective implementation of Commission decisions ordering Member States to recover unlawful and incompatible State aid (OJ 2007 C 272/4).
52. Procedure Regulation, Article 1(c).
53. Procedure Regulation, Article 1(f).

The recovery of unlawfully paid aid in accordance with Article 14 of the Procedure Regulation also requires that the Commission has taken a negative decision in accordance with Article 107(1) of the Treaty, and has thereby established that the aid measure is incompatible with the internal market.

The powers of the Commission to recover aid under Article 14 of the Procedure Regulation are subject to a limitation period of ten years.[54] The limitation period begins on the day on which the unlawful aid is awarded to the recipient.[55] In this context, the date of the award is treated as being the date of payment, and is thus not affected by when the decision to grant the aid is taken,[56] just as it is not relevant whether the aid is awarded individually or as part of an aid scheme.[57] On the same principle, the period of limitation for aid which is paid in instalments is calculated from the payment date for each instalment.

In certain circumstances the period of limitation can be interrupted or suspended, see the Procedure Regulation, Article 15(2). The interruption occurs whenever a measure is taken in relation to unlawful aid by the Commission or by a Member State on the prompting of the Commission. For example, such measure can take the form of the Commission's recommendation to the Member State concerning the support measure, or the Member State's legal steps taken to recover the aid.[58] After each interruption the 10 years limitation period starts again from the beginning. If the decision of the Commission is brought before the CJ, the period of limitation is suspended as long as the case is pending.[59]

Upon the expiry of the period of limitation, what was originally new unlawful aid changes its status to become existing aid.[60]

Implementation of the recovery decision

The Commission's decision on the recovery of unlawful aid is addressed to the Member State concerned, and as such it is binding on it.[61] The Member State is responsible for taking all the measures necessary to recover the aid

54. Procedure Regulation, Article 15(1).
55. Procedure Regulation, Article 15(2).
56. See Case T-254/00, *Hotel Cipriani*, para. 364.
57. See *Heidenhain:* European State Aid Law, 2010 p. 648.
58. In Case T-369/00, *Département du Loiret,* para. 82, it was recognised that a request by the Commission for information from a Member State is a measure which can interrupt the applicable period.
59. Procedure Regulation, Article 15(2).
60. Procedure Regulation, Article 15(3).
61. Article 288 of the Treaty.

paid to the recipient.[62] According to Article 14(3) of the Procedure Regulation, the repayment must be made without delay and in accordance with the procedures of the national law of the Member State concerned.[63] For this purpose, 'the Member States concerned shall take all necessary steps which are available in their respective legal systems, including provisional measures, without prejudice to Community law'.[64]

The actual implementation of the recovery demand is thus subject to the relevant national law. However, the national law must not make it impossible to seek recovery of the unlawful aid in practice,[65] for example because the Member State's provisions on payments made under beneficial legal acts prevent the implementation of the recovery decision. Where a Member State meets an unexpected or unpredictable problem in implementing the recovery decision, it cannot merely refrain from implementing the decision but must refer the matter to the Commission with a view to cooperating in order to overcome the problems.[66] In this context, administrative problems are not circumstances that can justify the failure to implement a recovery decision.[67]

If a Member State does not implement the recovery of incompatible aid in accordance with the Commission's decision, then either the Commission or another Member State can bring an action for breach of the Treaty directly before the CJ in accordance with Article 108(2), second paragraph, of the Treaty[68] and thereby move more rapidly than the longer procedure for cases of breach of the Treaty under Articles 258 and 259. According to the practice of the CJ, the only objection the Member State can make in such a case is to produce concrete evidence that it is absolutely impossible to recover the aid

62. Procedure Regulation, Article 14(1).
63. However, in connection with an appeal against the Commission's decision, the CJ can order the postponement of the implementation of the legal act which is being challenged; see Article 242 of the Treaty. In order to ensure the rapid execution of the repayment requirement, on the basis of Joined Cases T-244 and 486/93, *Deggendorf,* and Case C-355/95 P, *TWD,* the Commission can order the suspension of any payment of new aid to undertakings that have not repaid unlawful or incompatible State aid; see Report, State aid Scoreboard, COM(2007) 347 final, section 1.5.3.
64. Procedure Regulation, Article 14(3).
65. Case C-24/95, *Alcan,* para. 24; and Case C-5/89, *Commission* v *Germany,* para. 12.
66. Case C-507/08, *Commission* v *Slovenia,* para. 44; and Case C-214/07, *Commission* v *France,* paras 45 and 46.
67. Case C-280/95, *Commission* v *Italy*, para. 23.
68. Case C-232/05, *Commission* v *France,* commented on by *Antonis Metaxas:* Recovery Obligation and the Limits of National Procedural Autonomy, European State Aid Law Quarterly (2) 2007 pp. 407-415.

paid out from the recipient[69] This is interpreted restrictively by the CJ; for example, the financial collapse of an undertaking as a result of the recovery of incompatible aid is not an argument that justifies a Member State refraining from requiring the aid in question to be repaid.[70]

The Member State addresses the order for repayment to the recipient of the aid concerned, who is normally identified in the Commission's decision,[71] and it will normally be possible to make the identification without any problems. On the other hand, in some cases, if an undertaking or part of an undertaking has been sold or transferred, it can be difficult to establish to whom the Member State should address its recovery order.[72] However, if an undertaking which has received unlawful State aid is sold at the market price, the aid element is assessed at the market price and is included in the sales price, and the purchaser therefore does not benefit from a competitive advantage associated with receipt of the aid.[73] This means that a claim for repayment cannot be made against the purchaser unless it is proved that the purchaser has in fact had a competitive advantage associated with the aid, for example if the setting up of a hived-off company in order to carry on the business and to circumvent the obligation of the insolvent company to make a repayment.[74]

69. Case C-214/07, *Commission* v *France,* para. 44; Case C-261/99, *Commission* v *France,* para. 23; and Case C-404/97, *Commission* v *Portugal,* para. 39. See also Case 280/95, *Commission* v *Italy,* para. 13; and Joined Cases C-485 & 490/03, *Commission* v *Spain,* paras 72 and 74.
70. Case C-261/99, *Commission* v *France,* para. 15; and Case 52/84, *Commission* v *Belgium.*
71. For more details on the limits to the Commission's powers to identify debtors in repayment cases, see Case C-277/00, *SMI,* with commentary by *Gerrit Schohe:* May the Commission Select the Debtor of State Aid Payment? Where the Commission's Power over State Aids Events, European State Aid Law Quarterly (3) 2004 pp. 423-426; and *Andreas Knaul:* The SMI-Judgment – a New Course for Recovery of Illegal State Aid?, European State Aid Law Quarterly (3) 2004 pp. 427-430.
72. See *Christian Koenig:* Determining the Addressee of a Decision Ordering the Recovery of State Aid after the Sale of Substantial, European Competition Law Review 2001 pp. 238-248. See also Commission Decision 1999/720/EC, *GSW* (OJ 1999 L 292/27); Commission Decision 2000/567/EC, *SMI* (OJ 2000 L 238/50); and Commission Decision 2000/796/EC, *CDA* (OJ 2000 L 318/62). See also *Leigh Hancher, Tom Ottervanger & Piet Jan Slot:* EC State aids, 2006 paras 26-015 – 26-016; and *Heidenhain*: European State Aid Law, 2010 pp. 657-660.
73. Case T-291/06, *Operator ARP,* para. 67; and Case C-214/07, *Commission* v *France,* para. 58.
74. Case C-277/00, *Germany* v *Commission,* para. 86.

Possible exceptions to the obligation to repay
As stated above, the Commission can demand that unlawful and incompatible State aid should be recovered, as long as this is not contrary to general principles of Union law; see the Procedure Regulation, Article 14(1). In practice this primarily involves an assessment of whether an order to recover unlawful or incompatible State aid is contrary to the proportionality principle or the principle of legitimate expectations.

In so far as it is a logical consequence of the incompatibility of the unlawful aid with the internal market that it is sought to be recovered, and the recovery of payment has the sole purpose of restoring the *status ante quo*, in several cases the CJ has stated that the duty to repay should not, in principle, be a disproportionate burden in relation to the aims of the Treaty's provisions on State aid.[75] In these circumstances the Commission's order to repay will therefore comply with the proportionality principle.

The principle of legitimate expectations, meaning the principle that the expectation that a legal ruling is final, is sufficiently justified as to be entitled to legal protection under the control of the courts, is a principle that is recognised by the CJ as part of Union law.[76]

The problems that have been of particular concern in the area of State aid are whether, in cases of breach of the Treaty, the Member States can use the principle of legitimate expectations in order to justify not complying with a Commission decision to seek recovery of unlawfully paid aid, and whether, in connection with a case of annulment of an aid scheme, the recipient of the aid can claim legitimate expectations as the basis for revocation of the Commission's decision on the recovery of unlawful State aid.[77]

The possibility of a Member State relying on a recipient's legitimate expectation as a basis for not implementing recovery of incompatible State aid is closely linked to the question of the extent to which the Member State's law may impede the implementation of the recovery decision. As previously

75. Joined Cases T-298/97 and others, *Alzetta*, para. 169. See also, e.g. Case C-142/87, *Tubemeuse*, para. 66; and Case C-169/95, *Spain* v *Commission*, para. 47.
76. Joined Cases 205-215/82, *Deutsche Milchkontor*, para. 30; and Case 5/89, *Commission* v *Germany*, para. 13.
77. See *Krzysztof Jaros & Nicolai Ritter:* Pleading Legitimate Expectations in the Procedure for the Recovery of State Aid, European State Aid Law Quarterly (4) 2004 pp. 573-584.

stated, national law must be applied, subject to the reservation that recovery of payment must not be made impossible in practice.[78]

In connection with a prosecution for breach of the Treaty in Case C-5/89, *Commission* v *Germany*, Germany claimed that it was absolutely impossible to implement recovery of the aid, as such recovery would mean setting aside the principle of the protection of legitimate expectations, which was expressed in the relevant administrative law. According to the administrative law in question, the revocation of an unlawful beneficial administrative act requires weighing up the various interests involved, including the interests of the undertaking which has received the aid and the public interest of the Union in having the aid recovered, and that recovery of the aid should take place within one year of the administrative authority becoming aware of the circumstances constituting grounds for revocation – this deadline was exceeded in the actual case. In reply to this, the CJ stated that a Member State which has granted aid contrary to the procedural rules laid down in Article 108 may not rely on the legitimate expectations of recipients in order to justify a failure to comply with the obligation to recover the aid. If the CJ allowed this possibility, it would deprive Articles 107 and 108 of their intended effect, as the national authorities would be able to rely on their own unlawful conduct in order to prevent the effective implementation of the Commission's decisions in the area of State aid.[79] This means that a Member State cannot rely on the provisions, practice or circumstances in its national legal system as a basis for failing to fulfil its obligations under Union law.[80] Therefore, if the national legal system lays down a provision stating a period of limitation for the revocation of a beneficial administrative act, this provision must be applied in such a way that the recovery of unlawfully paid State aid is not made impossible in practice, and so that the interests of the Union are fully taken into consideration.[81]

In Case C-5/89, *Commission* v *Germany*, the CJ also ruled on the scope for the recipient to rely on legitimate expectations.[82] In this connection,

78. Case C-24/95, *Alcan,* para. 24; Case 94/87, *Commission* v *Germany,* para. 12; and Case C-5/89, *Commission* v *Germany,* para. 12.
79. Case C-5/89, *Commission* v *Germany,* para. 17.
80. Case C-5/89, *Commission* v *Germany,* para. 18.
81. Case C-5/89, *Commission* v *Germany,* para. 19.
82. See also Case 223/85, *RSV;* Case 310/85, *Deufil;* Case C-298/00 P, *Alzetta;* and Case T-55/99, *CETM.*

> the CJ held that a recipient of aid cannot have a legitimate expectation that the aid received is lawful unless the aid has been provided in compliance with the State aid procedure in Article 108 of the Treaty.[83] The CJ stated that a diligent businessman should normally be able to determine whether that procedure has been followed.[84] However, if the recipient of aid can point to extraordinary circumstances that would reasonably give rise to a legitimate expectation that the aid is lawful, the CJ would not exclude the possibility of the recipient being able to avoid having to make repayment. According to the practice of the CJ, if a long period elapses before the Commission takes a decision on the aid scheme, this can constitute such an extraordinary circumstance.[85] Thus, in Case 223/85, *RSV*, the CJ found that the two years and two months that had elapsed before the Commission took its decision meant that the plaintiff could have acquired legitimate expectations which prevented the Commission requiring the Dutch authorities seeking to recover the aid.[86] On the basis of the existing practice it seems that, in principle, it will only be possible to claim that there are legitimate expectations if it is the Union itself that has created the legitimate expectation of the recipient of aid.[87]

Where a recipient of aid receives compensation from the aid granting authority for the loss suffered as a result of the repayment of the aid which the undertaking in question had relied on, this compensation ought to be considered as State aid covered by Article 107 of the Treaty. Such compensation merely serves to compensate for the loss of the financial advantage which the undertaking received from the aid, and it therefore seems in itself to constitute State aid which is incompatible with Article 107 of the Treaty.[88] The alternative would mean that the Commission's scope for demanding the recovery of unlawful State aid would be nugatory, and the scope for getting round Article 107 would be strengthened.

83. Case C-24/95, *Alcan,* para. 25; and Case C-169/95, *Spain* v *Commission.*
84. Case C-5/89, *Commission* v *Germany,* para. 14. See also Joined Cases T-298/97 and others, *Alzetta,* para. 171.
85. Case 223/85, *RSV,* para. 17.
86. Case 223/85, *RSV,* para. 12.
87. See e.g. the Commission Decision C 45/07 of 28 October 2009 on the tax amortisation of financial goodwill for foreign shareholding acquisitions, paras 164-167 (OJ 2011 L 7/48); and Case C-297/01, *Sicilcassa,* paras 40-41.
88. Commission Decision 96/434/EC, para. 3.1 (OJ 1996 L 180/31). See also the Opinion of Advocate General Slynn in Joined Cases 106-120/87, *Asteris.*

2.8. Interested parties

According to Article 1(h) of the Procedure Regulation, *interested party* means 'any Member State and any person, undertaking or association of undertakings whose interests might be affected by the granting of aid, in particular the beneficiary of the aid, competing undertakings and trade associations.'

The rights of interested parties

The rights of interested parties in the Commission's investigation proceedings relating to aid measures are laid down in Article 20 of the Procedure Regulation. The precise extent of the rights depends partly on who the party is, and partly on the point in the process at which the interested party intends to exercise their rights.

According to Article 20(2) of the Procedure Regulation, interested parties have the possibility of informing the Commission of any alleged unlawful aid and any alleged misuse of aid.[89] Competitors, business organisations or one of the other Member States thus have the possibility of getting the Commission to assess whether an undertaking has received State aid in breach of the State aid provisions of the Treaty.

Interested parties do not have any opportunity to submit comments on a case during a preliminary examination.[90] The opposite applies in relation to the formal investigation procedure. Any interested party may submit comments pursuant to Article 6 following a Commission decision to initiate the formal investigation procedure; see Article 20(1) of the Procedure Regulation.[91] These comments are then forwarded to the Member State concerned with a view to obtaining its reactions. Interested parties are not entitled either to receive information about or to submit comments on any reaction by the Member State to their comments, nor are interested parties informed about the comments submitted by other interested parties.

89. On the legal protection of those who complain, see Case T-351/02, *Deutsche Bahn.* The decision is commented on by *Carsten Nowak:* Judicial Protection of Complainants in the Scope of EC State Aid Law: New Developments and Question Marks, European State Aid Law Quarterly (3) 2006 pp. 621-628.
90. However, see Case T-95/94, *Sytraval,* para. 78, where the GC found that, in certain circumstances, the Commission's duty to justify its decisions can require it to conduct an adversarial proceeding with a complainant.
91. In practice, a notice is published in the C series of the Official Journal, in which the State aid and the Commission's view on it is described, while interested parties are encouraged to submit comments on the case.

Where an interested party submits comments in a case concerning State aid, that party is entitled to receive a copy of the Commission's decision on the State aid. The recipient of the State aid is entitled to receive such a copy, whether or not it exercises its right to submit comments.[92]

Rights before the CJ and the GC

According to Article 263 of the Treaty, the positive and negative decisions which the Commission makes at the conclusion of a preliminary examination or a formal investigation procedure can be referred to the CJ or the GC with a view to having the decision overturned. The rights of Member States to bring an action are set out in Article 263, second paragraph, and the rights of other interested parties are set out in Article 263, fourth paragraph. In the case of Member States it is the CJ which has jurisdiction, and for natural and legal persons it is the GC that has jurisdiction.

Actions brought by natural and legal persons require either that the decision is addressed to the person in question or, if the decision is addressed to some other person or is made in the form of a regulation, that it directly and individually concerns that person.[93] In relation to the Commission's decisions on State aid it will thus be of decisive importance that the interested party is able to show that they are directly and individually affected, as the direct addressee for the Commission's decision will be the Member State concerned.[94] In this context, the recipient of State aid is considered to be directly and individually affected. Moreover, in the area of State aid, the CJ has identified persons, undertakings or associations as interested parties whose interests may be affected by the aid given, i.e. competing undertakings and trade organisations.[95]

92. Procedure Regulation, Article 20(1).
93. See Article 263, fourth paragraph, of the Treaty, as interpreted in Case C-25/62, *Plaumann.* See also Case C-198/91, *Cook,* paras 23-26; Case C-225/91, *Matra,* paras 17-20; Case C-78/03 P, *ARE,* paras 35-37; and Case T-395/04, *Air One,* where the GC went so far as to recognise the right of a potential competitor to bring an action. The decision is commented on by *Julie Bousin & Jorge Piernas,* European State Aid Law Quarterly (3) 2006 pp. 639-642, and confirmed in the GC's later decision in Case T-167/04, *Asklepios,* para. 50.
94. For further discussion of the rights of interested parties to bring an action, see *Michael Honoré:* The Standing of Third Parties in State Aid Cases, European State Aid Law Quarterly (2) 2006 pp. 269-284.
95. Case C-367/95 P, *Sytraval,* para. 41; Case 323/82, *Intermills,* para. 16; and Case T-167/04, *Asklepios,* para. 49.

Actions for annulment must be submitted within 2 months. This period runs from the date when the disputed legal act has been published in accordance with the formal requirements or the plaintiff has been informed or, in default of this, within two months after the plaintiff has become aware of the legal act.[96]

Actions for breach of the Treaty can be brought by the Commission or by the other Member States in cases where the Member State concerned does not fulfil its obligations under the Commission's decision; see Article 108(2), second paragraph. Other interested parties do not have this possibility, but must try to get an action for breach of the Treaty brought via their national authorities.

Rights before the national courts

The Commission has sole competence to asses the compatibility of a State aid with the internal market; in other words, only the Commission has jurisdiction to decide whether a State aid is covered by the prohibition in Article 107(1), and whether the exceptions in Article 107(2) and (3) apply.[97] Article 107(1) is therefore not directly applicable in national legal systems. However, the CJ has held that the provision can be relied upon in a national court to the extent that it has been put in concrete form by acts having general application provided for by Article 109 or by decisions, in particular cases under Article 108(2).[98] Under the authority of Article 109, the Council has adopted Regulation (EC) No 994/98 on the application of Articles 92 and 93 of the Treaty to certain categories of horizontal State aid.[99] On this basis the Commission has adopted the General block exemption Regulation on the compatibility of certain forms of aid with the State aid rules, as well as Regulation (EC) No 1998/2006 on *de minimis* aid.[100] These have direct effect in national law.

The CJ has also laid down that the standstill obligation in Article 108(3), third paragraph, has direct effect, so that the rights which the provision cre-

96. Article 263, fifth paragraph, of the Treaty.
97. Case C-119/05, *Lucchini,* para. 52; Joined Cases C-261/01 & 262/01, *van Calster*, para. 45; and Case T-73/98, *Prayon-Rupel,* para. 40.
98. Case 77/72, *Capolongo,* para. 6.
99. OJ 1998 L 142/1.
100. Commission Regulation (EC) No 800/2008 declaring certain categories of aid compatible with the common market in application of Articles 87 and 88 of the Treaty (General block exemption Regulation) (OJ 2008 L 214/3); and Commission Regulation (EC) No 1998/2006 on the application of Articles 87 and 88 of the Treaty to de minimis aid (OJ 2006 L 379/5).

ates must be protected by the national courts of the Member States.[101] This direct effect of the standstill obligation covers both notified and non-notified aid.[102] A competing undertaking which fulfils national requirements for bringing an action thus has the possibility of getting a national court to assess whether State aid has been paid in breach of the standstill obligation. In this connection, national courts can decide whether a measure should be categorised as State aid within the meaning of Article 107(1) of the Treaty, and national courts thus have jurisdiction to interpret the concept of State aid.[103] However, the national courts cannot decide whether the State aid measure in question is compatible with the internal market, as the Commission has sole jurisdiction to decide this. In the event of doubt about the categorisation of a measure, a national court can ask the Commission for further information on this, or refer the question to the CJ with a request for a preliminary ruling.[104]

If a national court finds that State aid is paid out in breach of the standstill obligation, the court concerned must take all the necessary measures that follow from the disregard for the Treaty provision, including seeking recovery of the aid paid out.[105] A Member State that breaches the standstill obligation may also risk being required to seek recovery of the aid in accordance with the national procedural rules, regardless of whether the Commission may later find that the aid in question is compatible with the internal market. The Commission's decision that a non-notified aid is compatible with the internal market does not mean that implementation measures that are unlawful because they have been taken in breach of the standstill obligation subsequently become lawful.[106] However, a national court does not have a duty to recover

101. Case 120/73, *Lorenz,* para. 8; with reference to Case 6/64, *Costa/ENEL.* For further discussion of certain aspects of the national enforcement of the State aid rules; see *Thomas Jestaedt, Jacques Derenne & Tom Ottervanger:* Study on the Enforcement of State aid Law at National Level, 2006; *Lovells:* 2009 update of the 2006 Study on the enforcement of State aid rules at National Level, 2009; and *Adinda Sinnave:* What to Expect from National Courts in the Fight against Unlawful State Aid, European State Aid Law Quarterly (1) 2005 pp. 1-2.
102. Case 120/73, *Lorenz,* para. 8.
103. Case C-39/94, *SFEI* v *La Poste,* para. 49; Case C-143/99, *Adria-Wien Pipeline,* para. 29; and Case C-368/04, *Transalpine Ölleitung,* para. 39. See also Commission notice on the enforcement of State aid law by national courts (OJ 2009 C 85/1).
104. Case C-39/94, *SFEI* v *La Poste,* para. 50; and Article 234 of the Treaty. See also the Commission's Notice on cooperation between national courts and the Commission in the State aid field (OJ 1995 C 312/8).
105. Case C-354/90, *FNCE,* para. 12; and Case C-39/94, *SFEI* v *La Poste,* para. 40.
106. Case C-368/04, *Transalpine Ölleitung,* para. 59. On the problems to which such a decision leads, see *Kurt Retter & Holger Bielesz:* Review of Judgment in Transalpine

all the unlawful aid if the Commission has taken a final decision on the compatibility of the aid,[107] but it does have a duty to require the aid recipient to pay interest for the period in which there was unlawful aid.[108]

Apart from seeking to have the prohibition of implementation enforced by a national court, a competing undertaking also has the possibility of challenging the administrative act whereby the Member State has granted the disputed aid, in accordance with the national administrative procedures. Finally, if a competitor suffers loss as a result of the damaging effects of the aid on competition, the competitor has the possibility of seeking compensation for such loss.[109]

On the other hand, the recipient of aid can try to challenge the Member State's demand for the recovery of unlawful aid by, for example, claiming that that it had a legitimate expectation that the aid was lawful, or that the aid measures are covered by one of the Commission's block exemption regulations. The recipient of aid also has the possibility of seeking compensation from the Member State for the damage the undertaking suffers from having to repay the aid. However, as mentioned above, in the EU context such compensation is also considered to be State aid.[110]

3. The prohibition of State aid in Article 107(1) of the Treaty

Article 107(1) of the Treaty states as follows: 'Save as otherwise provided in the Treaties, any aid granted by a Member State or through State resources in any form whatsoever which distorts or threatens to distort competition by favouring certain undertakings or the production of certain goods shall, in so far as it affects trade between Member States, be incompatible with the internal market.'

It follows from this provision that the application of the prohibition of State aid requires a number of conditions to be fulfilled. First there must be

Ölleitung in Österreich GmbH and Others, Case C-368/04, European State aid Law Quarterly (1) 2007 pp. 129-137.

107. Case C-199/06, *CELF,* paras 45-46. See further in *Thomas Jaeger:* The CELF-Judgement: A Precarious Conception of the Standstill Obligation, European State Aid Law Quarterly (2) 2008 pp. 279-289.

108. Case C-199/06, *CELF,* para. 52. See also *Christopher Vajda & Paul Stuart:* Effect of the Standstill Obligation in National Courts – all said after CELF? An English Perspective, European State Aid Quarterly (3) 2010 pp. 629-636.

109. *Michael Honoré & Nanna Eram Jensen:* Damages in State aid cases, European State Aid Law Quarterly (2) 2011 pp. 265-286.

110. See section 2.7.

some form of *aid*. Second, this aid must be *granted by a Member State or through State resources*. Third, the aid must *favour certain undertakings or the production of certain goods*. Fourth and finally, the aid must *affect trade* between Member States by *distorting competition* within the internal market.

All these conditions must be fulfilled before an aid measure can be characterised as *incompatible State aid* within the terms of the Treaty.[111] The first two conditions are decisive for whether a specific aid measure can be characterised as *State aid*, while the latter two conditions are decisive for whether aid can be characterised as incompatible with the internal market within the context of State aid law.[112] These conditions are intended to prevent the implementation of State aid which is contrary to the aims and principles of the Treaty. Once the incompatibility of State aid with the internal market has been established in principle, it then becomes possible to apply the provisions on exceptions in Article 107(2) and (3) and Article 108(2), third paragraph, so as to approve aid measures which, because of the purposes which they are intended to pursue, are nevertheless found to be compatible with the internal market.

3.1. The concept of *aid*

In order to be covered by the prohibition of State aid in Article 107(1) of the Treaty, the measure of the Member State must involve *aid*. The meaning of this term has been defined several times by the CJ and by the Commission, but without this having led to the establishment of an exhaustive definition. For example, the CJ has defined aid as including measures whereby a Member State independently and unilaterally makes financial means available to undertakings or gives them advantages which are intended to contribute to the implementation and realisation of the economic and social goals of the Member State.[113] In other decisions aid has been defined as a financial advantage to an undertaking which it would not have obtained under normal market conditions.[114] Even though it is not possible to give an exhaustive definition of the term, the decisions of the CJ and the Commission point to a number of characteristic elements of aid, which indicate whether a state measure involves aid within the meaning of Article 107.

111. Case C-345/02, *Pearle,* para. 32.
112. See *Leigh Hancher, Tom Ottervanger & Piet Jan Slot:* EC State aids, 2006 para. 3-011.
113. Case 61/79, *Denkavit,* para. 31.
114. Case C-39/94, *SFEI* v *La Poste,* para. 60.

The effect of aid

In establishing the scope of application of Article 107(1), the CJ starts from the position that the aim of the provisions on State aid is 'to prevent trade between Member States from being affected by benefits granted by the public authorities which, in various forms, distort or threaten to distort competition by favouring certain undertakings or the production of certain goods.'[115] The realisation of this aim requires the concept of aid to be interpreted sufficiently widely so that all the benefits that fulfil the relevant characteristics are covered by the definition of aid. The CJ has therefore stated that aid measures should be defined purely by their effects,[116] while the form in which the aid is given, and the aim or intention in giving the aid in question is not important.[117] The decisive factor is thus the financial effect of the benefit on the recipient's competitive position, in other words whether it gives the recipient a financial advantage which it would not be given under normal competitive conditions and which means that the recipient undertaking's financial position is improved so its competitive position is likewise improved in relation to its competitors.[118]

The form of the aid

Regardless of its form, a state measure that gives an undertaking a financial advantage will be covered by the concept of aid.[119] The concept of aid is therefore not limited to aid in the form of normal direct grants, but also covers more general forms of aid.[120] This means that all measures which, in one way or another, ease the burdens that are normally imposed on an undertaking's finances and which, without giving a subsidy as normally understood, are nevertheless of the same nature and have a corresponding effect,[121] are

115. Case 173/73, *Italy* v *Commission,* para. 26, and Case 387/92, *Banco Exterior,* para. 12.
116. However, this is modified in relation to compensation paid for the provision of services of general economic interest – see below.
117. Case 173/73, *Italy* v *Commission,* para. 27. See also Case C-75/97, *Maribel bis/ter,* para. 25; and Case C-81/10 P, *France Télécom,* para. 17.
118. When assessing whether an aid measure has a beneficial effect, the starting point is the competitive position that existed in the internal market before the disputed measure was adopted; see Case 173/73, *Italy* v *Commission,* para. 36.
119. Joined Cases 106-120/87, *Asteris,* para. 22; and Case C-140/09, *Fallimento Traghetti*, para. 34
120. Case 30/59, *Steenkolenmijnen,* p. 217, (on the interpretation of the ECSC Treaty); and Case C-387/92, *Banco Exterior,* para. 13.
121. Case C-387/92, *Banco Exterior,* para. 13; and Joined Cases T-204 and 270/97, *EPAC*, para. 65.

covered by the aid concept. When assessing an aid measure it is thus not necessary to distinguish whether, in principle, the aid is given the form of a direct grant to the undertakings, or whether the aid is provided in an indirect form, such as relief from taxes or duties, advantageous terms for loans, or investments in the company's capital, since all these forms of support are covered by the concept of State aid.[122]

For example, it is also not necessary to determine whether the financial advantage is granted to the undertaking by a reduction in investment or in operating costs.[123] However, when assessing whether a State aid can be approved, this distinction can be relevant, as investment support is more widely accepted than support for operation costs.

The broad definition of aid also means that it is not relevant to the assessment of aid whether the undertaking concerned receives the aid directly or indirectly.[124] Thus the concept of aid covers first, the financial advantage which is given to the direct addressee of the aid measure. Second, it covers the financial advantage which, because of the aid measure, is indirectly given to undertakings on the basis of their links with the direct recipient of the aid. For example, an exemption from a tax applied to bio fuels of agricultural origin will be a direct aid for the production of such fuels (to the producer), as well as an indirect aid for the production of the materials from which the bio fuels are produced (the suppliers).[125]

Finally, the particular legal basis for giving the aid is irrelevant. The prohibition of State aid in Article 107(1) of the Treaty covers, for example, aid provided on the basis of an administrative decision, aid provided on the basis of an agreement, and aid such as a tax advantage provided by legislation.

The purpose of the aid

The specific purpose for which a Member State provides aid is not a factor which can place a measure outside the scope of Article 107 of the Treaty. In Case 173/73, *Italy* v *Commission*, the CJ stated that Article 107 does not dis-

122. Case 323/82, *Intermills,* para. 31. As explained immediately below, the terms *direct* and *indirect* aid are used both in respect of the form in which the aid is provided and the recipient of the aid.
123. Case 173/73, *Italy* v *Commission,* which concerned the reduction of the textile industry's payments for social benefits.
124. However, whether or not the aid is directly addressed to an undertaking can be relevant in determining whether unlawful aid will be sought to be recovered or not, see e.g. Commission Decision 97/542/EC, *Biofuels* (OJ 1997 L 222/26).
125. Commission Decision 97/542/EC, *Biofuels* (OJ 1997 L 222/26).

tinguish between measures of state intervention by reference to their causes or aims but, as stated above, defines them in relation to their effects.[126] In this case, this meant that neither the possible fiscal nature of the disputed measure nor its social purposes were sufficient to put it outside the scope of the prohibition of State aid.[127]

However, the aim of an aid measure is relevant when assessing whether the exemptions in Article 107(2) and (3) can apply. When assessing whether an aid measure can be approved as being compatible with the internal market, an assessment is made of whether the negative effects of the measure can be counterbalanced by its furtherance of one of the other goals of the EU. In making an assessment under Article 107(1), of whether a measure involves aid, a clear distinction is made between, on the one hand, the measure's financial and competitive effects and, on the other hand, the purpose for which the aid is given.[128] The opposite approach would mean that the Member States could attempt to avoid the prohibition of State aid by claiming various praiseworthy purposes.

The intentions of the parties

The assessment of the aid is made independently of whether, subjectively, the parties intend either to give or to receive State aid.

> In the Commission Decision 92/11/EC, Toyota, the Commission fully accepted that the United Kingdom Government did not intend aid to be given to Toyota in connection with the transfer of a site, and that there was no evidence to suggest that Toyota requested State aid or intended to benefit directly or indirectly from State aid through the terms of transfer of the site. However, the Commission did not attach importance to the subjective intentions of the parties, but considered it crucial whether the terms and condition for the transfer of the site were contrary to normal business practice to such an extent that the transfer could be assumed to be State aid for the benefit of Toyota.[129] In this connection the Commission considered that the difference of £4.2 million between the sales price and

126. Case 173/73, *Italy* v *Commission,* para. 26; and the similar Case 78/76, *Steinike & Weinlig,* para. 21; and Case C-81/10 P, *France Télécom,* para. 17.
127. Case 173/73, *Italy* v *Commission*, para. 28. See also Case C-241/94, *France* v *Commission,* para. 21.
128. However, payment for carrying out services of general economic interest is subject to a special test; see the discussion of the *Altmark* case below.
129. See Part V of Commission Decision 92/11/EC, *Toyota* (OJ 1992, L 6/36).

the market price constituted incompatible State aid within the meaning of Article 107(1).

The existence of an advantage must be determined objectively and without regard to the reasons of the originator of the aid measures for giving the aid. Thus, the nature of the purpose of aid measures and their justification is not decisive for determining whether they constitute State aid, and such measures must only be defined according to their effects, without distinction as to their aims or reasons.[130]

Financial advantages
As shown by the Commission's decision in the *Toyota* case,[131] and confirmed by the CJ in, among others, Case C-39/94, *SFEI* v *La Poste*, what is crucial for the assessment of an aid measure is whether or not the undertaking to which the aid measure is addressed obtains a financial advantage which it would not have obtained under normal market conditions.[132] Aid measures are characterised by benefiting the recipient by giving a unilateral financial advantage. Such a financial advantage can be given, regardless of whether it corresponds to the actual cost to the state, and it is not relevant whether the recipient's position becomes better or worse, or is unchanged in relation to the situation which existed before the implementation of the aid measure.[133] What matters is only whether the aid measure in question, taken in isolation, benefits some undertakings rather than other undertakings which, with regard to the purpose of the measure in question, are in a corresponding factual or legal situation.[134]

If the recipient provides remuneration, this does not necessarily eliminate the beneficial element of the measure.[135] Where aid is given for remuneration which does not correspond to the value of the aid, but is insufficient or mere-

130. Case C-81/10 P, *France Télécom,* para. 17.
131. Commission Decision 92/11/EC, *Toyota* (OJ 1992, L 6/36).
132. Case C-39/94, *SFEI* v *La Poste,* para. 60; Joined Cases T-204 and 270/97, *EPAC,* para. 66; and Case C-140/09, *Fallimento Traghetti,* para. 34.
133. Case C-143/99, *Adria-Wien Pipeline,* para. 41; and Case 57/86, *Greece* v *Commission,* para. 10. See e.g. the Commission's decision in the Danish CO2 case, XXIIth Report on competition policy, 1993, para. 451, and Commission Decision 92/411/ECSC (OJ 1992 L 223/28).
134. Case C-143/99, *Adria-Wien Pipeline,* para. 41; Case C-88/03, *The Azores,* paras 54 and 56; and Case C-106/09 P & 107/09 P, *Gibraltar,* para. 75.
135. There is no requirement that the benefit should be given completely free or without the payment of a fee. See e.g. Case C-353/95 P, *Ladbroke SA.*

ly symbolic, the aid measure will still be characterised as unilateral. The same is the case if the nature of the consideration differs from what is usually given in a business transaction on normal market terms. For example, if the aid is given on condition that the undertaking carry out some restructuring,[136] create jobs, or reduce production capacity with the aim of realising the Member State's social and economic goals,[137] such remuneration will not be typical in relation to what is normal under market conditions and will not, of itself, place the aid outside the scope of Article 107.

Variance from normal market conditions

When assessing whether an undertaking receives a financial benefit which is covered by the definition of a State aid, it is decisive whether the benefit received is more than the undertaking could expect to receive under normal market conditions. In this connection it is necessary to establish what the normal conditions would be for the service in question. The answer to this depends on an economic analysis 'taking into account all the factors which an undertaking acting under normal market conditions should have taken into consideration when fixing the remuneration for the services provided'.[138]

> In Case C-39/94, *SFEI* v *La Poste*, the Commission considered that the cross-subsidies resulting from the provision of logistical and commercial assistance by a public undertaking to its subsidiaries, which are governed by private law and carry on an activity open to free competition, were capable of constituting State aid, provided that remuneration for the services was less than that which would have been demanded under normal market conditions.[139]

The assessment of whether an undertaking is given a unilateral advantage, and whether this advantage varies from normal market terms, is decided in accordance with the *market economy investor principle*.[140] According to this

136. Case 323/82, *Intermills,* where as consideration the undertaking was obliged to switch to a specific type of production.
137. Case 61/79, *Denkavit,* para. 31.
138. Case C-39/94, *SFEI* v *La Poste,* para. 61.
139. Case C-39/94, *SFEI* v *La Poste,* para. 62. See also Commission Decision 92/11/EC, *Toyota* (OJ 1992, L 6/36), and the XVIIth Report on competition policy, 1988, para. 220.
140. Case T-613/97, *Ufex,* both the judgment of 14 December 2000 and the judgment of 7 June 2006, which concerned logistical and commercial support given by a public undertaking which provides services of general economic interest within the postal

principle a measure does not constitute aid as long as the terms on which the public authority provides resources to an undertaking would be acceptable to a private investor under the conditions of the normal market economy. This principle is of particular importance in relation to financial transactions between the state and public undertakings (and between public undertakings themselves).[141] For example, such transactions may occur where a state participates in the financing of a public undertaking which provides financial support for a subsidiary which is in difficulties, or otherwise deals with a public undertaking.

In this context, the market economy investor principle can be used to distinguish between aid measures and transactions that are carried out on the normal terms of the market economy, as well as to quantify the amount of aid given.[142]

Measures that do not normally constitute aid

Repayment of unduly levied charges

According to the practice of the CJ, a Member State's repayment of a charge to an undertaking will not constitute State aid in all cases. This applies if the Member State has been required to repay a charge which has been collected and found to be contrary to Union law and which the taxpayer was therefore not required to pay.[143]

Such unduly levied charges must be repaid in accordance with the national law of the Member State.[144] In this connection there is no requirement for the Member States to take into account whether the taxpayer has suffered loss as a result of the tax obligation. However, the CJ does not regard it as incompat-

sector to a subsidiary which did not carry on business in an area reserved to a monopoly but rather in an area where there was competition. See also Case C-305/89, *Alfa Romeo;* and Case C-303/88, *ENI-Lanerossi.* Case T-613/97, *Ufex,* is commented on by *Claudia Berg:* The Chronopost Saga Continues: the Battle about the Concept of Cross-Subsidies in the Field of State Aid has entered its 17th Year, European State Aid Law Quarterly (2) 2007 p. 299.

141. In certain circumstances public undertakings are regarded as being part of the state, and can thereby risk giving aid which is covered by the prohibition of State aid in Article 107(1) of the Treaty; see below in section 3.2. See e.g. Case C-39/94, *SFEI* v *La Poste.*

142. For a further discussion of the market economy investor principle, see *Heidenhain:* European State Aid Law, 2010 pp. 24-26 and 73-76; and *Phedon Nicolaides & Eleonora Rusu:* Private Investor Principle: What Benchmark and Whose Money?, European State Aid Law Quarterly (2) 2011 pp. 237-248.

143. Case 61/79, *Denkavit,* para. 32.

144. Case 68/79, *Just,* paras 25 and 27.

ible with the Treaty if, under national law, it is possible to take account of the fact that it has been possible for the charges unduly levied to be incorporated in the prices of the undertaking liable for the charge and to be passed on to the purchasers.[145] Depending on the formulation of the national law, the taxpayer could demand that the charge paid in breach of the Treaty should be refunded, without regard for whether the taxpayer has suffered loss or has been able to pass on the burden to other undertakings or consumers, and thus without regard for whether the undertaking receives a financial advantage by the tax refund. Such a financial advantage is not covered by the provision on State aid which may seem inappropriate if, because of the framing of the tax provisions, some undertakings are favoured more than others.

Damages

The CJ has also considered whether a Member State's payment of compensation is permitted under the provisions on State aid. In its preliminary ruling in Joined Cases 106-120/87, *Asteris*, the CJ held that State aid is fundamentally different in its legal nature from damages which Member States may be ordered to pay to individuals in compensation for the damage they have caused to those individuals.[146] The aim of such compensation is in part to compensate the injured party for the losses caused, and in part to restore the injured party to the position it was in prior to the occurrence of the action which incurred liability. Thus the injured party is not given any financial advantage, and the compensation is not covered by Article 107(1).[147]

However, in certain circumstances compensation paid by a Member State can be covered by Article 107(1). This will be the case where the Member State gives an undertaking compensation for the loss of a financial advantage or right which in itself constitutes State aid.[148]

> This problem arose in Commission Decision 96/434/EC. The case concerned an Italian law which gave the state authority to provide financial help to undertakings whose insolvency had arisen from the obligation to repay aid which the Commission or the CJ had found to be in breach of Articles 107 and 108 of the Treaty. The provisions of the law did not necessarily lead to the transfer of new state resources to the

145. Case 68/79, *Just,* para. 26.
146. Joined Cases 106-120/87, *Asteris,* para. 23.
147. Joined Cases 106-120/87, *Asteris,* para. 24.
148. Commission Decision 96/434/EC (OJ 1996 L 180/31). See also *Leigh Hancher, Tom Ottervanger & Piet Jan Slot:* EC State aids, 2006 para. 3-006.

recipients, but it did mean that undertakings that had an obligation to repay incompatible aid could retain the advantages from the aid and avoid the repayment of the benefits they had obtained, contrary to EU law.[149] The law thus had the effect that there was not full implementation of the decisions of the Commission and CJ on the recovery of incompatible aid, and the unlawful advantages which the decisions were intended to annul were perpetuated.[150] The Commission therefore found that the provisions of the law were contrary to the Treaty's provisions on State aid.

In cases where an undertaking receives damages from a Member State on the grounds of a legitimate expectation of receiving State aid based on national law which the Commission has found to be incompatible with the internal market, and which must therefore be repaid, the corresponding arguments apply. A Member State's payment of damages in this situation will constitute State aid.[151] This is the case regardless of whether the payment is made voluntarily or it is made on the basis of a judgment of a national court of the Member State concerned.

Compensation

To a certain extent, both private and public undertakings can provide services in the common interest. This is on the basis of agreements or obligations laid down in law to provide certain services, for example in the fields of radio and television broadcasting, transport, telecommunications, postal services, pharmacies, energy supply etc.[152]

In connection with the transfer of the provision of such services, Member States often grant undertakings which provide these services special or exclusive rights, and in certain cases these undertakings receive financial support to cover the additional costs incurred by carrying out the obligations.

In Case C-53/00, *Ferring SA*, the CJ laid down that compensation paid to undertakings for the provision of services of general economic interest does not constitute aid within the meaning of Article 107(1) of the Treaty.[153] Such

149. Commission Decision 96/434/EC, part VI (OJ 1996 L 180/31).
150. Commission Decision 96/434/EC, part IV (OJ 1996 L 180/31).
151. See e.g. the case of *Spar Nord,* Skat Udland, 1995 p. 68, which did not constitute incompatible State aid, however, because of the lack of effect on trade.
152. Several of these sectors are now liberalised in whole or in part, and these are discussed in Chapter XI.
153. Case C-53/00, *Ferring SA,* para. 27. However, the GC has considered such compensation to be State aid within the meaning of Article 107(1) of the Treaty in

compensation is in the nature of a charge paid to the undertaking for the provision of the service in question.

Nevertheless this requires that the conditions laid down by the CJ in Case C-280/00, *Altmark*, are fulfilled.[154] The *Altmark* case thus establishes that compensation paid to undertakings for the provision of services of general economic interest does not constitute aid within the meaning of Article 107(1) if: 1) the recipient undertaking does actually have public service obligations to discharge, and the obligations are clearly defined; 2) the compensation is calculated on the basis of criteria which are established in advance in an objective and transparent manner; 3) the compensation does not exceed what is necessary to cover all or part of the costs incurred in the discharge of public service obligations;[155] and finally 4) the level of compensation is determined on the basis of an analysis of the costs which a typical undertaking would incur in discharging the obligations.

According to the decision of the CJ, a measure of a Member State which fails to comply with one or more of these conditions is considered to be State aid within the meaning of Article 107(1).[156] Thus, in relation to services of general economic interest, it is not the economic effect of the aid which is decisive to the assessment of the aid, but compliance with these four criteria.

among others, Case T-106/95, *FFSA,* paras 178 and 199; and Case T-46/97, *SIC*, para. 84.

154. Case C-280/00, *Altmark,* paras 89-93. For a discussion of this decision and its implications both for the law of State aid, public procurement and economic advantage, see*: Phedon Nicolaides:* Competition and Services of General Economic Interest in the EU: Reconciling Economics and Law, European State Aid Law Quarterly (2) 2003 pp. 183-210; *Adinda Sinnave:* State Financing of Public Services: The Court's Dilemma in the Altmark Case, European State Aid Law Quarterly (3) 2003 pp. 351-364; *Andreas Bartocsh:* Clarification or Confusion? How to Reconcile the ECJ's Ruling in Altmark and Chronopost, European State Aid Law Quarterly (3) 2003 pp. 375-386; *Noel Travers:* Public Service Obligations and State Aid: Is all really clear after Altmark?, European State Aid Law Quarterly (3) 2003 pp. 387-392; *Ulrich Schelle:* Bidding Procedures in the EC State Aid Surveillance over Public Services after Altmark Trans, European State Aid Law Quarterly (3) 2003 pp. 411-414; *Barbara Rapp-Jung:* The State Financing of Public Services – The Commission's New approach, European State Aid Law Quarterly (2) 2004 pp. 205-216; *Tilman Lüder:* Calculating Public service Compensation, European State Aid Law Quarterly (3) 2004 pp. 385-392; and *Bjørnar Alterskjær:* Interpretation of the Altmark Conditions: Case C-451/03, Servizi Ausiliari Dottori Commercialisti, European State Aid Law Quarterly (1) 2007 p. 73.

155. Case T-106/95, *FFSA,* para. 178; Case C-174/97 P, *FFSA,* para. 6; and Case C-53/00, *Ferring SA,* para. 27.

156. Case C-280/00, *Altmark,* para. 94.

For example, aid will be considered to be present in cases where the compensation is not calculated on the basis of criteria that are established in advance in an objective and transparent manner, regardless of whether the undertaking in fact receives a financial advantage.

In cases where compensation for the performance of services of general economic interest are regarded as aid covered by Article 107(1), it may be possible for the aid to be exempted from the prohibition of State aid by the application of the special provision in Article 106(2) of the Treaty.[157] This provision allows for exemption from the application of the provisions prohibiting State aid in relation to undertakings entrusted with the operation of services of general economic interest. However, this only applies in so far as the application of such rules does not obstruct the performance, in law or in fact, of the particular tasks assigned to them, and the development of trade must not be affected to such an extent as would be contrary to the interests of the EU.[158]

3.2. Aid granted by a Member State or through State resources

Article 107(1) only covers *aid granted by a Member State or through State resources*. According to the wording of the Article, these two criteria could appear to be alternative conditions. Nevertheless, according to the practice of the CJ, the application of Article 107(1) requires both criteria to be fulfilled. This means that aid must both be the consequence of the actions of a state and be financed from the state's resources.[159] Both of these conditions are interpreted broadly. As will be seen in the following, in certain circumstances

157. For more on this provision see Chapter X.
158. The approach of the Commission to the application of Article 107 and Article 106(2) in relation to the prohibition of State aid is set out in Communication from the Commission on the application of the European Union State aid rules to compensation granted for the provision of services of general economic interest (OJ 2012 C 8/4); Communication from the Commission – European Union framework for State aid in the form of public service compensation (2011) (OJ 2012 C 8/15); and Commission Decision 2012/21/EU of 20 December 2011 on the application of Article 106(2) of the Treaty on the Functioning of the European Union to State aid in the form of public service compensation granted to certain undertakings entrusted with the operation of services of general economic interest (OJ 2012 L 7/3). See also *Evelyn Regner:* Reform of the Legal Framework for Services of General Economic Interest: Where Do We Stand? What Should a Reform Look Like, European State Aid Law Quarterly (4) 2011 pp. 597-598.
159. Case C-379/98, *PreussenElektra,* para. 58.

private bodies can be considered as part of the state, and in certain circumstances private resources will be covered by the concept of State aid.

3.2.1. The State and State resources

The central organs of the state and other public authorities

The prohibition of State aid in Article 107(1) covers both aid provided by the central organs of the state and aid which is provided by the regional or local authorities of the state. In Case 248/84, *Germany* v *Commission*, the CJ thus rules that the prohibition covers aid which is granted by regional and local bodies of the Member States, whatever their status and description, and must be scrutinised to determine whether it complies with Article 107 of the Treaty.[160]

In this context, the concept of *state resources* should be understood in such a way that resources coming from the state treasury as well as public resources in a broad sense, such as resources from regional or local authorities, can be used to finance incompatible aid.

The financing of State aid can be on the basis of a direct grant from the state, or in the form of an actual or potential reduction in the income of the authority which provides the aid. However, the applicability of Article 107(1) does not seem to be conditional on the aid imposing a financial burden on the state.[161] Thus, for example, a guarantee by the state will be a potential financial burden on the state, but it will only be an actual burden if the guarantee is called upon.[162] Nor is it decisive for the evaluation of State aid whether the state resources used come from the general state budget, or from specially targeted taxes, or from contributions that are provided for by the act of an authority.[163]

160. Case 248/84, *Germany* v *Commission,* para. 17. See correspondingly Case T-358/94, *Air France,* para. 56.
161. Case 57/86, *Greece* v *Commission,* para. 12. However, see Case 82/77, *van Tiggele,* para. 52. For further a discussion, see *Leigh Hancher, Tom Ottervanger & Piet Jan Slot:* EC State aids, 2006 paras 3-018 – 3-022; and *Leigh Hancher:* Towards a New Definition of a State Aid under European Law: Is there a New Concept of State Aid Emerging?, European State Aid Law Quarterly (3) 2003 pp. 365-374, at pp. 368-370.
162. For more on state guarantees and their compliance with the regulation of State aid, see Commission Notice on the application of Articles 87 and 88 of the EC Treaty to State aid in the form of guarantees (OJ 2008 C 155/10), and the Corrigendum to it (OJ 2008 C 244/32) .
163. Case 47/69, *France* v *Commission;* and Case 1873/73, *Italy* v *Commission.*

Public and private bodies established or appointed by the state to administer aid

In Case 78/76, *Steinike & Weinlig*, the CJ stated that the prohibition in Article 107(1) covers 'all aid granted by a member state or through state resources without its being necessary to make a distinction whether the aid is granted directly by the state or by public or private bodies established or appointed by it to administer the aid.'[164] Such public or private bodies are thereby regarded as being a part of the state in the context of the law on State aid.

The resources of the public or private bodies concerned will be considered as state resources within the meaning of Article 107(1). For example, specially targeted taxes which are collected at the request of the state and paid into a fund which is then used finance aid will be considered State aid covered by Article 107(1).[165]

Private and public bodies subject to state control

The application of the provisions of Article 107(1) in cases where aid is provided by public or private bodies which have not been established or appointed by the state to administer the aid depends on whether the state has a *de jure* or *de facto* degree of control over or influence on the body concerned and the decision to provide aid, which is sufficient in order to regard the body as part of the state and the resources as state resources. In this context it must be shown that an aid-giving body could not have taken its decision to provide aid without having regard for the public authorities. Consequently, the aid has to be regarded as imputable to the State.[166]

> There is an example of this in Joined Cases 67, 68 and 70/85, *van der Kooy* v *Commission*, where the CJ stated that the undertaking Gasunie in no way enjoyed full autonomy in the fixing of gas tariffs, but acted under the control of and on the instructions of the public authorities, so it was clear that it could not fix the tariff without taking account of the

164. Case 78/76, *Steinike & Weinlig,* para. 21; Case C-305/89, *Alfa Romeo,* para. 13; and Case C-345/02, *Pearle,* para. 34.
165. Case 173/73, *Italy* v *Commission;* and Case 259/85, *France* v *Commission.*
166. Case C-126/01, *GEMO,* para. 24; Case C-345/02, *Pearle,* para. 35; and Case C-279/08 P, *NOx,* para. 103. For more on the requirement for imputability, see *Conor Quigley:* European State Aid Law and Policy, 2009 pp. 13-18; *Edoardo Gambaro, Allessandro Nucara & Luca Prete:* Pearle: so much Unsaid!, European State Aid Law Quarterly (1) 2005 pp. 3-15; and *Bo Vesterdorf:* A Further Comment on the New State Aid Concept as this Concept Continues to be Reshaped, European State Aid Law Quarterly (3) 2005 pp. 393-400.

> requirements of the public authorities.[167] This finding was sufficient to conclude that the establishment of the disputed tariff was the result of the conduct of the Dutch state, and was thus covered by Article 107(1).[168]

An undertaking or a body is considered as public, and can thus be part of the state within the meaning of Article 107(1), if the state directly or indirectly exercises dominant influence over it as a result of legal or actual control.[169]

Where the state exercises either *de jure* or *de facto* control over a public or private body, it is not necessary to distinguish whether the aid given is financed by public resources or from the body's own private resources. In this context the resources are regarded as being state resources for the purposes of Article 107(1) – regardless of their origin.[170]

In Case C-482/99, *Stardust Marine*, the CJ thus stated that Article 107(1):

> 'covers all the financial means by which the public authorities may actually support undertakings, irrespective of whether or not those means are permanent assets of the public sector. Therefore, even if the sums corresponding to the measure in question are not permanently held by the Treasury, the fact that they constantly remain under public control, and therefore available to the competent national authorities, is sufficient for them to be categorised as State resources'.[171]

However, this does not mean that all financial transactions of public undertakings in principle may involve State aid subject to Article 107(1). The provision of aid by public undertakings will only be covered by Article 107(1) if the aid is considered imputable to the state. The state must therefore have exercised its control in fact, for example by taking the initiative for the

167. Joined Cases 67, 68 and 70/85, *van der Kooy* v *Commission,* para. 37. See also Case C-44/93, *Namur,* para. 31; and Case C-345/02, *Pearle,* para. 35.
168. Joined Cases 67, 68 and 70/85, *van der Kooy* v *Commission,* para. 38.
169. With regard to undertakings, the definition of scope in the Transparency Directive can serve as an inspiration for the definition of a public undertaking in the context of State aid; see Directive 2006/111/EC on the transparency of financial relations between Member States and public undertakings as well as on financial transparency within certain undertakings, Article 2(b) (OJ 2006 L 318/17).
170. Joined Cases 67, 68 and 70/85, *van der Kooy* v *Commission,* where Gasunie and the state each financed half of the aid resources. In spite of this, the whole amount was considered as being covered by Article 107(1).
171. Case C-482/99, *Stardust Marine,* para. 37.

implementation of the aid measures or by otherwise being involved in its implementation.

The fact that a measure is decided by a public undertaking which is subject to public control is thus not in itself enough for the aid measure in question to be regarded as imputable to the state. In determining whether the aid is imputable to the state it is necessary to make a more detailed examination of whether the public authorities can, by one means or another, be considered as involved in the adoption of the measure in question.[172]

The broad interpretation of the concept of State aid prevents Member States from getting round the application of Article 107(1) by channelling their aid through a state controlled undertaking or fund, for example by requiring the state undertaking to invest in an undertaking which a private investor would not have invested in on the basis of normal commercial considerations.[173]

However, the problem of State aid not only arises when the State aid is channelled to other undertakings via a public undertaking,[174] but likewise where resources are transferred internally in a public undertaking from an activity in an area which is not subject to competition to a competitive area. For example, there was such cross-subsidisation in Case C-39/94, SFEI v *La Poste*, where part of the French state's payment to the French postal service for the conduct of the postal monopoly was used as a cross-subsidy to part of the undertaking's activities which lay outside the scope of the monopoly.[175]

3.2.2. European Union resources

The European Union has established a number of structural funds and aid programmes which provide financial support to undertakings in the Member States with a view to promoting specially chosen aims.[176]

Where undertakings receive such aid directly from the EU, the aid is not covered by the prohibition of State aid in Articles 107-109 of the Treaty. The basis for this is that the EU institutions are not regarded as part of the state,

172. Case C-482/99, *Stardust Marine,* paras 51 and 52. See e.g. the CJ's assessment in Case C-345/02, *Pearle,* paras 35-39.
173. Case C-305/89, *Alfa Romeo.*
174. Case C-305/89, *Alfa Romeo,* where it could not be characterised as normal commercial conduct that a state owned public undertaking invested in a financially weakened subsidiary.
175. On cross-subsidies between a reserved (non-competitive area) and an area subject to free competition, see also Case T-613/97, *Ufex,* paras 68-76.
176. E.g., undertakings can obtain support from the European Social Fund, European Regional Development Fund, the European Agricultural Guidance and Guarantee Fund, European Fisheries Fund, or from the LIFE Programme.

and the EU's resources are not considered to be state resources within the meaning of Article 107(1).[177]

In certain cases aid resources from the EU's aid programmes will be paid to the Member States with a view to the Member States being responsible for the administration and payment of EU aid. Such financial aid, which is wholly financed by the EU's aid programmes, but which is in fact paid to the undertakings by the Member States themselves will not, in principle, be covered by Article 107(1). However, such aid is likely to be regarded as Member State resources provided the payment of aid from the EU's aid programmes allows the Member States a certain measure of discretion with regard to the distribution of the aid.[178]

In other cases there is an obligation for Member States to co-finance projects etc., in order to be able to attract EU aid payments. The requirement for such co-financing follows directly from Union legislation and since the Member States have no choice but to provide the co-financing, the aid payments are in principle not imputable to the Member State and the aid is thus not covered by the Treaty provisions on State aid.[179] However, Article 12 of Council Regulation (EC) No 1260/1999 provides that co-financing via the EU's Funds must be compatible with the Treaty's State aid rules.[180] This means that where the EU and a Member State provide co-financing as mentioned above, the overall aid will be subject to the State aid rules, including the obligation to notify the aid, and the standstill obligation.[181]

If a Member State voluntarily combines means from the EU's aid programmes with its own means, the State aid rules must naturally be complied with.

Even though EU aid cannot be considered State aid within the meaning of Article 107(1), it is clear from several of the Commission's regulations and guidelines in the area of State aid that aid to undertakings which is financed

177. See Joined Cases 213-215/81, *BALM,* para. 22.

178. However, see the Opinion of Advocate General VerLoren van Themaat in Joined Cases 213-215/81, *BALM,* from which it was stated that in case where the Member States are given some discretion in relation to the allocation of EU resources, this can lead to favouring an undertaking within the meaning of Article 107(1). See *Leigh Hancher, Tom Ottervanger & Piet Jan Slot:* EC State aids, 2006 paras 3-032.

179. See Case C-460/07, *Puffer,* paras 69 and 70. See also *Conor Quigley:* European State Aid Law and Policy, 2009, p. 17; and *Leigh Hancher, Tom Ottervanger & Piet Jan Slot:* EC State Aids, 2006 para. 3-033.

180. Council Regulation (EC) No 1260/1999 laying down general provisions on the Structural Funds (OJ 1999 L 161/1).

181. *Heidenhain:* European State Aid Law, 2010 p. 18.

by EU resources must be included in the calculation of aid intensities and aid ceilings.[182] This is in line with the intention behind Article 12 of Council Regulation (EC) No 1260/1999, that the same aid ceilings and aid intensities apply to aid that is wholly financed by a Member State and aid that is partially financed from EU resources.[183]

3.2.3. Private resources

The prohibition of State aid in Article 107(1) of the Treaty presumes that a given amount of aid is given by the state and is financed from state resources. This means that aid given by private bodies or by public bodies that is financed by a body's private resources, and is provided without state intervention, for example the award of scholarships by a private trust fund, or a private parent company giving support to a financially weakened subsidiary, is not covered by Article 107(1).

However, on the basis of the above, it may be presumed that aid financed out of private resources that is given by a private or public body will fall within the scope of the prohibition of State aid in the following situations: first, where the body in question has been established or appointed by the state to administer aid;[184] second, where it can be shown that the aid is imputable to the state;[185] and third, where the resources for the aid result from obligatory contributions required by law (as explained in the following section).

In these cases, it is considered that State aid is provided by the state through state resources within the meaning of Article 107(1), without it being

182. See e.g. Article 7 of Commission Regulation (EC) No 800/2008 (General block exemption Regulation) (OJ 2008 L 214/3), according to which, when assessing maximum aid intensities, the total amount of public aid must be taken into account, regardless of whether it is provided from local, regional, national or EU financial resources. See also the Community guidelines on State aid for environmental protection, para. 189 (OJ 2008 C 82/1), according to which the aid ceilings apply whether the aid is wholly financed from national resources or partially financed by the EU
183. *Heidenhain:* European State Aid Law, 2010 pp 18-19.
184. Case 78/76, *Steinike & Weinlig,* para. 21; it is not necessary to distinguish between aid given by such a body and aid given by the state.
185. Case C-482/99, *Stardust Marine;* and Case C-342/02, *Pearle.* See e.g. Commission Decision 82/73/EEC, *Gasunie* (OJ 1982 L 37/29); and the later Joined Cases 67, 68 and 70/85, *van der Kooy,* where the CJ did not find that it was necessary in order for Article 107(1) to apply that there should be a requirement that aid from a private body should be financed via public resources, if the resources in question had been allocated as a consequence of an act of the state; see para. 37.

necessary to determine whether the resources are derived from private or public means.

> Case 290/83, *CNCA*, concerned a public agricultural credit fund, *Caisse nationale de crédit agricole* (CNCA). CNCA had decided to give a 'solidarity grant' of FRF 1.5 billion to those French farmers who were worst off. This aid was to be financed from the operating profit which CNCA had accumulated in the previous years. In this connection, the CJ held that aid which, like the solidarity grant concerned, was agreed and financed by a public body and which could only be implemented with official approval, is covered by Article 107(1).[186]

3.2.4. Aid provided on the basis of the legislation of a Member State

It is also possible that undertakings may receive a financial advantage on the basis of Member State legislation in circumstances other than those referred to in the preceding section. However, Article 107(1) does not apply if undertakings receive such advantage without state resources being directly or indirectly involved.[187] Though, in certain circumstances the national provisions will involve a transfer of state resources from a body which falls within the definition of a state body, with the consequence that the measure may be brought within the scope of application of Article 107(1). Examples are given below of situations which have been referred to the CJ on whether the legislation in a Member State involves State aid subject to Article 107(1).

Taxes

The revenues which a state obtains on the basis of obligatory taxes which are imposed on undertakings and private individuals are considered to be state resources for the purposes of Article 107(1). This also applies where tax is paid directly to a publicly controlled fund, where the resources cannot be said to come directly from the state treasury.[188] Such resources could therefore be used to provide State aid in breach of Article 107(1) of the Treaty.[189]

186. Case 290/83, *CNCA*, para. 15. See also Case T-358/94, *Air France,* where the GC regarded aid which was financed by voluntary contributions by private investors who could, at any time, demand payment, as State aid.
187. Case C-379/98, *PreussenElektra,* para. 58.
188. Case 173/73, *Italy* v *Commission,* para. 16, concerning a partial reduction of the social burdens of the textile industry. In this cases the CJ stated: 'As the funds in question are financed through compulsory contributions imposed by state legislation and as, as this case shows, they are managed and apportioned in accordance with the

An aid measure does not lose the character of a gratuitous advantage by the fact that it is wholly or partially financed by contributions imposed by the public authority and levied on the undertakings which receive the aid, so that the contributions made correspond to the advantages which the undertakings receive from the aid.[190]

If a public or private body provides aid which is exclusively financed by voluntary contributions from private undertakings or persons, this aid will not be covered by Article 107(1).[191] Where the Commission has required an aid measure to be terminated, and the measure has been continued by national employers' organisations using means which undertakings have provided 'voluntarily' through a national insurance scheme, the Commission found that this was indirect aid.[192]

> In Case 290/83, *CNCA*, voluntary payments to a state-controlled fund, which were thereafter given to undertakings, were also regarded as State aid covered by Article 107(1). However, in this case it was decisive to the assessment of the aid that the state controlled the use of the resources so the resources could be considered as state resources for the purpose of Article 107(1).

Social regulation

In several cases the CJ has had occasion to assess the compatibility of national social provisions with the rules on State aid, and on these occasions it has shown itself reluctant to characterise the easing of social burdens as State aid.

provisions of that legislation, they must be regarded as state resources within the meaning of Article 92 [now Article 107], even if they are administered by institutions distinct from the public authorities.' See also Case 259/85, *France* v *Commission,* which concerned aid to the French textile industry financed via tax-like duties collected on every delivery of domestically produced textile goods.

189. Case C-126/01, *GEMO*; Case 259/85, *France* v *Commission;* Joined Cases 67, 68 and 70/85, *van der Kooy;* and Joined Cases C-78-83/90, *Compagnie commerciale de l'Ouest,* para. 35.
190. Case 78/76, *Steinike & Weinlig,* para. 22.
191. See *Marco M. Slotboom:* State Aid in Community Law: A Broad or Narrow Definition?, European Law Review 1995 pp. 289-301, at p. 296, note 57, which refers to the Commission's decision in the *Milchföderungsfonds* case (OJ 1985 L 35/85). However, such measures can be covered by Article 101 of the Treaty.
192. Xth Report on competition policy, 1981 paras 163 and 220.

In Joined Cases C-72 and 83/91, *Sloman Neptun*, the CJ considered a German arrangement for merchant vessels which were entered in the German international shipping register. The arrangement allowed seafarers who were citizens of a third country and who had neither permanent abode nor residence in Germany not to be covered by German collective employment agreements, and to be subject to working conditions and rates of pay which were considerably less favourable than those applicable to German seafarers. In this way the arrangement made it possible for German shipping companies to reduce their costs for wages and social contributions, while the German state lost tax revenue.

The CJ examined whether this arrangement involved giving advantages which could be considered to be aid given through state resources.[193] The CJ ruled that the arrangement did not constitute State aid within the meaning of Article 107(1), as neither by its purpose nor its general scheme was the arrangement intended to create an advantage for the shipping companies which could be an additional burden for the state. The arrangement only involved a change, to the advantage of the ship owners, of the framework which applied to contracts between the undertakings and their employees. The CJ found that the consequences of the arrangement in relation to the calculation of social contributions, and the loss of tax revenue because of the lower wages, were inseparable from the arrangement and were therefore not a means for providing the undertakings concerned with a particular advantage.[194] On this basis the CJ concluded that the arrangement did not constitute State aid within the meaning of Article 107(1).[195]

Protection of employees

In Case C-189/91, *Kirsammer-Hack*, the CJ considered whether the prohibition of State aid applied to a law excluding small businesses from a national system of protection of workers against unfair dismissal. In the event of socially unjustified dismissals, small businesses were not obliged to pay compensation or to bear the legal expenses incurred in proceedings concerning the dismissal of workers.

The CJ held that the exclusion of small businesses from the protection system in question did not entail any direct or indirect transfer of state

193. Joined Cases C-72 and 73/91, *Sloman Neptun,* para. 20.
194. Joined Cases C-72 and 73/91, *Sloman Neptun,* para. 21.
195. Joined Cases C-72 and 73/91, *Sloman Neptun,* para. 22. See also Joined Cases C-52-54/97, *Viscido,* paras 14 and 15.

resources to those businesses.[196] The arrangement only established a special legal framework for working relationships between employers and employees in small businesses and avoided imposing financial burdens on those businesses which might hinder their development. The CJ therefore ruled that the arrangement did not constitute aid within the meaning of Article 107(1) of the Treaty.[197]

Minimum price harmonisation

Sometimes Member States impose price controls by laying down special maximum or minimum prices for certain products. Despite their general character, such price controls will often have a selective effect, so that some undertakings, products or business sectors will be favoured. Minimum prices laid down by law can favour the seller, as sellers will be guaranteed minimum prices for their products, while maximum price harmonisation can favour buyers by giving them lower costs. On the face of it there does not seem to be any reason to exclude such price controls from the Treaty's prohibition of State aid.

The Commission has found that State aid exists within the meaning of Article 107(1) of the Treaty in cases where, in a particular business sector, a Member State lays down minimum prices which are higher than the market prices. Among other things, this has been the case in connection with a German draft law on the setting of a minimum price for electricity supplies from renewable energy sources, where the Commission found that this was State aid covered by Article 107(1).[198]

However, the CJ has adopted a different approach. The key point, for deciding whether a maximum or minimum price established by law is covered by the prohibition of State aid or not, has been whether the benefit has been financed from state resources.

In Case 82/77, *van Tiggele*, the CJ was asked whether a Dutch provision on minimum prices, for the domestic sale of spirits, should be regarded as a State aid which was incompatible with the internal market. The CJ stated that Article 107(1) does not cover measures which, with a view to favouring distributors of a product, lay down fixed minimum prices for

196. Case C-189/91, *Kirsammer-Hack,* para. 17
197. Case C-189/91, *Kirsammer-Hack,* para. 18.
198. However, the arrangement was approved by the Commission; XXth Report on competition policy, 1991, para. 291.

sales at the retail level which only impose a burden on consumers.[199] The CJ justified this on the grounds that the advantages which the minimum prices gave to distributors were neither directly nor indirectly provided by state resources within the meaning of Article 107(1).[200]

Case C-379/98, *PreussenElektra*, concerned a German law on the input of electricity from renewable energy resources to the public grid. This law contained provisions requiring private electricity supply companies to buy electricity produced in their supply areas from renewable energy, and to pay a minimum tariff for this laid down by law, which was higher than the true economic value of this kind of electricity. The law also contained a provision on the allocation of the consequent financial burden between the electricity supply companies and upstream private electricity network operators, so that in some circumstances the private electricity network operators, in this case *PreussenElektra*, would have to pay compensation to secondary electricity supply companies for the additional costs which were a consequence of the obligation to buy the electricity at the minimum price determined by law. The question was whether this arrangement amounted to State aid within the meaning of Article 107(1).[201]

In its decision the CJ again emphasised that only advantages granted directly or indirectly through State resources are to be considered aid within the meaning of Article 107(1).[202] In relation to the case before it, the CJ commented that the obligation imposed on private electricity supply undertakings to purchase electricity produced from renewable energy sources at fixed minimum prices did not involve any direct or indirect transfer of State resources to undertakings which produce electricity from renewable energy sources.[203] Nor could the allocation of the financial burden constitute a direct or indirect transfer of State resources.[204]

In these circumstances the CJ found that the fact that the purchase obligation was laid down by law and led to an unquestioned advantage for

199. Case 82/77, *van Tiggele,* para. 24.
200. Case 82/77, *van Tiggele,* para. 25. However, the measure did constitute a measure with an equivalent effect to a quantitative restriction, and was therefore contrary to Article 28 [then Article 30].
201. Case C-379/98, *PreussenElektra,* para. 56.
202. Case C-379/98, *PreussenElektra,* para. 58.
203. Case C-379/98, *PreussenElektra,* para. 59.
204. Case C-379/98, *PreussenElektra,* para. 60.

certain undertakings did not mean that it could be characterised as State aid for the purposes of Article 107(1).[205]

In the context of the law on State aid there thus seems to be a decisive difference between whether the aid is financed through obligatory taxes imposed by public authority or even the potential recipients of the aid, or whether the aid is financed by the state laying down minimum prices which are only a burden on the consumer. In the latter case, according to the practice of the CJ this is not State aid within the meaning of Article 107(1).

3.3. Selectivity

In order for a State aid measure to be characterised as incompatible with the internal market, as laid down in Article 107(1), the measure must favour *certain undertakings* or the *production of certain goods*. The purpose of this criterion is first and foremost to exclude the application of the State aid provisions to the general economic measures of the Member States, and thus limit such general measures to those measures which selectively favour certain undertakings. If an aid measure is general it can be adopted and implemented as part of the powers of a Member State to implement the economic policy which it considers appropriate. On the other hand, if the measure is selective, it may fall within the scope of the prohibition of State aid.

The application of the selectivity criterion therefore requires first, that there is a definition of what is meant by *undertakings* and *production of certain goods* for the purposes of Article 107(1), and second, that it is established under what circumstances a measure is deemed to favour *certain* undertakings or the production of *certain* goods, and is therefore regarded as selective.

3.3.1. Undertakings and productions of goods

The concept of undertakings

The CJ has defined the concept of an *undertaking* as covering any entity engaged in an economic activity, regardless of its legal status and the way in which it is financed.[206] In accordance with this definition, which applies to

205. Case C-379/98, *PreussenElektra,* para. 61. See also para. 66.

206. Case C-244/94, *FFSA*, para. 14; Case C-364/92, *Eurocontrol,* para. 18, which concerned Articles 102 and 106 (then Articles 86 and 90).

competition law in general, Article 107 thus covers undertakings in a broad sense.[207]

In this context, any activity which consists of offering goods or services in the market consists of an economic activity.[208] It is not necessary to separate the activity that consists of the purchase of goods and the activity that consist of their subsequent use in order to determine whether an activity is an economic activity. It is thus the economic or non-economic use of the goods that necessarily determine the nature of the activity.[209]

All undertakings that carry on an economic activity covered by the Treaty can potentially receive State aid in breach of Article 107(1), regardless of whether the commercial activity is of an economic, cultural or other character, and regardless of whether the undertaking operates in the retail, manufacturing or service sector.[210]

Article 107(1) covers both aid to private and public undertakings. This follows from the practice of the CJ, as well as from the Transparency Directive[211] and Article 106 of the Treaty which states that public undertakings are subject to the competition rules of the Treaty.[212]

An undertaking need not be carried on for profit in order to be covered by the rules on State aid.[213] It is thus sufficient that the undertaking in fact carries on some economic activity.[214] This means that non-profit organisations will also be covered by the concept of an undertaking.

There are no particular requirements as to the legal form of an undertaking. Public limited companies, private limited companies, trusts, mutual institutions, one man businesses etc. are all covered by the concept of an undertaking. Also, for public bodies it is irrelevant to the definition of an undertak-

207. Case C-41/90, *Höfner & Elser,* para. 21; and Joined Cases C-159 and 160/91, *Poucet,* para. 17.
208. Case T-155/04, *Eurocontrol,* para. 50; and Case T-81-83/07, *Jan Rudolf Maas,* para. 178.
209. Case C-113/07 P, *Selex,* para. 102; and Case C-205/03, *FENIN*, para. 26.
210. On the definition of the concept of an undertaking in special areas, see*: Maria Kleis & Phedon Nicolaides:* The concept of undertaking in education and public health systems, European State Aid Law Quarterly (3) 2006 pp. 505-508.
211. Directive 2006/111/EC on the transparency of financial relations between Member States and public undertakings as well as on financial transparency within certain undertakings (OJ 2006 L 318/17).
212. Though with the reservation for the undertakings referred to in Article 106(2).
213. Case C-41/90, *Höfner & Elsner,* paras 19-23, concerning a public employment agency; and Case C-244/94, *FFSA*, concerning a public organ which administered an old age pension arrangement.
214. Case C-437/09, *AG2R*, para. 65.

ing whether the body is an independent legal entity or whether it is part of the central government administration.[215]

However, the concept of an undertaking in competition law does not include the exercise of public authority or the carrying out of tasks of a social nature. Where there is a transfer of resources between state bodies in connection with their exercise of authority, this will not be affected by the prohibition of State aid in Article 107(1).[216]

Production of certain goods

The provisions on State aid apply to aid that is provided for the *production of certain goods*, including aid to certain sectors, for example the motor car or textile industries. The provision covers all production carried out by the entities which are covered by the concept of an undertaking defined immediately above.[217]

Private households

Aid to private households or social benefits paid to individuals are not covered by the Treaty provisions on State aid. However, there could be State aid within the scope of Article 107(1) if certain undertakings were to derive ultimate financial advantage from the aid, so as to constitute indirect aid to the undertaking, regardless of whether an individual consumer or person is the direct recipient.

3.3.2. General and selective measures

The economic measures of the Member States will often lead to a direct or indirect reallocation of resources which will benefit some undertakings rather

215. Case 118/85, *Commission* v *Italy,* para. 13; Case C-69/91, *Decoster,* para. 15; and Case C-92/91, *Taillandier,* para. 14.
216. Case C-364/92, *Eurocontrol,* which concerned Article 102 [then Article 86], where the CJ found that the provision of navigation services by Eurocontrol in order to ensure the safety of air traffic was the exercise of authority and thus Eurocontrol as not an undertaking within the meaning of Article 102; see Article 106. In its decision, among other things the CJ emphasised Eurocontrol's powers of enforcement, and the fact that Eurocontrol had a duty to provide its services to all airlines, whether or not they had paid a fee for the service.
217. Commission Decision 80/932/EEC (OJ 1980 L 264/28); and Case 203/82, *Commission* v *Italy,* where a greater reduction in employers' health insurance contributions for female employees than for male employees could favour certain productions of goods in Italy in which there was a preponderance of female workers, such as the textile, clothing, footwear and leather sectors.

than others, and thereby distort the competitive situation. However, this fact does not necessarily mean that the measure is covered by the prohibition of State aid in Article 107(1). The application of the State aid rules requires that the measure should be selective in the sense that the measure favours *certain* undertakings or the production of *certain* goods.

This requirement for selectivity means that, in indicating those who may be entitled to aid, the measure should contain an element of specificity or discrimination. Within the context of a given legal arrangement the measure must favour certain undertakings in comparison with other undertakings which, given the purpose of the measure in question, are in a comparable legal and factual situation.[218] Measures which benefit all the undertakings of a Member State, without distinction, or measures which make a distinction, but on an objective basis, will not be covered by the State aid prohibition.[219]

This definition is important, as distortions of competition which are the result of selective measures are covered by Article 107(1), while distortions of competition which are the result of general measures are covered by the harmonisation provisions in Articles 116 and 117 of the Treaty.[220] The application of the correct Treaty provision is important, as the different Treaty provisions apply different legal remedies.

General measures

In order for a measure to be regarded as general, it must be open to all economic agents operating within the legal order which constitutes the reference framework for the assessment of selectivity, without regard to the size, nature, regional location or sector, and give the undertakings equal access to the measure.[221]

218. Joined Cases C-106/09 P & 107/09 P, *Gibraltar,* para. 75; sag Case C-88/03, *The Azores,* paras 54 and 56; and Case C-143/99, *Adria-Wien Pipeline,* para. 41.
219. Case C-143/99, *Adria-Wien Pipeline,* para. 36.
220. According to the Commission, the economic argument for distinguishing between general and selective measures is based on the economic point of view that selective aid measures have a more direct and immediate effect on competition between Member States than general measures; see the Second Survey on State aid in the European Union in the Manufacturing and Certain Other Sectors, 1991 p. 4 et seq. On the delimitation of Articles 107-108 in relation to Articles 116 and 117, see *Leendert A. Geelhoed:* The demarcation of State aid and regulatory charges, European State Aid Law Quarterly (3) 2005 pp. 401-406.
221. Commission Notice on the application of the State aid rules to measures relating to direct business taxation, para. 13 (OJ 1998 C 384/3).

Such measures, for example a Member State's reduction of interest rates, the structure of the tax system (e.g. the rules for depreciation or the remission of tax debts), the system for social security contributions (e.g. employers' and employees' financing of social benefits), or the decisions of the authorities concerning infrastructure, are usually considered to be part of a Member State's general economic and social policy.

In special cases the general measures of a Member State can mean that certain undertakings or sectors derive a greater benefit from the measures than other undertakings in the Member State. For example, where a Member State introduces general reductions in payroll taxes, or gives a subsidy for the employment of the long-term unemployed, on the face of it this will benefit labour-intensive undertakings or sectors, while all things being equal more favourable tax rules for depreciation will benefit capital-intensive undertakings with substantial assets which qualify for depreciation. In the same way, tax incentives to promote investments in environmental protection, research and development, or training can benefit undertakings which undertake such investments. Where such advantages are merely a consequence of an arrangement which has been put together on the basis of proper objective criteria, it will not be considered to be selective in the context of State aid.[222]

The situation is different where the extent of a measure is reduced *de facto* by, for example, discretionary allocation by the state. The measure thereby acquires a selective element so that certain undertakings, sectors or regions can be given an advantage. If there is such a selective element, a measure which is expressed in general terms can be covered by the prohibition of incompatible State aid.[223]

On the basis of the above, it must be assumed that an aid measure must be considered general in relation to the State aid rules if it is phrased as being generally applicable and the allocation of aid is based on objective criteria, without the authorities being given discretionary powers in relation to it.

Selective measures

Selective measures are characterised by the fact that they do not apply to all the undertakings or industrial sectors which ought, in principle, to benefit from the measure if the character of the Member State's economic system is

222. Commission Notice on the application of the State aid rules to measures relating to direct business taxation, para. 14 (OJ 1998 C 384/3). For example, this argument was tried in Joined Cases T-92 & 103/00, *Territorio Histórico de Álava,* para. 50.

223. Case C-241/94, *France* v *Commission,* para. 23. This was the case in Joined Cases T-92 & 103/00, *Territorio Histórico de Álava,* para. 58

taken into account.[224] A measure will be characterised as a selective measure if it favours a specific sector, region, undertaking or group of undertakings.

The selectivity criterion is interpreted very broadly. For example, an aid measure that favours small and medium sized enterprises will be characterised as selective, even though the measure is general in terms of not being limited in respect of sectors or regions.[225] This will apply even if, for example, small and medium sized enterprises represent up to 95 % of all undertakings in the Member State concerned.[226] Aid for exports is also regarded as being selective within the meaning of Article 107(1), even if all exporting undertakings in the Member State can in principle benefit from the measure.[227] According to the practice of the CJ, the same applies to aid measures which are targeted at sectors which are exposed to international competition.[228]

An aid measure can selectively favour a specific sector, such as the shipbuilding sector or the transport sector.[229] In this context the term 'sector' is interpreted broadly. Thus, the Commission has found that the specially favourable treatment of the manufacturing sector, compared with the service sector, stated in the Irish corporation tax law meant that the measure was characterised as selective within the meaning of Article 107(1).[230]

Aid measures with a limited geographic extent of a local or regional nature can also be characterised as selective.[231] However, such measures will often have a purely local competitive effect and will therefore not actually or po-

224. *Marco M. Slotboom:* State Aid in Community Law: A Broad or Narrow Definition?, European Law Review 1995 pp. 289-301, at p. 297.
225. Commission Regulation (EC) No 70/2001 on the application of Articles 87 and 88 of the EC Treaty to State aid to small and medium-sized enterprises. See also Joined Cases T-92 and 103/00, *Territorio Histórico de Álava,* para. 40.
226. See *Henrik Mørch & Lena Sandberg:* Forbudet mod uforenelig statsstøtte i EF-Traktatens artikel 91(2), UfR 1995 B.301, at p. 307.
227. Joined Cases 6 and 11/69, *Commission* v *France,* paras 20 and 21; and Case 57/86, *Greece* v *Commission,* para. 8.
228. Case C-75/97, *Maribel bis/ter.*
229. Case 248/84, *Germany* v *Commission,* para. 18; and Case C-75/97, *Maribel bis/ter,* para. 33. See also Case 173/73, *Italy* v *Commission,* concerning aid which benefited the textile industry; and Case C-143/99, *Adria-Wien Pipeline,* where undertakings which produced goods were favoured in relation to undertakings which provided services.
230. Commission Decision E/2/98, *Ireland* (OJ 1998 C 395/19). The Decision was discussed in the XXVIIIth Report on competition policy, 1999, para. 210.
231. Case 248/84, *Germany* v *Commission,* concerning regional aid programmes that benefited undertakings that invested in Nord-Rhein-Westfalen.

tentially affect trade between Member States, as referred to in Article 107(1).[232]

However, the fact that a measure only grants benefits in one part of a Member State's territory is not in itself enough for the measure to be regarded as selective.[233] The definition of the reference framework for selectivity need not necessarily consist of the whole of the territory of the Member State in question, but in certain cases it can be a limited part of the territory. Thus, in Case C-88/03, *The Azores*, the CJ established that it is possible that an infra-State body enjoys a legal or factual status which makes it sufficiently autonomous in relation to the central government of the Member State, with the result that, by the measures it adopts, it is that body and not the central government which plays a fundamental role in the definition of the political and economic environment in which undertakings operate.[234]

For a measure to be regarded as having been adopted in the exercise of sufficiently autonomous powers, the CJ requires:

1. That the aid decision must have been taken by a regional or local authority which has, from a constitutional point of view, a political and administrative status separate from that of the central government;
2. The aid decision must have been adopted without the central government being able to directly intervene as regards its content; and
3. The financial consequences of a reduction of the national tax rate for undertakings in the region must not be offset by aid or subsidies from other regions or the central government.[235]

232. See the Commission's assessment of tax deductions for reserves which Sparekassen Nordjylland was allowed to make in connection with the takeover of Himmerlandsbanken, Skat Udland, 1995 p. 68.
233. Case C-88/03, *The Azores,* para. 57.
234. Case C-88/03, *The Azores,* para. 58. The case is commented on by *Carsten Zatschler:* Review of the Judgment in Case C-88/03, Portugal v. Commission (Azores Tax Regime), European State Aid Law Quarterly (4) 2007 p. 779. See also *Phedon Nicolaides:* Developments in Fiscal Aid: New Interpretations and New Problems with the Concept of Selectivity, European State Aid Law Quarterly (1) 2007 p. 43.
235. Case C-88/03, *The Azores,* para. 67. In the case in question only the first of these conditions was fulfilled and the arrangement was therefore regarded as selective; see paras 69-85. See also Joined Cases C-106/09 P & 107/09 P, *Gibraltar,* commented on by *Pierpaolo Rossi-Maccanico:* Gibraltar and the Unsettled Limits of Selectivity in Fiscal Aids, European State Aid Law Quarterly (1) 2009 pp. 63-72.

If these criteria are met, the regional environment is then taken as the point of reference for whether the aid measure constitutes a benefit for some undertakings in relation to other undertakings which are in a corresponding legal and factual situation.

The assessment of selectivity
When assessing the general or selective character of an aid measure the Commission first examines how the measure is framed, and then it looks at its actual effect. It will often be clear from the aid measure whether it is intended to favour certain undertakings or sectors where, for example, it is directed at small and medium sized enterprises or at a specific undertaking.

Where the selective element of a measure is not immediately apparent, it is necessary to make a more detailed assessment of whether the measure, as part of a particular legal arrangement, can favour certain undertakings or the production of certain goods in relation to other undertakings which are in a corresponding legal and factual situation.[236]

Thus, it is possible that, after a more detailed analysis, measures which appear to be general are shown to involve differences of treatment which mean that the measure will be considered selective for the purposes of Article 107(1).[237] This will be the case both where the measure allows certain discretionary powers to the authorities which administer the aid scheme in question and where the effect of the measure is to favour certain undertakings, unless such difference in treatment is justified by reasons relating to the nature and general scheme of the system of which it is part.[238]

> In Case C-241/94, *France* v *Commission*, the CJ assessed a general aid measure which allowed special discretionary powers to the authority which was to administer the aid scheme. In this case, a fund was empowered to co-finance measures for following up social programmes that had been drawn up by undertakings with employment problems. The interventions of the fund were not restricted to certain sectors, regions or categories of undertaking, but the fund had certain powers of discretion

236. Case C-88/03, *The Azores,* paras 54 and 56; Joined Cases C-106/09 P & 107/09 P, *Gibraltar,* para. 75; Case C-143/99, *Adria-Wien Pipeline,* para. 41; and similarly Case C-75/97, *Maribel bis/ter,* paras 28-31.
237. This was the case in Joined Cases T-92 & 103/00, *Territorio Histórico de Álava,* para. 58.
238. Case C-53/00, *Ferring SA,* para. 17; and Case C-143/99, *Adria-Wien Pipeline,* para. 42.

over, among other things, the choice of who should benefit, the amount of the aid and the conditions under which aid was provided.[239] The aid scheme was therefore considered to be selective within the meaning of Article 107(1).[240]

In Commission Decision 80/932/EEC, the Commission considered an Italian arrangement for the partial takeover by the State of the contributions to health insurance schemes of manufacturing undertakings and certain undertakings in the service sector; the Commission considered that this arrangement was selective. The arrangement provided for a greater reduction of employers' contributions for the health insurance of female employees than the contributions paid in respect of male employees. The measure thus supported those parts of the Italian manufacturing sector in which female employment was preponderant, such as the textile, clothing, footwear and leather sectors.[241] Despite the general nature of its wording, the actual effect of the measure thus favoured some sectors over others, and it was therefore regarded as selective for the purposes of Article 107(1).

Corresponding considerations applied in connection with a proposed amendment to the Danish Law on electricity supply. This amendment gave electricity companies the possibility of taking account of their losses in the electricity prices, and was in principle applicable to the whole electricity supply sector. In practice it was only the SEAS company which was able to fulfil the conditions of the law for including losses in their electricity prices. The amendment to the Law on electricity supply was therefore regarded as selective.[242]

239. Case C-241/94, *France* v *Commission,* paras 22 and 23.

240. Case C 241/94, *France* v *Commission,* para. 24. Case C-295/97, *Piaggio*, para. 39; and Joined Cases T-92 and 103/00, *Territorio Histórico de Álava,* paras 33 and 35.

241. Commission Decision 80/932/EEC (OJ 1980 L 264/26); and Case 203/82, *Commission* v *Italy.* See also Joined Cases T-92 and 103/00, *Territorio Histórico de Álava,* para. 39.

242. See *Henrik Mørch:* Summary of the most important recent developments, Competition Policy Newsletter (4) 1995 pp. 47-51, at p. 49; and see Commission Decision 2001/605/EC (OJ 2001 L 212/34), concerning a Spanish aid arrangement for the acquisition of commercial vehicles which was found to be selective, as the potential recipients of the aid had in fact to be natural persons and undertakings engaged in transport operations, either on their own account or for hire or reward; see para. 23 of the Decision.

The Member States' legal orders may sometimes include provisions which selectively favour certain undertakings, other than in connection with taxation or the payment of social benefits.

> For example, this was so in Case C-295/97, *Piaggio*, which concerned an arrangement whereby large industrial undertakings in difficulties which owed particularly large debts to certain, mainly public, classes of creditors could depart from the normal law of insolvency.[243] Subject to the discretion of the relevant government minister, such undertakings could obtain permission to continue trading in circumstances which would not have been allowed under the generally applicable insolvency law. In these circumstances the arrangement was regarded as selective within the meaning of Article 107(1).[244]

According to the CJ, selectivity will not to exist if an aid arrangement, that may well constitute an advantage for the recipient, can be justified by the nature or general scheme of the arrangement.[245] In assessing whether an aid arrangement is selective, the Commission must thus establish how the general rules are framed and investigate how far an exception or differentiation within this system for the benefit of certain undertakings or the production of certain goods can be justified by the nature of the system.

Under special circumstances it will be justifiable to treat certain sectors, regions or undertakings differently, on the basis of an aid measure.

> The possibility for this was made clear in Case 173/73, *Italy* v *Commission*, which concerned an Italian measure whereby there was a partial reduction of employers' social payments for family allowances to the advantage of all employers in the textile sector which, for a three year period, eased the social burdens of the exempt undertakings. The contributions of these undertakings were reduced from 15 % to 10 %. In respect of this the CJ stated: 'It must be concluded that the partial reduction of social charges pertaining to family allowances devolving upon employers in the textile sector is a measure intended partially to exempt undertakings of a particular industrial sector from the financial

243. Case C-295/97, *Piaggio,* para. 37.
244. Case C-295/97, *Piaggio,* para. 39.
245. Case C-143/99, *Adria-Wien Pipeline,* para. 42; Joined Cases C-106/09 P & 107/09 P, *Gibraltar,* para. 145; and Case C-88/03, *The Azores,* para. 52. See also Case 173/73, *Italy* v *Commission,* para. 33; and Case C-53/00, *Ferring SA,* para. 17.

charges arising from the normal application of the general social security system, without there being any justification for this exemption on the basis of the nature or general scheme of this system.'[246]

In Joined Cases T-92 and 103/00, *Territorio Histórico de Álava*, in respect of a tax measure, the GC stated that the measure could be justified on the basis of the nature or overall structure of the tax system, and that the measure concerned reflected consistency with the internal logic of the tax system in general.[247] As an example of this, the GC stated that the progressiveness of the tax which was justified by the system's aim of redistribution would not constitute State aid under Article 107(1).[248]

If the elective element of a measure can be justified in accordance with the above, the measure will not constitute an advantage amounting to a State aid within the meaning of Article 107(1). There is no such advantage where the difference in treatment is justified by reasons relating to the logic of the system.[249]

3.4. Aid which distorts or threatens to distort competition, and which affects trade between Member States

The prohibition of State aid in Article 107(1) only applies to aid measures to the extent that the aid distorts or threatens to distort competition, and affects trade between Member States. These two criteria are closely linked to each other.[250] Thus, if an undertaking receives aid, with the effect that the undertaking's position is strengthened in relation to other undertakings with which the recipient undertaking competes in trade within the internal market, the CJ presumes that the criteria for the existence of incompatible State aid are fulfilled.[251]

Both the criteria of distortion of competition and the element of effect on trade are broadly interpreted by the CJ and the Commission, and in practice it does not require much for these criteria to be met. Article 107(1) does not re-

246. Case 173/73, *Italy* v *Commission,* para. 15 See also Case C-143/99, *Adria-Wien Pipeline.*
247. Joined Cases T-92 and 103/00, *Territorio Histórico de Álava,* para. 60. In this connection see also Case C-75/97, *Maribel bis/ter,* para. 39.
248. Joined Cases T-92 and 103/00, *Territorio Histórico de Álava,* para. 60.
249. Case C-53/00, *Ferring SA,* para. 17.
250. The condition relating to distortion of competition and the effect on trade is also closely connected with the selectivity criterion. The distorting effect of a measure on competition will thus depend on whether the aid is given selectively.
251. Case 730/79, *Philip Morris,* para. 11.

quire that the distortion of trade or the effect on trade should be appreciable. However, in the experience of the Commission, aid below a certain level does not affect trade or distort competition sufficiently for the criteria to be regarded as having been met. For this reason, the Commission adopted Regulation (EC) No 1998/2006 on the application of Articles 107 and 108 of the Treaty to *de minimis* aid, according to which aid below a certain threshold is not considered as fulfilling the criteria in Article 107(1), and does not therefore fall within the scope of the provision.[252]

3.4.1. Aid which distorts or threatens to distort competition

The prohibition of State aid in Article 107(1) only applies to aid measures which distort or threaten to distort competition within the internal market. Aid which gives a selective advantage will by its very nature mean that competition will be distorted, as the aid will improve the financial position of those who receive it in relation to their competitors, which will normally result in an improvement in the recipients' competitiveness and market position.[253] The Commission interprets the term *competitiveness* as meaning an undertaking's ability to compete on a global level. This means that an undertaking must constantly adjust to the economic changes and new conditions which apply to a market. In the longer term it means that the undertaking's revenues must cover its production costs, and give a sufficient margin for investment and return on capital so as to secure the continued existence of the undertaking.[254] Therefore, if it can be shown that an undertaking's competitiveness and market position are strengthened on the basis of an aid measure which selectively benefits the undertaking in question, and this undertaking competes with other undertakings within the internal market, it can justifiably be assumed that competition is distorted.[255]

252. Commission Regulation (EC) No 1998/2006 of 15 December 2006 on the application of Articles 87 and 88 of the Treaty to de minimis aid (OJ 2006 L 379/5).
253. Case 730/79, *Philip Morris,* where the State aid was to contribute to an increase in the undertaking's production capacity by restructuring the production units. The undertaking's ability to supply the trade would thus be increased, which would improve its market position in relation to its competitors, and thus distort competition.
254. See Written Question No 562/80 by Mr Fernandez to the Commission*:* The concept of competitiveness as understood by the Commission (OJ 1980 C 283/7).
255. Case 173/73, *Italy* v *Commission;* Case C-142/87, *Tubemeuse.* See also, e.g. *Tourisme social en Belgique* which granted associations organising leisure activities aimed at giving underprivileged persons access to tourism infrastructure, which could distort competition in the hotel trade as apart from their social role of promoting low-

Competitive effect

The State aid provisions prohibit both State aid which actually distorts competition and State aid that threatens to distort competition within the internal market.[256] In addition to this, State aid can distort actual and potential competition for example by reducing actual or potential competitors' possibilities for maintaining or increasing market shares, or preventing the entry of new competitors to the market. It is therefore sufficient for the criteria to be met that there is potential competition and that the aid can potentially distort this competition,[257] and it is thus not a requirement that the aid should in fact have affected competition.[258]

Competition can exist between national competitors or between competitors from different Member States. In assessing whether an aid measure distorts competition, the starting point must be the competitive situation which existed in the internal market before the adoption of the measure in question.[259]

In addition to the effect on competition for the aid recipient's actual and potential competitors, State aid can have a competitive effect on the aid recipient's suppliers and customers. Aid measure can thus have a downstream effect on competition for undertakings that buy the products of the aid recipient.[260] This applies in particular where an undertaking buys the aid recipient's products and may obtain an indirect advantage in the form of lower prices. Correspondingly, an aid measure can have an upstream effect, as it can give the aid recipient's suppliers an indirect financial advantage in the form of increased supplies to the aid recipient.[261]

The fact that the competitors of an undertaking which receives aid have themselves received – possibly unlawful – aid cannot alter the assessment of whether the aid in question is compatible with the Treaty. In other words, a

budget tourism and holidays for workers, the centres also operated traditional hotels which were in direct competition with others in the same category; see XXVIth Report on Competition Policy 1996, 1997 para. 173.

256. Case T-214/95, *VLM*, para. 44.
257. Joined Cases C-62/87 and C-72/87, *Walloon Regional Executive* v *Commission,* para. 15. See *Franz Philipp Sutter:* The Adria Wien Pipeline Case and the State Aid Provisions of the EC Treaty in the Tax matters in European Taxation, 2001, pp. 239-250, at p. 243.
258. Case T-214/95, *VLM,* para. 67.
259. Case 173/73, *Italy* v *Commission,* para. 36.
260. Commission Decision 72/253/EEC (OJ 1972 L 164/22); and Commission Decision 84/508/EEC (OJ 1984 L 283/42).
261. Commission Decision 97/542/EC, *Biofuels* (OJ 1997 L 222/26).

Member State cannot justify an infringement of the State aid provisions on the grounds that other Member States have likewise infringed the State aid provisions.[262] This also applies where a Member State provides compensation for legal differences between the Member States.[263] Such measures do not result in the smoothing out of distortions of competition, but rather in the accumulation of distortions.

Evidence of distortions of competition

The presumption that State aid distorts competition seems to mean, on the face of it, that the Commission need not make a detailed assessment of the potential effect of the aid on competition in the sectors where there is trade between Member States.[264] However, according to the practice of the CJ, the Commission must make a certain analysis of the criteria and give a statement of reasons which show the distorting effect on competition of aid measures, also in cases where it appears from the circumstances in which aid is given, that it can distort competition.[265] The requirements to be satisfied by the statement of reasons depend on the circumstances of each case.[266] However, the Commission's decision must at least state which circumstances distort competition in the actual case,[267] as well as contain information which enables the CJ to exercise control of legitimacy. It must also be possible for the addressee of a Commission decision to confirm that the decision has a proper basis.[268] The Commission must therefore define the relevant geographic market and the relevant product market within which the distortion of competition may occur, as well as the period within which the distortion of competition takes place, though without making an analysis of the same thoroughness as is required in connection with Articles 101 and 102, or the Merger Control

262. Case T-214/95, *VLM,* para. 54; and Case 78/76, *Steinike & Weinlig,* para. 24.
263. Case C-6/97, *Italy* v *Commission,* para. 19; and see *Franz Philipp Sutter:* The Adria Wien Pipeline Case and the State Aid Provisions of the EC Treaty in Tax Matters, European Taxation 2001 pp. 239-250, at p. 243.
264. This is because, as noted initially, trade between Member States may be assumed to be affected where an undertaking which receives aid participates in trade between Member States.
265. Joined Cases 296 and 318/82, *Leewarder Papierwarenfabriek,* para. 24.
266. Joined Cases 296 and 318/82, *Leewarder Papierwarenfabriek,* para. 19.
267. Joined Cases T-92 and 103/00, *Territorio Histórico de Álava,* para. 69; and Joined Cases C-15/98 and C-105/99, *Italy and Saedegna Lines* v *Commission,* para. 66.
268. Joined Cases 296 and 318/82, *Leewarder Papierwarenfabriek,* paras 19 and 24.

Regulation.[269] In addition to this, depending on the circumstances, the Commission may assess the market position of the aid recipient, including the size of the undertaking's market share, the volume of trade in the product which the undertaking produces, and the general circumstances, structure and situation of the relevant market.[270] It is sufficient that the Commission demonstrates the probability that the aid will have a distorting effect by showing that in the actual circumstances the aid can lead to a distortion of competition,[271] while it is not necessary to give evidence about what distortion of competition the aid will in fact cause.[272] If the Commission were obliged to give evidence about the actual effect of aid which has already been given, this would benefit the Member States that have provided aid in breach of notification and standstill obligations, at the expense of those Member States that give notification of proposed aid.[273]

For the definition of the relevant market, the staring point will normally be the demand substitution between products.[274] This starting position is modified where a market capable of being distorted has not yet been established. However, Article 107 is also applicable where a market is only of a potential nature, as the aid may prevent new competitors entering the market, regardless of the fact that there may not yet be competition there.[275]

The relevant product market covers both goods and services that are delivered to or demanded from the recipient undertaking, as well as goods which are produced on the basis of these goods and services, and goods which are substitutable for them due to their characteristics, price or intended use.[276]

269. Case 730/79, *Philip Morris,* paras 8-13, where the CJ rejected Philip Morris' claim that the Commission should have undertaken the same assessment as in cases under Articles 101 and 102.
270. Joined Cases 296 and 318/82, *Leewarder Papierwarenfabriek,* para. 24.
271. Joined Cases T-92 and 103/00, *Territorio Histórico de Álava,* para. 70.
272. Joined Cases T-92 and 103/00, *Territorio Histórico de Álava,* para. 77; and Case T-55/99, *CETM* v *Commission,* para. 103.
273. Joined Cases T-92 and 103/00, *Territorio Histórico de Álava,* para. 77; and Case C-301/87, *Boussac,* para. 33.
274. See the Commission Notice on the definition of relevant market for the purposes of Community competition law, para. 15 et seq (OJ 1997 C 372/5) . The procedure for determining the relevant market set out in the Notice can in part be used as the basis for assessment in State aid cases; see note (1) of the Notice.
275. Joined Cases C-62/87 and C-72/87, *Walloon Regional Executive* v *Commission,* para. 15.
276. Commission Notice on the definition of relevant market for the purposes of Community competition law, para. 7 (OJ 1997 C 372/5). See also Commission Decision 72/253/EEC (OJ 1972 L 164/22).

Thus, the scope of the prohibition of State aid is not limited to measures that affect competition between two products that are in direct competition with each other, as is the case, for example, with different makes of cars. In this context it is sufficient to establish that competition between two products that are substitutable is affected, as might be the case with car transport and railway transport.[277]

The relevant geographic market is defined as 'the area in which the undertakings concerned are involved in the supply and demand of products or services, in which the conditions of competition are sufficiently homogeneous and which can be distinguished from neighbouring areas because the conditions of competition are appreciably different in those area.'[278] The relevant geographic market need not necessarily consist of a significant part of the internal market in order for Article 107(1) to apply. However, where aid to local or regional undertakings can only be assumed to affect competition in the local or regional area of the recipient undertakings, it is unlikely to affect trade between Member States.[279]

Competition within the internal market can be distorted even if the undertaking receiving the aid exports nearly all its production to third countries.[280] This can be the case where undertakings from the EU compete outside the internal market as well as inside it.

> In Case 142/87, *Tubemeuse*, the CJ stated that, 'having regard to the interdependence between the markets on which Community undertakings operate, it is possible that aid might distort competition within the Community, even if the undertaking receiving it exports almost all its production outside the Community. The exportation of part of the undertaking's production to non-member countries is only one of a number of circumstances which must be considered.'[281]

In the same way, aid to undertakings in third countries could affect competition within the internal market, and such aid must therefore also be assessed under the provisions on State aid.

277. See *Franz Philipp Sutter:* The Adria Wien Pipeline Case and the State Aid Provisions of the EC Treaty in Tax Matters, European Taxation 2001 pp. 239-250, at p. 243.
278. Commission Notice on the definition of relevant market for the purposes of Community competition law, para. 8 (OJ 1997 C 372/5).
279. Commission Decision 2001/605/EC, para. 29 (OJ 2001 L 212/34).
280. Case C-142/87, *Tubemeuse,* para. 35.
281. Case C-142/87, *Tubemeuse,* para. 32.

3.4.2. *Aid that affects trade between Member States*

Even though an aid measure distorts competition, it will only be covered by the State aid prohibition in Article 107(1) if it affects trade between Member States. Where the aid only affects trade internally within a Member State, or a Member State's trade with a third country, the Treaty provisions on State aid are not applicable. In such cases it is the Member State's own competition law and international trade agreements which govern the issue of State aid. The criterion of affecting trade thus contributes to the allocation of competences between the EU and the Member States.

Just as in relation to Articles 101 and 102, the term *trade* is interpreted broadly, and covers all economic transactions between Member States, such as the exchange of goods, services and capital. An effect on trade will normally be revealed by an artificial fall or an artificial increase in the imports or exports of the Member States.

As earlier stated, the condition on the effect on trade between Member States is interpreted broadly. Thus in Case 730/79, *Philip Morris*, the CJ held that when State aid strengthens the position of an undertaking compared with other undertakings competing in trade within the EU, that trade must be regarded as affected by that aid.[282]

The presumption previously referred to, that State aid distorts competition, thus leads to the presumption that such distortion of competition also affects trade between Member States, where it can be shown that the undertaking receiving the aid participates in trade within the EU.

However, it is not enough for the Commission merely to show that the undertaking in question participates in trade within the EU. The Commission has to show that it is probable that the aid actually or potentially involves an effect on trade between Member States.[283] However, this does not mean that the Commission has to show empirical evidence of the effect of the aid on trade within the EU,[284] but in its decision the Commission must clearly state the facts which mean that the aid can affect trade between Member States.

The effect of State aid on trade between Member States will particularly depend on the exports of the undertaking in question to the other Member States.[285] However, trade within the EU is not only considered to be affected

282. Case 730/79, *Philip Morris,* para. 11. See also Case C-42/93, *Spain* v *Commission,* para. 21.
283. Case C-142/87, *Tubemeuse.* See e.g. Case 730/79, *Philip Morris,* para. 11.
284. See *Franz Philipp Sutter:* The Adria Wien Pipeline Case and the State Aid Provisions of the EC Treaty in Tax Matters, European Taxation 2001 pp. 239-250, at p. 243.
285. Joined Cases 296 and 318/82, *Leewarder Papierwarenfabriek.*

when the undertaking receiving the aid itself directly participates in trade between Member States. If the products which are produced by the undertaking receiving the aid are the subject of cross-border trade, it does not matter whether it is the undertaking receiving the aid itself which is involved in the trade. A Member State's aid to an undertaking can thus mean that its domestic production is maintained or even increased so that the opportunities for undertakings established in the other Member States to export their products to that Member State will be reduced. Such aid can reduce the potential market for imports of products from other Member States, and can therefore affect trade between Member States and distort competition.[286]

Trade between Member States will also be affected within the meaning of Article 107(1) where the undertaking receiving aid exports (nearly) all its production to countries outside the EU.[287]

State aid for direct investments in third countries can likewise affect trade between Member States within the meaning of Article 107(1).288

Member States sometimes give financial incentives to influence undertakings as to where they locate their activities. This occurs particularly at regional level where, for example, a local government authority may seek to attract or retain commercial undertakings. If an undertaking moves from one Member State to another, this will in itself affect trade between Member States, both because of the change in manufacturing location, and because of the changes to the supply network to the undertaking.[289]

Trade between the Member States will not be affected, within the meaning of Article 107(1), if the aid only has a local effect.

> For this reason the Commission assessed that the unlawful tax deduction which Sparkassen Nordjylland was allowed to make in connection with the takeover of Himmerlandsbanken was not covered by the provisions of the Treaty. The aid measure could be considered State aid, but because of the local character of the undertaking, with its activities geographically

286. Case 102/87, *France* v *Commission,* para. 19. See correspondingly Case C-303/88, *ENI-Lanerossi,* para. 27; and Joined Cases T-298/97 and others, *Alzetta,* para. 91.
287. See Case C-142/87, *Tubemeuse,* where the Tubemeuse company exported 90 % of its production to third countries, para. 32.
288. XXIXth Report on competition policy, 2001 para. 260.
289. See Commission Decision 87/573/EEC (OJ 1987 L 347/64).

limited to North Jutland, where there were no foreign banks active, it did not affect trade within the meaning of Article 107(1).[290]

However, aid measures which do not affect cross-border trade can be covered by national rules on State aid.

Trade between Member States can also be affected if, in connection with internal infrastructure projects, the market conditions for domestic undertakings are improved, giving them a dominant position so as to make it difficult for foreign undertakings to penetrate the market.[291]

In several cases the CJ has rejected arguments that the fact that aid is of a modest extent, or that the undertaking receiving the aid is of a modest size, automatically means that trade between Member States will not be affected in one of the ways described above.[292] The CJ's practice thus does not leave room for the requirement that the effect on trade must be appreciable before Article 107(1) is applicable.[293]

3.4.3. The de minimis rule

As stated above, the application of the provision in Article 107(1) does not necessarily require that an aid measure affects competition and trade appreciably.[294] The CJ has not formulated an appreciability requirement as in the case of Article 101, but on the contrary in several cases it has held that even very small amounts of aid are incompatible with the internal market within the meaning of Article 107(1).[295]

The fact that the criterion for the effect on competition and trade between Member States is interpreted relatively broadly means that the Member States

290. Skat Udland 1995 p. 68. See also Case C-280/00, *Altmark,* paras 78-82
291. See *Franz Philipp Sutter:* The Adria Wien Pipeline Case and the State Aid Provisions of the EC Treaty in Tax Matters, European Taxation 2001 pp. 239-250, at p. 243.
292. Case C-142/87, *Tubemeuse,* paras 42 and 43; and Case C-113/00, *Spain* v *Commission,* para. 33.
293. Case C-303/88, *ENI-Lanerossi,* para. 27, where the CJ stated that even relatively modest aid can affect trade between Member States when there is intense competition in the sector concerned. See also Case 259/85, *France* v *Commission,* para. 24; Case C-173/03, *Heiser,* paras 32-35; Case C-42/93, *Spain* v *Commission,* para. 21; and Case 234/84, *Meura,* para. 22.
294. Joined Cases T-92 and 103/00, *Territorio Histórico de Álava,* para. 78; Case C-142/87, *Tubemeuse,* paras 42 and 43; and Case T-55/99, *CETM* v *Commission, para. 23.*
295. Case C-303/88, *ENI-Lanerossi,* para. 27; Case C-42/93, *Spain* v *Commission,* para. 21; and Case 234/84, *Meura,* para. 22.

have an obligation to notify numerous small aid measures. In order to reduce the administrative burden of this mass of notifications, and recognising that the Commission does not consider that aid measures without appreciable effect are covered by the State aid prohibition, in 1992 the Commission introduced a *de minimis* rule. This rule was originally adopted as a part of the framework provisions on State aid to small and medium sized enterprises before, in 1996, being separated out into a special *de minimis* notice.[296] The *de minimis* rules, previously laid down administratively, are now codified in Commission Regulation (EC) No 1998/2006 on the application of Articles 107 and 108 of the Treaty to *de minimis* aid.[297]

As a starting point, the *De minimis* Regulation covers horizontal aid to undertakings in all the sectors that are covered by the Treaty. However, certain forms of aid are excluded from the scope of the Regulation. This includes aid to undertakings in the fisheries and aquaculture sectors; aid to undertakings involved in the primary production of certain agricultural products; certain forms of aid for undertakings involved in the processing and marketing of agricultural products; the coal sector; aid to undertakings which carry out the transport of goods for hire or reward, for the purchase of road freight transport vehicles; aid for export-related activities; aid contingent upon the use of domestic products over imported products; and aid to undertakings in financial difficulties.[298]

The *de minimis* provision is based on the assumption that State aid of below a certain amount does not affect trade between Member States and/or distort or threaten to distort competition, and does not therefore fulfil the criteria for the prohibition in Article 107(1).

296. Community guidelines on State aid for small and medium-sized enterprises (SMEs), para. 3.2 (OJ 1992 C 213/2); and Commission notice on the *de minimis* rule for State aid (OJ 1996 C 68/9).

297. OJ 2006 L 379/5. The Commission Regulation was adopted under the authority of Council Regulation (EC) No 994/98 (OJ 1998 L 142/1). The original *de minimis* regulation, Commission Regulation (EC) No 69/2001 (OJ 2001 L 10/30), entered into force on 2 February 2001 and applied up to 31 December 2006. The *de minimis* provision is discussed by *Michael Berghofer:* The new de minimis regulation: enlarging the sword of Damocles?, European State Aid Law Quarterly (1) 2007 pp. 3-11. See also Commission Regulation (EU) No 360/2012 On the application og Articles 107 and 108 og the Treaty on the Functioning of the European Union to de minimis aid granted to undertakings providing services of general ecconomic interest (OJ 2012 L 114/8).

298. Article 1 of Regulation (EC) No 1998/2006 (OJ 2006 L 379/5).

In establishing this amount, the Regulation distinguishes between road transport undertakings and other undertakings. In principle, the total *de minimis* aid to an individual undertaking may not exceed a value corresponding to a cash payment of EUR 200,000 over a three year period.[299] However, this amount differs in relation to undertakings in the road transport sector, where the total *de minimis* aid to an individual undertaking may not exceed a value corresponding to a cash payment of EUR 100,000 over a three year period.[300] This means that an undertaking may receive aid corresponding to EUR 200,000 (or EUR 100,000 in the road transport sector) without the aid having to be notified to the Commission.[301] If an aid measure leads to the threshold being exceeded, the aid measure as a whole must be notified to the Commission with a view to getting the Commission's approval.[302] In this context, EU resources which are used to finance Member States' aid are included in the calculation of the accumulated aid, even though such resources are not considered to be state resources for the purpose of Article 107(1).[303]

4. Approval of State aid

An aid measure that fulfils all the criteria in Article 107(1) and which is therefore covered by the prohibition of State aid is in principle considered to be incompatible with the internal market. However, in Article 107(2) and (3) there are lists of situations which exhaustively state in what special circumstances the Commission *can* (Article 107(3)) or *must* (Article 107(2)) approve an aid measure as being compatible with the internal market. There is a similar provision in Article 108(2), third paragraph, whereby the Council may approve an aid measure as being compatible with the internal market.[304] In accordance with the practice of the CJ, these exemptions are interpreted restrictively.[305]

299. If aid is given in some other form than as cash, the aid must be calculated as the gross cash equivalent of the aid; Regulation (EC) No 1998/2006, Article 2(3).
300. Regulation (EC) No 1998/2006, Article 2(2).
301. Regulation (EC) No 1998/2006, Article 2(1). In relation to groups of companies, it will be the accumulated aid paid to the group as a whole which is relevant for the application of the *de minimis* provision.
302. Regulation (EC) No 1998/2006, Article 2(2).
303. Regulation (EC) No 1998/2006, Article 2(2). See the discussion in section 3.2.2.
304. Under Article 107(3)(e) the Council may also, on a proposal from the Commission, approve other categories of aid than those listed in the Article.
305. Case T-106/95, FFSA, para. 172.

The overall aim of the Commission in the area of State aid is to confirm and strengthen the application of the provisions on State aid both by effective control of the Member States' aid measures, and by the effective enforcement of the Treaty's provisions on State aid, with a view to reducing the extent of aid provided by the Member States and thereby limiting distortions of competition in the internal market.

On the basis of the European Council's encouragement, in March 2005, for State aid to be reduced and to be better targeted with a view to achieving the goals of growth and employment under the Lisbon Strategy,[306] in 2005 the Commission presented its 'State aid action plan – Less and better targeted State aid : a roadmap for State aid reform 2005-2009'.[307] The guidelines laid down for the reform include: less and better targeted State aid; a more refined economic approach; more effective procedures and better enforcement, predictability and transparency; and shared responsibility between the Commission and the Member States.

Following the European Council's encouragement for there to be less and better targeted State aid, the Member States have targeted more than 90 % of their State aid to horizontal goals of general interest, rather than to supporting individual undertakings or sectors. The total amount of the State aid provided by the Member States in 2010 is estimated to have been EUR 73.7 billion (0.6 % of the EU's GDP), and it has been more or less stable at 0.6 % of GDP

306. The Lisbon Strategy, adopted at the Extraordinary Meeting of the European Council in Lisbon on 23-24 March 2000, Council/00/900, is a strategy aimed at making the EU the most competitive and dynamic knowledge-based economy in the world by 2010. The Lisbon Strategy has now been replaced by the Europe 2020 Strategy, adopted by the Council on 17 June 2010, which seeks to ensure that the EU is a knowledge-based, sustainable and inclusive economy which is capable of providing high levels of productivity and employment and characterised by social cohesion. See the Communication from the Commission: EUROPE 2020 A strategy for smart, sustainable and inclusive growth (COM(2010) 2020 final).

307. COM(2005) 107 final of 7 June 2005. This Action Plan is discusses by *Neelie Kroes:* Reforming Europe's State Aid Regime: an Action Plan for Change, European State Aid Law Quarterly (3) 2005 pp. 387-390; *Andreas Bartosch:* Comment on Commissioner Kroes' New State Aid Action Plan, European State Aid Law Quarterly (3) 2005 pp. 391-392; *Chrisitan Koenig & Oliver C. Füg:* How to Put the EC State Aid Action Plan into Action – Rendering the Market Failure Test Operational, European State Aid Law Quarterly (4) 2005 pp. 591-592; and *Paul Heidhues & Rainer Nitsche*: Comments on state aid reform: Some implications of an effects-based approach, European State Aid Law Quarterly (1) 2006 pp. 23-34.

since 2008.[308] In addition, in 2010 the Commission approved crisis-related aid of EUR 383.8 billion (3.1 % of the EU's GDP).[309]

The high level of total State aid within the EU reflects the fact that, despite its policy aims, the Commission largely approves the Member States' provision of State aid. This approval practice is based on the fact that it is to a certain extent regarded as legitimate to use aid in support of purposes which have a high priority in the EU.[310] For example, this is the case in relation to aid for small and medium sized enterprises, environmental protection, research and development and innovation, employment, regions and culture. At the same time, in its State aid action plan the Commission has listed a number of areas that are prioritised with regard to the goals of the Lisbon Strategy. These priority areas are: innovation and research and development; creating a better business climate and stimulating entrepreneurship; investing in human capital; high quality services of general economic interest; better prioritisation through simplification and consolidation; a focused regional aid policy; encouraging an environmentally sustainable future; and setting up modern transport, energy and information and communication technology infrastructures.

The Commission's approach in regard to approving the State aid measures of the Member States is based on two significant requirements. First, the aid must promote the aims and interests of the *EU*.[311] This means that the interests of the Member State in giving the aid and the interests of the recipient in receiving it are irrelevant. Second, the aid must be *necessary* for promoting the aims and interests in question.[312] This requirement means that if, without the intervention of the Member State, market forces can promote the aims and interests to a sufficient degree, aid for the promotion of these aims cannot be approved. The aid must thus attempt both to make good an identified market failure and encourage the undertaking that receives the aid to change its conduct in such a way that it initiates an activity which it would not otherwise

308. State aid Scoreboard (COM(2011) 848 final), pp. 5 and 6.
309. State aid Scoreboard (COM(2011) 848 final), p. 9.
310. Article 107(2) and (3) lists a number of overriding purposes which mean or which can mean that a State aid measure is compatible with the internal market.
311. Case 730/79, *Philip Morris,* paras 16 and 17.
312. Case 730/79, *Philip Morris,* para. 17. See also Commission Decision 98/251/EF (OJ 1998 L 103/28), on a proposal by Austria to give aid to Hoffmann-La Roche for the development of a medicine. At the time when it was proposed to give Hoffmann-La Roche research and development aid, the development project had already been brought to a successful conclusion, so the Member State was unable to show that the aid was necessary.

have done without the aid, or which it would only have carried out in a more limited or to a different extent.[313] At the same time, the aid must be proportionate to its aim.

The Commission's approach to the application of the State aid rules in relation to the various industrial, environmental and social policy aims which can, under certain circumstances, be legitimately promoted via State aid are to some extent expressed in the adoption of the block exemption regulations,[314] and to some extent in the publication of a number of soft law instruments in the form of guidelines, notices and framework provisions,[315] which the Commission has adopted in order to give some predictability about what State aid measures are likely to be approved. Thus, the Commission has adopted guidelines on the application of the State aid rules in relation to aid for rescuing and restructuring undertakings which are in financial difficulties, aid for measures for environmental protection, and aid for research and development.[316] In connection with the financial crisis the Commission has used a number of temporary guidelines, of which among others the banking rules are still in force.[317]

313. A non-paper from DG Competition: Common principles for an economic assessment of the compatibility of State aid under Article 87(3).
314. Commission Regulation (EC) No 1998/2006 on the application of Articles 87 and 88 of the Treaty to *de minimis* aid (OJ 2006 L 379/5); and Commission Regulation (EC) No 800/2008 declaring certain categories of aid compatible with the common market in application of Articles 87 and 88 of the Treaty (General block exemption Regulation) (OJ 2008 L 214/3).
315. For a more detailed discussion of soft law and the legal significance of its measures, see *Linda Senden:* Soft Law in European Community Law, 2004; *Michelle Cini:* The Soft Law Approach: Commission rule-making in the state aid regime, Journal of European Public Policy Vol. 8(2) 2001 pp. 192-207; *Mona Aldestam* in *Ulrika Mörth (ed.):* Soft Law in Governance and Regulation, 2004, Chapter 2. See also Case C-69/05, *Commission* v *Luxembourg;* and Case T-198/01, *Technische Glaswerke.*
316. Community guidelines on State aid for rescuing and restructuring firms in difficulty (OJ 2004 C 244/2); Community guidelines on State aid for environmental protection (OJ 2008 C 82/1); and Community framework for State aid for research and development and innovation (OJ 2006 C 323/1). When the Commission assesses whether State aid is compatible with the internal market, it uses the substantive rules which applied at the time when the aid was given; see Commission notice on the determination of the applicable rules for the assessment of unlawful State aid (OJ 2002 C 119/22). This approach is in line with the established practice of the courts, see e.g. Case T-357/02, *Freistaat Sachsen,* para. 94.
317. Communication from the Commission on the application, from 1 January 2012, of State aid rules to support measures in favour of banks in the context of the financial crisis (OJ 2011 C 356/7).

Just as the Commission has a positive view of certain purposes of State aid, there are also some purposes for State aid which are automatically considered incompatible with the internal market. This applies in particular to aid which is aimed at promoting an undertaking's exports. Measures which are aimed at supporting the operation of an undertaking are also considered, in principle, to be incompatible with the internal market.

4.1. Aid for exports

The kinds of aid which are considered to be aid to export-related activities include 'aid directly linked to the quantities exported, to the establishment and operation of a distribution network or to other current expenditure linked to the export activity.'[318] The aim of such aid is to directly influence competition between the undertaking receiving the aid and its actual and potential competitors. The harmful effects of State aid for exports are therefore clear. For this reason the Commission regards export aid for trade between the Member States as incompatible with the internal market, as the export aid is clearly contrary to the goals of the EU. For this reason export aid is not covered by the *De minimis* Regulation.[319] For the same reason the Commission considers export aid as not suitable for exemption from the prohibition of State aid, regardless of the intensity or form of the aid, or what other aims or reasons there may be for the aid.[320]

4.2. Operating aid

An undertaking which receives operating aid is relieved of the expenses which it would normally have to bear in its day-to-day management and its usual activities.[321] The Commission interprets operating aid broadly and in this respect, for example, aid for advertising campaigns and aid for market research are considered to be operating aid.[322] Aid of this kind has a direct effect on production costs and sales prices and therefore in principle it distorts competition within the business sector where it is granted.[323] For this reason

318. Article 1(d) of Commission Regulation (EC) No 1998/2006 (OJ 2006 L 379/5).
319. Article 1 of Commission Regulation (EC) No 1998/2006 (OJ 2006 L 379/5).
320. VIIth Report on competition policy, 1978, para. 242. This view was acknowledged by the CJ in Joined Cases 6 and 11/69, *Commission* v *France*. The case concerned a French preferential rate for rediscounting on the export of goods, with the aim that the exported goods could compete with the domestically produced goods in the other Member States.
321. See the definition of operating aid in Case T-459/93, *Siemens,* para. 48.
322. Case T-459/93, *Siemens.*
323. Commission Decision 92/398 (OJ 1992 L 207/47).

operating aid will, in principle, not be exempted under Article 107(3), as such aid will not promote the purposes referred to in the provision.[324] When such aid comes to an end, the undertaking is back where it was before, without the aid having contributed to the promotion of the EU's aims or interests.

However, in special circumstances operating aid could be covered by Article 107(3), as long as the aid is used for the promotion of one of the legitimate purposes of aid referred to above. The Commission has therefore exceptionally approved operating aid, on condition that the aid is necessary, temporary and in principle degressive, and that the aid only compensates for the additional costs incurred by the undertaking from the pursuit of the purpose in question. Such approvals have primarily concerned operating aid in the area of energy saving, among other things in the form of tax advantages, as well as operating aid for the treatment of waste.

4.3. Investment aid

In contrast to aid for exports and operating aid, investment aid will often contribute to the promotion of the EU's aims and interests. Aid for investment gives undertakings a financial incentive to make investments which are necessary for bringing them into line with the applicable laws, such as investing in environmental protection measures which go beyond the applicable laws. For this reason investment aid will, to a large extent, be approved by the Commission.

The assessment of whether an aid measure is investment aid or operating aid is made in an EU context. It is thus irrelevant how national tax or accounting rules classify the aid.

4.4. Possibilities for approval

4.4.1. Article 107(2)

Article 107(2) states that certain forms of aid *are* compatible with the internal market. According to this provision, this includes certain forms of aid of a social character, certain forms of aid to make good damage caused by natural disasters,[325] and certain forms of aid for areas of Germany affected by the division of Germany. What these forms of aid have in common is that they all have the aim of re-establishing the financial and competitive situation of aid recipients prior to them being affected by the relevant event. The aid must

324. Case T-459/93, *Siemens,* para. 48. See also Case C-86/89, *Italy* v *Commission,* para. 8.
325. See e.g. XXIVth Report on competition policy, 1995, para. 354, concerning aid given because of flood damage caused by the Meuse going over its banks.

therefore not go beyond what is necessary to re-establish the aid recipient's financial position.[326]

When applying Article 107(2), the Commission's powers are limited to establishing whether the aid measure satisfies the conditions for being covered by the exemption. If this is confirmed, the Commission must approve the measure, unless the Commission finds that the measure is not proportionate to the aim pursued, or is not compatible with the general principles of Union law or with the other provisions of the Treaty. This means that the Commission does not have any discretion to refuse approval.[327]

4.4.2. Article 107(3)

Article 107(3) gives the Commission the possibility of approving State aid for promoting development in certain regions or certain areas of the economy, as well as for the realisation of important projects of common European interest, and to promote and conserve culture.[328]

The Commission has wide discretion in deciding whether an aid measure can be approved in accordance with Article 107(3). The assessment of an aid measure's compatibility or lack of compatibility with the internal market raises a number of problems which involve considerations of a technical and a political nature, as well as consideration for the overall economic situation.[329] In this connection, the Commission has to take as its starting point an assessment of the need for the aid in an EU context. This assessment covers not only the need to achieve the economic goals of the EU, but also the need to achieve other goals which are important to the EU.[330] In this connection the Commission weighs the negative effects of the aid on trade and competition against the positive effect on the achievement of the EU's goals.[331]

The Commission cannot approve an aid measure which conflicts with one of the other provisions of the Treaty. Regardless of whether an aid measure could be exempted from the prohibition of State aid, it cannot be approved if,

326. See *Heidenhain:* European State Aid Law, 2010 p. 148.
327. Case 730/79, *Philip Morris,* para. 17. For further discussion of the exemption provisions see *Heidenhain:* European State Aid Law, 2010 pp. 147-149.
328. In relation to the provision on aid for culture in Article 107(3)(d), see e.g. Commission Decision 1999/133/EC, *CELF* (OJ 1999 L 44/37).
329. Case T-149/95, *Ducros,* para. 63.
330. See the Opinion of Advocate General Capotorti in Case 730/79, *Philip Morris.*
331. A non-paper from DG Competition: Common principles for an economic assessment of the compatibility of State aid under Article 87(3), p. 3.

for example, it conflicts with freedom of establishment or the right of free movement of goods.

4.4.3. Article 108(2), third paragraph

According to Article 108(2), third paragraph, when exceptional circumstances justify it, the Council may decide, unanimously, that an aid measure should be considered as compatible with the internal market. This applies regardless of the State aid assessment which may be made under the provisions in Article 107 or the regulations adopted in accordance with Article 109.

A Member State can submit a request to the Council for the application of Article 108(2), third paragraph, before the Commission decides that the aid in question is not compatible with the internal market. If the Commission has made such a decision on the incompatibility of the aid measure, the Council no longer has powers to apply Article 108(2), third paragraph, as a basis for declaring the State aid measure concerned to be incompatible with the internal market.[332]

The provision in Article 108(2), third paragraph, is not often used, but it has been used in a few cases to approve aid measures in the agricultural sector and the transport sector, among others.

332. Case C-110/02, *Commission* v *Council,* para. 33; and Case C-399/03, *Commission* v *Council.*

CHAPTER X

Public undertakings

Michael Steinicke

Bibliography: *Andreas Bala: Art. 90 Abs 2 im System unverfälschten Wettbewerbs, 1997; Rudolf Benesch: Die Kompetenzen der EG-Kommission aus Art. 90 Abs. 3 EWG-V, 1993; Blum & Logue: State Monopolies under EC Law, 1999; Christopher Bright: Article 90, Economic Policy and the Duties of Member States, European Competition Law Review 1993 p. 263; David Edwards and Mark Hoskins: Article 90: Deregulation and EC Law, Reflections arising from the XVI FIDE Conference, Common Market Law Review 1995 p. 157; Joseph Fesenmair: Öffentliche Dienstleistungmonopole im europäischen Recht, 1995; Andreas Heinemann: Grenzen staatlicher Monopole im EG-Vertrag, 1996; Jan Keller: Service Public und Art. 86 Abs. 2 EGV, 1999; Jose Luis Buendia Sierra: Exclusive Rights and State Monopolies under EC Law, 1999.*

1. Introduction

Over the last 25 years public undertakings have attracted considerable political attention. The number of cases which have been brought before the Court of Justice of the European Union (CJ) concerning the provisions on public undertakings has increased in line with this.

In principle, public undertakings are covered by the same provisions as private undertakings, in other words primarily Articles 101 and 102. This applies to public undertakings which operate independently of public authorities and on an equal footing with other undertakings in the market. However, it is only a minority of public undertakings that are independent of public authorities. Most public undertakings have a connection to a public authority in the way in which they benefit from special rights, for example concessions, legal monopolies and similar. This means that the majority of public undertakings do not operate on an equal footing with private undertakings, but have special advantages over competing undertakings. In the Treaty on the functioning of the European Union, Articles 106 and 37 contain provisions which are intended to ensure that competition is not distorted under the special conditions of competition which apply when one undertaking has been granted an exclusive right. While the subject of this chapter is public undertakings, Articles 106 and 37 apply equally to privately owned undertakings where they have been granted special or exclusive rights by a public authority. The granting of such rights makes these undertakings 'public' in the sense that by granting such rights the granting authority establishes and maintains some form of influence over such undertakings. This means that the public authority has the possibility of influencing the market and so Articles 106 and 37 are primarily aimed at the decisions of public authorities or the Member States.

To the extent that these privileged undertakings conduct themselves in a way which distorts competition independently and without reference to the exclusive or special right they have been granted, their conduct will not be governed by Article 106 or Article 37, but by the ordinary competition rules in Articles 101 and 102.

As stated, in this chapter the focus is on two of the Treaty's provisions, namely Article 37 and Article 106. These provisions govern the special situations where public entities do not act as administrative authorities, but rather as market participants. The aim of these provisions is to ensure that the Treaty provisions for securing the conditions of competition (i.e., the competition rules and the rules on freedom of movement) are also complied with in cases where there is a public undertaking, rather than the exercise of administrative authority.

2. Presentation of the provisions

Article 106(1) of the Treaty provides that a Member State may not enact or maintain any measure contrary to the rules in the Treaty in respect of such undertakings as the Member State grants special or exclusive rights, or in relation their conduct towards public undertakings. The provision refers in particular to infringements of the Treaty's competition rules and of the prohibition on discrimination in Article 18 of the Treaty.

According to Article 106(2), undertakings which have been entrusted with the operation of services of general economic interest or which have the character of a revenue-producing monopoly are subject to the rules of the Treaty, in particular to the rules on competition, in so far as the application of such rules does not obstruct the performance, in law or in fact, of the particular tasks assigned to them. It concludes by stating that the development of trade must not be affected to such an extent as would be contrary to the interests of the Union.

Finally, in Article 106(3) the Commission is given powers to address appropriate directives or decisions to Member States to ensure that the provisions of the Article are applied.

Article 37(1) of the Treaty, on State monopolies, states:

> 'Member States shall adjust any State monopolies of a commercial character so as to ensure that no discrimination regarding the conditions under which goods are procured and marketed exists between nationals of Member States.
>
> The provisions of this Article shall apply to any body through which a Member State, in law or in fact, either directly or indirectly supervises, determines or appreciably influences imports or exports between Member States. These provisions shall likewise apply to monopolies delegated by the State to others.'

Under Article 37(2), Member States must refrain from introducing any new measure which is contrary to the principles laid down in Article 37(1).

2.1. Terminology

The terminology used in the above provisions, as well as in a number of secondary acts of Union law, is very varied. For example, in relation to the exclusive right which is granted to undertakings, the terms used are 'exclusive right', 'legal monopoly', 'concession' etc. For the purposes of this presentation it has been decided to use uniform terms when referring to general circumstances. Thus, the terms used are: *privileged undertaking*, in relation to entities that have been granted rights; *privileged activity*, for the activity which benefits from protection; and *exclusive or special rights*, in respect of the right which is granted to privileged undertakings. In respect of specific rights, the terms used are those used in the particular provisions concerned.

3. The aims and structure of the provisions

Articles 106 and 37 differ in their formulation and in the contexts in which they apply, but they nevertheless have a sufficient degree of similarity in their content to enable them to be treated together here.

3.1. The application of Article 106 and Article 37

Article 345 of the Treaty in essence states that the Member States have the right to organise themselves as they wish. This means that the Member States can organise their undertakings as they find best. At the same time, the organisation of undertakings in the individual Member States must naturally comply with the Treaty's other rules on market conduct, i.e. in particular: the prohibition on discrimination on grounds of nationality (Article 18); the freedoms of movement (in particular Articles 34, 45, 49 and 56); the competition rules (Articles 101 and 102); and the rules on State aid (Articles 107 and 108).

Both Article 37 and Article 106 should be read in conjunction with Article 345 which states that the Treaty in no way affects the rules of Member States governing the system of property ownership. Thus the Treaty does not affect the right of Member States to organise an undertaking according to the legal form that each Member State may choose. Thus, in principle it is primarily the *activities* of the undertaking in question more than the *existence of a monopoly* which the Treaty regulates. This is also reflected in the wording of Article 37 in particular, which requires Member States to *adjust* any State monopolies of a commercial character and not to wind them up. Nor does the wording of Article 106 prevent Member States from organising their activities as they find most appropriate.

In its earlier practice the CJ established that the only thing that could be disputed in connection with a public authority's allocation of rights to undertakings was not the rights themselves or their form (the existence of sole rights), but only the illegal exercise of the sole right; see Case 155/73, *Sacchi*.

At the start of the 1990s this practice was modified so that even the right itself can now be found to be in breach of Article 106 or Article 37.[1]

Article 37 of the Treaty requires State monopolies of a commercial character[2] and undertakings with a state concession to comply with the prohibition on quantitative restrictions on imports.

As is clear from the wording of the provisions, the basic difference between Article 37 and Article 106 is that the rules on State monopolies of a commercial character contain an independent prohibition, while Article 106 refers to the Treaty's other provisions.

Both Article 37 and Article 106 cover both measures adopted at State level and regional and local measures.[3] Where references are made to the Mem-

1. Thus, see Case C-320/91, *Corbeau.*
2. In Case 6/64, *Costa* v *ENEL,* a commercial monopoly was defined as first, a monopoly which has as its object transactions regarding a commercial product capable of being the subject of competition and trade between Member States, and secondly it must play an effective part in such trade.
3. Case 30/87, *Bodson,* para. 13

ber States, they must be interpreted broadly so as to cover all levels of public authorities in the Member States.

While Article 37 imposes obligations on Member States in relation to monopoly undertakings, the provision does not contain any specific obligations for the undertakings themselves. Article 106(1) contains an obligation for the Member States, while Article 106(2) contains both an obligation and an exception for undertakings.

Article 37 is concerned exclusively with imports (and exports) of goods, whereas Article 106 refers to all the provisions of the Treaty, and in particular the competition rules and the prohibition of discrimination on grounds of nationality.

For both articles it is the case that all undertakings and bodies which have been granted a State concession are covered, regardless of their legal status.[4]

It is clear from Article 37 and Article 106 that the two provisions overlap each other to a considerable degree. The distinction between Article 37 and Article 106 is that Article 37 has a *lex specialis* function in relation to Article 106(1), but it is subordinate to Article 106(2).

3.2. Those to whom the provisions are addressed

Article 106(1) is addressed in particular to the Member States. However, it does not only refer to central government authorities, but also covers local and regional government bodies.[5] In addition, Article 106(2) also applies to the measures which the undertakings themselves adopt.

3.3. The application of Article 106

As is clear from the wording of Article 106, the provision contains no direct independent prohibition, but refers to other provisions of the Treaty, of which some are emphasised.[6] These emphasised provisions are the prohibition on discrimination in Article 18 and the competition rules. The practice has shown that the primary application of Article 106 has been in connection with problems involving abuses of dominant positions, i.e. in connection with Article 102.

4. Case 30/87, *Bodson,* para. 13.
5. Case 30/87, *Bodson.*
6. This indirect construction has been criticised several times; see e.g. *Gareth Davies* who directly states that ‘The Treaty, and society, would be better if it was gone’, p. 67 in *Kajewski, Neergaard & Van de Gronden (eds.):* The Changing legal framework for Services of General Interest in Europe, 2009.

Article 106 has also been applied in connection with other Treaty provisions, in particular Article 56 on freedom to provide services. In particular, Article 56 has been used in connection with Article 106(2) which provides for the application of the Treaty provisions to undertakings which have been entrusted with the provision of services of general economic interest.

4. Article 106(1)

4.1. Concepts

4.1.1. Special or exclusive rights

Some of the decisive concepts in Article 106 are *special or exclusive rights*. The CJ has not given a clear definition of theses terms, but there a number of indications for how they should be understood.

The CJ has not explicitly decided on the question of when an exclusive right exists. However, in the legal literature there is agreement that such a right exists when there is an exclusive right to carry on some specific activity, i.e. a legal monopoly.[7]

The right of exclusivity means that it is (only) the owner of the right who may carry on the activity in question. In principle it is irrelevant how the owner of the right in fact exercises this right. Thus, the owner of the right can make agreements with other undertakings for them to take on certain of the activities, as long as there is provision for this in the agreement with the entity granting the right.

It is more difficult to determine when a special right exists. The term *special right* has not been more precisely defined by the CJ.[8]

For a possible definition, reference can be made to the definition of the same term in Directive 2006/111, on the transparency of financial relations between Member States and public undertakings as well as on financial transparency within certain undertakings (as amended). 'Special rights' are defined there as: 'rights that are granted by a Member State

7. Inspiration can be drawn from Article 2(f) of Directive 2006/111, on the transparency of financial relations between Member States and public undertakings as well as on financial transparency within certain undertakings (as amended), in which exclusive rights are regarded as 'rights that are granted by a Member State to one undertaking through any legislative, regulatory or administrative instrument, reserving it the right to provide a service or undertake an activity within a given geographical area'.
8. However, in point 50 of his Opinion in Joined Cases 271, 281 and 289/90, *Spain, Belgium and Italy* v *Commission* (on telecommunications services), Advocate General Jacobs argued there must be special rights when a right is given to a limited number of undertakings.

to a limited number of undertakings, through any legislative, regulatory or administrative instrument, which, within a given geographical area:

- limits to two or more the number of such undertakings, authorised to provide a service or undertake an activity, otherwise than according to objective, proportional and non-discriminatory criteria, or
- designates, otherwise than according to such criteria, several competing undertakings, as being authorised to provide a service or undertake an activity, or
- confers on any undertaking or undertakings, otherwise than according to such criteria, any legal or regulatory advantages which substantially affect the ability of any other undertaking to provide the same service or to operate the same activity in the same geographical area under substantially equivalent conditions.'[9]

To the extent that authority can be found in secondary legislation, there can be special rights when more than one undertaking has been granted a right to carry on an activity in a given area, or where one or more undertakings has been granted advantages in relation to other undertakings, but where the right to carry on the activity in question is open to all undertakings.

The question could be asked whether there are certain limits as to the kinds of advantages that will result in the application of Article 106. For example, to what extent will Article 106 be applicable to a situation where the competitors of an undertaking are subject to certain administrative burdens to which the privileged undertaking is not subject? It must be assumed that the competitive advantage must be given to the privileged undertaking rather than to its competitors. Where the competitors are subject to burdens, it is possible that the Treaty's provisions on freedom of movement will apply instead. Furthermore, it must be considered how significant an advantage must be in order for Article 106 to be applicable. It is apparent from the definition in Directive 2006/111, on the transparency of financial relations between Member States and public undertakings, that a special right will exist where the competitive advantage which a privileged undertaking obtains means that competition is not on 'substantially equivalent conditions'. On this basis, the granting of minor advantages, which only have a limited significance for the competitive situation, would presumably not be enough for it to be found that a special right exists.

9. Directive 2006/111 Article 2(g).

Within the meaning of Article 106, the terms *special or exclusive rights* do not include intellectual property rights[10] or rights to practise a profession subject to authorisation.

4.1.2. The grant of a right

The grant of a special or exclusive right can be by means of traditional public law methods, such as by legislation or by an administrative decision, as well as by private law methods, such as by a contract. The assessment which is used for determining whether a right has been granted is thus functional and not formal. Where a grant is made in the form of a public law act, for example by legislation, there will clearly be a grant, in the sense of the wording of Article 106. Where a grant is made in the form of an agreement, it is decisive whether the grant is made on the basis of legislation or some other administrative act, and whether the measure making the grant is drawn up by a public authority or public undertaking. Where the grant is made by a public undertaking, this will probably not constitute a grant within the meaning of Article 106, since such a body will lack the powers of a public administrative body.

In Case 30/87, *Bodson*, the CJ considered whether the grant by local authorities of exclusive rights to provide funeral services was covered by Article 106. The CJ stated: 'As the Commission has rightly pointed out, Article 85 [now Article 101] of the Treaty applies, according to its actual wording, to agreements 'between undertakings'. It does not apply to contracts for concessions concluded between communes acting in their capacity as public authorities and undertakings entrusted with the operation of a public service', see the eighteenth paragraph of the judgment. In Case C-393/92, *Almelo*, the CJ had to consider whether an agreement entered into between a regional energy supplier and a local energy supplier for the exclusive supply of energy was covered by Article 106. The CJ stated: 'IJM has not been granted an exclusive concession giving it a monopoly in the supply of electricity within the territory covered by the concession. Secondly, the contracts giving rise to the dispute before the national court were concluded not between the public authorities and IJM but between a regional distributor and local distributors. Moreover, those contracts determine the conditions under which IJM supplies electric power to the local distributors, and do not have the effect of transferring to those distributors the public

10. There are several reasons why the term 'exclusive rights' does not cover the exclusive rights granted under intellectual property law. First, the rights referred to in Article 106 have a wider area of protection than intellectual property rights. Intellectual property rights protect individual trade marks or products, whereas Article 106 is directed at certain activities. Furthermore, the basic consideration of intellectual property law is consideration for undertakings and their possibilities of commercially exploiting the products they develop and their trade reputation, whereas the concern behind Article 106 is for the protection of the internal market as well as certain general interests of society; see Article 106(2).

service concession granted to the regional undertaking. The conditions of supply, in particular the exclusive purchasing clause, stem from the agreement between the parties and are not inherent in the territorial concession granted to IJM by the public authorities.'[11]

4.1.3. *Undertaking*

The concept of an undertaking is important for both Article 106(1) and (2). An 'undertaking' is defined in Union competition law as an entity which is engaged in some economic activity. The difficult point in this context is *economic activity*.

Activities which are carried on in the private market will often naturally be characterised as economic activities. However, there are a number of activities which, to a certain extent, *can* be undertaken by the private market, but the private market may not give the same results as are obtained when the performance of the tasks is under public control.

According to the case law, for example, the business of an employment agency is covered by the term 'economic activity', while air traffic control and environmental monitoring and control of harbours are not considered economic activities. The CJ has also stated that the services of providing insurance and pensions *can* be economic activities, depending on the way in which the individual arrangements are set up. The CJ has also stated that the fact that an entity makes purchases and thereby acts on the market using economic means, does not in itself mean that the public body in question qualifies as an undertaking. What is decisive for whether a purchase is regarded as part of the running of an undertaking is the subsequent use of the purchased product or service. If the product is to be part of a commercial arrangement and subsequently sold, the activity is regarded as an economic activity. If the product purchased is used in the ordinary running of the entity, and is thus not resold, the purchase will not in itself be regarded as an economic activity; see Case C-205/03 P, *FENIN*.

It is possible to classify the situations where the CJ has had to consider to what extent there were an economic activity, and thus an undertaking. First, there are individual services, which are characterised by being aimed at a specific person or a defined group of persons. Second, there are collective services which are characterised by the fact that the recipient of the service is society as a whole, and not an individual or group of individuals.

Most of the cases which the CJ has considered in the category of individual services have concerned various forms of insurance, though primarily pensions policies. See for example

11. Para. 31 of the judgment.

Case C-67/96, *Albany International*; Case C-244/94, *Fédération Francaise Societes d'Assurances*; Joined Cases C-159 and 160/91, *Poucet*; and Case C-218/00, *Cisal*. In these cases the CJ found that the most important factor in judging whether there was an economic activity was the element of solidarity, i.e. whether the insurance scheme was arranged so that there was no direct link between the premiums paid and the benefits obtained. When assessing other activities it can be expected that the degree of solidarity which characterises the activity will be decisive – in other words, whether the activity is carried on for the benefit of society, or whether there are exclusively individual arrangements between the service provider and the individual citizen.

The case law relating to collective service provision is dealt with primarily in two leading cases: Case C-364/92, *Eurocontrol*; and C-343/95, *Calí*. In the *Eurocontrol* case the CJ considered whether the activity of air traffic control was covered by the term 'economic activity'. The CJ found that it was not, and emphasised the nature of the activity, the aim of the activity, and the rules to which the activity was subject. The CJ stated that: 'Taken as a whole, Eurocontrol's activities, by their nature, their aim and the rules to which they are subject, are connected with the exercise of powers relating to the control and supervision of air space which are typically those of a public authority. They are not of an economic nature justifying the application of the Treaty rules of competition.'[12]

4.1.4. Public undertaking

The term 'public undertaking' is not defined in Article 106 or elsewhere in the Treaty. It can be said that a public undertaking will exist if the undertaking is in public or state ownership. It will not matter whether the undertaking is separated from the public authority as an independent legal person. Questions can arise where an undertaking is only partially in public ownership. The CJ has found it decisive whether there is a level of public control over the undertaking corresponding to the level of control which is required under Article 2 of Directive 2006/111, on the transparency of financial relations between Member States and public undertakings as well as on financial transparency within certain undertakings.[13] This means that an undertaking is public where a public authority can exercise direct or indirect control over the undertaking. There is an assumption that this is the case where a public authority: (1) directly or indirectly controls more than half of the undertaking's share capital; (2) controls more than half of the voting rights; or (3) can appoint more than half of the members of the undertaking's administration, management or supervisory bodies.

The decision whether an undertaking is a public undertaking should not be made on the basis of a formal interpretation, as this could lead to a risk of attempts at avoidance. Such

12. Case C-364/92, *Eurocontrol,* para. 30.
13. Joined Cases 188 to 190/80, *France, Italy and United Kingdom* v *Commission.*

attempts take one of two forms. First, the public authority could try to camouflage the economic activity as being the exercise of administrative authority, or seek to integrate the economic activity with the exercise of administrative authority; second, the public authority could outsource the activity to a private company, without maintaining any of the formal controls referred to above. However, regardless of the form of avoidance used, it will be caught by one of the Treaty's other provisions. As stated in Chapter 1, the exercise of public authority is covered by the Treaty provisions on freedom of movement, while the activities of private undertakings are directly covered by Articles 101 and 102.

4.2. The application of Article 106

Infringements of Article 106(1) can occur in many different circumstances. There follows a systematic presentation of groups of arrangements that are assumed to be in breach of Article 106, in combination with the other provisions of the Treaty.

4.2.1. The demand doctrine

There can be an infringement of Article 106 (in connection with Article 102) if the exclusive right covers an activity which is not effectively taken care of by the privileged undertaking. The doctrine was laid down in Case C-41/90, *Höfner*. In this case it was claimed by Höfner, that the State employment exchange could not meet the market demand for managers – a service that was provided by Höfner. The CJ held that it was contrary to Article 106, in conjunction with Article 102, to exclude private undertakings from providing this particular form of employment agency service, which consisted of arranging for the introduction of managers to vacant senior positions.

A similar, but not identical, problem is that of *special services*. The CJ has held that an exclusive right may not be expanded so as to cover special services which have not previously been offered; see Case C-320/91, *Corbeau*.

> In Case C-320/91, *Corbeau*, the CJ found that it was an abuse of a dominant position, and thus an infringement of Article 102 and Article 106, that an undertaking was prevented from providing a special service, so that an exclusive right was expanded to cover this service. The case concerned the Belgian postal monopoly. A businessman, Pierre Corbeau, offered a new postal service which consisted of collecting mail from the sender and delivering it before 12.00 on the following day. The Belgian postal authority argued that Corbeau's activity was covered by the postal monopoly and it was therefore not a lawful activity for Corbeau. In paragraph 19 of its judgment the CJ stated: 'the exclusion of competition is not justified as regards specific services dissociable from the service of general interest which meet special needs of economic operators and

> which call for certain additional services not offered by the traditional postal service, such as collection from the senders' address, greater speed or reliability of distribution or the possibility of changing the destination in the course of transit, in so far as such specific services, by their nature and the conditions in which they are offered, such as the geographical area in which they are provided, do not compromise the economic equilibrium of the service of general economic interest performed by the holder of the exclusive right.'

According to the practice of the CJ there are a number of conditions which must be fulfilled for a private undertaking to be able to claim that an exclusive right does not cover special services. *First*, the special service must not be connected with services of a general economic interest; *second*, the special services in question must meet a particular need of business; *third*, the special service must be a supplementary service which the privileged undertaking does not offer; and *fourth*, the special service may not, according to its nature or the terms under which it is provided, disturb the economic stability of the exclusive right.

4.2.2. Cross-subsidising

The activities which privileged undertakings have been granted the exclusive right to carry out will often be difficult to perform satisfactorily on market terms. Therefore the performance of these activities will often be made at a loss. As will be clear from the discussion below concerning Article 106(2), public undertakings are permitted to make some form of financial equalisation in order to cover for the loss-making privileged activity. This financial equalisation can be made by means of carrying out profitable activities alongside the privileged activities.

The CJ has held that it is an infringement of Article 106, in conjunction with Article 102, to transfer financial resources from a protected activity to an activity which is exposed to competition. Thus, for example, it is not permitted to transfer public funds paid to support a privileged activity to an activity which is carried out in a competitive market. If this happens, there will be distortion of the competition on the free market.

Cross-subsidising also takes place within undertakings which have not been granted special rights, and in this case the cross-subsidisation only has to be assessed in relation to Article 102. In contrast to cross-subsidising by a privileged undertaking, cross-subsidising by a private undertaking is only contrary to Article 102 if the transferred funds are used for *predatory pricing*.

The General Court has accepted the use of means set aside for privileged activities for the acquisition of undertakings on other markets which are exposed to competition; see Case T-175/99, *UPS*.

4.2.3. Expansion of the exclusive right

In Case 18/88, *RTT*, the CJ had to decide on a referral for a judicial ruling under Article 267 of the Treaty. The case concerned the Belgian telecommunications monopoly RTT. The Belgian supermarket chain, GB-Inno-BM, had sold telephones which were not approved by RTT. RTT wanted GB-Inno-BM to stop selling the non-approved telephones. GB-Inno-BM argued that Union law prevented RTT from maintaining its powers of approval, as this meant that RTT should approve the products of its competitors, and could therefore determine which products could be marketed. The CJ stated that:

> 'The Court has also held that an abuse within the meaning of Article 86 [now Article 106] is committed where, without any objective necessity, an undertaking holding a dominant position on a particular market reserves to itself an ancillary activity which might be carried out by another undertaking as part of its activities on a neighbouring but separate market, with the possibility of eliminating all competition from such undertaking.
>
> Therefore the fact that an undertaking holding a monopoly in the market for the establishment and operation of the network, without any objective necessity, reserves to itself a neighbouring but separate market, in this case the market for the importation, marketing, connection, commissioning and maintenance of equipment for connection to the said network.'[14]

The CJ has held that there can be cases where, as part as its exclusive right, a privileged undertaking carries out activities which can give rise to problems concerning its legal capacity. An example of this is where the privileged undertaking must approve products before they can be put on the market, but where the products in question compete with the privileged undertaking's own products.

> The first of these cases was Case C-260/89, *ERT*. In Greece, Elliniki Radiophonia Tiléorassi (ERT) had a monopoly for television broadcasting. The Greek authorities had give ERT an exclusive right to broadcast

14. Case 18/88, *RTT*, paras 18-19.

programmes produced by ERT itself and programmes produced by others. The CJ hinted, though without expressly stating, that the situation means that ERT had the possibility, and probably also the incentive, to prefer programmes it had produced itself rather than programmes produced by others. The CJ thus said: 'Article 90(1) [now: Article 106(1)] of the Treaty prohibits the granting of an exclusive right to transmit and an exclusive right to retransmit television broadcasts to a single undertaking, where those rights are liable to create a situation in which that undertaking is led to infringe Article 86 [now: Article 102] by virtue of a discriminatory broadcasting policy which favours its own programmes.'[15]

4.2.4. Essential facilities

Under Article 106 of the Treaty, abuse can take the form of denying other undertakings access to the facilities of the privileged undertaking. The problem is well known in American antitrust law[16] and is called the 'essential facilities doctrine'.

The essential facilities problem is often found in connection with undertakings that have a natural monopoly. Such a situation will exist where an undertaking owns a network (electricity grid, railway network etc.) or equivalent infrastructure (for example port facilities). The sectors in which such essential facilities are most important are the sectors that have traditionally been based on special and exclusive rights.

Certain sectors are characterised by the fact that participation in the market in question depends on access to such facilities. This refers in particular to the transport, telecommunications, and energy sectors, as well as television broadcasting. In addition there are a number of other sectors where essential facilities may not play such a decisive role, but where certain facilities are nevertheless significant. These include the postal sector and a number of other sectors where knowledge and products can constitute an essential part of the possibility of gaining access to the market.

The essential facility problem is not expressly regulated in EU law, but it arises as one of the relevant topics for the application of Article 106 and Article 102. The guidelines presented below are derived from the case law.

The starting point for competition law is that there should be freedom of contract for actors on the market. This means that undertakings have the right to choose with whom, when,

15. Case C-260/89, *ERT,* para. 37.
16. The doctrine was established in the case of *United States of America* v *Terminal Railroad Association,* 224 U.S. 383 (1912).

how and with what content they wish to enter into agreements. On this basis the essential facilities doctrine represents a departure from this principle. This necessarily means that it is only in exceptional circumstances that an undertaking can claim access to a competing undertaking's facilities. The reason why the principle of freedom of contract is departed from in special circumstances is that if competitors can be refused access to a facility which is essential for the performance of a service, then competition for the provision of the service is essentially excluded. It might be argued that freedom of contract should be so far reaching that a duty to enter into a contract should never be imposed. However, the principle of proportionality and certain interests of society mean that this approach is not appropriate. This is because the alternative to access to the essential facility is effectively either that an undertaking which wishes to operate on the market must establish its own network or infrastructure, or that such undertakings cannot gain access to the market. The principle of proportionality means that such a solution would impose a disproportionately large burden on a potential competitor, compared with the disadvantages and restriction on freedom of contract which a third party's access to the network would cause for the owner of the network. From the point of view of society it would be clearly undesirable to require the establishment of several networks since this would not be a sensible use of resources. One of the considerations which lies behind the European regulation of competition is that there should be an effective use of resources in the Member States. Where more networks are established than is necessary from the point of view of capacity, there will be a waste of resources. In addition to this, the establishment of several such networks would make it difficult for consumers to switch from one supplier to another, if the consumer so wished.

To the extent that a privileged undertaking is required to give access to an essential facility, it is possible to lay down a number of conditions for such access. Thus it will be required that access is given on reasonable terms. An important condition will be that access should be given on equal and non-discriminatory terms. This means that if access is granted to one undertaking, access must be granted to other undertakings on the same terms, so that the price for access will be the same for all third parties which wish to use the facilities. It must also be assumed that this non-discrimination also covers the undertaking which owns the essential facility.

In determining what can be considered an essential facility, various circumstances must be taken into consideration. There must be consideration of the importance of the facility for access to the market. As there is an obligation to enter into a contract, the obligation should only be imposed exceptionally. This means that the mere fact that access to the market is made *difficult* will not be sufficient to impose an obligation to enter into a contract. There must be an actual prevention of access to the market.

The conditions for imposing an obligation to enter into a contract in connection with access to an essential facility are:

1. The undertaking must be *dominant* on the downstream market in question;

2. For access to be granted, refusal of access must be connected with a high degree of probability that this will *eliminate competition* from the undertaking which seeks access;
3. Access must be necessary, meaning that *there is only this possibility for gaining access to the market*, and thus there is no alternative; and
4. It is not possible to give an *objective justification* for refusal.

4.2.5. Other infringements

Article 106(1) of the Treaty is most often applied in conjunction with Article 102, but sometimes with other provisions, including the rules on freedom of movement, in particular Article 56 on the freedom to provide services.

When applying Article 106(1) in conjunction with Article 56 the former often does not play such a major role as it does when used in conjunction with Article 102. There are examples of this in connection with the granting of public procurement contracts (see Chapter XII). Here Article 106 will often be applicable, but it will typically act to emphasise that Article 56 can apply; see Case C-410/04, *ANAV*, paragraph 23, and Case C-458/03, *Parking Brixen*, paragraph 52. The tendency for there to be limited application of Article 106 together other provisions, other than Article 102, is also seen in connection with, among other things, national gambling rules which have been referred to the CJ. In a number of these cases legislation has established legal monopolies or special rights for specific undertakings, in other words potential Article 106 situations. Nevertheless, only the rules on freedom of movement have been used in these cases.

5. Article 106(2)

Article 106(2) of the Treaty covers undertakings that have been entrusted with the provision services of general economic interest. Article 106(2) thus supports the prohibition in Article 106(1), but it covers a slightly different situation. At the same time Article 106(2) is distinguished by containing an exception from the Treaty's rules.

5.1. Services of general economic interest

The scope of Article 106(2) covers undertakings which have been entrusted with the provision of services of general economic interest. The conditions for this are fulfilled by entrusting the provision of the service in question by a legal act of a public authority.[17] Services of general economic interest are general services which are of interest to society at large. The CJ has established that services such as telecommunications services, air traffic control, employment exchanges, television broadcasting, postal services and electricity supply are considered to be activities of general economic interest. The Member States have wide discretion to determine what they consider to be a service of economic interest. In this connection, the Commission only has the right to question a Member State's designation in cases where there it is clearly wrong; see Case T-17/02, *Fred Olsen*, paragraph 216.

The importance of services of general economic interest has been increased by the inclusion of Article 14 in the Treaty. This provisions states: 'Without prejudice to Article 4 of the Treaty on European Union or to Articles 93, 106 and 107 of this Treaty, and given the place occupied by services of general economic interest in the shared values of the Union as well as their role in promoting social and territorial cohesion, the Union and the Member States, each within their respective powers and within the scope of application of the Treaties, shall take care that such services operate on the basis of principles and conditions, particularly economic and financial conditions, which enable them to fulfil their missions.' The provision is included in Part One of the Treaty under the heading of 'Principles', and this thereby emphasises that such services are important for the functioning of the Union. At the same time it must be assumed that the most important role of Article 14 is as a statement of policy, and that the provision is not intended to lead to any change in the actual practice concerning services of general economic interest.[18] The term 'services of general economic interest' is one that has attracted much attention over the last 10 years.[19]

5.2. Entrusted with the operation of services

The provision in Article 106(2) applies if a *right and a duty* is entrusted to an undertaking for the provision of a service of general economic interest. This can be entrusted by a central or local government entity. It is a condition that the right and duty should be entrusted by a *public authority*, but there is no requirement that it should be entrusted by means of legislation.[20] A right/duty can also be entrusted by an administrative agreement or by some other form of administrative measure. The entrusting of a right or duty on the basis of a

17. Case 127/73, *SABAM*, para. 20.
18. However, in the Lisbon Treaty it was made clear that it must be possible for such services to be provided on economic and financial terms which make it possible for them to achieve their purposes.
19. See e.g. *Kajewski, Neergaard & Van de Gronden (eds.):* The Changing legal framework for Services of General Interest in Europe, 2009.
20. Case 127/73, *SABAM*, para. 20.

purely private law agreement between a public authority and an undertaking does not constitute the entrusting of a right or duty for the purposes of Article 106(2).[21] However, there is nothing to stop a commercial undertaking which has been entrusted with the provision of a service of general economic interest, from being involved in the process by which the task has been entrusted; see Case T-17/02, *Fred Olsen*, paragraph 189.

It is assumed that participation in the ownership of a public company is also not regarded as having been entrusted, if the owner of shares does not have special influence on the running of the company (the traditional company law instruments are thus insufficient). Nor can EU legislative acts or general public licences be regarded as entrusting a right/duty for the purposes of Article 106(2).[22]

The granting of special or exclusive rights is not identical with entrusting an entity with the provision of services of general economic interest. These will often go together, so that a grant under Article 106(1) will be covered by the concept of entrusting the provision of a service under Article 106(2). However, in principle it is quite possible to grant an exclusive right which does not concern the provision of services of general economic interest, while it is also possible that entrusting to an undertaking the provision of services of general economic interest under Article 106(2) may not necessarily fulfil the conditions for being a grant of special or exclusive rights.

In order for an entity to be entrusted with the provision of services of general economic interest, the activity must be clearly defined. However, this does not exclude the possibility of subsequently changing the content of the obligation, at least as long as the changes are made between the parties, i.e. the public authority responsible and the privileged undertaking.[23] There is no obligation for the public authority to entrust the provision of services of general economic interest to an undertaking by using the public procurement rules. Such an obligation can be derived neither from the wording of Article 106(2) nor from the practice of the CJ; see Case T-17/02, *Fred Olsen*, paragraph 239.

21. Case C-393/92, *Almelo,* which concerned an agreement between a public body in its capacity as a supplier and a supplying undertaking; see especially para. 31.
22. See *Andreas Bala:* Art. 90 Abs. 2 im System unverfälschten Wettbewerbs, p. 62 and at p. 57. The background to this is that licences usually do not include an obligation to provide social services.
23. Case T-17/02, *Fred Olsen,* para. 202.

5.3. The exception in Article 106(2)

Article 106(2) provides that undertakings which have been entrusted with the provision of services of general economic interest must comply with the rules of the Treaty. At the same time the provision enables the use of an exception to this, to the extent that the service cannot be provided while complying with the Treaty's rules.

5.3.1. Conditions for exceptions

The practice shows that it is possible to exempt restrictions on competition from the Treaty's provisions, as long as the restrictions on competition are necessary: (1) for it to be possible to provide services of general economic interest; (2) so that the services can be provided on acceptable financial terms; (3) so that in this connection the undertaking can have the possibility for equalising differences between profitable and non-profitable areas; (4) to prevent 'cherry-picking' (i.e. where private undertakings cream off profitable areas of the market); or (5) if the restrictions on competition are necessary for complying with national law/special obligations. The most probable defences will involve the financial circumstances for the performance of the sole right and the question of compliance with existing national laws.

5.3.2. Special financial circumstances

The financial circumstances of a privileged undertaking are of particular significance in connection with the exemption provision in Article 106(2). It is established that where it is impossible for a privileged undertaking to provide services of general economic interest on acceptable financial terms, this is sufficient to justify an exemption from the Treaty's rules; see Article 106(2). The CJ has not defined more precisely what is meant by acceptable terms, but it is clear that it is not required that the privileged activity should merely break even. A privileged undertaking is thus entitled to obtain a certain profit from its activities.

The financial equalisation which is permitted in order to give undertakings acceptable financial conditions can be achieved in many ways. One possibility is for a public authority to compensate the privileged undertaking for the losses arising from the provision of services of general economic interest. Another possibility is to reserve some other profitable activity for the privileged undertaking, so that the undertaking can make an internal financial equalisation – a form of cross-subsidy which is legitimate. A third possibility is for undertakings which carry on activities within the sector in which the privileged undertaking has an exclusive right to be required to pay a fee for financing the privileged activity.

If a public authority provides a subsidy to a privileged undertaking, in certain situations this can be considered a State aid.[24] In this context, State aid is understood to be support provided on unilateral terms to the privileged undertaking. When financial aid is provided in connection with the equalisation of the loss which a privileged undertaking incurs through the provision of unprofitable services of general economic interest, the CJ has held that this is in accordance with the rules on State aid.[25]

> In the *Altmark* case, the CJ concluded that: 'public subsidies intended to enable the operation of urban, suburban or regional scheduled transport services are not caught by that provision [Article 107(1)] where such subsidies are to be regarded as compensation for the services provided by the recipient undertakings in order to discharge public service obligations. For the purpose of applying that criterion, it is for the national court to ascertain that the following conditions are satisfied:
>
> – first, the recipient undertaking is actually required to discharge public service obligations and those obligations have been clearly defined;
> – second, the parameters on the basis of which the compensation is calculated have been established beforehand in an objective and transparent manner;
> – third, the compensation does not exceed what is necessary to cover all or part of the costs incurred in discharging the public service obligations, taking into account the relevant receipts and a reasonable profit for discharging those obligations;
> – fourth, where the undertaking which is to discharge public service obligations is not chosen in a public procurement procedure, the level of compensation needed has been determined on the basis of an analysis of the costs which a typical undertaking, well run and adequately provided with means of transport so as to be able to meet the necessary public service requirements, would have incurred in discharging those obligations, taking into account the relevant receipts and a reasonable profit for discharging the obligations.'[26]

24. For more on State aid, see Chapter IX.
25. Case C-280/00, *Altmark*.
26. See also Case C-53/00, *Ferring;* and the Opinion of Advocate General Jacobs in Case C-126/01, *GEMO*.

With the *Altmark* case the relationship between Article 107 and Article 106(2) was made more complex. The background for this is that the test in *Altmark* uses criteria which are highly reminiscent of those found in the case law concerning Article 106(2). The Commission has been quite energetic in distinguishing between these two provisions; see the latest regulatory package of 20 December 2011, consisting of a Commission Decision, two Communications from the Commission, and a proposal for a *de minimis* Regulation.

A final condition for exemption from the rules of the Treaty is that the exemption must not be *contrary to the interests of the Union*. The 'interests of the Union' is not a well-defined term, but the CJ has expressed a view on it in certain cases, and in can be said in general to concern the functioning of the internal market.

6. Article 106(3)

In Article 106(3) it is provided that the Commission has powers to initiate certain measures addressed to the Member States. The provision supports the general and exclusive powers of the Commission on questions of competition in the EU.

The provision gives the Commission powers to ensure compliance with Article 106(1) and (2). The Commission can ensure this by addressing appropriate directives or decisions to the Member States. With reference to this provision the Commission has adopted several directives for the regulation of public undertakings and undertakings based on special or exclusive rights.

Thus, Directive 2006/111/EC, on the transparency of financial relations between Member States and public undertakings as well as on financial transparency within certain undertakings, and several directives on telecommunications (for example Directive 2008/63/EC and Directive 2002/77/EC) have been adopted under the authority of Article 106(3).

6.1. The adoption of directives and decisions

One of the most important questions in connection with the application of the powers in Article 106(3) concerns the limits to the Commission's powers under this provision on the one hand, and on the other hand the other powers of the Commission and of other institutions.

In practice it has been established that the Commission's powers under Article 106(3) (the adoption of directives and decisions) can be applied appropriately in different situations. Decisions can be used in the event of actual infringements of Article 106, whereas directives are of a more general character and are therefore addressed to the Member States in general, and not in relation to specific infringements.[27]

In addition to its powers under Article 106(3), the Commission can also bring proceedings for breach of the Treaty under Article 258, and it can also use its powers under Article 108 on State aid, and Article 103 concerning infringements of the general competition rules in Articles 101 and 102.

The Commission is allowed a broad scope in relation to the use of the powers given to it. According to the case law of the CJ, the Commission is not required to choose the procedure for breach of the Treaty under Article 258, rather than using any of its other powers. On the contrary, the Commission can initiate proceedings for infringements by making informal approaches to one or more of the Member States in question.

As for the Commission's powers to issue directives, directives issued under the authority of Article 106(3) are identical in form and effect to directives issued under other authority. On the other hand, the procedures for adopting such directives are not the same under the different sources of authority. Thus, Article 114 lays down procedural requirements, while Article 106(3) contains no formal conditions for the procedure for adoption. This can give rise to questions of legal certainty. It is perhaps questionable that the Commission can avoid the normal procedure by using Article 106(3).

This is why the Commission is reluctant about adopting legal acts under the authority of Article 106(3). Far fewer decisions and directives have been adopted under this provision than under the other provisions concerning the internal market. At the same time, when applying Article 106(3), the Commission often follows a procedure that gives a measure of legal certainty.

The Commission can start proceedings on its own initiative, but it can also start proceedings on the basis of a complaint or a reference from a third party. However, the Commission is not obliged to bring proceedings, and where a complaint is rejected by the Commission, the complainant does not have the possibility of having the rejection tried either under Article 263 or Article 265 of the Treaty.

Regardless of which methods the Commission uses for carrying out its tasks, under Article 296 a statement of reasons is required for acts adopted within the EU. The statement of

27. According to Article 288 of the Treaty, decisions are binding in their entirety upon those to whom they are addressed. A directive is binding, as to the result to be achieved, upon each Member State to which it is addressed, but it leaves to the national authorities the choice of form and methods for implementation.

reasons must be adapted to the nature of the act in question and must clearly state the reasons for which the institution in question has issued the legal act, so that the parties affected can know the basis for the act and so that a competent court can exercise its right of review.

There can be situations in which an infringement or a proposed regulatory initiative falls within the scope of two different authorising provisions, for example, an infringement of both the general competition rules and Article 106, or the regulation of the internal market in general and public undertakings in particular. In the first case both Article 103 and Regulation (EC) No 1/2003 can be used, and in the second case both Article 114 and Article 106(3) can be used as authority. In these cases the Commission can use Article 106(3), but it may be expected to use the other provisions for the purposes of legal certainty.

To the extent that legal acts are adopted on the wrong legal basis, these will be annulled in connection with a suit for annulment. It has been argued that the relationship between the different authorising provisions should be determined by a *lex specialis* assessment.[28] According to this view, the source of authority will often be Article 106(3), since this provision will be special in relation to the more general rules on competition or the internal market. Regardless of whether use of the *lex specialis* leads to the correct allocation, the Commission is still expected to be reluctant about using the authority of Article 106(3).

Where a decision is made concerning an actual infringement, the undertaking[29] which has committed an action which is contrary to competition law and the Member State in question have certain rights of appeal. These consist primarily of the use of different kinds of legal proceedings within the EU legal system.

6.2. The Directive on the transparency of relations between Member States and public undertakings

Directive 2006/111/EC, on the transparency of financial relations between Member States and public undertakings as well as on financial transparency within certain undertakings (with subsequent amendments), is intended to en-

28. See *Rudolf Benesch:* Die Kompetenzen der EG-Kommission aus Art. 90 Abs. 3 EWG-V, pp. 63-64.
29. In this context the party entitled to appeal is not a trade organisation, but only the undertakings that have committed the infringement.

sure that there is transparency about, among other things, financial support paid by the Member States to public undertakings.

Under the Directive, the primary obligation is for Member States to ensure that financial relations between public authorities and public undertakings are transparent, as provided in the Directive, so that the following are made clear:

a. what public funds are made available directly by public authorities to the public undertakings concerned;
b. what public funds made available by public authorities through the intermediary of public undertakings or financial institutions; and
c. the use to which these public funds are actually put.[30]

In the Directive a 'public undertaking' is defined as any undertaking, whether at State, regional or local level, 'over which the public authorities may exercise directly or indirectly a dominant influence by virtue of their ownership of it, their financial participation therein, or the rules which govern it'; see Article 2(1) of the Directive.

The definition of special or exclusive rights as set out in this Directive is presented in section 4.1.1 above.

7. State monopolies of a commercial character

7.1. Article 37 – aim and function

Article 37 of the Treaty contains a provision which has largely the same aim and focus as Article 106. Both provisions are directed at the carrying out of activities on the basis of special rights. Article 37(1) and (2) both have direct effect.[31]

7.1.1. Article 37 – in brief

According to its wording, Article 37 covers trade in goods, but not services. The term 'goods' includes electricity, waste and gas. In general it must be assumed that the definition of 'goods' for the purposes of Article 37 is identical with the definition under the other provisions of the Treaty.

Even though the prohibition in Article 37 covers hindrances to trade in goods, this does not mean that monopolies for the provision of services cannot be covered by Article 37, though only to the extent that such monopolies

30. Article 1 of Directive 2006/111/EC.
31. Case 59/75, *Manghera;* and Case 6/64, *Costa* v *ENEL.*

have an effect on imports or exports of goods.[32] According to the wording of the provision, the prohibition also concerns the conditions for the procurement and marketing of goods. However, the primary concern is trade in goods.

Goods that are directly imported from third countries are excluded from the provision. This only relates to products which are directly imported from third countries. According to well-established case law, goods which are lawfully imported into the EU and which are subsequently put on the market within the EU are considered to be EU goods, and they will thus be covered by Article 37.

7.2. Important concepts

7.2.1. State monopolies of a commercial character

The term *State monopolies of a commercial character* can be split into three parts: State, commercial character and monopoly.

The term *State monopolies of a commercial character* must also be set in the context of Article 37(1), second paragraph, where it is stated that the provisions of Article 37 apply to any body through which a Member State, in law or in fact, either directly or indirectly supervises, determines or appreciably influences imports or exports between Member States. It is also stated that the provisions apply to monopolies delegated by the State to others. It is not clear what the relationship is between the first and second paragraphs of Article 37(1), but it is assumed that the second paragraph should be seen as an explanation of the first paragraph.[33]

7.2.1.1. State

It has been argued by some people that the fact that Article 37 refers to State monopolies of a commercial character is evidence that it is only the State's (meaning the central administration's) allocations of rights which are covered by Article 37. This cannot be assumed to be the case. If one looks at other provisions in the Treaty where there is a direct reference to the 'State', it will be seen that in all cases this is considered to be a reference to public authori ties, often in the broadest sense.[34] It must therefore be assumed that the refer-

32. Case 30/87, *Bodson;* Case C-271/81, *Mialocq,* para. 10; and Case C-17/94, *Gervais,* paras 36-37.
33. See *Sierra:* Exclusive Rights and State Monopolies under EC Law, p. 79 et seq. As will be seen below, in certain cases unfortunately this 'explanation' leads to more confusion than clarification.
34. See, e.g., Case 45/87, *Commission* v *Ireland (Dundalk)*, where a local government authority was held liable for an infringement of Article 34, even though Article 34

ence in Article 37 to 'State monopolies of a commercial character' refers to all trade monopolies which are established by delegation by a public body.[35]

State monopolies of a commercial character can exist where a public authority owns a trading enterprise, but it must also be assumed to exist where an undertaking has been granted an exclusive right; see the term *monopoly*. This brings the scope of application of Article 37 into line with Article 106, both dealing with public undertakings and undertakings which have been granted special or exclusive rights.

7.2.1.2. Commercial character

The wording of Article 37 refers to undertakings of a commercial character. This means that buying and selling monopolies established by law will be covered by Article 37. Both wholesale and retail sales are covered by the provision.[36]

There can be no doubt that when there is a monopoly of a commercial character, this means that the entity must be an undertaking. It must further be assumed that the definition of *undertaking* which is used is that which is generally used in competition law; see above. This means that there must be an entity which carries on some economic activity.[37] It must also be assumed that where there is an entity which both exercises authority and conducts trade, this will be a monopoly of a commercial character under Article 37.[38] However, where there is a production monopoly this will probably not fall within the scope of Article 37.

7.2.1.3. Monopoly

At first sight, the term monopoly gives the impression that an entity must have exclusive rights. It must thus be assumed that the term *monopoly* in Article 37 covers the concept of a legal monopoly, in other words a right which has been granted such as e.g. a concession. The question is whether the term monopoly applies equally to *de facto* monopolies.

In this context a *de facto* monopoly can be defined as a monopoly which arises in some other way than through an express grant from a public authority. Some authors are of the view that such monopolies are covered by Article

refers to Member States, and even though the case was brought against a Member State (Ireland).

35. Case 30/87, *Bodson,* para. 13.
36. Case 90/82, *France* v *Commission.*
37. See section 4.1.3 in this chapter for a discussion of 'economic activity'.
38. Case C-387/93, *Banchero:* and Case 90/82, *France* v *Commission.*

37, but most authors do not believe that Article 37 applies to *de facto* monopolies.[39]

To the extent that *de facto* monopolies are covered by Article 37, a number of problems arise. For example, will it be sufficient if a public body exercises influence on an undertaking merely through administrative acts or through ownership of an undertaking which, by chance, had a *de facto* monopoly at a given time, or perhaps merely a dominant position on a market? If so, will Article 37 apply to situations where there is a markedly more distant influence on the market than is the case for Article 106? It cannot be assumed that Article 37 is aimed at this type of arrangement. In addition, in these situations there is a risk of conflict with the general rules of competition law as one moves away from the area of exclusive rights.

The statements of the CJ in Case 161/82, *Commission* v *France* indicate that there is a requirement for some form or other of exclusive right, which is traditionally understood to be a legal monopoly. However, the CJ also uses the term *de facto*, which indicates that forms of monopoly other than legal (*de jure*) monopolies can be included. In paragraph 17 of the judgment, the Commission's view is accepted that 'the French authorities, by the indirect means of an established administrative practice in relation to the grant of import licences, *de facto* conferred an exclusive right of import on production or insemination centres or bodies acting on their behalf or in conjunction with them.' The reference to *de facto* monopolies can be understood not as a reference to a *de facto* monopoly as such (understood as an actual or natural monopoly), but rather to the *de facto grant* of a monopoly. This must mean that there was not an actual instrument granting a monopoly, but rather an administrative practice which in effect meant that there was a legal monopoly. The CJ has not yet given an unambiguous answer to this question.[40] At the same time, the use of the word 'adjust' in the first paragraph of Article 37(1) suggests that Member States have the possibility of changing a monopoly. An effective change to a monopoly would only be possible in the case of a legal monopoly, as it is only in these cases that public authorities have sufficient influence to be able to 'adjust' a monopoly. If a Member State is to adjust a *de facto* monopoly or an undertaking which has a dominant position, this must be carried out under the provisions of Article 102 and not Article 37.

The term 'monopoly' must include the influence of the undertaking on the market in question (and which the State thereby has the possibility of influencing). However, the case law shows that it is not necessary for the whole

39. E.g. *Rolf-Dieter Theisen* does not believe that *de facto* monopolies are covered by Article 37, see Die Stellung der staatlichen Handelsmonopole nach dem EWG-Vertrag unter besonderer Berücksichtigung der Gegelung des Tabakmarkets, p. 74. Among those on the other side of the argument, *Sierra,* appears to believe that *de facto* monopolies are covered by Article 37, see Exclusive Rights and State Monopolies under EC Law, p. 86.
40. Case C-393/92, *Almelo,* paras 29-32. In this case the CJ also failed to give a clear statement on the question. Article 37 was not found to apply and there was no actual concession, but the link between these two circumstances in the judgment is not clear.

market to be reserved to the privileged undertaking for Article 37 to apply.[41] It must also be assumed that there is a requirement for there to be some entity which stands behind the right, i.e. a company or some other distinct entity. The term *monopoly* thus does not only refer to the *right*.

It has been established in the case law that it is not only monopolies that cover the whole of the territory of a Member State that are covered by Article 37, as local government monopolies are also covered.[42]

7.2.3. The concept of appreciability

The concept of appreciability is referred to in the wording of Article 37, 'or appreciably influences'. The concept can be understood in two ways. First, the State can exercise appreciable influence on a monopoly of a commercial character. Second, there can be a requirement for an appreciable influence on trade, i.e. a *de minimis* threshold. It is presumably the latter which is the correct understanding.[43] This means that not all monopolies of a commercial character will be covered by Article 37, but only those monopolies through which a Member State can appreciably influence imports or exports. If the influence on imports or exports is not appreciable, Article 37 will not apply.

There is no appreciability requirement in relation to Article 34, and this difference can be quite significant in practice. The CJ has not yet considered what criteria will be applicable to this appreciability evaluation under Article 37. One possibility could be the market share of the State monopoly, where this is an accurate reflection of the situation.[44]

41. Case 347/88, *Commission* v *Greece,* where it was found sufficient that 65 % of the market was reserved to the privileged undertaking.
42. Case 30/87, *Bodson.*
43. Case 347/88, *Commission* v *Greece,* para. 41, where the CJ held that Greece 'had the power to exert an appreciable influence on imports of petroleum products from other Member States'.
44. In Case 347/88, *Commission* v *Greece,* para. 41, the CJ stated that Greece had 'the exclusive right to import and market a quantity of petroleum products corresponding to 65% of the requirements of the domestic market. Accordingly … Greece had the power to exert an appreciable influence on imports of petroleum products from other Member States'. The CJ did not decide what percentage would be sufficient in order to be able to influence imports appreciably. It would only be very seldom that the CJ would have the opportunity for putting precise figures on appreciable influence, which means that the percentage in question cannot be used as a yardstick for appreciability.

7.2.2. Adjusting the monopoly

In accordance with Article 345 of the Treaty, Article 37 does not require State monopolies of a commercial character to be dissolved, but merely that they should be adjusted. However, it is difficult to say what is required for a monopoly to be adjusted to comply with Article 37. The requirement for adjustment is yet another of the terms used in the provisions which has given rise to questions of interpretation, both in practice and in the legal literature. The ultimate purpose of the adjustment must be that there should not be different treatment between undertakings in the Member States with regard to the conditions under which goods are produced and marketed.[45]

7.3. Measures which conflict with Article 37

7.3.1. General

Infringements of Article 37 are mostly made by the Member States; see the wording of the provision. However, there can also be situations where State monopolies of a commercial character infringe the provisions.

7.3.2. Discrimination

According to Article 37, the provision prohibits discrimination. The term 'discrimination' does not in itself raise any major problems in relation to Article 37, but there are certain unsettled questions in relation to the application of the prohibition of discrimination.

It is not clear from the practice of the courts whether it is only discrimination or whether other measures can be covered by Article 37. The wording gives the impression that it is only discrimination that is covered, but some statements by the CJ seem to indicate a wider interpretation of the meaning of restriction in Article 37.

> See, for example, Case 59/75, *Manghera*; and Case 86/78, *Peureux*. In the *Manghera* case the CJ stated that Article 37 'aims at ensuring compliance with the fundamental rule of the free movement of goods throughout the common market, in particular by the abolition of quantitative restrictions and measures having equivalent effect in trade between Member States.'[46] To the extent that the application of Article 37 is driven by a desire for a connection with the general provisions in Article 34, it will also be necessary for certain non-discriminatory measures to be covered by

45. See *Sierra:* Exclusive Rights and State Monopolies under EC Law, p. 91.
46. Case 59/75, *Manghera.*

Article 37. However, the CJ has primarily applied Article 37 to discriminatory measures.

7.3.2.1. The concept of discrimination in EU law

Traditionally, discrimination will be found to exist where there is an unjustified difference in treatment. It is assumed that there will be discrimination where equivalent situations are treated differently and where non-equivalent situations are treated in the same way. While this is a broad formulation, it works in practice. The only thing that is required for its application is a basis for comparison. If it can be said that there is equivalence in a given situation, this equivalence can be characterised by an object: a product, a service, or a person. In connection with Article 37, the discrimination must presumably be aimed at persons rather than products.

The practice of the courts provides a rather ambivalent contribution to the issue. The clearest example is the *Franzén* case,[47] and the cases on electricity and gas monopolies.[48] In paragraph 40 of the case *Franzén* the CJ stated as follows: 'Article 37 requires that the organization and operation of the monopoly be arranged so as to exclude any discrimination between nationals of Member States as regards conditions of supply and outlets, so that trade in goods from other Member States is not put at a disadvantage, in law or in fact, in relation to that in domestic goods and that competition between the economies of the Member States is not distorted'. The *Franzén* case seems to be focused on products. In contrast, in the electricity and gas monopoly cases the CJ found that the Treaty had been infringed, 'by the very existence of exclusive import rights in a Member State since economic operators in other Member States are thereby deprived of the possibility of offering their products to customers of their choice in the Member State concerned.'[49] Here the emphasis seems to be on undertakings rather than on products.

Reverse discrimination covers the situation where there is no discrimination against persons or products from other Member States, but rather in favour of them, so that a Member State's own citizens or products are put at a disad-

47. Case-189/95, *Franzén.*
48. Case C-157/94, *Commission* v *Netherlands;* Case C-158/94, *Commission* v *Italy;* and Case C-159/94, *Commission* v *France.*
49. Case C-157/94, *Commission* v *Netherlands,* para. 23.

vantage.[50] Reverse discrimination is not covered by Article 37. This is in line with the practice on Article 34.

Both direct (legal) and indirect (actual) discrimination are prohibited under Article 37, whereas non-discriminatory rules governing the formation and functioning of State monopolies of a commercial character are permitted.[51]

Given the provisions on discrimination and on appreciability of influence, it can be decisive whether Article 37 or Article 34 is applied to an actual case. The Member States have an interest in Article 37 being applied, as the prohibition is less strict on these points.

7.3.2.2. Discrimination by a Member State

According to the wording of Article 37, the Member States are covered by the provision. The measures which Member States can adopt may vary in character. Direct restrictions on imports of foreign goods are naturally covered. The same applies to the fixing of prices, rules restricting the scope for the marketing of imported goods, and establishing a special tax status for the monopoly. These rules can result in more favourable conditions for domestic goods than for imported goods. Depending on the circumstances, such measures may take the form of taxes or subsidies, so that other provisions of the Treaty may also be applicable. Where there is a conflict between such provisions, an assessment has to be made as to which provisions should apply. For more on this see section 7.5 below.

Apart from obvious discrimination which occurs via the rules which regulate a State monopoly of a commercial character, discrimination by Member States which is executed via a State monopoly of a commercial character will also be covered. Naturally, this presumes that it is possible to prove that it is the Member State that has initiated the measure. Where it is assessed that the measure can be ascribed to the undertaking, see below.

In connection with the review of Article 106, it was pointed out that in certain situations the monopoly itself can be prohibited. The same applies to Article 37. This will be the case if the monopoly itself (or the form or terms of the monopoly) means that there is a degree risk of discrimination by the undertaking. This was established in Case 59/75, *Manghera*.

50. Case 86/78, *Peureux,* paras 28-38.
51. This should be understood in the light of the fact that most of the other Treaty provisions not only prohibit discrimination, but also other forms of hindrances to the free movement of goods, persons and services. See, e.g., the provisions on freedom of movement for goods (Article 34) in Case 120/78, *Cassis de Dijon;* freedom of movement for persons in Case C-415/93, *Bosman;* and Case C-212/97, *Centros* on freedom of establishment (Article 49).

In this case, the Italian state tobacco monopoly had been granted the exclusive right to import tobacco products. The CJ stated that, according to Article 37 and the other provisions on freedom of movement of goods, Article 37(1) imposes an obligation to ensure compliance with the fundamental rules on the free movement of goods. This purpose would not be achieved if, in a Member State, free movement was not ensured for goods from other Member States, corresponding to the goods of the monopoly. The CJ concluded by stating that 'the exclusive right to import manufactured products of the monopoly in question thus constitutes, in respect of community exporters, discrimination prohibited by Article 37(1).'[52]

7.3.2.3. Discrimination by a monopoly

Privileged undertakings are not, in principle, referred to as being subject to Article 37, but it was clear from the earlier practice concerning Article 37 that a privileged undertaking can, in certain circumstances, be bound by the provision. This will be the case where the undertaking sets up hindrances to trade on its own initiative.[53] However, it is a condition that these hindrances should be derived from the monopoly. Where measures are taken by an undertaking on its own initiative, and where these are not based on the exclusive right, any breach of the Treaty provisions will be subject to some other Treaty provisions than Article 37 (presumably Article 102).

However, more recent practice has raised doubts about whether it is still possible to apply Article 37 to the measures of undertakings, regardless of whether or not they are based on a sole right.[54]

7.3.2. Article 37(2)

Article 37(2) deals with the situation where a State monopoly of a commercial character already exists. Article 37(2) prohibits Member States from 'introducing any new measure which is contrary to the principles laid down in

52. Case 59/75, *Manghera,* para. 12.
53. Case 91/78, *Hansen,* paras 13-14.
54. The view has been expressed from time to time that, regardless of whether the measures of a privileged undertaking are or are not based on a monopoly, Articles 101 and 102 should apply to the measures taken by the privileged undertaking. There is some support for this view in Case 30/87, *Bodson* and Case C-393/92, *Almelo.* Because of the differences between Article 37 and Article 102 it would be desirable if measures taken by an undertaking, but based on a sole right, were subject to Article 37.

paragraph 1 or which restricts the scope of the articles dealing with the prohibition of customs duties and quantitative restrictions between Member States.' Briefly, this must mean that the same restrictions that apply to existing monopolies apply equally to new monopolies. An important question in this context is whether the establishment of new monopolies can be said to be an expression of discrimination, or whether their establishment can be said to influence trade between Member States appreciably. If this is the case, Article 37(2) means that it is not permitted to establish new State monopolies of a commercial character.

It is possible to construe the provision in two ways. First, it can be understood as meaning that new measures may not be adopted within existing monopolies; and second, 'measure' can be understood as referring to a monopoly, so that the provision only (or primarily) concerns the setting up of new monopolies. The former must be the correct interpretation.

7.3.3. Observations on Article 37(3)

Article 37(3) contains a provision which is particularly addressed to agriculture. It is stated that: 'If a State monopoly of a commercial character has rules which are designed to make it easier to dispose of agricultural products or obtain for them the best return, steps should be taken in applying the rules contained in this Article to ensure equivalent safeguards for the employment and standard of living of the producers concerned.' There has been some discussion about whether this provision constitutes an exception to Article 37(1) and (2); this is not the case. Rather, the aim of the provision is to make it easier for national authorities to adopt measures to compensate for the effects which the abolition of the discrimination which a monopoly specifically implies may have on the employment and the standard of living of the producers concerned.[55]

7.4. Exceptions to Article 37

Article 37 is included in the part of the Treaty which deals with quantitative restrictions and the free movement of goods. It would be natural if the exceptions laid down in Article 36 were also to apply to measures which are covered by the prohibition in Article 37. However, the wording of Article 30 makes it clear that this is not the case. Article 36 refers explicitly to Articles 34 and 35, but not to Article 37. On the other hand, the CJ has held that, de-

55. Case 91/75, *Miritz*, para. 11.

pending on the circumstances, the exemption in Article 106(2) can be applicable to infringements of Article 37.[56]

7.5. The relationship between Article 37 and the other provisions of the Treaty

The scope of Article 37 overlaps with the scopes of a number of the other rules in the Treaty. It is therefore necessary to define the limits of Article 37 and these other Treaty provisions.

7.5.1. The relationship between Article 34 and State monopolies of a commercial character

Like Article 37, Article 34 contains a prohibition on quantitative restrictions. Previously, the CJ did not see a need to distinguish between the two provisions, so they could both be applied to the same circumstances.[57] However, more recent practice shows that there is a distinction between the scopes of two provisions.

In Case C-189/95, *Franzén*, the CJ distinguished between Article 34 and Article 37 as follows (paragraphs 35 and 36):

> 'Having regard to the case-law of the Court, it is necessary to examine the rules relating to the existence and operation of the monopoly with reference to Article 37 of the Treaty, which is specifically applicable to the exercise, by a domestic commercial monopoly, of its exclusive rights…
>
> On the other hand, the effect on intra-Community trade of the other provisions of the domestic legislation which are separable from the operation of the monopoly although they have a bearing upon it, must be examined with reference to Article 30 [now Article 36] of the Treaty'.[58]

This new approach respects the intended distinction between the two provisions. On the basis of the CJ's distinction between of the two provisions it must be assumed that an examination of whether the existence of a monopoly

56. Case C-157/94, *Commission* v *Netherlands;* Case C-158/94, *Commission* v *Italy;* and Case C-159/94, *Commission* v *France* – the electricity and gas monopoly cases.
57. Case 119/78, *Distilleries Peureux;* and Case 347/88, *Commission* v *Greece.*
58. On the *Franzén* case, see *P.J. Slot,* Common Market Law Review 1998 pp. 1183-1203.

is contrary to the Treaty must also take account of the rules governing the monopoly and its function.[59]

> In Case C-170/04, *Rosengren and Others*, the CJ again had to consider the Swedish monopoly on trade in alcohol. The CJ was specifically asked whether a prohibition on the import of alcoholic beverages for private consumption was contrary to Article 37. The CJ replied that this question should be assessed under Article 34, as the prohibition did not really concern the monopoly or its function; see paragraph 25.

In the *Franzén* case the CJ also stated that it is a condition for the application of Article 37 that the monopoly must pursue aims of a public interest.[60] As long as the activity is primarily commercial, it must be assumed that Article 34 applies, and not Article 37.

7.5.2. The relationship to the other Treaty provisions

In relation to the other provisions on freedom of movement there is a natural distinction in relation to the nature of the protected object, i.e. goods, services or persons. Where a case does not concern trade in goods, Article 37 will not apply.

Articles 30 and 110 of the Treaty include provisions on tax measures which constitute barriers to trade. Thus, Article 30 provides that customs duties and charges having equivalent effect are prohibited between Member States, while in Article 110 there is a prohibition of discriminatory internal taxation. The prohibition in Article 37 covers both these types of measures. The relationship between the provisions is that Article 37 applies to tax measures that relate to a monopoly, while Article 30 and Article 110 relate to other tax measures which constitute barriers to trade. There is thus nothing to prevent all three provisions being applied to the same case, but to different aspects of it.[61]

59. Case C-157/94, *Commission* v *Netherlands,* where in para. 24 it is stated: 'Since SEP's exclusive import rights are thus contrary to Article 37 [now: Article 37] of the Treaty, it is unnecessary to consider whether they are contrary to Article 30 [now: Article 34] or, consequently, whether they might possibly be justified under Article 36 [now: Article 36] of the Treaty.' See also Case C-158/94, *Commission v Italy;* and Case C-159/94, *Commission* v *France.* The quotation must be seen as a consequence of the fact that the provisions contain the same prohibition.
60. Case-189/95, *Franzén,* para. 39.
61. Case 91/75, *Miritz,* where the CJ refused to consider the compatibility of national measures with Article 30, as the tax measure in question was linked to a State

With regard to the competition rules in Articles 101 and 102, the CJ has not had to consider the relationship between these and Article 37 in an actual case. Cases could arise where both the competition rules and Article 37 could presumably apply. The most obvious would be situations where a State monopoly of a commercial character demonstrates such conduct as can be regarded as an abuse of a dominant position under Article 102. The CJ has held that conduct corresponding to an abuse of a dominant position can be contrary to Article 37.[62] On the other hand, in Case C-393/92, *Almelo* and Case 30/87, *Bodson* the CJ refused to apply Article 37 to restrictions on competition that were not directly related to the monopoly itself.

In relation to the provisions on State aid in Articles 107 and 108, both Article 37 and the rules on State aid apply to measures that fall within the scope of both provisions. This can occur where a national measure laid down by the monopoly has the character of a State aid. In such cases the measure can both fall within the prohibition in Article 107 and the prohibition in Article 37.

If a measure which is adopted by a State monopoly of a commercial character is not found to be contrary to Article 37, this does not mean that the measure cannot be independently tried under the rules on State aid.[63]

8. Other regulation

8.1. International regulation

In addition to the EU rules, there are also rules at international level on public undertakings and undertakings with special rights in the European Economic Area (EEA) and in the WTO agreements. In the EEA Agreement Article 16 and Article 59 contain provisions corresponding to Article 37 and Article 106. The provisions are practically identical.[64]

In the international trade cooperation under the WTO regime, the General Agreement on Tariffs and Trade 1994 contains a provision which is intended to cover the same circumstances as Article 37 and Article 106. This is in GATT 1994, Article XVII on State trading enterprises. Article XVII.1(a)

monopoly of a commercial character and it should therefore have been tried under Article 37. In contrast to this, see Case 45/75, *Rewe*, where the CJ applied both Article 110 and Article 37.

62. Case 91/78, *Hansen*.
63. Case 253/83, *Kupferberg*.
64. Under the EEA regime the Commission's powers of enforcement are given to the corresponding body – the EFTA Surveillance Authority. In the EEA regime the equivalent to the CJ is the EFTA Court.

provides that where a WTO member establishes a State enterprise, or grants to any enterprise exclusive or special privileges, the member must act in a manner consistent with the general principles of non-discriminatory treatment in GATT 1994. This is expanded in Article XVII.1(b) which provides that enterprises must make any purchases or sales solely in accordance with commercial considerations. Furthermore, WTO members must give enterprises of the other WTO members adequate opportunity to compete for participation in such purchases or sales. In Article XVII.1(c), it is provided that WTO members may not prevent any enterprise which is a public undertaking or has been granted privileges from acting in accordance with these principles. Article XVII.2 to 4 contains rules, for example, on exemption from the provisions in paragraph 1 in respect of imports of products for immediate or ultimate consumption in governmental use, an obligation to negotiate with a view to removing serious obstacles to trade in connection with such undertakings, as well as a number of formal obligations on the exchange of information between WTO members.

CHAPTER XI

The liberalised sectors

Bent Ole Gram Mortensen

Bibliography: *Christian Bergqvist: Mellem regulering og deregulering, 2007; Peter Cameron: Competition in Energy Markets, 2002; Peter Cameron: Legal Aspects of EU Energy Regulation, 2005; Eugene D. Cross: Electric Utility Regulation in the European Union, 1996; I.H.Ph. Diederiks-Verschoor: An Introduction to Air Law, 2006; Kjell A. Eliassen & Marit Sjøvaag (eds.): European Telecommunications Liberalisation, 1999; Peter Forsyth, Kenneth Button & Peter Nijkamp (eds.): Air Transport, 2002; Damien Geradin (ed.): The Liberalization of Electricity and Natural Gas in the European Union, 2001; Damien Geradin (ed.): The Liberalization of Postal Services in the European Union, 2002; Damien Geradin (ed.): The Liberalization of State Monopolies in the European Union and Beyond, 2000; Dieter Helm & Tim Jenkinson: Competition in Regulated Industries, 1998; Christopher W. Jones (ed.): EU Energy Law, Vols. I-II, 2010-11; Martha M. Roggenkam, Anita Rønne, Catherine Redgwell & Iñigo del Guayo: Energy Law in Europe, 2001; Luc Werring (ed.): EU Energy Law, Vol. III, 2006.*

This chapter is concerned with a number of commercial sectors which, in recent years, have been through a liberalisation process, among other things because of a number of measures adopted by the Union. The title of the chapter has been chosen in order to reflect this. The first section includes a general introduction to those elements of Union law that are dealt with in this chapter. This is followed by a number of sector-specific sections which look at the most important elements of concrete EU regulation. The sectors chosen for this review of specific sectors include energy (electricity and natural gas supplies), transport (air transport and railways) and communications (telecommunications and postal services). This is not an exhaustive listing of the sectors which can be categorised as liberalised sectors. Only those aspects which are concerned with Union law are dealt with. For further information about the implementation of the Union law for these sectors by the Member States, the reader is referred to the specialist works on the specific topics.

1. General cross-sectoral considerations

In post-war Europe there was a widespread assumption that market weaknesses in certain sectors were such as to make it necessary to use the involvement of public authorities, vertical integration and regulation of monopolies.

'Market weaknesses' means that the market was unable to function as an efficient allocator of welfare. This is based on the first principle of a welfare economy that market equilibrium is an effective method of allocation (Pareto optimality, i.e. that no participant in the market can be better off without at least one other participant being worse off).[1]

This has been the case for a number of undertakings in the sectors concerned with energy supply, communications and public transport. At the same time, these sectors have been seen as being of vital importance for society and for its economic development, so that society has had a strategic interest in these sectors. Public involvement in the running of these undertakings was assumed to be able to solve conflicts which could arise between private enterprise and the interests of society. This often resulted in the existence of a public monopoly, whether *de facto* or *de jure*, so that society was able to maintain a direct influence on these sectors.

The most direct way to obtain influence was through ownership. Full public ownership is not necessarily essential for obtaining influence equivalent to that of ownership.[2] The direct or indirect influence of the authorities can be achieved in many other ways, including ownership of a majority of the capital of a company, control of a majority of the voting rights, or the right to appoint a majority of the members of the board. This can be characterised as giving a dominant influence which is decisive in relation to the application of Article 106 of the Treaty on the Functioning of the European Union (TFEU or 'Treaty'). For detailed discussion of Article 106, see Chapter X on public undertakings.

The conditions or regulation connected with the public grant of exclusive rights can be concerned with the same considerations. Accordingly, Article 2(1)(b) of Directive 2006/111/EC defines a public undertaking as 'any undertaking over which the public authorities may exercise directly or indirectly a dominant influence by virtue of their ownership of it, their financial participation therein, or the rules which govern it.' Also, contractual terms can involve control over the performance of some particular task, for example

1. *Michael C. Blad & Hans Keiding:* Microeconomics, 1990.
2. Public ownership can exist both at national and at regional/local level.

through the tendering out of certain functions, while the responsibility for carrying out the functions remains with the public entity.[3]

The liberalised sectors have been and often still are characterised by involving major investments. Historically, vertical integration (the gathering together of functions that represent different links in the value chain[4]) and the status of a monopoly have been used to allow individual undertakings to secure their investments while consumers to bear the risk. The use of a monopoly can also afford protection against destructive competition. National monopolies have often been maintained by giving exclusive rights under public law to carry on a certain kind of undertaking. The term used in this connection is a *de jure* or legal monopoly. The same monopoly situation can exist without the granting of such exclusive rights, if an undertaking is in fact the only provider of a specific service in a specific geographic area; this is a *de facto* or an effective monopoly.

In the 1980s there was a certain amount of pressure to liberalise some of these industries. Monopolies (exclusive rights) came to be regarded as being inappropriate. This was a feeling felt across large parts of the world. In Europe, the United Kingdom set the ball rolling with a number of privatisations.[5] In other European countries the liberalisation process tended to take the form of doing away with exclusive rights and introducing the right of third parties to have access to a network.[6] Thus, the liberalisation of these sectors refers to many different phenomena. In itself, the expression *liberalisation* is not very precise. Basically it is an expression for the economic policy of freeing business life from restrictions. Among other things it can be understood as the complete or partial repeal of the exclusive rights of public authorities or special organisations to be engaged in a particular area – it is the opening up of markets. This can also be referred to as de-monopolising.[7] The

3. See *Hans Petter Graver:* Det offentlige og konkurranse i markedsstaten – særrettigheter og offentlig kontroll på de regulerte sektorer, Lov og Rett 2006 p. 579 et seq., in particular at p. 594, where the primary methods of control are listed: ownership, the use of directions under public law, and contracts.
4. The 'value chain' is the chain of activities which together create value for an undertaking and its owners; see *John Christensen et al.:* Virksomhedens økonomistyring, 2002 p. 12.
5. *Dieter Helm & Tim Jenkinson:* 'Introducing Competition into Regulated Industries, in *Dieter Helm & Tim Jenkinson (eds.):* Competition in Regulated Industries, 1998 p. 1.
6. See section 1.4.4 on third party access to networks.
7. The term is used by, among others, *Hans Petter Graver* in Lov og Rett 2006 p. 580.

term liberalisation is widely used together with other terms which relate to the increased use of market forces.

The term *tendering* is often used when private entities are involved in undertaking tasks such as production, supply and responsibility for personnel, while the public authorities retain responsibility for administrative tasks, management responsibility (defining quality and quantity), and any exclusive rights. Tendering typically involves *inviting offers*. This can be combined with a *control offer* from the public undertaking that has previously been responsible for carrying out the task. With *deregulation* there is usually the removal or reduction of parts of the public law regulation of a sector, for example, by opening up a market to competition. This does not necessarily mean an end to public ownership of undertakings. Even though the expression is a negation of regulation,[8] opening up for competition on a market will often be followed by an increased amount of legislation etc. in the sector, and is thus more in the nature of re-regulation. *Privatisation* consists of selling off public undertakings, publicly owned facilities and/or other assets, or merely giving up public engagement in a sector which is thus left to private participants. However, the term 'privatisation' sometimes has a broader meaning, where public authorities and undertakings allow private operators to perform individual elements of the value chain as an alternative to carrying out such tasks themselves. Finally, the management of public undertakings can be reorganised along the lines of *undertakings under private law*. Thus, a number of State-owned limited companies and mutually owned institutions have been set up, and local government authorities have, for example, organised rubbish collection in jointly owned partnerships, and supply companies have been organised by the establishment of holding companies. This process can be referred to as *corporatisation* or *demutualisation*.[9]

At Union level, true liberalisation can be said to have been introduced by the Single European Act of 1987 and the programme for the completion of the single market by 1 January 1993. In the EC Treaty then in force, there was a declaration on the establishment of the internal market in Article 3(1)(c). The Union's involvement in the liberalisation of sectors which have traditionally been public has to a large extent been driven by the desire to make these sectors part of the internal market. The establishment of the internal market had both the aim to further policy of integration and a desire to open a given market to competition.

8. In *Jørgen Dalberg-Larsen:* Om deregulering og regelsanering, in *Lis Frost (ed.):* Deregulering. Ret uden regler, 1990, the term deregulation is considered to be a vogue word of the 1980s which will nearly always refer to something which ought more correctly to be called *re-regulation.*
9. *Ian Duncan & Alan Bollard:* Corporatization & Privatization, 1992.

The liberalisation measures have had the aim of reducing the prices which European households and businesses (end users)[10] have had to pay for the goods and services which have traditionally been supplied by public undertakings. It can be said that this has had the aim of improving the efficient allocation of resources. The increased competition expected through liberalisation is the means for promoting improved efficiency. This can be seen both from the point of view of the welfare of society (better use of resources, improved competitiveness), and from the point of view of the end user (lower prices, better quality and service).

The political goals behind the liberalisation of traditional public sector undertakings can be other than purely considerations for improved efficiency. For example, there can be a desire to give consumers greater choice, and a desire to reduce the involvement of the public authorities in the supply of goods and services. Liberalisation in the form of increasing the freedom of the participants on a market can thus be both an end and a means.[11]

10. Consumers and undertakings which buy a service or product with a view to using it themselves can be classified as 'end users'. The use of the terminology varies somewhat in relation to different categories of users of a network and of the goods or services supplied thereby. In the area of telecommunications, Directive 2002/21/EC on a common regulatory framework for electronic communications networks and services (Framework Directive) and Directive 2002/22/EC on universal service and users' rights relating to electronic communications networks and services (Universal Service Directive) use the term 'end users' and uses 'consumers' to refer to non-commercial end users. Directive 97/67/EC on common rules for the development of the internal market of Community postal services and the improvement of quality of service uses the term 'users'. In the Electricity Directive and the Natural Gas Directive the terms 'system user' and 'final customer' are used. In the latest version the latter term has been supplemented by the terms 'household customer' and 'commercial customer' where the latter can also cover producers and wholesalers. Directive 2005/89/EC concerning measures to safeguard security of electricity supply and infrastructure investment, which otherwise in its terminology provisions refers to Electricity Directive, uses the term 'final customers' in its Article 3. Council Directive 2004/67/EC concerning measures to safeguard security of natural gas supply uses the terms 'customers and household customers' in its Article 4. In the area of railway infrastructure, Directive 2001/14/EC on the allocation of railway infrastructure capacity and the levying of charges for the use of railway infrastructure and safety certification exclusively uses the terms 'applicant' and 'railway undertaking'.
11. For a discussion of the competition law aspects of this, see *Olav Kolstad:* Fra konkurransepolitikk til konkurranserett. Samfunnsøkonomisk effektivitet i den konkurranserettslige analyse, 1998 p. 65 et seq. See also *P.J. Slot & A.M. Skudder:* Common

Today the systems of ownership in the liberalised sectors vary widely from country to country and from sector to sector. In several cases there will be a large well-established national operator which is publicly owned in whole or in part.[12] In other sectors there are local government owned, consumer owned and commercial participants. Finally, international undertakings are participating to an increasing extent in undertakings which were previously national monopolies (for example in the telecommunications and electricity supply sectors), which can still be under complete or partial public ownership. However, many national markets are still characterised by having one dominant participant in the shape of the previously public provider.

Even though the sectors covered by this chapter have traditionally been characterised by the existence of national or local monopolies, this has not necessarily meant that there has been a lack of cross-border exchange of services or goods. The participants on the market for the international exchange of goods or services have merely been restricted to national or local monopolies. Cooperation has been carried on a private law basis. Thus there have been both bilateral and multilateral cooperation agreements, often in connection with some trade organisation (for example the Universal Postal Union).

1.1. Which sectors are dealt with?

The sectors which have been selected for study in this chapter have been referred to as (half) public sectors. The terms *regulated undertakings* or *utility undertakings* are also often used of these sectors.[13]

What characterises the sectors dealt with here is that, at one or more steps in the value chain, they have facilities or systems that have the characteristics of a network.

Networks are often distinguished between *distribution networks* (local networks which serve individual customers), and *transmission networks* (trunk networks which link the distribution networks).

In the Commission's Green Paper of 21 May 2003 on services of general interest (COM(2003) 270 final) such sectors have been described as 'Services of general economic interest provided by large network industries'. The ex-

Features of Community Law Regulation in the Network-Bound Sectors, Common Market Law Review Vol. 38 2001 p. 120.

12. Such an undertaking is regarded as the *incumbent.*
13. The term *public utility* is often used. However, the use of this term is usually limited to the supply of telecommunications, electricity, gas and water.

istence of a network is obvious in connection with electricity supply, natural gas supply, the railways and parts of the telecommunications sector. These sectors have contiguous physical networks. These can be referred to as *physical networks*. Other systems, such as harbours and airports, and transmission masts can also constitute networks, on which the supply of the services in question depend, even though the systems may not be physically linked. The same considerations apply to the delivery points for the postal service (postboxes), sorting offices, and the distribution network (postal delivery workers). These have the character of a *non-physical network.*

In terms of cost, networks are characterised by having economies of scale, with cost regression as well as economies of scope. Furthermore, networks often have high sunk costs. Other parts of the value chain, i.e. those parts that have been exposed to competition as a result of liberalisation, can be seen to suffer from 'stranded costs'.

A sunk cost can be defined as a cost which has already been paid, and which cannot be varied.[14] They are, in any event, irrecoverable. Stranded costs, especially in relation to the utilities sectors, can be defined as 'those costs that the utilities are currently permitted to recover through their rates but whose recovery may be impeded or prevented by the advent of competition'.[15] For example, in the electricity supply sector stranded costs are found in the form of power stations that have been built during the period of monopoly, when all the costs could be passed on to the end users. Because of their choice of technology and overcapacity, some power stations can be unable to give a return on their investment on an open electricity market. Stranded costs can also arise in the form of contractual obligations for the purchase of electricity for which there is no longer certainty of there being sales.[16] Article 24 of Directive 96/92/EC concerning common rules for the internal market in electricity ('the first Electricity Directive') contained some transitional provisions relating to stranded costs.[17]

The existence of a network with sunk and stranded costs means that new participants will not necessarily be attracted to the market, even if there is a profitable market or ineffective competitors. The investments required for entering a market which is characterised by the existence of a network are often

14. *Robert S. Pindyck & Daniel L. Rubinfeld:* Microeconomics, 2001 p. 205.
15. *William J. Baumol & J. Gregory Sidak:* Transmission Pricing and Stranded Costs in the Electric Power Industry, 1995 p. 98.
16. On stranded costs, see *Peter Cameron:* Competition in Energy Markets, 2007 p. 432 et seq.
17. The possibility of transitional arrangements has not been carried forward in the third (and current) electricity directive.

considerable, especially if it is not possible to gain access to the networks of the established participants.

In addition to having a network, the provision of goods and services by the sectors dealt with in this chapter often cannot be stored, or can only be stored at great expense. A train or an aircraft which departs with unused capacity loses the capacity. Electricity can only be stored at great expense, and its production must be adjusted to consumption. There are typically wide variations of loading in the course of the day (rush hour, peak loading), the week and the year. If demand is always to be met, there must be a capacity which will be under-used at certain times of the day, week or year.

Finally, it is common to all the sectors that it is assumed that competition can be introduced in whole or in part in these sectors. This can be described as the competitive capacity of the market. The introduction of competition to a sector is often referred to as the initiation of competition, or simply liberalisation. The Union has sought and still seeks to introduce competition-based market regulation, in whole or in part, to the sectors which have been selected for discussion in this chapter. The network structure and the special interests in the sectors have meant that segments which are exposed to competition and segments that are not exposed to competition exist side by side in the individual sectors. Consideration for the existing participants and their investments (stranded costs) has mean that in many cases the opening of the market to competition has been done in stages.

In the electricity supply sector, it was directly stated in the first Electricity Directive that a certain percentage of the market should be opened to competition. The percentage level was raised in steps. From the start some end users (large commercial customers) were given the right to choose their suppliers. An end user who could chose their supplier was referred to as a *privileged customer*. The electricity market is now fully liberalised, and the distinction between privileged and non-privileged customers is only relevant where some customers are free to choose their supplier, while others are not.

Despite the complete or partial opening of markets, many liberalised sectors are still characterised by the presence of one or more national participants (previous monopolists), which still have a dominant position on the market which is at least linked to those segments of the market which are not open to competition.

It should also be noted that the content and purpose of the varying degrees of liberalisation can vary considerably from sector to sector.[18] It is also stated in the Commission's Green Paper on services of general interest that the Union has adopted different regulatory strategies for different network industries and services of general interest. This is because of the differences between the different sectors (notably in their profitability, their production structure, their capital intensity, their methods of service delivery, and their demand structure), and because these industries are at different stages of the liberalisation process.[19]

1.2. Facilities of special significance

Networks of the kind described above are called *essential facilities*. This term has its roots in US antitrust law and was introduced in a judgment of the Supreme Court. The term characterises facilities that are controlled by an individual supplier to the market, which cannot be substituted by some other solution, and which are of general importance to society. The importance of the facility (or infrastructure) consists in the fact that customers cannot be reached without using it. There will be no possibility of finding an alternative solution if the facility cannot be duplicated at a reasonable cost.[20]

The competition law interest in essential facilities concerns the right of access of market participants to facilities owned by another participant, even a competitor, as long as the facility in question is of particular importance for being able to operate on a given market. A right to such access has been developed in competition law in the *essential facilities doctrine*.

The doctrine can be stated as follows: 'Where facilities cannot practically be duplicated by would-be competitors, those in possession of them must allow them to be shared on fair terms.'[21] This obligation to make facilities available to others only concerns facilities which in practice cannot be duplicated. This is a description which, to a large extent, will only be applicable to the networks in the liberalised sectors.

18. For statements on this, see *Klaus J. Hopt*: Transsectoral Issues of Regulation, in *Jürgen Basedow et al. (eds.):* Economic Regulation and competition, The Hague 2002 p. 306.
19. COM(2003) 270 final, section 3.2, para. 71. These comments are made in relation to network access and interconnectivity, but they have wider applicability.
20. See *Daniel Glasl:* Draft Council Directive concerning licences to railway undertakings: A Contribution to the Current Debate, European Competition Law Review 1994 p. 307. For a short review of the term in relation to third party access and the rejection of its direct applicability at Community level, see *Friedrich von Burchard & Lutz Eckert:* Natural Gas and EU Energy Law, 1995 p. 102 et seq.
21. *A.D. Neale & D.G. Goyder:* Antitrust Laws of the United States of America, 1980 p. 62.

'Essential facilities' is a concept which is not directly found in the TFEU.[22] The General Court (formerly the Court of First Instance)[23] has applied the principle of a right of access to such facilities several times in relation to individual sectors.[24] The same applies to the Commission.

The Commission has dealt with this question in two cases concerning a right of access to the harbour at Holyhead in Wales (the *B&I* case and the *Sea Containers* case from 1992 and 1993) as well as a case concerning *Rødby Harbour* in Denmark in 1994.[25] For a short commentary on essential facilities, see *Antonio Capobianco*, E.L. Rev. 2001 pp. 548-564. It is in particular in connection the access to infrastructure facilities that most cases arise.

The principle has also been applied by the Court of Justice of the European Union[26] in connection with the prohibition of abuse of dominant position under Article 102 TFEU. There is thus a presumption that possession of an essential facility is an expression of the existence of a dominant position. On the basis of the presumption the CJ has considered a number of cases on the refusal to enter into trading relations. According to the cases, a product or service can only be regarded as essential if there is no actual or potential alternative.[27] In a case concerning a joint venture involving railways under Article 101 TFEU [then Article 85], it was further explained:[28]

> 'Consequently, with regard to an agreement such as that in the present case, setting up a joint venture, which falls within Article 85(1) of the Treaty [now Article 105(1) TFEU], the Court considers that neither the parent undertakings nor the joint venture thus set up may be regarded as being in possession of infrastructure, products or services which are 'necessary' or 'essential' for entry to the relevant market unless such

22. For a review of the rules in an EU context see *John Temple Lang:* Defining legitimate competition: Companies' duties to supply competitors and access to essential facilities, 18 Fordham Int'l L.J. 437.
23. Hereinafter referred to as the GC.
24. A non-exhaustive list of the cases includes Case T-504/93, *Tiercé Ladbroke* v *Commission;* and Joined Cases T-374/94, T-375/94, T-384/94 and T-388/94, *European Night Services* v *Commission.*
25. See the Commission's Decisions in Case 94/19/EC and Case 94/119/EC.
26. Hereinafter referred to as the CJ.
27. Joined Cases C-241/91 P and C-242/91 P, *Magill,* paras 53-54 (originally Case T-69/89 *RTE* v *Commission* and Case T-76/89 *ITP* v *Commission ;* and Case T-504/93, *Tiercé Ladbroke* v *Commission,* para. 131.
28. Joined Cases T-374/94, T-375/94, T-384/94 and T-388/94, *European Night Services and others* v *Commission,* para. 209.

> infrastructure, products or services are not 'interchangeable' and unless, by reason of their special characteristics – in particular the prohibitive cost of and/or time reasonably required for reproducing them – there are no viable alternatives available to potential competitors of the joint venture, which are thereby excluded from the market.'

These conditions are illustrated further in the *Bronner* case.[29] A publisher had a distribution network for its newspapers. The question was to what extent this publisher was required to give other publishers access to its network. The CJ accepted that there could be refusal of access to the network. The grounds for this were the existence of alternative means of distribution both actual (via the postal service, sales via shops and kiosks – paragraph 43) and potential (the possibility of building up its own network – paragraph 44). The CJ thus restricted the application of the essential facilities doctrine to situations where there are no other actual or potential distribution possibilities.

The competition rules of the TFEU thus contain provisions that can give a right of access to a competitor's network, as long as exclusion from the network would effectively exclude a participant from entering or remaining in the market.

Certain networks have the character of a natural monopoly. This means that the costs for the essential facilities for the distribution of, for example, energy are so great that, because of the economies of scale, it is only cost effective to have one set of facilities through which the service or product can be supplied.[30] The monopoly situation will normally concern the provision of the specific good or service. On the demand side there will usually be possibilities for substitution; for example different forms of transport can be substituted for each other.[31]

In *W. J. Baumol et al.*: Weak Invisible Hand Theorems on the Sustainability of Multiproduct Natural Monopoly, American Economic Review 1977 pp. 350-365, there is an alternative cost-related definition: 'By a natural monopoly we mean an industry whose cost

29. Case C-7/97, Bronner. For commentary on the case see *Leo Flynn:* Access to the Postal Network: the situation after Bronner, in *Damien Geradin (ed.):* The Liberalization of Postal Services in the European Union, 2002 p. 190 et seq.
30. Economies of scale mean that the average costs per unit supplied will fall as the capacity usage rises. The marginal costs are thus lower than the average costs.
31. There are not always substitution possibilities, and sometimes they are of such a different quality (for example with respect to the time required) that the possibility is not realistic.

function over some given set of products is such that no combination of several firms can produce an industry out-put vector as cheaply as it can be provided by a single supplier.'

The concept is linked to economic theory and as such is not a principle of competition law. The concept implies cost considerations in relation to the technology existing at the time. What is (economically) impossible or decidedly inappropriate seems to lie at the core of this. The way in which this fits with the concept of *essential facilities* is notable.

Not all infrastructures in the liberalised sectors have the character of networks which can be categorised as natural monopolies. This often depends on the specific market and the available technology. Until recently local fixed line telephone traffic (subscriber networks)[32] would perhaps have been considered a natural monopoly, since a nationwide duplication of such a network would normally be impossible.[33] The increased use of mobile telephony and the spread of the broadband network make it questionable whether the subscriber network is still a natural monopoly. For connections between two large urban areas or exchanges the existence of a natural monopoly has long been in doubt. Long distance telephony is no longer regarded as a natural monopoly. There can also be local differences to some extent. While natural gas transmission has been regarded as a natural monopoly in most of Europe, in Germany parallel or alternative connections have been established in some places.[34]

There can be other hindrances to the duplication of a set of installations, other than the purely economic. In some cases individual undertakings may have been granted exclusive rights. In other cases there are legislative barriers which may involve long-lasting procedures for the establishment of certain installations. For example, this will typically be the case for the building of a railway network or an electricity supply network carried by pylons. Among other things planning and environmental requirements for consultation and environmental impact assessment will complicate the establishment of such a network.

The terms *essential facilities* and *natural monopolies* are linked to infrastructures or networks in the liberalised sectors. In connection with the liberalisation of these sectors a distinction is often made between the infrastructure and

32. Subscriber links are the paired twisted wires constituting physical metallic leads which connect the terminal node of the subscriber to the main distributor of the local exchange or to an equivalent point on a fixed public telephone network.
33. The Commission's XXXI Report on Competition Policy, p. 34. However, this may change with the roll-out of fibre optic cables under the regime of the electricity supply undertakings.
34. *Christopher W. Jones:* EU Energy Law, Vol. I, 2010 p. 29.

the goods or services whose provision is dependent on the infrastructure in question.

There can be a distinction between goods and services. In the energy sector, electricity and gas are regarded as being goods, while the transport or transmission of these is considered to be a service.[35] In the transport and communications sectors all the relevant provision constitutes services.

1.3. The regulatory background

The powers of the Union in this area are derived in part from the general provisions of the TFEU (including Articles 14, 37, 101, 102 and 106),[36] in part from the articles dealing with transport (Articles 90-100), and in part from the articles dealing with trans-European networks (Articles 170-172).

In the Commission's Notice on the application of the competition rules to access agreements in the telecommunications sector – framework, relevant markets and principles (OJ 1998 C 265/2) some views are expressed which seem to have wider validity.[37] Thus it is assumed that the Union's competition rules and the sector-specific regulation constitute different sets of rules which apply independently of each other and which have different purposes and different means of enforcement. However, the competition rules are directly applicable,[38] and it is not possible to introduce provisions via sectoral regulation that conflict with the competition rules laid down in the Treaty. Also in other cases where EU law is observed, the competition rules must be complied with.[39] For example, as a consequence of this the rules in the telecommunications sector must be interpreted so as to be in accordance with the general competition rules.[40]

35. Case 6/64, *Costa* v *ENEL,* in which electricity was presumed to be a good. In relation to Article 34 TFEU [then Article 28], this was confirmed by the CJ in Case C-393/92, *Almelo and others* v *Energiebedrijf Ijsselmij*, para. 28 which refers to the Union's tariff nomenclature (code CN 27.16).
36. See Chapters II, V and IX for discussions on Articles 101, 102 and 106 respectively.
37. See *Pierre Larouche:* Telecommunications, in *Damien Geradin (ed.):* The Liberalization of State Monopolies in the European Union and Beyond, 2000 pp. 284-316; and *Laurent Garzaniti:* Telecommunications, Broadcasting and Internet: EU Competition Law and Regulation, 2000 sections 10-01 to 10-15.
38. Case 127/73, *BRT I.*
39. Case 66/86, *Ahmed Saeed* v *Silver Line Reisebüro.*
40. The Commission's Notice on the application of the competition rules to access agreements in the telecommunications sector – framework, relevant markets and principles, para. 58 (OJ 1998 C 265/2).

Whether a case involves public or private ownership is, in principle, not relevant to the application of the competition rules. This can be deduced from the principle of equal treatment expressed in Article 106 TFEU and the principle of neutrality expressed in Article 345 TFEU.

Conversely, there is nothing to prevent sector-specific provisions going further than the provisions that apply under the competition rules. However, the authority for this must be sought elsewhere.

The use of sector-specific regulation is characteristic for the liberalised sectors. Two main reasons can be given for this. First, there can be imperfect competition in a market so that for a period,[41] or perhaps permanently, it will not be possible to create a truly competitive market. This can be due to natural monopolies, for example, or the historical strength of the dominant participant on the market (depreciated investments etc.). Second, the choice of sector-specific regulation can be based on other considerations than effective competition, such as security of supply, environmental protection and, to some extent, consumer protection. Such considerations cannot necessarily be taken care of through general competition rules.

Article 103 TFEU contains a provision whereby the Council, acting by a qualified majority on a proposal from the Commission and after consulting the European Parliament, can issue appropriate regulations or directives to give effect to the principles set out in Articles 101 and 102 TFEU. This provision has been used in the air transport and railways sectors. Moreover, the Commission publishes notices giving its understanding of the competition rules and the related administrative procedures. Such notices have been issued for the telecommunications and postal services sectors. Neither the Council nor the Commission has issued such guidelines or legislation in the area of energy supply.[42]

A number of the most important provisions connected with liberalisation measures have been introduced via directives. These can be divided into two main groups:

41. If the imperfect competition is only temporary, one can imagine that the sectoral regulation – at least in respect of its competition law provisions – will later be repealed, and the sector will be subject to the general competition rules.
42. In the following sector-specific section there is an emphasis on sector-specific provisions. The application of the TFEU's general competition law provisions is only dealt with to a limited extent. For more detailed treatment of these, the reader is referred to the other chapters in this book.

- *Liberalising directives*: These have been issued under the authority of Article 106 TFEU, and are discussed in more detail in Chapter IX. In Article 106(1) it is stated: 'In the case of public undertakings and undertakings to which Member States grant special or exclusive rights, Member States shall neither enact nor maintain in force any measure contrary to the rules contained in the Treaties, in particular to those rules provided for in Article 18 and Articles 101 to 109.' The authority to issue directives or decisions is given in Article 106(3). For example, Directive 2002/77/EC on competition in the markets for electronic communications networks and services was issued under this authority. This authority has particularly been used in the telecommunications sector.
- *Harmonising directives*: These are issued under the authority of Article 114 TFEU, according to which: 'The European Parliament and the Council shall, acting in accordance with the ordinary legislative procedure and after consulting the Economic and Social Committee, adopt the measures for the approximation of the provisions laid down by law, regulation or administrative action in Member States which have as their object the establishment and functioning of the internal market'; see Article 114(1).[43] Directive 2009/72/EC concerning common rules for the internal market in electricity ('the Electricity Directive'), Directive 2009/73/EC concerning common rules for the internal market in natural gas ('the Natural Gas Directive'), Directive 2005/89/EC concerning measures to safeguard security of electricity supply and infrastructure investment, and Directive 97/67/EC on common rules for the development of the internal market of Community postal services and the improvement of quality of service are examples of this. In the telecommunications sector, where liberalising directives have also been issued, there are harmonising directives in the form of Directive 2002/21/EC on a common regulatory framework for electronic communications networks and services (Framework Directive), Directive 2002/19/EC on access to, and interconnection of, electronic communications networks and associated facilities (Access Directive) and Directive 2002/20/EC on the authorisation of electronic communications networks and services (Authorisation Directive). In addition to these, examples of measures adopted under the authority of Article 114 include: Regulation (EC) No 715/2009 on conditions for access to the natural gas transmission

43. A distinction is often made between total harmonisation and minimum harmonisation, as the two main variations. Other less used variations can be used.

networks; Regulation (EC) No 714/2009 on conditions for access to the network for cross-border exchanges in electricity; Decision No 676/2002/EC on a regulatory framework for radio spectrum policy in the European Community (Radio Spectrum Decision); and Decision No 128/1999/EC on the coordinated introduction of a third-generation mobile and wireless communications system (UMTS) in the Community.

The liberalising directives primarily identify and flesh out the rules of the TFEU. In particular the provisions in Article 102 and Article 106(1) TFEU are relevant. In contrast, the harmonising directives provide to a greater degree for the issuing of new obligations.[44]
Furthermore, a number of secondary legal acts have been issued under the authority of Article 91 in the transport section of the Treaty. These relate in particular to the railway sector. Article 100(2) has been used in the air transport sector.[45] Some secondary legal acts have also been issued under the authority of Article 352 TFEU, according to which, if action by the Union should prove necessary to attain one of the objectives of the Union and the Treaty has not provided the necessary powers, the Council, acting unanimously on a proposal from the Commission and after obtaining the consent of the European Parliament, shall adopt the appropriate measures.

Article 122(1) TFEU (formerly Article 100(1) of the EC Treaty), under which the Council, acting by a qualified majority on a proposal from the Commission, may decide upon the measures appropriate to the economic situation, in particular if severe difficulties arise in the supply of certain products (especially in the energy sector), has been used as authority for the issue of Directive 2004/67/EC concerning measures to safeguard security of natural gas supply.

1.4. Regulating the liberalised sectors

The liberalising process which is in progress is based to a high degree on the idea that the introduction of partial competition can lead to greater efficiency

44. Cf. *Bronner Leo Flynn:* Access to the Postal Network: the situation after Bronner, in *Damien Geradin (ed.):* The Liberalization of Postal Services in the European Union, 2002 p. 204.
45. Under Article 100(2) TFEU, The European Parliament and the Council, acting in accordance with the ordinary legislative procedure, may lay down appropriate provisions for sea and air transport.

on otherwise imperfect markets.[46] The background to this has also been the pressure within the EU to include traditional utilities sectors in the internal market.

There are considerations other than purely competition interests that are associated with the liberalised sectors. Thus, regulation of the energy and transport sectors is of significant importance to environmental policy. The networks and production facilities associated with these sectors also affect the landscape and thus have a planning dimension. Moreover, there are significant security aspects associated with carrying on undertakings in these two areas. These affect employees, consumers and the surrounding society. Security of supply in the energy sector also affects the electricity and natural gas sectors. Both the EU and the Member States are involved in regulating these areas. Such regulation both affects the market situation by acting as a barrier to entry to the market or by opening up the market. In some situations environmental and planning applications can take years. However, these areas of policy will not be discussed in this chapter.

In order to include the liberalised sectors in the internal market it is possible, in part, to use the general competition rules of the TFEU. The application of these is reviewed in brief in the individual sector sections below. However, the Union has primarily made use of framework regulation. This has mostly been expressed in sector-specific directives and regulations. These address various important and often overlapping problems and solutions for opening up public utilities to competition. Many of these problems will be discussed below.

Many directives and regulations have been amended several times. When, in the following, a reference is made to a directive or a regulation, this includes the subsequent amendments, unless it is made clear from the context that the reference is to the original version.

1.4.1. Exclusivity

Undertakings whose possible monopoly status or dominant position on a given market is due to a public grant of a right can be said to have exclusive rights. In relation to Article 106 TFEU, undertakings which enjoy such exclusive rights are referred to as *privileged undertakings*.

Exclusivity will have both a geographic limit (perhaps the territory of a Member State or part thereof) and a limit to one or more special business are-

46. There is disagreement between economists as to whether a competitive market necessarily gives rise to greater efficiency than a monopoly market. See the experiences referred to in *John J. Siegfried & Edwin H. Wheeler:* Cost Efficiency and Monopoly Power, Quarterly Review of Economics and Business Vol. 21 1981; and *Roger S. Frantz:* X-Efficiency: Theory, Evidence and Applications, 1997.

as – in the terminology of competition law, geographic markets and product markets respectively.

Exclusivity does not always occur as an exclusive right.[47] In certain areas a few undertakings in the same product market or the same geographic market can have a joint exclusive right. Article 106 TFEU has thus been used for the grant of rights to more than one undertaking. See Case 173/83 *Commission* v *France* (Waste oil), Case 66/86, *Ahmed Saeed Flugreisen*, and Case C-209/98 *Entreprenørforeningens Affalds/Miljøsektion* v *Copenhagen*. However, in relation to the liberalised sectors, exclusivity will usually be in the form of an *exclusive right*.

There is not uniformly used terminology in this area in the context of Community law. Privileged undertakings are sometimes referred to as licensed undertakings or public undertakings. The exclusivity which is granted is sometimes referred to as an exclusive right, a sole right or a licence.

Exclusivity for network energy industries has been referred to as area licences, for example the exclusive right to manage a distribution network in a given area. In contrast to this is a trading licence, which is more in the nature of an authorisation, for example to trade in electricity, but it does not imply any exclusivity. The concept of a licence also applies to rights to exploit natural resources, such as the mining of raw materials.

Exclusivity is not a situation which is prohibited in principle by the Community. On the other hand the Community does seek to regulate the exploitation of exclusivity. For the liberalised sectors the most important provision on this is Article 106(1) TFEU, according to which, in respect of public undertakings and undertakings to which they grant special or exclusive rights, the Member States must neither enact nor maintain in force any measure contrary to the rules contained in the Treaty. The term 'exclusive rights' is not defined in more detail in the Treaty.[48]

47. In *José Luis Buendia Sierra:* Exclusive Rights and State Monopolies under EC Law, 1999 p. 6, exclusivity seems to be linked to a 'single undertaking'.
48. The provision in Article 106(2) TFEU on undertakings entrusted with the operation of services of general economic interest, is dealt with below in section 1.4.6. The use of the term 'exclusive rights' in Article 106(1) is not the subject of a separate discussion. The expression is predominantly used in respect of rights granted under public law that are given to a few undertakings. In Directive 2008/63/EC of 20 June 2008 on competition in the markets in telecommunications terminal equipment, *special rights* are defined as 'rights that are granted by a Member State to a limited number of undertakings, through any legislative, regulatory or administrative instrument, which, within a given geographical area,

In secondary Community legislation the exploitation of exclusivity is regulated in relation to the liberalised sectors. Here there are also definitions of the concept of exclusivity. In the relation between a Member State and a privileged undertaking there are thus special provision in Article 2(1)(f) of Directive 2006/11/EC on the transparency of financial relations between Member States and public undertakings, as amended by Directive 2000/52/ EC, whereby 'exclusive rights' are defined as 'rights that are granted by a Member State to one undertaking through any legislative, regulatory or administrative instrument, reserving it the right to provide a service or undertake an activity within a given geographical area'. There is a similar definition in Article 1(5) of Directive 2002/77/EC on competition in the markets for electronic communications networks and services.

Exclusivity can also be based on a grant under private law, for example on the basis of intellectual property rights. By virtue of their ownership rights public authorities can grant exclusive user rights to undertakings (licensees). In several Member States this has been used in connection with the placing of networks alongside and over public roads.[49]

Exclusivity can be granted as part of planning, where a public authority lays down that there shall be a certain service on a certain route or area. Here, planning is used as an instrument to ensure a provision which might not otherwise be established to a sufficient extent, or perhaps to serve the general economic interest by excluding a competing network. An example could be a licence to serve a particular air transport route or railway line, or a licence to establish a natural gas distribution network in a limited area. Article 3(2) of the Electricity Directive includes explicit possibilities for using long term planning with regard to the fulfilment of environmental targets, security of supply, targets for the generation of energy from renewable sources, or energy efficiency through demand management.

a. limits to two or more the number of such undertakings, otherwise than according to objective, proportional and non-discriminatory criteria; or
b. designates, otherwise than according to the criteria referred to in point (a), several competing undertakings; or
c. confers on any undertaking or undertakings, otherwise than according to the criteria referred to in points (a) and (b), any legal or regulatory advantages which substantially affect the ability of any other undertaking to import, market, connect, bring into service and/or maintain telecommunication terminal equipment in the same geographical area under substantially equivalent conditions.'

There is a similar definition in Article 2(1)(g) of Directive 2006/111/EC.

49. In Germany licence fees are still collected for this. This has also been the case in certain areas in Denmark in connection with electricity supply, but is no longer so.

Article 4(4) of the Natural Gas Directive allows Member States to refrain from granting further authorisations to build and operate distribution pipeline systems in any particular area once such pipeline systems have been or are proposed to be built in that area and if existing or proposed capacity is not saturated. It is explicitly stated that this is for the purpose of the development of newly supplied areas and efficient operation generally.

A company which is granted such a licence will often be under an obligation to supply in the licensed area or provide some other stated minimum service of a route or extent.[50]

Exclusivity can be combined with various other instruments which secure a special market position for the undertaking with the exclusive rights. For example, this can concern an obligation to connect to a distribution network, with or without an obligation to accept supply of the service in question. End users can also be prohibited from securing the service for themselves by prohibiting or limiting the possibility for self-supply.

1.4.2. Cross subsidisation

In the liberalised sectors it is not unusual for finances from profitable areas of business to be transferred to other perhaps less profitable areas of business, or maybe one area of a business carries a smaller share of the shared costs than another area. In terms of competition law, this is cross subsidisation.

'Cross-subsidisation means that an undertaking bears or allocates all or part of the costs of its activity in one geographical or product market to its activity in another geographical or product market.'[51] Geographic markets exist when the same product or service is priced differently, depending on where it is sold. In relation to product markets, the possibility of cross subsidisation arises when there is complete or partial overlap of production of two products or services. Examples of this are travel by both economy and business class on the same aircraft, or the joint production of electricity and heating.

This definition is based on a cost-based understanding of cross-subsidies.[52] As appears from the quotation above, such cross subsidisation can occur in-

50. On obligations to supply, see section 1.4.6.1 of this chapter.
51. The definition comes from the Commission Notice on the application of the competition rules to the postal sector and on the assessment of certain State measures relating to postal services (OJ 1998 C 39/2).
52. The alternative to this is an *efficient pricing approach.* In relation to this, prices depend on customers' willingness to pay (price elasticity) in order to obtain optimal pricing (Ramsey pricing) and thereby maximise welfare. See *Giuseppe B. Abbamonte:* Cross-subsidisation and Community Competition Rules: Efficient Pricing versus Equity, European Law Review 1998 p. 418.

ternally within an undertaking. It can also take place between legal persons (companies) and within a corporate group. Cross-subsidisation can take place either through the incorrect allocation of costs, or by transferring surpluses or other resources. It is not always easy to determine with certainty whether there is cross-subsidisation.[53]

Cross subsidisation is not prohibited in principle in Community law.[54] In fact it can be an expression of perfectly normal practice. Thus it is not unusual for one market to contribute more to the shared costs than other markets. In business terms this can be rational in order to remain in or to break into a less profitable market, as long as the marginal costs are covered. However, where a participant on a market has a dominant position, cross subsidisation can be an expression for abuse of the dominant position. Likewise it can be an expression of discrimination and State aid contrary to the Treaty.

When there is public involvement in a sector, there will be a risk of confusion of the roles of administrative authority and owner. This makes it desirable for there to be a certain degree of transparency in the relationship between an authority and its undertakings.

1.4.2.1. From monopoly to market

When a sector is split into one or more parts which are open to competition and a part which is subject to a monopoly, there is a risk that funds obtained from the area of a *de jure* monopoly will be used to subsidise activities which are subject to competition in the same undertaking or same group of undertakings. The opposite, cross subsidisation from an activity that is subject to competition to a monopoly activity, is not normally regarded as a problem under competition law. Nor is cross subsidisation between monopoly activities seen as a problem. There is no risk of distortion of competition on monopoly markets.[55]

The term *cross subsidisation* is directly used in Article 31(3) of the Electricity Directive. In their internal accounting, integrated electricity companies have to keep separate accounts for each of their transmission and distribution activities, 'with a view to avoiding discrimination, cross subsidisation and distortion of competition'. There is a corresponding provision in Article 31(3) of the Natural Gas Directive, in relation to transmission, distribution,

53. See *Leigh Hancher & José Luis Buendia Sierra:* Cross-Subsidization and EC Law, Common Market Law Review Vol. 35 1998 p. 906 et seq.
54. *Giuseppe B. Abbamonte:* Cross-subsidisation and Community Competition Rules: Efficient Pricing versus Equity, European Law Review 1998 p. 423.
55. To a certain extent this form of cross-subsidising can be used to finance the obligation to supply. On this, see section 1.4.6.1.

LNG and storage activities. The requirement can be described as *unbundling of accounts* and is discussed in more detail below.

Cross subsidisation from a monopoly activity to an activity which is subject to competition can constitute abuse of a dominant position. For example, it can be used to support dumping prices (predatory pricing)[56] in the business area which is subject to competition or be used to prevent market entry by new participants (competition concerns). Equally, the possibility for such a (abnormally large) cross subsidy can be an indication that the monopoly is being exploited in order to take too high prices for the monopoly goods or services (consumer protection concerns). Such circumstances may not only be an expression of infringement of sector-specific provisions in secondary legislation, but they could also mean that there is a breach of the prohibition of abuse of dominant position. Article 102 TFEU does not have regard for whether the dominant position has arisen *de jure* or *de facto*.

In the area of postal services the question of cross subsidisation has been before the courts in connection with a merger in Case T-175/99, *UPS*. A postal undertaking (Deutsche Post) had possibly used funds obtained from an area where it had been granted exclusive rights to acquire a shareholding of 22.498 % in an undertaking (DHL), which operated in a part of the postal sector which was subject to competition

Two arguments were put forward for why this was contrary to Community law (paragraph 53):

‘a. the financing by Deutsche Post of the acquisition of its holding in DHL implies that it financed that acquisition from income obtained from its activities in the reserved letter market, thereby abusing its dominant position in that market; and

b. the future relationship between Deutsche Post and DHL will necessarily lead to cross-subsidisation of DHL’s activities in the liberalised parcel market by income obtained by Deutsche Post from the reserved market.’

Since the GC could not establish that the means which had been derived from the monopoly market had been obtained by an abuse of the

56. For a more detailed discussion of the link between cross subsidisation and predatory pricing, see *Leigh Hancher & José Luis Buendia Sierra:* Cross-Subsidization and EC Law, Common Market Law Review Vol. 35 1998 p. 912 et seq.

monopoly, there was no problem under competition law. The GC's central considerations in relation to argument a) were stated in paragraph 61: 'In the absence of any evidence to show that the funds used by Deutsche Post for the acquisition in question derived from abusive practices on its part in the reserved letter market, the mere fact that it used those funds to acquire joint control of an undertaking active in a neighbouring market open to competition does not in itself, even if the source of those funds was the reserved market, raise any problem from the standpoint of the competition rules and cannot therefore constitute an infringement of Article 82 EC or give rise to an obligation on the Commission to examine the source of those funds in the light of that article.'

The key question seems to be whether there has been an abuse of the monopoly market (the privileged activity). If this is not the case, funds obtained from activities on the monopoly market can be used to make acquisitions in the sector which is subject to competition. A different result could have given rise to a number of problems in relation to other and earlier acquisitions in the liberalised sectors.

As for distortion of competition in the market itself, this was not accepted by the GC, but again this is a question of evidence; see paragraph 64: 'As regards the applicant's second contention, to the effect that the future relationship between Deutsche Post and DHL would necessarily involve cross-subsidisation of DHL's business in the parcels market, it need merely be observed that it is clear from the undertaking given by Deutsche Post to the Commission, in response to the requirement to that effect imposed by the decision of 26 June 1998, that Deutsche Post is prohibited from engaging in any such cross-subsidisation, with the result that, for the purposes of this case, that question is academic. Consequently, if, in the future, the applicant were able to prove such cross-subsidisation on the part of Deutsche Post, it would be entitled to apply to the Commission or, by virtue of the direct effect of Article 82 EC, to the competent national court for appropriate penalties to be imposed.' In this case the GC did not consider the legality of the exclusive right itself under Article 106 TFEU or in relation to the provisions on State aid. Subsequently in amending Directive 2002/39/EC, an amendment was made to Article 12 of Directive 97/67/EC on postal services to the effect that 'cross-subsidisation of universal services outside the reserved sector out of revenues from services in the reserved sector shall be prohibited except to the extent to which it is shown to be strictly necessary to fulfil specific universal service obligations imposed in the competitive area'. The granting of exclusive or special rights for financing the provision of

> postal services was prohibited by Directive 2008/6/EC amending Directive 97/67/EC.

In a French case on postal services it was established that even covering all the costs would not necessarily exclude cross-subsidisation and State aid.

> In this case the French public postal undertaking, La Poste, had provided logistical support (including collection, sorting, distribution and delivery of letters etc.) as well as business support for Chronopost.[57] Chronopost was 66 % owned by La Poste. In this case the CJ stated that, even if it was accepted that Chronopost had paid all La Poste's costs for logistical and business support, this would not in itself be sufficient to show that there had not been some form of State aid. The CJ emphasised that 'La Poste might, by virtue of its position as the sole public undertaking in a reserved sector, have been able to provide some of the logistical and commercial assistance at lower cost than a private undertaking not enjoying the same rights'. The CJ went on to say that, on the contrary, 'it is precisely a relationship in which the parent company operates in a reserved market and its subsidiary carries out its activities in a market open to competition that creates a situation in which State aid is likely to exist.'

There are sector-specific provisions on cross subsidies in, for example, Article 3(1) of Regulation (EC) No 1775/2005 on conditions for access to the natural gas transmission networks, and Article 7(3) specifically states that undertakings must avoid cross-subsidisation between network users.

1.4.2.2. Joint production

Cross subsidisation occurs not only as a result of the exploitation of a dominant position on a market. There is often joint production (joint management or shared traffic) of several goods or services.

The decision as to whether cross subsidisation exists is usually based on questions of the allocation of costs. It can be understood as a requirement for there to be true cost allocation for the individual good or service. If there is not such a true allocation, this will prompt a suspicion of cross subsidisation. However, there is not one undisputed method for deciding the true cost allocation when there is joint production.

57. Joined Cases C-83/01 P, C-93/01 P and C-94/01 P, *Chronopost and others* v *Ufex and others,* which overturned the judgment of the GC in Case T-613/97, *Ufex.*

With joint production, some costs are specifically linked to a specific good or service (specific costs), while other costs are common for two or more goods or services (shared costs).[58] Two concepts have been developed with a view to using them to identify any cross subsidisation: incremental costs and the stand alone cost test. *Incremental cost* refers to the increase in costs caused by the production of a secondary good or service. *Stand alone costs* refers to the hypothetical costs which each good or service would have incurred if it had been produced on its own. If the price for a good or service is equal to or greater than the incremental cost (the floor) and less than the stand alone cost (the ceiling), the price is in the core area where cross subsidisation will not be found to exist; see the *Faulhaber* rule. However, this theory does not include any particular requirements as to the allocation of costs.[59]

Under another cost-based method, the *fully distributed cost* method (FDC) also known as *fully allocated costs*, the costs are allocated systematically according to a key. If such an allocation system is not used, or if some specific good or service bears a significant part of the shared costs, there can be cross subsidisation. This method seems to be preferred by the Commission.[60] For the liberalised sectors the share of costs which an individual good or service (i) must bear under the FDC method can be described by the following model:

$$FDC i = AC i + f i CC.$$

AC*i* represents the specific costs for i, and f*i*CC is the part of the shared costs (CC) attributable to i. The shared costs can thus be allocated according to different principles, including i's share of the total production costs of the under-

58. In accounting terminology a distinction is often made between *joint costs,* which refers to the shared costs for two goods or services which are necessarily produced together, and *common costs* where the same input is used is used for the production of two goods or services. See *David Heald:* Contrasting approaches to the 'problem' of cross subsidy, Management Accounting Research Vol. 7 1996 p. 54. In this chapter the term *shared costs* is used for both concepts.
59. For more on cost-based methods and the terms referred to above see*: Giuseppe B. Abbamonte:* Cross-subsidisation and Community Competition Rules: Efficient Pricing versus Equity, European Law Review 1998 p. 416 et seq.; *Leigh Hancher & José Luis Buendia Sierra:* Cross-Subsidization and EC Law, Common Market Law Review Vol. 35 1998 p. 906 et seq.; and in particular *David Heald:* Contrasting approaches to the 'problem' of cross subsidy, in Management Accounting Research Vol. 7 1996 p. 56 et seq.
60. *Giuseppe B. Abbamonte:* Cross-subsidisation and Community Competition Rules: Efficient Pricing versus Equity, European Law Review 1998 p. 423.

taking (e.g. calculated on the basis of the distance travelled or the time taken), i's share of the total income of the undertaking, or i's share of the total specific costs. Such pricing models are practical in the sense that they are, to a certain extent based on objective accounting data from the individual undertaking. However, these objective data are historical, and it has been argued that the method does not give any incentive for efficiency improvements.[61]

In the absence of such a key, it will often be a highly complex task to establish whether there has been cross subsidisation.

The questions of costs connected with joint production are closely related to questions on the payment for access to a network. In the now repealed Directive 97/33/EC on interconnection in Telecommunications with regard to ensuring universal service and interoperability through application of the principles of Open Network Provision, in Annex V, a number of examples are given of costing standards which could be used in connection with interconnection (network access) in the telecommunications area: 'fully distributed costs, long-run average incremental costs, marginal costs, stand-alone costs, embedded direct costs, etc., including the cost base(s) used, i.e. historic costs (based on actual expenditure incurred for equipment and systems) or forward-looking costs (based on estimated replacement costs of equipment or systems).'[62] In respect of interconnection, in recital 10 of the Directive it is stated that 'whereas flexibility in the methods of charging for interconnection traffic should be possible, including capacity-based charging; whereas the level of charges should promote productivity and encourage efficient and sustainable market entry, and should not be below a limit calculated by the use of long-run incremental cost and cost allocation and attribution methods based on actual cost causation, nor above a limit set by the stand-alone cost of providing the interconnection in question; whereas charges for interconnection based on a price level closely linked to the long-run incremental cost for providing access to interconnection are appropriate for encouraging the rapid development of an open and competitive market.' Here it seems that the forward looking long-run average incremental costs (FL-LRAIC) should be the floor, while the direct costs (stand alone costs) should be the ceiling for the price calculation for the interconnection service in question.[63]

The aim of cross subsidisation can be related to the undertaking, for example the desire to strengthen competitiveness in certain areas of the market, or to penetrate these areas. These instances will often fall under the prohibition of agreements which restrict competition or abuse of a dominant position. However the aim can also be politically based, and can be determined by the authority which regulates or maybe owns the participant in question. For example, the aim can be to maintain uniform pricing for the same goods or ser-

61. *Christian Bergqvist:* Mellem regulering og deregulering, 2007 p. 348 et seq.
62. 'Marginal costs' refers to the costs of producing a single additional unit.
63. See also COM(99) 539 final.

vices for different groups of customers or in different geographic areas, where the costs for the provision of the goods or services differ (geographical equalisation).

In connection with the liberalised sectors, cross-subsidies could be used as sources of finance for maintaining the provision of services that are not, in themselves, profitable, or for keeping prices low to ensure supplies to groups of the population which would not otherwise be able to afford to buy the services. This can be done by introducing price ceilings. Similarly, cross-subsidies can be used to reduce prices in geographical areas in which the provision of a given service would have higher costs than in other areas. This can result, for example, in there being different prices in different areas, according to their population densities.

Financing is generally via an exclusive right, reserving certain profitable activities to an undertaking which has an obligation to perform some unprofitable provision of goods or services.[64] To a certain extent political motivations for such transfers have been the reasons why certain sectors have been granted exclusive rights, or access to the market has been otherwise restricted.[65] Cross subsidisation is thus a source of financing in connection with providing services of general economic interest, as discussed below.

There is a particular variant in the electricity supply sector where, under Article 15(3) of the Directive on the internal market in electricity, the Member States must require systems operators to give priority to production facilities which use renewable energy when allocating loading between production facilities. Member States can also give priority to the combined production of heat and electricity.[66] This has particular regard for environmental considerations.

1.4.3. Division between undertakings subject to competition and monopoly undertakings etc.

The fact that not all parts of traditionally vertically integrated sectors are regarded as being capable of being subject to competition, or if is merely that it

64. On cross subsidisation and EU law see *Leigh Hancher & José Luis Sierra:* Cross-Subsidization and EC Law, Common Market Law Review Vol. 35 1998; and *Giuseppe B. Abbamonte:* Cross-subsidisation and Community Competition Rules: Efficient Pricing versus Equity, European Law Review, 1998.
65. *Alberto Heimler & Paolo Saba:* Role and Enforcement of Competition Policy in Regulated Sectors, in Proceedings of the OECD/World Bank Conference on Competition and Regulation in Network Industries, OECD 1995 pp. 75 and 78.
66. See Article 16 of Directive 2009/28/EC.

is not wished to subject them to competition, makes it necessary to introduce a separation between what is to be subject to competition and what is not to be subject to competition. For example, control of a network is often put into a separate network undertaking or organisation.

Control of access to a network can perhaps be given to a system operator or infrastructure manager. This task can be given to a network undertaking as an independent undertaking. The Directive on the internal market in electricity and the Directive on the internal market in natural gas contained requirements for *system operator*, while Directive 2001/14/EC on the allocation of railway infrastructure capacity and the levying of charges for the use of railway infrastructure and safety certification refers to an *infrastructure manager*.

This form of separation of activities is often referred to as 'unbundling'. The separation can often be between different links in the value chain[67] and will therefore be vertical.[68] In the terminology of competition law one can say that the value chain represents different product markets. In the liberalised sectors there will be one or more markets for the good or service which is actually demanded by the end user (energy, transport, communications), and correspondingly one or more product markets for the facilities that are necessary for the provision of that good or service (e.g. access to a network).

The provisions on unbundling have the same aims as the general competition rules which prohibit the abuse of a dominant position. However, the provisions on unbundling are more far-reaching since, on the one hand they involve structural requirements, and on the other hand they are imposed regardless of whether there has been abuse. The thinking behind the unbundling provisions is to limit the effects on competition of some of the less desirable incentives which exist in vertically integrated corporate structures. First, there is the incentive to favour companies which are part of the same corporate group. Such incentives are usually linked to control of a network. A vertically integrated company that controls a network can favour giving associated companies access to the network. In addition, network companies automatically acquire information about other market participants' turnover and cus-

67. This splitting up of the tasks will not necessarily be noticed by the individual consumer, who often buys a single package of services that in fact consists of several different services.
68. There are also examples of horizontal separation, e.g. the separation between goods and passenger traffic on the railways. The two business areas are very different, apart from the fact that they use shared facilities, including the railway network. This horizontal division is thus not necessarily dependent on a division between an undertaking which is subject to competition and a monopoly undertaking.

tomers. Network companies can pass this information on to associated companies which thereby obtain a competitive advantage by acquiring insight into the commercially confidential information of their competitors. Furthermore, vertically integrated companies can exploit the monopoly advantages of control of the network by cross-subsidising the activities of associated companies which are exposed to competition.

A requirement for vertical unbundling is often introduced in connection with the liberalisation of public sectors. There can be unbundling at various levels. For example, there can be unbundling at the following levels:

- Accounting (separating different operating divisions)
- Management (functional)
- Organisational (legal personality, incorporation)
- Ownership.[69]

These four levels are often perceived as expressing some form of progression. However, this is not necessarily the case. Requirements for management unbundling are not necessarily met by organisational or ownership unbundling.

Accounting unbundling consists of a requirement for keeping separate accounts for the different links of the value chain. It is primarily a method for obtaining greater transparency. It should not be possible to hide any abuse of a dominant position or cross subsidising in accounts which separate out the individual areas of the business. See, for example Article 11 of Directive 2002/21/EC (the Framework Directive), Article 31(3) of the Natural Gas Directive, and Article 31(3) of the Electricity Directive. Article 11 of the Framework Directive has been upgraded to the level of organisational unbundling; see below.

Management unbundling refers to the situation where the management of one undertaking may not be subject to the instructions of another undertaking. This will typically be the case where a link in the value chain which is not subject to competition may not be managed by an undertaking which is subject to competition. This can be significant for example in relation to undertakings that administer access to networks or have responsibility for sys-

69. The division of ownership is not included by all writers. See *Peter Cameron:* Competition in Energy Markets, 2007 p. 32 et seq. However, Cameron subsequently referred to the significance of ownership. The first unbundling provisions are described in more detail in the Commission's Note of DG Energy & Transport on Directives 2003/54/EC and 2003/55/EC on the Internal Market in Electricity and Natural Gas of 16 January 2004.

tems. There was an example of management unbundling in Article 7(6) of the first Electricity Directive 96/92/EC.

Organisational unbundling refers to separation into independent legal entities. There are examples of this in Article 8 of Directive 2002/77/EC on competition in the markets for electronic communications, and Article 11 of Directive 2002/21/EC (the Framework Directive).[70] Organisational unbundling does not prevent the existence of corporate groups, where a parent company owns subsidiary companies which together represent a vertical structure. One of the key issues about the corporate group model is the possibility of an undertaking which is subject to competition and which is in the same corporate group as a monopoly undertaking having access to better and quicker information than its competitors (asymmetric information). This is normally assumed to give rise to market failure. This can arise, for example, in connection with customer databases shared between an electricity supplier which is subject to competition and an undertaking which is responsible for a distribution network.

Ownership unbundling means a prohibition of overlapping ownership interests, and thus it is a hindrance to the corporate group model. However, neither organisational nor ownership unbundling prevent an overlap between the decision makers of the individual participants. The property laws of the Member States are not affected by various Treaties; see Article 345 TFEU, and there is debate as to the extent to which requirements for ownership unbundling can be included in secondary legislation.[71]

The provision in Article 345 TFEU established the Member States' freedom to determine the rules governing the system of property ownership in their territories. Among other things, a Member State can determine that certain undertakings must be operated and owned by public authorities. However, this freedom is not total. Where public ownership leads to a distortion of competition, it must be possible for the Union to regulate the scope for public ownership. Among other things, the CJ has established a requirement for the separation of commercial activities from the exercise of administrative authority, so that a public authority has only limited scope for operating and undertaking that is subject to competition while being responsible for administrative tasks in the same area. See the

70. Article 11 of Directive 2002/21/EC (the Framework Directive) is an example of a provision where there was originally only a requirement for accounting unbundling, but which was later amended and upgraded to a requirement for organisational unbundling.
71. In the case law of the CJ, property rights are regarded as a fundamental principle. See Case C-491/01, *British American Tobacco,* para. 149; Joined Cases C-20/00 and C-64/00, *Booker Aquaculture,* para. 69; Case C-368/96, *Generics,* para. 79; and Case 44/79, *Liselotte Hauer,* para. 15.

discussion of Case C-18/88, *RTT*; and Joined Cases C-46/90 and C-93/91, *Lagauche*, in section 1.4.5.2.

It is now the prevailing view that Article 345 TFEU cannot be relied on in support of an absolute prohibition of Union intervention in property rights, and that Article 345 does not prevent some reorganization of an industrial sector, even if the reorganisation makes changes to the ownership of assets and capital.[72] Article 345 does not exclude the Member States' rules governing their systems of property ownership from the scope of Union law,[73] but it presumably means that the Union cannot force a Member State to privatize publicly owned undertakings. However, ownership unbundling does not amount to a direction to privatise. According to the third liberalisation package, ownership unbundling means that the same legal person may not both control the infrastructure and an undertaking that is subject to competition.[74]

Nevertheless, there are examples of ownership unbundling in national regulation of the liberalised sectors.[75]

In Commission Decision of 20 March 2001 relating to a proceeding under Article 82 of the EC Treaty (Case COMP/35.141 – *Deutsche Post*) (OJ 2001 L 125/27), Deutsche Post accepted the obligation to separate its mail order parcels business in an independent company. The risk of cross subsidisation was therefore limited. In this connection, the unbundling requirement was not directly derived from public regulation, but was the result of conditional obligations in connection with a concrete case. The case is also discussed in the section on postal services (section 4.2.1.1).

In the case of publicly owned undertakings it can also be desirable to separate the operator which carries on the business from the regulatory authority. This form of unbundling can reduce the risk of the abuse of power in favour of the authority's own operators. There is an example of this in Article 22 of Directive 97/67/EC on postal services, which requires the regulatory authorities for the postal sector to be legally separate from and operationally independent of the postal operators.

72. Case C-491/01, *British American Tobacco,* para. 147; and Joined Cases 56/64 and 58/64, *Consten and Grundig*.
73. See Case 182/83, *Fearon,* para. 7; and Case C-302/97, *Konle,* para. 38.
74. 'Control' is defined in accordance with its definition in Article 3(2) of Regulation (EC) No 139/2004 on the control of concentrations between undertakings (the EC Merger Regulation).
75. This is the case with regard to the transmission system operator in the area of electricity and natural gas.

1.4.4. Access to networks

In connection with network industries, where a network constitutes an essential facility or a natural monopoly, the exposure to competition of part of the value chain will usually involve all participants having access to the network, regardless of whether it is owned by a participant on the market exposed to competition. This is referred to as *third party access*.[76] Without access to the network and other technical installations, a potential market participant is effectively denied access to the market. On markets characterised by the existence of networks, there will thus often be at least two kinds of market:

- A market for the provision of goods or services to end users, and
- A market for access to the network.

The general competition rules of the Treaty apply to access to the network. In particular, the prohibition of abuse of a dominant position will be relevant, because of the nature of the network as a natural monopoly. Usually the sector-specific provisions will to some extent address the question of access to the network. However, these must not be contrary to the Treaty's competition rules, and the Treaty provisions apply in parallel.

Provisions on third party access are often associated with an obligation to give equal treatment in connection with access to a network. In such cases the owner of the network cannot have better or cheaper access to the network than those who do not own the network. In this connection the term *common carrier* is often used.[77]

According to the common carrier concept in its classical form, if there is a lack of capacity, new suppliers must be allowed access on an equal footing with existing suppliers, leading to a form of rationing. However, this solution is not always used. See below in the discussion on regulated access.

The requirement for equal treatment does not prohibit giving special priority on proper grounds. For example, this may involve giving priority in an electricity supply network to electricity from generators using renewable energy

76. For a general presentation of this, see *Marcel Haag:* Der Netzzugang Dritter aus der Sicht des Europäischen Wettbewerbsrecht, in *Jürgen Schwarze (ed.):* Der Netzzugang für Dritte im Wirtscarftsrecht, 1999 p. 57 et seq.
77. The term is derived from the transport sector. There is an example of this in Article 320(1) of the Electricity Directive, which requires third party access to the transmission and distribution systems based on published tariffs, applicable to all eligible customers and applied objectively and without discrimination between system users.

or waste or producing combined heat and power, see Article 15(3) of the Electricity Directive, or giving priority between passenger and goods traffic on the railways, see Article 20 of Directive 2001/14/EC on the allocation of railway infrastructure capacity.

Imposing an obligation on a common carrier can be seen as a counterpart to any exclusive right which an undertaking may have been granted (for example in the form of permission to carry on a natural monopoly), or it may just be imposed as a step in the liberalisation process.

The requirements for equal treatment are supplemented by the prohibitions in the Treaty on discrimination on the grounds of nationality and the provisions on abuse of a dominant position. What is special about such requirements which are found in sector-specific legislation is that they also apply to participants whose networks are essentially intended for their own use as well as, where this is only partly the case, to their own use in relation to access for third parties.

Conditions are often imposed to the effect that the terms for access to a network must be equitable.

The regulation of third party access in the EU is sometimes takes the form of negotiated access and sometimes regulated access. Negotiated access respects the principle of individual agreements, which may need to be renewed with each new use of the network. There is an example of this in Article 19(3) of the Natural Gas Directive in relation to storage of natural gas. The requirement for negotiated access will often be a minimum requirement so that a Member State can instead choose to give users the greater protection which lies in regulated access.[78] Conversely, *regulated access* means that the price is determined in advance by the undertaking providing the service. This latter recalls the common carrier. On this there are provisions in Article 32 of the Electricity Directive and Article 18 of the Natural Gas Directive (transmission and distribution systems). Correspondingly in the area of telecommunications Regulation (EC) No 2887/2000 on unbundled access to the local loop and Article 9(4) in Directive 2002/19/EC (the Access Directive) there are provisions on standard terms for access to networks.

In principle, the provisions on regulated access will be accompanied by provisions whereby lack of capacity will be a proper reason for refusing access. See for example Article 21 of the Natural Gas Directive and Article 32 of the Electricity Directive. When there is lack of capacity the existing capacity must be shared out. A pro rata system, first-come-first-served, and auc-

78. For example, in Article 19(4) of the Natural Gas Directive there is also the possibility of choosing regulated access.

tions are different ways of allocating capacity. Likewise, network rights can be linked to supply contracts (merit order).[79] In the area of energy supply, where the provision of energy using the network is more or less homogeneous, there can be a certain amount of equalisation on either side of a bottleneck.[80] For example, a system operator can implement upward or downward adjustments of production, or there can be a set-off in the case of natural gas, so that only the net amount can be transmitted through the bottleneck.[81] There is great uncertainty as to whether the various methods in their different variations can be in breach of Article 102 TFEU.[82]

Agreements for the establishment and use of networks should be interpreted in the light of Articles 101 and 102 TFEU. There can very well be conduct which restricts competition in breach of the competition rules. There is especially a need for care in connection with the allocation of capacity when there are bottlenecks. These often occur in physical networks in connection with cross-border connections, and often with divided ownership. When establishing new capacity, long-term contracts are often entered into on the use of the capacity. The Commission will not necessarily intervene against such agreements if they can be considered to improve the overall competitive situation, for example by increasing capacity.

An example of this is the *Viking Cable* case. A Norwegian electricity supply company and a German electricity supply company agreed to establish and operate a new undersea cable between Norway and Germany for the transmission of high voltage electricity. The establishment of such a cable required a major capital investment, and the parties wanted to secure their investment by a 25 year agreement which included exclusive use of the cable. However, unused capacity could be disposed of on the spot market (Nord Pool) for 24 hours at a time. In an interim statement, the Commission found that the notified agreement was not contrary to Article 101 TFEU (then Article 81 of the EC Treaty), and it emphasised in particular the increase in capacity and the significant investment required.[83]

79. This is the case in connection with an electricity trader on the Nordic electricity exchange (Nord Pool). Transmission capacity is bought together with the current.
80. Those parts of the network where the capacity is less than the demand.
81. In the nature of things, the same cannot occur in the areas of transport and telecommunications.
82. *Michael Albers:* Competition Law Issues Arising from the Liberalization Process, in *Damien Geradin (ed.):* The Liberalization of Electricity and Natural Gas in the European Union, 2001 p. 7 et seq.
83. Notice on Case COMP/E-3/37.921 *Viking Cable* (OJ 2001 C 247/11). The Commission also stated, though without giving any grounds, that there was not a breach of the prohibition of abuse of dominant position. However, the cable was not laid as the parties later cancelled their agreement.

In a corresponding case concerning a gas pipeline,[84] established as a joint venture, in its approval the Commission emphasised the furthering of competition in the linking of otherwise technically isolated markets and on the freedom of the participants to transfer their transmission rights. A provision on joint marketing of the transmission capacity which restricted competition was of less importance in the overall picture.

When there is limited capacity there is a question of whether priority should be given to prior users of the facility. Regulation (EEC) No 95/93 on common rules for the allocation of slots at Community airports authorises giving such priority to owners of existing slots, provided they have been used; see Article 8. In contrast, Regulation (EC) No 714/2009 on conditions for access to the network for cross-border exchanges in electricity contains a principle whereby problems of capacity restrictions in a network must be resolved by means of transaction-based methods, i.e. methods which do not involve a choice between the contracts of the individual market operators. This could involve compensation.

In some cases, the owners of rights to allocated capacity are prohibited from re-selling their capacity. In the area of railways there is such a prohibition in Article 13(1) of Directive 2001/14/EC on the allocation of railway infrastructure capacity. On the other hand, there can be a certain amount of exchange or transfer of capacity (landing and take-off slots) in the area of air transport; see Article 8(1)(a) of Regulation (EEC) No 95/93.

There are variations as to whether the EU lays down a specific form for dealing with third party access, or leaves it to the Member States to decide. Third party access is often accompanied by a requirement for the Member States to set up or appoint some kind of out-of-court dispute settlement authority to deal with disagreements about third party access or the conditions for such access. There are examples of this in Article 32(2) of the Electricity Directive and Article 21(6) of Directive 2001/14/EC on the allocation of railway infrastructure capacity. Such dispute settlement bodies are normally required to be impartial; see the examples referred to in the energy sector, where it is a requirement of Article 3(13) of the Electricity Directive.

Commission Recommendation 98/257/EC on the principles applicable to the bodies responsible for out-of-court settlement of consumer disputes lays down four principles which ought to apply to the settlement of disputes by consumer bodies; these are: independence, transparency, the adversarial principle, and effectiveness. In relation to the principle of independence, it is important that a person appointed to settle disputes cannot be dismissed

84. Between the United Kingdom and Belgium – referred to in the Commission's XXV Report on Competition Policy, 1995 p. 125 et seq.

during their period of office (if a single individual) and that a body of several persons should include an equal number of representatives from the commercial sector and consumers.

In some cases the Union has also regulated the Member States' scope for introducing *price regulation*. Price regulation and the possibilities for third party access are closely linked. An unrealistically high price for third party access will have the same effect of restricting competition as a refusal of third party access.

Among other things, price regulation has been introduced in the area of telecommunications in Article 13 of Directive 2002/19/EC on access to, and interconnection of, electronic communications networks and associated facilities (Access Directive), which allows for cost-based pricing in connection with interconnection.[85] There is another example in Article 3 of Regulation (EC) No 1775/2005 on conditions for access to the natural gas transmission networks, which states that tariffs for access to networks must 'reflect actual costs incurred, insofar as such costs correspond to those of an efficient and structurally comparable network operator and are transparent, whilst including appropriate return on investments, and where appropriate taking account of the benchmarking of tariffs by the regulatory authorities.'

Benchmarking is a term which is increasingly used to refer to a form of comparison whereby supervisory authorities use a comparison of undertakings that are not subject to competition, or where it is assumed that competition is not optimal. Used in connection with a special price regulation, benchmarking can identify the least cost effective undertakings and can apply special incentive regulation to them, for example by setting price or income ceilings to prevent them covering their cost levels or profits hitherto.

1.4.4.1. Direct lines

The establishment of direct lines between a provider and end users, outside the normal network (network by-pass) can be used as an alternative to third party access. This means that the natural monopoly is not absolute. For example, both the Electricity Directive and the Natural Gas Directive provide for the establishment of direct lines.[86] In Germany connections have been es-

85. See section 4.1.3.3 for a more detailed discussion.
86. Article 38 of the Natural Gas Directive and Article 34 of the Electricity Directive. 'Direct line' means a connection between a seller of a good or service and a customer for such good or service which is outside or complementary to the interconnected system. 'Direct line' is defined in Article 2 of each of these directives.

tablished to some extent by others than network and transmission undertakings, so that end users can be supplied outside the distribution or transmission network. In connection with the possibility of establishing direct lines, Member States are required lay down criteria for the issue of authorisations for setting up or managing such direct lines that must be objective, transparent and non-discriminatory.

1.4.4.2. Transit

Transit is understood as the carrying of a good or service for the fulfilment of transactions where none of the parties to the agreement buy or produce the good or service in an area through which the good or service is carried. In the EU, the regulation of transit is relevant where one Member State is the country of origin or the country where the good or service is received, while the good or service crosses the territory of a Member State which is neither the country of origin nor the country where the good or service is received.[87] The provisions on access to networks in connection with transit are relevant where two participants would not be able to trade together without using network facilities in a third Member State. It is thus relevant to electricity supply, natural gas supply, telecommunications and railways.

The concepts of transit and rights of transit have been discussed for centuries. Thus, Grotius (Hugo de Groot) argued in the 17th century that there was a general right of transit over the territory of another country.[88] The right of transit has also been dealt with in international agreements; see the Barcelona Convention on Freedom of Transit (1921) and Article V in the General Agreement on Tariffs and Trade (GATT). In the area of energy; see also Article 7 in the Energy Charter Treaty.[89]

Transit can take place via an interconnected network. However, in a physical network transit will usually be carried through some trunk lines in the network, referred to as the transmission lines.[90] In addition to this there will often be special transnational connections which link national networks. Access to these will also be necessary for transit.

87. See, e.g. the definition in Article 2(1) of the Electricity Directive and Article 2(1) of the Natural Gas Directive.
88. *Hugo Grotius:* De Jure Belli ac Pacis II, 2, 13 (1625), as translated in Classics of International Law, 1925 pp. 196-197.
89. *Martha M. Roggenkamp:* Transit of Network-bound Energy: the European Experience, in *Thomas Wälde (ed.):* The Energy Charter Treaty, 1996.
90. This is the terminology used, e.g. in the areas of electricity and natural gas.

In Union law, access to transit is regulated by a number of sector-specific directives. In the area of the railways, the transit provisions are built into Directive 91/440/EEC on the development of the Union's railways, which deals with the ordinary provisions on third party access. The same is the case with the Directive on access to communications networks. In the areas of electricity and natural gas transit was dealt with in Directive 90/547/EEC on the transit of electricity through transmission grids and Directive 91/296/EEC on the transit of natural gas through grids. In these two sectors the transit markets were opened to competition before the national markets, which was presumably why the transit provisions were included in separate directives. See now the two market directives as well as the Regulation on the network for cross-border exchanges in electricity[91] and the Regulation on access to the natural gas transmission networks.[92] These are discussed in sections 2.1.3.3 and 2.2.3.1.

Access to transit can be limited to special networks or special participants. In the railways sector the right of transit is limited to the special groups of participants who have general third party access rights in the Member State where they are established, the destination Member State or the transit Member State, in accordance with Directive 91/440/EEC on the development of the Community's railways.

1.4.4.3. Expansion of capacity

From the financial point of view, the owners of a network ought to scale their network with a view to maximising their own profit. For a private network owner the most appropriate capacity will not necessarily coincide with what is the most appropriate capacity for society as a whole. For example, lack of capacity in a given network can be an expression of an inappropriate situation for the general economic interest.

If a network is owned by a commercial undertaking there can be a need to ensure the appropriate capacity for society by other means. For example, payment can be given for the maintenance of a certain capacity on a given network. This is seen in the air transport and railways sectors.

If an expansion of capacity requires the expansion of a physical network, or other structural changes, it can be necessary to make a full analysis. In connection with overloaded railway capacity, according to Articles 22, 25 and 26 of Directive 2001/14/EC, the infrastructure manager has to make a capacity analysis and prepare a capacity enhancement plan.

91. Regulation (EC) No 714/2009 on conditions for access to the network for cross-border exchanges in electricity and repealing Regulation (EC) No 1228/2003. This also referred to as the Cross-border Regulation.
92. Regulation (EC) No Regulation (EC) No 715/2009 on conditions for access to the natural gas transmission networks and repealing Regulation (EC) No 1775/2005.

Another possibility is for Member States to require capacity to be increased. Article 21(2) of the Natural Gas Directive contains authority for Member States to take measures to ensure that a network owner who refuses third party access to the network on the grounds of lack of capacity or a lack of connection makes the necessary enhancements to capacity. However, this presumes that it is economic to do so or that a potential customer is willing to pay for the enhancements.

1.4.5. Management of networks

In connection with the management of a network there are a number of tasks which must be taken care of in relation to the use of the network, cooperation with foreign network managers, decisions relating to disturbances of supply, and planning future network capacity. Such tasks are usually the responsibility of the owner of the network, a public authority or an independent undertaking. To a certain extent the EU has regulated the performance of these tasks separately for the liberalised sectors.

An example of this is the regulation of infrastructure management in the railway sector. According to Directive 2001/14/EC, infrastructure managers have powers and responsibilities with regard to cooperation with other infrastructure managers (Article 15), with regard to lack of capacity (Articles 21-22), with regard to disturbances of service (Article 29), and with regard to planning capacity enhancement (Articles 25-26).

There is another example in the Electricity Directive and the Natural Gas Directive which contain requirements for the establishment of, among other things, transmission systems operators whose tasks include allocation of loading and access to networks, as well as interconnection, expansion and security of supply.

1.4.5.1. Unbundling

In some cases the requirement for the establishment of such network managers is combined with a requirement for unbundling. There is an example of a requirement for management unbundling in the railways sector in the requirement that the collection of charges should be carried out by a charging body that is independent in its legal form, organisation and decision-making from any railway undertaking; see Article 4(2) of Directive 2001/14/EC.

An alternative to having a private undertaking as the network manager is to allocate these tasks to a public authority. In the electricity supply sector the organisation of the system operator function varies. There are cases where the function is the responsibility of undertakings with predominantly private ownership, of public undertakings, and of public authorities.

1.4.5.2. Authorities

The boundaries between the tasks of a public supervisory authority and the carrying on of an undertaking are often unclear. Where an actual undertaking has been carried on by an administrative authority it has been natural for certain sector-specific administrative decisions to be taken by the same administrative authority as that which carries on the undertaking. Where the carrying on of the business has been separated out to be carried on by an independent private law entity, but is in fact carried on by a state-owned monopoly, certain supervisory tasks and powers have a tendency to go with the new legal entity. But at the moment when parts of the business of the state-owned undertaking become subject to competition, it is highly questionable for the state-owned participant to exercise administrative authority which can have an influence on the conditions of competition.[93]

In a number of areas the CJ has found that this combining of tasks is a breach of Article 102 TFEU.[94] In Case C-67/96, *Albany International* v *Stichting Bedrijfspensioenfonds Textielindustrie*, which concerned the possibility for the public authorities to give a pension fund the exclusive right to administer a supplementary pension scheme in a particular industrial sector, the CJ accepted, on the basis of a number of specific reasons (see in particular paragraphs 116-122 of the judgment), that the pension fund in question could exercise administrative authority, without this being contrary to Articles 102 and 106 TFEU (then Articles 82 and 86 of the EC Treaty).

There is thus a requirement to separate commercial activities and the exercise of authority (where a public authority operates on a market that is subject to competition). According to the CJ's decision in Case C-18/88, *RTT*, it is contrary to Articles 102 and 106 TFEU (then Articles 82 and 86 of the EC Treaty) for a public undertaking to operate on a market while it has powers to supervise and grant licences to other operators on that market. According to the CJ's decision in Joined Cases C-46/90 and C-93/91, *Lagauche*, this is not contrary to Article 106 TFEU (then Article 86 of the EC Treaty) as long as the decision does not involve the exercise of any discretion.

93. From the point of view of administrative law it is altogether questionable to give administrative authority to undertakings which are organised in the form of private law entities.
94. Case C-18/88, *Régie des télégraphes et des téléphones (RTT)* v *GB-Inno-BM;* Case C-202/88, *France* v *Commission;* Case C-260/89, *ERT*; Case C-91/94, *Tranchant and another*. Case C-18/88 and Case C-260/89 are discussed in Chapter X on Public Undertakings, section 4.2.3.

Regardless of whether network management is delegated to a special organisation or authority, secondary EU legislation can impose requirements regarding the confidential treatment of commercial information both by the manager and by the undertaking which owns the essential facilities. See, for example, Articles 8 and 11 of the Natural Gas Directive.

1.4.6. Public obligations

The aims of the Community include more than just consideration for the internal market and the promotion of competition. A number of the Treaty articles contain provisions concerning other and possibly even conflicting interests. The term 'services of general economic interest' has a special position in the EC Treaty, as appears from Article 14 TFEU (originally inserted as Article 16 in the EC Treaty by the Treaty of Amsterdam: 'Without prejudice to Article 4 of the Treaty on European Union or to Articles 93, 106 and 107 of this Treaty, and given the place occupied by services of general economic interest in the shared values of the Union as well as their role in promoting social and territorial cohesion, the Union and the Member States, each within their respective powers and within the scope of application of the Treaties, shall take care that such services operate on the basis of principles and conditions, particularly economic and financial conditions, which enable them to fulfil their missions.'

A corresponding term is used in Article 106(2) TFEU: 'Undertakings entrusted with the operation of services of general economic interest or having the character of a revenue-producing monopoly shall be subject to the rules contained in this Treaty, in particular to the rules on competition, in so far as the application of such rules does not obstruct the performance, in law or in fact, of the particular tasks assigned to them. The development of trade must not be affected to such an extent as would be contrary to the interests of the Community.'

These services of general economic interest differ from other and ordinary services by the fact that they are considered by the public authorities to be necessary, regardless of whether the ordinary market incentives will be sufficient to ensure their supply.[95] Services of general economic interest have been defined as services of a commercial character which serve general pub-

95. Communication from the Commission – Services of general interest in Europe of 19.01.2001 (OJ 2001 C 17/4).

lic purposes.[96] In a case concerning the electricity supply sector,[97] the CJ stated that the aim of Article 106(2) TFEU [then Article 90(2) of the EC Treaty] is 'to reconcile the Member States' interest in using certain undertakings, in particular in the public sector, as an instrument of economic or fiscal policy with the Community's interest in ensuring compliance with the rules on competition and the preservation of the unity of the common market.'[98]

The terminology can differ. The term 'universal service obligation' is used in the Communication from the Commission – Services of general interest in Europe of 19.01.2001. Regulation (EEC) No 95/93 on common rules for the allocation of slots at Community airports uses the term 'public service obligations'. Article 3.9 of the Electricity Directive refers to 'universal service and public service obligations'. According to Article 3(2) in the Electricity Directive and in the Natural Gas Directive, 'public service obligations' may relate to 'security of supply, regularity, quality and price of supplies and environmental protection, including energy efficiency, energy from renewable sources and climate protection.' The concept of public service obligation is derived from French administrative law.[99] In relation to electricity supply, the content of the term has been described as:[100]

> 'Le principe de service public a à la fois des fondements juridiques (continuité de service, égalité d'accès et neutralité), économiques (planification, économies publiques) et sociales (pressions syndicales, problèmes d'emploi et le développement de 'l'Etat-providence').'
>
> The expression 'special service obligations' has also been used in this context.[101]

The same term is used in the railway sector in Article 2(e) of Regulation (EC) No 1370/2007 on public passenger transport services by rail and by road. Here it is stated that public service obligations include requirements to provide transport services that an operator would not provide if it were considering its own commercial interests.

96. European Economic and Social Committee statement of 17.07.2002 on 'Services of general economic interest', and Communication from the Commission – Services of general interest in Europe of 19.01.2001 (OJ 2001 C 17/4).
97. Case C-159/94, *France* v *Commission,* para. 55.
98. On public undertakings in general, see Chapter X.
99. *Rosa Greaves:* EC Transport Law, 2000 p. 20.
100. *Jacques Asscher & Guy-Martial Weijer:* Energie et protection de l'environment dans la perspective européenne, Report to the FIDE Congress 1996 p. 238. The concept can be interpreted very broadly, and has been so by the CJ.
101. *William J. Baumol & J. Gregory Sidak:* The Pricing of Inputs Sold to Competitors, Yale Journal on Regulation Vol. 11 1994 pp. 171-202.

The concept of a public service obligation can naturally be abused by Member States to promote the interests of their national participants on markets which are subject to competition. If so, this would be a breach of the general provisions of the Treaty. Individual liberalising directives can include provisions on notification in order to make the Commission's control of this easier. There are examples of this in Article 3(15) of the Electricity Directive and Article 3(11) of the Natural Gas Directive, according to which the Member States must inform the Commission of all measures adopted to fulfil universal service and public service obligations. Notification must be given whether or not such measures require a derogation under the Directive. The Member States must inform the Commission subsequently every two years of any changes to such measures.

1.4.6.1. Obligations to supply

One of the general economic interests is the obligation to provide a particular good or service to a particular area at an affordable price and of a uniform quality, regardless of the profitability of the particular activity – an obligation to supply. Regardless of whether the goods or services are provided by a public undertaking or on a commercial basis, there is a need to ensure their availability to all citizens. In this context citizens are protected in their role as consumers, and the obligation to supply thus takes on the character of consumer protection, even if the obligation to supply extends to end users who use the goods or services as part of their commercial undertaking.

The obligation to supply has been accepted in Article 36 of the Charter of fundamental rights of the European Union: 'The Union recognises and respects access to services of general economic interest as provided for in national laws and practices, in accordance with the Treaties, in order to promote the social and territorial cohesion of the Union.'[102] However, the expression is not enshrined in the EC Treaty. Instead the obligation is derived from the expression 'services of general economic interest'. According to the White Paper on services of general interest, the term 'services of general interest' is broader than the term 'services of general economic interest' and covers 'both market and non-market services which the public authorities class as being of general interest and subject to specific public service obligations.'[103]

102. As published in OJ 2007 C 303/1.

103. Communication from the Commission – White Paper on services of general interest, COM(2004) 374 final, which merely repeats para. 16 from the Commission's Green paper on services of general interest, COM(2003) 270 final.

In other contexts the expression 'universal services' is used. This concept can be understood as a requirement to supply goods or services at affordable prices to all customers who demand them (the principle of universality), without discrimination as to geographic location (the principle of equality) and on a permanent basis (the principle of continuity).[104] Barry M Mitnik calls this the 'Public Interest Concept'.[105] He quotes Charles Phillips[106] on the special obligations developed under the Common Law for regulated sectors of industry: 'Obligations were to serve all who request service; to give safe and adequate service; to serve all on an equal basis, forbidding unjust discrimination; and to require only a 'just and reasonable' price for services.' The concept can be seen as a subset of the public service obligation. Some directives, for example in the telecommunications sector, often lay down minimum requirements for universal service/the public service obligation.

There is an example of this in Article 3(1) of the Directive 97/67/EC on common rules for Community postal services, which states that 'Member States shall ensure that users enjoy the right to a universal service involving the permanent provision of a postal service of specified quality at all points in their territory at affordable prices for all users.' Correspondingly, Directive 2002/22/EC on universal service and users' rights relating to electronic communications networks and services (Universal Service Directive) states that 'Member States shall ensure that the services set out in this Chapter are made available at the quality specified to all end-users in their territory, independently of geographical location, and, in the light of specific national conditions, at an affordable price.' However, it is not necessarily all end users who are protected by the obligation to supply. For example, the guarantee of supply may be limited to ordinary household users, in other words, non-commercial customers. The Electricity Directive thus only requires Member States to en-

104. *Damien Geradin & Christophe Humpe:* The Liberalization of Postal Services in the European Union: An Analysis of Directive 97/67, *Damien Geradin (ed.):* The Liberalization of Postal Services in the European Union, 2002 p. 93 et seq. The extent of the principle of equality is limited. In Article 12 of Directive 97/67/EC on common rules for Community postal services, there is only a requirement for tariffs to be 'transparent and non-discriminatory'. There is not a requirement for there to be uniform tariffs, regardless of the geographic location of the user. On the other hand Member States can impose a requirement for the use of the same tariff for the whole of their national territory. Other possibilities for Member States to impose universal services are found in Article 9 of the Natural Gas Directive.

105. *Barry M. Mitnick:* The Political Economy of Regulation, 1980 p. 243 et seq.

106. *Charles Franklin Phillips:* The Economics of Regulation: Theory and Practice in the Transportation and Public Utility Industries, 1965 pp. 80-83. See in particular the section on 'Obligations', p. 81 et seq.

sure that all household customers are covered by the obligation to supply; see Article 3(3).[107]

The concept of *affordability* has been developed in connection with the regulation of telecommunications. It has also subsequently been introduced in the postal services sector. It involves a requirement that a good or service of general economic interest must be offered at an affordable price, so that it is available to all.[108] In Article 3(3) of the Electricity Directive and of the Natural Gas Directive, the term 'reasonable' is used about prices for universal services supplied to household customers. This is supplemented by a requirement for price transparency.

In other contexts there is a requirement for cost sharing. In Article 6 of Directive 2002/77/EC on competition in the markets for electronic communications networks and services it is required that any 'national scheme pursuant to Directive 2002/22/EC, serving to share the net cost of the provision of universal service obligations shall be based on objective, transparent and non-discriminatory criteria and shall be consistent with the principle of proportionality and of least market distortion'.

In other situations it is up to the Member States themselves to define what the terms mean. For example, that is the case in the natural gas sector,[109] where, according to Article 3(3) of the Natural Gas Directive, the Member States must 'take appropriate measures to protect final customers, and shall, in particular, ensure that there are adequate safeguards to protect vulnerable customers.'[110] The Member States are subject to a number of minimum requirements for national protection, including requirements, for transparency, notice of changes to conditions of supply, and prohibitions on the charging of fees for change of supplier; see Annex 1 to the Directive.

According to Article 3(2) of the Electricity Directive, the Member States may impose public service obligations on undertakings operating in the electricity sector, 'which may relate to security, including security of supply, regularity, quality and price of supplies and environmental protection, including energy efficiency, energy from renewable sources and climate protection.' There is a restriction on the considerations which can be taken into account which acts as an upper limit.

107. In Article 2(10) 'household customers' are defined as 'customers purchasing electricity for their own household consumption, excluding commercial or professional activities.'
108. See the Commission's Green paper on services of general interest, COM(2003) 270 final.
109. *P. J. Slot & A. M. Skudder:* Common Features of Community Law Regulation in the Network-Bound Sectors, Common Market Law Review Vol. 38 2001 p. 123.
110. Article 3(8) of the Electricity Directive also contains a provision on addressing energy poverty, including in the broader context of poverty. This must be seen as an expression that electricity supply is a basic welfare service.

In certain situations the obligation to supply can be given to a supplier which has special obligations.

According to Article 3(3) f the Electricity Directive, Member States may appoint a supplier of last resort. In particular in the area of electricity supply, the CJ has made decisions which could indicate that the Member States have considerable freedom to define the content of the public service obligation.[111]

Requirements can be laid down for uniform charging rates (geographical equalisation) as part of an obligation to supply. Article 12 of the Postal Services Directive implies that Member States may lay down requirements for uniform postal rates. However, there is no obligation to do so. Here the question arises as to whether a requirement for uniform rates excludes the possibility of making individual agreements, primarily for discounts for large customers. This must be assumed to be the allowed, unless specifically stated otherwise. Article 12 of the Postal Services Directive explicitly states that the application of a uniform tariff does not exclude the right of universal service providers to conclude individual agreements on prices with customers. This opens the possibility of granting discounts for large customers.

1.4.6.2. Exclusivity and the obligation to supply

The obligation to supply has often been linked to the allocation of exclusive rights (*de jure* monopoly), or the existence of a natural or institutional monopoly. If a monopoly undertaking is made subject to an obligation to supply, this can be seen as an expression of taking care of services of general economic interest. In this connection an exclusive right can be granted with a view to ensuring the provision (financing) of the obligation. This implies that parts of the area covered by the exclusive right are profitable or can be made so, and that by means of cross subsidisation that can be (part) financing of the area where there is an obligation to supply. Without there being an exclusive right, other suppliers could establish competing undertakings in the profitable areas (skimming) and thereby deprive the undertaking with an obligation to supply of the possibility of obtaining a surplus which can be used to cover the deficit arising from supplying the unprofitable areas.

111. *P. J. Slot & A. M. Skudder:* Common Features of Community Law Regulation in the Network-Bound Sectors, Common Market Law Review Vol. 38 2001 p. 124, which refers to the four judgments of the CJ in: Case C-159/94, *France* v *Commission;* Case C-158/99, *Thermenhotel Stoiser Franz and others* v *Commission;* Case C-159/99, *Commission* v *Italy;* and Case C-160/99, *Commission* v *France.*

In parts of sector-specific legislation special provisions have been introduced on the financing of the extra costs of obligations to supply. In the telecommunications sector the Member States are required to revoke all special or exclusive rights. Instead, a sharing mechanism can be set up to cover the supplementary expenses for the provision of the obligatory services on the basis of contributions from all providers of services; see Article 13 of Directive 2002/22/EC (the Universal Service Directive), and Articles 7 and 9 of the Postal Services Directive. In the air transport sector, Member States can issue temporary exclusive licences on the basis of open offers to ensure regular services on certain routes, so as to ensure sufficient service of the market.

However, an obligation to supply is not necessarily linked to exclusive rights. In Community law there is nothing in principle to prevent a Member State from imposing on individual undertakings or groups of undertakings such obligations to supply, without them at the same time being granted an exclusive right. However, the obligation to supply must not be contrary to the general principles of Community law, for example the discrimination principle.

1.4.6.3. Financial compensation

An alternative to granting exclusive rights as a source for financing an obligation to supply is financial compensation from public funds (State aid or aid from other public bodies). Aid can be given from the state treasury (for example by subsidies or other financial advantages such as tax reliefs), contributions from market participants (for example a fund for the supply obligation), averaging of tariffs (for example nationwide uniform tariffs, despite significant variances in the cost of providing the service), and financing on the basis of social solidarity (for example national insurance contributions).

According to Articles 12 and 13 of Directive 2002/22/EC (the Universal Service Directive), it is possible to provide public aid in the telecommunications sector if the responsibility for the obligation to supply imposes an unreasonable burden. This Directive uses a part arrangement where the participants who do not have an obligation to supply help to bear the costs of the obligation to supply. This method is also found in Articles 7 and 9 of the Postal Services Directive. In the postal services sector compensation using public means is also a possibility; see Article 7(1) of the Postal Services Directive.

In other areas there can be an obligation to submit such service provision to a tender. This is the case with air transport; see Article 174 of Regulation (EC) No 1008/2008 of the European Parliament and of the Council of 24 September 2008 on common rules for the operation of air services in the Community.

It has been questioned whether aid for carrying out an obligation to supply constitutes State aid. The answer is: Yes. Over-compensation will clearly be State aid.

In the *Altmark* case,[112] the CJ held that State aid which had the aim of enabling the fulfilment of obligations to supply (in the case in question urban, suburban or regional transport services) did not fall within the prohibition of State aid under Article 107(1) TFEU (the Article 87(1) of the EC Treaty), in so far as such aid should be seen as being compensation for discharging public service obligations. However, for such compensation to escape classification as State aid, a number of conditions must be satisfied:

- 'First, the recipient undertaking must actually have public service obligations to discharge, and the obligations must be clearly defined ...
- Second, the parameters on the basis of which the compensation is calculated must be established in advance in an objective and transparent manner ...
- Third, the compensation cannot exceed what is necessary to cover all or part of the costs incurred in the discharge of public service obligations, taking into account the relevant receipts and a reasonable profit for discharging those obligations ...
- Fourth, where the undertaking which is to discharge public service obligations, in a specific case, is not chosen pursuant to a public procurement procedure which would allow for the selection of the tenderer capable of providing those services at the least cost to the community, the level of compensation needed must be determined on the basis of an analysis of the costs which a typical undertaking, well run and adequately provided with means of transport so as to be able to meet the necessary public service requirements, would have incurred in discharging those obligations, taking into account the relevant receipts and a reasonable profit for discharging the obligations.'

However, it can be relevant where the aid comes from.

The *PreussenElektra* case[113] concerned the German law, *Stromeinspeisungsgesetz*, on the purchase by electricity supply undertakings of electricity generated from hydraulic energy, wind energy, solar energy, gas from waste dumps and sewage treatment plants, or products or residues and biological waste from agriculture and forestry work, which was paid for by consumers. The law also laid down minimum prices for

112. Case C-280/00, *Altmark Trans and another* v *Nahverkehrsgesellschaft Altmark and another.*
113. Case C-379/98, *PreussenElektra* v *Schhleswag.*

the electricity produced by such methods. The minimum prices were higher than the real economic value of the electricity. The CJ found that in the case in question the prohibition on State aid in Article 107(1) TFEU was not applicable, since there was not a transfer of State funds.

The referring national court had asked whether Article 107 TFEU (then Article 92 of the EC Treaty) should be interpreted so that the concept of State aid should also include national arrangements that only regulated the allocation of costs between undertakings at different levels of production involving purchase obligations and minimum payments, when this in fact led to an allocation of costs, without the undertaking which had to make payments receiving a return.

The disputed provision in Paragraph 2 of the *Stromeinspeisungsgesetz* provided that electricity supply undertakings were obliged to purchase the electricity produced in their area of supply from renewable energy sources and to pay for it in accordance with the provisions of Paragraph 3. According to this provision, a minimum price was laid down for electricity from certain forms of renewable energy. The price was based on a percentage of the average income per kilowatt from the electricity supply company's supply of electricity to the end user. After receiving many complaints from electricity supply companies, the Commission had informed the German Federal Finance Minister of its concern with regard to the question of whether, after a number of amendments which extended the scope of its application, the *Stromeinspeisungsgesetz* was still compatible with the provisions on State aid in the EC Treaty. However, the Commission's approach did not lead to any amendment of the German law.

In relation to the prohibition on State aid, the CJ argued that the obligation to purchase at fixed minimum prices, and the sharing out of the financial burden which the purchase obligation meant for the private electricity supply companies, between these and other private undertakings, did not constitute a direct or indirect transfer of State resources within the meaning of Article 87(1). It was thus somewhat surprisingly established that the German purchase obligation did not fall foul of the prohibition on State aid.

It was not disputed before the CJ that the obligation to buy electricity made from renewable energy at fixed minimum prices would give producers of this form of electricity a financial advantage, as it gave them risk-free higher earnings than they would otherwise have been able to obtain.

In paragraph 58 of its judgment the CJ noted that the distinction in Article 107(1) TFEU [then Article 92(1) of the EC Treaty] between 'aid granted by a Member State and aid granted through State resources' did not mean that all the benefits which were granted by a State constituted aid, regardless of whether they were financed by State resources or not. The distinction was merely intended to bring within that definition both advantages which are granted directly by the State and those granted by a public or private body designated or established by the State. In this particular case the CJ commented in paragraph 59 of its judgment that the obligation imposed on private electricity supply undertakings to purchase electricity produced from renewable energy sources at fixed minimum prices did not involve any direct or indirect transfer of State resources to undertakings which produced that type of electricity. Furthermore, the CJ found that the allocation of the financial burden arising from that obligation for those private electricity supply undertakings as between them and other private undertakings could not constitute a direct or indirect transfer of State resources (paragraph 60). Under these circumstances the CJ did not find that the fact that the purchase obligation was laid down in law, nor that it meant that there was an undoubted benefit for certain undertakings, gave the measure the character of a State aid within the meaning of Article 107(1) TFEU.

1.4.6.4. Price regulation

The pricing of such obligatory service provision will often be subject to regulation, whether or not there is an associated exclusive right. Technically, such obligation to provide a service can be imposed under public law (by a regulation) or it can be provided under private law (through a publicly owned undertaking or contractually, by an undertaking that is granted permission to exploit public rights).

As a rule it is up to the Member State to decide whether to introduce price regulation. However, in certain cases such a duty can be implicit. Thus, Article 12 of Directive 97/67/EC on postal services requires that prices must be affordable and must be such that all users have access to the services provided, that prices must be proportionate to costs, and must be transparent and non-discriminatory. This must be presumed to require some form of national regulation.

Article 12 of the Postal Services Directive implies that individual Member States may lay down requirements for uniform postal rates. However, it is explicitly stated that such a requirement does not prevent an undertaking entering into individual agreements with users on postal rates. This allows for special discount agreements with large customers.

1.4.7. Authorisations

In a number of secondary legal acts there is a requirement that the Member States should establish procedures for granting authorisations.

Authorisation refers to public regulation of access to the market. There are often specific requirements as to persons or undertakings which carry on some particular profession. Such procedures can be called authorisation, approval, consent, grant, registration, permission, licence, concession, certification and so on. The word used is often determined by tradition. The word used does not indicate any special categorisation. Authorisations can reflect some special qualification, as in many of the liberal professions and in skilled trades, or there can be special organisational requirements, or authorisation can relate to special requirements as to the participant's financial standing. A requirement for authorisation can also be used as a means for ensuring that the norms of public law are complied with. The loss of authorisation can be a supplement to punishment by fine.

Authorisation normally only involves a right to carry on some particular business. It does not the same as giving a right, for example, to use essential facilities. Article 4(4) of Directive 95/18/EC on the licensing of railway undertakings specifically states that a licence does not in itself entitle the holder to have access to the railway infrastructure.

Authorisations which involve an exclusive right in a certain geographic area are often, though far from always, called a concession.[114] Territorial concessions are thus normal in connection with the establishment of a distribution network or, for example, the exploitation of sea areas for (wind) energy purposes. In addition to these procedures for authorisations, there are a number of conditions for licences connected with planning and environmental law. These will not be discussed in this chapter.

The requirement for the establishment of authorisation procedures is found in, among others, the Electricity Directive, Regulation (EC) No 1008/2008 on common rules for the operation of air services in the Community, and Directive 95/18/EC on the licensing of railway undertakings. In other sectors it is up to Member States themselves to decide whether to introduce authorisation procedures. See Article 4 of the Natural Gas Directive which refers to this explicitly.[115] The regulation can be function-specific, so that the requirements can differ at different stages of the value chain. Thus it is quite normal for there to be requirements for authorisation for carrying on an undertaking

114. In para. 2.4 of the Commission Interpretative Communication on Concessions under Community Law (OJ 2000 C 121/2), concessions are defined as 'acts attributable to the State whereby a public authority entrusts to a third party – by means of a contractual act or a unilateral act with the prior consent of the third party – the total or partial management of services for which that authority would normally be responsible and for which the third party assumes the risk.'

115. If the matter is not explicitly dealt with, the assumption is that national law can be used to determine whether an authorisation procedure is used, as long as it does not otherwise conflict with Community law.

which involves public obligations, while authorisation is not always necessary for those parts of the liberalised sectors which are subject to competition.

In connection with liberalisation, an authorisation procedure without an exclusive right (an authorisation procedure) has been established as an alternative to a tendering procedure. The authorisation procedure means that all can seek authorisation to carry on the relevant kind of undertaking. The capacity in the sector in question is thus determined by the market participants and the incentives that influence them. In a tendering procedure it is up to the Member State, through its offering for tender the establishment of new capacity, which will at least in part determine the size of the overall capacity in a given area. It will be normal for a sector which is subject to market conditions to use authorisation procedure. However, a tendering procedure could be used in a transitional phase or as a supplement, for example to ensure security of supply.

There is an example of the use of a tendering procedure as a transitional arrangement in Article 4 of the first Electricity Directive, Directive 96/92/EC concerning common rules for the internal market in electricity, which provided for a tendering procedure as an alternative to an authorisation procedure. In Article 6 of the second Electricity Directive the tendering procedure was done away with. However, according to Article 7 of the second Electricity Directive, Member States can use a tendering procedure with a view to fulfilling their obligations concerning security of supply, and in the interests of environmental protection and the promotion of infant technologies. This provision has been carried forward in Article 8 of the present Electricity Directive.

In the telecommunications sector it is acknowledged that the Member States can use tendering in the allocation of frequencies and telephone numbers etc. Among other things, this has been used in connection with the Universal Mobile Telecommunications System (UMTS) network.

Provisions on authorisation procedures often contain administrative law provisions intended to prevent unequal treatment or other improper conduct in general. There is a requirement that the Member States' criteria for the grant of authorisations must be objective and non-discriminatory. Such provisions can be combined with a requirement that the procedures for the grant of authorisations should be made public, that reasons should be given for refusals and that the possibility of an appeal should be included. See Article 4 of the Natural Gas Directive, for example.

1.4.8. Transparency

There is a requirement for transparency in a number of secondary acts. The aim is to act as a support for the other goals that are built into the rules. Transparency is a tool which is intended to reveal or to make it more difficult for there to be unlawful restrictions of competition, or merely in appropriate measures which can be advantageously dealt with by legislation. Transparency thereby has a preventive effect. For example, provisions on transparency can be directed at unlawful State aid, abuse of dominant position, cross subsidisation or against measures which reduce the effectiveness of competition in general. Transparency provisions can have the aim of giving the authorities, customers and/or the general public insight into procedures.

Within the liberalised sectors the requirement for transparency is found in connection with the Member States' scope for imposing public service obligations on undertakings. There are examples of this in Article 3.2 of the Natural Gas Directive and Article 3.2 of the Electricity Directive. There can also be requirements relating to quality controls and their publication; see Article 16 of Directive 97/67/EC on postal services. The requirement can also be found in connection with the presentation of accounts. This can be seen in the unbundling of accounts, special requirements for making information public, independent auditing and supervision by public authorities, or by a requirement for compliance with some set of accounting rules. There is an example of this in Article 31(2) of the Natural Gas Directive, which refers to Directive 78/660/EEC. There is a requirement for the independent auditing of certain kinds of undertakings in Article 15 of the Postal Services Directive.

There are often transparency requirements for provisions on access to networks. One example is Article 18 of the Natural Gas Directive which requires the publication of tariffs. Similarly, there are such requirements in connection with the establishment of the criteria for granting and administering authorisations. There is an example of this in Article 4 of the Natural Gas Directive which requires the criteria and procedures for the granting of authorisations to be made public.

The prices for services in the liberalised sectors are also subject to the requirement for transparency. For example, this is the case with the prices for gas and electricity to industrial end users. In fact, the transparency requirements are set out separately in special legislation, Directive 2008/92/EC (formerly 90/377/EEC) concerning a Community procedure to improve the transparency of gas and electricity prices charged to industrial end-users.

According to its preamble, this Directive on price transparency is intended to ensure that competition is not distorted in the internal market, and to help obviate discrimination against users. The Directive is the culmination of earlier recommendations on increased price transparency for electricity and reports on the lack of the transparency.[116]

Article 1 of the Directive requires Member States to take steps to ensure that undertakings which supply gas or electricity to industrial end-users, submit information on:

- the prices and terms of sale of gas and electricity to industrial end-users,
- the price systems in use, and
- the breakdown of consumers by category and their respective market shares, in order to ensure that these categories are nationally representative.

This information has to be sent to Eurostat[117] and the competent authorities of the Member States within two months. Eurostat publishes the information in May and November of each year. Moreover, every two years undertakings which supply gas or electricity to industrial end users must submit information about the breakdown of consumers and the corresponding volumes by category of consumption. This information is not made public. In general, Article 4 of the Directive requires Eurostat not to disclose information supplied to it by undertakings which might, by its nature, be subject to commercial confidentiality. However, confidential statistical data can be published 'in an aggregated form which does not enable individual commercial transactions to be identified'. This ensures that undertakings do not feel a need to obscure information to protect their competitive situations. Once a year the Commission has to present a summary report on the operation of the Directive to the European Parliament, the Council and the Economic and Social Committee.[118]

In EU legislation transparency is not always expressed as a requirement. In certain cases the possibility of transparency requirements is left to the Member States. Thus, Article 9(1) of Directive 2002/19/EC (the Access Directive) does not impose a requirement for transparency in the telecommunications sector, but Member States are given the possibility of introducing such provisions for special kinds of undertakings.

At a more general level, in Directive 2006/111/EC on the transparency of financial relations between Member States and public undertakings as well as on financial transparency within certain undertakings ('the Transparency Directive'),[119] which was adopted under the authority of Article 106(3) TFEU, Article 1 lays down the general obligations of the Member States:

116. Council Recommendation 81/924/EEC on electricity tariff structures in the Community; and COM(84) 490 final, Commission Staff Report – The application of the Community' s energy pricing principles in Member States. See also *Eugene D. Cross:* Electric Utility Regulation in the European Union, 1996 p. 7.
117. The Statistical Office of the European Communities.
118. See COM(93) 666 final; and COM(96) 92 final.
119. Originally Directive 80/723/EEC.

'1. The Member States shall ensure that financial relations between public authorities and public undertakings are transparent as provided in this Directive, so that the following emerge clearly:
   a. public funds made available directly by public authorities to the public undertakings concerned;
   b. public funds made available by public authorities through the intermediary of public undertakings or financial institutions;
   c. the use to which these public funds are actually put.
2. Without prejudice to specific provisions laid down by the Community the Member States shall ensure that the financial and organisational structure of any undertaking required to maintain separate accounts is correctly reflected in the separate accounts, so that the following emerge clearly:
   a. the costs and revenues associated with different activities;
   b. full details of the methods by which costs and revenues are assigned or allocated to different activities.'

Originally the Transparency Directive did not cover the energy, transport, postal or telecommunications sectors. However this was changed by the introduction of a new Article 4 amending Directive 85/413/EEC. However, following the latest amendments by Directive 2005/81/EEC, the transparency requirements in Article 1(2) do not apply to undertakings whose annual net earnings are less than EUR 40 million in the two accounting years prior to a given year in which a special or exclusive right is granted by a Member State pursuant to Article 106(1) TFEU or is entrusted with the operation of a service of general economic interest pursuant to Article 106(2), if the public service compensation it receives in any form whatsoever, including subsidies, aid or compensation, is fixed for an appropriate period and according to an open, transparent and non-discriminatory procedure.

In relation to the individual end user, certain transparency requirements can be seen as an expression of consumer protection. This will be in accordance with Article 169 TFEU under which consumers have a right to information.

Special provisions which require the reporting of statistical information are used as control instruments. Also, there are requirements for the Member States to publish special arrangements in the Official Journal of the European Union. There are such requirements, for example, in connection with issuing or revoking authorisations and the imposition of an obligation to supply (for example in the area of air transport).

1.4.9. The cross-border provision of services

Under Article 170(1) TFEU, the Union is required to contribute to the establishment and development of trans-European networks in the areas of transport, telecommunications and energy infrastructures. Also, under Article 170(2) the Union has the aim – within the framework of a system of open and competitive markets – of promoting the interconnection and interoperability of national networks as well as access to such networks. Consideration for the realisation of the internal market for, among other things, networked services was one of the main motivations for the inclusion of this wording.[120] However, the planning, establishment and management of such networks does not appear to fall under the provisions of Article 154, and must therefore fall within the scope of the powers of the Member States.

Trans-European networks are one of the Union's policy areas; see Title XVI TFEU. According to Article 170, 'the Union shall contribute to the establishment and development of trans-European networks in the areas of transport, telecommunications and energy infrastructures.' The actions of the Union are to be aimed at promoting the interconnection and interoperability of national networks as well as access to such networks. The Treaty provisions are to be supplemented by guidelines to identify projects of common interest, the implementation of any measures that may prove necessary to ensure the interoperability of the networks, in particular in the field of harmonisation of technical standardisation, and support for projects of common interest; see Article 171 TFEU.[121] Among others, guidelines have been issued for the telecommunications sector.

Access to a network often requires a certain compatibility or technical harmonisation between the systems used in the Member States. If such do not exist, there will be technical barriers to trade. There is an example of a standardisation measure to remove such barriers in Regulation (EEC) No 3922/91 on the harmonization of technical requirements and administrative procedures in the field of civil aviation, as well as in the Framework Directive for telecommunications (Directive 2002/21/EC).

In other cases, with regard to enabling systems to be interoperable, the Member States are required to ensure the drawing up of technical rules containing minimum requirements for their construction and operation which

120. This part was included in connection with the signing of the Treaty on European Union, signed at Maastricht on 7 February 1992.

121. Rules for support are laid down in Regulation (EC) No 2236/95 laying down general rules for the granting of Community financial aid in the field of trans-European networks. An overview of supported energy projects (1995-2006) can be found at: http://ec.europa.eu/ten/energy/studies/doc/ten_e_financed_projects_95_06.pdf and correspondingly for transport (1983-2004) at: http://ec.europa.eu/ten/transport/actions/doc/1983_2004_supported_actions_en.pdf.

must be fulfilled in order to be linked to a network, and to make these available. These technical rules must be objective and non-discriminatory. They must also be notified to the Commission in accordance with Article 8 of Directive 98/34/EC laying down a procedure for the provision of information in the field of technical standards and regulations, as well as the rules for services in Europe's Information Society. See for example Article 6 of the Natural Gas Directive.

1.4.10. Public authorities

In several sectors there is a requirement that the Member States must establish a supervisory authority. This is often referred to as a *regulator*.

The requirement for the appointment of a regulator is often combined with a requirement for the regulator's independence from market participants, for example in the form of a separation between the management of undertakings and the exercise of authority. This is particularly relevant when some public authority is still a market participant. In general, in terms of administrative law, it is appropriate for the supervisory authority, in its composition, to be independent at the political level. In particular in the liberalised sectors there often appears to be some political interest in individual cases.

In the telecommunications sector, Article 3(2) of the Framework Directive (2002/21/EC) established that 'Member States shall guarantee the independence of national regulatory authorities by ensuring that they are legally distinct from and functionally independent of all organisations providing electronic communications networks, equipment or services.' Article 22, first paragraph, of the Postal Services Directive requires Member States to 'designate one or more national regulatory authorities for the postal sector that are legally separate from and operationally independent of the postal operators'. Article 35 of the Electricity Directive contains detailed requirements for the independence of regulatory authorities:

'4. Member States shall guarantee the independence of the regulatory authority and shall ensure that it exercises its powers impartially and transparently. For this purpose, Member State shall ensure that, when carrying out the regulatory tasks conferred upon it by this Directive and related legislation, the regulatory authority:

a. is legally distinct and functionally independent from any other public or private entity;
b. ensures that its staff and the persons responsible for its management:
   i. act independently from any market interest; and
   ii. do not seek or take direct instructions from any government or other public or private entity when carrying out the regulatory tasks. This requirement is without prejudice to close cooperation, as appropriate, with other relevant national authorities or to general policy guidelines issued by the government not related to the regulatory powers and duties under Article 37.

5. In order to protect the independence of the regulatory authority, Member States shall in particular ensure that:

a. the regulatory authority can take autonomous decisions, independently from any political body, and has separate annual budget allocations, with autonomy in the implementation of the allocated budget, and adequate human and financial resources to carry out its duties; and
b. the members of the board of the regulatory authority or, in the absence of a board, the regulatory authority's top management are appointed for a fixed term of five up to seven years, renewable once.

In regard to point (b) of the first subparagraph, Member States shall ensure an appropriate rotation scheme for the board or the top management. The members of the board or, in the absence of a board, members of the top management may be relieved from office during their term only if they no longer fulfil the conditions set out in this Article or have been guilty of misconduct under national law.'

There is a corresponding provision in Article 39 of the Natural Gas Directive.

The fact that a distinction is made between operations and the exercise of authority does not necessarily exclude the possibility of the authorities supervising the interests of the regulated undertakings on the grounds of *regulatory capture*.[122] It can be difficult to prove the existence of such circumstances, and a general legal protection normally merely consists of a requirement for proper conduct.

The requirement for the appointment of a regulator is often accompanied by an obligation for the Member States to inform the Commission about which authorities have been given responsibility for which tasks under the respective directives.[123]

A supervisory authority can exercise control both *ex ante* (for example by requirements for prior authorisation) and *ex post* (for example control after the event). In the electricity and natural gas sectors there is a minimum of *ex ante* approval of the methods used for the calculation of tariffs.

With the administration of a network and access to it, in certain sectors there is a requirement for there to be a special entity to administrate this (system administrator/ infrastructure manager). Such an entity can be a public authority. This is discussed in the section on the administration of networks above.

There can also be a requirement for the establishment of an *appeals procedure*. The provisions on this can be combined with rules on whether the

122. For further on this, see *Rauf Gönenc et al.:* The Implementation and the Effects of Regulatory Reform: Past Experience and current Issues, OECD 2000 p. 41 et seq.
123. See Article 22 of Directive 97/67/EC on postal services and Article 3(6) of the Framework Directive for telecommunications (Directive 2002/21/EC).

appeal tribunal must be a court or an administrative tribunal. Article 4(1) of the Framework Directive allows the use of a court. In some cases there will be a requirement for a dispute resolution authority for access to a network. See the section on access to networks above. It is possible for the appeal tribunal and the supervisory authority to be one and the same. Under Article 37(11) of the Electricity Directive, the regulator is also a dispute resolution authority. It is possible for the Member States to introduce other mechanisms, including mediation of disputes. Such provisions can be combined with a deadline for the appeal tribunal to decide on a dispute, if the parties have not reached an agreement beforehand, whereupon the case can be brought before a court by the complainant, i.e. the party seeking access to the network. The right of appeal can also cover other factors, such as the right of authorisation. See for example Article 4 of the Natural Gas Directive.

Secondary Community legal acts can include requirements for the application of administrative law rules. For example, in relation to the telecommunications sector, Article 4(1) of the Framework Directive provides that an appeal does not have suspensive effect for the decisions of a supervisory authority which are appealed against, unless the appeal body decides otherwise. There are also provisions on the duty of regulated undertakings to give such information to the supervising authority as is necessary for the authority to carry out its tasks. These are often linked to provisions on confidentiality. See for example Article 4 of the Framework Directive, and Article 16(2) of the Natural Gas Directive. Procedural deadlines can also be laid down for dealing with appeals. For example, there is a two month deadline in Article 37(11) of the Electricity Directive, though with the possibility of extending it.

1.4.11. Authority at the EU level

The Commission has a special role in the application of the general competition rules. As for sector-specific supervision, currently European supervisory authorities have not been set up for some of the liberalised sectors. However, discussions on this have particularly related to the telecommunications sector. In the air transport sector the European Aviation Safety Agency was set up on 28 September 2003. The Agency was set up to help the Commission with the introduction of common standards for civil aviation safety and environmental protection, using the *comitology procedure*.

For most of the liberalised sectors Community legislation contains special provisions on the use of the comitology procedure when laying down details for the implementation of the Union's basic legislation. In general the Commission will first decide, after consulting either an advisory committee or a regulatory committee composed of representatives from the Member States. The topics which are dealt with are often those which are relevant to cross-border transactions, such as quality standards. A comitology committee has been appointed in the telecommunications, postal services, railways, air transport and electricity supply sectors.[124]

1.4.12. Reciprocity

Different levels of market openness in the Member States have given rise to fears of the creation of unequal conditions for competition. The problem is that an undertaking in one Member State should not benefit from legal protection in its home market but while being able to act freely on more open neighbouring markets. In some liberalised sectors provisions on *reciprocity* have been introduced to limit this problem. This means that undertakings from one Member State can be refused access to a market in another Member State to the extent that the undertaking's national market is not open to participants from other Member States.[125]

The reciprocity clause has provoked much debate, as it seems to be contrary to the general Community law prohibiting discrimination.[126] The aim of such a provision has been to avoid imbalances between the undertakings of the different Member States due to Member States liberalising their electricity sectors at different speeds.[127]

Such provisions have primarily been used in the energy sector; see Article 33 of the Electricity Directive and Article 37 of the Natural Gas Directive, but they do not seem to be very relevant following a full opening up of a market.

124. See the Commission's Green paper on services of general interest, COM(2003) 270 final. See also Commission Decision 2001/546/EC setting up a consultative committee, to be known as the 'European Energy and Transport Forum'; and Article 11 of Regulation (EEC) No 2408/92 on access for Community air carriers to intra-Community air routes (now Article 25 in Regulation (EC) No 1008/2008. For a more detailed discussion of the concept of comitology, see *Helle Tegner Anker:* Comitology, in *Birgitte Egelund Olsen & Karsten Engsig Sørensen:* Regulation in the EU, 2006 p. 429 et seq.
125. *A. K. Klom:* Liberalisation of Regulated Markets and its Consequences for Trade: The Internal Market for Electricity as a Case Study, Journal of Energy & Natural Resources Law Vol. 14 No 1 1996 p. 2, where examples are given of a lack of reciprocity. Such provisions must presumably be interpreted restrictively, and thus cannot be used, e.g. in the absence of unbundling.
126. For a criticism of reciprocity clauses see *Bent Ole Gram Mortensen:* Elforsyning – Afvejning af hensyn til en sektor på vej mod det indre marked, 1998 p. 151 et seq.
127. See *A. Johnston:* Maintaining the Balance of Power: Liberalization, Reciprocity and Electricity in the European Community, Journal of Energy and Natural Resources Law Vol. 17 1999 pp. 121-150.

Article 33(2) of the Electricity Directive provides that 'contracts for the supply of electricity with an eligible customer in the system of another Member State shall not be prohibited if the customer is considered as eligible in both systems involved.' By contrast, under the Electricity Directive a Member State can introduce a provision to the effect that the State's own privileged customers can be protected from third party access to a network if the supplier comes from a Member State where the customer in question could not be privileged. Under Article 37(2) of the Natural Gas Directive third party access cannot be refused if the customer is considered to be privileged in both systems. The provision is not very clearly expressed and has been much criticised. Nevertheless, it seems that some Member States have made use of the opportunity.

Apart from this there are only corresponding provisions in the air transport sector. In Article 12 of Regulation (EEC) No 95/93 on common rules for the allocation of slots at Community airports there is a similar possibility of refusing to allocate slots where, in connection with the allocation of slots at airports, a third country does not grant Community air carriers treatment comparable to that granted by Member States to air carriers from that country. There is also a similar provision concerning computer reservation systems in Article 8 of Regulation (EC) No 80/2009 on a Code of Conduct for computerised reservation systems. According to this, the Commission may require all system vendors operating in the Union to treat air carriers of that third country in a manner that is equivalent to the treatment of Union air carriers in that third country

2. Energy

From the start, energy policy has been a key policy area for the Union. Two of the three founding treaties – the Treaty of the European Coal and Steel Community (ECSC Treaty)[128] and the Treaty establishing the European Atomic Energy Community (Euratom Treaty) – were specifically related to energy policy. Later the importance of coal as a source of energy was diminished by the availability of cheaper coal and natural gas.

Following the oil crises of the 1970s security of supply played an important role in the Union's energy policy. Since then, environmental protection has also become a key issue. In respect of competition, the efforts have been concentrated on including electricity and natural gas supply in the internal market, and at the same these sectors have been important areas for environmental regulation and regulation of security of supply.

128. The ECSC Treaty expired on 24 July 2002. However, coal remains an important source of energy both at EU and world level.

The Treaty contains no special exceptions for energy, including electricity and natural gas supply.[129] Thus the establishment of the internal market is also an important goal in the energy sectors. This is clear from Articles 194 and 26 TFEU. According to the original version of the latter provision (Article 14 of the EC Treaty, in the period up to 31 December 1992 the Community (as it then was) should have adopted measures a with a view to the gradual establishment of the internal market. The areas of energy ought thus by now to have been covered by the internal market. In principle, under the authority of Article 106(1) and (3) TFEU the Commission could have taken steps to prohibit existing monopolies. However, the Commission has never made use of Article 106(3) in the energy sectors, which has possibly delayed the liberalisation process.[130] Instead, the Commission has published a number of proposals for market directives.[131] In 1996 these proposals resulted in the adoption of the first Electricity Directive, and in 1998 in the adoption of the first Natural Gas Directive.[132] Both of these were issued as harmonising directives. Previously, in its Green paper – for a European Union energy policy (COM(94) 659 final), paragraph 70, the Commission had laid out its strategy for the development of the market, and listed the considerations which should be given priority:

'The integration of the market can be encouraged by regulation or liberalization of the market. It is in the Community's interest to limit Community regulation to the absolute minimum necessary to reconcile freedom of movement with the legitimate objectives of the Member States. In the field of energy, the essential and legitimate elements are:
- protection of public service missions;
- security of supply;
- environmental protection
- energy efficiency.'

According to the Commission, the method by which at least some of these goals were to be achieved was by exposing parts of the sectors concerned to competition.

129. *A.K. Klom:* Liberalisation of Regulated Markets and its Consequences for Trade: The Internal Market for Electricity as a Case Study, Journal of Energy & Natural Resources Law Vol. 14 No 1 1996 p. 8.
130. *P.J. Slot & A.M. Skudder:* Common Features of Community Law Regulation in the Network-Bound Sectors, Common Market Law Review Vol. 38 2001 p. 92 et seq.
131. COM(91) 548 final; and COM(93) 643 final.
132. Directive 96/92/EC concerning common rules for the internal market in electricity ('the first Electricity Directive'); and Directive 98/30/EC concerning common rules for the internal market in natural gas.

The Union does not have exclusive regulatory powers in the area of energy. It shares these powers with the Member States; see Article 5 TFEU. On the contrary, the activities of the Member States include 'the adoption of an economic policy which is based on the close coordination of Member States' economic policies, on the internal market and on the definition of common objectives, and conducted in accordance with the principle of an open market economy with free competition'; see Article 119(1) TFEU. The authority in Article 103(3)(c) TFEU, 'to define, if need be, in the various branches of the economy, the scope of the provisions of Articles 101 and 102' has been applied in the energy sector.

Under Article 194 TFEU, energy is now a special policy area. The policy areas included are: the functioning of the energy market; security of energy supply in the Union; energy efficiency; and the interconnection of energy networks.

From an overall perspective the two energy market directives are relatively broad minimum framework directives. This has allowed for somewhat different implementation measures in the Member States. Among other things these differences are reflected in a number of country reports.[133] In 2003 new directives were issued for both the electricity and natural gas sectors. These have led to increased liberalisation. Previously it had been clear that the first market directives did not sufficiently create an internal market for energy. The main problem was the uneven implementation of the market directives between the Member States, discriminatory methods applied to access to networks, especially in relation to cross-border links, and the continued market strength of the previous monopoly undertakings.[134]

In 2009, the Union adopted the third energy package, with a number of further measures, including:[135]

- Stricter requirements for unbundling of transmission system operators (TSOs) and activities that are open to competition. The requirements are the same for transmission companies in the electricity and natural gas sectors. The starting point is a requirement for ownership unbundling so as to prevent corporate group structures, but two other kinds of structure are allowed. First, the establishment of an ITO (independent transmission operator) structure is allowed. This arrangement involves management independence, including operational and network development decisions

133. *Damien Geradin:* The Liberalization of Electricity and Natural Gas in the European Union, 2001.
134. *Peter Cameron:* Legal Aspects of EU Energy Regulation, 2005 p. 9. This book contains a general review of the market directives for the electricity and natural gas sectors, as well as their implementation in a number of Member States.
135. For a review of the third energy package, see *Christopher W. Jones (ed.):* EU Energy Law, Vol. I, 2010.

being taken independently of group interests. This arrangement involves stricter supervision. Second, it is possible to use an ISO (independent system operator) structure, where there is merely a requirement for not very well defined independence from group interests. This arrangement must merely be more effective than the ITO structure. Furthermore, Article 9(9) of both the Electricity and the Natural Gas Directives contains a fourth possibility, the so-called ITO+ or 'unbundling à la carte' option. The requirements for this option are very vague, merely requiring arrangements that guarantee more effective independence than the ITO structure. However, it can be difficult to comply with this fourth option. It requires both that the arrangements should have been in place by 3 September 2009, and that the transmission system operators should have belonged to a vertically integrated undertaking. Distribution system operators (DSOs) that are part of a vertically integrated undertaking must be independent in legal form, organisation and decision making from activities not relating to distribution; see Article 26 of both the Electricity and the Natural Gas Directives. It is possible to combine TSOs and DSOs; see Article 29 of both the Electricity and the Natural Gas Directives.

- Stricter supervision among other things through the establishment of ACER – the EU Agency for the Cooperation of Energy Regulators, which builds further on previous cooperation.
- The establishment of European Networks of Transmission System Operators (ENTSOs). One has been established for electricity (pursuant to Article 5 of Regulation (EC) No 714/2009 on conditions for access to the network for cross-border exchanges in electricity), and one for natural gas (pursuant to Article 5 of Regulation (EC) No 715/2009 on conditions for access to the natural gas transmission networks). The role ENTSOs is to work on network development plans and to draw up detailed rules for networks and cross-border links.

In the following the electricity and the natural gas sectors will be reviewed in the light of the present market directives.

The two market directives for the electricity and natural gas sectors have been supplemented by: Directive 2005/89/EC concerning measures to safeguard security of electricity supply and infrastructure investment; Regulation (EC) No 715/2009 on conditions for access to the natural gas transmission networks; Regulation (EC) No 714/2009 on conditions for access to the network for cross-border exchanges in electricity; Regulation (EC) No 713/2009 establishing an Agency for the Cooperation of Energy Regulators; and Regulation (EU) No 994/2010 concerning measures to safeguard security of gas supply.

In addition, in the borderland between energy policy and environmental policy there are three directives which are important for electricity and natural gas supplies: Directive 2009/28/EC on the promotion of electricity produced from renewable energy sources in the internal electricity market; Directive 2004/8/EC on the promotion of cogeneration based on a useful heat demand in the internal energy market and amending Directive 92/42/EEC; and Directive 2003/87/EC establishing a scheme for greenhouse gas emission allowance trading within the Community. These will not be considered in detail in this chapter.[136]

2.1. Electricity supply

Electricity supply is traditionally divided into four parts: production, supplying, transmission and distribution. Participants in these stages in the value chain are referred to in the Electricity Directive[137] as *electricity undertakings*.

The term 'electricity undertaking' is not defined, in the Electricity Directive. However, the term is defined indirectly in connection with the definition, in Article 2(2), of an 'integrated electricity undertaking' which is defined as a 'vertically or horizontally integrated undertaking'. And both 'vertically integrated undertaking' and 'horizontally integrated undertaking' are defined.

Transmission and distribution are network functions, by means of which the electricity is physically distributed. These two functions are normally regarded as natural monopolies.[138]

Transmission means the transport of electricity on extra high-voltage and high-voltage interconnected systems with a view to its delivery to final customers (end users) or to distributors. *Distribution* means the transport of electricity on high-voltage, medium voltage and low voltage distribution systems with a view to its delivery to customers (end users). These terms are defined in Article 2 of the Electricity Directive.

In contrast to the network functions, both electricity generation and supply are regarded as being subject to competition. The EU's regulation bears the marks of this distinction.

136. For a discussion of these, see *Luc Werring (ed.):* EU Energy Law, Vol. III, 2006.
137. Directive 2009/72/EC concerning common rules for the internal market in electricity. This is the third such Directive, replacing Directive 2003/54/EC, which in turn replaced Directive 96/92/EC.
138. On natural monopolies in relation to electricity supply see, among others: *Michael Albers:* Competition Law Issues Arising from the Liberalization Process, in *Damien Geradin (ed.):* The Liberalization of Electricity and Natural Gas in the European Union, 2001 p. 4 et seq.

2.1.1. EU regulation

The electricity supply sector has been subject to several EU secondary legal acts. The primary set of rules is in the Electricity Directive, the current version of which dates from 2009. The provisions of this Directive were to be implemented by 3 March 2011, see Article 49 of Directive 2009/72/EC.

The electricity supply sector has also been subject to liberalisation in stages on the route to establishing the internal market for electricity.[139] The first stage was the implementation of Directive 90/547/EEC on the transit of electricity through transmission grids, and the first Directive (90/377/EEC) to improve the transparency of gas and electricity prices charged to industrial end-users. The second stage was the adoption of the first Electricity Directive. The third stage was the adoption of the second Electricity Directive which stated that all end users should have free access to markets by 1 July 2007.

The second Electricity Directive was not necessarily to be the last. Even though one could be tempted to regard the liberalisation process as having been completed with the formal full opening of the market, in practice the internal market for electricity does not function as a liberalised market. In its initiative with regard to the energy markets – An energy policy for Europe[140] – the Commission suggested that there would be further measures, including unbundling. The unbundling requirements were strengthened with the adoption of the third Electricity Directive (2009/72/EC).

The third Electricity Directive is a compromise, and it must be expected that there will at least be a fourth Electricity Directive. With a view to monitoring and evaluating the effect of the Electricity Directive, its Article 47 provides that the Commission must submit an overall progress report.

2.1.1.1. The Electricity Directive

The purpose of the Electricity Directive is to contribute to the establishment of a fully operational internal electricity market. The Directive regulates the generation, transmission, distribution and supply of electricity; see Article 1.

139. See COM(91) 548 final. See also *Herbert von Bose:* Die Richtlinienvorschläge der Kommission betreffend gemeinsame Vorschriften für den Erdgas-Binnenmarkt bzw. für Elektrizitäts-Binnenmarkt, in *Jürgen F. Baur (ed.):* Die Europäische Gemeinschaft und das Recht der leitungsgebundenen Energie, 1993 p. 44 et seq.; and *Wolfgang Hoffmann-Riem & Jens-Peter Schneider:* Wettbewerbs- und umweltorientierte Re-Regulierung im Großhandels-Strommarkt, in *Wolfgang Hoffmann-Riem & Jens-Peter Schneider (eds.):* Umwelt-politische Steuerung in einem liberalisierten Strommarkt, 1995 p. 45.

140. Communication from the Commission to the European Council and the European Parliament – an energy policy for Europe (COM(2007) 1 final).

On the other hand, the choice of fuel is not governed by the Directive; that is up to the Member States.[141]

According to the Electricity Directive, since 1 July 2007 customers have been free to choose which producer or supplier they wish to buy electricity from. Since 1 July 2007, all non-household customers have been eligible customers in another Member State.[142]

Article 19(1) of the first Electricity Directive contained a provision on a minimum percentage of the electricity market which each Member State was required to open. The share of the national market was calculated on the basis of the Community share of electricity consumed by final customers consuming more than 40 GWh per year (on a consumption site basis and including autoproduction), corresponding to 22 % of market opening. The first Electricity Directive did not distinguish between market opening at the wholesale level (purchases by distribution undertakings) and the final customer level. The Member States could therefore choose to fulfil their obligations under this part of the requirement for market opening either by including part of the purchases by distribution undertakings, part of the purchase by final purchasers, or a combination of both, corresponding to at least 22 % of the electricity market in a system with access. According to Article 19(3) of the first Electricity Directive, the only requirement for the Member States' regulation of market opening at wholesaler level was that distribution companies should have to be considered as eligible customers at least for the volume of electricity being consumed by their customers designated as eligible within their distribution system, in order to supply those customers. The market share calculated above the 40 GWh threshold (corresponding to an average of 25.37 % market opening) was subject in the first Electricity Directive to an ongoing adjustment, as three years after the entry into force of the Directive the basis for calculation was to be reduced to 20 GWh (corresponding to about 28 % market share), and after another three years to 9 GWh (corresponding to 33 % market opening).[143] However, the provisions on the sizes of market shares could not prevent participants who were not covered by national provisions on market opening from claiming that there was abuse of a dominant position under Article 82 of the EC Treaty (now Article 102 TFEU). This applied whether or not the national provisions were in accordance with the Directive.

In line with the Union's competition rules, the Electricity Directive does not contain any principles on pricing. In general the sector is regulated in accordance with the Treaty prohibition of abuse of a dominant position in Article

141. Among others, the EU's regulation of the electricity supply sector is discussed in *Christopher W. Jones:* EU Energy Law. The Internal Energy Market, Vol. I, 2010.
142. The term 'non-household customer' includes electricity producers and wholesalers.
143. See COM(1998) 212 final, p. 6. The Union's average market share was calculated at 34.53 % for 2003; see the Commission's Report of 29 October 2002 on the calculation of average market shares after the opening of the electricity market as laid down in Directive 96/92/EC concerning common rules for the internal market in electricity.

102 TFEU, including 'directly or indirectly imposing unfair purchase or selling prices or other unfair trading conditions'.[144] However, there are provisions in Articles 12 and 25 of the Electricity Directive which prohibit discrimination as between system users. This also includes price discrimination. On the other hand, the Member States are free to include such provisions as part of public service obligations; see Article 3 of the Electricity Directive.

Under Article 3(3) of the Electricity Directive, Member States must ensure that all household customers and, where Member States deem it appropriate, small enterprises, (meaning enterprises with fewer than 50 employees and an annual turnover not exceeding EUR 10 million), can enjoy universal service, meaning the right to be supplied with electricity of a specified quality within their territory at reasonable, easily and clearly comparable and transparent prices. See below on public service obligations.

Article 33(2) of the Electricity Directive allows for Member States to include requirements for reciprocity in their implementation of the Directive. The provision states that contracts for the supply of electricity to an eligible customer in the system of another Member State 'shall not be prohibited if the customer is considered as eligible in both systems involved.'[145] This special provision has lost its significance now that all end users can freely choose their suppliers.

Article 24, first and second paragraphs, of the first Electricity Directive allowed for the introduction of special transitional arrangements dealing with stranded costs.[146] Consideration is given on the one hand to investors (and their ability to continue to supply their customers), and on the other hand to the ability of new participants to enter the market. Such transitional provi-

144. *Michael Albers:* Competition Law Issues Arising from the Liberalization Process, in *Damien Geradin (ed.):* The Liberalization of Electricity and Natural Gas in the European Union, 2001 p. 5.
145. The possibility of introducing a reciprocity provision has been used in German law, among others, where until 31 December 2006 it was possible to refuse access to a network on the grounds of lack of reciprocity; see Article 4(2) in Gesetz vom 24.04.1998 zur Neuregelung des Energiewirtschaftsrecht, as amended on 26.08.1998. For a description, see *Christiane Nill-Theobald & Christian Theobald:* Grundzüge des Energiewirtschaftsrechts, 2001 p. 213 et seq.
146. See *Michael Albers:* Competition Law Issues Arising from the Liberalization Process, in *Damien Geradin (ed.):* The Liberalization of Electricity and Natural Gas in the European Union, 2001 p. 14 et seq.

sions must be evaluated against the rules on State aid.[147] These provisions have not been carried forward in the present Electricity Directive. On the other hand there is a possibility of exempting small isolated systems. This provision is now found in Article 26(1) of the current Directive.

2.1.1.2. The application of the general competition rules

As early as in Case 6/64, *Costa* v *ENEL*, the assumption that electricity is good was something which was disputed, because of its special physical nature. In relation to Article 36 TFEU (then Article 28 of the EC Treaty) this was confirmed in Case C-393/92, *Almelo and others* v *Energiebedrijf Ijsselmij*, paragraph 28, which refers to the Union's tariff nomenclature (code CN 27.16).[148] The competition rules must therefore be assumed to apply in principle to the electricity sector. In accordance with this, the Commission applies the competition rules to the energy sector.[149]

There has been a tendency for the security of supply aspect to be emphasised when applying the competition rules to the electricity supply sector. In the *Scottish Nuclear* Decision[150] the Commission emphasised that a long term contract with a take-or-pay clause[151] allowed the possibility of reliable production which could guarantee security of supply and energy independence.

> In connection with the prospective liberalisation of the British energy market, two independent vertically integrated electricity supply companies were set up in Scotland (Scottish Power and Scottish Hydro Electric), which were to compete with each other. At the same time, the Scottish

147. For a review of the Commission's approach see *Brice Allibert:* A Methodology for Analysing State Aid Linked to Stranded Costs, EC Competition Policy Newsletter No 3 2001 pp. 25-27.
148. The CJ has more recently repeated this in Case C-158/94, *Commission* v *Italy,* para. 17.
149. See the Commission's intervention in a dispute between an independent French producer and the two French and Italian electricity monopolists, discussed in the Commission's XXII Report on competition policy, para. 145. For a thorough review of the application of the Union's competition rules in the electricity supply sector, see *Christopher W. Jones (ed.):* EU Energy Law, Vol. II, 2011.
150. Commission Decision 91/329/EEC of 30 April 1991 in Case IV/33.473 – *Scottish Nuclear,* Nuclear Energy Agreement.
151. A take-or-pay clause means that the buyer is obliged to pay the full contractual amount, or a significant proportion of it, for the quantity contracted for, regardless of whether at the time of delivery the buyer is able to take the full quantity. The aim is to protect the investment linked to nuclear and natural gas power stations. These kinds of contracts are normal on the natural gas market, for example.

nuclear power stations were put into a separate company (Scottish Nuclear Limited) which only had a generating licence. An agreement was entered into between the three companies under which Scottish Power and Scottish Hydro Electric bound themselves to take the whole of the production from Scottish Nuclear's two nuclear power stations on the basis of a fixed purchase contract. On its side, Scottish Nuclear bound itself to maximise its production and not to supply to others than Scottish Power and Scottish Hydro Electric. The Commission considered that the agreement restricted competition. The Commission gave the agreement an individual exemption under Article 85(3) [now Article 81(3)] provided that the duration of the agreement was reduced from 30 years to 15 years. 30 years corresponds to the normal life of a nuclear power station.

Security of supply was also a weighty consideration in the Commission's Decision on an agreement for the supply of German coal in the *Jahrhundertvertrag* case[152]

The case concerned an agreement between a group of German coal producers (*Gesamtverband des deutschen Steinkohlenbergbaus*) and a group of German electricity generating stations (*Vereinigung Deutscher Elektrizitätswerke*) on the supply of German coal for the period 1991-1995. The German State was not a party to the agreement, but it had encouraged the agreement by, among other things, providing full cover for the extra costs of using German coal. This cover was provided in the form of direct compensatory payments and the restriction of imports of third-country coal and the issuing of import licences. In Germany there was an import limit on coal from third countries. Regardless of the role of the State, the agreement was regarded by the Commission as being an agreement under Article 101(1) TFEU (then Article 85(1) of the EC Treaty). Since the agreement aimed at dividing up the market, it was in breach of this provision. However, the Commission accepted an exemption under Article 81(3), since it increased the security of supply and thereby contributed to improve electricity production and distribution. With regard to the establishment of the internal market for energy, the permission was granted for a limited period and a limited quantity.

152. Notice of 29 June 1990 pursuant to Article 19(3) of Regulation No 17, concerning Case IV/33.151 – *Jahrhundertvertrag*. See also Commission Decision 93/126/EEC of 22 December 1992 in Case IV/33.151 – *Jahrhundertvertrag*.

In the *Pego* case,[153] in connection with the acceptance of 15 year exclusivity, the Commission especially took into account the liberalisation of the electricity sector which was about to take place in Portugal. There was thus an assessment under competition law of the effect on the market of the actual agreement. However, it also seems that the assessment indirectly took account of the fact that the capacity of the generating station was important to the fulfilment of the public supply obligation to which Electricidade de Portugal was subject. In other words weight was attached to security of supply.

> The case concerned an agreement between four large electricity supply companies from four different Member States: Electricidade de Portugal, National Power (UK), Electricité de France and Empresa National de Electricidad (Spain). The agreement concerned the construction and running of a power station in Portugal. The agreement contained a provision according to which the capacity of all the power station's capacity and production should be made available to Electricidade de Portugal for a 28 year period. After negotiations with the Commission the period of exclusivity was reduced to 15 years, after which Electricidade de Portugal could have first call on the electricity from the power station.

However, concern for security of supply cannot be extended so as to favour domestic end users, for example by cutting off foreign demand through export restrictions.

> This was the situation in a case concerning the interruption of exports to neighbouring countries by the Swedish State undertaking and electricity TSO, Svenske Kraftnët.[154] In periods of high domestic demand for electricity, the Swedish TSO interrupted exports of electricity to neighbouring countries with a view to being able to maintain Sweden as a unitary pricing zone.[155] This meant that electricity prices in Sweden were

153. Notice 93/C 265/03 of 30 September 1993, pursuant to Article 19 (3) of Council Regulation No 17 concerning a request for negative clearance or exemption pursuant to Article 85 (3) of the EEC Treaty – Case No IV/34.598 – *Electricidade de Portugal/Pego* project. The decision is referred to briefly in Cross: Electric Utility Regulation in the European Union, 1996 p. 199.
154. Commission Decision of 14 April 2010 – Case 39351 – *Swedish Interconnectors.*
155. Countries such as Denmark and Norway, which are part of the Nord Pool area together with Sweden, are divided into several pricing zones in order to be able to deal with the domestic physical limits to transmission capacity (bottlenecks). Sweden did not want to do the same, even though there are substantial bottlenecks in Sweden.

> lower in periods when exports were cut off, while the prices were correspondingly higher in the neighbouring countries.
>
> The Commission made it clear that there were come overriding principles involved, such as non-discrimination and the prohibition of export restrictions and, with reference to the case law of the CJ, it stated that the rules on abuse of dominant position also applied in such a case: 'It is useful to recall the general principle enshrined in Article 18 TFEU according to which any discrimination on the basis of nationality is prohibited. Moreover, Article 35 TFEU expressly prohibits quantitative restrictions on exports and all measures having equivalent effect. It is thus clear that a Member State would not be entitled to restrict exports of electricity so as to reserve such electricity for domestic consumption. Similarly, a dominant undertaking cannot seek to achieve the same objective through its conduct on the market without falling foul of Union competition rules.[156] Practices that do so are generally considered to have as their object the restriction of competition'.[157]
>
> Thereafter the Commission stated that the general conditions existed for the application of Article 102 TFEU, on abuse of dominant position.
>
> The Commission accepted a Swedish proposal to refrain from using export restrictions for an interim period of 10 years from 1 November 2011, and to start using pricing zones instead.

In a case in 2008, the Commission suspected that the German electricity supplier, E.ON, was abusing its dominant position by, among other things, adopting a special discounting strategy on the short term market (the power exchange EEX) and by abuse on the balancing market.[158]

> The Commission suspected that E.ON was limiting the supply of electricity from certain plants on the short term market EEX, in order to increase the spot price for electricity. On the German electricity balancing

Sweden has a large part of its generating capacity in the north, while a large part of electricity demand is in the south (Stockholm, Gothenburg, Malmö).

156. Joined Cases 56 and 58-64, *Établissements Consten* and *Grundig v Commission* [1966] ECR 299, p. 340.
157. Case 41-69, ACF *Chemiefarma* v *Commission,* para. 128; and Joined Cases 56 and 58-64, *Établissements Consten* and *Grundig* v *Commission,* paras 342 and 343.
158. Summary of Commission Decision of 26 November 2008 relating to a proceeding under Article 82 of the EC Treaty and Article 54 of the EEA Agreement (Cases COMP/39.388 – *German Electricity Wholesale Market* and COMP/39.389 – *German Electricity Balancing Market*) (notified under document number C(2008) 7367 final).

market, the concern was that E.ON was abusing its dominant position by increasing its costs with a view to favouring its production affiliate and passing the costs on to the end user, and preventing power producers from other Member States from exporting balancing energy into the E.ON balancing market. The case resulted in undertakings being given by E.ON.

It is especially in connection with the Member States' measures to promote renewable energy that there have been problems concerning State aid. The sector is specifically regulated by the guidelines on State aid for environmental protection. In relation to renewable energy, State aid can be provided in the following ways:

- Compensation for the difference between the production costs for renewable energy and the market price on any given day,
- Use of market mechanisms such as green certificates or a tendering procedure,
- Support for operating costs on the basis of the external environmental costs which society saves by virtue of the establishment of electricity generating capacity based on renewable energy, and
- Use of general support arrangements for environmental protection.

These provide for regressive support over a maximum of 5 years.

Case C-379/98, *PreussenElektra* v *Schhleswag,* concerned an obligation to buy electricity generated using renewable energy, where it was held that a specific arrangement involving consumer-financed support for renewable energy did not constitute State aid contrary to Article 107(1) TFEU (then Article 87(1) of the EC Treaty), even though it was a public law measure which provided for this support.[159] The decision raised the question of whether a corresponding obligation to purchase green certificates would also not be considered State aid. In connection with the *PreussenElektra* case, the Commission argued that the German arrangement was covered by the State aid provisions. It must now be considered extremely doubtful whether an obligation to purchase renewable energy will in future be considered to be State aid.

159. The case is discussed in section 1.4.6.3.

2.1.2. Authorisation procedures

The Electricity Directive lays down special requirements for authorisation procedures for new capacity (Article 7).[160] Transmission system operators and distribution system operators must be designated either by the Member State (by an administrative law measure, which is therefore like an authorisation), or by the Member State allowing those who are responsible for the relevant facilities to appoint the system operator (Articles 10 and 24). The latter procedure cannot be characterised as a true grant of authorisation. It is up to the Member States to determine whether other parts of the national electricity supply sector should be subject to authorisation requirements. This is discussed in the section dealing with access to networks. In addition to this, there can be special requirements for the establishment of a network supervisor and the unbundling of the network in relation to the other participants.

2.1.2.1. Electricity generation

The Electricity Directive contains a special chapter on electricity generation. According to Article 7, the Member States must adopt an authorisation procedure for the construction of new generating capacity. According to Article 8, a tendering system can be sued, specifically with regard to security of supply, the promotion of wholly new technology and environmental protection. Both approaches must be based on the criteria of objectivity, transparency and non-discrimination; see Article 7(4) and Article 8(1) and (3).

An authorisation procedure means that any undertaking can seek permission to build new generating capacity at any time. Article 7(2) lists the criteria which such a procedure can take account of. These *can* include: a) the safety and security of the electricity system, installations and associated equipment; (b) protection of public health and safety; (c) protection of the environment; (d) land use and siting; (e) use of public ground; (f) energy efficiency; (g) the nature of the primary sources; (h) characteristics particular to the applicant, such as technical, economic and financial capabilities; (i) compliance with measures adopted pursuant to Article 3, which refers to public service obligations, including customer protection and environmental protection; (j) contribution to the Union's target for the use of energy from renewable sources; and (k) the contribution of generating capacity to reducing emissions. Both consideration for the environment and security of supply are constant themes in the list.

160. In special cases there is a possibility of a tendering procedure in Article 8.

As indicated by the use of the word *can* indicates, this list is not exhaustive. There are thus plentiful opportunities for Member States to supplement the criteria for authorisation.

A requirement in the first Electricity Directive, to send notification to the Commission in the event of a refusal of a request to build new generating capacity, was not carried over into the second Electricity Directive. According to recital 30 of that Directive, this proved to be an unnecessary administrative burden. On the other hand, the administrative law requirement to give reasons for a refusal has been carried over; see Article 7(4) of the third Electricity Directive. Thus, Article 7(4) also states that the authorisation procedures and criteria must be made public.

Under a tendering procedure the Member States must designate an authority, public body or private body independent from electricity industry to be responsible for the tendering procedure. This can be a regulator. The tendering conditions must be transparent, in the form of a detailed description of the contract specifications and of the procedure to be followed, and invitations to tender must be published in the Official Journal of the European Union at least six months prior to the closing date for tenders, and an estimate of the expected need must be prepared and published every two years.

Under the first Electricity Directive the Member States were free to choose between an authorisation procedure and a tendering procedure. The basic difference between an authorisation procedure and a tendering procedure is that an authorisation procedure leaves the initiative for installing new generating capacity to the market participants, while a tendering procedure leaves the initiative to the responsible public authorities. With authorisation the initiative lies with the market participants who will only have financial incentives to expand or renew generating capacity as the expansion or renewal of capacity becomes profitable. Authorisation procedures should only be used if there is a demand driven need for new or expanded capacity. All applications for the establishment of generating capacity which fulfils the pre-established criteria must be approved. In a liberalised market the regulation of the amount of capacity is subject to market forces. If a participant thinks it is worth building new capacity, either to export electricity or to compete with existing participants in the market, an application for authorisation to build new capacity should not be refused on the grounds that there is a lack of domestic demand.[161] With a tendering procedure the public authority will be more inclined to look at the need for new capacity. This means that the authorisation procedure leads to competition both in relation to new and ex-

161. Environmental concerns are subject to national rules on the choice of fuel, emissions standards, quotas etc.

isting generating capacity, while the tendering procedure will have a tendency, at least in the short term, to protect the existing generating facilities from domestic competition.[162]

2.1.2.2. Network supervisor

Articles 10 and 24 of the Electricity Directive require the Member States to ensure that system operators are appointed for transmission networks (TSO) and for distribution networks (DSO). According to the Directive there is nothing to prevent a transmission network system operator and a distribution network system operator being part of the same corporate group. However, there is an unbundling requirement in Article 26. The systems operators are responsible for the operation, maintenance, management of energy flows and development of the network. Traditionally these functions have been dealt with in vertically integrated electricity companies, often by a network owner who was also engaged in electricity production.

In contrast to a natural gas network, an electricity network is characterised by the fact that electricity cannot be stored in the network. Input (production) and output (consumption) must always correspond largely to each other in order to maintain the frequency at 50 Hz. Systems operators seek, by means of dispatching and balancing, to compensate for lack of inputs or excess inputs. Interruption of supply to end users can also be used for this purpose.[163] A network can be described as being like connected tanks. As long as the transmission capacity between two tanks is sufficient, it does not matter to the balance of the system where the inputs and outputs take place. If the transmission capacity is insufficient, there will be bottlenecks.

According to Article 12(f) and Article 25(2), transmission and distribution system network operators can be independent participants or be owned by participants in the market, since 'related undertakings' must not be favoured.

Article 9 of the Electricity Directive lays down provisions on the unbundling of the ownership of transmission system operators in relation to generation and supply. There is no requirement for unbundling in relation to distribution. This is expressed as a prohibition of direct or indirect exercise of control. On the arrangements for ISOs and ITOs, see above.

The first Electricity Directive did not contain requirements for unbundling at the distribution level. However, Article 26 of the present Electricity Di-

162. Working Paper of the Commission on the Organisation of the Internal Electricity Market, SEC(95) 464 final, 22 March 1995.
163. Interruptions of supply can be necessary to avoid a system falling out of balance if there is an acute lack of current, or on the basis of agreements on interruptions, whereby a consumer is compensated for agreeing to interruption of supply if there is lack of current.

rective introduced unbundling requirements for distribution system operators, corresponding to organisational and management unbundling. However, in particular for distribution companies there is scope for Member States to introduce a *de minimis* provision in the form of a threshold of 100,000 customers or serving small isolated systems; see Article 26(4). Below this limit, a Member State can refrain from imposing requirements for unbundling. This thus avoids splitting up smaller electricity distributors between supply companies and network companies.

As part of the requirement for unbundling, system operators at both transmission and distribution levels are subject to a duty of confidentiality with regard to commercially sensitive information which they receive in the course carrying out their tasks; see Article 16 on transmission and Article 27 on distribution. Confidentiality is not just intended as a security against general publication, but includes a prohibition on passing on information about competitors' circumstances to market participants in the system operator's own corporate group.[164] Identical provisions in the two articles explicitly state that a system operator must 'prevent information about its own activities which may be commercially advantageous being disclosed in a discriminatory manner.' The fact a system operator can belong to the same corporate group as an electricity generating or supply company could give an incentive for discriminatory treatment of system users. The provisions make an exception for passing on information to the authorities; see Article 30(1). However, such authorities are themselves subject to a duty of confidentiality; see Article 30(2).

There is also a requirement for accounting unbundling for all electricity undertakings which are either vertically integrated or which carry on some non-electricity related activity alongside their electricity supply undertaking. Article 31 provides that the undertakings in question shall keep separate accounts for transmission and distribution activities and, where relevant, for non-electricity activities. Furthermore there is a requirement for all electricity supply undertakings to keep accounts in accordance with the relevant national implementing provisions for the Fourth Council Directive 78/660/EC based on Article 44(2)(g)(12) of the Treaty on the annual accounts of certain types of companies.

164. COM(91) 548 final – Proposal for a Council Directive concerning common rules for the internal market in electricity, and Proposal for a Council Directive concerning common rules for the internal market in natural gas.

2.1.3. Access to networks

In its Articles 16 to 20 the first Electricity Directive introduced a limited right to use others' electricity networks for certain electricity supply undertakings and end users in connection with entering into electricity supply agreements. The customers who thereby got access to networks and to trading rights were designated eligible customers.[165]

Access to networks was not absolute. Access covered those participants which, in connection with their compliance with the degree of market opening referred to, the Member States had categorised as eligible customers. Both distributors and final customers could be included in the calculation of the degree of market openness. According to Article 19(3) of the first Electricity Directive, all final customers consuming more than 100 GWh per year, on a consumption site basis and including autoproduction, must be covered by access to networks.[166] The first Electricity Directive included an automatic adjustment of this threshold value.

Commercial customers have been 'eligible customers' since 1 July 2004, and household customers have been 'eligible customers' since 1 July 2007; see Article 33. Thereby, all final customers are entitled to choose their suppliers.

Under Article 12(f) and Article 25(2) system operators must not discriminate between system users or classes of system users. This means that the Member States must also not require system operators to discriminate, for example by giving individual users or classes of users prior rights to network access over others, unless there is an exceptional situation which can justify such discrimination and which is expressly provided for in the Electricity Directive. Such exceptions are provided for in Article 15(3) and (4) as well as Article 25(4) (priority for certain forms of generation); see below.

2.1.3.1. Procedures for system access

Under Article 32 of the Electricity Directive, regulated third party access to networks is made obligatory. This right of access is based on published tariffs. The Member States must ensure that the tariffs for third party access, or the methods for their calculation, are approved prior to their entry into force. It is still possible to deny access by reference to lack of capacity. Substantiated reasons must be given for refusal of access. However, there is nothing to

165. See Article 19 of Directive 96/92/EC (the First Electricity Directive). The term 'eligible customer' was first used in Article 17.
166. It could thus be decisive for an undertaking's possibility of access to a network whether its undertaking was geographically concentrated or spread out over a number of production units.

prevent the grant of access rights. In this case it is up to the system operator to ensure that production and consumption are balanced on both sides of a bottleneck, where capacity is too low.

The first Electricity Directive distinguished between two possibilities for access to the network: *negotiated access* and *single buyer access*. Negotiated access meant that the more detailed conditions for access to a network were subject to a normal negotiating procedure. However, there was a requirement for the publication of recommended tariffs. Single buyer access meant that it was possible for a Member States appoint an undertaking as the sole undertaking for the territory covered by the system operator. The Member State could thereafter require the single buyer to buy the electricity for which an eligible customer had entered into a purchase agreement. A single buyer would thus retain control over the network, securing its status as a monopolist.

2.1.3.2. Direct lines

In order to be able to supply final customers a supplier is dependent either on being able to use an existing network or establish a direct line. Article 34 of the Electricity Directive ensures that every electricity producer can establish a direct line to supply their own premises, subsidiaries and eligible customers on the basis of objective and non-discriminatory criteria. However, Member States may refuse to authorise a direct line if granting such authorisation would be contrary to the provisions of Article 3. Article 3 deals with the possibility of imposing a public service obligation on an electricity undertaking and of departing from the provisions of the Directive if they hinder the fulfilment of the obligations imposed. Article 3 of the Electricity Directive refers to Article 106 TFEU. Only if the conditions in this provision are fulfilled can authorisation to establish direct lines be refused. Similarly, under Article 34(4) of the Directive, Member States may make authorisation to construct a direct line subject either to the refusal of system access on the basis of lack of capacity or the initiation of a dispute resolution procedure. This provision may be seen as an expression of concerns for environmental protection. Because they can disfigure the landscape, new installations can be prevented if they do not meet an actual need for capacity. If there is sufficient capacity, competition law measures will be sufficient to take care of competition concerns.

Article 34(3) of the Electricity Directive explicitly states that the possibility of supplying electricity through a direct line does not affect the possibility of supplying electricity in accordance with the right of third party access.

2.1.3.3. Cross-border connections

Access to cross-border connections (interconnections) is important for the establishment of the internal market for electricity. Such interconnections link the transmission networks of different Member States.

The Electricity Directive does not provide for specific methods for arranging the allocation of access to these interconnections. In most cases there will be times in the day or in the year when capacity is insufficient to meet demand. There will be a bottleneck and there will be a need to allocate a limited resource. According to Article 15(2) of the Directive, 'the use of interconnectors shall be determined on the basis of criteria which may be approved by the Member State and which must be objective, published and applied in a non discriminatory manner which ensures the proper functioning of the internal market in electricity.' The usual methods for making allocations are pro rata rationing and auctions. Other methods are first-come-first-served or linking network rights to contracts for supply (merit order). A special arrangement consists in giving free access to interconnections. The transmission system operators in question can be given the task of regulating both consumption and production on both sides of the bottleneck. This can be done by requiring producers to regulate production, possibly for payment. It is also possible that consumers will be offered payment for agreeing to an interruption of supply, in whole or on part. This will only be relevant to industrial undertakings which are heavy users of energy.

Problems arise concerning exclusive rights, especially in connection with the establishment of new interconnecting lines. Such agreements are often necessary in order to secure investment and thus the financing of such new lines. However, there is a problem in relation to Article 101 TFEU about how long such exclusivity may last. It must be assumed that the duration must be sufficient to secure the investment. See the cases referred to above on the application of the Treaty's general competition rules.

Regulation (EC) No 714/2009 on conditions for access to the network for cross-border exchanges in electricity (the 'CBT Regulation') introduced provisions on cost-related tariffs for access to national networks. Moreover, in Article 14(1) it introduced a prohibition of distance-related charges. This is an expression of a clear choice of charging principles. A tariff point system is preferred. Other measures, such as planning laws, may be used instead. On the other hand the prohibition of distance-related tariffs is presumably beneficial for the establishment of the internal market for electricity.

Under Article 15(1), transmission system operators must put in place co-ordination and information exchange mechanisms to ensure the security of the networks as part of congestion management. Article 16 states that network congestion problems must be addressed using non-discriminatory market based solutions which give efficient economic signals to market participants and transmission system operators. Network congestion problems should preferably be solved by using non-transaction based methods, i.e. methods that do not involve a selection between the contracts of individual market participants. One method will be to use regulatory powers on both sides of a bottleneck. Procedures to curtail transactions should only be used in emergencies where the transmission system operator must act rapidly, and where re-dispatching or counter-trading is not possible. Except in cases of force majeure, market participants who have been allocated capacity must be compensated for any curtailment to supply.

Article 17 of the CBT Regulation contains a special possibility for exempting new direct current interconnectors from the provisions of Article 6. This makes it possible to give special protection for the establishment of new interconnections if necessary.

2.1.3.4. Transit

The CBT replaced the Directive on the transit of electricity through transmission grids.[167] Until its repeal on 1 July 2004, this Directive required the Member States to take measures to ease the transit of electricity. Transit agreements were negotiated between the owners or those responsible for the network concerned and the companies which were responsible for the export and import of electricity in the Member States concerned.

Under Article 13 of the CBT Regulation, transmission system operators must receive compensation for costs incurred by hosting cross-border flows of electricity on their networks. This is to be paid by the operators of national transmission systems from which cross-border flows originate and the systems where those flows end. The compensation is not negotiable. It is the Commission which decides the compensation to be paid; see Article 13(4) of the Regulation. The costs-based compensation is to be determined 'on the basis of the forward looking long-run average incremental costs, taking into account losses, investment in new infrastructure, and an appropriate proportion of the cost of existing infrastructure, as far as infrastructure is used for the transmission of cross-border flows, in particular taking into account the need to guarantee security of supply'; see Article 13(6).

167. Directive 90/547/EEC on the transit of electricity through transmission grids (OJ 1990 L 313/90). This Directive was repealed in Article 29 of the second Electricity Directive.

2.1.4. Public service obligations

The Electricity Directive contains a number of special public service obligations. The provisions cover in part those concerns which *must* be the responsibility of the Member States and in part those that *can* be their responsibility.

The Member States must be responsible for consumer protection. Thus, Article 3(3)-(5) of the Directive imposes on Member States a general duty to ensure connections for supply to all household customers, and a genuine possibility for switching suppliers. The Member States are also given the possibility of extending consumer protection to cover small enterprises, (enterprises with fewer than 50 employees and an annual turnover not exceeding EUR 10 million),[168] appointing a supplier of last resort, and protecting final customers in remote areas.

The provision in Article 3(2) gives Member States the possibility of imposing public service obligations on electricity companies 'which may relate to security, including security of supply, regularity, quality and price of supplies and environmental protection, including energy efficiency, energy from renewable sources and climate protection.' However, such obligations must be clearly defined, transparent, non-discriminatory, and verifiable. The provision goes on to say that EU electricity companies must be guaranteed the equal access to national consumers, and: 'In relation to security of supply, energy efficiency/demand-side management and for the fulfilment of environmental goals and goals for energy from renewable sources, as referred to in this paragraph, Member States may introduce the implementation of long-term planning, taking into account the possibility of third parties seeking access to the system.'

There is still no clear practice concerning the application of Article 3(2) and the corresponding provision of the first and second Electricity Directives (also Article 3(2)). Despite the wording of the provision, it must be assumed that any application of the provision by a Member State would require the prior approval of the Commission.[169] The question of how Article 86(2) of the Treaty should be interpreted in relation to the electricity supply sector has been dealt with by the CJ in four cases on exclusive rights to import and ex-

168. However, even without this provision Member States could extend the obligation to supply. The obligation to supply can be extended beyond the stated size of undertaking.

169. *Piet Jan Slot* 2001 p. 24.

port electricity. These cases do not give much guidance, apart from the fact that the Commission has a significant burden of evidence.[170]

A special public service obligation for security of supply is imposed by the Directive on measures to safeguard security of electricity supply.[171] Article 1 lays down measures aimed at safeguarding security of electricity supply so as to ensure the proper functioning of the internal market for electricity and to ensure:

'a. an adequate level of generation capacity;
b. an adequate balance between supply and demand; and
c. an appropriate level of interconnection between Member States for the development of the internal market.'

The special provisions of this Directive are particularly aimed at the conditions governing networks and system operators and they are supplemented by Article 7 of the Electricity Directive which gives Member States the possibility of providing for new capacity in the interests of security of supply. The Directive on measures to safeguard security of electricity supply is also supplemented by the public service obligations in Article 3(2) of the Electricity Directive, whereby Member States can impose obligations on electricity undertakings with a view to security of supply, among other things.

Under Article 3 of the Directive on measures to safeguard security of electricity supply, Member States must take the necessary measures to promote a stable investment climate, define the roles and responsibilities of competent authorities, including regulatory authorities where relevant, and all relevant market actors[172] and publish information thereon.

According to the Directive, transmission and, where appropriate, distribution system operators must meet quality of supply and network security performance objectives. These objectives must be objective, transparent and non-discriminatory. They must be approved by the Member State in question and published. Interruption of supply in emergency situations must be based on predefined criteria relating to the management of imbalances by transmission system operators.

170. Cases C-157/94, C-158/94, C-159/94 and C-160/94, *Commission* v *The Netherlands, Italy, France and Spain* respectively.
171. Directive 2005/89/EC concerning measures to safeguard security of electricity supply and infrastructure investment.
172. The relevant market actors are, among others, transmission and distribution system operators, electricity producers, suppliers, and final customers.

As for investing in networks, pursuant to Article 6 of the Electricity Directive, Member States must establish a regulatory framework that facilitates maintenance and, where necessary, renewal of their networks. Member States must also provide investment signals for both the transmission and distribution system network operators to develop their networks in order to meet foreseeable demand from the market. In certain cases an individual project can be so important as to fall under the heading of 'projects of mutual interest' and may qualify for financial support from the EU under Article 171 TFEU.[173]

Article 5 of Directive 2005/89/EC, on measures to safeguard security of electricity supply and infrastructure investment, states that Member States must take appropriate measures to maintain a balance between the demand for electricity and the availability of generation capacity. The definition of 'balance between supply and demand' is given in Article 2, and it means 'the satisfaction of foreseeable demands of consumers to use electricity without the need to enforce measures to reduce consumption.' Named possible methods for maintaining a balance include: interruptible contracts, real-time demand management technologies such as advanced metering systems, energy conservation measures and tendering procedures.

2.1.5. Technical harmonisation

In order to ensure that all participants can be linked to a network, under Article 5 of the Electricity Directive the Member States must ensure that technical safety criteria are defined and that rules establishing the minimum technical design and operational requirements for connection to the system of generating installations, distribution systems, directly connected consumers' equipment, interconnector circuits and direct lines are developed and made public. These technical rules must ensure the interoperability of systems and be objective and non-discriminatory, and must be notified to the Commission in accordance with Article 8 of Directive 98/34/EC laying down a procedure for the provision of information in the field of technical standards and regulations.

173. See Decision 1229/2003/EC of the European Parliament and of the Council laying down a series of guidelines for trans-European energy networks and repealing Decision 1254/96/EC. See also Chapter 1, section 1.2.1.

2.1.6. Transparency

Together with Directive 90/547/EEC on the transit of electricity through transmission grids, the first Directive on price transparency[174] was implemented as part of the first phase of the liberalisation of the electricity sector. The Directive has been emended several times and was most recently adopted in partially amended form in 2008.[175] According to its preamble, the purpose of the Directive is to ensure that competition is not distorted in the internal market and to help obviate discrimination against users. Article 1 of the Directive requires the Member States to take the steps necessary to ensure that undertakings which supply gas or electricity to industrial end-users send information on the prices and terms of sale of gas and electricity to industrial end-users, as well as the price systems in use..

Article 31(2) and (3) of the current Electricity Directive states that, whatever their system of ownership or legal form, electricity undertakings must draw up, submit to audit[176] and publish their annual accounts in accordance with the rules of national law on the annual accounts of limited liability companies adopted pursuant to the Fourth Council Directive 78/660/EC on the annual accounts of certain types of companies. Companies which are not legally obliged to publish their annual accounts must keep a copy of them at the disposal of the public at their head office. In Article 19(3) there is a requirement for accounting unbundling. Thus, in their internal accounting electricity undertakings must 'keep separate accounts for each of their transmission and distribution activities as they would be required to do if the activities in question were carried out by separate undertakings, with a view to avoiding discrimination, cross subsidisation and distortion of competition. They shall also keep accounts, which may be consolidated, for other electricity activities not relating to transmission or distribution.' Moreover, the internal accounts must include a balance sheet and a profit and loss account for each activity.

2.1.7. Public authorities

Under Article 35 of the Electricity Directive, each Member State is required to appoint a single national regulatory authority (a regulator). In most Mem-

174. Directive 90/377/EEC concerning a Community procedure to improve the transparency of gas and electricity prices charged to industrial end-users.
175. Directive 2008/92/EC concerning a Community procedure to improve the transparency of gas and electricity prices charged to industrial end-users. The Directive is discussed generally in section 1.4.8.
176. According to Article 31(4), the audit must verify that the obligation to avoid discrimination and cross-subsidies is respected.

ber States this has led to the appointment of an independent regulator. Until 2004, Germany was an exception to this. Here the supervisory tasks were the responsibility of the ordinary competition authorities, as *ex post* control combined with widespread special regulation. This was much criticised by the other Member States. It is up to the Member States to ensure the independence of regulators. Article 35(4) and (5) of the Electricity Directive explicitly requires that the regulatory authority:

- is legally distinct and functionally independent from any other public or private entity;
- ensures that the management acts independently of any market interest;
- does not seek or take direct instructions from any government or other public or private entity when carrying out the regulatory tasks;
- can take autonomous decisions, independently from any political body, and has separate annual budget allocations, with autonomy in the implementation of the allocated budget, and adequate human and financial resources to carry out its duties; and
- and that the members of the board or top management are appointed for a fixed term of five up to seven years, renewable once.

Pursuant to Article 37 of the Electricity Directive, regulators have the following powers and duties, among others:

- fixing or approving transmission or distribution tariffs or their methodologies;
- ensuring compliance by electricity undertakings with their obligations under the Electricity Directive, including as regards cross-border issues;
- cooperating on cross-border issues with the regulatory authorities of neighbouring Member States and with the Agency for the Cooperation of Energy Regulators;
- complying with and implementing legally binding decisions of the Agency and of the Commission;
- reporting annually on its activities;
- ensuring that there are no cross-subsidies between transmission, distribution, and supply activities;
- monitoring and evaluating the investment plans of the transmission system operators;
- monitoring compliance with and reviewing the past performance of network security and reliability rules;

- monitoring the level of transparency, including of wholesale prices, and ensuring compliance of electricity undertakings with transparency obligations;
- monitoring the level and effectiveness of market opening and competition at wholesale and retail levels;
- monitoring the occurrence of restrictive contractual practices, including exclusivity clauses;
- helping to ensure that the consumer protection measures are effective and enforced;
- ensuring access to customer consumption data; and
- monitoring investment in generation capacities in relation to security of supply.

Also, Article 37(8) of the Electricity Directive states that the Member States must 'create appropriate and efficient mechanisms for regulation, control and transparency so as to avoid any abuse of a dominant position, in particular to the detriment of consumers, and any predatory behaviour.' Pricing is thus perhaps the most important task of the regulator who, under the Electricity Directive must at least have responsibility for fixing or approving the methodologies used to calculate or establish the terms and conditions for connection and access to national networks, prior to their entry into force. The Directive does not include requirements for the explicit approval by the regulator of electricity undertakings' individual prices. As for terms and conditions for connection and access to national networks, including transmission and distribution tariffs, as well as the provision of balancing mechanisms, the regulator must at least approve the methods used for the calculation or fixing of tariffs. This approval must be given before the tariffs become effective; see Article 37 of the Electricity Directive. There is thus a kind of *ex ante* control.

The Electricity Directive also gives regulators a role as a dispute resolution authority in relation to various matters. When acting as dispute settlement authority, the regulatory authority must in principle give a decision within two months after receipt of a complaint.

2.2. Natural gas

In contrast to electricity, natural gas (primarily methane) is a primary form of energy, even though there is often some form of refining prior to the gas being used. Natural gas is not necessarily as homogeneous a product as electricity. The calorific value can vary according to where it comes from. However, inputs to a network can be made on the basis of a measurement of the calorific value of the gas input, or it can be refined to a specific calorific value.[177]

The recovery and supply of natural gas are regulated by different sets of rules. This section only deals with the supply of natural gas, often referred to as *downstream*, as opposed to *upstream* which refers to natural gas from the gas well to the refinery.[178]

As for the downstream market, this is defined in Article 2 of the third and most recent Natural Gas Directive,[179] which lists a number of different functions. These represent different stages of the value chain and are to some extent subject to different frameworks.

In Article 2(1) of the Natural Gas Directive, *natural gas undertaking* is defined as: 'a natural or legal person carrying out at least one of the following functions: production, transmission, distribution, supply, purchase or storage of natural gas, including LNG, which is responsible for the commercial, technical and/or maintenance tasks related to those functions, but shall not include final customers.'[180]

Transmission is defined as: 'the transport of natural gas through a network, which mainly contains high-pressure pipelines, other than an upstream pipeline network and other than the part of high-pressure pipelines primarily used in the context of local distribution of natural gas, with a view to its delivery to customers, but not including supply.'[181] *Distribution* means 'the transport of natural gas through local or regional pipeline networks with a

177. If the calorific value varies too widely, this can give problems for gas installations which are optimised for a specific calorific value.
178. For a description of the Union's rules on the upstream sectors for hydrocarbons, see *Piet Jan Cross et al.:* EC Energy Law, in *Martha Roggenkamp et al.:* Energy Law in Europe, 2007 p. 336 et seq. Article 20 of the Natural Gas Directive contains provisions on access to upstream pipeline networks.
179. Directive 2009/73/EC concerning common rules for the internal market in natural gas. This was required to be implemented by 3 March 2011, from which date the old Directive 2003/55/EC was repealed. For general comments on the first Directive 98/30/EC, see *Eugene D. Cross et al.:* EC Energy Law, in *Martha Roggenkamp et al.:* Energy Law in Europe, 2001 p. 308 et seq. The second Natural Gas Directive is described in *Christopher W. Jones*: EU Energy Law, Vol. I, 2006; *Martha Roggenkamp et al.:* Energy Law in Europe, 2007 p. 364 ff.; and *Peter Cameron:* Competition in Energy Markets, 2007.
180. LNG is the abbreviation for 'liquefied natural gas'.
181. *Customers* means wholesale and final customers of natural gas and natural gas undertakings which purchase natural gas.

view to its delivery to customers,[182] but not including supply.' Both transmission and distribution are considered to be natural monopolies. The legal entities which are responsible for the transmission and distribution functions are referred to as *transmission system operators* and *distribution system operators* respectively.

A storage function will often be associated with a natural gas system, and this is the responsibility of *storage system operators*. This function is an essential part of a gas network and thus part of a natural monopoly. Most of these functions are performed by an integrated natural gas undertaking. These can be categorised as vertically integrated natural gas undertakings, which refers to a natural gas undertaking which performs two or more of the following functions: production, transmission, distribution, supply or storage of natural gas, and horizontally integrated natural as undertakings which performs at least one of the following functions: production, transmission, distribution, supply or storage of natural gas, together with an activity not related to natural gas.

2.2.1. Regulation under EU law

The primary regulation of competition in the natural gas sector is found in the Natural Gas Directive. The first Natural Gas Directive dated from 1998. In 2004 this was replaced by the second Natural Gas Directive, which was in turn replaced by the third Natural Gas Directive in 2009. The sector is also covered by Directive 2008/92/EC on a Community procedure to improve the transparency of gas and electricity prices charged to industrial end-users, which is discussed in section 1.4.8. The earlier Directive 91/296/EEC on the transit of natural gas through grids was repealed as from 1 July 2004, and this area is now covered by the Natural Gas Directive and by Regulation (EC) No 715/2009 on conditions for access to the natural gas transmission networks. Directive 2004/67/EC concerning measures to safeguard security of natural gas supply is also applicable.[183]

2.2.1.1. The Natural Gas Directive

The primary purpose of the Natural Gas Directive is to open the market for natural gas to competition. Thus, Article 18 of the first Natural Gas Directive

182. This primarily refers to end users, designated as 'final customers' in the Natural Gas Directive.
183. See *Christopher W. Jones:* EU Energy Law. The Internal Energy Market, Vol. I, 2010, for a commentary on the EU regulation of the natural gas market following the adoption of the third energy package.

provided that, after the entry into force of the Directive, the national gas markets should have a degree of openness corresponding to at least 20 % of the total annual gas consumption on the national gas market. This percentage was increased to 28 % five years after the entry into force of the Directive, and 33 % after ten years.

The Member States' abilities to reach these levels of market openness consisted mainly in regulating who could have free choice of their supplier, referred to as *eligible customers*. The Directive included minimum rules as to which customers should be *eligible*. If these minimum rules led to a greater degree of openness than the levels stated above, Article 18 gave the possibility of changing the minimum definition of eligible customers so that the level of market openness would be reduced to less than 30 % of the total annual gas consumption of the national market. This percentage was increased to 38 % five years after the entry into force of the Directive, and 43 % after ten years.

The second Natural Gas Directive moved this process on. Instead of regulating the degree of market openness, the starting point was the classification of customers. As from 1 July 2004, all non-household customers have had a free market. As from 1 July 2007, all customers have had a free market.

In common with the EU's competition rules, the third and current Natural Gas Directive does not contain any special principles for pricing. In general the sector is regulated in line with the Treaty's other prohibitions of abuse of a dominant position under Article 102 TFEU, including the prohibition of 'directly or indirectly imposing unfair purchase or selling prices or other unfair trading conditions.' However, the Natural Gas Directive contains provisions prohibiting discrimination between system users in Article 13(1) and Article 25(2). This also concern pricing discrimination.

In addition, the general competition rules apply to the natural gas sector. These are relevant in particular in relation to network access.[184]

Similarly to the Electricity Directive, the Natural Gas Directive contains a provision on reciprocity. Article 37(2) states that contracts for the supply of an eligible customer in the system of another Member State may not be prohibited if the customer is eligible in both systems.[185] The relevance of this provision has lapsed in connection with the implementation of full market opening.

184. For a comprehensive review of the application of the Union's competition rules to the natural gas sector, see *Christopher W. Jones (ed.):* EU Energy Markets, Vol. II, 2011.
185. Reciprocity is discussed in more detail in section 1.4.12.

2.2.1.2. Application of the general competition rules

Like the electricity sector, the natural gas sector is subject to the Union's general competition rules. However, over the years there have not been as many cases on natural gas as on electricity. In 2009, *E.ON Ruhrgas* and *GDF Suez* were each fined EUR 553 million in connection with an anti-competitive horizontal agreement on market sharing.[186]

In connection with the construction of a shared gas pipeline (the MEGAL pipeline), in 1975 the two parties (originally Ruhrgas and GDF) entered into an agreement not to sell gas transported over this pipeline in each other's home markets (Germany and France respectively). At that time the market had not been liberalised. Until 2000, GDF had a legal monopoly on the import of natural gas to France, and until 1998 Ruhrgas had a *de facto* monopoly in its supply area, via a set of agreements with other German supply undertakings. However, the parties maintained the market-sharing agreement after the market had been opened in 2000 by the first Natural Gas Directive (98/30/EC).

In relation to the German market, the Commission brought proceedings against RWE AG for abuse of its dominant position by denying third party access and by use of a margin squeeze.[187]

In relation to third party access, the Commission suspected that RWE may not have implemented an effective congestion management system to manage the scarce capacities on its network with a view to systematically excluding competitors from their network. Moreover, there were indications that RWE may have intentionally set its transmission tariffs at an artificially high level in order to squeeze RWE's competitors' margins (margin squeeze strategy). The case was settled after RWE had committed itself to selling its entire current German high-pressure gas transmission network.

2.2.2. Authorisation procedures

Under Article 4 of the Natural Gas Directive the Member States may decide whether to use an authorisation procedure. Where a Member State does have a system of authorisation, it must lay down objective and non-discriminatory criteria which are to be met by an undertaking applying for authorisation to build and/or operate natural gas facilities or for authorisation to supply natural gas. These criteria and procedures for granting authorisations must be made public. The reasons for any refusal to grant an authorisation must be given to the applicant, and there must be procedures enabling the applicant to

186. Decision IP/09/1099 of 8 July 2009.
187. Commission Decision of 18 March 2009 relating to a proceeding under Article 82 of the EC Treaty and Article 53 of the EEA Agreement (Case COMP/B-1/39.402 – *RWE Gas Foreclosure*) (OJ 2009/C 133/8).

appeal against such refusal. There are similar requirements in respect of direct lines. The Member States can introduce authorisation procedures for this. Under Article 24(2), the Member States or a designated competent authority must lay down the criteria for the grant of authorisations for the construction or operation of direct lines in their territory.

In the interests of the development of newly supplied areas and efficient operation generally, Article 4(4) provides a special possibility for Member States to refuse to grant a further authorisation to build and operate distribution pipeline systems in any particular area, once such pipeline systems have been proposed to be built in that area and if the existing or proposed capacity is not fully used.

However, as discussed below, a system operator is to be appointed for transmission, storage and/or LNG facilities. This can be under an administrative act of the Member State, or by the owners of the facilities in question appointing a system operator. In the latter case this can hardly be considered an authorisation procedure.

2.2.2.1. Network management

In contrast to the first Electricity Directive, the first Natural Gas Directive did not contain any requirement for the appointment of a system operator. However, in the second and third Natural Gas Directives there is a requirement for the establishment of a system operator function at both the transmission and the distribution levels.

Thus, Article 9 of the third Natural Gas Directive lays down that the owner of a transmission system must act as a transmission system operator (TSO) and is thus subject to the rules that apply to TSOs.[188] According to Article 13(1) and (2), the primary tasks of such system operators are to operate, maintain and develop reliable and efficient facilities to secure an open market, with due regard to the environment, and ensure adequate means to meet service obligations. A system operator may not discriminate between system users or classes of system users, and in particular not favour its related undertakings. Corresponding rules apply to distribution system operators. A system operator must also provide other system operators with sufficient information to ensure effective access to the system. There are special rules on network development (Article 22), ensuring compliance (Article 21), and supervision (Article 20). There are similar, if less strict rules for distribution system oper-

188. The deadline for implementing this specific requirement is 3 March 2012.

ators (Articles 24-27), and storage and LNG system operators (Articles 12-13).

2.2.2.2. Unbundling

Under Article 31 of the Natural Gas Directive, whatever their system of ownership or legal form, natural gas undertakings must draw up, submit to audit and publish their annual accounts in accordance with the rules of national law concerning the annual accounts of limited liability companies adopted pursuant to the Fourth Council Directive 78/660/EEC on the annual accounts of certain types of companies (unbundling of accounts). Undertakings which are not legally obliged to publish their annual accounts must keep a copy of these at the disposal of the public at their head office. In their internal accounting, integrated natural gas undertakings must keep separate accounts for each of their transmission, distribution, LNG and storage activities and, where relevant, consolidated accounts for other activities not relating to transmission, distribution, LNG and storage of natural gas, as they would be required to do if the activities in question were carried out by separate undertakings. The internal accounts must include a balance sheet and a profit and loss account for each activity. The aim of these provisions on the unbundling of accounts is to avoid discrimination, cross-subsidisation and distortion of competition.

The Natural Gas Directive now contains the same requirements for unbundling as the Electricity Directive. The unbundling requirement at the transmission level are either separation of ownership, ISO, ITO, or ITO+; see the introduction in section 2 above. At the distribution level there is are requirements for management and company unbundling.

2.2.3. Access to networks

The main provisions on network access were found in Chapter VI of the first Natural Gas Directive. According to Article 18, the Member States should state which customers were eligible, with a view to achieving the required minimum level of market openness. Regardless of their annual consumption, gas-fired power stations and other final customers with a consumption of more than 25 million cubic metres of gas per year per consumption location were eligible, whether or not they were otherwise covered by the market opening.

Under the second Natural Gas Directive, all customers have been eligible since 1 July 2007. Article 32 of the third and current Natural Gas Directive regulates third-party access. However, lack of capacity, the fulfilment of public service obligations or economic and financial difficulties with take-or-pay contracts are valid grounds for refusing access; see below. In this connection it is important to bear in mind that the Directive does not exclude long-term contracts as long as they comply with Union competition rules; see Article 32(3).

Article 35(2) of the Natural Gas Directive allows Member States to take measures to ensure that a natural gas undertaking which refuses access to a system on the basis of lack of capacity or a lack of connection makes the necessary enhancements as far as it is economic to do so or when a potential customer is willing to pay for them. The entitlement to do so becomes an obligation to do so, if the Member State has made use of the possibility in Article 4(4) of the Directive to decline to grant a further authorisation to build and operate distribution pipeline systems in a particular area if pipeline systems are already proposed to be built in that area.

2.2.3.1. Network access procedures

Under Articles 14 to 16 of the first Natural Gas Directive, Member States could generally choose between negotiated access and regulated access. Under Article 32 of the current Natural Gas Directive, Member States must use regulated network access. Only in relation to access to storage facilities and linepack,[189] can Member States still choose between negotiated and regulated access; see Article 33 of the Directive. Both procedures must be administered in accordance with objective, transparent and non-discriminatory criteria.

Article 48 allows for the possibility of derogating from the provisions on network access. Thus, a natural gas undertaking that has or expects to have serious economic and financial difficulties because of its take-or-pay commitments in connection with one or more gas-purchase contracts, can apply to the Member State in question or the designated competent authority for a temporary derogation from the provisions on network access. When deciding whether to grant such a derogation the Member State or the designated competent authority, must take into account a number of criteria including: the objective of achieving a competitive gas market; the need to fulfil public service obligations and to ensure security of supply; and the extent to which, when accepting the take-or-pay commitments in question, the undertaking could reasonably have foreseen that serious difficulties were likely to arise. In any case, it must be assumed that the natural gas undertaking will not have serious difficulties if the sales of natural gas do not fall below the level of minimum offtake guarantees in take-or-pay contracts for the purchase of gas,

189. *Linepack* means the storage of gas by compression in gas transmission and distribution systems.

or if the take-or-pay contract for the purchase of gas can be adapted or the natural gas undertaking is able to find alternative outlets. Reasons for a refusal must be given.

Under Article 36, major new gas infrastructures (i.e. interconnectors between Member States, LNG and storage facilities) may, upon request, be exempted from the provisions of Articles 32. The conditions for the application of this provision are, among other things, that the investment must enhance competition in gas supply and enhance security of supply, and that the level of risk attached to the investment is such that the investment would not take place unless an exemption were granted.

If an exemption is granted, the Member State or the designated competent authority must inform the Commission of its decision as soon as possible, and send all information relevant to the exemption. Within eight weeks (for a take-or-pay contractor) or two months (for new infrastructure) after receiving such notification, the Commission can require the Member State or the designated competent authority to change or revoke its decision. Likewise, the reasons for any exception allowed for take-or-pay contracts must be published in the Official Journal of the European Union.

Finally, Article 49(2) of the Natural Gas Directive provides that where a Member State qualifies as an emergent market, and where the implementation of this Directive would cause substantial problems, among other things the provisions on network access in Article 32 of the Directive may be derogated from. Such exemptions expire at the same time as the Member State is no longer considered to be an emergent market.

In accordance with Article 13(1) of the Natural Gas Directive, system operators for transmission, storage and/or LNG may not discriminate between system users or classes of system users, and particular may not favour its related undertakings. There is a similar provision relating to distribution system operators in Article 25(2).

Under Article 16 of the Natural Gas Directive, each transmission system operator and transmission system owner must preserve the confidentiality of commercially sensitive information obtained in the course of carrying out its activities, subject to any legal obligation to disclose information. This includes information received from third parties in connection with allocating or negotiating access to the system. For transmission system operators that are part of vertically integrated undertakings it is explicitly stated that they must not disclose any commercially sensitive information to the remaining parts of the undertaking, unless this is necessary for carrying out a business transaction. In this connection, Member States must ensure that the transmission system owner and the remaining part of the undertaking do not use joint services, such as joint legal services, apart from purely administrative or IT functions. There is a similar, though less strict, duty of confidentiality for distribution system operators in Article 27.

As from 1 July 2006, a Regulation on conditions for access to the natural gas transmission networks has been in force, with the aim of harmonising the setting of harmonised principles for tariffs, or the methodologies underlying their calculation, for access to the network, the establishment of third party access services and harmonised principles for capacity allocation and congestion management, the determination of transparency requirements, balancing rules and imbalance charges and facilitating capacity trading. The current, and second, Regulation (Regulation (EC) No 715/2009) applies to 'the transport of natural gas through a network, which mainly contains high pressure pipelines, other than an upstream pipeline network and other than the part of high pressure pipelines primarily used in the context of local distribution of natural gas, with a view to its delivery to customers, but not including supply'; see the definition of *transmission* in the Regulation. The Regulation also applies to high pressure pipelines linking local distributors to the gas network which are not primarily used for local distribution; see recital 6. The aim of the Regulation is to lay down non-discriminatory rules for access conditions to natural gas transmission systems, taking into account the specificities of national and regional markets with a view to ensuring the proper functioning of the internal gas market.

The Annex to the Regulation contains comprehensive guidelines to the Regulation, in order to contribute to harmonisation. The Commission may adopt Guidelines on certain issues; see Article 23(2) of the Regulation.

The Regulation does not apply to the Member States that have been granted a derogation under Article 49 of the Natural Gas Directive as an emergent market; see Article 30. Nor does the Regulation apply to interconnections between Member States and other substantial increases in capacity to the existing infrastructure or changes to such infrastructure which enable the development of new sources of supply of gas, to the extent that these are exempt under Article 36 of the Natural Gas Directive. Finally, those gas transmission networks that are exempt as a result of take-or-pay obligations are exempted from the provisions of the Regulation; see Article 48 of the Natural Gas Directive.

Article 13(1) of the Regulation lays down that tariffs must be transparent, take into account the need for system integrity and improvement, and reflect actual costs incurred, corresponding to those of an efficient and structurally comparable network operator, while giving an appropriate return on investment. There is a possibility for regulating authorities to approve other market-based tariff arrangements, such as auctions. According to Article 13, the tariffs applied must contribute to efficient gas trade and competition, while avoiding cross-subsidisation between network users and providing incentives for investment and maintaining or creating interoperability for transmission networks. Equally, tariffs for network access must not restrict market liquidity nor distort cross-border trade between different transmission systems. If a system operator offers the same service to different customers, it must be on the same terms and conditions.

System operators are subject to a number of requirements with regard to non-discrimination. Also, as part of the fulfilment of the aim of transparency, system operators must make public detailed information regarding the services they offer and the relevant conditions applied, together with the technical information necessary for network users to gain effective network access; see Article 18(1).

The Regulation also imposes special requirements for balancing rules and imbalance charges and trading of capacity rights.

Pursuant to Article 41(6) of the Natural Gas Directive, the regulatory authorities are responsible for fixing transmission tariffs or the methodologies used to calculate tariffs.

2.2.3.2. Direct lines

Article 38 of the Natural Gas Directive contains provisions on the establishment of direct lines. According to this, Member States must take measures to enable natural gas undertakings established within their territory to supply their customers through a direct line, so that any customer within their territory can be supplied through a direct line by natural gas undertakings.[190]

Where a Member State requires authorisation to establish or operate direct lines, the criteria for the grant of authorisation must be objective, transparent and non-discriminatory.

Member States can grant permission to establish a direct line if network access has been refused on the basis of Article 35, or if a dispute resolution procedure has been initiated under Article 41.

190. According to its wording, the provision only covers 'privileged' customers. However, since 1 July 2007, all customers have been 'privileged'; see Article 37 of the Natural Gas Directive.

In contrast to the Electricity Directive (Article 34(3)), the Natural Gas Directive does not explicitly provide that the possibility of supplying natural gas via a direct line should not affect the possibility of using a third party arrangement. It has been argued by *Friedrich von Burchard*[191] that this means that the Member States could introduce a rule that the possibility of establishing a direct line should exclude the possibility of third party access. This argument is rejected by *Moen & Dyrland*,[192] among other things on the grounds that third party access is the primary rule in the Natural Gas Directive, whereas the establishment of direct lines is secondary, and can be made conditional on refusal of access to the existing network.

2.2.3.3. Transit

Up until 1 July 2004, Directive 91/296/EEC on the transit of natural gas through grids governed access to the overall high-pressure network for natural gas transmission. Since then access to transmission networks has been governed by the general provisions of the Natural Gas Directive and, since 1 July 2006, by the Regulation on conditions for access to the natural gas transmission networks, as discussed above (originally Regulation (EC) No 1775/2005).

Separate legislation for cross-border transmission, such as that introduced for the electricity sector in the CBT Regulation, has not been introduced for the natural gas sector.

2.2.4. Public service obligations

Under Article 3 of the Natural Gas Directive, with regard for the general economic interest, Member States may impose public service obligations on undertakings operating in the gas sector which may relate to security, including security of supply, regularity, quality and price of supplies, and environmental protection, including energy efficiency and climate protection. Such obligations must be clearly defined, transparent, non discriminatory, and verifiable. Furthermore, any subsequent changes to them must be notified every two years to the Commission.

This makes it possible for Member States to use long term planning as a means for ensuring the fulfilment of public service obligations in relation to

191. *Friedrich von Burchard:* Netzzugang im Bereich der Gasversorgung, in *Jürgen Schwarze (ed.):* Der Netzzugang für Dritte im Wirtscharftsrecht, 1999 p. 201.
192. *Ketil Bøe Moen & Sondre Dyrland:* EU's gassmarkedsdirektiv, 2001 pp. 130-131.

security of supply. However, account should also be taken of the possibility that third parties may seek access to the system.

In relation to distribution, Member States can derogate from the provisions in Article 4 (on objective and non-discriminatory criteria for authorisation procedures), if the application of these provisions would, in law or in fact, hinder the performance of the obligations imposed on natural gas undertakings in the general economic interest, and where the development of trade is not affected to such an extent as to be contrary to the interests of the Union; see Article 3(10).

Article 3(3) of the Natural Gas Directive contains a provision on *universal services*. According to this provision, Member States must take appropriate measures to protect final customers and to ensure high levels of consumer protection and, in particular, they must ensure that there are adequate safeguards to protect vulnerable customers. In this context, the Member States can take appropriate measures to protect customers (end users) in remote areas who are connected to the gas system.[193] For this purpose, Member States can appoint a supplier of last resort for customers connected to the gas network. The Member States can thus impose on distribution undertakings or suppliers an obligation to supply to customers in a given area and/or of a particular category. Tariffs for such supplies can also be regulated, for example by ensuring equal treatment of the customers concerned. Compared with the equivalent provision in the Electricity Directive, the consumer protection seems weak. Clearly, natural gas is not considered such an essential service as electricity.

The provisions are supplemented by Directive 2004/67/EC concerning measures to safeguard security of natural gas supply which, in Article 4(1), requires Member States to comply with *security of supply standards*, for ensuring protection for household customers to an appropriate extent, at least in the event of a partial disruption of national gas supplies during a nationally determined peak periods, and periods of exceptionally high gas demand during the coldest weather periods.

2.2.5. Technical harmonisation

Under Article 8 of the Natural Gas Directive, Member States must ensure that technical safety criteria are defined and that technical rules establishing the

193. Article 3(4) of the Natural Gas Directive includes an obligation to take measures to address energy poverty. This must be seen as an expression that electricity supply is a basic welfare service.

minimum technical design and operational requirements for connection to the system of LNG facilities, storage facilities, other transmission or distribution systems, and direct lines, are developed and made public. These technical rules must ensure the interoperability of systems and shall be objective and non-discriminatory. They must be notified to the Commission in accordance with Article 8 of Directive 98/34/EC laying down a procedure for the provision of information in the field of technical standards and regulations and of rules on Information Society Services.

2.2.6. Transparency

The first Directive on price transparency[194] was introduced together with Directive 91/296/EEC on the transit of natural gas through grids as part of the first phase of the liberalisation of the electricity sector. According to its preamble, the purpose of the Directive was to ensure that competition was not distorted in the internal market, and to help obviate discrimination against users. Article 1 requires Member States to take the steps necessary to ensure that undertakings which supply gas or electricity to industrial end-users, send to industrial end-users information about the prices and terms of sale of gas and electricity, and the price systems in use. Only gas that is distributed through a piped network is covered. The Directive covers all industrial applications, though not customers who use gas for generating electricity in public power stations, for non energy-related applications (such as the chemicals industry), or in quantities of over 4,000,000 Gj per year. Information is given on the basis of a number of standard users.

2.2.7. Public authorities

Under Article 21(1) of the first Natural Gas Directive, Member States had to ensure that parties negotiated for network access in good faith and that no party abused its negotiating position to prevent a positive outcome of the negotiations. The Directive did not include a specific requirement for the appointment of a regulatory authority. However such a provision was introduced in the second Natural Gas Directive, and is now in Article 39 of the third and current Natural Gas Directive.

Pursuant to Article 39 of the Directive, the regulatory authority must exercises its powers impartially and transparently. Member States must ensure

194. Directive 90/377/EEC concerning a Community procedure to improve the transparency of gas and electricity prices charged to industrial end-users. This Directive has now been replaced by Directive 2008/92/EC, which is discussed in section 1.4.8.

that regulatory authorities are legally distinct and functionally independent from any other public or private entity; that their staff and management act independently from any market interest, and do not seek or take direct instructions from any government or other public or private entity when carrying out their regulatory tasks. Moreover, Member States must ensure that regulatory authorities can take autonomous decisions, independently from any political body, with separate annual budget allocations, autonomy in the implementation of the allocated budget, and adequate human and financial resources to carry out their duties.

Regulatory authorities also have general responsibility for ensuring non-discrimination, effective competition and the efficient functioning of the market.

Pursuant to Article 41 of the Directive, the duties of regulatory authorities include:

- fixing or approving, in accordance with transparent criteria, transmission or distribution tariffs or their methodologies;
- ensuring compliance of transmission and distribution system operators, and where relevant, system owners, as well as of any natural gas undertakings, with their obligations under the Directive;
- cooperating on cross-border issues with the regulatory authorities of other Member States;
- submitting annual reports;
- ensuring that there are no cross-subsidies between transmission, distribution, storage, LNG and supply activities;
- monitoring and evaluating the investment plans of the transmission system operators;
- monitoring compliance with network security and reliability rules;
- monitoring the level of transparency, including of wholesale prices;
- monitoring the occurrence of restrictive contractual practices, including exclusivity clauses;
- monitoring and reviewing the access conditions to storage, linepack and other ancillary services; and
- ensuring access to customer consumption data.

The regulatory authority also acts as a dispute resolution authority. In particular, this task covers disputes concerning the conditions for and denial of network access within the scope of application of the Directive. The regulatory authority must decide within two months of receiving a complaint. This period can be extended by up to two months if the regulatory authority needs further information. This period can be extended further with the agreement of the complainant. Such a decision has binding effect unless and until it is reversed on appeal. Bringing a complaint before the regulatory authority does not exclude the application of other legal remedies in accordance with Community law.

Article 30 of the Natural Gas Directive provides that, to the extent necessary for carrying out their functions, the Member States and the competent authorities designated by them have a right of access to the accounts of natural gas undertakings. These authorities must treat commercially sensitive information as confidential. However, the Member States can provide for the disclosure of such information where this is necessary for the competent authorities to carry out their functions.

3. Transport

Transport is one of the original policy areas of the Union. Article 90 TFEU, in Title VI – Transport, states: 'The objectives of the Treaties shall, in matters governed by this Title, be pursued within the framework of a common transport policy'. At a general level, transport can be divided between land, sea and air transport. The EU has issued legislation in all three areas. The sectors chosen for study in this chapter, air transport and railways, thus represent only part of the total body of EU regulation on transport.

Article 58(1) TFEU states that 'Freedom to provide services in the field of transport shall be governed by the provisions of the Title relating to transport.' This refers to Articles 90 to 100 TFEU. This provision does not prevent the other provisions of the Treaty concerning the other freedoms applying to the area of transport.[195] This primarily means that restrictions on domestic traffic are not covered by the provisions on the free movement of services. As long as it has not otherwise been provided for in secondary legislation, Member States are thus free regulate the right to offer services in this area, including granting exclusive rights. However, the grant of exclusive

195. See the judgment of the CJ of 23 April 1991 in Case C-466/98, *Commission* v *United Kingdom,* para. 40; Case C-467/98, *Commission v Denmark,* para. 123; Case C-468/98, *Commission* v *Sweden,* para. 114; Case C-469/98, *Commission* v *Finland,* para. 119; Case C-471/98, *Commission* v *Belgium,* para. 132; Case C-472/ 98, *Commission* v *Luxembourg,* para. 123; Case C-475/98, *Commission* v *Austria,* para. 131; and Case C-476/98, *Commission* v *Germany,* para. 145.

rights to a company which is clearly not able to meet the demand could constitute an abuse of a dominant position.[196]

Article 91 TFEU gives authority to lay down special provisions in this area:

'1. For the purpose of implementing Article 90, and taking into account the distinctive features of transport, the European Parliament and the Council shall, acting in accordance with the ordinary legislative procedure and after consulting the Economic and Social Committee and the Committee of the Regions, lay down:
   a. common rules applicable to international transport to or from the territory of a Member State or passing across the territory of one or more Member States;
   b. the conditions under which non-resident carriers may operate transport services within a Member State;
   c. measures to improve transport safety;
   d. any other appropriate provisions.
2. When the measures referred to in paragraph 1 are adopted, account shall be taken of cases where their application might seriously affect the standard of living and level of employment in certain regions, and the operation of transport facilities.'

Article 91 TFEU has been used as authority for issuing a number of directives for the railway sector.

Also, under Article 100(2) TFEU, the European Parliament and the Council may 'lay down appropriate provisions for sea and air transport. They shall act after consulting the Economic and Social Committee and the Committee of the Regions'. This division of the area of transport can be seen as recognition that sea and air transport are already regulated by a large number of international agreements. This provision has been particularly applicable to air transport.

The Union's competition rules now apply to the whole area of transport, including air transport.[197]

The procedural rules are in Regulation (EC) No 1/2003 on the implementation of the rules on competition laid down in Articles 81 and 82 of the Treaty (now Articles 101 and 102 TFEU).

Previously the transport sector differed in that the general Regulation No 17/62 did not apply to it. Thus, Article 1 of Regulation No 141/62 stated that the transport sector was not covered by Regulation No 17/62.

196. Case C-41/90, *Höfner,* para. 31; and see *Hans Petter Graver* in Lov og Rett, 2006 p. 593.
197. Joined Cases 209 to 213/84, *Lucas Asjes and others* (the *Nouvelles Frontières* case).

3.1. Air transport

In the years following the Second World War European, air transport developed through cooperation between the authorities and the air transport companies. There was a need for public involvement in civil airports, which would sometimes share their facilities with military air bases. The public authorities often favoured one particular airline which may have been wholly or partly owned by the state – the so called *flag carrier*. Among other things, this gave rise to a number of bilateral agreements between states, under which a particular international route would be served by one airline from each of the parties to the agreement – a duopoly. Such agreements often included market sharing and pricing agreements.[198]

Since 1944 international air transport has been covered by the Chicago Convention (Convention on International Civil Aviation). This Convention secured sovereignty over its own airspace for each state. However, the Convention did not succeed in establishing multilateral agreements on the exchange of air transport rights.[199]

Many European airlines still have something of the character of a national flag carrier. These airlines often use one or more of the airports in their home country as a 'hub'. Passengers are flown to these hubs with a view to transiting to other destinations. This is the 'hub and spoke' system.[200]

The Treaty has included transport policy ever since the Treaty of Rome. However, originally air transport was not included. Liberalisation measures have appeared in several waves. Since 1997 the market within the EU has been totally deregulated. However, in relation to third countries the market is still characterised by the existence of bilateral agreements, even though attempts have been made to replace these with common EU-wide agreements.

Modern air transport is dependent on the existence of airports which have the necessary facilities for handling aircraft, cargo, passengers and their baggage. Transport will often be between two towns. Where a town can only realistically be served by one airport, that airport can be characterised as an es-

198. See *Ben van Houtte:* Air Transport, in *Damien Geradin (ed.):* The Liberalization of State Monopolies in the European Union and Beyond, 2000 p. 67 et seq.

199. *Jesper Fredborg Huric Larsen & Susanne Storm:* Flybonusprogrammer som et konkurrencebegrænsende element mellem luftfartsselskaber i Europa, Nationaløkonomisk Tidsskrift 140 2002 p. 164. The Chicago Convention entered into force in 1947, replacing the Paris Convention of 1919 and the Havana Convention of 1928.

200. *The Nordic competition authorities:* Competitive Airlines. Towards a more vigorous competition policy in relation to the air travel market, 2002 pp. 5 et seq., 13 et seq. and 46 et seq.

sential facility.[201] At the same time, the hub and spoke system creates a structure like a network with considerable market strength for the company that operates the hub.[202]

Airport capacity is also to some extent a limited resource. In modern scheduled traffic arrivals and departures should preferably be scheduled so as to limit the waiting time of transit passengers. However, this leads to there being peak loading of airports. Airspace is also a limited resource. For safety reasons aircraft must follow fixed routes. These routes constitute a network whose limited capacity is used by allocating slots. Airspace is under the control of the Member States. The lack of harmonisation and cooperation (for example in the form of one or more cross-border network administrators) has meant that, even on short flights between European airports, civil aircraft have to change altitude, change radio wavelength to a new controlling authority, and make major detours. In an attempt to do away with these problems, the Union introduced the Single European Sky initiative.

3.1.1. EU regulation

The liberalisation of the air transport sector has taken place in stages. There have been three 'packages' with regulation for the sector in 1987, 1990 and 1992. In the first package the Commission was given the powers to act against conduct that restricted competition in the air transport sector, in the same way as on other markets. This was the adoption of Regulation (EEC) No 3975/87 laying down the procedure for the application of the rules on competition to undertakings in the air transport sector.[203] The market for international flights within the Union was opened in January 1993. The market was further opened by the second package. The third package, from 1992 with a deadline for implementation in April 2007, introduced, among others, Regulation (EEC) No 2407/92 on licensing of air carriers. With the implementation of the third package, the sector is considered as being liberalised within the EU.

Regulation (EEC) No 2407/92, together with Regulation (EEC) No 2408/92 on access for Community air carriers to intra-Community air routes and Regulation (EEC) No 2409/92

201. Only the largest urban centres can support two or even three commercial airports. *Bailey & Williams,* 1988 p. 184.
202. *The Nordic competition authorities:* Competitive Airlines. Towards a more vigorous competition policy in relation to the air travel market, 2002 p. 6, and for a general discussion of the character of networks in the air transport sector, see p. 41 et seq.
203. This is now regulated in Regulation (EC) No 1/2003.

on fares and rates for air services, have been gathered together in Regulation (EC) No 1008/2008 on common rules for the operation of air services in the Community.

It is characteristic for the air transport sector that only regulations are used. There is no consolidating or overall market directive. Instead the sector has been liberalised by using measures which regulate specific elements, primarily concerned with market access, consumer protection and safety. The almost exclusive use of regulations to implement liberalisation has made national implementation by the Member States unnecessary.

In particular in connection with access to airspace, a number of regulations have been issued with the aim of improving the use of airspace and relations between civil and military flights.

See Regulation (EC) No 549/2004 laying down the framework for the creation of the single European sky (the Framework Regulation), Regulation (EC) No 551/2004 on the organisation and use of the airspace in the single European sky (the Airspace Regulation), and Regulation (EC) No 2150/2005 laying down common rules for the flexible use of airspace.

As for market access, among other things there are rules on computer reservation systems, the issue of licences to air carriers and access to routes within the Union. These issues are discussed below. Safety is regulated by rules on the investigation of civil aviation air accidents and incidents, and on the establishment of the European Aviation Safety Agency. These are also discussed below.

Consumer protection is regulated in particular by:

- Regulation (EC) No 261/2004 establishing common rules on compensation and assistance to passengers in the event of denied boarding and of cancellation or long delay of flights, and
- Regulation (EC) No 2027/97 on air carrier liability in the event of accidents, as amended by Regulation (EC) No 889/2002.

There are also special rules on consumer protection in Directive 90/314/EEC on package travel, package holidays and package tours. These will not be subject to detailed study in this chapter.[204]

204. In Denmark the Directive on package tours has been implemented by Law No 472 of 30 June 1993 on package tours.

Regulation (EC) No 261/2004 lays down minimum rules for compensation for passengers with valid tickets and reservations[205] who are turned away because of overbooking, cancellation or extended delays. The provisions apply to passengers for a flight departing from an airport in the EU, or passengers flying with an airline based in the EU and flying to an airport situated in the EU.

Overbooking means that the number of passengers with confirmed reservations who have properly checked in by the deadline before departure exceeds the number of places available on the flight in question. This is a normal practice for airlines. This is because there are usually a number of passengers with valid tickets and reservations who do not show up.

Cancellation refers to a flight which is planned but not carried out, and for which there is at least one reservation.

Delays are divided into different categories, depending on the length of delay, the duration of the flight, and whether it is within the EU or not. There are consequences when there are delays of more than 2 to 4 hours.

The principle with overbooking is that the airline must first try to find volunteers to change their reservation, for payment of compensation. Where this is not possible, a passenger who is turned away must be able to choose between a refund for the unused portion of a ticket, transport as soon as possible, and the rerouting of their journey. In addition to this, such passengers are entitled to meals and hotel accommodation, as well as to make two free telephone calls, telefaxes or e-mails. In addition, compensation must be paid for passengers turned away in accordance with the following:

- EUR 250 for flights up to 1,500 km,
- EUR 400 for all flights within the Union of more than 1,500 km, and for all other flights of between 1,500 and 3,500 km, and
- EUR 600 for all other flights.

Such compensation does not exclude claims for other kinds of compensation, such as under Regulation (EC) No 2027/97, as discussed below.

In Case C-344/04, *The Queen on the application of IATA and another* v *Department for Transport*, the CJ held that the standard measures prescribed in Article 6 of Regulation No

205. Article 3(3) contains an exception for specially cheap or gratis tickets that cannot be obtained by the general public.

261/2004 do not prevent the passengers concerned – should a delay also cause them damage giving entitlement to compensation – from being able to bring actions for compensation under the conditions laid down by the Montreal Convention.

In the event of a cancellation there is a fixed right to a refund, meals and hotel accommodation. However, any compensation depends on whether due notice has been given to passengers and any event of *force majeure*. There are corresponding rights to meals and hotel accommodation in the event of delay, and for delays of at least 5 hours there is a right to a refund for the unused portion of the ticket. On the other hand there is no right to compensation for delays.

By virtue of an amendment in Regulation (EC) No 889/2002, Regulation (EC) No 2027/97 implements certain uniform rules for international air transport which were agreed in the Montreal Convention in 1999.[206] These provisions relate to liability for death or injury, for goods, delays for passengers or baggage, or loss of or damage to baggage. In principle, national procedures apply to the satisfaction of claims for compensation.

The Regulation and the Convention do not provide any upper limit for liability for compensation in the event of a passenger's death or injury. On the other hand there is a lower limit of 100,000 SDR (special drawing rights), where there is strict liability. Above this level there is a presumption of liability. There is also a deadline for the payment of an advance on compensation of 15 days after it is established who is entitled to compensation. In the event of death, the advance must be at least 16,000 SDR.

When passengers are delayed there is a fixed duty for airlines to pay compensation. The liability is limited to 4,150 SDR. There is also a duty to pay compensation for delays to baggage. However, an airline is not required to pay if it has adopted the necessary measures or if it was impossible to take the necessary measures. Liability for delays to baggage is limited to 1,000 SDR. There is the same limit to liability for destroyed, lost or damaged baggage. For baggage that has been checked-in there is strict liability, unless there are defects in the baggage. For non-checked baggage there is liability equivalent to the standard for negligence. For damage to checked baggage, passengers must make their claims in writing within 7 days, and for delays within 21 days from the date on which the baggage was made available to the passenger. There is a deadline of two years from the date on which the flight landed or ought to have landed for bringing a claim for compensation.

206. OJ 2001 L 194/39.

At international level there are also rules on the payment of compensation in the event of an accident in the Convention for the Unification of Certain Rules Relating to International Carriage by Air, Signed at Warsaw on 12 October 1929, and the amendment to it signed at the Hague on 28 September 1955, as well as the convention entered into on 18 September 1961 in Guadalajara (together called the 'Warsaw Convention'). This applies throughout the world. The introduction of the Montreal Convention's provisions for EU airlines was because the Warsaw Convention's compensation rules were considered too low, given modern economic and social norms.

3.1.1.1. The application of the general competition rules

The CJ's decision in Joined Cases 209 to 213/84, *Lucas Asjes and others* (the *Nouvelles Frontières* case) established that Articles 81 and 82 of the EC Treaty also apply to air transport. Air transport now falls under Regulation (EC) No 1/2003.[207]

The general competition rules have been applied in a number of cases. Some of them are discussed in the following.

> In 2001 *SAS* and *Maersk Air* were fined EUR 39,375,000 and EUR 13,125,000 respectively by the Commission for entering into a secret agreement on market sharing. This came to light in connection with dealing with notification of a cooperation agreement between the two companies on codesharing and frequent flyer programmes. In connection with the entry into force of the cooperation agreement, Maersk Air had withdrawn from the Copenhagen-Stockholm route, leaving SAS with a monopoly. Correspondingly SAS had withdrawn from the Billund-Frankfurt route leaving Maersk Air with a monopoly. SAS also stopped flying on the Copenhagen-Venice route which Maersk Air had started serving. These measures were an expression of a more comprehensive market sharing agreement which covered future flying of both domestic and international routes to and from Denmark. SAS appealed to the GC against the amount of the fine in Case T-241/01.
>
> In Commission Decision 2000/74/EC of 14 July 1999 (IV/D-2/34.780 – *Virgin/British Airways*), where Virgin had brought a claim against British Airways (BA), BA had been fined EUR 6,800,000 for abuse of a dominant position by using loyalty based commission arrangements in trade with travel agents. The commission paid was based on the increase in the travel agents' sales of BA tickets compared with the previous year.

207. Regulation (EC) No 1/2003 is discussed in detail in Chapter VII. Air transport was previously covered by Regulation (EEC) No 3975/87 laying down the procedure for the application of the rules on competition to undertakings in the air transport sector.

Commission Decision 92/213/EEC of 26 February 1992 (IV/33.544 – *British Midland* v *Aer Lingus*) concerned the situation where Aer Lingus had excluded British Midland from interlining cooperation[208] on the Heathrow-Dublin route. This was regarded as abuse of a dominant position and Aer Lingus was fined EUR 750,000.[209]

The definition of the relevant market for passenger traffic can give rise to problems. In general business passengers are more focused on short travelling times and avoiding transit arrangements than tourist passengers. However, the distinction between the two groups of passengers is not clear cut. Many business travellers are increasingly focusing on price. In this connection, in defining the relevant market for air transport the Commission has discussed dividing passenger groups on the basis of their focus on time. See, for example Commission Decision of 11.08.1999 in case M/JV-19 – *KLM-Alitalia,* para. 21, and Commission Decision of 12.01.2001 in case M.2041 – *United Airlines/US Airways,* para. 18. However, in neither of these cases did the Commission find that such a definition was decisive. As for transit (one-stop) as an alternative to direct connections (non-stop), this distinction is most relevant on shorter routes. See Commission Decision of 12.01.2001 in case M.2041 – *United Airlines/US Airways,* para. 13-17, and Commission Decision 2002/746/EC of 5 July 2002 (COMP/37.730 – *Austrian Airlines/Lufthansa*), para. 53.

Regulation (EEC) No 3976/87 on the application of Article 85(3) of the Treaty to certain categories of agreements and concerted practices in the air transport sector has given the Commission authority to issue block exemptions regulations in accordance with Article 101(3) TFEU. According to Article 2(2), as amended by Regulation (EEC) No 2411/92, the Commission may adopt such regulations in respect of agreements, decisions or concerted practices concerning any of the following:

- joint planning and coordination of airline schedules,
- consultations on tariffs for the carriage of passengers and baggage and of freight on scheduled air services,

208. This means the possibility of one airline issuing tickets for the flights of another airline. This enables passengers to travel with a single set of documents between two destinations which are not served by a single airline, either directly or by changing flights, enabling the passenger to travel more quickly by taking the first flight, regardless of which airline is flying.
209. OJ 1992 L 96/34.

- joint operations on new less busy scheduled air services,
- slot allocation at airports and airport scheduling; the Commission must take care to ensure consistency with the Code of Conduct adopted by the Council,

The most important of these block exemption regulations was Regulation (EEC) No 1617/93 on the application of Article 85(3) of the Treaty to certain categories of agreements and concerted practices concerning joint planning and coordination of schedules, joint operations, consultations on passenger and cargo tariffs on scheduled air services and slot allocation at airports.[210] Following its latest amendment (by Regulation (EC) No 1105/2002) the Regulation expired on 30 June 2005. It was replaced by Regulation (EC) No 1459/2006 on the application of Article 81(3) of the EC Treaty (now Article 101(3) TFEU) to certain categories of agreements and concerted practices concerning consultations on passenger tariffs on scheduled air services and slot allocation at airports. This was a transitional regulation, various parts of it expiring at the end of 2006, and other parts expiring in the course of 2007.

There have been other block exemption regulations. Regulation (EEC) No 2671/88 on certain categories of agreements between undertakings, decisions of associations of undertakings and concerted practices concerning joint planning and coordination of capacity, sharing of revenue and consultations on tariffs on scheduled air services and slot allocation at airports, Regulation (EEC) No 2672/88 on certain categories of agreements between undertakings relating to computer reservation systems for air transport services, and Regulation (EEC) No 2673/88 on certain categories of agreements between undertakings, decisions of associations of undertakings and concerted practices concerning ground handling services all expired on 31 January 1991.

The rules of the Treaty on State aid are also generally applicable to the air transport sector. The Commission has issued Community guidelines on the financing of airports and start-up aid to airlines serving regional airports.[211]

> In Commission Decision 2003/637/EC of 30 April 2003 on State aid from Austria to Austrian air carriers, certain forms of State aid were considered to be covered by Article 107(2)(b) TFEU (then Article 87(2)(b) of the EC Treaty), to make good the damage caused by natural disasters or exceptional circumstances, following the closing of airspace for some time after the terrorist attacks of 11 September 2001. However, a number of losses in the following period, which were only indirectly related to the closure of the airspace, could not be compensated for.

210. This included *interlining* – see the definition above.
211. OJ 2005 C 312/1.

In Commission Decision 2003/196/EC of 11 December 2002 concerning a State aid scheme which France proposed to implement to assist French airlines, the Commission referred to its own Communication of 10 October 2001[212] on the repercussions of the terrorist attacks in the USA on the air transport industry, stating that the terrorist events of 11 September 2001 could qualify as exceptional circumstances in accordance with Article 87(2)(b) of the EC Treaty (now Article 107(2)(b) TFEU). In the case it was clear that the security measures made it more difficult for airlines to operate. However, the extra costs involved in this did not fall within the terms of the Treaty provision. Since the Commission found that the State aid in question was too much, the arrangement in question was found to be incompatible with the Treaty.

3.1.1.2. Bilateral agreements

Air traffic between the Union and third countries is to a certain extent regulated by bilateral agreements between the two countries between which the flights are made. It is not contrary to EU law for individual Member States to enter into such agreements, but they cannot enter into agreements which breach the competition rules of the EC Treaty.[213] This was the case in a number of decisions which the CJ decided on 5 November 2002, concerning the infringement of the right of establishment when entering into bilateral 'open skies' agreement between a number of Member States and the USA.[214]

Towards the end of and after the Second World War, a number of countries which subsequently became Member States of the EU entered into bilateral agreements with the USA on air traffic; these were referred to as the Bermuda Agreements. In 1992 the USA took the initiative to enter into new bilateral agreements with as many of the EU's Member States as possible. These agreements included free access to all air routes, unlimited route and traffic rights, and the possibility for agreeing common codes. Moreover, the agreements contained a provision whereby the USA could refuse to issue licences or technical approval to airlines which may have been designated by a Member State, but where a significant part of the ownership of the airline was not held by, and effective control was not exercised by the citizens of that Member State. Previously granted licences or technical approval

212. COM(2001) 574 final.
213. Case C-66/86, *Ahmed Saeed;* and *The Nordic competition authorities:* Competitive Airlines. Towards a more vigorous competition policy in relation to the air travel market, 2002, p. 29.
214. Case C-467/98, *Commission* v *Denmark;* Case C-468/98, *Commission* v *Sweden;* Case C-469/98, *Commission* v *Finland;* Case C-471/98, *Commission* v *Belgium;* Case C-472/98, *Commission* v *Luxembourg;* Case C-475/98, *Commission* v *Austria;* and Case C-476/98, *Commission* v *Germany.*

could be revoked, suspended or restricted. Such measures could not be taken against airlines whose control rested with the Member State in question or its citizens.

In these cases, it was argued that the provisions in Article 351 TFEU (then Article 234 of the EC Treaty) applied, under which the rights and obligations arising from agreements concluded before 1 January 1958 or, for acceding States, before the date of their accession, between one or more Member States on the one hand, and one or more third countries on the other, are not affected by the provisions of the then EC Treaty. The CJ rejected this argument on the basis that in all cases there had been later amendments which 'replaced' the agreements previously entered into, even though these previous agreements contained similar clauses.

As for freedom of establishment in Article 49 TFEU (previously Article 52 of the EC Treaty), the CJ found that the clause in the bilateral agreements which gave the USA the right to exclude EU airlines that were not controlled by the Member State in question or its citizens, was contrary to Article 49 TFEU.[215]

Regulation (EC) No 847/2004 on the negotiation and implementation of air service agreements between Member States and third countries sets out the conditions under which Member States can enter into negotiations with third countries on new air transport agreements or amendments to existing agreements. Among other things, there is a requirement to notify the Commission and a prohibition on the introduction of more restrictive agreements than those existing. It is a general wish of the Commission that common EU agreements should be made in this area.

The possibility of taking action against State aid from third countries is governed by Regulation (EC) No 868/2004 concerning protection against subsidisation and unfair pricing practices causing injury to Community air carriers in the supply of air services from countries not members of the European Community.

An air transport agreement was entered into between the EU and the USA in April 2007 to replace the previous bilateral agreements between the USA and the individual Member States. The agreement enters into force on 30 March 2008 and it will constitute the first phase in the establishment of open skies between the Member States and the USA. Under the agreement, there will be a reduction of the restrictions on market access and capacity.[216]

215. The Commission has described the consequences of the decisions in these cases in COM(2002) 649 final.

216. The agreement is published in OJ 2007 L 134/4. See also Council Decision 2007/339/EC on the signature and provisional application of the Air Transport Agreement between the European Community and its Member States, on the one hand, and the United States of America, on the other hand.

3.1.1.3. Pricing regulation

Regulation (EC) No 1008/2008 on common rules for the operation of air services in the Community provides that airlines can freely set their own prices; see Article 22(1).

However, under public service obligations referred to in Article 16, it is still possible for a Member State to lay down requirements with regard to pricing.

3.1.2. Authorisation procedures

Regulation (EC) No 1008/2008 on common rules for the operation of air services in the Community requires airlines established in the Union to be licensed. Thus, an undertaking that is established in the Union may only carry air passengers, mail and/or cargo for remuneration and/or hire if the undertaking has been granted the appropriate operating licence; see Article 3(3). The Regulation does not cover carriage by air of passengers, mail and/or cargo, performed by non-power driven aircraft and/or ultra-light power driven aircraft, or local flights not involving carriage between different airports (round trips). In respect of these, Member States are free to introduce national authorisation requirements or not. The possession of a licence is important for access to a network; see below.

The authority to issue a licence lies with the Member States. The Regulation provides that, as a condition for issuing or renewing a licence, an undertaking's principal place of business and its registered office, if any, must be located in the licensing Member State, and its main occupation must be air transport, in isolation or combined with any other commercial operation of aircraft or repair and maintenance of aircraft; see Article 4(1). It is also a requirement under Article 4(2) that a majority of the undertaking is owned and continues to be owned by Member States and/or nationals of Member States, subject to agreements and conventions to which the Union is a contracting party. There is an exemption for existing airlines which have been given special dispensation under previous legislation. Decisions to grant or revoke operating licences must be published in the Official Journal of the European Communities.

In Article 5 there are special provisions to ensure that licensed airlines have sufficient financial solidity for their operations to be carried on properly. This includes submitting audited annual accounts and informing the licensing authority of new routes. Accident insurance cover is also required in order to obtain a licence; see Article 7.

Article 8 of the Regulation prevents a Member State making ownership of aircraft a condition for granting or maintaining an operating licence, but a

Member State may require that a licensed air carrier has one or more aircraft at its disposal.

Under the Regulation on air navigation services in the single European sky[217] all forms of air services in the Union are subject to certification by the Member States. See also Regulation (EC) No 1794/2006 laying down a common charging scheme for air navigation services, and Directive 91/670/EEC on mutual acceptance of personnel licences for the exercise of functions in civil aviation.

3.1.3. Network access

The main provisions on network access are in Regulation (EC) No 1008/2008 on common rules for the operation of air services in the Community. The Regulation deals with both scheduled flights and charter flights, but only scheduled flights within the Union. The Regulation distinguishes between Community air carriers[218] and others. According to Article 15 of the Regulation, only Community air carriers can have traffic rights on routes within the Union.

> In Case C-92/01, *Stylianakis* v *Elliniko Dimosio*, the CJ held that Article 3(1) of Regulation (EEC) No 2408/92 (now Article 15(1) in Regulation (EC) No 1008/2008) prevents measures being taken by a Member State whereby flights to other Member States are generally subject to higher airport taxes than those which are imposed on domestic flights in the Member State in question, unless it can be shown that the taxes relate to services provided at the airports which are necessary for passengers, and the costs of services for passengers travelling to other Member States are higher than the costs of the services which are necessary for passengers on domestic routes.

When there is serious congestion or environmental problems the Member State concerned can restrict traffic; see Article 9. This may not lead to discrimination or unreasonable distortion of competition.

217. Regulation (EC) No 550/2004 on the provision of air navigation services in the single European sky.
218. A 'Community air carrier' is defined as an air carrier with a valid operating licence granted by a competent licensing authority in accordance with Chapter II of Regulation (EC) No 1008/2008; see Article 2(11) of the Regulation.

Access to routes between the EU and third countries is regulated bilaterally. The conditions for being able to open a route are linked to a nationality criterion. There are no reciprocity conditions at EU level.[219]

Fees for overflying etc. are harmonised through Regulation (EC) No 1794/2006 of laying down a common charging scheme for air navigation services. This lays down the guiding principles for the calculation of fees for overflying and entry of airspace.

Airspace constitutes an overall 'network' for air traffic. Without access to airspace services cannot be provided. Regulation (EC) No 549/2004 laying down the framework for the creation of the single European sky (the framework Regulation) was adopted in accordance with the Union goal of establishing an internal market. This Regulation starts from the position that airspace is a limited resource which must be regulated in order to achieve its effective exploitation. Article 6 of Regulation (EC) No 551/2004 on the organisation and use of the airspace in the single European sky (the airspace Regulation) provides for an air traffic management network in the form of an authority responsible for air traffic management (ATM). This function is the responsibility of Eurocontrol (www.eurocontrol.int/). More detailed provisions are laid down in Regulation (EU) No 677/2011 laying down detailed rules for the implementation of air traffic management (ATM) network functions and amending Regulation (EU) No 691/2010.

There is a special network problem related to the allocation of slots. Flag carriers have traditionally been allocated the most sought after slots (an equally limited resource) in their home airport(s). They are allowed to renew these from year to year, provided that their use of them has been above 80 %; see Articles 8 and 10 of Regulation (EEC) No 95/93 on common rules for the allocation of slots at Community airports.[220] These are referred to 'grandfathered rights'. Since in most of the major airports there are only a limited number of slots available, it can be difficult for other operators to obtain attractive landing and take-off rights, which make it difficult for new operators to penetrate the market. This is why terms which deal with the allocation of slots are so important in merger decisions. The provision can give airlines in-

219. *P.J.G. Kapteyn & P. VerLoren van Themaat:* Introduction to the Law of the European Communities, 1998 pp. 1202-1203.

220. A special Article 10a was inserted in Regulation (EC) No 894/2002 amending Council Regulation (EEC) No 95/93 on common rules for the allocation of slots at Community airports, under which air carriers were entitled to the same slots during for the summer of 2002 and winter of 2002/2003 as had been allocated to them as of 11 September 2001 for summer 2001 and winter 2001/2002.

centives to keep flying on otherwise unprofitable routes in order to prevent competitors taking over desirable slots.

Regulation (EEC) No 95/93 contains rules for the allocation of slots at Community airports. Certain airports are designated as coordinated airports or fully coordinated airports. This involves the appointment of airports coordinators. To some extent it is possible for individual airlines to exchange slots, to transfer them within the same corporate group in connection with a merger, or to use them for other routes or other kinds of flights; see Article 8 of the Regulation. This possibility can give the allocated slots the character of a valuable asset.

Computerised reservation systems used in the airline industry can also be characterised as essential facilities. In this area Regulation (EC) No 80/2009 on a Code of Conduct for computerised reservation systems applies.

A computerised reservation system is a system which contains information about, among other things, airline timetables, spare capacity, ticket prices and associated services. There can be associated services for making reservations or issuing tickets; see Article 2. In the Nordic countries the Amadeus system is widely used.

According to Article 3 of Regulation (EC) No 80/2009 , there is a prohibition on unreasonable conditions, on requiring customers to take other services (tied sales), on requirements for exclusive arrangements and on the payment of commission for promoting the sales of tickets of a particular airline. There are equivalent rules for parent carriers in Article 10. Under Article 8 it is possible to exclude non-EU airlines from such systems if the company or the third country from which it comes does not allow corresponding access to their computerised reservation system. There is thus a level of reciprocity.

Another essential facility is *ground handling*.[221] Major airlines often have their own ground handling services. When there is only one ground handling company at a given airport, it will both have a dominant position and it will also often represent vertical integration. The independent airlines will thus become the customers of their competitor, with the risk of abuse of a dominant position. Directive 96/67/EC lays down the framework for the restrictions which the Member States can introduce on the right to provide these services, including the airlines' own provision of these services.

221. The term covers a long list of activities that are carried out in airports in connection with the arrival and departure of aircraft, including dealing with passengers, goods and mail, as well as a number of tasks related to aircraft. The term is defined in more detail in Directive 96/67/EC on access to the groundhandling market at Community airports.

Bonus flying arrangements constitute a special problem in competition law. This refers to the giving of special points in connection with the purchase of flights. These points can later be redeemed for other flights, hotel accommodation etc. Their existence can act as a barrier to the entry of new market participants.[222] In some cases access to a programme has been used to reduce the effect of these programmes on restricting competition.[223] See the Commission's Decision of 16.01.1996 on the cooperation between *SAS* and *Lufthansa*.

3.1.4. Public obligations

According to Article 16(1) of Regulation (EC) No 1008/2008 on common rules for the operation of air services in the Community, a Member State may impose a public service obligation for the provision of scheduled air services serving a peripheral or development region in its territory or on a thin route. It is a requirement that the route must be vital for the economic development of the region in question. The provision has the character of a universal service. The obligation can relate to matters such as continuity, regularity, capacity and pricing. The imposition of the obligation is subject to prior consultations with the other Member States concerned and after having informed the Commission and the airports and air carriers already operating on the route. The Commission will publish the existence of the public service obligation in the Official Journal of the European Communities. There is a requirement to use a tendering process and a possibility of making compensation for the provision of the public service.

The Community guidelines on financing of airports and start-up aid to airlines departing from regional airports (OJ 2005 C 312/1) apply when assessing the compatibility of State aid with the EU's State aid rules.

3.1.5. Technical standards

Regulation (EEC) No 3922/91 on the harmonization of technical requirements and administrative procedures in the field of civil aviation implement-

222. An example of this is Eurobonus, which is a programme run by SAS. In Norway there is a prohibition on the earning of any form of bonus points, and in Sweden there is a prohibition on giving bonus points on domestic routes which are served by more than one airline.
223. See Commission Decision of 16 January 1996 on Case IV/35.545 – *Lufthansa/SAS*. For a review of the problem see *Susanne Storm:* Air Transport Policies and Frequent Flyer Programmes in the European Community – a Scandinavian Perspective, Unit of Tourism Research at Research Center Bornholm, Report No 14/1999.

ed the Community's joint aviation requirements (JARs) for technical safety standards. The JARs are prepared by the Joint Aviation Authorities (JAA), which is a group of European civil aviation authorities. The JARs have led to harmonisation of standards for, among other things, the approval and certification of airline personnel, aircraft and airlines. In 2004 and 2007 the JAA stopped being responsible for tasks relating to aviation skills and tasks on operational questions and certification of personnel, as these tasks were taken over by the European Aviation Safety Agency (EASA), which is an EU agency.[224]

Further standards have been adopted by the European Parliament and the Council under the authority of Article 100(2) TFEU.

According to Articles 6 and 7 of Regulation (EEC) No 3922/91, an aircraft that is operated under a licence from one Member State in accordance with the common technical standards and administrative procedures can be operated under the same conditions in the other Member States, without further technical requirements or evaluations by another Member State. The Member States must recognise the certification granted under the Regulation by another Member State or by a body acting on its behalf, to bodies or persons under its jurisdiction and under its authority, who are concerned with the design, manufacture and maintenance of products, and the operation of aircraft.

The European Organisation for the Safety of Air Navigation (Eurocontrol)[225] is the body which, in accordance with the International Convention Relating to Co-operation for the Safety of Air Navigation, is appointed to adopt the necessary measures to solve safety problems in relation to European air traffic. It draws up the Eurocontrol standards which constitute the obligatory elements concerning the physical properties, form, materials, performance, personnel and procedural issues whose uniform application is recognised as being of significant importance for the implementation of an integrated system of air traffic services.

There has been a CJ decision on whether Eurocontrol should be considered as a public authority or a private undertaking. This was in Case 364/92, *Eurocontrol*, where the CJ found that the tasks of the organisation concerning control and safety were typically the tasks of public bodies.

224. The JAA is now responsible for a training office and for contacts with JAA members in non-EU countries. For a more detailed review of the rules of the two organisations see http://www.jaa.nl/ and http://www.easa.eu.int/level1/index.php.
225. http://www.eurocontrol.int.

> The case arose over a complaint of abuse of a dominant position in connection with Eurocontrol's pricing of route charges.[226]

In Article 3 of the now repealed Directive 93/65/EEC on the definition and use of compatible technical specifications for the procurement of air-traffic-management equipment and systems, the Commission was authorised, using special procedures, to adopt the Eurocontrol standards and subsequent Eurocontrol amendments to those Eurocontrol standards, compliance with which was mandatory under Community law. However, Directive 93/65/EEC only dealt with the obligations of procurement authorities, and for this reason it has been replaced by the Interoperability Regulation,[227] which also concerns the obligations of air navigation service providers, airspace users, industry and airports. In its Annex II the Regulation lists requirements for a number of essential systems and procedures which must be complied with in the European air traffic system. It is also possible to lay down Community specifications, possibly in the form of obligatory standards or by the new method. There is also a requirement for the use of an EC declaration of conformity or suitability for use of constituents linked to the Regulation.

3.1.6. Safety

Directive 94/56/EC establishing the fundamental principles governing the investigation of civil aviation accidents and incidents lays down requirements for the investigation of every accident or serious incident. The Member States are responsible for this.

Directive 2003/42/EC on occurrence reporting in civil aviation established a framework for reporting occurrences such as operational interruptions, defects, faults or other irregular circumstances that have or may have influenced flight safety without resulting in an accident or serious incident covered by Directive 94/56/EC. The Directive requires the Member States to introduce an obligatory reporting system. Databases must be established for recording the information assembled. All bodies that have responsibility for making rules for civil aviation safety or for investigating air accidents or serious incidents in the Union have access to these databases.

Regulation (EC) No 216/2008 on common rules in the field of civil aviation and establishing a European Aviation Safety Agency has the primary

226. The case is commented on in *Niels van Antwerpen:* The Single European Sky, Air & Space Law, Vol. 27/2, 2002.
227. Regulation (EC) No 552/2004 on the interoperability of the European Air Traffic Management network.

aim of maintaining a high uniform level of civil aviation safety in the Union. The Regulation defines an overall requirement for airworthiness, which is described in more detail in its Annex I. To enforce this requirement, each aircraft must be issued with an individual certificate of airworthiness. Certification is evidence of an aircraft's airworthiness.

The European rules are to some extent the implementation of common European rules established by the Cyprus Agreement of 1990 on joint European aviation requirements. This set up the Joint Aviation Authorities (JAA) which has laid down safety requirements. The Chicago Convention also contains provisions on safety requirements. For a more detailed discussion of safety requirements, see *Manuhutu* 2000.

The Commission has special powers to ban air carriers from operating in European airspace. See Regulation (EC) No 2111/2005 on the establishment of a Community list of air carriers subject to an operating ban within the Community and on informing air transport passengers of the identity of the operating air carrier, and repealing Article 9 of Directive 2004/36/EC; and Regulation (EC) No 474/2006 establishing the Community list of air carriers which are subject to an operating ban within the Community referred to in Chapter II of Regulation (EC) No 2111/2005 of the European Parliament and of the Council. Finally, there is Regulation (EC) No 300/2008 on common rules in the field of civil aviation security establishes common rules in the field of civil aviation security, the main objective of which is to establish and implement appropriate Community measures to prevent acts of unlawful interference (for example, terrorism) against civil aviation. The common basic standards for air security are based on the current recommendations of the European Civil Aviation Conference (ECAC), and are laid down in detail in an Annex to the Regulation. Each Member State is responsible for preparing and implementing a national security training programme for civil aviation, and must ensure that the airports and airlines that provide services from that State prepare, implement and maintain appropriate security programmes for such airports and airlines in order to fulfil the national security programme for civil aviation. These programmes must be laid before the supervisory authority for approval, and are monitored by that authority.

Pursuant to Regulation (EC) No 300/2008 (or its predecessors) the Commission has issued Regulation (EU) No 185/2010 laying down detailed measures for the implementation of the common basic standards on aviation security, Regulation (EC) No 1217/2003 laying down common specifications for national civil aviation security quality control programmes, and Regulation (EC) No 1486/2003 laying down procedures for conducting Commission inspections in the field of civil aviation security.

Special insurance requirements are laid down in Regulation (EC) No 785/2004 on insurance requirements for air carriers and aircraft operators. In October 2006 an agreement was entered into between the EU and the USA on the transfer of air passenger name records (the PNR Agreement). The Agreement was renewed in 2007.[228]

3.1.7. Transparency

In the civil aviation sector, Regulation (EC) No 437/2003 on statistical returns in respect of the carriage of passengers, freight and mail by air lays down that the Member States must transmit to the Statistical Office of the European Communities a large amount of information about developments of passenger, freight and mail traffic. The aim is to support the implementation of the common air traffic policy.

The Regulation is supplemented by Regulation (EC) No 1358/2003 implementing Regulation (EC) No 437/2003 on statistical returns in respect of the carriage of passengers, freight and mail by air and amending Annexes I and II thereto.

3.1.8. Public authorities

Europe's airspace is characterised by being subject to regulations and controls by national authorities. Apart from Luxembourg, all Member States have their own civil aviation authorities which control their own airspace.[229] This has been seen as one of the most important reasons for why there is such an unsatisfactory use of airspace capacity in parts of Europe. These bottlenecks regularly lead to major delays to air traffic and an increased risk of collisions. With a view to increasing capacity the EU has launched an initiative under the heading of 'The Single European Sky'.[230]

In particular in the field of safety, the European Aviation Safety Agency has been set up;[231] see Regulation (EC) No 216/2008. Its tasks are particularly concentrated on certification of airworthiness and environmental certification.[232]

228. See Council Decision 2007/551/FUSP/RIA.
229. In Denmark it is the Danish Civil Aviation Administration (CAA-DK).
230. For a description of this see *Niels van Antwerpen:* The Single European Sky, Air & Space Law, Vol. 27/2, 2002.
231. http://www.easa.eu.int
232. See also Regulation (EC) No 488/2005 on the fees and charges levied by the European Aviation Safety Agency.

In connection with accidents, according to Article 6 of Directive 94/56/EC establishing the fundamental principles governing the investigation of civil aviation accidents and incidents, each Member State must have a permanent civil aviation body capable of acting as in investigation commission, functionally independent of the national aviation authorities, and responsible for airworthiness, certification, air traffic control, licensing, etc.

3.2. Railways

Since the end of the 1980s Europe's railways have be subject to regulatory liberalisation. This has by no means been the most comprehensive liberalisation of a regulated sector. Nevertheless it is remarkable how little competition has developed in this market. To some extent new participants may have been deterred because of the high costs of rolling stock and personnel required to get established. At the same time it seems that the traditional national undertakings prefer to cooperate rather than compete.[233]

The market in railways sector differs between passenger and goods services. On the passenger side the authorities are often contractors for a certain (politically determined) provision of passenger transport. Competition between train operators is often for public contracts (tendering). There is significant competition in relation to private cars and buses. In the area of goods traffic, there is direct competition for the transport of freight with other train operators and other forms of transport. The businesses of the two areas have little in common. However, passenger traffic and goods traffic compete with each other for access to the networks which they both use. The same applies to some other related facilities (for example shunting yards), and certain traction power, including engine drivers, can cover both areas.

Even though the existence of railway lines is a common requirement for both categories of railway traffic, they do not have the same network requirements. The convenience of passengers makes different demands than the needs of goods traffic. If these differences are not reflected in the pricing, there can be cross subsidisation between the two business areas.

There has been a considerable need for liberalisation. In particular in the area of goods traffic in Europe the railways have had difficulty competing with road haulage. From 1970 to 1998 the railways' share of the freight market fell

233. *Andre Meyer:* Rail Transport, in *Damien Geradin (ed.):* The Liberalization of State Monopolies in the European Union and Beyond, 2000 p. 113.

from 21.1 % to 8.4 %; this reflects a fall in the total volume of freight carried at a time when the total market for freight had strong growth.[234]

In addition to the transport policy interests, the railways have been the subject of growing interests from the point of view of environmental and climate change policy, because of the growth in emissions from European traffic. The preamble to Directive 2008/57/EC on the interoperability of the rail system within the Community refers to the Kyoto Protocol and the European Union's undertaking to reduce its gas emissions. This goal requires a change in the balance between different forms of transport, and therefore an improvement in the competitiveness of the railways.

3.2.1. EU regulation

The regulation of the different competition law aspects of the railways has been made in several steps. In 1969 the Council issued Regulation (EEC) No 1191/69 on action by Member States concerning the obligations inherent in the concept of a public service in transport by rail, road and inland waterway, as well as Regulation (EEC) No 1192/69 on common rules for the normalisation of the accounts of railway undertakings.

At the end of the 1970s and beginning of the 1980s a number of regulations and decisions were issued on the accounting systems and annual accounts, costing principles, and commercial independence of railway undertakings.[235]

The most important legislation for the liberalisation of the railways was first adopted at the beginning of the 1990s, and was realised by Directive 91/440/EEC on the development of the Community's railways (as amended by Directive 2007/58/EC); Directive 95/18/EC on the licensing of railway undertakings (as amended by Directive 2004/49/EC); and Directive 2001/14/EC (as amended by Directive 2007/58/EC) on the allocation of railway infrastructure capacity and the levying of charges for the use of railway infrastructure and safety certification (previously Directive 95/19/EC). The

234. Commission White Paper – European transport policy for 2010: time to decide, COM(2001) 370 final, p. 27.
235. Regulation (EEC) No 2830/77 on the measures necessary to achieve comparability between the accounting systems and annual accounts of railway undertakings; Regulation (EEC) No 2183/78 laying down uniform costing principles for railway undertakings; Decision 82/529/EEC on the fixing of rates for the international carriage of goods by rail; and Decision 83/418/EEC on the commercial independence of the railways in the management of their international passenger and luggage traffic. These have now been replaced.

Railway Safety Directive was adopted in 2004.[236] The aim of the Directive is to harmonise different safety rules. Among other things, the intention is to create equal conditions for all railway undertakings; see recital 15.

The sector-specific EU regulation is a very limited minimum liberalisation which gives only poor opportunities for enforcing competition in the Member States that choose minimum implementation. However, this has not prevented some Member States from creating some competition by putting out to tender some routes which can be considered as public services.

Directive 91/440/EEC (as amended by Directive 2001/12/EC) defines two fundamental types of undertaking:

- *Railway undertaking* means 'any public or private undertaking licensed according to applicable Community legislation, the principal business of which is to provide services for the transport of goods and/or passengers by rail with a requirement that the undertaking must ensure traction; this also includes undertakings which provide traction only'. Such an undertaking can also be referred to as an operator. In principle such an undertaking is subject to competition.
- *Infrastructure manager* means 'any body or undertaking responsible in particular for establishing and maintaining railway infrastructure. This may also include the management of infrastructure control and safety systems. The functions of the infrastructure manager on a network or part of a network may be allocated to different bodies or undertakings'. This is a network undertaking or network owner, which in reality administers a natural monopoly.

In its white paper 'European transport policy for 2010: time to decide', the Commission announced further opening of the internal market for passenger transport by rail, while ensuring that public service obligations are carried out. Furthermore, in its Communication on the Consumer Policy Strategy 2002-2006, the Commission set the goal of ensuring a high level of consumer protection in the area of transport. Subsequently on 26 September 2007, the European Parliament adopted the EC's third railway package consisting of the following legal acts:

236. Directive 2004/49/EC on safety on the Community's railways and amending Council Directive 95/18/EC on the licensing of railway undertakings and Directive 2001/14/EC on the allocation of railway infrastructure capacity and the levying of charges for the use of railway infrastructure and safety certification.

- Directive 2007/58/EC of the European Parliament and of the Council of 23 October 2007 amending Council Directive 91/440/EEC on the development of the Community's railways and Directive 2001/14/EC on the allocation of railway infrastructure capacity and the levying of charges for the use of railway infrastructure. The deadline for implementation was 4 July 2009.
- Directive 2007/59/EC of the European Parliament and of the Council of 23 October 2007 on the certification of train drivers operating locomotives and trains on the railway system in the Community. The deadline for implementation was 4 December 2009.
- Regulation (EC) No 1370/2007 of the European Parliament and of the Council of 23 October 2007 on public passenger transport services by rail and by road. The Regulation entered into force on 3 December 2009. The provisions in Regulation (EEC) No 1191/69 have been repealed, but continued to apply to freight services for three years after the entry into force of Regulation (EC) No 1370/2007.
- Regulation (EC) No 1371/2007 of the European Parliament and of the Council of 23 October 2007 on rail passengers' rights and obligations. The Regulation entered into force on 3 December 2009.

Since, for the most part, the provisions do not take effect before the end of 2009, the rules will not be subject to further analysis in this chapter.

In addition, the Commission has pointed out that the integration of the European railway systems requires further technical harmonisation so that the equipment of the different national systems can operate together.

3.2.1.1. The application of the general competition rules

As stated above, the competition rules of the Treaty apply to the railways sector. However, there is an exception in Regulation (EC) No 169/2009 applying rules of competition to transport by rail, road and inland waterway.

The Regulation applies to 'agreements, decisions and concerted practices which have as their object or effect the fixing of transport rates and conditions, the limitation or control of the supply of transport, the sharing of transport markets, the application of technical improvements or technical co-operation, or the joint financing or acquisition of transport equipment or supplies where such operations are directly related to the provision of transport services and are necessary for the joint operation of services by a grouping within the meaning of Article 4 of road or inland waterway transport undertakings, and to the abuse of a dominant position on the transport market'. The

Regulation also applies to undertakings carried on by recipients of aid in the transport sector, when such undertakings have the aims or effects referred to.

Articles 3 and 4 of the Regulation make special exceptions in relation to the prohibition of agreements that restrict competition in Article 101(1) TFEU for defined technical agreements and groups of small and medium-sized undertakings.

> In the case of *Commission* v *Union internationale des chemins de fer*, the Commission applied Regulation (EEC) No 17/62 to a leaflet concerning railway tickets, on the assumption that Regulation (EEC) No 1017/68 (now Regulation (EC) No 169/2009) did not apply. This view was rejected by the GC (Case T-14/93) and later by the CJ (Case C-264/95 P). Exemptions have also been given under Regulation (EEC) No 1017/68 (now Regulation (EC) in Commission Decision 93/174/EEC concerning tariff structures in the combined transport of goods, and Commission Decision 94/594/EC concerning a joint venture. Likewise the Commission has applied the Regulation in a case on the abuse of a dominant position in connection with different tariff treatment of containers, depending on whether they were unloaded in German ports or ports in other Member States (Commission Decision 94/210/EC). This case resulted in a fine on Deutsche Bahn of EUR 11 million. This decision was upheld by the GC in Case T-229/94, and an appeal dismissed by the CJ in Case C-436/97.

3.2.1.2. Pricing

Article 95(1) TFEU contains an overall prohibition against price discrimination so that, in the case of transport within the Union there is a prohibition of 'carriers charging different rates and imposing different conditions for the carriage of the same goods over the same transport links on grounds of the country of origin or of destination of the goods in question.' This provision is supplemented by Article 96(1) TFEU, under which the 'imposition by a Member State, in respect of transport operations carried out within the Union, of rates and conditions involving any element of support or protection in the interest of one or more particular undertakings or industries shall be prohibited, unless authorised by the Commission.' These provisions are expressed in more detail in EEC Council Regulation No 11 (of 1960) concerning the abolition of discrimination in transport rates and conditions, in implementation of Article 79 (3) of the Treaty establishing the European Economic Community. Article 4(1) of Regulation 11/1960 repeats the prohibition in Article 75(1) of the Treaty, and in Article 4(2) it is more specifically stated that the fixing, by tariff or otherwise, of transport rates and conditions which, when applied, would constitute discrimination within the meaning of paragraph 1 is also prohibited.

In addition, Article 18 of Regulation 11/1960 contains provisions for intervention and the imposition of sanctions. There are also provisions on the Member States' supervisory responsibilities, the obligation of freight companies and the providers of transport services to make notifications, rules on the burden of evidence, requirements concerning the use of transport documentation, and the Member States' obligations to notify.

There is no specific price regulation regime under EU law. However, Article 5 of Directive 91/440/EEC on the development of the Community's railways does require Member States to take measures to ensure that the goal of railway undertakings is to provide efficient and appropriate services at the lowest possible cost for the quality of service required. At the same time it states that railway undertakings must be managed according to the principles that apply to commercial companies.

3.2.2. Authorisation procedures

The general rules on the licensing of railway undertakings are in Directive 95/18/EC on the licensing of railway undertakings. This Directive requires the Member States to introduce a licensing system. Under Article 1(2) of the Directive (as amended by Directive 2001/13/EC) Member States can exempt a number of undertakings from the cope of the Directive, as follows:

- undertakings which only operate rail passenger services on local and regional stand-alone railway infrastructure;
- railway undertakings which only operate urban or suburban rail passenger services;
- railway undertakings whose activity is limited to the provision of regional rail freight services that are not covered by the scope of Directive 91/440/EEC; and
- undertakings which only carry out freight operations on privately owned railway infrastructure that exists solely for use by the infrastructure owner for its own freight operations.

Railway undertakings which fulfil the requirements laid down have a right to a licence; see Article 4(3) of Directive 95/18/EC. Conversely, there is a prohibition on the issue or extension of validity of a licence for undertakings which do not fulfil the requirements; see Article 4(2). A licence is valid throughout the territory of the Union; see Article 4(5) (as inserted by Directive 2001/13/EC).[237]

The requirements which it is necessary to fulfil in order to obtain a licence as a railway undertaking are laid down in Articles 6 to 9 of the Directive. These include good repute, financial fitness, professional competence and insurance cover for civil liability. Among other things, the requirement for good repute includes that the undertaking must not have been declared bankrupt, or have been convicted of serious offences of a commercial nature or against specific legislation applicable to transport, or have been convicted of serious or repeated failure to fulfil social, labour or tax law obligations. As for financial fitness, an applicant railway undertaking must show that it will be able to meet its actual and potential obligations for a period of twelve months. The requirements for professional competence relate to management, personnel, organisation and the physical assets.

The Member States otherwise lay down regulations on technical standards and operations, safety, health, social insurance, workers' rights and consumer protection.

3.2.2.1. Unbundling

Article 6 of Directive 91/440/EEC requires for the unbundling of accounts for business relating to the provision of transport services and accounts for business relating to the management of railway infrastructure. The provision also allows for organisational unbundling. Article 9(4) (inserted by Directive 2001/12/EC) includes further requirements for the publication of profit and loss accounts and either balance sheets or annual statements of assets and liabilities by railway undertakings; funds paid for activities relating to the provision of passenger transport services as public service remits must be shown separately.

Under Article 6 (as amended by Directive 2001/12/EC) there is a prohibition on public funds paid for the provision of transport services being transferred to the management of railway infrastructure, and vice versa. However, there is not a specific prohibition of cross subsidisation if it does not involve public funds.

237. It is explicitly stated in Article 4(4) that a licence does not itself entitle the holder to have access to the railway infrastructure. However, this is not the starting point in connection with authorisations; see section 1.4.7.

3.2.2.2. Independence between the State and railway undertakings

Article 4 of Directive 91/440/EEC requires there to be a separation between the State and railway undertakings with regard to management, administration and internal control over administrative, economic and accounting matters. Railway undertakings must hold independent assets, budgets and accounts which are separate from those of the State. This requirement can be satisfied by incorporation.

3.2.3. Access to networks

The rules on third party access to railway networks do not give an unconditional right of access. There are several forms of restriction. Thus, the regulation is primarily aimed at transport provided over longer distances. Railway undertakings whose activities only cover towns, suburbs and regional transport are not covered by Directive 91/440/EEC; see Article 2.[238] Only railway undertakings which are established or which wish to become established in a Member State are covered by the Directive.

Pursuant to Directive 2004/51/EC amending Directive 91/440/EEC, since 1 January 2007, the railway undertakings covered by Article 2 of Directive 91/440/EEC have had access on reasonable terms to all the Member States' infrastructure, with a view to the provision of all forms of railway freight services.

The Trans-European Rail Freight Network consists of the following elements; see Article 10a of Directive 91/440/EEC (as inserted by Directive 2001/12/EC):

a. Railway lines as indicated in the maps in Annex I.
b. Diversionary routes, where appropriate, particularly around congested infrastructure within the meaning of Directive 2000/14/EC. When these routes are offered, overall journey times must be safeguarded as far as possible.
c. Track access to terminals serving or potentially serving more than one final customer and to other sites and facilities, including feeder lines to and from these.
d. Track access to and from ports as listed in Annex I, including feeder lines.

Article 6(3) of Directive 91/440/EEC (as amended by Directive 2001/12/EC) contains a special provision whereby the Member States must 'take the measures necessary to ensure that the functions determining equitable and non-discriminatory access to infrastructure, listed in Annex II, are entrusted

238. Railway undertakings whose operations are limited to providing shuttle services for road vehicles through the Channel Tunnel are excluded from the scope of the Directive.

to bodies or firms that do not themselves provide any rail transport services. Regardless of the organisational structures, this objective must be shown to have been achieved.'

Annex II contains the following list of essential functions referred to in Article 6(3):

- Preparation and decision-making related to the licensing of railway undertakings including granting of individual licenses,
- Decision-making related to the path allocation, including both the definition and the assessment of availability and the allocation of individual train paths,
- Decision-making related to infrastructure charging,
- Monitoring observance of public service obligations required in the provision of certain services.

There is no requirement that such a body may not to be part of a corporate group with or even be part of a railway undertaking. There is nothing to prevent an infrastructure manager being given the functions referred to in Article 6(3).

Access to a network is given by the allocation of a *train path*, meaning the infrastructure capacity needed to run a train between two places over a given period. In principle, network access is given in the form of annual timetables. The transition to as new timetable takes place at midnight on the second Saturday in December.[239] Annex III of Directive 2001/14/EC sets out the schedule for the allocation process. In principle a train path is only allocated for a period corresponding to the timetable period; see Article 13(2). However, framework agreements can be made for the allocation of capacity to an applicant for five years or more if special commercial contracts, investments or risks justify this; see Article 17 of the Directive. This possibility should be seen against the background of the major investment which is often needed in equipment and personnel to penetrate a new market. Framework agreements may not exclude other applicants or services from using the relevant infrastructure. Finally, infrastructure managers can grant *ad hoc* requests; see Article 23. These relate to applications for individual train paths (for example for freight trains). Infrastructure managers must respond to *ad hoc* requests within five working days.

If a railway network does not have sufficient capacity to meet all the requests received, the infrastructure manager must attempt, through consultation with the applicants, to achieve a resolution; see Article 21 of Directive

239. Commission Decision 2002/844/EC of 23 October 2002 amending Directive 2001/14/EC in respect of the date for changing the working timetable for rail transport.

2001/14/EC. In this situation the infrastructure manager may, within reasonable limits, offer capacity which differs from that which has been applied for. The applicants must be consulted. A dispute resolution system must be made available to resolve disputes within 10 working days.

If attempts to coordinate do not make it possible to satisfy all applications for capacity to a sufficient extent, the infrastructure manager must declare that that element of the infrastructure is congested; see Article 22 of Directive 2001/14/EC. In this situation the infrastructure manager must carry out a capacity analysis. This situation can be resolved either through the imposition of infrastructure charges, see Article 7(4), or if this cannot solve the problem, by using priority criteria. The priority criteria must take account of the importance of a service to society and the effects of prioritising on other Member States; see Article 22. Finally, it is possible that capacity use can be improved by re-routing services, re-scheduling services, speed alterations and infrastructure improvements; see Article 25.

There are similarities between infrastructure managers and system operators in the energy supply sector. This is apparent from the powers and tasks which are given to infrastructure managers in Directive 2001/14/EC. These include cooperation with other infrastructure managers (Article 15), tasks related to lack of capacity (Articles 21-22), tasks related to disruptions to services (Article 29), and planning tasks relating to capacity enhancement plans (Articles 25-26).

Train paths may not be assigned; see Article 13 of Directive 2001/14/EC which prohibits any trading in infrastructure capacity.

Annex II of Directive 2001/14/EC lists the services which must be provided to railway undertakings in connection with third party access to a network. This also indicates what are considered to be the essential facilities in this sector:

Services to be supplied to the railway undertakings

1. The minimum access package must comprise:
   a. handling of requests for infrastructure capacity;
   b. the right to utilise capacity which is granted;
   c. use of running track, points and junctions;
   d. train control, including signalling, regulation, dispatching and the communication and provision of information on train movement;
   e. all other information required to implement or operate the service for which capacity has been granted.
2. Track access to services facilities and supply of services must comprise:
   a. use of electrical supply equipment for traction current, where available;
   b. refuelling facilities;
   c. passenger stations, their buildings and other facilities;

d. freight terminals;
e. marshalling yards;
f. train formation facilities;
g. storage sidings;
h. maintenance and other technical facilities.

3.2.3.1. Access to other than the track

In connection with access to the rail network, there has been a debate about whether anything other than access to the track and the facilities connected with it could constitute essential facilities in the eyes of the law. In the *European Night Services* case,[240] concerning a joint venture under Article 101 TFEU (then Article 81 of the EC Treaty), in connection with the setting of a condition the Commission assumed that the provision of the locomotive, train crew and train path constituted essential facilities. The case was brought before the GC which rejected the idea that locomotives and personnel could be essential facilities. However, the GC did note that in this case competitors without locomotives would be unable either to penetrate the relevant market or to continue operating on it. In particular in relation to locomotives, the GC emphasised that in the case in question the Commission had not shown that the necessary locomotives could not be bought or leased on the market. Moreover, the GC argued that the fact that the notifying undertakings had been the first to acquire the locomotives in question did not mean that they were alone in being able to do so.[241] In the case in question the Commission's original decision was annulled by reference to the insufficiency of investigations. From this it must be assumed that, in connection with the interpretation of Directive 91/440/EEC,[242] there must be overwhelming obstacles to acquiring locomotives for these to be regarded as essential facilities.

In particular in respect of computer reservation systems, Regulation (EC) No 80/2009 on a Code of Conduct for computerised reservation systems has

240. Commission Decision 94/663/EC of 21 September 1994 on Case IV/34.600 *European Night Services,* para. 81.
241. Joined Cases T-374/94, T-375/94, T-384/94 and T-388/94, *European Night Services and others* v *Commission,* para. 212 and paras 215-216.
242. *Horn Normand:* Comments, in *Damien Geradin (ed.):* The Liberalization of State Monopolies in the European Union and Beyond, 2000 states at p. 134, that it was precisely the fear of creating a precedent of a right to locomotive facilities which was the reason for bringing the Commission's Decision before the GC. For a further comment on the case, see *Andre Meyer:* Rail Transport, in *Damien Geradin (ed.):* The Liberalization of State Monopolies in the European Union and Beyond, 2000 p. 122 et seq.

laid down special rules, among other things for railway products. The Regulation is discussed above in connection with air transport in section 3.1.3.

3.2.3.2. Pricing

For access to a railway network, Article 8 of Directive 91/440/EEC states that the fee for use of the railway infrastructure (user fee) must be laid down by Member States after consulting the infrastructure manager. The second paragraph of Article 8 states that the user fee must be calculated so as to avoid any discrimination between railway undertakings. The Article also lists the criteria which can be taken into account when setting the fee.

The list of criteria includes the total mileage travelled, the composition of the train and any specific requirements in terms of factors such as speed, axle load and the degree or period and frequency of use of the infrastructure.

This list does not exhaust the Member States' possibilities for laying down criteria. According to Article 4 of Directive 2001/14/EC, provided that an infrastructure manager is independent of any railway undertaking with regard to legal form, organisation or decision-making functions, the Member State may delegate price setting powers to the infrastructure manager.[243] Otherwise, except for the collection of fees, such powers can be given to an independent charging body. In this connection there is a requirement for the use of uniform and non-discriminatory charges for the same mode of transport in the same markets. Competing railway undertakings must compete on equal terms.

The principles for charging set out in Article 7 of Directive 2001/14/EC are that charges for the minimum access package and track access to service facilities must be set at the cost that is directly incurred in operating the train service. Among other things charges may reflect the scarcity of capacity, environmental costs, performance incentives, reservations and discounts; see Articles 7, 9, 11 and 12.

3.2.3.3. Transit

In the railways sector, transit rights are restricted to special international groupings which have access and transit rights in the Member States where their constituent railway undertakings are established, as referred to in Article 10 of Directive 91/440/EEC.

243. Thus the minimum requirement on accounting unbundling in Article 6 of Directive 91/440/EEC does not extend to the delegation of pricing competence.

3.2.4. *Public service obligations*

Regulation (EC) No 1370/2007 on public passenger transport services by rail and by road contains special provisions on public service obligations in the railway sector.

Article 2 of the Regulation defines the concept of a public service obligation for the purposes of the railway sector as:

> 'a requirement defined or determined by a competent authority in order to ensure public passenger transport services in the general interest that an operator, if it were considering its own commercial interests, would not assume or would not assume to the same extent or under the same conditions without reward'

The provision of such a public service is to be compensated, but the compensation 'may not exceed an amount corresponding to the net financial effect equivalent to the total of the effects, positive or negative, of compliance with the public service obligation on the costs and revenue of the public service operator'; see Article 2 in the Annex to Regulation (EC) No 1370/2007. However, these rules do not cover 'general rules on financial compensation for public service obligations which establish maximum tariffs for pupils, students, apprentices and persons with reduced mobility'; see Article 3(3). Such general rules must be notified in accordance with Article 108 TFEU.

According to Article 5 of Directive 91/440/EEC, the requirement that railway undertakings must be managed according to the principles that apply to commercial companies also applies to their public services and to public services contracts which they conclude with the competent authorities of the Member State.

3.2.5. *Technical harmonisation*

The commercial operation of railway traffic on the trans-European network requires, among other things, coordination between the specifications of the infrastructure and the rolling stock, and it also requires the effective coordination of the information and communication systems of the various infrastructure managers and the train operators. Technical harmonisation is therefore an important area for the creation of an internal market for railway traffic. The existence of many separate technical systems acts as a barrier. Thus it is not unusual that when a train crosses a national border it must change its locomotive. The areas in which there is a need for technical harmonisation include:

- Track gauges (Portugal, Spain and Finland differ from the rest of the EU),[244]
- Electric current etc. (there are major national differences),
- Signals,
- Safety systems,
- Seat reservation systems, and
- Licensing of locomotive drivers (licences often only cover one country, and training is the responsibility of individual train operators).

The need for harmonisation resulted in Directive 2001/16/EC on the interoperability of the trans-European conventional rail system and Directive 96/48/EC on the interoperability of the trans-European high-speed rail system. Both these directives have been replaced by Directive 2008/57/EC on the interoperability of the rail system within the Community, which provides for technical specifications for interoperability (TSIs). These specifications are drawn up under a mandate from the Commission by The European Railway Agency.[245]

Under the authority of Article 6(1) of Directive 2008/57/EC (formerly Directive 96/48/EC) the Commission has laid down specifications for interoperability.[246]

In Article 7 of Directive 2001/16/EC the Member States are given the possibility of derogating from the TSIs.[247]

> Article 7 of Directive 2001/16/EC lists the following situations in which there may be a derogation:

244. The different track gauges were, among other things, a deliberate military strategic choice. New high-speed lines are being built in Spain using gauge the normally used in the EU.
245. The European Railway Agency was set up under Regulation (EC) No 881/2004 establishing a European Railway Agency (Agency Regulation).
246. Commission Decision 2002/735/EC concerning the technical specification for interoperability relating to the rolling stock subsystem of the trans-European high-speed rail system referred to in Article 6(1) of Directive 96/48/EC; Commission Decision 2008/231/EC – operation subsystem; Commission Decision 2008/284/EC – energy subsystem; Commission Decision 2008/217/EC – infrastructure subsystem; Commission Decision 2006/860/EC – control-command and signalling subsystem; and Commission Decision 2002/730/EC – maintenance subsystem.
247. Article 9 of Directive 2008/57/EC on the interoperability of the rail system within the Community contains much the same provision.

'a. for a proposed new line, for the upgrading of an existing line, or for any element referred to Article 1(1) at an advanced stage of development or the subject of a contract in course of performance when these TSIs are published;
b. for any project concerning the renewal or upgrading of an existing line where the loading gauge, track gauge, space between the tracks, or electrification voltage in these TSIs is not compatible with those of the existing line;
c. for a proposed new line or for the proposed renewal or upgrading of an existing line in the territory of that Member State when its rail network is separated or isolated by the sea from the rail network of the rest of the Community;
d. for any proposed renewal, extension or upgrading of an existing line, when the application of these TSIs would compromise the economic viability of the project and/or the compatibility of the rail system in the Member State;
e. where, following an accident or a natural disaster, the conditions for the rapid restoration of the network do not economically or technically allow for partial or total application of the relevant TSIs;
f. for wagons from or going to third countries the track gauge of which is different from that of the main rail network of the Community.'

In all cases the Member State concerned must serve prior notice of its intended derogation to the Commission and must forward to it a file setting out the TSIs or the parts of TSIs that it does not wish to be applied as well as the corresponding specifications that it does wish to apply.

3.2.6. Transparency

Regulation (EC) No 91/2003 on rail transport statistics lays down reporting obligations in relation to data on passenger and goods transport by railway. The data are to be used by the Commission in order to monitor the development of the common transport policy, include transport safety.

The provisions are supplemented by Regulation (EC) No 332/2007 on the technical arrangements for the transmission of railway transport statistics.

3.2.7. Public authorities

Article 30 of Directive 2001/14/EC lays down requirements for the establishment of a regulatory body to act as an appeal body (dispute resolution authority) in relation to the infrastructure manager. This body must be independent of the infrastructure manager and operationally independent of the authorities that award contracts for public services. The regulatory body has the power to request relevant information from the infrastructure manager, applicants and any third party involved. The regulatory body is required to decide on any complaints within two months from receipt of all information. A decision of the regulatory body is binding on all parties. However, decisions of the regulatory body are subject to judicial review.

Responsibilities for establishing safety standards and rules, as well as for monitoring and enforcing such standards and rules are a matter for public authorities which must be dealt with by the Member States or by independent bodies; see Article 7 of Directive 91/440/EEC. The aim is to prevent the use of such rules for discrimination with regard to network access.

The infrastructure manager and any charging body are subject to duty of confidentiality with regard to commercially confidential information; see Articles 4 and 6 of Directive 2001/14/EC.

4. Communication

Both postal and telecommunications services have previously primarily been national monopolies. These have often been owned by the State and have been organised as administrative entities. To some extent the traditional market actors are still dominant on the national markets, among other things because of their control over existing networks.

Both sectors are characterised by the fact that those parts of the networks that are still in the nature of a monopoly service have become very limited.

4.1. Telecommunications

In historical terms national telecommunications monopolies were the main actors on the EU's telecommunications market up until the 1980s.[248] They cooperated bilaterally. The alternative to these monopolies was to provide telecommunications services for one's own use, and this was only a realistic possibility for the largest entities. Where the national telecommunications undertakings had an exclusive right to establish (and own) telecommunications infrastructure, those entities that wanted to provide their own telecommunications services had to lease network capacity from the relevant monopolist. The costs of this were often very high compared to equivalent prices in the USA, especially for cross-border connections. This has been one of the

248. *Kjell A. Eliassen & Marit Sjøvaag:* European Telecommunications Liberalisation, 1999 p. 9 et seq.

major motivations behind the Union's liberalisation measures in this area.[249] Relatively early on the Commission succeeded in establishing its right to use its authority under Article 106(3) TFEU in the telecommunications sector.[250] In contrast to the other liberalised sectors, the telecommunications sector is still characterised by being regulated in part by liberalising directives.

The telecommunications sector has been subject to a number of changes in recent years. Telecommunications undertakings that were previously organised as national monopolies have increasingly been organised as limited companies under private law and are now often parts of multinational telecommunications giants. In this connection the EU has been active in promoting liberalisation and in setting the framework for competition. Already in 1984 the Council published its Recommendation 84/549/EEC concerning the implementation of harmonization in the field of telecommunications (OJ 1984 L298/49).[251] This was followed up by the Commission's Green Paper COM(87) 290 final. Regulation has developed at different speeds.[252] 1 January 1998 was the deadline for Member States to remove the last obstacles to consumers being able to be offered telecommunications services on competitive markets.[253] In 2002 there was a whole package of new telecommunications directives, dealing with both the technical and market aspects of development. These impose strict limits on the scope for Member States to restrict competition, for example by favouring a national operator.

249. *Pierre Larouche:* Telecommunications, in *Damien Geradin (ed.):* The Liberalization of State Monopolies in the European Union and Beyond, 2000 p. 16.
250. Commission Decision 82/861/EEC Case IV/29.877 – *British Telecommunications.* The Decision was subsequently referred to the CJ, with a claim for annulment. In Case 41/83, *Italy* v *Commission,* the CJ found in favour of the Commission, and the Commission's powers in this area were therefore confirmed. See also the later Case C-202/88, *France* v *Commission.* See *P.J. Slot & A.M. Skudder:* Common Features of Community Law Regulation in the Network-Bound Sectors, Common Market Law Review Vol. 38 2001 p. 92.
251. There was also liberalisation of a specific segment of the market via Directive 88/301/EEC on competition in the markets in telecommunications terminal equipment. See also Council Recommendation concerning the implementation of harmonization in the field of telecommunications (COM(80) 422 final).
252. The development of Union regulation of the telecommunications sector is described in *Pierre Larouche:* Competition Law and Regulation in European Telecommunications, 2000 pp. 1-36.
253. Some Member States were allowed limited extensions to the deadlines in Directive 96/19/EC and Directive 96/2/EC. Extensions were granted to Ireland (Decision 97/114/EC), Portugal (Decision 97/310/EC), Luxembourg (Decision 97/568/EC), Spain (Decision 97/603/EC) and Greece (Decision 97/607/EC).

As part of the Lisbon strategy, the Commission published a Communication 'i2010 – A European Information Society for growth and employment' (COM(2005) 229 final), and a Communication on the review of the EU Regulatory Framework for electronic communications networks and services (COM(2006) 334 final). Among other things, changes were made in 2009.

4.1.1. EU regulation

At the international level the Union is bound by its obligations under the WTO Telecommunications Agreement.[254] This is made clear in Council Decision 97/838/EC concerning the conclusion on behalf of the European Community, as regards matters within its competence, of the results of the WTO negotiations on basic telecommunications services. In the area of networks, the Union's policy is expressed in Decision 1336/97/EC on a series of guidelines for trans-European telecommunications networks. This lays down the goals and priorities and the main lines of action which it is proposed to implement for a trans-European network for telecommunications infrastructure. These guidelines also set out concrete projects of common interest.

The framework for the EU's telecommunications sector now consists of a liberalisation directive – Directive 2002/77/EC on competition in the markets for electronic communications networks and services – which replaced the previous Directive 90/388/EEC on competition in the markets for telecommunications services. In addition to this, Directive 2002/21/EC provides a common regulatory framework for electronic communications networks and services (Framework Directive).[255] This is supplemented by three specific directives: Directive 2002/20/EC on the authorisation of electronic communications networks and services (Authorisation Directive); Directive 2002/19/EC on access to, and interconnection of, electronic communications networks and associated facilities (Access Directive); and Directive 2002/22/EC on universal service and users' rights relating to electronic communications networks and services (Universal Service Directive). There are also: Directive 2002/58/EC[256] concerning the processing of personal data and the protection of privacy in the electronic communications sector (Directive on privacy and electronic communications); Decision No 676/2002/EC on a regulatory framework for radio spectrum policy in the European Community (Radio

254. Agreement on Telecommunications Services (Fourth Protocol to General Agreement on Trade in Services, Geneva 15 February 1997). The WTO Agreement is discussed in more detail in *Raj Bhala & Kevin Kennedy*: World Trade Law, 1998 p. 1289.
255. This Directive replaced earlier directives on open network provision (the ONP rules).
256. This replaced Directive 97/66/EC.

Spectrum Decision); and Decision No 128/1999/EC on the coordinated introduction of a third-generation mobile and wireless communications system (UMTS) in the Community; as well as Decision No 710/97/EC on a coordinated authorization approach in the field of satellite personal-communication services in the Community, also issued under the authority of Article 114 TFEU (the Article 95 of the EC Treaty).

Together with the classic telecommunications services, Directive 2002/77/EC includes the dissemination and broadcasting of radio and television programmes under the general heading of electronic communications services and electronic communications networks. This is a reaction to the coalescing of technologies in the areas of IT, media and telecommunications

R-LAN systems[257] are not directly covered by Community regulation. However, in its Recommendation 2003/203/EC on the harmonisation of the provision of public R-LAN access to public electronic communications networks and services in the Community, the Commission recommended that, in connection with the Framework Directive and the Authorisation Directive, Member States' measures should make it possible to offer public R-LAN access for public electronic communications networks in the 2.4 GHz band and the 5 GHz band.

The present rules primarily cover the circumstances concerning transmission, while content is regulated under other sets of rules. These cover, for example, electronic commerce and television broadcasting.[258] However, this chapter does not include a discussion of these special rules.

4.1.1.1. The application of the general competition rules

The general competition rules of the Treaty apply to the telecommunications sector. The Commission has issued both guidelines for the application of the general competition rules to the telecommunications sector in 1991, and a more specific Notice on the application of the competition rules to access agreements in the telecommunications sector in 1998.

257. Radio Local Area Networks. These create wireless broadband access to the internet and possibly also local area networks. For example, they are used in airports and main railway stations.
258. See Directive 2010/13/EU on the coordination of certain provisions laid down by law, regulation or administrative action in Member States concerning the provision of audiovisual media services (Audiovisual Media Services Directive), and Directive 2000/31/EC on certain legal aspects of information society services, in particular electronic commerce, in the Internal Market (Directive on electronic commerce).

The nature of guidelines means that the first set of guidelines referred to does not actually create rights which can be enforced through the courts, nor do they bind the GC and the CJ. Among other things, they contain guidelines for the calculation of the relevant market and give examples of the application of Articles 101 and 102 TFEU to the telecommunications sector.

The second Notice from 1998 is discussed in more detail below in the section on access to networks.

For an example of the application of the general competition rules, see Case C-52/09, *Konkurrensverket* v *TeliaSonera Sverige*, on the application of the general provisions on abuse of a dominant position in connection with the fixing of resale prices for ADSL connections in the wholesale market in relation to retail prices; and Case C-280/08, *Deutsche Telekom* v *Commission* on largely the same topic.

4.1.2. Authorisation procedures

Article 2 of Directive 2002/77/EC on competition in the markets for electronic communications networks and services prohibits Member States from granting or maintaining in force exclusive or special rights for the establishment and/or the provision of electronic communications networks, or for the provision of publicly available electronic communications services.

The Member States are primarily required to make use of general authorisations[259] rather than individual authorisations; see Article 2(4) of Directive 2002/77/EC and Article 3 of the Authorisation Directive (2002/20/EC). More detailed provisions on this obligation are given in the Authorisation Directive. There should thus be freedom to offer electronic communications networks and services. However, Article 3 of the Authorisation Directive does refer to the possibility of restricting this in accordance with Article 46(1) of the Treaty (now Article 52(1) TFEU) on grounds of public policy, public security or public health.

Annex A of the Authorisation Directive sets out the conditions which may be attached to a general authorisation. This list is exhaustive; see Article 6 of the Directive.[260]

259. A 'general authorisation' is defined in Article 2 of the Authorisation Directive (2002/20/EC) as 'a legal framework established by the Member State ensuring rights for the provision of electronic communications networks or services and laying down sector specific obligations that may apply to all or to specific types of electronic communications networks and services.'
260. However, special rules apply to providers of public service obligations.

Among other things, the list covers conditions similar to the requirements of public service obligations, including financial contributions to the funding of universal service, interoperability of services and interconnection of networks, accessibility of numbers from the national numbering plan to end-users, environmental and town and country planning requirements, 'must carry' obligations, and general requirements for administrative charges and financial and technical guarantees which are necessary to ensure that the infrastructures function correctly. Article 10 contains a consultation procedure in connection with failures to comply with conditions. This includes a deadline for obligatory consultation.

An undertaking that requests access to a network or interconnection need not be authorised to operate in the Member State where access or interconnection is requested if it is not providing services and does not operate a network in that Member State; see Article 3(1) of the Access Directive (2002/19/EC).

Member States can lay down requirements for an authorisation procedure, but this is subject to strict limits; see Article 3(3) of the Authorisation Directive.

In connection with granting authorisations and user rights, Article 15(1) of the Authorisation Directive lays down requirements for transparency, according to which Member States must ensure that all relevant information on rights, conditions, procedures, charges, fees and decisions concerning general authorisations and rights of use is published and kept up to date in an appropriate manner so as to provide easy access to that information for all interested parties.

4.1.2.1. Telephone numbers and radio frequencies

In the area of telecommunications, special user rights are associated with telephone numbers etc. and radio frequencies. Their use is necessarily based on a certain measure of exclusivity. Decision No 676/2002/EC on a regulatory framework for radio spectrum policy in the European Community contains rules for the Union's radio frequency policy. At the European level the European Conference of Postal and Telecommunications Administrations (CEPT)[261] prepares measures for the technical harmonisation of the use of radio frequencies across the Union's borders. This can be based on a mandate from the Commission; see Article 4(2) of the Decision No 676/2002/EC.

In addition to administration fees, charges can be made for the use of radio frequencies and numbers, as a means of ensuring the optimal use of such resources. Such fees should not prevent the establishment of innovative services and competition on the market. Certain telephone numbers and radio

261. CEPT covers 48 European countries (www.cept.org).

frequencies have a special economic value. It is recognised that the Member States can use tendering procedures or similar procedures for their allocation. In connection with Decision No 128/1999/EC on the coordinated introduction of a third-generation mobile and wireless communications system (UMTS) in the Community, some Member States raised considerable licence fees via auctions, while others did not require payment for such licences. These differences have been criticised as it is possible that they can distort competition.[262]

The Authorisation Directive only applies to the allocation of rights to use radio frequencies in so far as this use involves the provision of an electronic communication network or service which is normally provided for payment. The basic principle is that the number of user rights can only be limited where this is necessary to ensure the effective use of radio frequencies; see Articles 7 and 5(5) of the Authorisation Directive, and Article 4 of Directive 2002/77/EC. Article 13 of the Authorisation Directive allows Member States 'to impose fees for the rights of use for radio frequencies or numbers or rights to install facilities on, over or under public or private property which reflect the need to ensure the optimal use of these resources.' In addition to the auctions referred to above, the provision also allows for the possibility of charging, for example, local government licence fees in connection with the laying of a network along or over public roads.

The Member States are neither obliged to allocate nor prevented from allocating the right to use numbers in the national numbering plan[263] or allocating licences to install facilities to other undertakings than providers of electronic communications networks and services. However, according to Article 10 of the Framework Directive (2002/21/EC), Member States must ensure that national regulatory authorities control the assignment of all national numbering resources and the management of the national numbering plans. Member States must also ensure that adequate numbers and numbering ranges are provided for all publicly available electronic communications services. National regulatory authorities must establish objective, transparent and non-discriminatory assigning procedures for national numbering resources.

It is permitted to recover administration fees from providers of electronic communications services in order to finance the activities of the national reg-

262. *P.J. Slot & A.M. Skudder:* Common Features of Community Law Regulation in the Network-Bound Sectors, Common Market Law Review Vol. 38 2001 p. 105.

263. A national plan for the numbering and addressing of telephones, ISDN and mobile communications can e.g. be based on recommendations from the International Telecommunication Union.

ulatory authorities in administering the licensing system and the allocation of user rights. Such fees should only cover the actual administration costs of these activities.

The Framework Directive contains provisions on non-discrimination in connection with the allocation of radio frequencies for electronic communication services (Article 9(1)) and the assignment of all national numbering resources (Article 10(1)).

4.1.2.2. Unbundling

Article 8 of Directive 2002/77/EC lays down a requirement for the organisational unbundling of an undertaking that provides public electronic communications networks and cable television networks. However, this is based on the assumption that such an undertaking is controlled by a Member State or benefits from special rights, is dominant in a substantial part of the internal market for the provision of public electronic communications networks and/or publicly available telephone services, and operates a cable television network which has been established under special or exclusive right in the same geographic area.

According to Article 13 of the Framework Directive, there is a requirement for general accounting unbundling by undertakings that provide public communications networks or publicly available electronic communications services and which have special or exclusive rights for the provision of services in other sectors in the same or another Member State, for the activities associated with the provision of electronic communications networks or services, to the extent that this would be required if these activities were carried out by legally independent companies. It is stated that it must be possible to identify all elements of cost and revenue, with the basis of their calculation and the detailed attribution methods used, related to activities associated with the provision of electronic communications networks or services including an itemised breakdown of fixed asset and structural costs. Alternatively, there must be structural separation for the activities associated with the provision of electronic communications networks or services.

4.1.3. Access to networks

There can be a debate about the extent to which there is still a natural monopoly in the telecommunications sector. These days, communications can be transmitted by many means (cable, satellite, radio masts). In recent years many new service providers have entered the market. In the area of transmission, undertakings in the electricity and railways sectors have begun to offer services on networks which they have established for their own use. Mobile telephone companies have established parallel networks of radio masts. At a technical level, technologies in the IT, media and telecommunications sectors have converged so that their signals can be sent using the same networks, whether these consist of cable connections, radio waves, fibre optic technology or other electro-magnetic networks. If there is still a natural monopoly in the telecommunications sector it consists of the local fixed networks with junctions that lead to individual households (subscriber networks or 'local loops'). The continued existence of natural monopolies depends to a great extent on the costs of duplicating networks or on competition between different kinds of networks (fixed as against mobile networks).

For a period it will often be the previous national monopoly undertakings that control parts of the network, including the local loop, which in places seems still to have the character of a natural monopoly. Among other things, the rules on network access in the early phases of liberalisation ensured that entrants to the market could have access to the established network, so as to ensure the rapid development of a competitive market.

In assessing whether third party access to a network should be granted, Article 14 of the Framework Directive uses the term *undertakings with significant market power*. According to Article 14(2), this is a position equivalent to dominance, whether held individually or jointly with others.[264] According to Article 15, at the latest on the date of entry into force of the Directive (24 April 2002), the Commission had to publish guidelines for market analysis and the assessment of significant market power. In relation to undertakings with significant market power, Member States had the possibility, but not the obligation, of introducing provisions on network access, whether access or interconnection. Such a requirement for network access is referred to as an obligation of non-discrimination; see Article 10 of the Access Directive (2002/19/EC). It would only exceptionally be possible for a Member State to impose on an undertaking which does not have significant market power an obligation to give other undertakings access to its network.

Access means the making available of facilities and/or services to another undertaking, under defined conditions, on either an exclusive or non-exclusive basis, for the purpose of providing electronic communications services. *Interconnection* means the physical and logical linking of public communications networks used by the same or a different under-

264. See also Commission guidelines on market analysis and the assessment of significant market power under the Community regulatory framework for electronic communications networks and services (OJ 2002 C 165/6).

taking in order to allow the users of one undertaking to communicate with users of the same or another undertaking, or to access services provided by another undertaking.

4.1.3.1. The Access Directive

Within the framework of the Framework Directive, the Access Directive (2002/19/EC) lays down harmonised rules for how the Member States can regulate access to and interconnection with electronic communications networks and associated facilities between public networks. The main provision is in Article 4, where it is stated that operators of public communications networks 'have a right and, when requested by other undertakings so authorised, an obligation to negotiate interconnection with each other for the purpose of providing publicly available electronic communications services, in order to ensure provision and interoperability of services throughout the Community.'

Under Article 5, the national regulatory authorities must ensure adequate access and interconnection, and interoperability of services. The aim is to promote efficiency, sustainable competition, and give maximum benefit to end-users. With this aim, the national regulatory authorities are empowered to impose a number of obligations on operators (Article 8). These obligations include transparency in connection with interconnection and network access (Article 9), non-discrimination between the subsidiaries of a network owner and competing companies (Article 10), accounting unbundling (Article 11), service obligations (Article 12), and price controls and cost accounting obligations (Article 13), and where these means fail to achieve Effective competition, by operational unbundling (Article 13a).

The obligation of non-discrimination can be combined with a requirement for the publication of a reference offer; see Article 9(4) of the Access Directive. This means that the right will effectively be altered from being negotiated access to regulated access. Regulatory authorities may impose obligations for transparency by requiring operators to make public information, such as accounting information, technical specifications, network characteristics, terms and conditions for supply and use and prices; see Article 9(1) of the Access Directive. Regulatory authorities may also impose obligations for accounting separation; see Article 11. Moreover, where a market analysis indicates that a lack of effective competition means that an operator may sustain prices at an excessively high level, price controls may be introduced, allowing the operator a reasonable rate of return on adequate capital employed, taking into account the investment made by the operator and any risks specific to a particular new investment network project; see Article 13 of the Access Directive.

4.1.3.2. The general competition rules

The provisions in Articles 101 and 102 TFEU apply in parallel with these rules. An undertaking might thereby be able to obtain third party access to a network and other essential facilities, regardless of whether the Member State in question has made use of the provisions in Article 10 of the Framework Directive. In this connection the 1998 Notice on the application of the competition rules to access agreements in the telecommunications sector – framework, relevant markets and principles applies.[265] This was issued under the old provisions for the telecommunications sector. Among other things, the Notice addresses questions concerning essential facilities. According to paragraph 149 of the Notice, the Commission considers that competition rules and sector specific regulation form a coherent set of measures to ensure a liberalised and competitive market environment for telecommunications markets in the Community.

In particular the Treaty prohibition on the abuse of a dominant position is probably applicable in connection with access to networks and other essential facilities. Paragraph 52 of the 1998 Notice states that some 'incumbent [telecommunications operators] may be tempted to resist providing access to third party service providers or other network operators, particularly in areas where the proposed service will be in competition with a service provided by the [telecommunications operator] itself. This resistance will often manifest itself as unjustified delay in giving access, a reluctance to allow access or a willingness to allow it only under disadvantageous conditions.'

This is expanded on in paragraph 95, where it is stated that '[d]ominant [telecommunications operators] have a duty to deal with requests for access efficiently: undue and inexplicable or unjustified delays in responding to a request for access may constitute an abuse. In particular, however, the Commission will seek to compare the response to a request for access with:

a. the usual time frame and conditions applicable when the responding party grants access to its facilities to its own subsidiary or operating branch;
b. responses to requests for access to similar facilities in other Member States;
c. the explanations given for any delay in dealing with requests for access.'

4.1.3.3. Price controls

In relation to public undertakings which are vertically integrated, the Member States must ensure that those that provide electronic communications net-

265. OJ 1998 C 265/2. See also the Commission's Guidelines on the application of EEC competition rules in the telecommunications sector (OJ 1991 C 233/2).

works and have a dominant position do not discriminate in favour of their own activities. This requirement indicates that they must act as a common carrier.

There is a more indirect pricing requirement in Article 4 of Regulation (EC) No 2887/2000 on unbundled access to the local loop, on charging for unbundled access to the local loop. According to this, the national regulatory authority must ensure that charging for unbundled access fosters 'fair and sustainable competition'. However, this is combined with a requirement in Article 3(3) that notified operators[266] must set prices for unbundled access to the local loop[267] and related facilities on the basis of cost-orientation. If the national regulatory authority determines that the local access market is sufficiently competitive, it must relieve the notified operators of these price control obligations; see Article 4(4)

Article 13 of the Access Directive provides that national regulatory authorities may impose obligations relating to the cost orientation of prices and cost accounting systems for the provision of specific types of interconnection and/or access, where a market analysis indicates that a lack of effective competition means that the operator concerned can sustain prices at an excessively high level, or apply a price squeeze, to the detriment of end-users.

In connection with obligations concerning cost recovery and pricing controls under Article 13 of the Access Directive, national regulatory authorities must have regard both for consumers and for service providers. Primarily, it must be ensured that the mechanisms used 'promote efficiency and sustainable competition and maximise consumer benefits'. The authorities may take account of prices available in comparable competitive markets. For calculating the cost of efficient provision of services, the national regulatory authorities are explicitly authorised to use cost accounting methods which are independent of those used by an undertaking. This allows for the use of benchmarking. Where the implementation of a cost accounting system is mandated in order to support price controls, a description of the cost accounting system must be made publicly available. It is the operator which has the burden of proving that charges are derived from costs including a reasonable rate of return on investment, and the regulatory authorities may require an operator to adjust its prices. At the same time, the national regulatory authorities must take into account the investment

266. A 'notified operator' is an operator of a fixed public telecommunications network which the national regulatory authorities have designated as having a significant market power on the market for fixed telecommunications networks and services. The provisions concerning significant market power are in Article 14 of the Framework Directive.
267. Unbundled access to a local loop means that other service providers than the owner of the network have access to the local loop, with a view to creating competition in this market segment.

made by operators and allow them a reasonable rate of return on the capital employed, taking into account the risks involved.

With Regulation (EC) No 717/2007 on roaming on public mobile telephone networks within the Community and amending Directive 2002/21/EC (the Roaming Regulation), a limit was introduced to the amount which the owner of a mobile network can charge the customers of a third party network in connection with mobile calls (wholesale charges), and a limit to how much the owner of a network (home provider) can take for its own customers' use of visited networks.[268]

4.1.4. Public service obligations

The Universal Service Directive (2002/22/EC) lays down the rights of end-users and the corresponding obligations of undertakings that provide publicly available electronic communications networks and services. The Directive also lays down an obligation for universal services in the form of minimum services of a given quality, to which all end-users have a right of access, at reasonable prices and without regard to national circumstances.

The Universal Service Directive contains a number of provisions to ensure that end-users have access to a number of services 'independently of geographical location'; see Article 3(1). This must mean that these services must be offered throughout the territory of the Member State. This has regard for regional policy. These service obligations and other consumer protection provisions cover the following:

- The provision of a fixed public telephone network by at least one undertaking. This includes allowing end-users to make and receive local, national and international telephone calls, facsimile communications and data communications (Article 4);
- A comprehensive telephone directory, the right to be listed in such directory and a directory enquiries service (Articles 5 and 25);
- The possibility of making emergency calls from public pay telephones without having to use any means of payment (Articles 6 and 26);
- Special measures for disabled users; and

268. The regulation was a response to the high level of the charges payable by users of public mobile telephone networks when travelling abroad. The excessive retail charges resulted from both high wholesale charges levied by the foreign host network operators and, in many cases, from high retail mark-ups charged by the customers' own network operators; see Recital 1 of the Regulation.

– Number portability (Article 30).

In addition, the national regulatory authorities can impose obligations on undertakings to ensure that public pay telephones are provided (Article 6). The Member States may require service providers to apply uniform charges throughout their territory (geographical equalisation), or to comply with price caps; see Articles 8 and 9.

According to Articles 12 and 13, it is up to the individual regulatory authority to decide whether compensation is paid for the provision of the obligations imposed. If such compensation is paid, it can either be paid out of public funds, or the costs can be allocated between the providers of electronic communications networks and services. In principle, only the net additional costs can be compensated for. Any commercial advantage of the obligation to supply must be set off.[269]

Member States may designate one or more undertakings to guarantee the provision of on or more of the universal services referred to in Articles 4 to 7. However, Article 8 does not allow a Member State to impose additional obligations on a service provider over and above those referred to.[270]

Article 6 of Directive 2002/77/EC provides that any national scheme to share the net cost of the provision of universal service obligations must be based on objective, transparent and non-discriminatory criteria and be consistent with the principle of proportionality and of least market distortion. Where universal service obligations are imposed on undertakings providing electronic communications services, this must be taken into consideration in calculating any contribution to the net cost of universal service obligations.

4.1.5. Technical harmonisation

The establishment of the internal market for telecommunications requires there to be technical standardisation. Thus, the harmonisation of interfaces between terminal equipment and networks is a means for promoting competitive markets both for terminal equipment and network services. This has been implemented by a number of harmonising directives. The first was Directive 86/361/EEC on the initial stage of the mutual recognition of type approval for telecommunications terminal equipment, followed by Directive 91/263/EEC on the approximation of the laws of the Member States concerning telecommunications terminal equipment, including the mutual recognition of their

269. Case C-222/08, *Commission* v *Belgium*.
270. Case C-16/10, *The Number (UK)* v *British Telecommunications*.

conformity. On the basis of these, and following up on them, a large number of standards have been established, primarily in conjunction with the new method for regulating standards.

These have concerned the integrated services digital network (ISDN),[271] cellular digital land-based mobile communications (GMS),[272] land-based public radio paging (ERMES – European Radio Messaging System),[273] digital European cordless telecommunications (DECT),[274] and mobile and wireless communications system (UMTS – Universal Mobile Telecommunications System).[275]

Furthermore the use of the emergency call number (112) and the prefix for making international calls (00) were harmonised.[276] Article 17 of the Framework Directive now contains provisions on standardisation. Under this the Commission has prepared a list of standards and/or specifications which will form the basis for the promotion of a harmonised provision of electronic

271. Council Recommendation 86/659/EEC on the coordinated introduction of the integrated services digital network (ISDN) in the European Community; Council Resolution of 18 July 1989 on the strengthening of the coordination for the introduction of the Integrated Services Digital Network (ISDN) in the European Community up to 1992; and Council Resolution of 5 June 1992 on the development of the integrated services digital network (ISDN) in the Community as a European-wide telecommunications infrastructure for 1993 and beyond (OJ 1992 C 158/1).
272. Council Recommendation 87/371/EEC on the coordinated introduction of public pan-European cellular digital land-based mobile communications in the Community; Directive 87/372/EEC on the frequency bands to be reserved for the coordinated introduction of public pan-European cellular digital land-based mobile communications in the Community; and Council Resolution of 14 December 1990 on the final stage of the coordinated introduction of pan-European land-based public digital mobile cellular communications in the Community (GSM) (OJ 1990 C 329/25).
273. Council Directive 90/544/EEC on the frequency bands designated for the coordinated introduction of pan-European land-based public radio paging in the Community; and Council Recommendation 90/543/EEC on the coordinated introduction of pan-European land-based public radio paging in the Community.
274. Council Recommendation 91/288/EEC on the coordinated introduction of digital European cordless telecommunications (DECT) into the Community; and Directive 91/287/EEC on the frequency band to be designated for the coordinated introduction of digital European cordless telecommunications (DECT) into the Community.
275. Decision No 128/1999/EC of the European Parliament and of the Council on the coordinated introduction of a third-generation mobile and wireless communications system (UMTS) in the Community.
276. Council Decision 91/396/EEC on the introduction of a single European emergency call number.

communications networks, electronic communications services and the associated facilities and services.[277] To a significant extent standardisation is carried out with the involvement of the international standards organisations. However, according to Article 17(7) of the Framework Directive, this does not apply in respect of any of the essential requirements, interface specifications or harmonised standards to which the provisions of Directive 1999/5/EC apply.

At international level the International Telecommunication Union (ITU) has been a forum for technical harmonisation.

4.1.6. Public authorities

The overall provisions are in Article 3 of the Framework Directive, according to which the Member States must ensure that each of the tasks assigned to national regulatory authorities in the Framework Directive and the specific directives is undertaken by a competent body. Member States must guarantee the independence of national regulatory authorities by ensuring that they are legally distinct from and functionally independent of all organisations providing electronic communications networks, equipment or services. If a Member State retains ownership or control of undertakings providing electronic communications networks and/or services, it must ensure effective structural separation of the regulatory function from activities associated with ownership or control. This must be understood as a requirement for both management and organisational unbundling.

The regulatory authority also acts as a dispute resolution body in relation to network access; see Article 20 of the Framework Directive. The Member States can choose to make use of other mechanisms, including mediation. However, there is a deadline of four months within which the regulatory authority must make a decision concerning a dispute, unless the dispute has been brought before the courts by the party seeking redress, i.e. the party seeking network access. According to the wording of the provision, the bringing of a case before the courts by others than the party seeking redress cannot exempt the regulatory authority from taking a decision. The decision of the national regulatory authority must be made available to the public, subject to the requirements of business confidentiality.

Article 4 of the Framework Directive requires Member States to ensure that effective mechanisms exist at national level under which any user or un-

277. List of standards and/or specifications for electronic communications networks, services and associated facilities and services (OJ 2002 C 331/32).

dertaking providing electronic communications networks and/or services who is affected by a decision of a national regulatory authority has the right of appeal against the decision to an appeal body that is independent of the parties involved. This body can be a court or an administrative tribunal. An appeal against a decision of a regulatory authority does not have suspensive effect, unless the appeal body decides otherwise.

Article 5 of the Framework Directive also contains administrative law provisions on the obligation of regulated undertakings to provide the information necessary for the regulatory authorities to carry out their tasks. The requirements for information must be reasonable in relation to the tasks carried out. There is also a duty of confidentiality by the regulatory authorities in relation to the information provided. This duty is subject to national rules and it also applies to the Commission.

4.2. Postal services

The postal sector has traditionally been characterised by the existence of national state participants which have been protected in whole or in part by a legal monopoly. These state undertakings did not compete with each other. To the extent that their monopolies were not absolute, there could be limited competition from private undertakings. It was first in the 1990s that individual European countries independently began to open their postal sectors to competition. This occurred in Sweden and Finland, among others.

Postal deliveries can be divided into three stages:[278]

- Collection (clearance) and rough sorting of post,
- Transport of the rough-sorted post from one area to another, and
- Detailed sorting and delivery.

It is normal for a postal service to be involved in all three stages. Thus this is a vertically integrated sector. However, the transport of the rough-sorted post from one area to another is to a large extent done by sub-contractors (common carriers), including railway companies, airlines and road haulage companies. To the extent that there are essential facilities in the postal sector, this is mainly at the delivery stage, where a duplication of the non-physical distri-

278. *James I. Campbell Jr.:* Evolution of Terminal Dues and Remail Provision in European and International Postal Law, in *Damien Geradin (ed.):* The Liberalisation of Postal Services in the European Union, 2002 p. 3 et seq.

bution network (postmen/women) can be economically non-viable, especially in thinly populated areas.

These parts of the postal services have typically been monopolised, among other things on the grounds that this is necessary to maintain a reasonable postal service at a reasonable and often uniform price. As certain parts of the business have been more profitable than others, there has traditionally been cross-subsidisation between the more profitable and less profitable business segments.

At Union level, the general rules of the Treaty have been applied to the sector.[279] On 11 November 1992 the Commission published a Green Paper on the Development of the Single Market for Postal Services, and this was followed on 2 June 1993 by the Commission's Guidelines for the Development of Community Postal Services. In 1997 there was the Postal Services Directive.[280] This Directive was issued under the authority of Article 114 TFEU, and introduced a minimum framework for the liberalisation of the postal sector; see Article 26 of the Directive.

The Postal Services Directive has been amended three times.[281]

4.2.1. Regulation under EU law

For many years the national state monopolies have cooperated. Special sets of rules (The Universal Postal Convention, since 1874) have been developed by the Universal Postal Union, and the WTO rules are also relevant.[282] International cooperation in the form of cost-sharing between the collection of post in one country and its delivery in another is regulated by the Universal Postal Convention.[283]

279. See Case C-320/91, *Corbeau;* and Joined Cases C-147/97 and C-148/97, *Deutsche Post.*
280. Directive 97/67/EC on common rules for the development of the internal market of Community postal services and the improvement of quality of service. Later amended by Directive 2002/39/EC.
281. By Directive 2002/39/EC; Regulation (EC) No 1882/2003; and Directive 2008/6/EC.
282. These rules are not dealt with in this chapter. For further information the reader is referred to *David Luff:* International Regulation of Postal Services: UPU vs. WTO Rules, in *Damien Geradin (ed.):* The Liberalisation of Postal Services in the European Union, 2002.
283. See *James I. Campbell Jr.:* Evolution of Terminal Dues and Remail Provision in European and International Postal Law, in *Damien Geradin (ed.):* The Liberalisation of Postal Services in the European Union, 2002 for a description of the development of cost allocation for international mail.

The regulation in the Union has the character of a minimum requirement for liberalisation and service levels. The most important directive is Directive 97/67/EC on common rules for the development of the internal market of Community postal services and the improvement of quality of service (the Postal Services Directive).[284]

According to the definition in Article 2 of the Postal Services Directive, *postal services* involves 'the clearance, sorting, transport and delivery of postal items', which means items addressed in their final form in which they are to be carried by the universal service provider. In addition to items of correspondence, *postal items* includes books, catalogues, newspapers, periodicals and postal packages containing merchandise with or without commercial value. The Member States are entitled to organise the siting of letter boxes on public highways, the issue of postage stamps and the registered mail service used in the course of judicial or administrative procedures in accordance with their national legislation; see Article 8 of the Directive.

The European Parliament and the Council adopted Directive 2008/6/EC amending Directive 97/67/EC with regard to the full accomplishment of the internal market of Community postal services. The main purpose of the amendment was to do away with exclusive rights in the area of postal services, thereby making postal services part of the internal market. It includes special scope for financing to guarantee the provision of a universal service, where necessary. The provisions of the Directive had to be implemented by 31 December 2010. However, a number of Member States have been given extensions until 31 December 2012.[285]

4.2.1.1. The application of the general competition rules

The sector-specific rules are supplemented by the Notice from the Commission of 6 February 1998 on the application of the competition rules to the postal sector and on the assessment of certain State measures relating to postal services (OJ 1998 C 39/2), which contains the Commission's interpretation of the relevant Treaty provisions and guiding principles which the Commission uses when applying the competition rules of the Treaty to cases in the postal sector.

Among other things, this concerns topics such as the granting of exclusive rights, abuse of dominant position in connection with a granted exclusive right, and cross-subsidisation.

284. The Postal Services Directive expires at the end of 2008, unless it is extended.
285. These are Cyprus, Czech Republic, Greece, Hungary, Latvia, Lithuania, Luxembourg, Malta, Poland, Romania and Slovakia.

In the area of postal services the general competition rules have given rise to a number of cases:

> In its Decision of 20 March 2001 (*Deutsche Post AG I*) the Commission gave its first formal decision on abuse of dominant position in the postal sector. Deutsche Post was fined EUR 24 million for having protected the market for commercial parcel services by using a long-term arrangement with loyalty rebates. The complainant (United Parcel Service) also claimed that Deutsche Post had undertaken cross-subsidisation to finance its activities on the market for commercial parcel services, which was subject to competition, enabling Deutsche Post to undercut prices by using revenues from its monopoly on the market for letters. The Commission did not impose any fine in connection with this, as it found that the cost calculations which were intended to show that there had been under-pricing were insufficiently developed. In connection with this case, Deutsche Post undertook to separate its commercial parcel services in an independent company (unbundling). This company could buy services from Deutsche Post at market prices, and Deutsche Post undertook to provide the same services to other providers of commercial parcel services at the same prices (non-discrimination).
>
> In Commission Decision of 25 July 2001 *(Deutsche Post AG II),* it was claimed that Deutsche Post had abused is dominant position on the German market. In connection with received international mail, Deutsche Post had discriminated between different customers, refused to provide delivery services/carriage, charged excessive prices and restricted the development of the German market for international mail and the British market for mail to Germany. The fine on Deutsche Post was set at a symbolic EUR 1,000, because of the legal uncertainty which existed at the time of the offences.
>
> In the Commission's Decision of 5 December 2001 the Belgian postal service *(De Post/La Poste)* was fined EUR 2.5 million for abuse of its dominant position. The Belgian postal service had exploited its monopoly on letter postal services to make a reduction in rates conditional on customers also entering into contracts on the market which was open to competition, where a private Belgian undertaking operated a special document exchange system between undertakings.

State aid in the postal services sector has also been dealt with by the CJ in Joined Cases C-83/01, C-93/01 and C-94/01, *Chronopost and others*, which concerned cross-subsidisation. This case is discussed above in section 1.4.2.1.

4.2.1.2. Unbundling

Article 14 of the Postal Services Directive contains a requirement for the unbundling of accounts. Thus, a distinction must be made between the services covered by the reserved sector and the non-reserved services. Separate accounts must be kept for the services within the reserved sector and for the non-reserved services. The provision should be seen from the perspective of competition law. The aim is to prevent cross-subsidisation from an activity which is covered by an exclusive right to an activity carried on in a market which is open to competition. The Commission considers it essential to avoid cross-subsidisation, which leads to unfair competition, if the postal sector is to develop.[286]

Paragraph 3.1 of the Notice of 6 February 1998 from the Commission on the application of the competition rules to the postal sector and on the assessment of certain State measures relating to postal services defines cross subsidisation:

> 'Cross-subsidisation means that an undertaking bears or allocates all or part of the costs of its activity in one geographical or product market to its activity in another geographical or product market.'

According to paragraph 3.4 of the Notice, postal operators which have been granted special or exclusive rights may not 'use the income from the reserved area to cross-subsidise activities in areas open to competition'.

One of the problem areas is the allocation of the direct costs and the common and overhead costs of the operator. In paragraph 3.4 of the Notice it is stated that the prices of competitive services must, in principle, be at least equal to the average total costs connected with the provision of the service. This includes 'the direct costs plus an appropriate proportion of the common and overhead costs of the operator'. It has been argued that in a later decision the Commission has adopted a less strict approach to the allocation of common costs.[287] The Postal Services Directive (Article 14) also uses the distinction between costs

286. Notice of 6 February 1998 from the Commission on the application of the competition rules to the postal sector and on the assessment of certain State measures relating to postal services, para. 3.1.
287. Commission Decision 2001/354/EC of 20 March 2001 relating to a proceeding under Article 82 of the EC Treaty [now Article 102 TFEU] (Case COMP/35.141 – Deutsche Post AG) (OJ 2001 L 125/27). See the discussion in *Damien Geradin & Christophe Humpe:* The Liberalisation of Postal Services in the European Union: An Analysis of Directive 97/67, in *Damien Geradin (ed.):* The Liberalisation of Postal Services in the European Union, 2002 p. 113 et seq. Decision 2001/354/EC is

which can be directly assigned to a particular service and common costs which cannot be directly assigned to a particular service. Common costs must be allocated on the basis of an analysis of the origin of the costs themselves, on the basis of an indirect linkage to another cost category, or in the absence of anything better, on the basis of a general allocation key.

In connection with a merger, the question of cross-subsidisation from a monopoly business to a business which was subject to competition was tried in Case T-175/99, *UPS*. A postal services undertaking had possibly used means obtained in an area where it had been granted exclusive rights in order to acquire a shareholding in an undertaking that operated in a sector of the postal market that was open to competition. As the GC could not establish that these means had been acquired by an abuse of the monopoly, there was not an issue under competition law. This case is discussed in more detail above, in the general discussion of cross-subsidisation.

4.2.2. Authorisation procedures

For postal services that are not covered by an exclusive right (see below), Article 9 of the Postal Services Directive allows Member States to introduce national requirements for authorisation. This applies where it is necessary in order to guarantee compliance with a number of essential requirements. These include a number of non-economic considerations listed in Article 2 (as amended by Directive 2008/6/EC:

'Essential requirements: general non-economic reasons which can induce a Member State to impose conditions on the supply of postal services. These reasons are the confidentiality of correspondence, security of the network as regards the transport of dangerous goods, respect for the terms and conditions of employment, social security schemes, laid down by law, regulation or administrative provision and/or by collective agreement negotiated between national social partners, in accordance with Community and national law and, where justified, data protection, environmental protection and regional planning. Data protection may include personal data protection, the confidentiality of information transmitted or stored and protection of privacy.'

The list must be assumed to be exhaustive. Such requirements for authorisation can also cover postal services which are not covered by a universal service obligation.

discussed above and in the Commission's XXXI Report on Competition Policy, p. 32.

4.2.3. Access to networks

According to Article 11 of the Postal Services Directive, the European Parliament and the Council, acting on a proposal from the Commission, must adopt such harmonisation measures as are necessary to ensure that users and the universal service providers have access to the public postal network under conditions which are transparent and non-discriminatory.

In the postal sector, access to a network is joined together with the universal service obligation referred to below, which benefits both end users and other market participants. The universal service obligation, as an instrument for network access, is particularly relevant for overseas mail.

There is some uncertainty about how this right of network access is to be interpreted. From the perspective of consumer protection, network access can be understood as a legal right to be able to use the postal network, both as a sender and a receiver. However, such rights are to a large extent already protected by the universal service obligation. From a competition point of view, network access can be understood as the right of one undertaking to have access to the network of another undertaking. In this connection, one can envisage that a postal services undertaking will use the traditional postal service to provide for delivery in more thinly populated areas, where the duplication of the distribution network is associated with relatively high costs.[288] That part of the network could perhaps be considered as an essential facility. The lack of access to it could constitute an abuse of a dominant position under Article 82 of the EC Treaty. The Commission will use this provision against competitors, provided the necessary conditions are fulfilled.[289] These conditions are illustrated by the *Bronner* case, which is dealt with above in section 1.2.

4.2.4. Public service obligations

Article 3 of the Postal Services Directive defines the public service obligation of the Member States. In their respective territories, the Member States must ensure that users enjoy the right to a universal service involving the permanent provision of a postal service of specified quality at affordable prices for

288. *Damien Geradin & Christophe Humpe:* The Liberalisation of Postal Services in the European Union: An Analysis of Directive 97/67, in *Damien Geradin (ed.):* The Liberalisation of Postal Services in the European Union, 2002 p. 103 et seq.

289. Notice of 6 February 1998 from the Commission on the application of the competition rules to the postal sector and on the assessment of certain State measures relating to postal services, para. 2.8.

all users.[290] They must establish collections and deliveries in accordance with the needs of users, with at least one collection and one delivery each weekday (5 days a week), with deliveries to the residences of all natural and legal persons. This obligation must at least cover the collection and distribution of postal items up to two kilograms, and postal packages up to 10 kilograms. For postal packages from other Member States the delivery obligation is for packages up to 20 kilograms. In this connection it is a requirement that one or more national universal service providers is appointed.

The quality of the service is sought to be ensured by establishing standards. These quality standards include routing times and the regularity and reliability of services. For domestic services these standards are set by each Member State, and for cross-border services within the Union, they are set by the European Parliament (published as an annex to the Directive; see Article 16). For these standards, independent performance monitoring must be carried out and reports published at least once a year. More technical standards are left to the European Committee for Standardization (CEN) to prepare, on the basis of mandates given in accordance with Information Procedure Directive.[291]

4.2.4.1. Pricing regulations

Article 12 of the Postal Services Directives provides that a number of conditions must be applied to the pricing of services covered by the universal service obligation:

- prices must be affordable and must be such that all users have access to the services provided,
- prices must be geared to costs; Member States may decide that a uniform tariff should be applied throughout their national territory,[292]
- the application of a uniform tariff does not exclude the right of universal service providers to conclude individual agreements on prices with customers,[293]

290. This principle is similar to the public service obligation in the telecommunications sector.
291. Directive 83/189/EEC laying down a procedure for the provision of information in the field of technical standards and regulations. Directive 83/189/EEC has now been replaced by Directive 98/34/EC.
292. It is quite normal for the same postal charges to be payable regardless of the distance the postal item is transported, and regardless of the costs differences related to population density.

- tariffs must be transparent and non-discriminatory,
- whenever universal service providers apply special tariffs, for example for services for businesses, bulk mailers or consolidators of mail from different customers, they must apply the principles of transparency and non-discrimination with regard both to the tariffs and to the associated conditions. The tariffs must take account of the avoided costs, as compared to the standard service covering the complete range of features offered for the clearance, transport, sorting and delivery of individual postal items and, together with the associated conditions, must apply equally both as between different third parties and as between third parties and universal service providers supplying equivalent services. Any such tariffs must also be available to private customers who post under similar conditions, and
- cross-subsidisation of universal services outside the reserved sector out of revenues from services in the reserved sector is prohibited except to the extent to which it is shown to be strictly necessary to fulfil specific universal service obligations imposed in the competitive area.[294]

The Directive does not contain any provisions on the pricing of services which fall outside the scope of the universal service obligation. Subject to respect for the general provisions of Community law, the Member States can either let pricing be unregulated, or they can lay down national provisions.

The pricing provisions in Article 12 of the Postal Services Directive leave a number of points unclear. Thus, the term 'affordable' is not defined. In the Preface to the Notice of 6 February 1998 from the Commission on the application of the competition rules to the postal sector and on the assessment of certain State measures relating to postal services, there is a reference to 'prices everyone can afford'. This is also not very precise. It must be up to the Member States to interpret this requirement in the first instance.

For terminal dues (the remuneration of universal service providers for the distribution of incoming cross-border mail comprising postal items from another Member State or from a third country), the Member States are required to encourage their universal service providers to set terminal dues in relation to the costs of processing and delivering incoming cross-border mail in the receiving Member State, having regard for the quality of the service, and the

293. It must be assumed that such individually set charging rates (primarily for large customers) will not be an expression of discriminatory charges.
294. The last two indents were added by the amending Directive 2002/39/EC and were to be implemented by the Member States by 31 December 2002.

terminal dues must be transparent and non-discriminatory. These requirements seem to have been satisfied to some extent by the Reims II Agreement.[295]

The general competition provisions of the Treaty apply in parallel with these special provisions. Among other things, these have been applied to pricing agreements on cost allocation in connection with cross-border postal services.

A number of the traditional postal services of EU and EEA Member States have entered into the Reims II Agreement, which lays down the price which the postal service in the country of origin pays to the postal service in the destination country to deliver the post to the recipient (terminal dues). The Reims II Agreement linked terminal dues to the domestic postal charges in the receiving country and the quality of service provided by the postal service which delivers the post. According to the Agreement, the terminal dues were to be increased each year for four years until (unless they were reduced as a sanction for failure to live up to the required service level) they reached 80 % of the domestic charges in 2001. On a couple of points the Agreement was granted exemptions under Article 81(3) of the EC Treaty.[296]

Abuse of a dominant position is also a possibility in a sector which usually has a national operator with certain exclusive rights. On this topic, see this book's chapter on Article 102 TFEU.[297]

4.2.4.2. Exclusive rights

Until its amendment by Directive 2008/6/EC, Article 7 of the Postal Services Directive (1997/67/EC) gave the Member States the possibility of giving uni-

295. Renewed Notification of an Agreement on Terminal Dues (REIMS II) between Postal Operators (Case No IV/36.748 – *REIMS II*) (OJ 1998 C 53/3).
296. See the Commission's Decision of 15 September 1999 in Case IV/36.748. *Reims II* is discussed in *Damien Geradin & Christophe Humpe:* The Liberalisation of Postal Services in the European Union: An Analysis of Directive 97/67, in *Damien Geradin (ed.):* The Liberalisation of Postal Services in the European Union, 2002 p. 109 et seq. For a description of terminal dues and their development, see *James I. Campbell Jr.:* Evolution of Terminal Dues and Remail Provision in European and International Postal Law, in *Damien Geradin (ed.):* The Liberalisation of Postal Services in the European Union, 2002 p. 26 et seq.
297. For a specialised presentation of this topic, in relation to the postal sector, see *J. Derenne & C. Stockford:* Abuse of Market Power in Postal Services: Lessons from the Commission's Decisional Practice and Court of Justice, in *Damien Geradin (ed.):* The Liberalisation of Postal Services in the European Union, 2002; and *S. Baker & J. Dodgson:* Market Definition in Postal Services, in *Damien Geradin (ed.):* The Liberalisation of Postal Services in the European Union, 2002.

versal service providers exclusive rights to handle certain categories of letter post, if it was necessary for the maintenance of the universal service. After 2006, the possibility of awarding exclusive rights was restricted to a very limited part of the area served.

The idea of the exclusive right was that surpluses obtained from the area of the exclusive right could be used to cross-subsidise other commercially unprofitable parts of the universal service. An example of cross-subsidisation in the postal sector is the transfer of means from profitable distribution activities in urban areas to unprofitable post distribution in rural areas.[298]

The possibility of awarding exclusive rights has now been replaced by the possibility of paying compensation; see below.

The exercise of exclusive rights in relation to Article 86 of the EC Treaty was tried in Case C-320/91, *Corbeau*[299] and Joined Cases C-147/97 and C-148/97, *Deutsche Post*. These have given extended application to exclusive rights. For a criticism of this, see *Damien Geradin & Christophe Humpe*: The Liberalisation of Postal Services in the European Union: An Analysis of Directive 97/67, in *Damien Geradin* (ed.): The Liberalisation of Postal Services in the European Union, 2002 p. 97 et seq.

4.2.4.3. Financial compensation

An alternative to or supplement to allowing the holder of an exclusive right to cross-subsidise is the payment of financial compensation. Article 7 and 9 of the Postal Services Directive allows for the possibility of paying support from public means by establishing a compensation fund financed by all postal services providers or users. The condition for the use of such a compensation fund is that the universal service obligations represent an unfair financial burden for the universal service provider. The compensation fund can be used to finance the services covered by the universal service obligations in Article 3.

The fund is financed by making the grant of authorisations conditional on making contributions to the fund. The costs are thereby shared with undertakings which do not have universal service obligations. The compensation fund must be administered by a body independent of the beneficiary or beneficiaries. Likewise, the Member States must ensure that the principles of transpar-

298. This example is given in Notice of 6 February 1998 from the Commission on the application of the competition rules to the postal sector and on the assessment of certain State measures relating to postal services, para. 3.2.
299. In contrast to the GC's decision in Case T-175/99, *UPS*, in the *Corbeau* case the court did not decide on the possibility of the privileged undertaking acting on markets which were open to competition.

ency, non-discrimination and proportionality are respected. However, there do not seem to be any special control mechanisms established in this area.[300]

4.2.5. Public authorities

Article 22 of the Postal Services Directive contains a requirement for each Member State to designate one or more national regulatory authorities for the postal sector. The regulatory authorities must be legally separate from and operationally independent of the postal operators – an unbundling requirement.

The Member States must also ensure the existence of a competent body to supervise the accounting requirements set out in Article 14 of the Directive. The body must be independent of any universal service provider. There does not appear to be anything to prevent this body being the same as the national regulatory authority.

The Directive provides for a complaints procedure to be set up in connection with refusals to grant authorisation under Article 9, and in connection with users' complaints, particularly in cases involving loss, theft, damage or non-compliance with service quality standards; see Article 19.

Under Article 15 of the Postal Services Directive, the financial accounts of all universal service providers must be drawn up, submitted to audit by an independent auditor and published in accordance with the relevant Community and national legislation relating to commercial undertakings. The publication requirement also applies to the quality standards; see Article 18.

Finally, under Article 9 of the Postal Services Directive, a Member State must give reasons for refusing authorisation under Article 9.

300. See *Damien Geradin & Christophe Humpe:* The Liberalisation of Postal Services in the European Union: An Analysis of Directive 97/67, in *Damien Geradin (ed.):* The Liberalisation of Postal Services in the European Union, 2002 p. 102 et seq., which is critical of this in relation to an earlier formulation.

CHAPTER XII

Public procurement

Michael Steinicke

Bibliography: *Sue Arrowsmith: The Law of Public and Utilities Procurement, 2005; Christopher Bovis: EC Public Procurement: Case Law and Regulation, 2006; Simon Evers Hjelmborg, Peter Stig Jakobsen & Sune Troels Poulsen: Public Procurement Law – the EU directive on public contracts, 2006.*

1. Introduction

1.1. History and background

Public procurement in the EU is regulated at two levels. First, the private law contracts of public authorities are subject to the general rules of the Treaty on the functioning of the European Union, primarily the rules on freedom of movement. In a number of cases the Court of Justice of the European Union (CJ) has ruled on the compatibility of measures which national authorities have laid down in connection with public procurement. In this context it has been established that it is not compatible with the rules on freedom of movement for discriminatory conditions to be applied to the granting of public contracts. Thus, it is not permitted to require that the goods in question must be from some specific source, or that the workers employed in the provision of a service must be of a specific nationality.[1] The rules on freedom of movement apply regardless of whether the secondary rules on public procurement (i.e. the public procurement directives – see below) apply.[2]

1. Some of the leading cases on freedom of movement and public procurement are: Case C-243/89, *Commission* v *Denmark* (the bridge over the Great Belt – *Storebælt*), Case 45/87, *Commission* v *Ireland* (Dundalk), and Case C-113/89, *Rush Portugesa and others*.
2. This is seen in Case C-324/98, *Telaustria*, and Case C-59/00, *Vestergaard*.

Depending on the circumstances, the competition rules (in Articles 101 and 102 of the Treaty) can be applicable to public procurement.[3] However, these provisions do not apply to the conduct of public bodies which place orders (contracting authorities), as the rules are only binding on undertakings, and public authorities are not considered to be undertakings merely because they make purchases on the market; see Case C-205/03 P, *FENIN*. However, in connection with public procurement, the competition rules are applicable to relations between suppliers. This means that the rules cover the situation where an agreement is made between tenderers that one particular tenderer will win the contract (collusive tendering). Under such an agreement the other tenderers will often push up the prices for their tenders so the favoured tenderer will give the lowest bid, and this will often be enough to win the contract.

Already by the end of the 1960s it was clear that the Treaty rules on public procurement were not sufficient to ensure the removal of all the obstacles to a free market for such contracts. On this basis, from the beginning of the 1970s the regulation of public procurement by means of directives was initiated. The first directives took effect from 1970, but the first of the directives as we know them today (Directive 71/305/EEC concerning the co-ordination of procedures for the award of public works contracts) took effect from 1971. The next directive to see the light of day was Directive 77/62/EEC coordinating procedures for the award of public supply contracts, which was adopted in 1977. After that there was a gap of more than ten years before the regulation of public procurement was addressed again. This occurred at the end of the 1980s, when there was a focus both on the adoption of the first of two control directives, and on the first directive for entering into public procurement contracts for the provision of services.[4] At the beginning of the 1990s there was a considerable increase in regulatory activity. This was against the background of the White Paper on the Internal Market of 1985, which lead to the adoption of the Single European Act. This White Paper identified a number of areas which needed to be strengthened if the internal market was to function optimally – areas that included public procurement. This process culminated in 1992 and 1993 when most of the present regulation was laid down with the adoption of four substantive directives; the three classic directives (Directives 92/50/EEC, 93/36/EEC and 93/37/EEC on the coordination

3. See section 10 in this chapter.
4. Directive 89/665/EEC 989 on the coordination of the laws, regulations and administrative provisions relating to the application of review procedures to the award of public supply and public works contracts supplemented by Directive 92/13/EEC. These have been amended by Directive 2007/66/EC.

of procedures for the award of public service contracts, public supply contracts and public works contracts respectively) and Directive 93/38/EEC on the procurement procedures of entities operating in the water, energy, transport and telecommunications sectors – the utilities procurement Directive. Towards the end of the 1990s minor amendments were made to these four directives by Directive 97/52/EC (amending the classic directives) and Directive 98/4/EC (amending the utilities procurement Directive).

In 1996 the Commission published a Green Paper – Public Procurement in the European Union: Exploring the way forward,[5] which addressed a number of problems related to public procurement. The Green Paper was followed by a further Communication from the Commission.[6] This follow-up document presented a number of initiatives for changing the existing regulation. These initiatives were in part prompted by the responses to the Green Paper.

The first proposals for new directives governing public procurement were presented in the Proposal for a Directive on the coordination of procedures for the award of public supply contracts, public service contracts and public works contracts (COM(2000) 275 final) and the Proposal for a Directive coordinating the procurement procedures of entities operating in the water, energy and transport sectors (COM(2000) 276 final); these were adopted as Directive 2004/17/EC coordinating the procurement procedures of entities operating in the water, energy, transport and postal services sectors, and Directive 2004/18/EC on the coordination of procedures for the award of public works contracts, public supply contracts and public service contracts respectively. To a large extent the core of the procurement rules remains the same. However, some changes have occurred. The biggest changes included greater focus on electronic means of communication, the introduction of new forms of tendering, the introduction of better possibilities for taking account of non-economic factors, the introduction of rules on framework agreements, and the consolidation of the three classic directives as one directive, the structuring of the directive to match the chronology of the procedure.

The development of Union procurement law took a further step forward with the Green Paper on the modernisation of EU public procurement policy – Towards a more efficient European Procurement Market (COM(2011) 15 final). Here the focus was on improving the framework for innovation, improving the business environment, encouraging wider use of green public procurement and generally improving the existing procurement rules. In De-

5. COM(96) 583 final.
6. COM(98) 143 final.

cember 2011 the work on the Green Paper resulted in a draft for a new Public Sector Directive (COM(2011) 896 final) and a new Utilities Directive (COM(2001) 895 final). It is intended that the new directives should be adopted in the course of 2012.[7]

1.2. The aim

The aim of the public procurement directives is to ensure that undertakings in the internal market have the possibility of participating in competition for the award of public contracts and have the opportunity of having public contracts awarded to them. This is shown in, among other things, Case C-243/89, *Commission* v *Denmark* (the bridge over the Great Belt – *Storebælt*), in which regard for competition was seen as being the basis for the principle of equal treatment which, according to the CJ, exists in public procurement law and is the fundamental principle in this field of law. The shaping of the public procurement directives was and is intended to give the contracting authority the possibility of making advantageous agreements. The competitive situation which arises from inviting offers should lead to lower priced bids, which is naturally to the advantage of purchasers. However, the benefit which the purchasers are expected to obtain is only secondary to the primary purpose of the directives, which is to open the market for public procurement to interested undertakings within the EU.

The means by which this goal is achieved is a set of rules which are intended to remove the protectionism which it is assumed characterised the making of public procurement contracts prior to the establishment of the internal market. In the view of the European institutions, contracting authorities have had a tendency to choose tenderers from their own area/Member State when allocating public contracts. This tendency has meant that it has been difficult for undertakings from other Member States to gain access to the markets for public supplies. On this basis the European institutions have adopted a set of rules to ensure, on the one hand that there is no discrimination between undertakings, and on the other hand to achieve a certain measure of transparency in connection with the making of public contracts.

7. In addition to the procurement rules referred to there are special directives for defence procurement; see Directive 2009/81/EC on the coordination of procedures for the award of certain works contracts, supply contracts and service contracts by contracting authorities or entities in the fields of defence and security. See also the Proposal, in December 2011, for a Directive on the award of concession contracts (COM(2011) 0897 final).

1.3. Description of the tendering procedure

Public procurement can take many different forms, depending on which type of procurement procedure is chosen, how the selection of undertakings is arranged, the criteria chosen for the award of a contract etc. Regardless of these differences, it is possible to give a basic description of what generally characterises public procurement procedures.

The process starts with the publication of a contract notice, which has the aim of informing the market about the task for which offers of supply are sought. The contract notice must give the necessary information to enable potential tenderers to get an impression of the task. Following this contract notice, interested undertakings must be given further information about the tendering procedure and the contract for which tenders are sought. This information can be given at different points in the procedure. The most important source of this information is the tender documentation which is given to the undertakings or which is made fully available to them on a website. The process consists of assessing the suitability of undertakings for taking on the task in question, an assessment of the offers made, and ends with the award of the contract to the undertaking which has submitted the best offer.

In the following, there is a more detailed description of the individual elements of the tendering procedure.

2. The obligation to invite offers

There is no general obligation of public authorities to offer their procurements to public competition. Public authorities decide for themselves whether to invite tenders for carrying out a task, or whether to carry it out themselves. However, under certain conditions, public bodies have an obligation to put a task out to tender.

2.1. Exhouse contracting

The obligation to submit procurements to public competition depends first of all on whether there is a mutual contract. The public procurement directives only regulate agreements between two separate entities, as it is not possible to enter into an agreement with oneself. From this comes the in-house rule, whereby only purchases which are made outside the contracting authority are subject to the rules of public procurement. The principle rule is that purchases which are made within the same legal entity are not subject to the rules of public procurement. However, there can be situations where an entity is of such a size, with a number of divisions that are sufficiently separate from each other, so as to be considered different entities for the purposes of the public procurement directives, so that one division's purchases from another division can be considered to be third party purchases. There can also be exceptions to the principle that purchases made outside the legal entity are subject to the rules of public procurement. In special cases the CJ has held that in some situations two different legal entities can be considered as being one. The conditions for this are that the contracting authority has a significant degree of control over the selling entity, and that most of the business of the selling entity is carried on together with the contracting authority.[8]

Case C-107/98, *Teckal*, concerned the award of a contract for the provision of heating services without following public procurement procedures. The award was made to an independent legal person, but one which was controlled by the local government authority which made the award. The CJ ruled that, in principle, when a public entity makes a purchase from another legal person there is a third party purchase. However, the position can be different if 'the local authority exercises over the person concerned a control which is similar to that which it exercises over its own departments and, at the same time, that person carries out the essential part of its activities with the controlling local authority or authorities'.[9] However, this extension of the rule was subsequently limited so that the in-house rule only applies to bodies which are wholly publicly owned; see Case C-26/03, *Stadt Halle*. Thus where an undertaking is partly privately owned, the *Teckal* rule does not apply.

In a surprising decision made in the summer of 2009, the CJ ruled that, subject to certain conditions, an agreement between various public entities (non-institutionalised horizontal cooperation) could be entered into without carrying out a procurement procedure. It is not entirely clear what these conditions are, as the CJ referred to a number of factors in its reasoning, without specifically identifying which of them were decisive to the decision in the case. It must be assumed that, if an agreement is entered into without any form of participation by a private undertaking, and as long as the purpose of the agreement does not go further than carrying out a task for consideration in pursuit of the public interest, it will be possible to enter into an agreement without carrying out a procurement procedure.[10]

2.2. Threshold values

In addition to the condition that there must be a third party purchase, there is also no obligation to comply with the public procurement rules unless the expected value of the contract exceeds the financial limits laid down in connection with the directives – the threshold values. These values are laid down for

8. This practice has been much debated, as it can be said to stretch the concept of in-house purchasing quite far.
9. Case C-107/98, *Teckal,* para. 50.
10. Case C-480/06, *Commission* v *Germany.* See also Commission Staff Working Paper concerning the application of EU public procurement law to relations between contracting authorities ('public-public cooperation') (SEC(2011) 1169 final).

the different kinds of purchase (i.e. services, goods and public works contracts) and are laid down by the Commission for two years at a time and can be found on the website of the European Commission.[11] The threshold values relate to the expected value of the contract, exclusive of VAT. For public works contracts the threshold is around EUR 5.0 million, while it is a somewhat lower for purchases of goods and services at EUR 400,000. These are the thresholds for local government authorities. For state purchases the thresholds are lower.

On the basis of these thresholds it could be advantageous for a contracting authority to have a contract categorised as a public works contract, rather than contract for goods or services. The contracting authority must make a genuine valuation of the expected value of the proposed purchase. It is naturally contrary to the rules for the contracting authority deliberately to make an incorrect valuation (setting the value of the contract below the threshold) with a view to avoiding the use of the public procurement procedure. Nor can the contracting authority satisfy the requirements by making a rough estimate of the value of the contract; it is required to demonstrate sufficient thoroughness in assessing the expected value of the contract.

One popular method for keeping the value of a purchase below the threshold values is to split up the contract so as to produce several contracts, each of a lower value. With a view to preventing such an avoidance of the procurement obligations, a rule in the directives provides that, if there is such a splitting up of the contract, the contract values must be added together so as to determine whether the purchase is subject to the procurement rules.[12] Even though the aim of the provision is in accordance with the idea behind the procurement directives, it can be difficult to determine which contacts should be added together. Where several identical contracts are entered into at the same time, there will be an assumption that this is to avoid the procurement rules. However, there can be other situations where the connection between the contracts is not so obvious. In assessing whether contracts have been artificially divided, account must be taken of the content of the contracts, their timing, and other relevant circumstances.

After the entry into force of the WTO's procurement rules[13] (Agreement on Government Procurement – GPA),[14] the threshold values are expressed in Special Drawing Rights (SDRs) in addition to the euro and national curren-

11. The current rules apply for the period 1.1.2012 to 31.12.2013.
12. See Article 9(3) of Directive 2004/18/EC.
13. From 1 January 1996,
14. On the GPA, see section 12 below.

cies. This is because of the harmonisation of the European threshold values with the international values in the GPA. Thus the threshold values relate both to purchases under the EU regime and under the WTO regime.

3. Contracting authorities

The entities that are covered by the procurement directives, the contracting authorities, are defined in Article 2(1)(a) of Directive 2004/17/EC and Article 1(9) of Directive 2004/18/EC. The Directives are binding on public authorities, including state, regional or local authorities, as well as on bodies governed by public law and associations of such authorities.

The term *public authorities* naturally covers state and regional/local administrative bodies. In addition to true administrative authorities, other entities which are linked to the public sector are covered. The assessment of this is based on a functional interpretation; see Case 31/87, *Beentjes*.

Bodies governed by public law are entities that 1) meet a need of the general public in a non-commercial capacity, 2) are independent legal persons, and 3) are controlled in some form or other by a public authority or some other legal person governed by public law. These conditions are cumulative, i.e. they must all be fulfilled in order for an entity to be categorised as a body governed by public law. The concept is one that has frequently been considered by the CJ.[15]

For example, the condition of meeting the needs of the general public has been found to be fulfilled where the authority in question is responsible for forestry management, refuse collection, running a university, printing services, environmental management, running a housing association, conducting the business of an undertaker, as well as certain forms of trading in real property and property management. Furthermore, arranging trade fairs has been accepted as meeting the needs of the general public; see Joined Cases C-223/99 and C-260/99, *Agorá*. In this case the activity was carried on in such a way that it was found to meet the needs of the general public but in a commercial area, so the undertaking fell outside the definition of a public law body. Among other things, the CJ emphasised that the undertaking was administered according to the criteria of performance, efficiency and cost-effectiveness. It also found that the undertaking operated in a competitive en-

15. See e.g. Case C-360/96, *Arnhem,* Case C-44/96, *Mannesmann Anlagebau,* Case C-306/97, *Connemara Machine Turf,* Case C-380/98, *Cambridge University,* Joined Cases C-223/99 and C-260/99, *Agorá,* Case C-237/99, *Commission* v *France,* Case C-373/00, *Adolf Truly,* and Case C-393/06, *Ing. Aigner.*

vironment. However, this was not decisive in itself but, together with the way in which the activities were carried on, the CJ found that there was an undertaking of a commercial character.

It will often not be difficult to determine whether an entity is a legal person. An undertaking will often be organised as one of the known forms of corporation. However, there can be cases where it is not obvious whether an entity is a legal person. In these cases the CJ must use a concrete evaluation to establish whether the undertaking is a legal person, presumably by seeing whether the entity has legal capacity etc. To determine whether there is a dominant influence over the body in question, and in particular over its purchasing, the procurement directives lay down three different criteria, of which one must be fulfilled. First, there can be a dominant influence by a contracting authority if the authority, directly or indirectly, holds the majority of the undertaking's subscribed capital, or controls the majority of the votes attached to shares issued by the undertaking, or can appoint more than half of the undertaking's administrative, management or supervisory body.

3.1. Specific points on the Directive 2004/17/EC

The bodies referred to above are found in Directive 2004/17/EC coordinating the procurement procedures of entities operating in the water, energy, transport and postal services sectors and by Directive 2004/18/EC on the coordination of procedures for the award of public works contracts, public supply contracts and public service contracts. In addition to these bodies there are further groups of private entities that are bound by Directive 2004/17/EC. The reason for this expansion of the scope of the Directive is that there are differences between the different Member States (possibly by chance) as to whether utilities undertakings are organised as public or private undertakings.

For private undertakings it is not so important which links they have to public bodies (which is important under Directive 2004/18/EC), but rather which activities they undertake. Private undertakings will be covered by the purchasing procedures in the Directive 2004/17/EC if they operate in the water, energy, transport and postal services sectors.[16]

16. In addition, there are stricter requirements in relation to private utilities undertakings, if these have been granted certain rights in connection with their activities, e.g. special or exclusive rights.

4. Preparation of the contract notice

4.1. General

A number of steps must be taken before a contract notice is issued, including making a description of what is to be purchased, so that undertakings which may be interested in tendering can participate in the competition for the order and so the competing undertakings have a clear idea about the procurement procedures chosen and thus understand the basic principles of the competition.

As part of the preparations it is often necessary to use the services of a technical adviser, as the contracting authority does not always have the necessary specialist knowledge to prepare the contract notice on their own. In this connection, there can be a problem if the technical adviser then wants to take part in the competition for the order. This is a problem, as the adviser can have obtained a competitive advantage, and be in a stronger competitive situation than other tenderers. The possibility for using technical advisers is dealt with in more detail below, in the section on the principle of equal treatment.

4.2. Specification of the object of the contract

The specification of the object of the contract is made on the one hand, by categorising the nature of the product required, and on the other hand by giving a detailed description of what is wanted.

The first specification is made with reference to various standard nomenclatures. Those primarily used are the CPV nomenclature and the CPC nomenclature,[17] which classify different kinds of goods and services by number.

> In Case C-76/97, *Walter Tögel*, the CJ held that the CPV is intended only to be used for drawing up notices and other communications published in connection with public tendering procedures. Thus, the designations of services listed in Annex I A, and Annex I B (to Directive 92/50/EC) must be made on the basis of the CPC nomenclature; see paragraphs 35-37 of the *Tögel* case. Article 1(14) of Directive 2004/18/EC states that, in the event of differences between the CPV nomenclatures and CPC nomenclatures, the CPC nomenclature takes precedence.

17. CPV stands for Common Procurement Vocabulary. CPC is the Central Product Classification of the United Nations.

The second specification is a detailed description of what goods or services are required. The object of a contract can be described in two different ways: either by the contracting authority's function-based description of the goods or services required, or by reference to technical specifications, including standards. The first possibility was introduced in Directive 2004/18/EC, on the basis that there had been a lack of a possibility to draw up a specification other than by reference to standards etc. As for the second possibility (reference to technical specifications), the Directive establishes a hierarchy for which technical specifications are to be used, and when. This hierarchy means that, where possible, European or international technical specifications are to be used. If no European specifications exist, then national technical specifications can be used, as long as these give a better description. If it is not possible to find national standards, then other national specifications can be used.

In recent years the possibility of focusing on function when describing a task has led to increased attention to the concept of functional requirements. These are not defined in the procurement rules, but the Danish *Udbudsrådet* (Procurement Council) has stated that in such procurements (functional procurements) the contracting authority does not give a detailed description in advance of how the task is to be performed, but lays down a number of functional requirements (goals) instead.[18] Thus it is not the activities to be carried out during the contractual period that are described, but the desired outcome. This is naturally reflected in the way in which the task is specified and the functional, goal-oriented elements will predominate in the contract.

In principle, it is not permitted to describe the object of a contract by reference to a trade mark or the specific manufacturer of a product. This is because reference to a specific trade mark or manufacturer will give an advantage to the undertaking that produces the product in question, as the reference product can easily be understood as being the product required. Other products will thus start with a competitive handicap in relation to the reference product. On the other hand, it can be an obvious and convenient way for a purchaser to describe a task by referring to a product which is well known on the market and which has a number of the characteristics which the purchaser wants. On this ground it is sometimes possible to use specific products or trade marks as a reference point. This is possible where a sufficiently precise and intelligible description of the subject-matter of the contract is not otherwise possible. A condition for the use of a trade mark as a reference

18. See para. 2.1 of Udbudsrådet's analysis of functional procurements, 9 November 2010.

point is that it must be accompanied by the words 'or equivalent'. This is to indicate that the product named merely represents the desired characteristics of the subject-matter of the contract, and that it is not necessarily the reference product itself that is required, but merely a product which has the same characteristics.

> The CJ has considered this provision in a few cases. In Case 45/87, *Commission* v *Ireland (Dundalk)*, an Irish local government authority had made a purchase in connection with the improvement of the water supply installations. In describing the installations, and specifying certain pipes, a reference had been made to a special Irish standard. In its judgment, the CJ held that the public procurement directives did not apply, but that Article 34 of the Treaty did.[19] The CJ held, with general applicability to all provisions on technical specifications, that a contracting authority may not reject an offer merely because it does not formally comply with the stated specification, but it is obliged to examine whether the product offered can in fact comply with the specifications. Case C-353/93, *Commission* v *Netherlands (UNIX)*, concerned the purchase of a meteorological station, where the contracting authority had described the operating system by reference to the trade mark UNIX. The contracting authority had not added 'or equivalent' after the reference, which in itself meant that the reference was in breach of the procurement rules. The CJ did not consider in more detail whether the requirements of necessity or adequacy were fulfilled in the case in question, but as there was apparently a possibility of describing the operating system objectively, the conditions for using the 'or equivalent' provision would not have been fulfilled. It is not enough that an objective description would have led to greater costs for the contracting authority than a reference to a product that was well known on the market. This decision was followed in Case C-328/96, *Commission* v *Austria (UNIX II)* and in Case C-59/00, *Vestergaard*.

The use of standards has the clearly positive aspect that it is possible to find objective references that are known by the whole market. However, there are also disadvantages connected with the use of technical specifications. First, the whole process of drawing up standards requires detailed work and takes a

19. The procurement took place before the current public procurement directives were adopted, and as water supply was excluded from the directive on public works procurement, the purchase fell outside the scope of the public procurement directives.

long time.[20] This means that when a standard is finally adopted it may not represent the latest technological developments in the area in question.[21]

Second, by referring in particular to trade marks and suchlike, it is not clear to the interested undertakings precisely which characteristics are decisive for the subject-matter of the contract. Standards are often formulated as a description of the characteristics of the products in question. In such a case it is primarily the most important qualities of the product which characterise the standard. With references to trade marks and suchlike, there is not only a reference to the product's characteristics, but also to its design, composition etc. This means that where there is merely a reference to a trade mark, it is not always clear which specific characteristics of the reference product are required for the subject-matter of the contract. It will often be assumed that the functional characteristics must be decisive for the reference and must be equally decisive for whether a product offered is regarded as having the desired characteristics.

In US public procurement law there is a requirement that a contracting authority that uses reference products (i.e. trade marks etc.) must clearly state which specific characteristics of the reference product it requires in the subject-matter of the contract. If there is not a reference to specific characteristics, the contracting authority cannot refuse offered products by reference to the fact that they do not meet these specific requirements if the products offered are in other respects in accordance with the reference product. It is possible that the CJ will apply what can be called the *relevance criterion* to establish which characteristics of a reference product must be understood as being decisive. Under this criterion it would be decisive whether the desired qualities were relevant to the subject-matter of the contract. For example, it would have been difficult to argue, in comparing the products offered and the Irish standard for water pipes which was the point in dispute in the *Dundalk* case referred to above, that the design of the pipes was decisive for whether the products were regarded as being in accordance with the reference product.

4.3. Publication

A requirement for establishing a competitive bidding procedure is that undertakings on the market should have the possibility, in one way or another, of being made aware that tenders are being invited. This is done by publishing a contract notice in the Official Journal of the European Union, S series. There

20. For further on standards and their formation, see *Christian Joerges, Karl-Heinz Ladeur & Ellen Voss (eds.):* Integrating Scientific Expertise into Regulatory Decision-Making.
21. This has been decisive for the fact that rules on technical specifications are not included in the Danish Law on public procurement, in spite of this law's wide-ranging approximation to the public procurement directives.

are different kinds of notices, of which the notice at the commencement of the procurement procedure is one. There are special requirements for the framing of all forms of notices in the Official Journal.[22]

Publication in the Official Journal is only a requirement if the threshold values for the different kinds of contracts are exceeded.

In addition to publication in the Official Journal, there is a possibility of publishing in Tenders Electronic Daily (TED) which is an electronic medium which contains the same information and has the same function as series S of the Official Journal. Contracting authorities are permitted to publish contract notices in other national and international media. However, such advertising must first be made after the notice required by the directives has been sent to the Publications Office for the Official Journal, and the national advertisement may not contain information which is not given in the notice published in the Official Journal.

4.3.1. Requirements for publication

The public procurement directives contain a number of specific requirements for the publication of contract notices which must be communicated as part of the procurement process. Thus, for each type of procurement there are different requirements as to the content of the contract notice in the Official Journal. In addition to the publication of contract notices, the contracting authority must also publish a *prior information notice*. A prior information notice is a notice about proposed purchases for the forthcoming year.[23]

In addition to these requirements at the start of the procurement procedure, there are also requirements for publication when the procurement procedure is completed. The form of publication for this is also determined by the forms in annexes to the directives.

4.4. Determination of the type of task

Which type of task is involved is decisive for the application of the public procurement directives. Public contracts are divided into three categories: public supply contracts, public service contracts and public works contracts. This division is relevant in two respects. First, there are different threshold values for the different types of tasks; see above. Second, to some extent different rules apply to the different tasks.

22. See Regulation (EC) No 1564/2005 establishing standard forms for the publication of notices in the framework of public procurement procedures.
23. See Article 38 of Directive 2004/18/EC.

The assessment of whether a contract concerns a public service or a public construction work is based on the nature of the task in question. Thus it must be considered whether what is being bought is a service or building or construction work. The distinction is usually not difficult, as most services are not confusable with building or construction work. For example, the collection of rubbish for a local government authority or providing public transport for a local government authority has no points of similarity with construction work. On the other hand, in a few cases there can be doubt about whether a task constitutes building renovation (a service) or building and construction work. In these cases help is presumably obtainable from the CPC nomenclature, which has a detailed list of what constitutes a service and what constitutes building and construction work. Moreover, in Annex I to Directive 2004/18/EC there is a list of main groups of building and construction tasks. Where there is a conflict between two types of tasks, the categorisation will be made in favour of a task being a building and construction task. This is on the basis of the provision in Article 1(2)(d) of the Directive, according to which a task will be considered to be a service if it is not regarded as either a contract for the supply of goods or a public works contract.

The distinction between public supply contracts, public service contracts and public works contracts seldom causes problems.

> There is an example in Case C-331/92, *Casino*. The contract involved the installation of a casino and certain building and construction services. However, the greater part of the value of the contract concerned the management of the casino, so the contract was not considered a public works contract. Another example is the distinction between goods and services. Buying standard software for computers is considered to be a purchase of goods, whereas buying specially tailor-made software is considered to be a purchase of services.

Another problem which often arises is the question of how mixed contracts should be treated. A mixed contract can be a contract which concerns both the provision of goods and services. An example of a mixed contract can be one for the purchase of computers and computer training. For such contracts it is clearly important to determine how the contract is to be classified, as this is relevant for which rules will apply to the contract notice. The main rule is that the financial value of each task should be assessed (i.e. the value of the goods bought and the value of the services bought), and the category of task which represents the greater financial value in the contract determines which rules apply. If the value of the goods bought in a mixed contract constitutes

EUR 2 million, while the value of the services constitutes EUR 1 million, the contract is considered to be a public supply contract, and it must thus be dealt with according to the rules for this in Directive 2004/18/EC.

In a couple of cases the CJ has had to rule on a related question. In these cases the situation was not whether a contract was for goods or services, but whether an agreement concerned participation in a company or a purchase agreement, since the agreements included elements of both aspects. If an agreement is a purchase agreement, then the procurement directives should apply. The CJ ruled that in such cases the starting point must be the same considerations as apply to contracts both for purchases of goods and purchases of services. The CJ stated that if an agreement (dealing both with the formation of a company and purchases of goods) constitutes an indivisible whole, the nature of the contract is to be determined by looking at the central subject-matter of the agreement. In Joined Cases C-145 og 149/08, *Hotel Club Loutraki*, the CJ found that there was effectively an agreement for participation in a company, whereas in Case C-215/09, *Mehiläinen Oy*, the contract was not an indivisible whole, and the part of the contract which concerned purchases whose value exceeded the threshold should be put out to tender in accordance with the requirements of the procurement directives.

If an undertaking is a supplier or service provider for the purposes of Directive 2004/17/EC coordinating the procurement procedures of entities operating in the water, energy, transport and postal services sectors, the undertaking will be covered by the rules of the Directive, and third party contracts will thus be subject to the rules on public procurement. Such service providers are concerned with energy and water supply, and postal services and transport.

The distinction between the different kinds of contracts is naturally relevant within the scope of Directive 2004/17/EC, in the same way as under Directive 2004/18/EC. In order to maintain the logic of having two separate directives, there must be differences between their provisions. Among other things, these differences consist of differences in the subjects to which the rules apply, differences in the right to use tendering with negotiation with prior publication, and other matters. The special circumstances which apply under Directive 2004/17/EC are dealt with in this chapter where the individual themes in question are discussed.

4.5. Documentation for contract notices

There are certain requirements for the contents of the documents which form the basis of the contract notice. First there is a requirement that the documentation (i.e. the materials which give a more detailed description of the subject matter of the contract) must be sufficiently detailed to enable interested parties to prepare an offer that can satisfy the conditions of the contracting authority. Second, the offer must also be clear and comprehensible, and it must be in accordance with the contract notice.

The liability for any lack of clarity in the contract notice or in offers naturally rests with the party which has prepared the material in question. If the contracting authority's framing of the contract notice is inadequate on one or more points, it will not be to the disadvantage of the tenderer if, as a result of this, the tenderer has to establish its own assumptions or correct the wrong information given by the contracting authority.

The possibility of providing supplementary information or for correcting the documentation is reviewed below in the section on making the award of the contract and the section on the prohibition of negotiation.

4.6. Electronic contract notices

Until the adoption of the latest public procurement rules there was insufficient regulation and a lack of clarity on the use of electronic means of communication. Previously electronic communication could be used to some extent, but the rules were not properly adapted to the technical reality.

Under Article 42(1) of Directive 2004/18/EC, it is possible to communicate by mail, by fax, by electronic means and even in some cases by telephone. For electronic communications there are some special requirements, including requirements as to information, and requirements that the tools for communicating electronically must be non-discriminatory, generally available and interoperable with information and communication technology products in general use; see Article 42(4) and (5) of the Directive.

In addition to the general rules for electronic communication, Directive 2004/18/EC (and Directive 2004/17/EC) contains rules on public procurement procedures that can be conducted entirely electronically. First, Article 33 of Directive 2004/18/EC describes a procedure for dynamic purchasing systems. Briefly, this procedure involves establishing a list of undertakings with a standing indicative tendering procedure, and when the contracting authority makes a specific purchase it initiates a mini-tender among the participants on the list. Second, contracting authorities can conclude a tendering competition by means of a fully electronic reverse auction where the tenderers can compete each other on price and other elements; see Article 54.

Finally, Article 38(5) and (6) allows for the possibility of reducing the time limits in connection with tendering by the use of electronic communication.

4.7. Deadlines

The public procurement directives lay down deadlines for submitting offers, submitting application for admission to the procurement procedure etc. The minimum time limit for receipt of requests to participate in a procurement procedure is 37 days from the date on which the contract notice is published. In the case of restricted procedures, the minimum time limit for the receipt of tenders is 40 days from the date on which the invitation is published. In the case of open procedures, the minimum time limit for the receipt of tenders is 52 days from the date on which the contract notice is published. In special situations where a rapid process can be used in connection with restricted procedures and negotiated procedures, the deadlines can be reduced to 15 days for the receipt of requests to participate,[24] and 10 days for the submission of a tender.

If the contracting authority has given a prior information notice, the deadlines for submitting offers and for requesting admission to participate in a procurement procedure can be shortened. In connection with open tendering procedures, restricted procedures and negotiated procedures, the deadline can be reduced to 36 days.

5. Types of contract

It is possible to enter into different types of contract. The traditional contracts are sales contracts in which the product in question, the quantity and the price are determined in advance. However, it is also possible to enter into contracts in which the final quantity is not predetermined – framework contracts. In addition to this it is also possible to make concession contracts. A concession contract is an agreement which has the same characteristics as traditional contracts, but where the payment consists of the right to carry on a particular activity, possibly in conjunction with paying for the right.

In addition to contracts for outright sales, the Directive also covers contracts for the leasing of goods.

5.1. Framework agreements

The procurement directives allow for the possibility of entering into framework agreements; see Article 32 of Directive 2004/18/EC. Even though it had been possible to use framework agreements for several decades, it was first in

24. The deadline of 15 days can be reduced to 10 days if the notice is sent in compliance with specific electronic formats; see Article 38(8) of Directive 2004/18/EC.

Directive 2004/18/EC that there have been express rules on this. A framework agreement is a contract like an ordinary sales contract, except that the quantity to be sold is not fixed. Thus, in the same way as with ordinary contracts, a framework agreement lays down all the circumstances which are considered necessary for the purchase, except the quantity required. Framework agreements are entered into in situations where, over a given period (for up to 4 years), a contracting authority *may* need to make purchases, or where it is certain that purchases will be made but where the quantity cannot be determined in advance. To the extent that the contracting authority wishes to make purchases of the product in question during the lifetime of the agreement, this purchase will be made in accordance with the conditions of the framework agreement, just as in the case of a traditional sales contract. If the contracting authority does not wish to make a purchase, for example if it happens that there is not the need which the contracting authority expected, the contracting authority can merely refrain from using the agreement. The contracting authority cannot decide to make a purchase from another supplier during the lifetime of the agreement, but if the need arises, it must make purchases from the designated undertaking. There are two types of framework agreement; see Article 32. First, there are agreements with a single economic operator. The use of such agreements is relatively unproblematic and follows the rules described above. Second, it is possible to enter into parallel framework agreements, where an agreement is entered into with three or more economic operators. Where this model is used the criteria for awarding the specific contract must be established in the framework agreement. There are two possible ways of awarding specific contracts: either by application of the terms laid down in the framework agreement without reopening competition, or after having established a competition between the suppliers who are parties to the framework agreement.

In addition to standing agreements in the form of framework agreements, there are also option agreements. Option agreements differ from framework agreements by the fact that option agreements are linked to a traditional main agreement for supply or provision, where the contracting authority has the option or right to increase the purchased quantity. Framework agreements usually stand alone.

5.2. Concession contracts

A concession contract is an agreement by which the payment for supply consists either of the right to provide the goods or services in question, or this right is combined with some payment. The Directive 2004/18/EC contains provisions on concession contracts for services and for building and construction works. It is stated in Article 17 that the Directive does not apply to public service contracts. In contrast, public works contracts are covered.[25]

Only few of the provisions of the Directive apply to concession contracts for public works. Thus, it is not required to issue contract notices, but the contracting authority may merely announce that a contract has been entered into. In certain situations there are further requirements as to the process for making contracts. First, the contracting authority may require the concessionaire to award contracts for up to 30 % of the total value of the work for which the concession contract is to be awarded, to third parties, and second, a contract notice is required if the concessionaire is a contracting authority.

Even though Directive 2004/18/EC does not contain any comprehensive rules on concession contracts, this does not mean that there is no regulation of concession contracts. Such contracts are subject to the Treaty rules (such as the rules on freedom of movement) and the general principles of Union law. This means that contracting authorities have a general obligation to comply with the principles of equal treatment and transparency. Over the years the CJ has developed a comprehensive body of case law on this, some of which is referred to in Communication from the Commission on Public-Private Partnerships and Community Law on Public Procurement and Concessions (COM(2005) 569 final).[26]

6. Forms of public procurement procedures

Contracting authorities have the possibility of using different kinds of public procurement procedures. *Open procedures* and *restricted procedures* are available to all contracting authorities under both Directive 2004/17/EC and Directive 2004/18/EC. In contrast to this, it is only exceptionally possible to use *negotiated procedures* under Directive 2004/18/EC. Directive 2004/17/EC gives wider scope for the use of negotiated procedures. It is also possible to use design contests, dynamic purchasing systems, competitive dialogue and electronic auctions. The use of these procedures is also subject to conditions.

The open procedure is characterised as being a procedure whereby any interested economic operator may submit a tender, while the restricted proce-

25. Articles 56-65 of Directive 2004/18/EC.
26. In December 2011 the Commission published a Proposal for a Directive on the award of concession contracts (COM (2011) 897 final).

dure is defined as a procedure in which only those economic operators invited by the contracting authority may submit a tender.[27]

Negotiated procedures are procedures whereby the contracting authorities consult the economic operators of their choice and negotiate the terms of the contract with one or more of these.[28] This procedure has two variants. First, there is the negotiated procedure *with* prior publication, and second there is the negotiated procedure *without* prior publication. The negotiated procedure with prior publication can be freely used for purchases made under Directive 2004/17/EC, but can only exceptionally be used under Directive 2004/18/EC. The occasions where an exception may apply are discussed below in the section on exceptions.

According to the directives, a design contest is a procedure which is only used in special situations.[29] Design contests are defined as procedures which enable a contracting authority to acquire, mainly in the fields of town and country planning, architecture and engineering, or data processing, a plan or design selected by a jury after being put out to competition.[30] Design contests are often used in connection with architectural designs. Several of the characteristics for other procurement procedures do not apply to design contests. For example, design contests are not determined by the traditional award criteria, which concern the most financially advantageous tender or the lowest price (on these, see the next section). In principle there is no restriction on the reasons for choosing a winning design in such a contest. However, the criteria for judgement must be made clear in the published invitation to take part in the contest. One of the special characteristics for design contests is that there are rules governing the composition of the jury. A jury must be composed of natural persons who are independent of the participants in the contest. If a particular professional qualification is required for participants in a contest (for example qualifications as an engineer), then at least a third of the members of the jury must have that qualification or an equivalent qualification.

Electronic auctions are not strictly speaking a tendering procedure, but really a method for concluding a procedure. The procedure is as follows: the procedure is implemented as normal as an open procedure or a restricted procedure, and in some cases as a negotiated procedure, or a mini-tender proce-

27. Article 1(11)(a) and (b) of Directive 2004/18/EC.
28. Article 1(11)(d) of Directive 2004/18/EC.
29. See Articles 60-66 of Directive 2004/17/EC and Articles 66-74 of Directive 2004/18/EC.
30. See Article 1(10) of Directive 2004/17/EC and Article 1(11)(e) of Directive 2004/18/EC.

dure with dynamic purchasing systems and framework agreements, until the point where the award of a contract is made. Instead of making the award, an electronic auction is initiated in which the participating tenderers have the possibility of underbidding each other on price, and perhaps on other factors which it is suitable to submit to auction.

Dynamic purchasing system is the term used for a procedure where, via a tendering process, a contracting authority lists a number of undertakings which have submitted indicative tenders. If a contracting authority wants to make a specific purchase, the contract is entered into after a tendering process involving the undertakings on that list.

Another procurement procedure which was introduced by Directive 2004/18/EC, but which is very similar to a procedure which has been contained in previous public procurement directives (the negotiated procedure) is *competitive dialogue* (Article 29). A competitive dialogue is a procedure where it is possible to conduct negotiations between contracting authorities and tendering undertakings on the basis of initial offers. However, this possibility only exists where there is a contract which is considered to be 'particularly complex'. This can relate to contracts where it is either not possible to specify the tasks (under Article 23 of the Directive), or where the legal or financial consequences cannot be determined.

7. Selection and award

Two evaluations must be made in connection with every procurement procedure. First, it is necessary to assess the qualifications of the undertakings which wish to participate in the tendering process. This part of the process is referred to as the selection of the candidates (selection phase). Second, an assessment is made of the tenders made in order to choose the offer which best fulfils the requirements of the contracting authority. This part of the process is referred to as the award of the contract (award phase).

7.1. Selection of candidates – procedures and criteria

The rules for the selection of candidates are set out in Articles 45-52 of Directive 2004/18/EC and Articles 52-54 of Directive 2004/17/EC. The various procurement procedures thus contain the same elements (selection and award), but these elements may be applied at different points in the process and in different ways, depending on the procedure used.

In the case of open procedures, the selection often takes place immediately prior to the award; in other words, the award process is a continuation of the selection process.

The selection is made on the basis of a number of selection criteria published in the contract notice. These criteria must relate to the qualifications and capacities of undertakings, and must either concern an undertaking's financial, economic, technical or professional qualifications. This list is exhaustive, so it is not possible to take other circumstances than those named into account. The directives list a number of examples of evidence of these circumstances. In relation to evidence of technical or professional qualifications, this list is exhaustive, but for economic and financial standing the list is not exhaustive. Thus, depending on the type of task involved, the contracting authority can require evidence of the educational and professional qualifications of the service provider or contractor, a list of the most significant tasks carried out, an indication of the technicians or technical bodies involved, a statement of the average annual manpower of the service provider or contractor, a description of the quality control measures, information about the implementation of controls and information about any subcontractors. It is not possible to require other information than that stated in the directives. Evidence of financial and economic standing is not restricted in the same way to the evidence listed in the provisions of the directives (appropriate statements from banks or evidence of relevant professional risk indemnity insurance, presentation of balance-sheets or a statement of the undertaking's overall turnover). Contracting authorities can therefore also demand other evidence to demonstrate an undertaking's financial and economic standing.

In addition to the rules on selection criteria, there are also a number of other rules which make it possible to eliminate undertakings which it may be assumed do not, have the qualifications to undertake the task for which tenders are invited. For this reason, an undertaking which is subject to bankruptcy or insolvency proceedings can be excluded from tendering. Furthermore, any candidate which has been found guilty of criminal acts which can give rise to doubts about the professional conduct of the candidate, or which is guilty of grave professional misconduct (though not necessarily in court proceedings) can be excluded. Finally, it is possible to exclude candidates which have not fulfilled obligations relating to the payment of taxes or social security contributions, or which have given incorrect information in connection with the procurement procedure. Directive 2004/18/EC introduced a requirement whereby contracting authorities *must* reject undertakings which have been found guilty of money laundering, corruption, fraud (within the meaning of the Convention relating to the protection of the financial interests of the European Communities) or organised crime; see Article 45(1).

The rejection of an applicant or tenderer from participating in a competitive tendering procedure on the basis of an old conviction, or otherwise because of historical circumstances that not longer apply, can be regarded as contrary to the proportionality principle. For this reason the practice has been developed in some Member States whereby a tenderer can make good its status by adopting measures to correct improper commercial conduct, for example by paying compensation to undertakings that may have suffered loss by the improper commercial conduct, and putting in place internal procedures to prevent a repeat of such conduct. The core of these cases is that when an economic operator has cleaned up its situation (so-called 'self-cleaning'), a contracting authority cannot reject an undertaking from participating in a competitive tendering procedure, regardless of Article 45 of Directive 2004/18/EC. The Commission appears to have accepted that there is such a practice in the Member States.[31]

An undertaking can submit evidence of the capacity of another undertaking and rely on this, as long as the first undertaking can make use of the capacity in question, for example by being part of the same corporate group. Other connections between candidates and third party undertakings can also satisfy the requirements, as long as the candidate can show that it has access to sufficient resources to fulfil the contract for which a tender is sought.[32]

If a contracting authority does not find that the documentation submitted for the assessment of a candidate undertaking is sufficient, it can ask the undertaking to submit supplementary information.

The situation can arise where too many qualified candidates seek to tender for a contract. A contracting authority can limit the number of participants in a tendering procedure to a given number, though not fewer than five tenderers for a restricted procedure, and three tenderers for a negotiated procedure or competitive dialogue. If a contracting authority wishes to have a limited group of tenderers, this must be made clear in the contract notice, including the maximum number of applicants who will pre-qualify.

The two selection situations can be referred to as *qualitative* (the initial assessment of the candidates' qualifications) and *quantitative* (the subsequent restriction of the number of qualified candidates) selection.

31. See the Green Paper on the modernisation of EU public procurement policy – Towards a more efficient European Procurement Market (COM (2011) 15 final). In Article 55(4) of the draft for a new Public Sector Directive (COM (2011) 896 final) there is a provision which, if the draft is adopted, would expressly give this possibility to economic operators.
32. Case C-389/92, *Ballast Nedam I;* Case C-5/97, *Ballast Nedam II;* and Case C-176/98, *Holst Italia.*

Where a quantitative selection is to be made, on the basis of a contracting authority's restriction of the number of participants in the tendering, this can be done in several ways. There is nothing in the public procurement directives which directly states how this selection must or may be made. However, there is a requirement that the criteria used must be objective and non-discriminatory. A number of suggestions have been made in the legal literature as to which methods should be used. First, there can be a *proportionate* application of the selection criteria which are the basis of the ordinary selection. Second, selection can be made so that the undertakings which can give the *best competition* are selected. Finally, but least probable, the quantitative selection can be made by the *drawing of lots*.

7.2. Award of the contract – procedures and criteria

The criteria for the award of a contract are aimed at establishing the framework for assessing tenders and for choosing the tender which is regarded as best and should therefore be awarded the contract. The public procurement directives have two different award criteria. First, there is the criterion of the *lowest bid*, and second there is the criterion of the *most economically advantageous bid.* In principle, the first criterion is both easy to define and to apply. According to this criterion, it is simply the offer that has the lowest overall price which wins the competition and is awarded the contract. This model has been fundamental not only for the public procurement directives, but also for a number of other procurement and tendering rules around the world.

The second criterion is more complex. Here the competition will be decided in favour of the tenderer that has given the most economically advantageous offer. The criterion takes account of other circumstances, and elements other than price can be relevant to the award of the contract. In buying a product, a contracting authority can attach importance to e.g. the quality of the product and the delivery schedule, as well as the price. Thus, the tender which best fulfils these three criteria will win the contract. It is clear that the assessment of the most economically advantageous offer is more difficult to make. This criterion gives the contracting authority wide discretion in its choice of supplier. The fact that a tenderer has given the best price does not necessarily mean it must be awarded the contract. If the tenderer has submitted an offer based on low quality and long delivery deadlines, the contract can be awarded to another tenderer who has offered a better *overall* solution.

The CJ has laid down conditions which must be fulfilled before a specific criterion can be used when awarding a contract on the basis of the most economically advantageous offer. These conditions are: 1) the criterion must be linked to the subject-matter of the contract; 2) the criterion must not confer an unrestricted freedom of choice on the contracting authority; 3) the criterion must be expressly mentioned in the contract documents or the tender notice; and 4) the criterion must comply with all the fundamental principles of Union law, in particular the principle of non-discrimination.[33]

As the contracting authority has increased discretion in awarding a contract on the basis of the most economically advantageous offer, the award phase becomes less transparent. This is because it is more difficult for the participating undertakings (and anyone other than the contracting authority) to predict which offer should be awarded the contract, since, as can be seen above, the assessment can be complex. In order to counter this uncertainty about the result of the procedure, there is a rule in the directives that the contracting authority must, if possible, give weightings to the different sub-criteria. This weighting can be expressed in percentages or otherwise. For a tender where the sub-criteria are price, quality and delivery time, the weighting could be expressed as follows: price 40 %, quality 35 % and delivery time 25 %. It is also possible to express the weightings within a range, for example: price 40-45 %.

If it is not possible to give weightings to the sub-criteria, the contracting authority must at least give a ranking of the sub-criteria, for example: 1 price, 2 quality and 3 delivery time. Such prioritising does not give a great deal of transparency for tenderers, since in the above ranking there can be wide differences in the weightings which lie behind the rankings. The ranking given in the example could apply to a weighting of price 40 %, quality 35 % and delivery time 25 %; but it could equally apply to a weighting of price 85 %, quality 10 % and delivery time 5 %. An offer that is primarily based on a low price may not do well in the first situation, whereas it would have a markedly better chance of being awarded the contract in the second situation.

The criteria for the award of the contract must be published in the initial contract notice. If the contracting authority wishes to award on the basis of the most economically advantageous offer, this must be stated in the contract notice, whereas the sub-criteria (quality, price etc.) need not necessarily be made public before the confirmation of the invitation to bid. With the open procedure, the invitation to bid is included in the contract notice, but with a restricted procedure, negotiated procedures with prior notice, and competitive dialogue, the contracting authority can delay making public the sub-criteria until the qualification of the candidates for the tendering procedure is decided. If a contracting authority nevertheless publishes the sub-criteria in the

33. Case C-513/99, *Concordia,* para. 64.

contract notice, even though it is not required to do so until qualification of the candidates for the tendering procedure is decided, it will be bound by the sub-criteria, and will not be able to change them later. This is because undertakings will to some extent express their interest on the basis of the sub-criteria by which the contract will be awarded. If an undertaking has low price products, which are also of a lower quality, it will be more interested in (have a better chance of winning) a tender procedure which is decided on the basis of the most economically advantageous offer if price is the most important criterion than if quality is the most important criterion.

7.2.1. Abnormally low tenders

Contracting authorities may reject tenders if they appear to have an abnormally low price.[34] However, a contracting authority must follow certain formal rules before making a final rejection. If a contracting authority believes that a tender is abnormally low, the tenderer must be given an opportunity to give details of the constituent elements of the tender, before it is rejected. The provision has been included in order to give contracting authorities the possibility of rejecting abnormally low tenders, but it is possible that in certain situations there can be an obligation to reject abnormally low tenders in certain situations, as there could otherwise be a possibility of an evasion of the procurement rules by a contracting authority.[35]

The CJ has laid down a more detailed procedure for the rejection of abnormally low tenders.[36] The four steps of the procedure are as follows: first, the contracting authority must identify suspect tenders; second, the contracting authority must allow the undertakings concerned to demonstrate the genuineness of their tenders by asking them to provide the details which it considers appropriate; third, the contracting authority must assess the merits of the explanations provided by the persons concerned; and fourth, the contracting authority must take a decision as to whether to admit or reject the tenders.

Under the provisions of Article 55(3) of Directive 2004/18/EC, a contracting authority may reject a tender that is abnormally low because the tenderer has obtained unlawful State aid.

34. Article 57 of Directive 2004/17/EC and Article 55 of Directive 2004/18/EC.
35. The contracting authority's favoured supplier could thus submit a tender with an abnormally low price and be certain of being awarded the contract. Once the contract has been awarded, the tenderer and the contracting authority can adjust the price to a more realistic level.
36. Joined Cases C-285/99 and C-286/99, *Impresa Lombardini,* para. 55.

7.3. Selection or award

In a number of cases the CJ has held that a distinction must be drawn between the selection of candidates for tendering and the award of the contract. This has the practical (and obvious) significance that the selection criteria must be used in connection with the selection, and the award criteria must be used in connection with the award. In addition to this, the distinction means that the same criterion cannot be used twice in connection with the same procurement procedure. In other words, if in connection with the selection of candidates a contracting authority has required evidence of an undertaking's experience related to a specific kind of task in connection with a contract, the contracting authority cannot use this same criterion (experience) when awarding the contract.

In Case C-532/06, *Lianakis*, the CJ emphasised as a general point that the two parts of the procurement procedure (selection and award) have different purposes, and the criteria and the conditions that apply to the two parts of the procedure are, in principle, different. In Case C-315/01, *GAT*, the CJ stated that a simple list of references to the tasks carried out by a supplier, which only contains the names and number of the suppliers' previous customers without other details relating to the deliveries made to those customers, cannot provide any information to identify the offer which is the most economically advantageous, and therefore cannot constitute an award criterion (para. 66). In the same case the CJ held that a criterion according to which a tenderer's offer may be favourably assessed only if the product which is the subject of the offer is available for inspection by the contracting authority within a radius of 300 km of the authority cannot constitute an award criterion (para. 72). The CJ referred to the decision in the *Beentjes* case concerning the distinction between selection criteria and award criteria, but did not go further in relation to the actual provisions. It could have been natural for the CJ to have made a categorical rejection of lists of references for use as allocation criteria, since these have already been named as potential selection criteria; see Article 48(2)(a) of Directive 2004/18/EC. However, the CJ chose not to use such an approach, which may indicate that one cannot totally exclude the possibility of the use of such lists of references. In any case, it must be assumed that it will only be seldom that lists of references will be such that they will be able to identify the most economically advantageous contract.

7.4. Non-financial criteria

It has previously been unclear to what extent it is possible to use non-economic criteria in connection with the selection of candidates or the award of contracts. Non-economic criteria are those which do not concern economic or commercial factors, such as regard for the environment, social concerns or consumer concerns. The CJ has not yet given a clear ruling on this question but more recent decisions, as well as the Commission's interpretative communications on social and environmental considerations,[37] suggest that there is now some clarity on the question.

The reason for being careful about allowing non-economic and non-commercial considerations to play a role in connection with public procurement is that the aim of the public procurement directives is to prompt contracting authorities to use a *commercial* approach and considerations in connection with public procurement, and abstain from using non-commercial considerations which are the basis of their work as public authorities.

Social and environmental concerns can be protected in many other ways. In relation to the formulation of public procurement contracts such concerns can be included in various ways. First, such considerations can be included as requirements for the contract, in other words the goods or services to be bought can be described so as to fulfil a number of different environmental requirements.[38] Second, such considerations can be taken care of, for example, by including social requirements in connection with the selection of undertakings accepted as candidates for tendering. It has been pointed out, both by the CJ and the Commission, that in order to apply non-economic criteria for the selection of candidates or the award of contracts, it must be possible to use these criteria to assess the suitability of an undertaking to carry out a specific task, or to asses the economic advantages of a tender. If the social require-

37. In 2001 the Commission published Interpretative communication COM(2001) 566 final, on the Community law applicable to public procurement and the possibilities for integrating social considerations into public procurement (OJ 2001 C 333/27) and Interpretative communication COM(2001) 274 final, on the Community law applicable to public procurement and the possibilities for integrating environmental considerations into public procurement (OJ 2001 C 333/12). The communications merely review (though in more detailed form than earlier communications) the CJ's practice in the area, and conclude that the scope for applying social and environmental considerations is limited by the rules on selection and award criteria.
38. See e.g. Case C-513/99, *Concordia,* where a number of environmental requirements had been made with regard to the buses that were to be procured.

ments of a contracting authority cannot do this, such considerations cannot be used as criteria for selection or award.[39]

A third way of implementing these considerations is by making the fulfilment of these requirements a contractual obligation for being considered for award of the contract. In other words, to win the contract, evidence must be given that certain contractual requirements (for example social requirements) will be fulfilled.

There has been discussion about the extent to which it is possible to include non-economic considerations as contractual requirements and, in extension of this, the extent to which it is possible to exclude offers which do not fulfil such requirements. In Case 31/87, *Beentjes*, and later in Case C-225/98, *Commission* v *France*, the CJ has allowed that it was possible to lay down such requirements in public procurement contracts as long as these have been stated in advance in the contract notice and as long as the requirements are non-discriminatory.[40]

There is a question as to whether such requirements can be the only requirements that can be made in connection with laying down non-economic contractual requirements. It has been argued that not all non-economic requirements should be allowed to form the basis of exclusion from public procurement business. The argument behind this is that the public procurement directives are intended to direct contracting authorities towards a more commercial purchasing policy, so it would be contrary to this purpose to allow contracting authorities to attach decisive weight to non-commercial factors. It could be argued that, in extension of the two requirements referred to above, the consideration which is to be taken account of should have a *certain relevance* to the subject matter of the contract in question. Thus, extreme requirements which have no connection with the task should be excluded, while requirements that are intended to protect concerns which have a natural connection to the task or contract could be maintained. However, so far there has not been support for this view in the practice of the CJ.

39. On the possibility of including environmental concerns for awarding a contract, see Case C-513/99, *Concordia.*
40. The CJ uses the terms 'special' or 'additional' criteria, which can be misunderstood as referring to selection of award criteria. This is not the case; see above.

8. Exceptions

8.1. General

There are a number of exceptions to the main rules laid down in the public procurement directives. These exceptions give contracting authorities the opportunity to use less strict procedures in certain cases. As is generally the case with exceptions under Union law, these exceptions must be interpreted restrictively, and the contracting authority has the burden of proof for showing that the conditions for granting the exceptions have been fulfilled.

There are two kinds of exceptions in relation to the public procurement directives. First, there are the exceptions which lead to total exclusion from the scope of the public procurement directives. Second, there are exceptions which affect the procedure for the entering into contracts.

8.2. The defence exception

Directive 2004/18/EC makes clear that its provisions apply to public contracts awarded by contracting authorities in the field of defence, except for contracts subject to Article 346 of the Treaty. This is in Article 10 of the Directive.

Article 346 of the Treaty states that the provisions of the Treaty do not preclude any Member State taking 'such measures as it considers necessary for the protection of the essential interests of its security which are connected with the production of or trade in arms, munitions and war material; such measures shall not adversely affect the conditions of competition in the common market regarding products which are not intended for specifically military purposes'. Article 346 also states that no Member State is obliged to supply information, the disclosure of which it considers contrary to the essential interests of its security.

In connection with Article 346 there is a category of products which are referred to as *dual use products*. These are products the use of which can be both military (and are thus covered by the provision) and civil (and thus fall outside the scope of the provision). Examples of dual use products can be explosives which can both be used for military purposes and for example for the demolition of buildings etc. It is not clear whether these products are covered by Article 346 of the Treaty. The scope of application of the provision in relation to dual use products can be delimited in two ways. One possibility is that dual use products fall within the scope of Article 346, to the extent that the proposed procurement is intended for military use. The other possibility is that only products which have a military use are covered by Article 346. When considered in relation to the CJ's established practice on exceptions (that they should be interpreted restrictively), it must be assumed that the CJ will choose the latter possibility, whereby only products which have a military use are covered by Article 346 and are therefore outside the scope of the public procurement directives.

Directive 2009/81/EC was adopted to govern public procurement in the fields of defence and security. The provisions of this Directive are very similar to the corresponding provisions and procedures laid down in Directive 2004/18/EC. However, there are a few differences, for example the stricter rules on the use of subcontractors in Article 21.

8.3. Negotiated procedures

Negotiated procedures can be seen as an exception, as the use of this form of procedure leads to a decidedly less strict procedure than is the case with open procedures or restricted procedures.

There are two forms of negotiated procedures: negotiated procedures *with* and *without* prior publication of a contract notice; see the section of different kinds of procedures above. The first of these can be freely used for procurements made under Directive 2004/17/EC, whereas under Directive 2004/18/EC the procedure can only be used as an exception. Negotiated procedures *without* prior publication of a contract notice can only be used as an exception.

Negotiated procedures *with* prior publication of a contract notice can be used as an exception where:[41]

- In connection with an open procedure or a restricted procedure, offers are made that are irregular tenders or are unacceptable under national provisions,
- Contracts for works are performed solely for purposes of research, testing or development and not with the aim of ensuring profitability or recovering research and development costs,
- The nature of the works, supplies, or services or the risks attaching thereto do not permit prior overall pricing, and
- The nature of the services to be provided is such that contract specifications cannot be established with sufficient precision to permit the award of the contract by selection of the best tender according to the rules governing open or restricted procedures.

41. Article 30 of Directive 2004/18/EC.

In the following situations negotiated procedures *without* prior publication of a contract notice can be used:[42]

- When no tenders or no suitable tenders or no applications have been submitted in response to an open procedure or a restricted procedure, provided that the initial conditions of contract are not substantially altered,
- When tenders are made which are not in accordance with requirements or are not acceptable, provided that the initial conditions of contract are not substantially altered, and provided that the procedure after negotiation covers all the undertakings which fulfil the conditions, which are qualified according to the rules on selection, and as long as these undertakings have submitted tenders in the initial tendering that are in accordance with the formal requirements of the tendering procedures,
- When the products involved are manufactured purely for the purpose of research, experimentation, study or development,
- Insofar as is strictly necessary when, for reasons of extreme urgency brought about by events unforeseeable by the contracting authorities in question, the time limit for other tendering procedures cannot be complied with,
- When, for technical or artistic reasons, or for reasons connected with the protection of exclusive rights, the contract may be awarded only to a particular economic operator,
- For additional deliveries by the original supplier which are intended either as a partial replacement of normal supplies or installations or as the extension of existing supplies or installations, and
- For new tasks which are a repetition of corresponding tasks and which are awarded to the undertaking which was awarded the original contract by the same contracting authority, provided that the repeat tasks are in accordance with the original project, and the contract for the work was entered into in accordance with open or restricted procedures.

In addition to these situations, under Article 40(3)(h) to (l) of Directive 2004/17/EC and Article 31(3) of Directive 2004/18/EC (negotiated procedure after a design contest) there are other possibilities for using negotiated procedures, for example for supplies quoted and purchased on a commodity market.

There is no specific procedure to be used in negotiated procedures. This is in spite of the fact that the reason why there is a limited entitlement to use the

42. Article 31 of Directive 2004/18/EC.

procedure is the lack of transparency in connection with negotiation. However, it must be assumed that there can be a requirement for a written record in connection with the exchange of information, and that the principles of equal treatment and transparency (see below) must be observed in all phases of the negotiations. It is the contracting authority which must lay down the procedure for the negotiations, and the procedure must be laid down before the negotiations are started.

8.4. Accelerated procedure

If it is not possible to carry out a tendering procedure by complying with the usual time limits, the contracting authority may use shorter time limits. The time limits may be reduced so that the deadline for the receipt of requests to participate may be 15 days from the date on which the contract notice is published, and the time limit for the receipt of tenders can be reduced to 10 days from the date of the invitation to tender.

This exception allowing the use of shorter time limits can only be used as long as it is not circumstances which are under the control of the contacting authority which have necessitated the use of the accelerated procedure.

8.5. Special provisions on the provision of services

8.5.1. The distinction between A and B services

There is not a full tenderingobligation for all services. Services where it can be expected that there will be competition for the award of a contract are subject to the full tendering obligation. Services which are not to any significant extent represented on the private market are not subject to the full tendering obligation, but they are subject to the provisions on the use of technical specifications and to the rules on the subsequent publication of information about contracts entered into; see Article 21 of Directive 2004/18/EC. The services which are subject to a full tendering obligation (so-called 'A services') include maintenance and repair services, land and air transport, transport of mail, telecommunications services, financial services, computer services, research and development, accounting and auditing, market research and opinion polling, management consultancy, engineering, advertising, building cleaning services and property management, publishing and printing, sewerage services and waste disposal. The group of 'B services', which are not subject to a full tendering obligation, include hotel and restaurant services, railway transport, water transport services, supporting and auxiliary transport services, legal services, personnel placement and supply services, investigation and security services, education and vocational education services, health and social services, recreational, cultural and sporting services, and other services that are not covered by the other categories. This categorisation applies both to services under Directive 92/50/EEC relating to the coordination of procedures for the award of public service contracts and Directive 93/38/EEC coordinating the procurement procedures of entities operating in the water, energy, transport and telecommunications sectors.[43] If a contract for the provision of services contains both A and B services, the contracting authority must add together all the A services and all the B services and assess whether the total value of the A services exceeds the total value of the B services. Only if the A services represent the majority of the value of the contract will the contract be subject to a full tendering obligation.[44]

8.5.2. The exclusive right exception

Directive 2004/18/EC contains a provision which, under special circumstances, exempts a contract from the full tendering obligation; see Article 18.

The Directive does not apply to public service contracts awarded by a contracting authority to another contracting authority on the basis of an exclusive right which they enjoy pursuant to a published law, regulation or administrative provision which is compatible with the Treaty.

8.5.2.1. Conditions

There are several conditions which must be fulfilled before this provision can be applied. First, the body which has been granted the exclusive right must itself be a contracting authority. Second, the contract must be awarded on the basis of the exclusive right. Third, the exclusive right must have been granted in accordance with a published law, regulation or administrative provision. Fourth, the published law, regulation or administrative provision must be compatible with the Treaty.

The question concerning the contracting authority is described in brief above, and it is applicable in connection with the application of Article 18 of Directive 2004/18/EC.

The award must thus be made to the undertaking which has the exclusive right to carry out the service in question. It must be assumed that it is the public body which itself determines which services are considered suitable for being carried out via an exclusive right. This is supported by Article 345 of the Treaty which provides that the Treaty does not concern itself with how

43. In Case C-76/97, *Walter Tögel,* it was made clear that it is the CPC nomenclature that determines which category a service should be placed in under Directive 92/50/EEC.
44. See also Case C-411/00, *Swoboda.*

Member States govern the system of property ownership, in other words the form in which public undertakings are carried out.[45]

The exclusive right need not be granted by central government (i.e. at ministerial level), but can also be granted by local or regional authorities.

The Commission has stated[46] that the term *exclusive right* should be interpreted narrowly, because the article in question is an exception. Sole or exclusive rights concern a monopoly situation where the supplier in question is the only one in the given geographic area which may provide the service in question. It is likewise assumed by the Commission that the exclusive right can be granted by the authority which awards the contract which is thus not subject to the public procurement procedures. It is further assumed by the Commission that the body can first be set up and the exclusive right provisions can then be made public.

It is possible that guidance on the definition of an exclusive right can be obtained from Article 106 of the Treaty, on public undertakings and undertakings to which Member States grant special or exclusive rights. For further on this, see Chapter X.

It is also a condition that the exclusive right must be pursuant to a published law, regulation or administrative provision. There are two parts to this condition. First, measures under which an exclusive right is granted must be made public. The reason for this is that it must be possible for the public to be aware of the grant of the exclusive right. Second, the grant must be made under a law, regulation or administrative provision, which is a requirement based on a desire to signal that this does not relate to an award under private law of the kind which is covered by the Directive, but a grant under public law.

The last condition is that the exclusive right must be compatible with the Treaty. It could be said that this condition is superfluous, since all legal acts of the Member States must be compatible with the Treaty. Nevertheless, the EU's legislators have chosen to emphasise this explicitly in the provision. The provisions of the Treaty which will be most relevant in this respect are Article 34 (on the free movement of goods), Article 45 (on the free movement of workers), Article 49 (on the right of establishment) and Article 56 (on freedom to provide services). These provisions mean that there must not

45. However, this rule is not without exceptions; see the practice concerning Article 106 of the Treaty on undertakings granted special or exclusive rights.
46. A letter of 7 December 1995 from Directorate General XV to the Netherlands Representative at the EU; see the guidelines of the Danish Competition Authority on the EU's public procurement rules.

be discrimination between domestic undertakings and goods, and undertakings and goods from other Member States. Another relevant provision is the general prohibition on discrimination on the grounds of nationality in Article 18. Finally, the Treaty's competition rules must be respected, primarily Article 106 on public undertakings and undertakings to which Member States grant special or exclusive rights.

9. General principles

The public procurement directives provide that contracting authorities must comply with the principle of equal treatment which is a part of public procurement law. In addition to this express obligation, contracting authorities are also required to comply with a number of other general principles of Union law. This is backed up by a number of decisions by the CJ. In particular, these principles are the principles of transparency, non-discrimination, proportionality and the mutual recognition.

9.1. The principle of equal treatment

The principle of equal treatment is the most important and the most often relied upon principle in public procurement law. The content of the principle is not described in more detail in the public procurement directives, but there have been many cases on the subject. As with the other principles, the principle of equal treatment must be complied with in all phases and situations involving public purchasing. It would be going too far, in this context, to list all the situations in which the principle of equal treatment is relevant. For this reason the following is structured so as to focus on a number of areas in which the application of the principle of equal treatment is the primary legal basis. Where the principle of equal treatment most often comes into play is in connection with the prohibition on negotiation, reserved contracts, rules on technical dialogue and in connection with cancelled procedures.

9.1.1. The prohibition on negotiation

As a consequence of the principle of equal treatment, there is a prohibition on contracting authorities *negotiating* with tenderers in connection with open procedures and restricted procedures. The prohibition was originally derived from the principle of equal treatment, see Case C-243/89, *Commission* v *Denmark*, and is now reflected in Article 2 of Directive 2004/18/EC. As the prohibition is derived from a general principle, there are no specific guidelines for the application of the prohibition. In order to actualise the prohibition, the Commission and the Council have issued a joint statement which to some extent clarifies the content of the prohibition:

> 'The Council and the Commission state that in open and restricted procedures all negotiations with candidates or tenderers on fundamental aspects of contracts, variations in which are likely to distort competition, and in particular on prices, shall be ruled out; however, discussions with candidates or tenderers may be held but only for the purpose of clarifying or supplementing the content of their tenders or the requirements of the contracting entities and provided this does not involve discrimination.'[47]

By and large, the joint statement has been relied upon by the authorities which apply the law, without them questioning its legal value. For example, several Advocates General have referred directly to the joint statement, while the CJ has merely used terminology corresponding to that used in the statement. Against this background it is natural that analyses in the legal literature of the prohibition on negotiation have largely been based on the joint statement and its terminology.

The CJ has dealt with the prohibition on negotiation in a few cases. In Case C-243/89, *Commission* v *Denmark*, the CJ held that it was not permitted to negotiate with a tenderer on the basis of a tender which did not comply with the tender conditions; see below. In Case C-87/94, *Commission* v *Belgium (Walloon buses)* the CJ held that the Belgian contracting authority had breached the public procurement rules by allowing certain amendments to be made to a tender.

9.1.1.1. Fundamental aspects

It is clear from the joint statement that it is not permitted to negotiate about the fundamental aspects of a contract. No definition is given of *fundamental aspects*, but they must be assumed to be aspects that are relevant either to the award of the contract or to the tender procedure in general. The term 'fundamental aspects' should not be interpreted as referring only to aspects which concern decisive elements of the contract. It must be assumed that less important elements which nevertheless have some weight in the tendering procedure are also covered.

47. OJ 1994 L 111/114. The statement is in the nature of soft law, and it is therefore difficult to be certain of its legal weight. It must be assumed that there is not an obligation to follow it word for word, but there may be an obligation to take account of the statement when interpreting the prohibition. On its legal authority, see among others Case C-292/89, *Antonissen,* and Case 322/88, *Grimaldi.*

The CJ has not expressly ruled on the question of fundamental aspects, but it did make an implicit evaluation of this in Case C-87/94, *Commission* v *Belgium*. The case concerned a contract for the supply of a number of buses. One of the tenderers sent some corrections to its tender to the contracting authority. These corrections related to fuel consumption, the frequency of engine replacement and some comments on technical quality. The tenderer had given figures for fuel consumption of 54 litres per 100 km, and had stated that there was a possibility of obtaining a reduction in fuel consumption of 5-8 %. In a later submission the tenderer corrected the consumption figure to a reduction of 16.7 %. There was clearly an amendment to the tender, and it was relevant whether this amounted to a fundamental change. As stated, the CJ did not expressly address this question, but since, on the one hand the fuel consumption influenced the ranking between tenders, and on the other hand it had a significant financial effect on the cost of running the buses, it must have been a fundamental aspect.

9.1.1.2. Price

It is clear from the joint statement that price plays a special role in connection with tenders. This is because price is the most important competitive parameter and, regardless of which criteria are chosen for the award of a contract, price will always have a high priority in public procurement procedures (see the award criteria: lowest price or most economically advantageous tender). On this basis there is particular sensitivity about negotiations on price. In principle, negotiation on price is not permitted.[48] This means that if, in certain circumstances negotiation is permitted, this may be on condition that there is no negotiation on price.

9.1.1.3. Clarification or negotiation

In the joint statement it is stated that there may be discussions with candidates or tenderers, but only for the purpose of *clarifying* or *supplementing* tenders and not for negotiation. The basic difference is that clarifying or supplementing does not result in changes being made to the tender documentation or to the offer, but is merely a confirmation of matters which are stated in the tender documentation or offer. In contrast, negotiation leads to or is intended to lead to changes in the existing documentation.

Thus, where there is confirmation, either in the form of clarification or supplementation or otherwise, discussions are permitted as long as they do not result in unequal treatment.

See Case C-87/94, *Commission* v *Belgium*, referred to in the section above. In this case the tenderer had initially indicated a reduction in fuel consumption of 5 to 8% in relation to the

48. In the joint statement it is said that negotiation 'in particular on prices, shall be ruled out'.

consumption indicated in its tenders, but had later changed this to a reduction of 16.7 %. In respect of this, in his Opinion, Advocate General Lenz made some general comments on the terms ‘amendments’ and ‘clarifications’. He said that from a semantic point of view the term ‘clarifying’, which is used in the joint statement of the Council and the Commission, should be understood as referring to information about details which describe the subject matter more clearly or define it more precisely. The other term used in the joint statement, namely ‘supplementing’, was understood by Advocate General Lenz to refer to the addition of information which was not previously available. What the two terms have in common is that they do not refer to the replacement of information that has already been given, but rather the confirmation of the information in one or another way.[49]

9.1.1.4. Permitted negotiations

The wording of the joint statement leaves the impression that negotiations can be permitted in certain circumstances. The possibility for this is naturally greatest in the case of negotiations on non-fundamental aspects; see above. However, if it is possible to negotiate lawfully, certain formal requirements must be laid down concerning the communication of information in connection with the negotiations. First, all information must be given in writing. This is to ensure the greatest possible transparency in connection with negotiations which are otherwise not particularly transparent. Second, all tenderers must have the same possibilities of amending their tenders. This is based on the principle of equal treatment.

9.1.1.5. The scope for making corrections

Apart from the possibility of making clarifications and for conducting lawful negotiations, there is also a limited possibility of making corrections to the tender documentation or to tenders. The right to make such corrections is shown by, among other things, the decision of the General Court (GC) in Case T-19/95, *Adia Interim*. The GC stated that there is no obligation on the contracting authority to make corrections, but merely a right to do so if some fault is sufficiently apparent. The GC stated that ‘even though the selection committee detected the presence of a systematic calculation error, it was unable to ascertain its exact nature or cause’.[50] Thus the contracting authority has a right to make a correction as long as it is not only clearly apparent, but it is also apparent how the fault has occurred.[51]

49. Point 37 of the Advocate General’s Opinion.
50. Case T-19/95, *Adia Interim,* para. 47.
51. See also the Opinion of the Advocate General in Case 87/94, *Commission* v *Belgium.*

9.1.2. Reservations

Reservations (or provisos) are yet another area of public procurement law where there are no express rules, and where the principle of equal treatment therefore plays an important role. *Reservations* refers to situations in which a tender contains conditions which differ from the conditions which the contracting authority has laid down in the contract notice. In other words, the tender differs from the basis for competition which the contracting authority has laid down in the conditions in the contract notice. The basic position in the law is that if a tenderer has included reservations in its tender, then the tender cannot be included in the competition for the award of the contract. The reason for this is that a tenderer should not be able to obtain a competitive advantage by breaching the rules for the competition which have been laid down by the contracting authority. There are differences about what can be accepted as a reservation, and not least differences as to the strength and effect on a tender which various reservations can have. Therefore in practice not all reservations necessarily lead to the exclusion of a tender. The inclusion of reservations in a tender, and the strength which any reservation may be thought to have, is at the risk of the tenderer.

The factors which may lead to the rejection of a tender are as follows: 1) reservations concerning fundamental aspects; 2) unclear reservations; and 3) reservations in cases where the contracting authority has given prior notice of refusal to accept reservations. As a starting point a tender that contains reservations is considered to be *unconditional.*

The first of these situations is related to the concept of fundamental aspects, as this is known from the joint statement and in the practice on the prohibition of negotiation. It is thus undisputed that where a reservation concerns fundamental aspects of the contract, the contracting authority cannot take the tender into account. Unclear reservations cannot be accepted, because of the lack of clarity about the consequences of the reservation in the tender, so it is not immediately possible to make the necessary adjustment in order for the tender to be compared with the other tenders and be included in the competition for the contract. If a contracting authority has given prior notice that it will refuse to accept reservations, this must be considered as one of the rules of the tendering process, so that tenders with reservations must be rejected.

It appears from the above that in certain situations it is possible to consider a tender even if it contains a reservation. However, a condition for the admission to the competition of a tender with a reservation is that the reservation must be priced; in other words, an evaluation must be made of the price effect of the reservation and this effect must be calculated against the price tendered.

Where there is no obligation on a contracting authority to exclude a tender from the procurement procedure on the basis of a minor reservation, the contracting authority may nevertheless choose to exclude such tender. In other words, the contracting authority has *a right but not a duty* to exclude tenders with 'minor' reservations.

The CJ has ruled that it is not possible to negotiate away reservations in a tender, with a view to making the tender conditional.[52]

The question of fundamental aspects has not had such great importance in connection with negotiations, as the main rule is that all negotiations, regardless of whether they concern fundamental aspects or non-fundamental aspects, are prohibited; see the prohibition of negotiations. On the other hand, the distinction between fundamental aspects and non-fundamental aspects has greater significance in connection with reservations, as the distinction determines whether a contracting authority *can* or *must* reject a tender with a reservation.

9.1.2.1. Variant tenders

In public procurement competitions which are awarded according to the criterion of the most economically advantageous tender, it is possible to take variant offers into consideration. When using this criterion, the contracting authority must state in the contract notice whether variant offers will be considered or not; see Article 24 of Directive 2004/18/EC.[53] The condition for taking variant tenders into consideration is that the variant tenders should fulfil the minimum requirements laid down by the contracting authority.

The contracting authority must state in the contract notice the minimum requirements which any variant tenders must satisfy, whether there are any *specific* requirements for such tenders, and if so what these requirements are.

It can be debated whether the minimum requirements must be expressly stated as being minimum requirements, or whether a less express presentation is sufficient. It must be assumed that the minimum requirements must at least be presented in such a way that tenderers should be able to understand that they are minimum requirements, and be able to establish the content of such requirements.

52. Case C-243/89, *Commission* v *Denmark*.
53. The wording of this provision differs from that of the previous formulation. Previously the contracting authority had to state if a variant tender would *not* be accepted. If nothing was stated, a variant tender could thus be considered. The new formulation removes any doubt which could have arisen previously. Previously, if the contracting authority had not said anything in the contract notice (because the question was not considered), variant tenders could nevertheless be submitted.

In Case C-421/01, *Traunfellner*,[54] the contracting authority had referred in the contract notice to a provision of national legislation requiring an alternative tender 'to ensure the performance of work which is qualitatively equivalent to that for which tenders are invited'. There was not otherwise any minimum requirement laid down for variant tenders. In other words, there were no concrete minimum requirements the fulfilment of which was necessary for a variant tender to be considered. In this connection the CJ stated:[55] 'This being so, it is clear from the very wording of the second paragraph of Article 19 of the Directive that, where the contracting authority has not excluded the submission of variants, it is under an obligation to set out in the contract documents the minimum specifications with which those variants must comply. Consequently, the reference made in the contract documents to a provision of national legislation cannot satisfy the requirement laid down in the second paragraph of Article 19 of the Directive'. The CJ expanded on this by pointing out that: 'Tenderers may be deemed to be informed in the same way of the minimum specifications with which their variants must comply in order to be considered by the contracting authority only where those specifications are set out in the contract documents. This involves an obligation of transparency designed to ensure compliance with the principle of equal treatment of tenderers, which must be complied with in any procurement procedure governed by the Directive'.[56]

Neither the provisions in Article 24 of Directive 2004/18/EC nor any other provision in the Directive contain any definition of a variant tender. Nor has the CJ defined the term. As the term suggests, a variant tender will differ in one or more points from other tenders. However, there are both qualitative and quantitative limitations in the rules on variant tenders. The quantitative limitation means that, unless variant tenders are accepted, a tenderer cannot submit more than one tender. The qualitative limitation means that a variant tender contains a proposal for a different solution to the kind of solution which is suggested in the contract notice.

The CJ has pointed out that a distinction must be made between two different types of variant tenders. First, there is an *obligatory* variant tender.

54. On this case, see *Martin Dischendorfer:* The Assessment of variants under the EC Public Procurement Rules: The Traunfellner Case, Public Procurement Law Review 2004 NA 67.
55. Case C-421/01, *Traunfellner,* paras. 27-28.
56. Case C-421/01, *Traunfellner,* para. 29.

Such a tender is a necessity for a tender to be conditional. It is thus a requirement from the contracting authority that tenderers should find alternative solutions to a specific point in the contracted task in order for a tender to be conditional. Second, there can be *optional* variant tenders, and it is typically these that are referred to when the term 'variant tender' is used. This kind of variant tender means that the tenderer submits a tender with an alternative solution to the 'ordinary solutions' which are suggested by the contract notice.

As stated, a variant tender is a tender which differs from the conditions of the contract notice. As can be seen, there are major similarities in the descriptions of reservations and variant tenders. It is also clear from the legal literature that it is not easy to draw the boundary between these two types of departures from the conditions of the contract notice and the other tender material. Below there is a review of a possible procedure for distinguishing between reservations and variant tenders. The reason why it is necessary to make the distinction is that there are different consequences connected with the use of reservations and variant tenders.

To distinguish between reservations and variant tenders, the following assessment can be used. First, an assessment can be made as to whether minimum requirements and other conditions for variant tenders are laid down in the tendering documentation. If such conditions are not laid down, the tenderer does not have the possibility of submitting a variant tender, and any departures in the tender from the conditions in the tendering documentation must be treated as reservations. Second, the next assessment (where there is a possibility of submitting a variant tender) is based on whether the difference of the tender from the requirements in the tendering documentation concerns the content of the task or merely a number of less important provisions and elements of the contract. One way to assess this can be the extent to which it is possible to put a price on the stated changes. Where there is a greater or more fundamental difference between the requirements in the tendering documentation and the tender, and where these are difficult to put a price on, this suggests that the case concerns a variant tender.

9.1.3. Technical dialogue

The situation with contracting authorities will often be such that the personnel who are employed by the public authority will not have sufficient expertise to lay down the technical specifications and the needs which the subject matter of the procurement is to satisfy, or the professional expertise to draft the tendering documentation. For this reason a contracting authority will often engage a technical adviser to undertake professional evaluations. Obviously, this technical advice will precede the publishing of the contract notice. The use of a technical adviser is not in itself a problem, but it can be a problem if technical advisers themselves decide to tender for the contract they have been associated with as advisers. The problem is that the advisory function often gives the adviser important insight into the needs of the contracting authority in relation to the contract in question, and the adviser will often have a major influence on how the goods or services to be bought are to be specified. This gives rise to a potential risk that, via their roles in the initial phases of the tendering process, advisers acquire a number of competitive advantages. Such advantages can conflict with the contracting authority's obligation to ensure equal treatment of all tenderers. This means that in some situations it can be necessary to exclude an adviser from participation in a tendering procedure, as competition would otherwise be distorted.

> In Joined Cases C-21/03 and C-34/03, *Fabricom*, the CJ stated that a contracting authority may not automatically exclude from tendering an undertaking that has acted as an adviser in the preparation of a public procurement. There must at least be a possibility for the undertaking to provide evidence that its participation in the tendering process will not influence the competition.

However, there is also another form of conflict of interest which is of major importance in connection with public procurement. This can be referred to as *general conflict of interest*.[57] The basis for this kind of incapacity is that, in addition to the principle of equal treatment, there is also a requirement for professional competence. This form of incapacity is referred to neither in the enacting terms nor in the preambles of the public procurement directives.

9.1.4. Cancellation

A practice has developed whereby it is not in all circumstances that a contracting authority can cancel a procurement procedure that has been initiated. A contracting authority can have many good grounds for cancelling a procurement procedure; for example the authority's needs may have changed, or budget cuts can mean that it does not have the financial resources to make the planned purchase. On the other hand there are circumstances which argue against an unconditional right to cancel a procurement procedure. The prima-

57. This kind of disqualification is not directly regulated in Directive 2004/18/EC. However, there is a prospect of the introduction of such rules in the proposed new procurement directive; see Article 21 of the draft.

ry argument is consideration for tenderers. The preparation of a tender can be costly, both with regard to personnel resources and time. It has thus been considered necessary to protect tenderers against arbitrary cancellations of procurement procedures. The CJ has adopted an interpretation which gives contracting authorities a broad right to cancel.

> According to the practice of the CJ, it is not contrary to the rules on public procurement to cancel a procedure if there is only one tender judged to be suitable; see Case C-27/98, *Metalmeccanica Fracasso*. In Case C-92/00, *Hospital Ingenieure Krankenhaustechnik Planungs-Gesellschaft*, the CJ held that there are limits to a contracting authority's possibilities for cancelling (withdrawing) a public procurement procedure. What was decisive for the possibility of cancellation was the general principles of Union law and the provisions of the Treaty on freedom of movement, particularly the principles of equal treatment, the principle of transparency and the prohibition of discrimination on the grounds of nationality. With these principles as the only restriction, the CJ may be said to have accepted that there is a broad right to cancel.

9.2. The transparency principle

The principle of transparency is an important part of the legal basis for public procurement, and it is expressly referred to in Article 2 of Directive 2004/18/EC. In recent years the transparency principle has been of growing importance to the law on public procurement. In contrast to the principle of equal treatment, the transparency principle is expressed in a large number of the provisions in the public procurement directives, even where these do not expressly refer to the principle. For this reason the transparency principle, as default principle, will not have quite the same significance as the principle of equal treatment – the transparency principle is to a great extent already provided for in the provisions of the directives.

The transparency principle also seems to be of growing importance in relation to public purchases made outside the scope of the public procurement directives. This is because the CJ as established that the transparency principle must also be complied with for purchases that are undertaken below the threshold values or otherwise outside the scope of the directives. The CJ has not expressly defined what this principle consists of, but it is possible to obtain interpretative guidance from the cases in which the CJ has laid down the existence of the transparency principle. It has done so in, among others, Case C-275/98, *Unitron*; Case C-324/98, *Telaustria*; Case C-231/03, *Coname*; and Case C-458/03, *Parking Brixen*. In these cases the CJ held that the transparency principle means that a contracting authority is bound to inform the market (or parts thereof) about proposed purchases so that potential suppliers have the opportunity to be considered for the contract. It must be assumed that there is an obligation to publish notice of the proposed procurement before carrying it out. The Commission has published an interpretative communication on the Union law applicable to contract awards which are not or not fully subject to the provisions of the public procurement directives (OJ 2006 C 179/2). In addition to this, contracting authorities are required to ensure that the procedure is implemented transparently, so that it is easier to monitor.

9.3. Other principles

Contracting authorities must respect a number of other principles in addition to the principle of equal treatment and the transparency principle. These principles are generally applicable in Union law, even though they can take a particular form when applied in connection with public procurement, because of the special character of this area of law.

It must be assumed that the *principle of non-discrimination* does not play a major independent role in connection with public procurement. This is because this principle and the principle of equal treatment overlap to a large extent. Since the principle of equal treatment is well-embedded in public procurement law, and the case law has been built on the basis of this principle, it will presumably be applied more frequently than the principle of non-discrimination.

Specifically in relation to public procurement, the *proportionality principle* means that contracting authorities may not adopt measures which go further than is necessary in order to achieve the intended aims of the measure. More specifically, this means that every time a contracting authority makes a choice in connection with a purchase, it must choose the solution which helps the achievement of the aim, without restricting competition, and without making it difficult for suppliers to take part in the competition for the award of the contract.

The *principle of mutual recognition* is relevant in connection with public procurement in that a contracting authority may not reject candidates or tenders merely by reference to the fact that these cannot deliver some particular form of (national) documentation. Thus there is a requirement that contracting authorities must make a concrete evaluation of the qualifications, candidates, documentation etc.

In addition to these principles there are a number of other principles that are relevant to public procurement to a greater or lesser extent. For example this includes the *principle of conformity* and the *principle of impartiality*. The principle of conformity is not referred to by the CJ, but it is the basis of the whole concept of public procurement: that a procurement procedure is initiated where a tender is to be submitted on the basis of tender documentation, and where neither the documentation nor the tenders may be altered in the course of the procurement procedure.

10. Procurement and the competition rules

As previously stated, the procurement rules are not formally linked to the Treaty rules on competition but are based on the rules on freedom of movement. However, it is beyond doubt that the procurement rules have some close resemblances to the competition rules. For example, there is some overlap of the aims of traditional competition law and the aims of the procurement rules.[58] There are many issues where procurement law and competition law touch or overlap, but it lies outside the scope of this treatment to deal with all of these.[59] However, the aim of the following is to identify some of the most important points of conflict between the traditional competition rules, including the State aid rules, on the one hand and the procurement rules on the other hand.

10.1. Procurement and the competition rules

In recent years there has been considerable focus on the relationship between the procurement rules and the competition rules (in particular Articles 101 and 102 of the Treaty). This relationship is particularly complex, and the complexity is only increased by the fact that there has not been any uniform approach in the way in which the case law has developed in these two areas of the law.

The basic approach is that the competition rules can be applied alongside the procurement directives. It is essential for the application of the competition rules that the general conditions for applying them should have been fulfilled. This means, to start with, that there must be an assessment of whether the contracting authority should be regarded as an undertaking for the purposes of the competition rules. According to the established case law, this must be determined according to whether the activities in question are to be

58. See e.g. *Grith Ølykke:* Abnormally low tenders, Chapter 2, and *Albert Sanchez Graells:* Public procurement and EU competition law, p. 83 ff.
59. For a more detailed review of the relationship of the procurement rules and the competition rules, see *Albert Sanchez Graells:* Public procurement and EU competition law.

regarded as economic activities. The CJ has established that what is decisive for whether a specific public procurement is to be regarded as an economic activity is whether the subsequent use of the product is associated with a commercial activity. Specifically, this mean that the great majority of purchases made by State, regional or municipal authorities will not be subject to the competition rules, as the subsequent use of purchases will not be commercial. It will potentially be different in relation to public law entities that are characterised by the fact that they often also undertake commercial activities and thus can potentially be regarded as undertakings in the eyes of competition law, and thus subject to Articles 101 and 102.

Article 11 of Directive 2004/18/EC allows certain kinds of contracting authorities (central purchasing bodies) to carry out procurements on behalf of other contracting authorities. Depending on the circumstances, this activity – acting on behalf of other contracting authorities – can be regarded as an economic activity, so that such entities will be subject to the competition rules.

If a contracting authority is in fact regarded as an undertaking subject to the competition rules, the prohibitions in Articles 101 and 102 can be applicable. However, a further challenge to the application of these prohibitions is that procurement procedures themselves are of a peculiar nature and unlike traditional agreements, so there can be some doubt about the application of the rules. The legislator has framed the procurement rules so as to focus largely on ensuring equal treatment and the transparency of the process, so there will seldom be any aspect of the award of a contract that will be covered by the provisions of competition law. There can potentially be competition law problems related to the provisions of the contracts entered into or to abnormal pricing in connection with predatory pricing by a tenderer.

One of the greatest challenges in the relationship between the procurement rules and the competition rules is the interaction between them during a procurement procedure. Situations can arise in which the two sets of rules lead to differing results, or where the conditions for what is acceptable differ.

The following examples can be given of this. First, Article 4 of Directive 2004/18/EC allows tenderers to organise themselves as a consortium with a view to submitting a tender. At the same time, competition law sets some clear restrictions on the possibility of forming a consortium. There thus appears to be a lack of cohesion or balance between the procurement rules and the competition rules. Second, it can be argued that the possibility of conducting an electronic auction pursuant to Article 54 of Directive 2004/18/EC to some extent makes it easier for undertakings to coordinate a concerted practice. This is because the provision on electronic auctions makes strict demands for transparency with regard to tenderers. In this situation the core principle of procurement law (on transparency) can make it easier to coordinate tendering, contrary to Article 101 of the Treaty.

The above describes some of the challenges that can arise from the conflicting aims of procurement law and competition law, and it can be seen from this that the most important issue in this area is the possibility of concerted practices between tenderers. This problem is not substantially different from the traditional scope of Article 101, so the reader is referred to the general chapters on this provision, and in particular the chapters on Article 101 in general and on horizontal agreements.

10.2. Procurement and the State aid rules

There are several facets to the relationship between the procurement rules and the State aid rules. First, there is the question of what role the State aid rules play in connection with procurements subject to the procurement directives, and second there is the question of what role procurement plays under the State aid regime.

As discussed in section 7.2.1, the State aid rules are directly referred to in Article 55 of Directive 2004/18/EC, in connection with abnormally low tenders.

Other than in Article 55, the State aid rules are to some extent applicable to the conduct of a procurement procedure. The problems associated with the State aid rules that arise in connection with procurement procedures are often very limited. This is because of the requirement in State aid law that there must be an economic advantage for an undertaking that receives payment for a contract. It is the established assumption in State aid law that if a contract is entered into after a competitive tendering procedure, there will not be an advantage within the meaning of Article 107. This is because the market mechanism (the competitive situation) will mean that any over-payment that would constitute State aid will not be relevant under the procurement procedures: A tendered price that is too high will not be competitive against the other tenders submitted in the procurement procedure. The winning bid will be often contain the lowest price which is (by definition) at the market level and therefore not an expression of an illegitimate economic advantage.

One of the biggest challenges in the overlap between the State aid rules and the procurement rules is the lack of coordination or convergence between the two sets of rules. The clearest expression of this is the problem that can potentially arise in connection with an attempt to apply the provisions simultaneously; when awarding a contract, a contracting authority must simultaneously comply with the procurement rules and the State aid rules. The means for avoiding State aid are in principle the same as are required under the procurement rules, namely that there must be competitive tendering. The problem in this connection is that the kinds of procurement procedures that are acceptable under the State aid rules are not always in line with what is allowable under the procurement rules. This is a problem in practice since a contracting authority can naturally only hold one procurement procedure for one contract, and should preferably be able to use a procedure that is acceptable under both sets of rules.[60]

11. Enforcement

11.1. General

The public procurement directives are a set of EU rules, and the final interpretation of these rules is a matter for the CJ. Since the CJ has limited capacity for dealing with cases, the EU institutions have adopted two directives to ensure the enforcement of the rules at national level. These two directives are referred to as the Remedies Directives.[61] The Remedies Directives were amended by Directive 2007/66/EC. This Directive has introduced striking new perspectives to the possibilities for enforcement. In particular it has introduced the possibility of declaring a contract to be 'ineffective'; see Article 2d of the Directive. What this means is that it is now possible to have a contract made invalid in practice, which is a very powerful sanction.

These directives require the introduction of measures by the Member States to ensure minimum review procedures for undertakings that feel a need to complain on the basis of a contracting authority's conduct of a procurement procedure. Such measures may include the setting up of special review bodies. However, the requirement can also be satisfied by providing the same guarantees via the ordinary court system if the Member State so wishes.

It is a general requirement of the enforcement system that the Member States' enforcement measures must ensure that decisions taken by bodies re-

60. For more on these problems see *Phedon Nicolaidis:* State Aid, Advantage and Competitive Selection: What is a Normal Market Transaction?, European State Aid Law Quarterly 2010 p. 65 and *Michael Steinicke:* Public contracts through procurement – can there still be state aid?, in Konkurrensverket: Pros and cons of competition in/by the public sector, 2009 p.139.

61. Directive 89/665/EEC on the coordination of the laws, regulations and administrative provisions relating to the application of review procedures to the award of public supply and public works contracts, and Directive 92/13/EEC coordinating the laws, regulations and administrative provisions relating to the application of Community rules on the procurement procedures of entities operating in the water, energy, transport and telecommunications sectors.

sponsible for review procedures can be effectively enforced.[62] Behind this provision lies the effectiveness principle, which means that the sanctions and enforcement measures of the Member States must be effective and must have deterrent effect.

One of the requirements that must be satisfied in national law is that it must be possible to cancel unlawful decisions taken in connection with public procurement, including the removal of discriminatory technical, economic or financial specifications in the invitation to tender, the contract documents or in any other document relating to the contract award procedure; see Article 2(1)(b) of Directive 89/665/EEC.

It is also laid down that it must be possible under national law to take interim measures with the aim of correcting an alleged infringement or preventing further damage to the interests concerned.

Finally, it must be possible to obtain an award of damages for persons harmed by an infringement. This is discussed further below. The question of what consequences interim measures or cancellation will have is a matter for national law.

11.2. Damages

The powers to grant damages and the conditions which must be fulfilled in order to obtain damages are determined under national law. In spite of this, the CJ does have certain requirements for national rules on damages in order to ensure that enforcement and the possibility of obtaining damages are applied in such a way as to ensure effective and non-discriminatory sanctions.

Detailed requirements with regard to damages are laid down in Article 2(7) of Directive 92/13/EC,[63] where it is stated that: 'Where a claim is made for damages representing the costs of preparing a bid or of participating in an award procedure, the person making the claim shall be required only to prove an infringement of Union law in the field of procurement or national rules implementing that law and that he would have had a real chance of winning the contract and that, as a consequence of that infringement, that chance was adversely affected.' It must be assumed that the provision does not lay down any conditions as to what form of infringement leads to liability for damages. In the same way that national rules on liability for damages are applied, it

62. Article 2(7) of Directive 89/665/EEC.

63. The provision concerns the requirements for obtaining damages in relation to the procurement procedures of entities operating in the water, energy, transport and telecommunications sectors, but it must be assumed to apply equally to the award of public supply and public works contracts.

must be assumed that the establishment of the basis for damages is also a matter for national law.

As for the type of damages that can be awarded, the provision must be understood so that it is not only when it is possible to show positively that damage has been suffered that damages may be obtainable. There can also be liability for damages where the contracting authority has infringed the rules so that any real chance of winning the award of a contract ceases to exist.

It is required of national rules on the award of damages that they must not make it more difficult for undertakings from other Member States to obtain damages than undertakings from the same Member State as the contracting authority. And in general it must not be unreasonably complicated to obtain damages.

12. Other rules on public procurement

12.1. General

The EU's rules on public procurement are the most important rules on public procurement within the EU. However, there are also other rules which supplement the directives in the different national legal systems as well as rules relating to the obligations which the Member States have accepted with regard to third countries, in particular agreements entered into via the EU.

12.2. WTO rules: The Government Procurement Agreement

There are many organisations which regulate trade between countries, both regionally and globally. The regulation which is most relevant to the EU and to the individual Member States is the World Trade Organization's Agreement on Government Procurement (GPA). The GPA is a bilateral agreement, which means that only Members of the WTO which are party to the GPA are governed by its provisions.[64]

Public procurement became part of the GATT system[65] in connection with the Tokyo Round. The negotiations resulted in the Government Procurement Code at the end of the 1970s, which was the first attempt at an agreement on public procurement, and during the Uruguay Round this was replaced by the

64. In contrast to bilateral agreements, most agreements under the WTO regime are, in principle, multilateral agreements, which means that as soon as a country becomes a Member of the WTO it automatically signs up to the multilateral agreements.
65. GATT stands for the General Agreement on Tariffs and Trade. Together with a number of individual agreements, including the GPA, the GATT Agreement constitutes the legal basis for the WTO.

GPA. Prior to the adoption of this explicit regulation of public procurement, public procurement was exempted from the general obligations laid down in the GATT Agreement. The obligations of the Members under this Agreement (for example, non-discrimination) expressly exclude public procurement situations. Instead, corresponding provisions have been introduced in the GPA.

The GPA contains a long list of provisions which essentially correspond to the provisions in the public procurement directives. These include rules on selection of candidates and award of contracts, as well as rules on the use of technical specifications etc.[66]

66. For more on the GPA see *Sue Arrowsmith:* Government Procurement in the WTO, and *Birgitte Egelund Olsen* et al.: WTO law from a European perspective, Chapter 12.

Numbering of TFEU before and after the Amsterdam and Lisbon Treaties

Before 1/5 1999	**1999-2009**	**After 1/12 2009**
Art.2	Art. 2	Art. 3 TEU
Art. 3	Art. 3	Art. 3-6 and Art. 8
Art. 3a	Art. 4	Art. 119
Art. 3b	Art. 5	Art. 5 TEU
Art. 3c	Art. 6	Art. 11
Art. 5	Art. 10	Art. 4 TEU
Art. 6	Art. 12	Art. 18
Art. 6a	Art. 13	Art. 19
Art. 7a	Art. 14	Art. 26
Art. 8	Art. 17	Art. 20
Art. 12	Art. 25	Art. 30
Art. 30	Art. 28	Art. 34
Art. 34	Art. 29	Art. 35
Art. 36	Art. 30	Art. 36
Art. 48	Art. 39	Art. 45
Art. 52	Art. 43	Art. 49
Art. 59	Art. 49	Art. 56
Art. 73b	Art. 56	Art. 63
Art. 85	Art. 81	Art. 101
Art. 86	Art. 82	Art. 102
Art. 90	Art. 86	Art. 106
Art. 92	Art. 87	Art. 107
Art. 93	Art. 88	Art. 108
Art. 94	Art. 89	Art. 109
Art. 95	Art. 90	Art. 110
Art. 100	Art. 94	Art. 115

Art. 100a	Art. 95	Art. 114
Art. 101	Art. 96	Art. 116
Art. 168a	Art. 225	Art. 256
Art. 169	Art. 226	Art. 258
Art. 170	Art. 227	Art. 259
Art. 173	Art. 230	Art. 263
Art. 222	Art. 295	Art. 345

Table of Cases

European Court of Justice

Court of First Instance

Table of Commission Decisions

Merger Decisions

Other Commission Decisions

Index